# Human-Centric, Sustainable, and Resilient Organizations in the Digital Age

Alper Erturk
*Australian University, Kuwait*

Mehtap Özşahin
*Gebze Technical University, Turkey*

Vladimir Simovic
*Institute of Economic Sciences, Serbia & Australian University, Kuwait*

IGI Global
Scientific Publishing
Publishing Tomorrow's Research Today

Vice President of Editorial — Melissa Wagner
Managing Editor of Acquisitions — Mikaela Felty
Managing Editor of Book Development — Jocelynn Hessler
Production Manager — Mike Brehm
Cover Design — Phillip Shickler

Published in the United States of America by
IGI Global Scientific Publishing
701 East Chocolate Avenue
Hershey, PA, 17033, USA
Tel: 717-533-8845
Fax: 717-533-8661
Website: https://www.igi-global.com E-mail: cust@igi-global.com



Library of Congress Cataloging-in-Publication Data

Names: Ertürk, Alper, 1973- editor.
Title: Human-centric, sustainable, and resilient organizations in the digital age / edited by Alper Ertürk, Mehtap Ozsahin, Vladimir Simović.
Description: Hershey, PA : IGI Global Scientific Publishing, [2025] | Includes bibliographical references and index. | Summary: "This is a comprehensive book that explores the concepts of digitalization, sustainability, resilience and human orientation from the business perspective in the Industry 5.0 era"-- Provided by publisher.
Identifiers: LCCN 2024054364 (print) | LCCN 2024054365 (ebook) | ISBN 9798369381816 (hardback) | ISBN 9798369381823 (paperback) | ISBN 9798369381830 (ebook)
Subjects: LCSH: Organizational resilience. | Business--Data processing.
Classification: LCC HD58.9 .H84 2025 (print) | LCC HD58.9 (ebook) | DDC 658.4/013--dc23/eng/20250203
LC record available at https://lccn.loc.gov/2024054364
LC ebook record available at https://lccn.loc.gov/2024054365

British Cataloguing in Publication Data
A Cataloguing in Publication record for this book is available from the British Library.

# Table of Contents

# Detailed Table of Contents



As the world enters Industry 5.0, universities must evolve as educators, innovators, and societal leaders. This chapter examines the impact of Industry 5.0 on higher education, emphasizing advanced technologies, interdisciplinary collaboration, and human-centric approaches. It highlights the integration of AI, robotics, and data analytics in research, teaching, and operations, stressing the need to bridge the digital divide, train faculty in emerging tools, and foster lifelong learning through microcredentials. The CDIO framework is revisited, aligning with Industry 5.0's ethical and interdisciplinary demands. University-industry partnerships are essential for aligning curricula, fostering innovation, and providing practical learning opportunities. The chapter underscores the role of universities in promoting sustainability, ethics, and community engagement to ensure technology serves societal well-being. Recommendations include adopting smart campus technologies, supporting entrepreneurship, and advocating for equitable, ethical, and technology-driven educational policies.



Industry 5.0 represents a significant shift, combining human creativity with advanced technologies to achieve sustainable and human-centered industrial practices. Universities play a critical role in this transformation by encouraging innovation, interdisciplinary research, and collaboration with industry, all while incorporating sustainability into their operations. This chapter investigates how universities advance the Sustainable Development Goals (SDGs) by implementing initiatives such as green campuses, smart technologies, and ISO standards that promote sustainable practices. It focuses on current sustainability practices in universities worldwide, such as renewable energy adoption, waste reduction, and project-based learning. Key challenges such as financial constraints, cultural resistance, and skill gaps are addressed through solutions such as public-private partnerships, green bonds, and adaptive curricula. The chapter concludes with policy recommendations for incentivizing sustainable infrastructure, developing global research networks, and implementing sustainability KPIs.

The first three industrial revolutions facilitated the transition from manual production to automation, while Industry 4.0 has supported the concept of smart manufacturing aimed at flexible and efficient production of goods. This transformation has been made possible through Cyber-Physical Systems (CPS), enabling real-time communication and collaboration. However, this shift raises concerns about the dehumanization of work, as modern systems heavily rely on mechanization and data-driven processes. This has driven Industry 5.0, which aims to harmonize human skills with intelligent systems by blending the efficiency of automation with human cognitive abilities to create a more balanced and flexible industrial paradigm. In this book chapter, a bibliometric analysis of studies conducted from the inception of Industry 5.0 in 2019 to the present has been performed, and the topic has been discussed in depth. It also examines emerging trends, highlights dominant research areas, explores methodological frameworks, and summarizes existing findings on the topic.



In the emerging world researchers put forward the idea of industry 5.0, focusing on the concept of human centricity, sustainability and resilience approaches in the organizations. Industry 5.0 includes technological advancement along with giving importance to the human capital. During the past, the industrial revolution emphasized the productivity, production quality and growth of business. There was less importance for the human capital and employees well being in the changing industrial style giving importance to the human capital, by integrating technological advancements. It is recognised for the societal values that are embedded, the whole industry 5.0 revolves around sustainability, human centric and resilience in the organization. In this book chapter we explore the concept and applicability of these topics. The book chapter used literature review method and case study analysis for thorough understanding of the subject.



Human -centric innovation is paramount in building sustainable organizations in the era of Industry 5.0. As businesses transition from purely technology-driven models to those that integrate human creativity and advanced technologies, a new paradigm emerges—one that places human well-being, ethical considerations, and sustainability at its core. This article delves into how organizations can leverage human-centric innovation to create more sustainable business practices, addressing environmental, social, and economic challenges. It discusses strategies such as empowering employees through inclusive decision-making, adopting design thinking to foster sustainable product development, and using digital tools that enhance both productivity and human health. By embracing a human-centered approach, organizations can achieve a balance between technological advancement and alignment with broader

are highly influential. Thematic analysis highlights "citizenship pressure," "interpersonal deviance," and "employee silence" as motor themes, while basic themes include work-family conflict, turnover intention, job stress, and burnout. Issues like "facades of conformity" and "impression management" are classified as niche or emerging themes. This study enriches the understanding of CCB research and offers insights for future studies.



Within the framework of digital transformation, this chapter examines the relationship between innovative work behavior, technostress, and digital leadership. It examines how innovation is encouraged by digital leadership while tackling issues like technostress, brought on by the usage of new digital technologies. According to the study, effective digital leadership reduces the negative consequences of technostress while simultaneously fostering innovative work behaviors of employees. Additionally, it explores the mediating role of technostress, which, depending on how employees handle the demands of the digital workplace, can either impede or strengthen the beneficial role of digital leadership in fostering innovation.



Intensification of the use of digital technologies and communication channels in business practice significantly influences corporate reputation building and maintaining, by enabling more efficient reaching of target audiences and greater interactivity in communication. In the digital age, the practice of managing corporate reputation implies the continuous monitoring of various digital channels such as social media, and data analysis based on advanced analytics and artificial intelligence. As the increasing number of corporate communication and relation building practices takes on digital forms, with the intensification of this field in practice, the volume of research is also increasing. Therefore, the focus of this chapter is on providing a comprehensive overview of this topic, by conducting a systematic review of the relevant literature and by indicating the dominant areas of research, methodological frameworks that are applied for data collection and analysis and existing findings related to it.



The adoption of the innovative perspective of Industry 5.0 at the highest level in organizations is important for ensuring sustainability in every field and the board of directors' role becomes increasingly important in improving companies' sustainability performance. This chapter first presents the theoretical and conceptual background of Industry 5.0 and sustainability, the role of boards of directors in sustainability, and corporate sustainability reporting. Then, the findings of an empirical study that examine the impact

Research on organizations in the Western Balkans has grown significantly over the past 30 years, highlighting the need for a comprehensive review. This bibliometric study examines the state of organizational research by performing bibliometric analysis, identifying research clusters through co-word analysis, and conducting trend topic analysis to uncover emerging themes. Using VOSviewer and Biblioshiny, the study analyzes 1,037 papers from the Scopus database. Findings reveal consistent growth in publications, especially after 2015. Co-word analysis identifies five major research clusters: SMEs, Kosovo, Serbia, entrepreneurship, and innovation. Future research is recommended to explore how businesses prepare for potential EU integration, the role of institutional support or voids in entrepreneurship rates, the effects of brain drain on organizations in the Western Balkans, and the dynamics of returnee entrepreneurs. This study provides valuable insights into the intellectual structure and trends in organizational research in the region and offers a foundation for future studies.



Transferring cultural heritage to younger generations plays an important role in shaping and guiding the future of societies. In this context, the "Historical Game Journey (HGJ)" project, which is based on Information Technology (IT) infrastructure, was developed to transfer historical knowledge and cultural heritage awareness to young generations through gamification. The aim of this study is to design and develop a smart scepter as a prototype that will help children find targets during the tour within the scope of HGJ's IT infrastructure. Three different designs were prepared using the Design Thinking Approach, and the most suitable one was selected by conducting a survey with the students who will use the scepter. The scepter and the developed IT infrastructure can be utilized, with minor adjustments, in museums, orienteering competitions, tourist areas, and military campuses. Additionally, it is anticipated that the database created by tracking the smart scepter will contribute to smart city applications.

# Preface

The journey toward a human-centric, sustainable, and resilient future in the digital age is both an exciting and challenging endeavor. In this edited volume, *Human-Centric, Sustainable, and Resilient Organizations in the Digital Age*, we explore the critical intersections of digitalization, sustainability, resilience, and human orientation within the evolving framework of Industry 5.0.

This book builds upon the academic and practical contributions of the 19th International Strategic Management Conference, themed "Planning for Industry 5.0: Human-Centric, Sustainable, and Resilient Organizations," while also welcoming insights beyond the conference's selected papers. As editors, we were driven by the need to offer a forward-thinking guide to the theories, practices, and strategic pathways for designing organizations that are not only prepared for the Industry 5.0 era but are also deeply attuned to the broader goals of sustainability, human well-being, and long-term resilience.

Industry 5.0 does not merely follow Industry 4.0 as a chronological progression; it represents a transformative vision that builds on the technological foundations of its predecessor while addressing the critical imperatives of environmental stewardship, social responsibility, and economic circularity. Unlike Industry 4.0, which emphasized productivity and efficiency through automation and smart technologies, Industry 5.0 elevates human-centricity and sustainability as its cornerstones. The transition requires us to reimagine the role of technology—not just as a tool for economic gain, but as an enabler of holistic, inclusive, and resilient systems that benefit both society and the environment.

This book provides a comprehensive analysis of Industry 5.0 and its impact across a broad spectrum of organizations, from businesses to non-profit entities, government institutions, and diverse industries such as healthcare, education, tourism, banking, logistics, and beyond. It delves into the strategies necessary for fostering organizations that prioritize adaptability, human engagement, and environmental accountability.

The chapters in this volume offer a mix of theoretical frameworks, empirical research, and real-world applications that equip business leaders, entrepreneurs, policymakers, and academics with the insights needed to thrive in this new paradigm. Our contributors examine diverse themes such as digital transformation, resilience in the face of disruption, and the interplay between technological innovation and human-centric values.

We are confident that the findings and perspectives presented in this book will have far-reaching implications for both research and practice. As Industry 5.0 gains traction, it poses unique challenges and opportunities for organizations worldwide, particularly in regions such as the Middle East, Europe, and Asia, where the rapid pace of technological adoption is reshaping economic and societal landscapes.

This book is intended for a wide audience, including academic researchers, university professors, students, and industry practitioners eager to understand the evolving dynamics of digital transformation and its intersection with sustainability and resilience. By addressing the core principles of Industry 5.0, we hope to inspire meaningful action, foster innovative solutions, and lay the groundwork for a future where technology and humanity work hand in hand for a better tomorrow.

We extend our deepest gratitude to the contributors who shared their expertise and to all those who supported the realization of this book. We trust that this work will serve as a valuable resource for advancing knowledge and practice in human-centric, sustainable, and resilient organizations.

## ORGANIZATION OF THE BOOK

### Chapter 1: Shaping the Future of Universities in the Age of Industry 5.0

In this chapter, the important catalyst power of universities in shaping the future is discussed in a holistic perspective. In the new age of Industry 5.0, the role of universities, as the crucial actors of information and knowledge creation and dissemination, extends far beyond educating students as future leaders and professionals. The workforce in the near future will be required to have more than technical skills; it will require creativity, emotional intelligence, adaptability, and a deep understanding of complex systems (UNESCO, 2020). As such, universities are expected to shape the future of work, innovation, and societal progress by becoming the architects of the future, fostering interdisciplinary research, promoting collaboration with industries, and leading sustainable development (Brynjolfsson & McAfee, 2014). Nevertheless, universities must also confront significant challenges, including the digital divide, ethical considerations, and the need for continuous faculty development to keep pace with technological advancements

### Chapter 2: Sustainable Universities as Catalysts for Industry 5.0 Transformation

This chapter explores the pivotal role of universities in driving Industry 5.0 transformation, blending human creativity with cutting-edge technologies to promote sustainability and human-centered practices. The discussion delves into how universities actively advance the Sustainable Development Goals (SDGs) by implementing green campuses, adopting renewable energy solutions, integrating smart technologies, and adhering to ISO standards for sustainable operations. The authors examine diverse global initiatives such as waste reduction and project-based learning while addressing challenges like financial limitations, cultural resistance, and skill gaps. By advocating solutions such as public-private partnerships, green bonds, and adaptive curricula, the chapter outlines strategies for overcoming obstacles and concludes with policy recommendations for fostering sustainable infrastructure, global research networks, and effective sustainability metrics.

### Chapter 3: Pioneering Sustainability through Industry 5.0 with a Human-Centric Approach: A Bibliometric Analysis

This chapter provides an in-depth bibliometric analysis of Industry 5.0 research, tracing its development since 2019. It contextualizes Industry 5.0 as a paradigm that harmonizes automation with human creativity and cognitive skills, aiming to address the dehumanization concerns associated with earlier industrial revolutions. By analyzing trends and dominant research themes, the authors highlight the shift toward human-centric and sustainable industrial practices. Methodological frameworks and key findings are presented to offer a comprehensive understanding of how Industry 5.0 can balance technological advancements with ethical and social priorities.

## Chapter 4: Resilience and Human-Centric Perspectives for Organizations in Industry 5.0

This chapter highlights the integration of human-centricity, resilience, and sustainability into Industry 5.0 organizations. Through a combination of literature review and case study analysis, the authors explore how technological advancements, coupled with a renewed emphasis on human capital, redefine organizational practices. The discussion underscores the importance of embedding societal values into industrial processes and offers insights into the practical applications of these principles in fostering sustainable and resilient organizations.

## Chapter 5: Human-Centric Innovation: Building Sustainable Organizations for Industry 5.0

Focusing on human-centric innovation, this chapter underscores its critical role in creating sustainable organizations in the Industry 5.0 era. It examines how businesses can transition from purely technology-driven models to approaches that prioritize human well-being and ethical considerations. Strategies such as inclusive decision-making, design thinking for sustainable product development, and the integration of digital tools are discussed to demonstrate how organizations can align technological advancements with broader societal goals, achieving sustainable growth in a connected world.

## Chapter 6: Human-Centric Digital Workplace: Designing for Employee Wellbeing and Productivity

This chapter explores the transformation of workplaces into digital ecosystems that prioritize employee well-being alongside productivity. Drawing on Self-Determination Theory, the authors highlight the critical elements of autonomy, competence, and relatedness in fostering healthier and more engaged workforces. By addressing challenges like digital exhaustion and diversity, the chapter proposes solutions such as AI, virtual reality, and individualistic work design to create sustainable and supportive digital workplaces.

## Chapter 7: Leveraging Technology for Employee Well-Being and Organizational Resilience

The authors examine how advanced IT solutions can enhance employee well-being while fostering organizational resilience. The chapter emphasizes the importance of human-centric design in creating supportive networks that build community and workplace flexibility. It also addresses the challenges of sustaining human connections in socially distanced environments and offers guidelines for developing durable and sustainable technologies that prioritize employee welfare.

### Chapter 8: Towards Sustainable and Human-Centered Organizations through the Prevention of Compulsory Citizenship Behaviors: A Bibliometric Analysis

This chapter investigates the role of human-centered approaches in fostering sustainable organizations while addressing the negative impacts of compulsory citizenship behaviors (CCB). Through a bibliometric analysis of CCB research, the authors identify key trends, influential contributors, and emerging themes such as citizenship pressure and employee silence. The findings provide valuable insights into how organizations can mitigate the adverse effects of CCB to enhance sustainability and employee well-being.

### Chapter 9: Exploring the Interplay between Technostress, Digital Leadership, and Innovative Work Behavior

This chapter explores the complex relationship between technostress, digital leadership, and innovative work behavior in the context of digital transformation. The authors highlight how effective digital leadership can mitigate the adverse effects of technostress while fostering innovation. The chapter also discusses the dual role of technostress, which can either hinder or enhance the beneficial impacts of leadership, offering practical insights for navigating the digital workplace.

### Chapter 10: Evaluating Corporate Reputation in the Digital Environment: Insights from a Systematic Literature Review

Focusing on the digital age's impact on corporate reputation, this chapter provides a systematic review of literature on digital communication and reputation management. The authors identify key research areas, methodologies, and findings, emphasizing the role of advanced analytics and AI in monitoring digital channels. The chapter offers valuable insights into how organizations can effectively build and maintain their reputations in a highly interconnected digital environment.

### Chapter 11: Board Structure and Sustainability Performance: A Study on Turkish Manufacturing Companies

This chapter investigates the relationship between board structure and sustainability performance within Turkish manufacturing companies. Drawing on data from 166 firms, the authors reveal how board size and gender diversity positively influence sustainability outcomes. The findings underscore the importance of integrating Industry 5.0 principles at the highest organizational levels to drive corporate sustainability.

### Chapter 12: The Effect of Servant Leadership on Organizational Citizenship Behavior in NGOs, Psychological Capital as A Mediator

This chapter examines the interplay between servant leadership, psychological capital, and organizational citizenship behavior (OCB) in NGOs. Using quantitative research methods, the authors demonstrate that servant leadership positively influences OCB, with psychological capital acting as a mediator. The findings offer actionable insights for fostering high OCB levels in NGOs, emphasizing leadership styles that prioritize employee development and well-being.

### Chapter 13: A Thematic Analysis of Literature on the Startup Assessment Criteria: Startup Success Factors Revisited

This chapter explores the complexities of assessing early-stage startups, particularly due to limited data and the unpredictability of success. A thematic literature review synthesizes key determinants of startup success, including the entrepreneurial team, market conditions, innovation potential, financials, and strategic readiness. The chapter introduces a practical framework for funders, incubators, and accelerators to systematically evaluate startups while enabling startups to self-assess and improve.

### Chapter 14: Organizational Research in the Western Balkans: A Comprehensive Bibliometric Review

This bibliometric study examines 30 years of organizational research in the Western Balkans, analyzing 1,037 Scopus-indexed papers using tools like VOSviewer and Biblioshiny. Findings highlight growth in publications post-2015 and identify five research clusters: SMEs, Kosovo, Serbia, entrepreneurship, and innovation. Emerging themes include preparation for EU integration, institutional support's role in entrepreneurship, the effects of brain drain, and returnee entrepreneur dynamics. The chapter offers insights into regional organizational research trends and serves as a foundation for future studies.

### Chapter 15: Smart Guider on Historical Game Journey: Smart Scepter Design with Design Thinking Approach

This chapter introduces the "Historical Game Journey (HGJ)" project, designed to transfer cultural heritage through gamification. Using a Design Thinking approach, a smart scepter prototype was developed to help children navigate historical sites within the HGJ framework. Student surveys informed the selection of the final design. The scepter's database tracking capabilities could also benefit applications in museums, tourist sites, and smart city initiatives.

## CONCLUSION

In compiling this volume, we aimed to bring together a diverse collection of studies that exemplify the evolving dynamics of innovation, organizational research, and cultural transformation in both theoretical and practical realms. Each chapter offers a unique perspective, from revisiting critical success factors in startups to exploring the organizational landscapes of emerging regions and leveraging gamification to preserve cultural heritage. The contributions highlight not only the global interconnectedness of contemporary challenges but also the critical role of creativity, technology, and localized understanding in addressing them.

As editors, we hope this book serves as a valuable resource for scholars, practitioners, and policymakers alike, inspiring further inquiry and collaboration across disciplines. The insights shared here underscore the necessity of adaptive strategies, evidence-based frameworks, and innovative solutions to navigate the complexities of our rapidly changing world. Ultimately, it is through such collective efforts that we can unlock the full potential of human ingenuity and drive meaningful progress.

We invite you, the reader, to explore these chapters with curiosity and an open mind, and we look forward to seeing how the ideas presented here may inform and shape the next wave of research, practice, and innovation.

**Alper Erturk**
*Australian University, Kuwait*

**Mehtap Özsahin**
*Gebze Technical University, Turkey*

**Vladimir Simovic**
*Institute of Economic Sciences, Serbia & Australian University, Kuwait*

# Chapter 1
# Shaping the Future of Universities in the Age of Industry 5.0

**Isam Zabalawi**
https://orcid.org/0009-0008-6181-4602
*Australian University, Kuwait*

**Helene Kordahji**
https://orcid.org/0009-0003-9870-9922
*Australian University, Kuwait*

## ABSTRACT

*As the world enters Industry 5.0, universities must evolve as educators, innovators, and societal leaders. This chapter examines the impact of Industry 5.0 on higher education, emphasizing advanced technologies, interdisciplinary collaboration, and human-centric approaches. It highlights the integration of AI, robotics, and data analytics in research, teaching, and operations, stressing the need to bridge the digital divide, train faculty in emerging tools, and foster lifelong learning through microcredentials. The CDIO framework is revisited, aligning with Industry 5.0's ethical and interdisciplinary demands. University-industry partnerships are essential for aligning curricula, fostering innovation, and providing practical learning opportunities. The chapter underscores the role of universities in promoting sustainability, ethics, and community engagement to ensure technology serves societal well-being. Recommendations include adopting smart campus technologies, supporting entrepreneurship, and advocating for equitable, ethical, and technology-driven educational policies.*

## 1. INTRODUCTION

### 1.1 Overview of Industry 5.0

As we stand on the cusp of the next industrial revolution—Industry 5.0—the world is witnessing an unprecedented convergence of advanced technologies, human ingenuity, and a renewed emphasis on societal well-being. Unlike its predecessor, Industry 4.0, which focused on automation, digitization, and

DOI: 10.4018/979-8-3693-8181-6.ch001

efficiency, Industry 5.0 heralds an era of enhanced collaboration between humans and machines, where personalization, sustainability, and innovation take center stage (McKinsey Global Institute, 2021). This revolution transcends the traditional pursuit of economic expansion, setting its sights on tackling some of humanity's most pressing challenges. It aspires to create a more sustainable world by combating climate change, fostering responsible and ethical use of emerging technologies, and ensuring that the benefits of innovation are shared equitably across societies (World Economic Forum, 2020).

Universities, as centers of knowledge creation and dissemination, are poised to play a pivotal role in shaping this future. The rapid pace of technological advancement, particularly in artificial intelligence (AI), robotics, and data analytics, is reshaping industries, economies, and societies. The workforce of tomorrow will need more than technical skills; it will require creativity, emotional intelligence, adaptability, and a deep understanding of complex systems. As such, universities must evolve to become incubators of innovation, fostering not only technical expertise but also the human-centered values that underpin Industry 5.0 (Tao, Zhang, & Nee, 2019).

In this new paradigm, the role of universities extends far beyond educating future employees. They must become architects of the future, embracing interdisciplinary research, fostering collaboration with industries, and driving sustainable development. Universities are tasked with shaping the future of work, innovation, and societal progress. This demands a radical rethinking of how education is delivered, how research is conducted, and how universities engage with the wider community.

Industry 5.0 marks a significant shift from the automation and efficiency-driven focus of Industry 4.0 to a more human-centered approach. While Industry 4.0 leveraged technologies such as the Internet of Things (IoT), big data, and artificial intelligence (AI) to enhance automation, Industry 5.0 integrates these technologies more deeply into our lives with a renewed emphasis on personalization, sustainability, and societal well-being as depicted in Figure1.

Central to Industry 5.0 is the concept of human-robot collaboration, where machines enhance human capabilities rather than replace them. Personalization is also a key theme, as industries move away from mass production toward customized, consumer-centric solutions. Additionally, sustainability is a core driver, with innovations aimed at reducing environmental impact and promoting the circular economy. The focus on societal well-being is reflected in efforts to use technology for the greater good, addressing issues such as climate change, healthcare, and social equity (Barata & Kayser, 2023).

## 1.2 Relevance to Higher Education

As Industry 5.0 continues to evolve, its impact on higher education is both profound and inevitable. Universities, as engines of innovation and thought leadership, are at the forefront of preparing students to thrive in a world shaped by these new industrial dynamics. The role of higher education is no longer confined to equipping students with technical skills; it must now also prepare graduates to navigate complex societal challenges, contribute to sustainable development, and work in harmony with intelligent systems (Hashim et al, 2024).

Universities need to adapt their curricula to emphasize not only technical expertise but also creativity, adaptability, emotional intelligence, and ethical decision-making—qualities that are vital in Industry 5.0. Teaching and learning methodologies must also evolve. AI-driven adaptive learning platforms, personalized education pathways, and virtual reality (VR) environments that simulate real-world scenarios are becoming crucial for providing students with experiential learning opportunities.

The research agendas of universities are equally impacted. In an era of human-machine collaboration, universities must champion research that integrates technological innovation with sustainability and societal goals. This requires interdisciplinary collaboration, where fields like AI, robotics, environmental science, and ethics converge to address issues ranging from climate change to social inequality. By fostering environments where this type of research can thrive, universities will help shape the ethical, sustainable, and human-centered technological advancements that are at the heart of Industry 5.0.

In summary, Industry 5.0 challenges universities to rethink their roles as educators, researchers, and innovators. To remain relevant and influential in this new industrial era, universities must not only embrace technological advancements but also align their missions with the broader goals of societal well-being, sustainability, and ethical innovation.

*Figure 1. Highlights of Industry 5.0 compared to Industry 4.0*

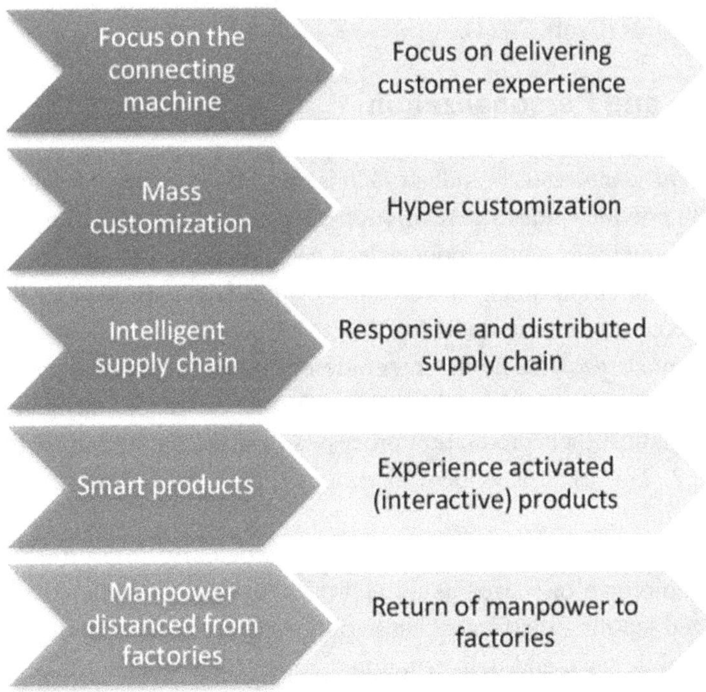


## 2. KEY TRENDS IN INDUSTRY 5.0

### 2.1 Human-Centric Technology

One of the defining aspects of Industry 5.0 is its emphasis on human-centric technology—a fundamental shift from the automation and efficiency-driven focus of Industry 4.0. While Industry 4.0 prioritized digital transformation through technologies like the Internet of Things (IoT), big data, and artificial intelligence (AI), Industry 5.0 aims to harness these technologies to enhance human capabilities rather than replace human labor.

In this new paradigm, collaboration between humans and machines is key. AI, robotics, and smart systems are no longer just tools for optimizing processes; they are now intelligent partners that assist humans in achieving more creative, innovative, and personalized outcomes. By integrating AI-driven tools and robots into everyday workflows, Industry 5.0 enables humans to focus on tasks that require critical thinking, emotional intelligence, and innovation while leaving repetitive or data-intensive tasks to machines. For example, in sectors like healthcare, AI systems assist doctors by analyzing vast amounts of patient data and suggesting personalized treatments (Brynjolfsson & McAfee, 2014). In manufacturing, robots work alongside human workers to create customized products tailored to individual consumer preferences.

The human-centric nature of Industry 5.0 also underscores the importance of ensuring that technology development aligns with human values. Technology must be designed to improve the quality of life, create meaningful work experiences, and contribute to societal well-being rather than displacing workers or perpetuating inequalities (Croft, 2024).

## 2.2 Customization and Personalization

One of the most significant trends in Industry 5.0 is the shift from mass production to customization and personalization. In previous industrial revolutions, efficiency and scalability were achieved through standardized production methods, with products designed to cater to the masses. However, Industry 5.0 takes a different approach, emphasizing the creation of products and services that are tailored to the unique needs and preferences of individuals (Croft, 2024).

This shift has been made possible by the integration of AI, data analytics, and robotics into production systems. Companies can now gather and analyze customer data to understand specific preferences and demands and then adjust their production processes in real-time to deliver personalized solutions as depicted in Figure 2. This trend is evident in various sectors, including manufacturing, healthcare, retail, and even education.

In education, this trend towards personalization is particularly impactful. Traditional education models, which often employ a one-size-fits-all approach, are being challenged by the capabilities of AI-driven, personalized learning platforms. These platforms use data analytics to track each student's progress, identify learning gaps, and deliver tailored content that adapts to the individual's pace and style of learning. This not only enhances the learning experience but also improves student outcomes by ensuring that each learner receives the support they need to succeed.

Customization and personalization also extend beyond products and services to how industries and institutions interact with their stakeholders. The ability to offer personalized customer experiences, employee training programs, and learning environments has become a competitive advantage in the Industry 5.0 era, fostering deeper connections and better outcomes (Rijwani et al, 2024).

*Figure 2. Customization with AI*

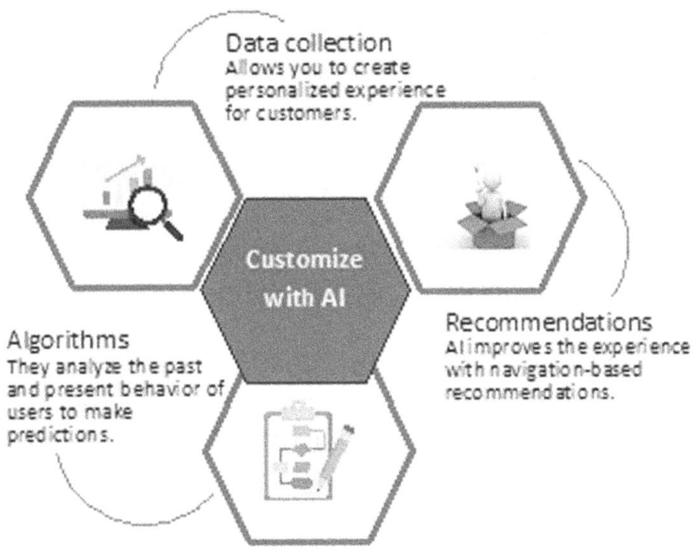


## 3. UNIVERSITIES AS INNOVATORS AND FACILITATORS OF CHANGE

### 3.1 Role of Universities in Preparing the Future Workforce

As the world enters the era of Industry 5.0, the role of universities has never been more critical. Higher education institutions are not only responsible for equipping students with the knowledge and skills needed for the current workforce but also for preparing them to thrive in a rapidly changing environment where human-machine collaboration, innovation, and adaptability are key (Hashim et al, 2024). To meet the demands of Industry 5.0, universities must align their curricula, research, and training to ensure graduates are ready to take on the challenges of this new industrial age as depicted in Figure 3.

**Curriculum Alignment:** Industry 5.0 requires a multidisciplinary approach that integrates technical skills with human-centered values. Engineering and computer science programs, for example, must now incorporate elements of ethics, sustainability, and human-robot collaboration into their coursework. Business programs need to emphasize data-driven decision-making, AI literacy, and strategic innovation alongside traditional management theories. The integration of soft skills such as creativity, problem-solving, critical thinking, and emotional intelligence is equally important, as these attributes are crucial for navigating the complex, interconnected systems that will define Industry 5.0.

**Research Innovation:** Universities are also at the forefront of driving the technological innovations that underpin Industry 5.0. Collaborative research projects between academia and industry can accelerate the development of new technologies that address real-world problems, such as climate change, healthcare disparities, and resource management. Furthermore, research in areas such as AI ethics, machine learning, and sustainable systems must be prioritized to ensure that Industry 5.0 progresses in a responsible and ethical manner.

**Hands-on Training:** Universities need to offer experiential learning opportunities that go beyond the classroom. Internships, co-ops, and industry partnerships will provide students with practical experience in human-machine collaboration, data analytics, and emerging technologies. Project-based learning, which involves students working on real-world problems, can also help them develop the critical thinking and problem-solving skills necessary for success in Industry 5.0.

The transformation of engineering education is crucial, as engineers will be at the core of Industry 5.0 advancements. Universities must focus on teaching students how to work in interdisciplinary teams, leverage AI tools to design innovative solutions, and create sustainable technologies that benefit society. In essence, the university of the future must not only be a place where knowledge is transferred but also where the workforce of tomorrow is shaped through a combination of theory, practice, and innovation (Carayannis & Morawska, 2023).

*Figure 3. Graduate attributes*

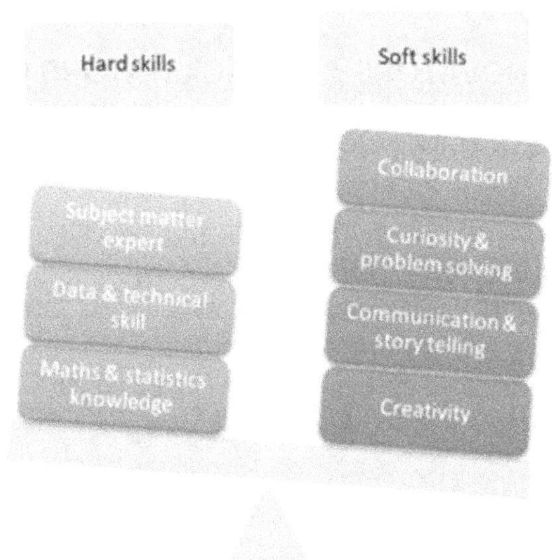

### 3.2 Emphasis on Lifelong Learning

In the age of Industry 5.0, lifelong learning is no longer a choice but a necessity. The rapid pace of technological change means that knowledge and skills can become obsolete within a few years. As industries evolve, professionals will need to continuously update their skills and knowledge to stay relevant in their fields. This requires universities to rethink their educational models, moving beyond the traditional four-year degree to embrace flexible, continuous learning opportunities that span an individual's career.

Universities must act as facilitators of lifelong learning by offering a wide range of learning formats, including short courses, microcredentials, and online learning platforms that cater to the needs of professionals at different stages of their careers. Flexible learning paths will allow individuals to upskill or reskill as technological advancements reshape their industries. For example, an engineer who graduated a decade ago may need to learn new AI tools to remain competitive in the job market.

The growing importance of microcredentials in lifelong learning cannot be overstated. Microcredentials offer a way for learners to gain specific skills quickly and efficiently, without committing to a long-term degree program. These bite-sized qualifications can be stacked over time, allowing learners to build a portfolio of competencies that reflect their professional growth and the evolving demands of Industry 5.0. This modular approach to education aligns perfectly with the fluid nature of today's job market, where the ability to quickly adapt to new tools and processes is highly valued (Shanahan & Organ, 2022).

Moreover, universities need to foster a culture of continuous learning among their graduates. This includes instilling a mindset that learning is not confined to formal education but is an ongoing process. Universities can achieve this by creating alumni networks and learning communities where professionals can collaborate, share knowledge, and access ongoing educational resources.

Partnerships with industries are essential to support lifelong learning. By working closely with employers, universities can identify the skills gaps that exist in the workforce and tailor their lifelong learning programs accordingly. For example, an AI-driven manufacturing company might collaborate with a university to develop specialized courses that teach employees how to use new AI technologies. This partnership benefits both the employees, who stay relevant in their roles, and the company, which gains a more skilled workforce (Carayannis & Morawska, 2023).

In conclusion, universities must embrace their role as lifelong educators, not only for current students but for professionals throughout their careers. By offering flexible, accessible learning opportunities, universities can ensure that their graduates remain competitive and capable in the face of continuous technological change (Shanahan & Organ, 2022).

## 4. AI AND DATA ANALYTICS IN THE CONTEXT OF INDUSTRY 5.0

### 4.1 AI-Driven Research and Learning

Artificial intelligence (AI) is one of the most transformative technologies shaping Industry 5.0, and its potential to revolutionize research and learning in universities is vast. By leveraging AI-driven tools as depicted in Figure 4, universities can enhance the quality and efficiency of both their academic research and educational offerings, empowering students and faculty to achieve more innovative, impactful outcomes (Croft, 2024).

AI in Research: AI's ability to process large datasets, identify patterns, and generate insights far exceeds the capabilities of traditional research methodologies. In fields such as engineering, medicine, and environmental science, AI-powered simulations, predictive models, and machine learning algorithms can accelerate research by automating time-consuming tasks, enabling researchers to focus on analysis and innovation. For example, AI-driven computational models in engineering can simulate real-world scenarios, optimizing designs before physical prototypes are constructed. Similarly, in the medical field, AI systems can analyze vast amounts of genetic or clinical data to identify potential treatments for diseases faster than human researchers alone (Hashim et al, 2024).

Moreover, AI facilitates interdisciplinary research, a crucial component of Industry 5.0. AI tools can analyze data across multiple fields, identifying connections between seemingly unrelated disciplines, enabling researchers to collaborate on complex, multifaceted problems. By breaking down traditional academic silos, AI empowers universities to foster cross-disciplinary innovation that addresses global challenges such as climate change, sustainability, and healthcare.

In addition to supporting research, AI plays a critical role in personalizing the learning experience. AI-powered learning platforms can tailor educational content to individual students' needs, ensuring that each learner progresses at their own pace and according to their unique learning. These platforms use algorithms to assess a student's strengths, weaknesses, and learning preferences, providing real-time feedback and recommendations for improvement. This level of personalization enhances student engagement and helps improve learning outcomes by addressing knowledge gaps more effectively.

For faculty, AI can assist in creating adaptive curricula that evolve based on student performance and feedback. AI tools can analyze data from previous courses to identify which teaching methods are most effective, helping instructors refine their approaches and improve course content over time. This creates a continuous feedback loop, where data from student interactions is used to enhance teaching strategies and better align them with the needs of the students (Carayannis & Morawska, 2023).

*Figure 4. 10 AI tools for researchers*

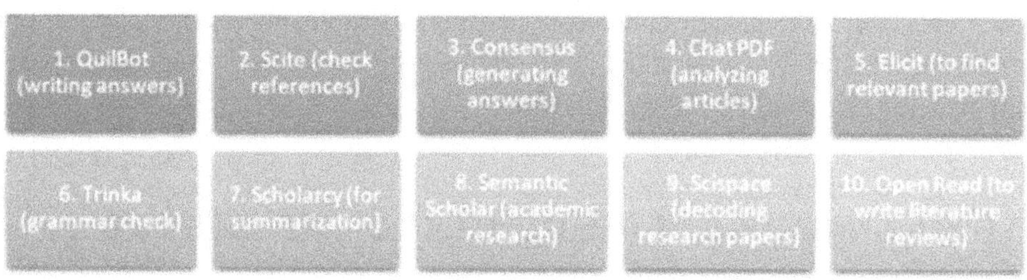

## 4.2 Data-Driven Decision Making

In the context of Industry 5.0, universities must also harness the power of data analytics to drive institutional effectiveness. Data-driven decision making enables universities to optimize operations, improve the student experience, and ensure that resources are allocated efficiently to meet both academic and administrative goals as depicted in Figure 5 (McKinsey Global Institute, 2021).

**Operational Management:** One of the most immediate benefits of data analytics is its ability to improve operational efficiency. Universities generate vast amounts of data across various departments, including student admissions, financial aid, course enrollment, campus services, and facilities management. By analyzing these datasets, universities can gain insights into patterns and trends that help them make more informed decisions. For example, predictive analytics can forecast student enrollment trends, enabling better planning for resource allocation, staffing, and campus infrastructure.

**Data Analytics:** Can also improve campus sustainability initiatives, an important aspect of Industry 5.0. By tracking energy consumption, waste management, and resource usage, universities can implement data-driven strategies to reduce their environmental footprint and promote sustainable practices. For instance, smart campus systems powered by IoT devices can monitor energy use in real time, allowing universities to adjust heating, cooling, and lighting systems based on occupancy patterns to minimize waste.

**Personalized Learning Paths:** Beyond operational efficiency, data analytics plays a crucial role in enhancing the student experience. By analyzing student performance data, universities can create personalized learning paths that adapt to the needs and aspirations of individual students. For example, learning management systems can track student progress, engagement, and performance across multiple courses, providing advisors and instructors with actionable insights to support each student's academic journey (Croft, 2024).

Universities can use data analytics to identify at-risk students early, allowing for timely interventions that improve retention and graduation rates. This proactive approach ensures that students receive the support they need, whether it's through academic advising, tutoring, or mental health services. Furthermore, data-driven insights can inform course design and curriculum development, ensuring that programs remain relevant and aligned with the demands of Industry 5.0.

**Strategic Planning and Institutional Improvement:** Data analytics can also enhance institutional planning and development. By analyzing trends in student demographics, employment outcomes, and alumni engagement, universities can better align their programs with industry needs and societal expectations. Data-driven insights enable institutions to track the success of new initiatives, assess the impact of policies, and ensure continuous improvement in both academic and administrative functions (Hashim et al, 2024).

Moreover, by combining data analytics with AI, universities can use predictive modeling to anticipate future challenges and opportunities. For example, predictive analytics can help universities understand which areas of study will be most in demand in the coming years, allowing them to adapt their offerings accordingly. Similarly, AI-driven analytics can forecast labor market trends, helping universities align their programs with the evolving needs of Industry 5.0 (Barat & Kayser, 2023).

*Figure 5. Leveraging data visualization for enhanced decision-making*

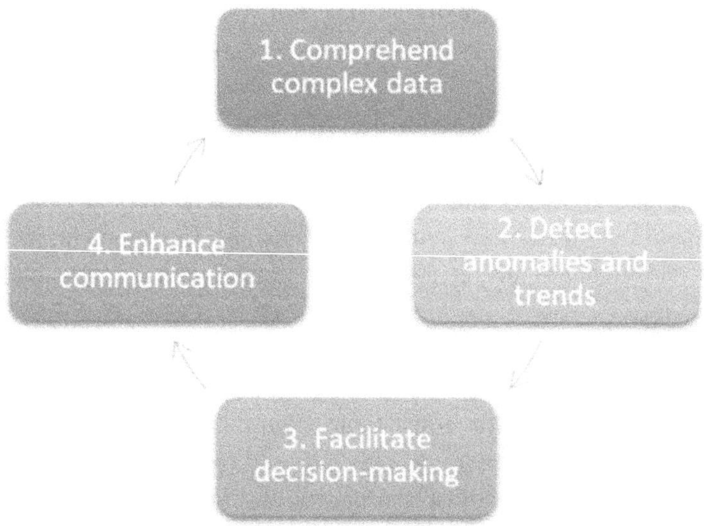


## 5. TECHNOLOGICAL INNOVATIONS IN EDUCATION

### 5.1 Human-Machine Collaboration in Learning

The concept of human-machine collaboration is a central theme of Industry 5.0, and its potential to transform education is immense. In the classroom, robotics, artificial intelligence (AI), and other advanced technologies can work alongside educators and students to create more interactive, personalized, and effective learning experiences. AI-driven learning platforms can assess each student's progress, learning style, and areas of difficulty, allowing for tailored educational content that meets individual needs as depicted in Figure 6. For example, AI systems can adjust the pace of lessons, recommend additional resources, or even suggest alternative explanations for complex topics based on a student's performance. This level of customization helps ensure that no student is left behind, while also challenging high achievers to reach their full potential.

Robotics and AI can also enhance hands-on learning. In fields such as engineering, healthcare, and robotics, students can interact with AI-driven systems and robots to simulate real-world scenarios. This allows students to develop practical skills in a controlled, low-risk environment before applying them in real-world settings. For instance, medical students might practice surgical techniques using AI-powered robotic systems, while engineering students can design and test prototypes using AI-driven simulations. Moreover, human-machine collaboration can foster greater engagement and interactivity in the classroom. AI-driven teaching assistants can provide real-time feedback on student work, answer questions, and offer additional support outside of class hours (Croft, 2024).

*Figure 6. Features of AI based learning platform*

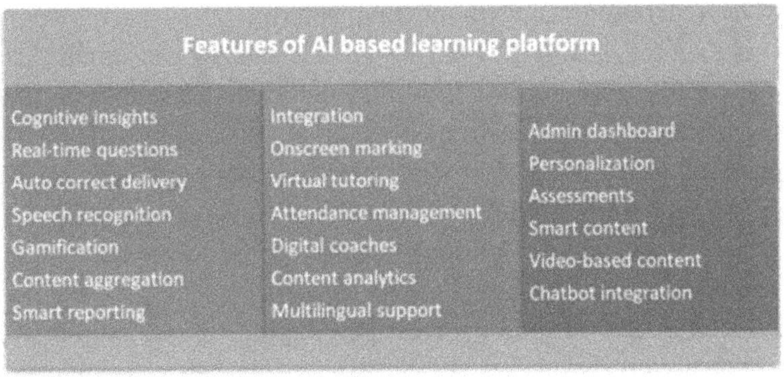


## 5.2 Smart Campuses

As universities strive to create more efficient, sustainable, and student-centered environments, the concept of the smart campus has emerged as a key technological innovation. Smart campuses leverage IoT (Internet of Things), AI, and data analytics to optimize the use of resources, improve the student experience, and promote sustainability.

At the core of a smart campus is the ability to collect and analyze data from various systems—such as energy management, security, transportation, and student services—to create a more connected and responsive campus environment. For example, IoT sensors can monitor building occupancy, temperature, and lighting to optimize energy usage in real time, ensuring that resources are used efficiently while reducing the university's environmental footprint. AI systems can predict and manage energy needs, adjusting heating, cooling, and lighting based on class schedules and student movements, further enhancing sustainability efforts.

Smart campuses also enhance safety and security. AI-driven surveillance systems, smart lighting, and real-time data analytics can improve campus security by detecting unusual patterns and responding to emergencies more quickly. For example, IoT-enabled security cameras can monitor activity across campus, while AI algorithms analyze the footage to identify potential threats or abnormal behaviors.

In addition to operational efficiency, universities can use data analytics to personalize student services, such as academic advising, career counseling, and mental health support. For instance, predictive analytics can identify students who may be at risk of academic failure or drop-out, enabling early interventions. Moreover, mobile apps can be used to streamline student interactions with campus services, from scheduling appointments to accessing learning materials, dining services, and campus transportation (Zhang & Aslan, 2021).

## 5.3 Virtual and Augmented Reality (VR/AR)

One of the most exciting technological innovations in education is the use of virtual reality (VR) and augmented reality (AR) to create immersive learning experiences. These technologies allow students to engage with educational content in new and dynamic ways, offering hands-on, experiential learning opportunities that go beyond traditional textbooks and lectures.

In fields such as engineering, healthcare, and design, VR and AR can simulate real-world scenarios, giving students the chance to practice skills and explore concepts in a safe, controlled environment. For example, in engineering education, VR environments can be used to simulate the design and testing of complex systems, allowing students to experiment with different materials, structures, and processes before implementing them in real life. Similarly, in healthcare education, medical students can use VR to simulate surgeries, patient interactions, and emergency response scenarios, honing their skills without the risks associated with real-world practice.

AR technology also enhances learning by overlaying digital content onto the real world, allowing students to interact with both physical and virtual objects simultaneously. For instance, architecture students might use AR to visualize and manipulate 3D models of buildings in real-world environments, while biology students could use AR to explore anatomical structures in a more interactive, engaging way.

Beyond these specialized fields, VR and AR can be integrated into a wide range of disciplines to enhance engagement and understanding. For example, history students could use VR to virtually explore historical sites, while art students might use AR to analyze famous works in greater detail. These immersive experiences allow students to engage with content in a more meaningful way, making abstract concepts more tangible and accessible.

In an increasingly digital world, universities are exploring ways to create more immersive online learning experiences. VR-based classrooms can simulate in-person interactions, allowing remote students to engage with their peers and instructors as if they were physically present. This not only improves the quality of online education but also expands access to educational opportunities for students who may not be able to attend traditional, on-campus classes (Zhang & Aslan, 2021).

# 6. THE FUTURE OF RESEARCH IN UNIVERSITIES

## 6.1 Interdisciplinary Research

In the age of Industry 5.0, universities are uniquely positioned to lead the charge in addressing some of the most complex and pressing challenges of our time. As these challenges—ranging from climate change and sustainability to ethical AI development and innovation—often transcend the boundaries of individual disciplines, interdisciplinary research has become critical to finding effective solutions. No single field of study can provide the knowledge and tools necessary to solve such multifaceted problems, making collaboration across various academic domains essential (Hashim et al, 2024).

Universities must foster environments that encourage cross-disciplinary research, where experts from engineering, computer science, social sciences, healthcare, business, and environmental studies can work together on common problems. For example, addressing sustainability challenges requires not only expertise in engineering and environmental science but also an understanding of economic systems, public policy, and social behavior. Similarly, the development of ethical AI systems demands collaboration between technologists, ethicists, legal scholars, and psychologists to ensure that algorithms are designed and implemented in ways that benefit society and protect individual rights.

Industry 5.0 places a significant emphasis on human-centric technology, sustainability, and ethical innovation. By breaking down the traditional silos that separate academic disciplines, universities can create more dynamic research ecosystems, where diverse perspectives and expertise come together to drive innovation and societal impact.

Moreover, interdisciplinary research often leads to breakthroughs and innovations that would be difficult or impossible to achieve within the confines of a single discipline. For example, the convergence of robotics, AI, and healthcare has led to the development of AI-driven diagnostic tools, robotic surgeries, and personalized medicine—advances that are transforming the field of medicine. In a similar vein, collaboration between environmental scientists, engineers, and urban planners is helping cities design smart, sustainable infrastructure that addresses the challenges of urbanization and climate change.

Universities that promote interdisciplinary research can serve as incubators for innovation, where students and faculty collaborate on projects that not only advance academic knowledge but also contribute to solving real-world problems (Rijwani et al, 2024).

## 6.2 AI-Enhanced Research Methodologies

One of the most transformative trends shaping the future of research in universities is the integration of AI-enhanced research methodologies. Artificial intelligence is revolutionizing how researchers approach problem-solving, allowing them to analyze vast datasets, conduct simulations, and generate insights at a scale and speed that were previously unimaginable as illustrated in Figure 7.

- **Handling Large Datasets:** In today's data-rich world, the ability to process and analyze massive amounts of information is critical for advancing research. AI-powered tools, such as machine learning algorithms, can quickly sift through large datasets, identifying patterns, trends, and anomalies that would take human researchers months or even years to detect. This capability is especially valuable in fields such as genomics, environmental science, and social sciences, where researchers are often confronted with complex, multi-dimensional datasets.

For example, in climate science, AI can analyze satellite imagery, weather data, and environmental sensors to monitor changes in the Earth's ecosystems, predict natural disasters, and assess the effectiveness of sustainability initiatives. Similarly, in healthcare, AI algorithms can analyze genetic data, patient records, and clinical trials to identify correlations and trends that can lead to new treatments or preventive measures (Zhang & Aslan, 2021).

- **Simulations and Modeling:** AI is also transforming how universities conduct simulations and modeling. In engineering, for instance, AI can be used to simulate the performance of materials and structures under various conditions, allowing researchers to test and refine designs before building physical prototypes. This not only speeds up the research process but also reduces costs and environmental impact.

In the life sciences, AI-driven simulations are being used to model biological processes at the molecular level, leading to breakthroughs in drug discovery, personalized medicine, and biotechnology. By creating virtual models of cells, tissues, and organs, researchers can test the effects of new drugs or treatments without the need for costly and time-consuming clinical trials. This accelerates the research timeline and allows scientists to explore a wider range of possibilities (Rijwani et al, 2024).

- **Generating Insights:** Beyond data analysis and simulations, AI is increasingly being used to generate novel insights and hypotheses. AI systems can autonomously explore data to uncover relationships and suggest potential avenues for further research, making it easier for researchers to identify promising areas of inquiry. For example, in physics, AI has been used to analyze particle collision data from experiments at CERN's Large Hadron Collider, leading to new insights into the fundamental nature of matter.

AI's ability to generate insights extends beyond the sciences. In the humanities and social sciences, AI can analyze large corpora of text, images, and historical data to reveal patterns in language use, cultural trends, or social behaviors over time. This has opened up new possibilities for research in fields like linguistics, anthropology, and history, where traditional methods of analysis were often limited by the sheer volume of data.

- **Ethical Considerations in AI Research:** While AI presents exciting opportunities for advancing research, it also raises important ethical questions. Universities must lead the way in ensuring that AI-enhanced research is conducted in an ethical and transparent manner. This includes addressing issues such as algorithmic bias, data privacy, and the potential for AI to perpetuate inequalities or cause harm. By developing ethical frameworks for AI research and promoting responsible AI use, universities can ensure that technological advancements serve the public interest.

*Figure 7. AI-enhanced research methodologies*

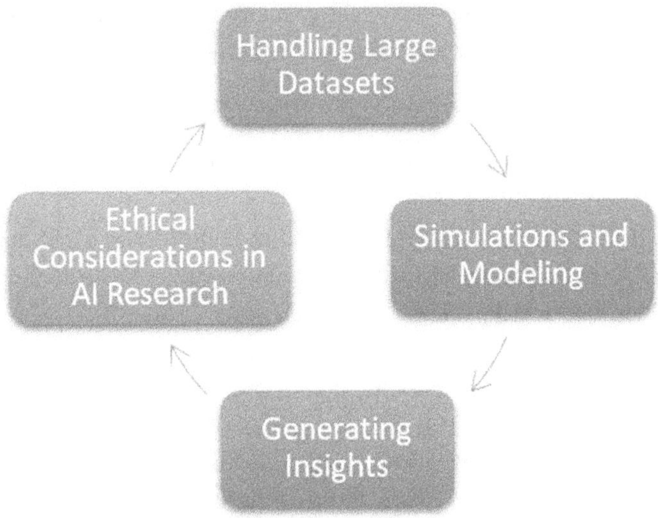


## 7. RETHINKING CURRICULA AND TEACHING METHODOLOGIES

### 7.1 Focus on Innovation, Creativity, and Soft Skills

As universities adapt to the needs of Industry 5.0, there is a growing recognition that technical skills alone are not sufficient to prepare students for the complexities of the future workforce. In this new era, creativity, innovation, collaboration, and emotional intelligence are just as important as proficiency in AI, robotics, or data analytics. These skills are essential for navigating the human-centric approach that Industry 5.0 emphasizes, where technology is used not just for efficiency but to improve societal well-being, drive personalized solutions, and foster sustainability.

Universities must rethink their curricula to ensure that students develop these critical soft skills alongside their technical competencies. Innovation and creativity can be fostered through project-based learning, where students are encouraged to think critically and devise novel solutions to real-world problems. Encouraging experimentation, risk-taking, and problem-solving in diverse teams prepares students for the dynamic challenges of Industry 5.0.

Collaboration and emotional intelligence are equally essential, as Industry 5.0 emphasizes human-machine partnerships and cross-disciplinary teamwork. In this context, universities should design courses that promote collaboration across different fields, encouraging students to work with peers from other disciplines. For example, an engineering student might collaborate with a business student to develop an AI-driven product that addresses both technical challenges and market viability. Emotional intelligence, including empathy, adaptability, and communication, is crucial for effective teamwork and leadership in such interdisciplinary contexts.

Additionally, teaching methodologies must encourage lifelong learning and adaptability. In a rapidly changing technological landscape, students need the skills and mindset to continuously update their knowledge throughout their careers. Embedding the principles of lifelong learning into university programs will ensure that graduates are not only ready for the workforce but are also prepared to evolve with it (Shanahan & Organ, 2022).

## 7.2 Integration of AI and Digital Tools in Teaching

The integration of AI and digital tools into the teaching and learning process is a core component of Industry 5.0's impact on education. Universities must embrace these technologies to create more interactive, personalized, and effective learning environments.

One of the most powerful applications of AI in education is its ability to personalize the learning experience. AI-driven learning platforms can analyze student performance data to identify individual learning patterns, strengths, and weaknesses. This enables the creation of customized learning paths tailored to each student's unique needs. For instance, students who struggle with specific concepts can receive additional exercises and resources, while those who excel can be challenged with more advanced material. This level of personalization not only enhances learning outcomes but also improves student engagement and motivation (Ajani, Gamede & Bansal, 2024).

AI can also support adaptive learning systems, where the content dynamically adjusts in real time based on the learner's progress as depicted in Figure 8. For example, AI algorithms can assess how well students are grasping a subject and adjust the difficulty level of exercises, accordingly, ensuring that each learner is challenged without becoming overwhelmed. AI tutors or virtual teaching assistants can provide real-time feedback, answer questions, and offer support to students outside of traditional class hours, providing a more flexible and responsive learning environment.

Incorporating digital tools such as virtual laboratories, simulations, and online collaboration platforms into curricula is also key to preparing students for Industry 5.0. For example, engineering students can use AI-powered simulations to test their designs in virtual environments, while medical students can practice procedures using AI-driven virtual patients. These technologies not only make learning more engaging but also provide practical, hands-on experiences that are critical for mastering complex skills (Ajani, Gamede & Bansal, 2024).

*Figure 8. Benefits of adaptive learning*

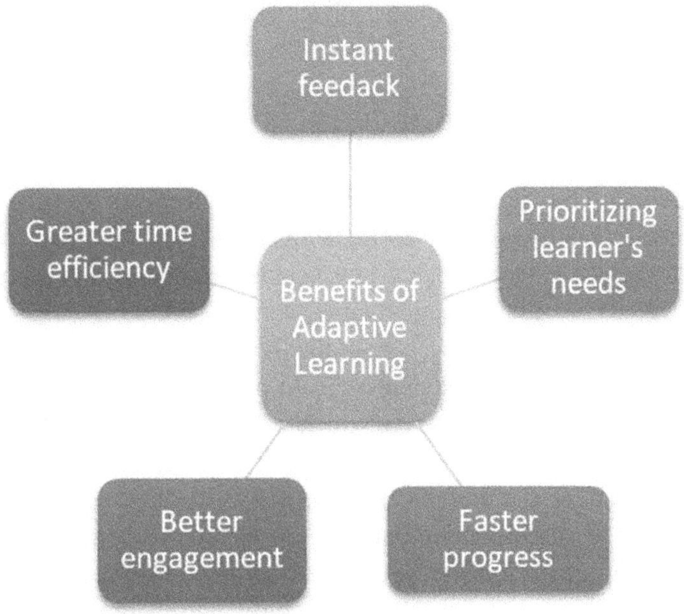


## 7.3 CDIO Approach in Industry 5.0

The "Conceive, Design, Implement, Operate" (CDIO) approach, which is widely used in engineering education, is well-suited to the demands of Industry 5.0. The CDIO framework provides a structured method for teaching students how to design and implement complex systems, and it can be enhanced with AI and other Industry 5.0 technologies to prepare students for the challenges they will face in the future workforce.

In the context of Industry 5.0, the CDIO model can be augmented with AI-driven tools to help students better understand and manage the complex interactions between human, technological, and environmental systems. For example, during the "Conceive" phase, students can use AI to gather and analyze large datasets to inform the conceptual design of their projects. AI tools can help identify trends, simulate potential outcomes, and suggest innovative solutions based on real-world data.

During the "Design" phase, AI-driven simulations can allow students to visualize and test their designs in virtual environments. This gives them the ability to identify potential design flaws early in the process, saving time and resources. The "Implement" phase can incorporate robotics, automation, and smart technologies, teaching students how to integrate cutting-edge Industry 5.0 tools into real-world applications. Finally, in the "Operate" phase, students can learn how to manage the systems they have created, using AI and IoT tools to monitor performance, optimize processes, and ensure sustainability.

The CDIO approach also emphasizes collaboration and teamwork, mirroring the interdisciplinary nature of Industry 5.0. Students are encouraged to work in teams that bring together diverse skill sets and perspectives, allowing them to practice the kind of cross-disciplinary problem-solving that will be crucial in the Industry 5.0 workforce. By incorporating AI, robotics, and other digital tools into the CDIO framework, universities can ensure that their graduates are not only skilled in technical problem-solving but also adept at navigating the broader ethical, societal, and environmental implications of their work.

## 8. COLLABORATION BETWEEN UNIVERSITIES AND INDUSTRY

As Industry 5.0 redefines the workforce, collaboration between universities and industries has become increasingly important. University-industry partnerships also foster research and innovation that can directly contribute to societal and technological advancement as depicted in Figure 9.

- **Practical Exposure and Internships**: One of the most significant benefits of university-industry partnerships is the opportunity for students to gain practical experience through internships and cooperative education programs. These real-world experiences provide students with valuable exposure to the technologies, methodologies, and collaborative practices used in today's industries, particularly in sectors impacted by Industry 5.0, such as manufacturing, healthcare, and technology. Universities can strengthen these partnerships by embedding industry-based projects into their curricula. For instance, engineering students might collaborate with local manufacturers to develop AI-driven systems, or business students could work with tech startups on market strategies for personalized products. These hands-on projects, co-developed with industry partners, not only enhance students' employability but also contribute to solving real-world problems faced by companies (Mitchell & Guile, 2021).
- **Research Partnerships**: University-industry collaboration is equally vital for advancing research and innovation. By aligning academic research with industry needs, universities can contribute directly to the development of new technologies and processes that will define the future of Industry 5.0. These partnerships foster a culture of innovation where cutting-edge ideas are tested and refined in real-world settings. Industries benefit from access to the latest academic research and technologies, while universities gain insights into the challenges and demands faced by businesses.
- **Industry-Specific Education and Training Programs:** Tailoring academic programs in partnership with industries ensures that graduates have the knowledge and skills required to meet evolving market demands. This might include incorporating emerging technologies such as AI, data analytics, robotics, and the Internet of Things (IoT) into existing courses or developing entirely new programs that focus on specialized areas such as sustainable manufacturing, personalized healthcare, or ethical AI. For example, a university's engineering program could partner with an automotive manufacturer to offer courses in autonomous vehicle technology, while a business school could collaborate with a tech company to create a curriculum on data-driven decision-making. These programs would be continuously updated based on feedback from industry partners, ensuring that graduates are equipped with the most relevant and up-to-date skills (Lantada, 2022).
- **Workforce Development and Continuing Education:** Universities can play a key role in providing continuing education programs and professional training that allow employees to upskill or reskill as new technologies emerge. For instance, a manufacturing company transitioning to AI-driven production might partner with a university to offer specialized training for its employees in areas such as robotics, data analytics, or AI integration. Similarly, healthcare providers adopting

personalized medicine technologies could collaborate with universities to develop training programs that teach healthcare professionals how to use AI tools for patient diagnosis and treatment.

Universities that offer flexible learning options, such as microcredentials, online courses, and certificate programs, can cater to the needs of both current students and working professionals. Moreover, these partnerships can result in shared resources, such as specialized research labs or innovation hubs where students, academics, and industry professionals collaborate on joint projects. This fosters an ecosystem of learning, innovation, and growth that benefits both academia and industry.

*Figure 9. Industry-academia collaboration*

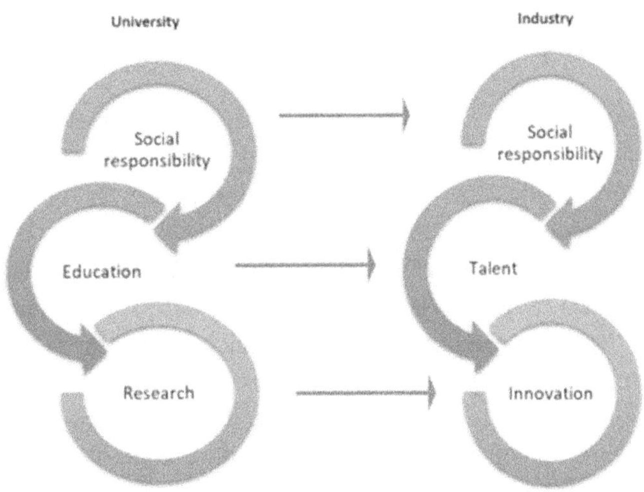


## 9. THE ROLE OF UNIVERSITIES IN PROMOTING SOCIAL RESPONSIBILITY

### 9.1 Education for Sustainability and Ethics

Higher education institutions are not only responsible for preparing students for the workforce but also for instilling values that emphasize the responsible and ethical use of technology. As society becomes more reliant on AI, robotics, and other advanced systems, universities must ensure that their graduates are equipped with a deep understanding of the ethical implications of these technologies and their potential impact on the environment and society.

Universities must play an active role in embedding sustainability and ethics across all disciplines, particularly in fields like engineering, business, and computer science, where technological innovation is at the forefront. For example, programs focused on AI and robotics should include discussions on the ethical considerations surrounding automation, privacy, data **security**, and algorithmic bias. Students need to understand the societal implications of their work, including how technology can contribute to inequality or exacerbate environmental degradation if not used responsibly.

Furthermore, universities should lead efforts to integrate sustainability principles into their curricula, ensuring that future generations of professionals prioritize the development of sustainable technologies and practices. This might involve offering specialized courses on renewable energy, circular economy models, and sustainable urban development, or incorporating sustainability into existing programs. For instance, engineering students could design products or systems with sustainability in mind, learning how to minimize resource use and reduce waste, while business students might explore strategies for creating environmentally responsible supply chains.

In this regard, universities serve as ethical stewards, guiding technological development toward goals that benefit society and the planet. By fostering a culture of sustainability and ethical responsibility, universities can help shape the next generation of leaders who will ensure that technological progress aligns with the long-term well-being of humanity and the environment (Rame, Purwanto & Sudarno, 2024).

## 9.2 Community Engagement and Societal Well-Being

Beyond preparing students for the workforce, universities play a pivotal role in addressing broader societal challenges, such as healthcare, social justice, and environmental sustainability. As centers of research and innovation, universities can contribute to the development of solutions that improve societal well-being and promote community engagement.

One of the most important ways universities can fulfill this responsibility is by promoting community-focused research and outreach programs. Universities have the capacity to engage with local communities, governments, and NGOs to tackle pressing issues such as healthcare disparities, environmental degradation, and social inequality. By partnering with community organizations, universities can ensure that their research is grounded in real-world problems and directly contributes to societal progress.

For example, universities can collaborate with local healthcare providers to develop AI-driven solutions for improving patient outcomes, particularly in underserved communities. Similarly, partnerships with environmental organizations can enable universities to conduct research on sustainable resource management, biodiversity conservation, and climate change mitigation. These initiatives not only contribute to scientific advancement but also provide tangible benefits to society.

Additionally, universities have a responsibility to foster a sense of social justice among students and faculty. In the context of Industry 5.0, where technology is reshaping the workforce and economic systems, universities must address the potential for job displacement, inequality, and the digital divide. By promoting research and education that focus on equity and access, universities can help ensure that the benefits of Industry 5.0 are distributed fairly across society (Rame, Purwanto & Sudarno, 2024).

Universities should also encourage student-led initiatives that contribute to community well-being. These might include volunteer programs, social entrepreneurship projects, or sustainability efforts that address local or global challenges. By providing students with opportunities to engage with real-world problems, universities can empower them to become active contributors to societal change, both during their studies and in their future careers (Martini, Bellisario & Coletti, 2024).

## 10. CHALLENGES AND OPPORTUNITIES

### 10.1 Digital Divide and Access to Technology

As universities embrace advanced technologies to prepare students for Industry 5.0, they must also confront the challenge of the digital divide. The increasing reliance on AI, data analytics, robotics, and other emerging technologies in education and research has the potential to exacerbate existing inequalities, particularly for students and communities with limited access to these resources. Ensuring equitable access to technology is essential if universities are to fulfill their role as inclusive institutions that provide opportunities for all.

Students from disadvantaged backgrounds may lack access to the necessary digital tools, including laptops, high-speed internet, and even basic digital literacy. This disparity creates unequal learning environments, where some students have the technological resources to thrive while others are left behind. Universities must take proactive steps to bridge this digital divide, ensuring that all students have the tools and support they need to succeed in a technology-driven world.

To address this challenge, universities can implement programs that provide low-cost or subsidized access to devices, software, and internet services for students in need. Additionally, establishing digital literacy programs can help students from diverse backgrounds acquire the skills required to navigate advanced learning platforms and AI-driven tools. Universities can also create more public digital spaces such as smart classrooms, computer labs, and digital resource centers that are accessible to all students, providing equal opportunities for engagement with technology (Ajani, Gamede & Bansal, 2024).

Partnering with industries, governments, and non-profit organizations can further assist universities in reducing the digital divide. These collaborations can fund initiatives that ensure students and faculty have access to the latest technologies and can use them effectively to enhance learning outcomes and innovation.

### 10.2 Faculty Training and Development

As technology becomes increasingly integrated into the fabric of education and research, faculty training and development is crucial. For universities to fully leverage the potential of Industry 5.0 technologies—such as AI-driven learning platforms, virtual and augmented reality, and robotics—faculty must be equipped with the necessary skills to integrate these tools into their teaching and research practices.

However, many faculty members may be unfamiliar with the rapidly evolving technological landscape, leading to a skills gap that hinders the effective use of these tools in the classroom. This is particularly true in fields where digital tools are transforming traditional methodologies, such as in engineering, healthcare, business, and the social sciences. For instance, professors who are experts in their academic fields may lack the digital proficiency to employ AI systems in course design or data analytics in research projects.

Universities must invest in continuous professional development programs that upskill faculty in the use of advanced technologies. Workshops, certifications, and hands-on training sessions can be implemented to ensure faculty members are not only comfortable using these tools but also able to apply them effectively in ways that enrich students' learning experiences. These programs should be flexible and tailored to meet the varying levels of technological proficiency among faculty members, ensuring that everyone can benefit regardless of their starting point.

## 10.3 Funding and Resource Allocation

Integrating advanced technologies such as AI, IoT, robotics, and virtual/augmented reality into educational and research programs requires substantial investments in infrastructure, training, and software. These technologies also need to be updated regularly to keep pace with the rapid advancements in the field, placing additional strain on university budgets.

Universities must carefully consider how to allocate their resources in ways that maximize impact while maintaining financial sustainability. Strategic planning is essential to ensure that investments in technology are aligned with institutional goals and deliver long-term value. For instance, universities may need to prioritize the development of smart classrooms, AI-driven learning platforms, or research centers that focus on areas of high societal impact, such as sustainability or healthcare.

To meet these financial demands, universities can explore diverse funding sources, including partnerships with industries, government grants, and philanthropic support. Collaborations with the private sector, for example, can provide funding for cutting-edge technology, while government programs may offer grants for research and development projects that align with national priorities. Additionally, alumni networks and **corporate** sponsors can be engaged to support specific initiatives, such as scholarships, innovation labs, or sustainability projects (Ramu, 2019).

Universities may also need to reimagine their revenue generation models, particularly by expanding online education and lifelong learning programs. By offering microcredentials, certificate programs, and professional development courses, universities can tap into new revenue streams while providing valuable services to working professionals looking to upskill or reskill in the era of Industry 5.0.

Finally, it is important for universities to adopt cost-effective strategies for resource allocation. This might include sharing resources with other institutions through consortiums, adopting cloud-based services to reduce infrastructure costs, and utilizing open-source software to lower expenses.

# 11. RECOMMENDATIONS

## 11.1 Strategies for Universities

To successfully adapt to the demands of Industry 5.0, universities must adopt innovative strategies that integrate new technologies, foster interdisciplinary collaboration, and promote human-centered approaches in education and research. Below are several practical recommendations for universities to embrace Industry 5.0 principles in both their educational programs and operational practices:

1. **Integrate Human-Centered Technologies into Curricula:** Universities should prioritize the integration of AI, robotics, IoT, and other advanced technologies across disciplines. Courses that combine technical expertise with creativity, emotional intelligence, and ethical responsibility should be introduced to prepare students for the human-centric nature of Industry 5.0. This can include AI-driven personalized learning platforms and collaborative problem-solving projects that simulate real-world challenges
2. **Promote Interdisciplinary Research and Education:** Universities should break down academic silos and foster interdisciplinary collaboration. Research programs and curricula should encourage students and faculty from different fields—such as engineering, social sciences, healthcare, and

business—to collaborate on projects that address complex societal challenges like sustainability, healthcare, and ethical AI development. Interdisciplinary labs, research centers, and joint programs can facilitate these partnerships.

3. **Emphasize Lifelong Learning and Microcredentials:** To keep pace with the rapid technological advancements of Industry 5.0, universities should offer flexible learning opportunities beyond traditional degree programs. Microcredentials, certificates, and online learning platforms tailored to professionals seeking to upskill or reskill should be an integral part of the university's offerings. These programs can ensure that graduates and working professionals remain competitive in a constantly evolving job market.
4. **Invest in Smart Campus Infrastructure:** Universities should invest in smart campus technologies that leverage IoT, AI, and data analytics to create efficient, sustainable, and student-centered environments. Smart systems can optimize energy usage, enhance security, and improve resource management. Additionally, universities should develop digital platforms that offer seamless integration of campus services and personalized support for students.
5. **Upskill Faculty in Emerging Technologies:** Faculty development programs should be a priority. Universities need to offer ongoing training for instructors to familiarize them with AI-driven teaching tools, virtual and augmented reality, data analytics, and robotics. This can be achieved through workshops, certification programs, and collaborations with industry experts. Faculty who are comfortable with these technologies will be better equipped to guide students in mastering the skills required for Industry 5.0.
6. **Enhance Industry Collaboration:** Establishing and strengthening partnerships with industries is vital for keeping curricula and research aligned with real-world needs. Universities should co-design programs with industry experts, offer internships, and involve students in industry-based projects. These collaborations can also provide access to the latest technologies and insights while facilitating the transition of research from academia to practical applications.
7. **Foster a Culture of Innovation and Entrepreneurship:** Universities should create environments that encourage students to innovate and pursue entrepreneurial ventures. This can be achieved by establishing incubators, innovation hubs, and funding opportunities for student startups. By fostering entrepreneurial mindsets, universities can equip students to become leaders and innovators in Industry 5.0.

## 11.2 Policy and Governance

For universities to fully embrace Industry 5.0 principles, educational policymakers and governments must play an active role in supporting this transition. The following are key recommendations for how policy and governance can enable universities to thrive in the Industry 5.0 era:

1. **Develop Supportive Educational Policies**: Governments should develop policies that encourage universities to integrate emerging technologies into their curricula and research. This could include financial incentives for universities that adopt AI, robotics, and data analytics in their programs, as well as grants and funding for research in human-machine collaboration, sustainability, and ethical innovation.

2. **Create National Frameworks for Lifelong Learning:** Policymakers should support lifelong learning initiatives by creating national frameworks for microcredentials and continuing education. These frameworks should provide guidelines for accrediting microcredential programs, ensuring they meet industry standards and are recognized by employers. This will encourage universities to offer short, flexible courses that align with market needs, while also helping professionals stay competitive in the workforce.
3. **Support University-Industry Collaboration:** Governments should encourage partnerships between universities and industries by providing incentives for collaborative research and innovation projects. Tax credits, public-private research grants, and innovation hubs supported by government funding can accelerate technology transfer from academia to industry. These initiatives will ensure that the latest research is applied in real-world contexts and that universities remain aligned with the needs of the modern workforce.
4. **Invest in Smart Campus Infrastructure and Digital Equity:** To help universities become more efficient and sustainable, governments should provide funding for the development of smart campus infrastructures that use IoT, AI, and renewable energy. Additionally, policymakers must address the digital divide by investing in digital equity programs that ensure all students, regardless of socioeconomic background, have access to the technology and resources necessary for success in a digitally driven world.
5. **Foster International Collaboration:** Policymakers should encourage universities to engage in international collaborations that promote the exchange of ideas, research, and technologies related to Industry 5.0. Governments can support joint research initiatives, international student and faculty exchanges, and partnerships with foreign universities. These collaborations will not only enhance the global competitiveness of universities but also ensure that students are exposed to diverse perspectives and cutting-edge research in global innovation.
6. **Establish Ethical Guidelines for Emerging Technologies:** Governments and policymakers should work with universities and industries to create ethical frameworks for the development and deployment of advanced technologies. These guidelines should address key issues such as AI transparency, data privacy, algorithmic bias, and the societal impact of automation. Universities can play a role in helping shape these policies through research and thought leadership in ethical technology use. By fostering supportive policies and governance frameworks, educational policymakers and governments can empower universities to fully embrace Industry 5.0, driving both technological innovation and societal progress.

## REFERENCES


Ajani, O. A., Gamede, B. T., & Bansal, R. (2024). Challenges and Opportunities of Integrating Industry 5.0 and Emerging Technologies in Higher Education for Enhancing Employability Skills. In Chakir, A., Bansal, R., & Azzouazi, M. (Eds.), *Industry 5.0 and Emerging Technologies. Studies in Systems, Decision and Control* (Vol. 565). Springer., DOI: 10.1007/978-3-031-70996-8_11

Barata, J., & Kayser, I. (2023) Industry 5.0 – Past, Present, and Near Future. *Procedia Computer Science*. vol 219: 778-788. ISSN 1877-0509. https://doi.org/DOI: 10.1016/j.procs.2023.01.351

Brynjolfsson, E., & McAfee, A. (2014) The second machine age: Work, progress, and prosperity in a time of brilliant technologies. W W Norton & Co. The second machine age: Work, progress, and prosperity in a time of brilliant technologies.

Carayannis, E. G., & Morawska, J. (2023). University and Education 5.0 for Emerging Trends, Policies and Practices in the Concept of Industry 5.0 and Society 5.0. In Machado, C. F., & Davim, J. P. (Eds.), *Industry 5.0*. Springer., DOI: 10.1007/978-3-031-26232-6_1

Croft, D. (2024) Guide: Industry 5.0. *Learn Lean* Sigma. [online] Available at: https://www.learnleansigma .com/guides/industry-5-0/

Hashim, M., Tlemsani, I., Mason-Jones, R., Matthews, R., & Ndrecaj, V. (2024) Higher education via the lens of industry 5.0: Strategy and perspective. *Social Sciences & Humanities Open*. vol 9. ISSN 2590-2911. https://doi.org/DOI: 10.1016/j.ssaho.2024.100828

Lantada, A. D. (2022). Engineering Education 5.0: Strategies for a Successful Transformative Project-Based Learning. In Bouezzeddine, M. (Ed.), *Insights Into Global Engineering Education After the Birth of Industry 5.0.*, DOI: 10.5772/intechopen.102844

Martini, B., Bellisario, D., & Coletti, P. (2024). Human-Centered and Sustainable Artificial Intelligence in Industry 5.0: Challenges and Perspectives. *Sustainability (Basel)*, 16(13), 5448. Advance online publication. DOI: 10.3390/su16135448

McKinsey Global Institute (2021) *McKinsey Global Surveys, 2021: A Year in Review*. mckinsey-global-surveys-2021-a-year-in-review.pdf

Mitchell, J., & Guile, D. (2021). Fusion skills and industry 5.0: conceptions and challenges. In Bouezzeddine, M. (Ed.), *Insights Into Global Engineering Education After the Birth of Industry 5.0.*, DOI: 10.5772/intechopen.100096

Rame, R., Purwanto, P., & Sudarno, S. (2024) Industry 5.0 and sustainability: An overview of emerging trends and challenges for a green future. *Innovation and Green Development*. 3(4). ISSN 2949-7531. https://doi.org/DOI: 10.1016/j.igd.2024.100173

Ramu, NB (2019) Management Challenges and Opportunities of Industry 5.0. *India's Changing Paradigm: Skills and Entrepreneurship for Global Competitiveness*. 62-68 (PDF) Management Challenges and Opportunities of Industry 5.0

Rijwani, T., Kumari, S., Srinivas, R., Abhishek, K., Iyer, G., Vara, H., Dubey, S., Revathi, V., & Gupta, M. (2024). Industry 5.0: A review of emerging trends and transformative technologies in the next industrial revolution. *International Journal on Interactive Design and Manufacturing*. Advance online publication. DOI: 10.1007/s12008-024-01943-7

Shanahan, B. W., & Organ, J. (2022) Harnessing the Benefits of Micro Credentials for Industry 4.0 and 5.0: Skills Training and Lifelong Learning. *IFAC-PapersOnLine*. 55(39):82-87. ISSN 2405-8963. https://doi.org/DOI: 10.1016/j.ifacol.2022.12.015

Tao, F., Zhang, M., & Nee, A. Y. C. (Eds.). (2019). *Digital Twin Driven Smart Manufacturing*. Academic Press., DOI: 10.1016/B978-0-12-817630-6.00014-X

World Economic Forum. (2021) *Annual Report 2020-2021*. Annual Report 2020-2021 | World Economic Forum

Zhang, K., & Aslan, A. B. (2021) AI technologies for education: Recent research & future directions. *Computers and Education: Artificial Intelligence*. vol 2. ISSN 2666-920X. https://doi.org/DOI: 10.1016/j.caeai.2021.100025

# Chapter 2
# Sustainable Universities as Catalysts for Industry 5.0 Transformation

**Jean H. El Achkar**
*Australian University, Kuwait*

## ABSTRACT

*Industry 5.0 represents a significant shift, combining human creativity with advanced technologies to achieve sustainable and human-centered industrial practices. Universities play a critical role in this transformation by encouraging innovation, interdisciplinary research, and collaboration with industry, all while incorporating sustainability into their operations. This chapter investigates how universities advance the Sustainable Development Goals (SDGs) by implementing initiatives such as green campuses, smart technologies, and ISO standards that promote sustainable practices. It focuses on current sustainability practices in universities worldwide, such as renewable energy adoption, waste reduction, and project-based learning. Key challenges such as financial constraints, cultural resistance, and skill gaps are addressed through solutions such as public-private partnerships, green bonds, and adaptive curricula. The chapter concludes with policy recommendations for incentivizing sustainable infrastructure, developing global research networks, and implementing sustainability KPIs.*

## 1. THE EVOLUTION OF INDUSTRY 5.0

Industry 5.0 signifies a fundamental change in the industrial sector, where human intellect is flawlessly combined with cutting-edge technology like artificial intelligence (AI), the Internet of Things (IoT), robotics, and big data analytics (Ghobakhloo et al., 2024). This phase follows the progression from Industry 1.0, which introduced mechanization, to Industry 2.0 with mass production, Industry 3.0 with automation, and Industry 4.0 with digitalization (Atif, 2023). Industry 5.0 diverges by prioritizing the harmonious integration of human creativity and technical innovation rather than merely focusing

DOI: 10.4018/979-8-3693-8181-6.ch002

on automation and efficiency (Xu et al., 2021). The vision entails a future where humans and robots cooperate, employing their strengths to attain unparalleled productivity, innovation, and sustainability.

The fundamental elements of Industry 5.0 signify a transition towards a more human-centered and sustainable industrial ecosystem (Martini et al., 2024). This transformation centers on resource efficiency, requiring industries to reduce operational costs while minimizing waste across the product lifecycle. This entails implementing innovative methods that optimize resource utilization, ensuring minimal environmental impact while maintaining productivity. Businesses within the Industry 5.0 paradigm must synchronize their operational strategies with sustainable practices, prioritizing resource efficiency. Figure 1 illustrates the core components of Industry 5.0, highlighting the balance between human ingenuity, advanced technologies, and sustainability. These elements are essential in shaping the future of industrial ecosystems, where efficiency, ethical governance, and innovation converge to meet the challenges of modern industries.

*Figure 1. Core components of industry 5.0*

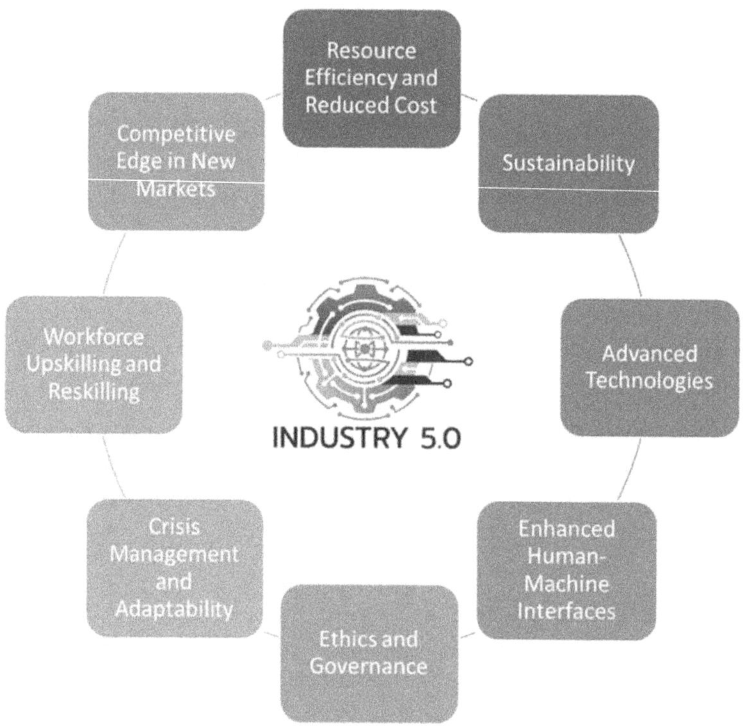


Upskilling and reskilling the workforce are pivotal elements of Industry 5.0 (Sachan et al., 2024). As advanced technologies such as AI, IoT, and robotics become more integrated into industrial processes, it is urgent to equip the human workforce with the requisite skills to collaborate with machines. Industry 5.0 envisions a future in which humans and machines collaborate, with humans focusing on tasks that require creativity, complex decision-making, and problem-solving rather than being replaced by technology. Continuous education and training initiatives will be crucial for employees to succeed in this context, facilitating their adaptation to positions that complement and improve technological progress.

The shift to Industry 5.0 provides a competitive advantage in emerging markets. The capacity for swift innovation, adapting to changing customer needs, and creating customized products affords companies a competitive edge (Elangovan, 2021). By developing the synergistic potential of human-machine interactions, businesses can react promptly to market fluctuations, provide personalized products, and exploit new opportunities emerging from technological progress. Incorporating sophisticated analytics and AI can expand market forecasting, improve customer engagement, and optimize product development processes, allowing businesses to maintain a competitive edge.

Developing enhanced interfaces is integral to this human-machine collaboration (Rani et al., 2024; Yang et al., 2024). Unlike in previous industrial revolutions, where machines operated independently of human input, Industry 5.0 promotes a more symbiotic relationship. Developing insightful interfaces that bridge the gap between human cognition and machine operation is central to achieving this. These interfaces empower workers to harness the full potential of automation and AI while maintaining control over key strategic and ethical decisions. The goal is to improve efficiency and enhance human capabilities, allowing for unmatched levels of innovation and productivity.

The technological foundation of Industry 5.0 is comprised of radical technologies such as AI, IoT, robotics, and machine learning, facilitating real-time data processing, intelligent decision-making, and autonomous operations. In contrast to Industry 4.0, which prioritized these technologies within industrial processes, Industry 5.0 underscores the collaborative integration of these technologies with human insight and intuition (Panagou et al., 2024). In this framework, machines serve as automation tools and collaborators that augment human creativity, offering novel opportunities for innovation, design, and problem-solving.

The ability to navigate unforeseen challenges, including natural disasters or supply chain disruptions, is essential in this era of swift transformation (Agrawal et al., 2024). Crisis management and adaptability are imperative elements of Industry 5.0, wherein enterprises must exhibit resilience during global crises. Organizations can use AI and predictive analytics to formulate more resilient risk management strategies, guaranteeing readiness for potential disruptions (Ivanov, 2023; Leng et al., 2023). Adaptability is incorporated into business models, facilitating swift modifications in production, supply chains, and workforce management to mitigate the effects of unexpected challenges. In addition to these technological and strategic elements, cultural factors are crucial in driving organizational flexibility and performance during times of change, especially as businesses shift their Route to Market. COVID-19, digital-first realities, and lean structures underscore the need for cultural reassessment to build organizational resilience and adaptability (Saksena & Jha, 2024).

Furthermore, as technology's influence on decision-making expands, an escalating focus is on ethics and governance (Longo et al., 2020; Rehman & Umar, 2024). As businesses embrace more sophisticated technologies, ensuring these innovations are utilized responsibly and ethically is essential. Data privacy, AI governance, and human rights concerns must be resolved to prevent technological misuse. Transparent governance frameworks are crucial to guarantee that technological advancements serve societal interests while mitigating risks and adverse effects. The ethical implications of Industry 5.0 extend beyond simple regulatory compliance; companies must actively protect individual dignity and rights while fostering trust in technology.

Sustainability is a central focus of Industry 5.0 (van Erp et al., 2024). This period recognizes the critical need to balance technological progress and environmental, social, and economic viability. Sustainability in Industry 5.0 extends beyond the ordinary reduction of carbon footprints. It involves establishing robust systems and procedures that can effectively tackle the complex issues presented by climate change, resource depletion, and societal injustices. Furthermore, these systems and processes should be able to adapt and remain resilient in the face of such challenges.

Sustainable universities are key drivers of Industry 5.0, advancing innovation through interdisciplinary research, sustainability-focused curricula, and ethical governance. They prepare future generations for human-machine collaboration by fostering technical expertise, creativity, and adaptability. This chapter explores how universities catalyze Industry 5.0 by adopting ISO-aligned sustainability practices, such as energy management and social responsibility while leveraging smart campuses, renewable energy, and project-based learning. It emphasizes key performance indicators like energy efficiency, waste reduction, and social equity. Financial, cultural, and educational barriers are addressed, with actionable policies proposed to position universities as leaders in sustainability and Industry 5.0 transformation.

## 2. THE ROLE OF UNIVERSITIES IN INDUSTRY 5.0

Universities play a transformative role in advancing Industry 5.0 by integrating sustainability, fostering innovation, and preparing future generations for human-machine collaboration. This section explores the multifaceted contributions of universities in promoting sustainable development goals (SDGs), revolutionizing education, driving research and innovation, and fostering interdisciplinary collaboration to address the complex challenges of Industry 5.0.

### 2.1. Promoting Sustainable Development Goals (SDGs)

Today, universities should make significant progress toward sustainability, maintaining their commitment to high-quality education while remaining financially viable and responsible. Their mission-driven approaches to education will contribute to SDGs such as quality education, economic growth, and innovation (Alcántara-Rubio et al., 2022; Cuesta-Claros et al., 2024). Universities must take a balanced approach to "shareholderism" and "stakeholderism", which benefits both shareholders and the community (Mayer, 2020). Universities are crucial in integrating Industry 5.0 into higher education. Awareness in this industry is emerging but limited, requiring innovative methods for effective implementation. Emphasizing human-centric elements, Industry 5.0 enhances operational efficiency, growth, and sustainable development. It offers strategic opportunities for resilience and sustainability, focusing on societal and environmental contributions. A tetra-dimensional empirical model that universities and other institutions should follow covers theoretical, application, technical, and practice dimensions for integration (Mohamed Hashim et al., 2024). The theoretical dimension focuses on developing frameworks that incorporate sustainability and human-centric technologies. The application dimension involves introducing practical and applied courses that engage students with real-world Industry 5.0 challenges. The technical dimension ensures that institutions provide access to the latest Industry 5.0 tools, technologies, and advanced manufacturing systems. Finally, the practice dimension stresses industrial partnerships to build and test sustainable solutions to boost economic growth and reduce inequality.

Figure 2 illustrates universities' vital role in advancing multiple SDGs through their core activities: High-Quality Education, Research and Innovation, Sustainable Campus Operations, Community Engagement, and Governance and Leadership. The figure highlights the primary SDGs addressed by these activities, showcasing how universities contribute to quality education, innovation and sustainable industry, responsible consumption, and climate action, among others. Universities balance technological innovation with social and environmental responsibility by fostering an environment that integrates Industry 5.0 principles (Pactwa et al., 2024). This places them as major drivers of sustainable development, enabling them to lead in creating resilient and inclusive futures.

*Figure 2. The role of universities in advancing Sustainable Development Goals (SDGs) through Industry 5.0*

## 2.2. Revolutionizing Education

As the world progresses toward Industry 5.0, universities are pivotal in cultivating the future workforce to address the changing requirements of this new industrial epoch. To achieve this function, universities must undergo significant transformations, particularly in educational program design and delivery. The transition is mainly built on integrating sophisticated technologies, multidisciplinary studies, and a strong emphasis on sustainability principles into curricula. Universities that promote a broad and innovative educational framework can better equip students to navigate and prosper in the intricate industrial landscape of the future (Tasdemir & Gazo, 2020).

Digital literacy is central to this transformation (Gutiérrez-Ángel et al., 2022). As Industry 5.0 progressively integrates human intelligence with advanced technologies, universities must guarantee that students develop strong digital competencies. These skills go beyond basic computer literacy and include experience in data analysis, machine learning, and the ethical implications of digital technologies. By integrating these skills across disciplines, universities can create a digitally literate workforce capable of responding to and supporting innovation.

Alongside digital competencies, interdisciplinary education is essential. Industry 5.0 requires people capable of transcending traditional silos, integrating skills from fields such as engineering, social sciences, business, and environmental studies. Universities can fulfill this requirement by creating inter/trans-disciplinary courses such as project-based learning (PBL) frameworks that encourage student collaboration. This fosters creativity and critical thinking while equipping students to address intricate, real-world issues necessitating a multifaceted viewpoint.

An essential element of aligning education with Industry 5.0 is the integration of sustainability principles into the fundamental university curricula. Students must be proficient in sustainability principles as the industrial landscape transitions to more sustainable and ethical production practices. Universities can spearhead this initiative by incorporating environmental stewardship, resource efficiency, and circular economy principles into their curricula. They adopt a generation of technologically proficient professionals dedicated to promoting sustainable innovation.

Moreover, universities can cultivate experiential learning environments that permit students to apply theoretical knowledge to practical, industry-relevant challenges. Students acquire practical experience with Industry 5.0 technologies and practices through internships, co-op programs, and industry partnerships. These experiences connect academic learning with the industrial environment, guaranteeing that graduates are adequately equipped to fulfill the demands of contemporary employers.

By adopting these transformative changes, universities can establish a vital position in sustainable innovation for Industry 5.0. They will produce graduates with the digital, technical, and sustainability skills essential for the future while facilitating the global transition towards more human-centered, sustainable industrial practices.

## 2.3. Research and Innovation

Within the paradigm of Industry 5.0, universities serve a crucial function as educational entities and hubs for research and innovation. Their contribution to sustainable technological advancements is essential in tackling global climate change and resource scarcity. By promoting interdisciplinary research, universities create innovative materials, processes, and systems that improve sustainability and resilience in various industries (Espina-Romero et al., 2023).

Universities advance sustainable technology by commanding innovations in environmentally friendly materials, renewable energy solutions, and energy-efficient systems. These innovations facilitate the global transition to more sustainable industrial practices. Furthermore, universities serve as centers for collaboration, fostering partnerships among academia, industry, and government to address intricate challenges through interdisciplinary research.

Universities facilitate research commercialization and introduce sustainable technologies to the market through innovation centers, technology transfer offices, and start-up incubators. This entrepreneurial ecosystem accelerates the integration of innovations that directly enhance sustainability in industries.

Universities are instrumental in tailoring solutions for pressing global issues, including smart cities, water purification technologies, and decentralized energy systems. Furthermore, the emphasis on human-centered innovation in Industry 5.0 corresponds with academic research prioritizing human health, well-being, and social equity. To progress in Industry 5.0, universities must invest in state-of-the-art research infrastructure, promote interdisciplinary collaboration, and assist researchers in advancing sustainable innovation.

## 2.4. Interdisciplinary Collaboration

The intricate challenges of Industry 5.0, including sustainability, technological integration, and social equity, necessitate solutions that exceed the boundaries of individual academic disciplines. Universities are ideally situated to promote interdisciplinary collaboration, uniting specialists from various domains such as engineering, environmental science, economics, and social sciences. This collaboration facilitates the creation of comprehensive solutions that tackle the complex challenges of contemporary industries.

Universities can bridge the gap between technical innovation and societal needs by encouraging multidisciplinary research and education, ensuring that Industry 5.0 developments are technologically sound, socially responsible, and environmentally sustainable. This strategy encourages inventive problem-solving by bringing together varied perspectives to address global concerns more cohesively and efficiently.

Universities gain advantages from their interdisciplinary environments, facilitating collaboration through joint research initiatives, multidisciplinary programs, and cooperative platforms. These initiatives facilitate collaboration among researchers and students across conventional boundaries, fostering innovation that echoes the interconnection of contemporary challenges.

# 3. ELEMENTS OF EDUCATION PROFILE IN INDUSTRY 5.0

In the framework of Industry 5.0, the educational landscape is experiencing a tremendous transformation to suit the demands of a fast-changing industrial sector (Mohamed Hashim et al., 2024). This transformation stresses the integration of human creativity with new technologies, resulting in a more holistic approach to education that values sustainability, innovation, and human-centered growth. Table 1 summarizes the main components that characterize this new educational paradigm.

*Table 1. Elements of education profile in Industry 5.0*

| Element | Education in Industry 5.0 |
|---|---|
| **Instructors** | Lectures focus on human-machine interaction technologies, demonstrating acceptance of behavior and fostering human-centric resilience in sustainable technologies. |
| **Content Delivery** | Impact-based learning is learner-centric, dynamic, customizable, and tailored to individual needs. |
| **Learning Process** | Independent learning is based on individual patterns rather than a standardized global approach. |
| **Universities' Learning** | Utilizes the human-machine learning association to consistently produce and disseminate knowledge. |
| **Student Nature** | Prepares students for lifelong learning, emphasizing skill acquisition over knowledge accumulation. Encourages participation in personalized education delivery and design. |
| **Platforms** | Integration of AI and green internet platforms. |
| **Learning Architecture** | Reusable, recyclable, and agile learning architecture. |
| **Assessment Methods** | Continuous and formative assessment methods focusing on real-world problem-solving and critical thinking skills. |
| **Collaboration** | Promotes interdisciplinary collaboration between students, faculty, and industry partners to solve complex problems. |
| **Research Opportunities** | Encourages student involvement in sustainability research projects and partnerships with industry for practical experience. |

continued on following page

*Table 1. Continued*

| Element | Education in Industry 5.0 |
|---|---|
| **Community Engagement** | Integrates community-based projects and service learning to foster social responsibility and real-world impact. |
| **Sustainability Integration** | Embeds sustainability principles across all courses and activities, emphasizing environmental stewardship and social equity. |
| **Technology Use** | Utilizes advanced technologies such as Virtual Reality (VR), Augmented Reality (AR), and simulation tools to enhance experiential learning and practical application. |
| **Global Perspective** | Encourages global learning experiences and exchanges to prepare students for international collaboration and diverse perspectives. |
| **Student Well-being** | Focuses on mental health, well-being, and holistic development as core components of the educational experience. |

In Industry 5.0, educators are essential in connecting human creativity with advanced technologies. They educate students on human-machine interaction while promoting adaptability and resilience in applying sustainable innovations. Education is shifting to impact-based learning, which is distinguished by dynamic learner-centric content and adaptable to individual requirements, resulting in a personalized and practical educational experience.

The learning process becomes gradually personalized, departing from uniform methodologies and acknowledging each student's strengths and preferences. This transition equips students for continuous learning, emphasizing the development of versatile skills rather than knowledge accumulation. Furthermore, students actively influence their educational trajectory, enhancing the learning experience's engagement and relevance.

Universities use the combination of human cognition and machine learning to continuously develop and share knowledge more effectively. Platforms incorporating AI and green technology provide a sustainable educational foundation, and adaptable learning frameworks allow institutions to adjust quickly to changing technological contexts.

Assessment methodologies in Industry 5.0 emphasize ongoing evaluation, focusing on practical problem-solving and analytical reasoning. This guarantees that students can effectively apply their knowledge in practical situations. Collaboration among students, faculty, and industry partners enhances the educational experience, facilitating the resolution of complex challenges through varied perspectives.

Research and community engagement are essential, with students involved in sustainability projects and practical initiatives promoting professional development and social responsibility. Incorporating sustainability into curricula enhances environmental and social equity, equipping students for responsible global citizenship.

Advanced technologies, including VR, AR, and simulation tools, revolutionize experiential learning by making complex concepts more understandable and applicable. A global perspective is emphasized, with universities providing opportunities for international collaboration to equip students for an interconnected world.

Ultimately, student well-being is central to this educational framework. By emphasizing mental health and comprehensive development, Industry 5.0 education equips students to be well-rounded and resilient, prepared to address the challenges of a swiftly evolving industrial environment.

## 4. IMPACT OF SUSTAINABLE UNIVERSITIES ON INDUSTRY 5.0

Sustainable universities are crucial in advancing Industry 5.0. These institutions are cultivating innovative solutions that harmonize technological progress with sustainability, shaping a future in which industry, society, and the environment coexist seamlessly. Figure 3 outlines these interconnected impacts, showcasing how sustainable universities contribute to a future that balances industry, culture, and environmental stewardship.

*Figure 3. The interconnected impacts of sustainable universities on Industry 5.0*

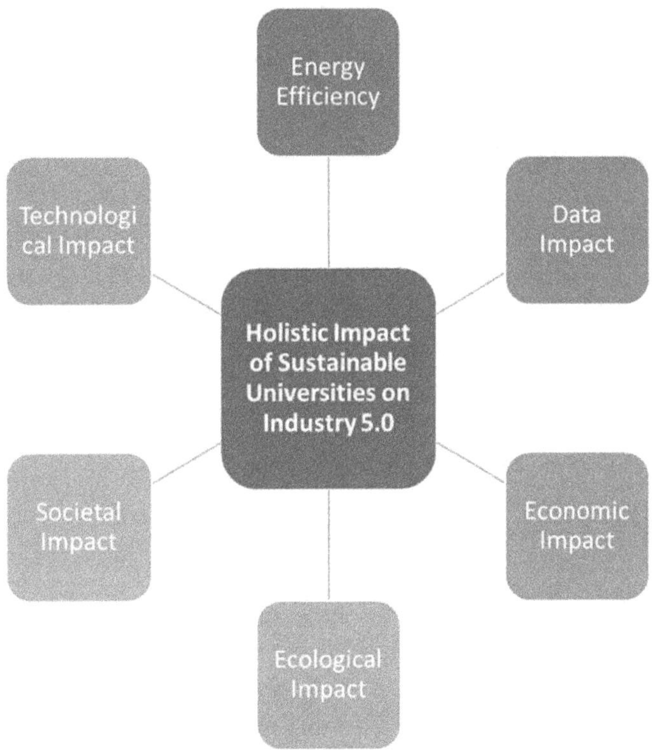


### 4.1. Energy Efficiency

Leading universities in sustainability emphasize the incorporation of renewable energy sources and the ongoing advancement of innovative, more efficient energy solutions. They actively reduce dependence on fossil fuels through initiatives prioritizing clean energy, including solar, wind power, and bioenergy. Investigation into alternative energy sources increases their capacity for innovation in this domain. Sustainable universities also employ intelligent energy management systems to optimize energy consumption throughout their campuses. Implementing smart grid technologies enhances energy distribution efficiency, whereas energy-efficient building designs and retrofitting initiatives substantially decrease energy consumption. Sustainable transportation systems, exemplified by carpooling and the heightened adoption of electric vehicles, underscore the dedication to energy efficiency and the mitigation of carbon emissions.

## 4.2. Data-Driven Impact

The success of Industry 5.0 depends on the efficient management and utilization of data, with sustainable universities playing a crucial role in promoting this initiative. Enhancing their data collection and analytical capabilities facilitates research and improves decision-making processes. These institutions advocate for ethical data utilization, prioritizing privacy and security in an increasingly digital landscape. Sustainable universities establish a benchmark for responsible data governance through frameworks that protect data privacy and implement stringent security measures. Furthermore, their capacity to utilize data analytics for predictive maintenance mitigates equipment failures, thereby ensuring the durability and efficacy of industrial operations.

## 4.3. Economic Contributions

Sustainable university practices provide substantial economic benefits for institutions and society. These universities reduce operational costs and optimize resource efficiency by utilizing economies of scale. Their emphasis on waste reduction and energy optimization increases profitability and attracts green investments (Lv et al., 2024). Moreover, by promoting innovation in the green economy, these universities generate new employment opportunities that correspond with the changing requirements of Industry 5.0. This dynamic economic model fosters enduring financial sustainability while facilitating the global transition to environmentally sustainable industries.

## 4.4. Environmental Advantages

Ecological preservation is a fundamental objective of sustainable universities, and their initiatives exemplify a significant model for Industry 5.0. Recycling and reuse initiatives are essential to these endeavors, especially in mitigating electronic waste (e-waste) (Mesjasz-Lech et al., 2024). Sustainable universities advocate circular economy principles that reduce waste and enhance resource efficiency. Green campus initiatives, encompassing biodiversity conservation efforts, reinforce their dedication to ecological stewardship. These practices lead to a substantial decrease in carbon footprints as sustainable universities proactively adopt strategies to mitigate emissions while improving the surrounding natural environment.

## 4.5. Contributions to Society

Sustainable universities significantly influence society by enhancing well-being and cultivating a culture of social responsibility (Michalos, 2022). By emphasizing the health and welfare of all stakeholders, they foster more resilient communities. The lifelong learning opportunities provided by these institutions enable individuals to consistently enhance the skills required to succeed in a changing industrial environment. Moreover, sustainable universities foster social equity and inclusion by ensuring equitable access to education and resources (Irizarry, 2022). They extend their influence beyond the campus through community outreach programs, engaging the broader public to promote positive social change. Their initiatives also enhance public health, as environmentally sustainable practices improve living conditions for society.

## 4.6. Technological Advancements

Sustainable universities lead in technological innovation, ensuring that advancements conform to ethical and environmental standards. By cultivating trust via transparency, these institutions promote the responsible integration of emerging technologies. Green technological architecture exemplifies sustainable universities, wherein systems are engineered to reduce environmental impact. AI is utilized for sustainable purposes, such as enhancing energy efficiency and waste management. Blockchain technology is examined for its capacity to improve supply chain transparency, guaranteeing adherence to sustainable practices across various industries (Movahed et al., 2024). Furthermore, advances in materials science drive the development of more environmentally sustainable products, which aids the industry's long-term prosperity.

In summary, sustainable universities are essential in promoting the principles of Industry 5.0 through technological innovation, environmental stewardship, economic resilience, and social well-being. By establishing benchmarks for sustainable practices in energy, data management, economics, ecology, society, and technology, these institutions guarantee that the industry's future aligns with sustainability objectives.

# 5. CURRENT PRACTICES IN UNIVERSITY SUSTAINABILITY

As key drivers of a sustainable future, universities are crucial in transitioning to Society 5.0 and Industry 5.0. This dual mission presents challenges and opportunities as universities cultivate the next generation of leaders capable of navigating technological advancements while embedding sustainability into every facet of society and industry (Husic, 2024). To promote sustainability, universities can implement various strategies, including investing in energy-efficient infrastructure, adopting waste reduction initiatives, fostering a paperless culture, and transitioning to renewables (Sugiarto et al., 2022). By creating sustainable campus environments, universities not only optimize resource use but also contribute to ecosystem regeneration, showcasing the benefits of sustainable practices to students, faculty, and the wider community. In addition, many sustainability initiatives reduced the environmental footprint and saved money (Farag & Aktas, 2024). However, balancing innovation with environmental sustainability presents complex challenges, particularly in governance, resource allocation, and fostering interdisciplinary collaboration. In this context, universities must lead technological progress and instill a sense of social responsibility and long-term ecological stewardship in their students and faculty. By advancing sustainable solutions alongside technological innovation, universities can position themselves at the forefront of both societal and environmental transformation. Moreover, they must create spaces for informed, complex, and accountable discussions about their role in shaping diverse futures on a shared planet (Stein, 2024).

One of the key challenges universities face in fostering sustainable development is effectively integrating sustainability into all academic and operational spheres. A recent study surveying students from 10 countries reveals that while students desire sustainability to be a part of every course, many are unaware of existing university initiatives due to inadequate communication. The study found no significant difference between public and private universities in raising awareness about Sustainable Development. This finding highlights the importance of improved funding, interdisciplinary collaboration, and locally adapted strategies to better engage students in sustainability efforts (ROSAK-SZYROCKA & KNOP, 2024).

Universities are also key players in promoting sustainable development through technological innovations. A study involving 513 students from 9 universities in the UAE introduced the Technology-Integration Framework for Education Sustainable Development. This study revealed that innovative technologies, such as Green Campus initiatives, Smart Education, Smart Campus facilities, and sustainability-focused curricula, have significantly raised students' awareness of sustainability practices. Integrating these technologies is instrumental in promoting Education for Sustainable Development (ESD) and building a sustainable future within higher education institutions (Shishakly et al., 2024).

In addition to smart technologies, universities are exploring innovative educational approaches to advance sustainability goals. At the Silesian University of Technology in Poland, a PBL approach has contributed to achieving SDGs by encouraging collaboration between students, researchers, and industry experts. An analysis of 108 interdisciplinary projects carried out between 2018 and 2021 revealed that the most frequently pursued goals were SDG 9 (Industry Innovation and Infrastructure), SDG 3 (Good Health and Well-Being), and SDG 12 (Responsible Consumption and Production). This highlights the importance of interdisciplinarity in addressing complex sustainability challenges and underscores PBL's effectiveness in fostering SDG-related outcomes in higher education (Podgórska & Zdonek, 2024).

Food waste is another critical area where universities can lead by example in sustainability efforts. A recent study investigates food waste within higher education institutions and its environmental, social, and economic implications. The causes of food waste, including over-supply, plate waste, inefficient food management, and lack of awareness, were examined, along with solutions like composting, reducing portion sizes, trayless dining, and educating students on sustainable practices. Drawing on case studies from universities across North America (Canada and the USA), Asia (China and Qatar), Southern Europe (Spain), and Africa (Nigeria and Ethiopia), the research underscores the need for universities to actively engage their communities in similar sustainability initiatives (Leal Filho et al., 2024).

Energy sustainability is also gaining attention in universities. At the University of Environment and Sustainable Development (UESD) in Ghana, a techno-economic analysis of rooftop solar photovoltaic (PV) systems was conducted to determine their feasibility and economic viability. The findings showed that solar PV generation is a sound investment, with a net present value of GHS 15.15 million, an internal rate of return of 21%, and a payback period of eight years. The university can reduce operational costs and carbon emissions by adopting solar energy, contributing to its environmental sustainability goals (Asante et al., 2024).

Another important dimension of university-led sustainability efforts is fostering entrepreneurship, focusing on SDGs. In India, research examined how university support, environmental concern, and SDG knowledge influence students' sustainability-driven entrepreneurial intentions. The study found that while university support positively impacts entrepreneurial intentions, students' understanding of SDGs was surprisingly low, which could hamper future efforts toward achieving these global goals. This highlights the critical need for universities to better educate students on SDGs to promote sustainable entrepreneurship (Sharma et al., 2024).

The importance of Education for Sustainable Development (ESD) extends beyond entrepreneurship, as illustrated by a study conducted in Somalia. Through a survey of 251 students, the study found a strong positive relationship between ESD and students' sustainable behavior. This research underscores the value of integrating ESD into higher education curricula to promote environmentally conscious practices among students, providing insights for academics, policymakers, and businesses seeking to advance sustainability in education and society (Abdullahi et al., 2024).

Several global examples demonstrate how universities are leading the charge toward sustainability. Since 2008, Copenhagen University has prioritized sustainability in its operations, focusing on responsible resource usage, climate change mitigation, and environmental consciousness (Campus, 2021). Stanford University has made sustainability a core element of its campus, adopting extensive water conservation measures, waste reduction initiatives, and sustainable transportation solutions. At the Massachusetts Institute of Technology (MIT), various groundbreaking initiatives in solar energy research and sustainable urban design have been developed to advance sustainability (*MIT Sustainability*, 2023). Erasmus University Rotterdam's Design Impact Transition (DIT) platform shows that the traditional university model, which focuses on objectivity and competition, falls short of advancing sustainability. It highlights the need for transformative, transdisciplinary, and action-oriented approaches to better support sustainability and drive institutional change (Loorbach & Wittmayer, 2024). Additionally, Qatar University has incorporated sustainability into its institutional policies and research projects (Zaidan et al., 2023), while the United Arab Emirates University recently launched the UAE's largest solar project in the education sector, fulfilling 25% of its electricity needs.

In the Gulf region, the Australian University in Kuwait (AU) has made notable progress in sustainability, actively contributing to several SDGs while promoting learning diversity and equity through its "Centre for Learning Differences." AU's commitment to sustainability extends beyond campus operations, as they are dynamically integrating sustainability principles into all new curricula, with a particular focus on PBLs (El Achkar & Alsaba, 2024). This approach warrants that students not only gain theoretical knowledge but also apply practical, sustainable solutions in real-world scenarios. In addition, AU continues to prioritize energy-efficient building construction, waste reduction measures, and adopting clean energy sources. The university also plays a vital role in community engagement, organizing public seminars and awareness campaigns, and fostering partnerships that strengthen local sustainability efforts while offering "public goods".

Through these examples, universities are key players in advancing sustainability and contributing to the global agenda of Industry 5.0. They can serve as models of resource optimization and ecological regeneration, inspiring students, faculty, and the broader community to embrace a sustainable future.

## 6. THE ROLE OF ISO STANDARDS IN ADVANCING UNIVERSITY SUSTAINABILITY

Within the framework of Industry 5.0, Sustainability in educational institutions has transitioned from a marginal issue to a fundamental component influencing the future of industries, economies, and societies. As centers of innovation and information, universities are uniquely positioned to lead sustainable development by adopting global standards that allow for effective oversight and management of their environmental, social, and economic impacts. ISO (International Organization for Standardization) standards offer a systematic and dependable framework for executing sustainable practices that correspond with global sustainability objectives and advance the overarching aims of Industry 5.0, including human-centric development, resilience, and technological innovation (Souza et al., 2024; Ulkhaq & George Joseph, 2024).

Table 2 outlines essential ISO standards universities may implement to systematically enhance and assess their sustainability performance (ISO, 2024). These standards, involving environmental management, energy efficiency, social responsibility, and compliance, provide extensive guidelines that can be customized to the specific requirements of educational institutions (Ab Wahid, 2019). By complying with these standards, universities can cultivate a culture of sustainability that impacts their operations, teaching, research, and community engagement (Budur et al., 2024).

*Table 2. ISO standards for monitoring sustainability in universities for Industry 5.0 transformation*

| ISO Standard | Title | Purpose | Application in Universities |
|---|---|---|---|
| **ISO 14001** | Environmental Management Systems (EMS) | Framework for managing environmental responsibilities systematically. | Helps universities develop environmental policies, manage resource use, and reduce environmental impacts. |
| **ISO 50001** | Energy Management Systems | Focuses on improving energy performance and reducing energy consumption. | Allows universities to manage and monitor energy use in buildings, transportation, and operations for better efficiency. |
| **ISO 26000** | Social Responsibility | Guides operating in a socially responsible manner. | Integrates social responsibility into university governance, teaching, and research while promoting community engagement. |
| **ISO 37101** | Sustainable Development in Communities | Guides sustainable development strategies in communities. | Supports the integration of sustainability in campus operations and promotes sustainable urban development within and around the university. |
| **ISO 14064** | Greenhouse Gas Emissions | Specifies principles for quantifying and reporting GHG emissions and removals. | Enables universities to measure their carbon footprint and manage GHG emissions, reducing overall climate impact. |
| **ISO 20400** | Sustainable Procurement | Guidance on integrating sustainability into procurement processes. | Ensures that goods and services procured by universities are produced sustainably and ethically, considering environmental and social impacts. |
| **ISO 9001** | Quality Management Systems | Ensures consistent quality in processes and services. | Improves sustainability-related processes in teaching, research, and campus operations while embedding sustainability objectives. |
| **ISO 45001** | Occupational Health and Safety Management | Prevents work-related injuries and ensures healthy workplaces. | Promotes a safe and healthy campus environment, contributing to overall sustainability by ensuring the well-being of students and staff. |
| **ISO 14040** | Life Cycle Assessment (LCA) | Provides a framework for assessing environmental impacts throughout a product's life cycle. | Assists universities in evaluating campus activities' environmental impact, such as construction, energy use, and waste management. |
| **ISO 37301** | Compliance Management Systems | Specifies requirements for developing and maintaining an effective compliance system. | Ensures universities adhere to environmental laws, regulations, and sustainability-related standards, fostering ethical and responsible practices. |

Implementing ISO standards enables universities to address Industry 5.0's demands by integrating social responsibility (ISO 26000) and sustainable procurement (ISO 20400). These standards emphasize human-centered, ethical, and sustainable innovation. ISO 14001 supports environmental management, reducing ecological impact (Gomes et al., 2023), while ISO 50001 enhances energy efficiency, and ISO

14064 enables monitoring of greenhouse gas emissions for carbon neutrality. ISO 26000 and ISO 37301 ensure that initiatives are socially responsible and legally compliant (Deus et al., 2015).

ISO 14040 promotes life cycle assessments, and ISO 20400 guides sustainable purchasing, ensuring universities align operations and supply chains with sustainability principles. These efforts contribute to SDGs and meet stakeholders' growing expectations for transparency and ethical practices.

In conclusion, adopting ISO standards positions universities as leaders in Industry 5.0 by fostering sustainability, aligning with global best practices, and cultivating a more equitable and resilient future.

## 7. OVERCOMING BARRIERS TO SUSTAINABILITY IN INDUSTRY 5.0

As universities take on a crucial role in advancing sustainability and preparing the workforce for Industry 5.0, several key challenges must be addressed to fully achieve these objectives. These challenges include securing financial resources, overcoming cultural resistance to change, and bridging the growing skills gap caused by rapid technological advancements. The following sections explore these barriers and present innovative solutions universities can adopt to maintain their leadership in both industry and society.

### 7.1. Financial Support and Necessary Materials

A primary challenge universities encounter in adopting sustainable practices is obtaining requisite funding and resources. Sustainability initiatives frequently necessitate significant initial investments, posing a considerable obstacle for numerous institutions. Nevertheless, several innovative solutions can assist in overcoming this challenge. Public-private partnerships provide an essential means to obtain financial backing and access to advanced technology, expertise, and industry knowledge. Such collaborations can advance the adoption of sustainable practices by distributing risks, costs, and benefits across various sectors.

Universities may also investigate grants, philanthropic contributions, and innovative financing strategies to alleviate initial costs. Revolving sustainability funds, in which savings from energy efficiency projects are reinvested in new sustainability initiatives, can provide a self-sustaining financial model. In addition, institutions can generate revenue by commercializing sustainable innovations in research laboratories, such as green technology, environmentally friendly materials, or sustainable energy systems. These entrepreneurial ventures generate revenue while establishing universities as leaders in the sustainable innovation marketplace (Hermundsdottir & Aspelund, 2021).

Green bonds constitute an innovative financing mechanism through which universities can secure capital for targeted sustainability initiatives, such as renewable energy installations, sustainable infrastructure, or comprehensive energy efficiency programs across the campus. By utilizing these emerging financial instruments, universities can surmount the cost obstacles linked to sustainable transformations and serve as models for integrating environmental and economic sustainability.

### 7.2. Resistance to Change

Cultural and institutional opposition to change constitutes a substantial obstacle to implementing sustainable practices (Madrid-Guijarro & Duréndez, 2024). Transitioning to more sustainable practices frequently necessitates significant alterations in mindset and behavior throughout the entire university ecosystem, which can be challenging. This resistance can be mitigated through a gradual and inclusive strategy. By incrementally implementing sustainability initiatives and demonstrating their concrete advantages, universities can generate momentum and gradually transform the cultural paradigm.

An effective strategy involves engaging stakeholders at all levels, including students, faculty, administrative staff, and external partners. Implementing educational and awareness initiatives, along with transparent communication regarding the enduring value and advantages of sustainability efforts, can cultivate a collective commitment. Incentive programs that reward sustainable practices, such as decreasing energy usage or advocating recycling, can also foster behavioral change.

Furthermore, universities can foster a "sustainability mindset" by integrating sustainability principles into the institution's mission and vision. This cultural transition can be aided by demonstrable leadership commitment, as evidenced by green building certifications or prominent sustainability programs, indicating that sustainability is a top priority.

Universities could investigate gamification strategies that render sustainable behaviors enjoyable and rewarding. Competitions that encourage departments or student groups to minimize energy consumption or implement environmentally sustainable practices can foster a communal spirit centered on sustainability. Digital platforms and mobile applications that monitor and encourage sustainable practices can enhance the involvement of the university community in these initiatives.

### 7.3. Competency Deficiencies in Industry 5.0

Industry 5.0 highlights the increasing skill gaps within the workforce due to rapid technological advancements. To address these discrepancies, universities must align their educational programs with the market's changing demands. This necessitates a progressive approach to education and training, wherein specialized programs are developed to give students the skills essential for success in the Industry 5.0 era.

Universities can accomplish this by collaborating with industry stakeholders to co-develop curricula and training programs that meet the specific skill requirements for emerging roles. This partnership guarantees academic curricula correspond with practical industry requirements, providing students with practical learning in contemporary technologies.

Furthermore, universities can significantly contribute to developing soft skills essential for Industry 5.0, including adaptability, critical thinking, and interdisciplinary collaboration. Incorporating PBL into the curriculum enables students to address real-world issues within varied teams, thereby cultivating essential skills. This equips students to transcend conventional disciplinary limits and address intricate challenges through innovative and comprehensive methods.

Universities should proactively anticipate emerging roles and job markets. With the advancement of Industry 5.0, novel career trajectories will arise, including AI ethicists, human-machine interaction specialists, and sustainability data analysts. Universities must anticipate future developments and adequately prepare students by adapting their programs. Finally, as there will be a gradual need for continuing learning that enables the workforce to acclimate to the future industry, universities should examine the provision of upskilling and reskilling programs for existing professionals (Padmaja & Mukul, 2021).

Table 3 presents the key challenges and solutions, providing a concise overview of how universities can drive sustainability in the Industry 5.0 landscape. By overcoming financial barriers, addressing resistance to change, and closing skill gaps, universities can position themselves as crucial enablers of Industry 5.0. Universities will continue advancing industry and society through strategic partnerships, innovative educational models, and a commitment to sustainability.

*Table 3. Key challenges and solutions for universities in advancing sustainability and Industry 5.0*

| Challenge | Description | Solutions |
|---|---|---|
| **Financial Support** | Lack of funding and resources for sustainability projects. | - Public-private partnerships<br>- Grants, green bonds, revolving funds<br>- Commercializing innovations |
| **Resistance to Change** | Institutional resistance to adopting sustainable practices. | - Gradual implementation<br>- Stakeholder engagement<br>- Incentives and gamification |
| **Skill Gaps** | Gaps in workforce skills due to rapid Industry 5.0 advancements. | - Specialized training<br>- Industry-aligned curricula<br>- Project-based learning (PBL) |
| **Emerging Job Markets** | Preparing students for new roles in Industry 5.0. | - Adapting programs for future job roles<br>- Upskilling and reskilling initiatives |

## 8. PROSPECTS FOR THE FUTURE

Universities are well-positioned to lead the global sustainability agenda as they evolve within the framework of Industry 5.0, incorporating innovative governance structures, cutting-edge technologies, and increased international collaboration. By embracing these forward-thinking strategies, universities can increase their impact, ensuring sustainability remains a core pillar of higher education. The following sections examine vital areas where universities can effect meaningful change in the future.

### 8.1. Policy and Governance

Universities should assume a more pivotal role in promoting sustainability, not only through their research and educational initiatives but also by adopting governance frameworks that emphasize sustainability. A notable advancement is the creation of positions such as the Chief Sustainability Officer (CSO) to spearhead sustainability initiatives. Internal policies incorporating sustainability into all facets of campus operations, including procurement and energy consumption, will be imperative. Furthermore, universities must implement adaptable governance frameworks that facilitate ongoing enhancement and adjustment to emerging environmental challenges.

Governments and regulatory agencies will progressively offer incentives for sustainable innovation. Through financial assistance, subsidies, and tax incentives, these institutions can assist universities in surmounting funding obstacles and expediting the implementation of sustainable technologies and practices. Policymakers may establish frameworks that promote universities as centers for sustainability research, where innovation benefits both the campus and broader societal objectives.

### 8.2. Technology Integration

The ongoing incorporation of advanced technologies will characterize the future of sustainability in higher education. Artificial intelligence, blockchain technology, and the Internet of Things will progress beyond fundamental operational roles to become integral to research methodologies, student education, and university administration. AI-driven analytics will refine resource management and decision-making, whereas blockchain could improve transparency in areas ranging from academic credentialing to sustainability reporting. Furthermore, intelligent campus solutions will advance into more complex systems that independently regulate energy usage, waste, and water, diminishing universities' environmental impacts.

As technology advances, universities will be experimental platforms for innovations, facilitating pilot projects that educate the academic community and various industries on sustainable practices.

### 8.3. International Collaboration

In the future, global alliances will be increasingly vital. Universities will progressively engage with international networks to exchange best practices, research, and technological innovations, thereby expediting global advancements in sustainability. Cross-border educational initiatives will cultivate a global perspective in students, equipping them for a career environment that increasingly prioritizes sustainability across various sectors.

International collaboration encompasses joint research initiatives targeting global environmental issues, including climate change and resource scarcity. This will enable institutions to consolidate resources, recruit elite talent, and develop scalable shared solutions globally.

### 8.4. Sustainability-Related KPIs and Impact Assessment

Future universities must enhance their sustainability metrics to conform to global standards (Jiang & Kurnitski, 2023). Instruments such as Environmental, Social, and Governance (ESG) rankings, Sustainalytics, and Global Reporting Initiative (GRI) reporting will advance in sophistication, allowing universities to benchmark their progress with greater efficacy (Zhutiaeva et al., 2023). These systems will enable universities to evaluate their environmental impact as well as their contribution to social and economic sustainability. Moreover, AI and blockchain-enabled automated reporting platforms may enhance transparency, alleviate administrative burdens, and deliver real-time insights into sustainability performance. Establishing explicit Key Performance Indicators (KPIs) aligned with local and global sustainability goals will enhance universities' stakeholder accountability and facilitate quantifiable advancements (Hristov & Chirico, 2019).

## 9. POLICY RECOMMENDATIONS

Universities must implement targeted policy interventions to fully embrace their role as sustainability and Industry 5.0 leaders. Figure 4 provides a visual summary of these key policy recommendations, highlighting the crucial areas where intervention is necessary to support universities in advancing their sustainability initiatives and contributing to Industry 5.0. These recommendations aim to help universities overcome financial, technological, and educational barriers while fostering long-term partnerships and accountability. The suggested policies below outline specific steps that governments, institutions, and industries can take to accelerate the adoption of sustainable practices in higher education.

*Figure 4. Key policy recommendations for universities in Industry 5.0 and sustainability*

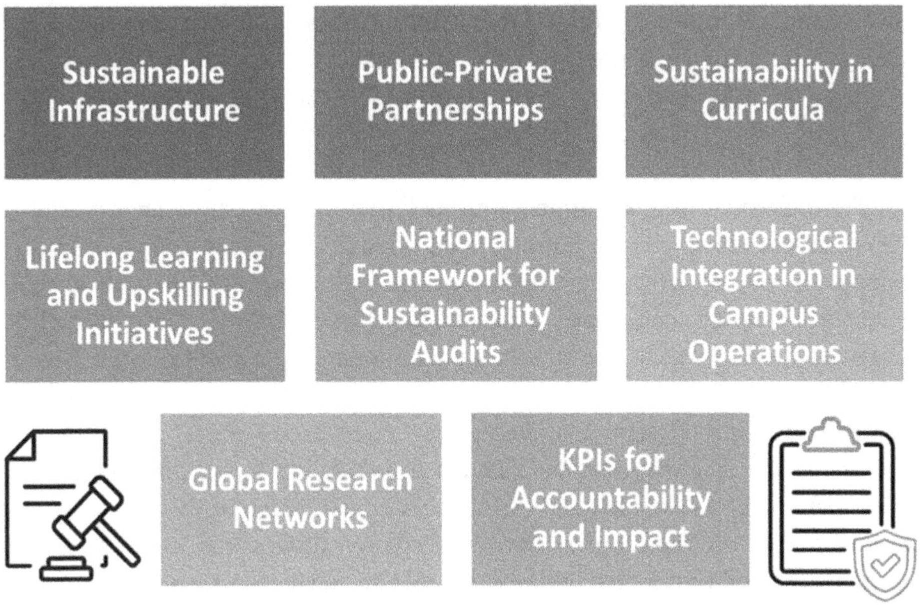


a) **Incentivize Sustainable Infrastructure:** Governments and international funding organizations should prioritize the allocation of grants and subsidies exclusively for developing sustainable infrastructure in universities. This may encompass financing for sustainable building certifications, renewable energy implementations, and advanced waste management systems. Implementing a policy framework that provides financial incentives for institutions to adopt green solutions and energy-efficient designs will encourage mass participation.

b) **Promote Public-Private Partnerships:** To address financial challenges, policies should facilitate public-private partnerships, enabling universities to collaborate with industries possessing both economic and technical expertise. Governments may provide tax incentives to private entities collaborating with universities on sustainability initiatives, thus distributing the financial burden and fostering technological innovation.

c) **Mandate Sustainability in Curricula:** Educational policies must necessitate the incorporation of sustainability concepts across disciplines within university curricula, extending beyond environmental science to encompass business, engineering, and social sciences. Policies could mandate minimum standards for sustainability-related coursework, guaranteeing that all students graduate with a fundamental comprehension of sustainability principles and their application to their respective disciplines.

d) **Advocate for Lifelong Learning and Upskilling Initiatives:** Governments should endorse establishing lifelong learning programs centered on sustainability and technological progress. Policies that finance upskilling and reskilling programs for professionals undergoing mid-career transitions will guarantee that the existing workforce adjusts to the requirements of Industry 5.0. These programs may be implemented through collaborations between universities and industries, supported by government incentives for adopters or providers of these initiatives.

e) **Establish a National Framework for Sustainability Audits:** A uniform, nationwide framework for sustainability audits in higher education should be formulated, mandating universities to periodically evaluate and publicly disclose their sustainability performance. This framework may be linked to eligibility for government funding and incentives for universities that surpass specific sustainability criteria.
f) **Facilitate Technological Integration in Campus Operations:** Governments should create digital innovation funds for universities to promote incorporating advanced technologies such as AI and IoT in campus operations. These funds may be allocated to execute smart campus solutions that enhance resource management, energy efficiency, and waste minimization. Furthermore, policies should advocate for implementing blockchain in sustainability reporting to improve transparency and data integrity.
g) **Enhance Global Research Networks:** International policy frameworks ought to promote the establishment of global research consortia dedicated to sustainability. Governments could provide financial support to universities engaged in these networks, facilitating the dissemination of knowledge, research outcomes, and exemplary practices. Furthermore, international academic mobility programs emphasizing sustainability-oriented initiatives should be enhanced to promote collaboration among institutions across various regions.
h) **Implement KPIs for Accountability and Impact:** Policymakers should require the adoption of standardized sustainability KPIs in higher education institutions. Mandating universities to report on these indicators and compare them to international standards enables governments to enhance transparency and accountability. These metrics may encompass environmental factors, such as energy and water consumption, alongside social sustainability indicators, including diversity and inclusion within the institution.

## 10. RESEARCH LIMITATIONS AND IMPLICATIONS

This chapter investigates the role of universities in advancing Industry 5.0 through sustainability, interdisciplinary collaboration, and technology integration. However, its emphasis on existing frameworks such as ISO standards and the SDGs may not adequately account for differences in resources, cultural settings, and governance structures between regions and organizations. Furthermore, the rapid expansion of Industry 5.0 technologies may lead to the need for periodic updates to insights, necessitating continued research to identify emergent patterns.

Despite these constraints, the findings highlight the importance of adaptable governance and dynamic curricula in ensuring universities remain leaders in Industry 5.0. Greater collaboration among academics, industry, and government is required to bridge theory and practice. Furthermore, global frameworks, such as ISO standards, must be tailored to local requirements.

## 11. CONCLUSIONS AND PERSPECTIVES

As universities worldwide embrace their roles as Industry 5.0 catalysts, they must continue to evolve as engines of sustainability, technological innovation, and social progress. Integrating advanced technologies with human ingenuity and creativity forms the basis of Industry 5.0. Universities are not just reacting to this shift but actively driving it forward by pioneering sustainable solutions, interdisciplinary collaboration, and human-centered development.

At the heart of this transformation is the university's ability to flesh out a digitally literate and environmentally conscious workforce. Universities equip students with the skills they need to thrive in a future where collaboration between humans and machines is critical by integrating sustainability principles into curricula and encouraging interdisciplinary research. This is no longer an option; it is required to address the complex issues of climate change, resource depletion, and social inequality. In this context, educational reform must continue emphasizing technical proficiency and the ethical and social responsibilities accompanying technological advancement.

The future of sustainability in higher education depends on integrating cutting-edge technologies that improve campus operations, streamline resource management, and enable transparency in sustainability reporting. Universities are uniquely positioned to serve as test beds for innovative solutions, from AI-powered analytics that optimize energy consumption to blockchain systems that improve supply chain accountability. By pushing the limits of what is possible, universities can set the standard for sustainable practices in industries and governments.

The global nature of Industry 5.0 necessitates that universities look beyond regional perspectives and encourage international collaborations. Universities can increase their impact and accelerate progress toward common goals by collaborating on research, providing global learning opportunities, and launching cross-border sustainability initiatives. This international collaboration will not only drive technological and social innovation but will also produce a generation of leaders prepared to face the dynamic and interconnected challenges of the twenty-first century.

Despite the promise of Industry 5.0, universities must still overcome significant challenges, such as financial constraints, cultural resistance, and a growing skills gap. Universities can secure the resources they need to move their initiatives forward by implementing innovative funding mechanisms such as public-private partnerships, green bonds, and commercializing sustainable innovations. Furthermore, universities can ensure that their communities remain agile and future-ready by encouraging a "sustainability mindset" and promoting ongoing upskilling and reskilling programs.

The path forward is clear. Universities must continue to promote sustainability, leverage technology, and foster global collaboration to survive and thrive in the age of Industry 5.0. As institutions of knowledge and innovation, they are responsible for shaping tomorrow's workforce and the future of industry and society. Finally, we must ask ourselves: How can universities continue to push the boundaries of innovation while ensuring that the future we shape is equitable, sustainable, and resilient for all? This question remains at the heart of the Industry 5.0 revolution, inspiring us to rethink the role of education as we mold a better future.

## REFERENCES


Ab Wahid, R. (2019). Sustaining ISO 9001-based QMS in higher education: A reality? *The TQM Journal*, 31(4), 563–577. DOI: 10.1108/TQM-12-2018-0185

Abdullahi, A. M., Hussein, H. A., Ahmed, M. Y., Hussein, O. A., & Warsame, A. A. (2024). The impact of education for sustainable development on university students' sustainable behavior: A case study from undergraduate students in Somalia. *Frontiers in Education*, 9, 1413687. Advance online publication. DOI: 10.3389/feduc.2024.1413687

Agrawal, S., Agrawal, R., Kumar, A., Luthra, S., & Garza-Reyes, J. A. (2024). Can industry 5.0 technologies overcome supply chain disruptions?—A perspective study on pandemics, war, and climate change issues. *Operations Management Research : Advancing Practice Through Research*, 17(2), 453–468. DOI: 10.1007/s12063-023-00410-y

Alcántara-Rubio, L., Valderrama-Hernández, R., Solís-Espallargas, C., & Ruiz-Morales, J. (2022). The implementation of the SDGs in universities: A systematic review. *Environmental Education Research*, 28(11), 1585–1615. DOI: 10.1080/13504622.2022.2063798

Asante, K., Gyamfi, S., Amo-Boateng, M., & Peprah, F. (2024). Techno-economic analysis of solar PV electricity generation at the university of environment and sustainable development in Ghana. *Energy Reports*, 11, 659–673. DOI: 10.1016/j.egyr.2023.12.028

Atif, S. (2023). Analysing the alignment between circular economy and industry 4.0 nexus with industry 5.0 era: An integrative systematic literature review. *Sustainable Development (Bradford)*, 31(4), 2155–2175. DOI: 10.1002/sd.2542

Budur, T., Abdullah, H., Rashid, C. A., & Demirer, H. (2024). The Connection Between Knowledge Management Processes and Sustainability at Higher Education Institutions. *Journal of the Knowledge Economy*. Advance online publication. DOI: 10.1007/s13132-023-01664-4

Campus, G. (2021, January 19). *About Sustainability 2030*. University of Copenhagen. https://sustainability2030.ku.dk/ucphs-approach/

Cuesta-Claros, A., Bonar, G., Malekpour, S., Raven, R., & Kestin, T. (2024). Uncovering perspectives on SDG integration for university transformations. *International Journal of Sustainability in Higher Education*, 25(6), 1252–1278. DOI: 10.1108/IJSHE-03-2023-0111

de Deus, R. M., de Castro, R., Vieira, K. R. O., Leite, A. E., & Jabbour, C. J. C. (2015). The journey to sustainable universities: Insights from a Brazilian experience. *International Journal of Business Excellence*, 8(2), 146–159. DOI: 10.1504/IJBEX.2015.068205

El Achkar, J. H., & Alsaba, M. (2024). *DYNAMIC INTEGRATION OF SUSTAINABILITY AND CLIMATE CHANGE IN ENGINEERING CURRICULA VIA CDIO. 20th International CDIO Conference*, Tunisia.

Elangovan, U. (2021). *Industry 5.0: The Future of the Industrial Economy*. CRC Press., DOI: 10.1201/9781003190677

Espina-Romero, L., Guerrero-Alcedo, J., Goñi Avila, N., Noroño Sánchez, J. G., Gutiérrez Hurtado, H., & Quiñones Li, A. (2023). Industry 5.0: Tracking Scientific Activity on the Most Influential Industries, Associated Topics, and Future Research Agenda. *Sustainability (Basel)*, 15(6), 6. Advance online publication. DOI: 10.3390/su15065554

Farag, K., & Aktas, C. B. (2024). A survey of the most prevalent sustainability initiatives at universities. *International Journal of Sustainability in Higher Education, ahead-of-print*(ahead-of-print). DOI: 10.1108/IJSHE-07-2023-0285

Ghobakhloo, M., Iranmanesh, M., Fathi, M., Rejeb, A., Foroughi, B., & Nikbin, D. (2024). Beyond Industry 4.0: A systematic review of Industry 5.0 technologies and implications for social, environmental and economic sustainability. *Asia-Pacific Journal of Business Administration, ahead-of-print*(ahead-of-print). DOI: 10.1108/APJBA-08-2023-0384

Gomes, L. P., Caetano, M. O., Brand, S. M., Dai-Prá, L. B., & Pereira, B. N. (2023). Maintenance of an environmental management system based on ISO 14001 in a Brazilian private university, seeking sustainable development. *International Journal of Sustainability in Higher Education*, 24(2), 361–381. DOI: 10.1108/IJSHE-07-2021-0298

Gutiérrez-Ángel, N., Sánchez-García, J.-N., Mercader-Rubio, I., García-Martín, J., & Brito-Costa, S. (2022). Digital literacy in the university setting: A literature review of empirical studies between 2010 and 2021. *Frontiers in Psychology*, 13, 896800. Advance online publication. DOI: 10.3389/fpsyg.2022.896800 PMID: 36176798

Hermundsdottir, F., & Aspelund, A. (2021). Sustainability innovations and firm competitiveness: A review. *Journal of Cleaner Production*, 280, 124715. DOI: 10.1016/j.jclepro.2020.124715

Hristov, I., & Chirico, A. (2019). The Role of Sustainability Key Performance Indicators (KPIs) in Implementing Sustainable Strategies. *Sustainability (Basel)*, 11(20), 20. Advance online publication. DOI: 10.3390/su11205742

Husic, D. W. (2024). Reframing sustainability initiatives in higher education. *Sustainable Earth Reviews*, 7(1), 5. DOI: 10.1186/s42055-024-00076-9

Irizarry, J. L. (2022). Integrating Mindfulness in Public and Nonprofit Education Programs to Foster Social Equity. *Public Integrity*, 24(4–5), 504–516. DOI: 10.1080/10999922.2022.2034356

*ISO - International Organization for Standardization*. (2024). https://www.iso.org/home.html

Ivanov, D. (2023). The Industry 5.0 framework: Viability-based integration of the resilience, sustainability, and human-centricity perspectives. *International Journal of Production Research*, 61(5), 1683–1695. DOI: 10.1080/00207543.2022.2118892

Jiang, Q., & Kurnitski, J. (2023). Performance based core sustainability metrics for university campuses developing towards climate neutrality: A robust PICSOU framework. *Sustainable Cities and Society*, 97, 104723. DOI: 10.1016/j.scs.2023.104723

Leal Filho, W., Ribeiro, P. C. C., Setti, A. F. F., Azam, F. M. S., Abubakar, I. R., Castillo-Apraiz, J., Tamayo, U., Özuyar, P. G., Frizzo, K., & Borsari, B. (2024). Toward food waste reduction at universities. *Environment, Development and Sustainability*, 26(7), 16585–16606. DOI: 10.1007/s10668-023-03300-2 PMID: 37362965

Leng, J., Zhong, Y., Lin, Z., Xu, K., Mourtzis, D., Zhou, X., Zheng, P., Liu, Q., Zhao, J. L., & Shen, W. (2023). Towards resilience in Industry 5.0: A decentralized autonomous manufacturing paradigm. *Journal of Manufacturing Systems*, 71, 95–114. DOI: 10.1016/j.jmsy.2023.08.023

Longo, F., Padovano, A., & Umbrello, S. (2020). Value-Oriented and Ethical Technology Engineering in Industry 5.0: A Human-Centric Perspective for the Design of the Factory of the Future. *Applied Sciences (Basel, Switzerland)*, 10(12), 12. Advance online publication. DOI: 10.3390/app10124182

Loorbach, D. A., & Wittmayer, J. (2024). Transforming universities. *Sustainability Science*, 19(1), 19–33. DOI: 10.1007/s11625-023-01335-y

Lv, X., Wang, Y., Liu, L., & Yin, S. (2024). Digital green innovation economy for Industry 5.0. *Sustainable Economies*, 2(1), 1. Advance online publication. DOI: 10.62617/se.v2i1.8

Madrid-Guijarro, A., & Duréndez, A. (2024). Sustainable development barriers and pressures in SMEs: The mediating effect of management commitment to environmental practices. *Business Strategy and the Environment*, 33(2), 949–967. DOI: 10.1002/bse.3537

Martini, B., Bellisario, D., & Coletti, P. (2024). Human-Centered and Sustainable Artificial Intelligence in Industry 5.0: Challenges and Perspectives. *Sustainability (Basel)*, 16(13), 13. Advance online publication. DOI: 10.3390/su16135448

Mayer, C. (2020). *Shareholderism Versus Stakeholderism – a Misconceived Contradiction. A Comment on "The Illusory Promise of Stakeholder Governance" by Lucian Bebchuk and Roberto Tallarita* (SSRN Scholarly Paper 3617847). DOI: 10.2139/ssrn.3617847

Mesjasz-Lech, A., Kemendi, Á., & Michelberger, P. (2024). Circular manufacturing and Industry 5.0. Assessing material flows in the manufacturing process in relation to e-waste streams. *Engineering Management in Production and Services*, 16(1), 114–133. DOI: 10.2478/emj-2024-0009

Michalos, A. C. (2022). Corporate Social Responsibility in Universities and Sustainable Development. In Poff, D. C. (Ed.), *University Corporate Social Responsibility and University Governance* (pp. 75–104). Springer International Publishing., DOI: 10.1007/978-3-030-77532-2_4

*MIT Sustainability*. (2023). https://sustainability.mit.edu/about

Mohamed Hashim, M. A., Tlemsani, I., Mason-Jones, R., Matthews, R., & Ndrecaj, V. (2024). Higher education via the lens of industry 5.0: Strategy and perspective. *Social Sciences & Humanities Open*, 9, 100828. DOI: 10.1016/j.ssaho.2024.100828

Movahed, A. B., Movahed, A. B., & Nozari, H. (2024). Opportunities and Challenges of Smart Supply Chain in Industry 5.0. In *Information Logistics for Organizational Empowerment and Effective Supply Chain Management* (pp. 108–138). IGI Global. DOI: 10.4018/979-8-3693-0159-3.ch006

Pactwa, K., Woźniak, J., Jach, K., & Brdulak, A. (2024). Including the social responsibility of universities and sustainable development goals in the strategic plans of universities in Europe. *Sustainable Development, n/a*(n/a). DOI: 10.1002/sd.2924

Padmaja, V., & Mukul, K. (2021). Upskilling and Reskilling in the Digital Age: The Way Forward for Higher Educational Institutions. In *Transforming Higher Education Through Digitalization*. CRC Press. DOI: 10.1201/9781003132097-15

Panagou, S., Neumann, W. P., & Fruggiero, F. (2024). A scoping review of human robot interaction research towards Industry 5.0 human-centric workplaces. *International Journal of Production Research*, 62(3), 974–990. DOI: 10.1080/00207543.2023.2172473

Podgórska, M., & Zdonek, I. (2024). Interdisciplinary collaboration in higher education towards sustainable development. *Sustainable Development (Bradford)*, 32(3), 2085–2103. DOI: 10.1002/sd.2765

Rani, S., Jining, D., Shoukat, K., Shoukat, M. U., & Nawaz, S. A. (2024). A Human–Machine Interaction Mechanism: Additive Manufacturing for Industry 5.0—Design and Management. *Sustainability (Basel)*, 16(10), 10. Advance online publication. DOI: 10.3390/su16104158

Rehman, A., & Umar, T. (2024). Literature review: Industry 5.0. Leveraging technologies for environmental, social and governance advancement in corporate settings. *Corporate Governance: The International Journal of Business in Society, ahead-of-print*(ahead-of-print). DOI: 10.1108/CG-11-2023-0502

Rosak-Szyrocka, J., & Knop, K. (2024). Sustainable development Universities—Opportunities & challenges on the road to society 5.0 from the key stakeholder perspective. *PLoS One*, 19(8), e0308929. DOI: 10.1371/journal.pone.0308929 PMID: 39146253

Sachan, R., Chauhan, K., & Agarwal, V. (2024). Outlook on Upskilling and Reskilling Capacities for Industry 5.0. In Shrivastava, R., & Jain, K. (Eds.), *Humanizing Businesses for a Better World of Work* (pp. 1–16). Emerald Publishing Limited., DOI: 10.1108/978-1-83797-332-320241001

Saksena, G., & Jha, A. (2024). Culture Essentials for Industry 5.0. In Sushil, N. R., & Joshi, R. (Eds.), *Flexibility, Resilience and Sustainability* (pp. 77–92). Springer Nature., DOI: 10.1007/978-981-99-9550-9_5

Sharma, L., Bulsara, H. P., Trivedi, M., & Bagdi, H. (2024). An analysis of sustainability-driven entrepreneurial intentions among university students: The role of university support and SDG knowledge. *Journal of Applied Research in Higher Education*, 16(2), 281–301. DOI: 10.1108/JARHE-11-2022-0359

Shishakly, R., Almaiah, M., Lutfi, A., & Alrawad, M. (2024). The influence of using smart technologies for sustainable development in higher education institutions. *International Journal of Data and Network Science*, 8(1), 77–90. DOI: 10.5267/j.ijdns.2023.10.015

Souza, M. A., González, M. O. A., & de Pinho, A. L. S. (2024). Maturity Model for Sustainability Assessment of Chemical Analyses Laboratories in Public Higher Education Institutions. *Sustainability (Basel)*, 16(5), 5. Advance online publication. DOI: 10.3390/su16052137

Stein, S. (2024). Universities confronting climate change: Beyond sustainable development and solutionism. *Higher Education*, 87(1), 165–183. DOI: 10.1007/s10734-023-00999-w

Sugiarto, A., Lee, C.-W., & Huruta, A. D. (2022). A Systematic Review of the Sustainable Campus Concept. *Behavioral Sciences (Basel, Switzerland)*, 12(5), 130. DOI: 10.3390/bs12050130 PMID: 35621427

Tasdemir, C., & Gazo, R. (2020). Integrating sustainability into higher education curriculum through a transdisciplinary perspective. *Journal of Cleaner Production*, 265, 121759. DOI: 10.1016/j.jclepro.2020.121759

Ulkhaq, M. M., & George Joseph, R. S. (2024). Students' attitudes towards campus sustainability: A comparison among three universities in Sweden. *Environment, Development and Sustainability*, 26(6), 16289–16313. DOI: 10.1007/s10668-023-03295-w

van Erp, T., Carvalho, N. G. P., Gerolamo, M. C., Gonçalves, R., Rytter, N. G. M., & Gladysz, B. (2024). Industry 5.0: A new strategy framework for sustainability management and beyond. *Journal of Cleaner Production*, 461, 142271. DOI: 10.1016/j.jclepro.2024.142271

Xu, X., Lu, Y., Vogel-Heuser, B., & Wang, L. (2021). Industry 4.0 and Industry 5.0—Inception, conception and perception. *Journal of Manufacturing Systems*, 61, 530–535. DOI: 10.1016/j.jmsy.2021.10.006

Yang, J., Liu, Y., & Morgan, P. L. (2024). Human–machine interaction towards Industry 5.0: Human-centric smart manufacturing. *Digital Engineering*, 2, 100013. DOI: 10.1016/j.dte.2024.100013

Zaidan, E., Belkhiria, E., & Wazen, C. (2023). Universities of the Future as Catalysts for Change: Using the Sustainable Development Goals to Reframe Sustainability – Qatar University as a Case Study. In Al-Maadeed, M. A. S. A., Bouras, A., Al-Salem, M., & Younan, N. (Eds.), *The Sustainable University of the Future: Reimagining Higher Education and Research* (pp. 1–23). Springer International Publishing., DOI: 10.1007/978-3-031-20186-8_1

Zhutiaeva, S. A., Usanov, A. Yu., & Selezneva, A. V. (2023). ESG Rankings to Confirm the Commitment of Universities to the SDGs. In Rumyantseva, A., Anyigba, H., Sintsova, E., & Vasilenko, N. (Eds.), *Finance, Economics, and Industry for Sustainable Development* (pp. 235–243). Springer Nature Switzerland., DOI: 10.1007/978-3-031-30498-9_21

# Chapter 3
# Pioneering Sustainability Through Industry 5.0 With a Human-Centric Approach:
## A Bibliometric Analysis

**Ebru Beyza Bayarcelik**
https://orcid.org/0000-0003-4886-5719
*Maltepe University, Turkey*

**Fulya Taşel**
https://orcid.org/0000-0001-6959-5776
*Maltepe University, Turkey*

## ABSTRACT

*The first three industrial revolutions facilitated the transition from manual production to automation, while Industry 4.0 has supported the concept of smart manufacturing aimed at flexible and efficient production of goods. This transformation has been made possible through Cyber-Physical Systems (CPS), enabling real-time communication and collaboration. However, this shift raises concerns about the dehumanization of work, as modern systems heavily rely on mechanization and data-driven processes. This has driven Industry 5.0, which aims to harmonize human skills with intelligent systems by blending the efficiency of automation with human cognitive abilities to create a more balanced and flexible industrial paradigm. In this book chapter, a bibliometric analysis of studies conducted from the inception of Industry 5.0 in 2019 to the present has been performed, and the topic has been discussed in depth. It also examines emerging trends, highlights dominant research areas, explores methodological frameworks, and summarizes existing findings on the topic.*

## 1. INTRODUCTION

For centuries, humans relied on their own skills and the assistance of animals for production. However, in 1877 the introduction of water and steam as new energy sources is an important turning point in industrialization, known as the First Industrial Revolution. These new energy sources revolutionized

DOI: 10.4018/979-8-3693-8181-6.ch003

manufacturing by increasing efficiency in less time and driving rapid economic growth. The Second Industrial Revolution, or Industry 2.0, emerged in the 1870s with the adoption of electricity in factories. The introduction of electricity in production enabled mass production through assembly lines, which led to faster production processes and lower costs. At the end of the 1960s, the integration of electronic and information technologies in production came into play with Industry 3.0. This era introduced partial automation, with electronic systems transforming factory operations and is an important foundation for modern manufacturing. Subsequently, Industry 4.0 integrates information technologies and operational infrastructures within the framework of a cyber-physical system so that machines can interact and communicate independently with one another. The development of the first three industrial revolutions took approximately 100 years, while the emergence and advancement of the Fourth Industrial Revolution occurred within 40 years, marking significant progress in production methods and economic growth. Now, we are moving into Industry 5.0 which emphasizes human-centered innovation, sustainability, and resilience as its core principles. Industry 4.0 is a German initiative aimed at revolutionizing manufacturing technologies by leveraging cyber-physical systems (CPS) to bridge between virtual environment and tangible, real-world environments. The primary goal of this strategy is to promote digital production by leveraging the Internet of Things, along with advanced value chains and business models (Bayarçelik & Bumin Doyduk, 2020). Industry 4.0 necessitates the comprehensive adoption of latest technologies into business world, such as Assembly 4.0 systems, which propel research efforts aimed at boosting productivity and profitability. Artificial intelligence (AI), big data, digital twins, blockchain, electric vehicles, 3D scanning-printing, augmented reality (AR) and automation-robotics are the leading innovations that are driving this new industry era. While Industry 4.0 shares certain familiarities with earlier industrial revolutions, it stands out for its transformative impact on industry, can be defined by greater connectivity, innovation, and making decisions based on collected data analysis. Growing customer demand and market competition have driven the manufacturing industry to improve its production systems (Ciucu-Durnoi, Delcea, Stănescu, Teodorescu, & Vargas, 2024). Industry 5.0 emerged after the rapid digitalization of various sectors by the advancement of Industry 4.0. Industry 5.0 aims to unite human creativity with advanced machines, enhancing efficiency through skill-based task assignments, enabling mass customization, improving production quality, and fostering economic growth while emphasizing sustainable prosperity and the well-being of industrial workers. Industry 5.0 is first proposed by Michael Rada, that aims to raise welfare, create innovative products and produce high quality, specialized products through systematic waste prevention techniques and logistical efficiency designs (Youssef & Mejri, 2023; Xun, Lu, Vogel-Heuser, & Wang, 2021). Özkeser (2019) stated that the main differences between Ind 4.0 and Ind 5.0 are the creation of working environments where employees and robots complement each other. This enhanced collaboration allows individuals to express their creativity through the production of personalized goods and services. It focuses on providing more tailored products, driven by active user involvement in their design (Özkeser, 2018). The birth of Ind 5.0 is driven by the need to combine human creativity with advanced technologies, such as collaborative robotics and AI, to achieve manufacturing that is both resource-efficient and socially responsible. The progress of industry from Ind 1.0 to Ind 5.0 is given in Figure 1, highlighting the increasingly shorter time intervals between each successive revolutionary phase.

*Figure 1. Roadmap from industry 1.0 to 5.0. (Demir, Döven, & Sezen, 2019)*

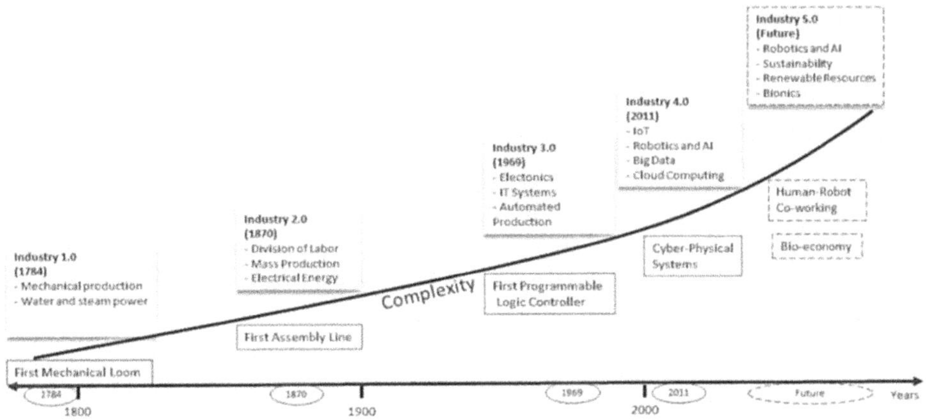


## 2.THE GLOBAL SPREAD OF INDUSTRY 4.0

Industry 4.0 was first introduced in Germany and has since gained widespread international interest. In 2011, in order to increase its competitiveness in the global market and to achieve higher efficiency and productivity, Germany has adopted the Industry 4.0 approach as its high-tech strategy, where new technologies will be incorporated into every stage of production. This initiative has spurred similar movements globally. By 2016, Industry 4.0 had become a central topic at the World Economic Forum, illustrating its significance on the global stage. Germany further strengthened its commitment with the "High-Tech Strategy 2020," allocating billions of euros to technological advancements as part of a broad innovation agenda (Kagermann, Wahlster, & Helbig, 2013).

Following Germany's lead, other nations adopted their own Industry 4.0 strategies. France launched "La Nouvelle France Industrielle" in 2013 to prioritize industrial policy initiatives (European Commission, 2016), while the UK introduced the "Future of Manufacturing" plan, envisioning industrial growth policies through 2050. In the USA, the "Advanced Manufacturing Partnership" (AMP) was developed to support the next era of manufacturing, with strong backing from the "Industrial Internet Consortium" (Rafael, Shirley, & Liveris, 2014). In Asia, South Korea introduced its "Innovation in Manufacturing 3.0" plan, emphasizing advancements in four key areas, while China announced, "Made in China 2025" and the "Internet Plus" plan to accelerate digital manufacturing. Also in 2015, the Japanese government launched the "5th Science and Technology Basic Plan with the goal of building a world-leading Super Smart Society" (Office, 2015), while Singapore allocated $19 billion to its "Research, Innovation and Enterprise 2020 Plan" in 2016 (Foundation, 2016). Where it once took over a century for the textile machine to disseminate globally, the internet achieved the same in just 15 years. Likewise, Industry 4.0's adoption is expected to accelerate rapidly. This transformation has not only been embraced by developed countries but also by emerging economies, including Turkey, which is advancing from Industry 2.0 toward Industry 3.0.

Industry 4.0 is the integration of industrial and societal outputs using advanced technologies such as "autonomous robots, simulation, horizontal and vertical integration, cybersecurity" to improve production and business processes (Mrugalska & Wyrwicka, 2017).

## 3.THE DEVELOPMENT OF INDUSTRY 5.0 WORLDWIDE

Industry 5.0 can be seen as building on the technology-based digital transformation of the recently developed Industry 4.0. While Industry 4.0 aims to increase economic growth and productivity through automation and digital transformation of processes to become human-independent, it has often ignored environmental and social issues (Santhi and Muthuswamy, 2023).

This has raised concerns about the negative impacts of technology, such as job loss and increased social inequality. In contrast, Industry 5.0 is a human-centered approach that aims to drive digital transformation towards sustainability goals. Industry 5.0 aims not only to view industries as sources of economic wealth, but also as new systems that protect the environment, promote social welfare and play an important role in solving societal problems (Sindhwani et al., 2022).

Industry 5.0 is a new phenomenon in the preliminary phases of its evolution, is rapidly evolving and aims to reduce concerns about unemployment crises and human resistance to technology that emerged during the Industry 4.0 era. However, for businesses trying to shape their future digitalization strategies under the influence of Industry 4.0, they are faced with issues such as how necessary Industry 5.0 is or how fast it should be realized. In order to create a sustainable world prioritized by Industry 5.0 and to meet the goals of a people-centered approach and more flexible industry, it is inevitable to conduct research on the effective management of digitally transforming industries. Achieving these goals requires a comprehensive review and broad understanding of the mechanisms, policies and regulatory frameworks for the effective transfer, integration and management of new technologies within the business ecosystem (Ghobakhloo et al.,2024).

Among the first publications on Industry 5.0 was Sachsenmeier's 2016 article "Industry 5.0-The Relevance and Implications of Bionics and Synthetic Biology". He argued that bionics, the precursor of synthetic biology, will lead this fifth industrial transformation, just as digital technologies did for Industry 4.0 (Sachsenmeier, 2016).

On the other hand, Özdemir and Hekim (2018) come up with something new by seeing Industry 5.0 as a developmental step built on Industry 4.0 technologies. They suggested that both large and small companies or entities engage in similar types of innovation processes, which should be leveraged to democratize knowledge as a result of technology consumption. In addition, this study critically refutes the digitalization approach that ignores humans.

From 2019 to 2020, a new perspective on Industry 5.0, which envisions human-machine symbiosis in production and leads to the concept of "symbiotic factories", has started to emerge. Although Industry 4.0 focuses on full automation, Industry 5.0 integrates human skills with advanced technologies and machine vision to meet the demands for more collaborative, personalized and customized products. This human-centered vision aims to increase production efficiency while enhancing human work experience. This shift reflects the understanding of the value of labor, competicies and talent in optimizing production efficiency and overall performance (Longo et al., 2020; Aslam et al., 2020).

In 2020, the European Commission started to recognize that Industry 4.0 does not encompass a sustainable and human-centered approach and that a new approach is needed as an extension of Industry 4.0 aimed at addressing socio-environmental challenges. In early 2022, the Commission criticized Industry 4.0 for being incompatible with Europe's future goals, such as tackling the climate crisis and social challenges, and instead advocated Industry 5.0 as a new perspective for industrial development. This vision seeks to prioritize societal well-being and ecological preservation while promoting adaptability in the highly integrated business environment. The European Commission does not see Industry 5.0 as a different industrial revolution or a substitute for Industry 4.0. Rather, it is seen as a regulatory framework designed to guide the acceleration and the consequences of digital transformation in the context of Industry 4.0. The key differences include a balance between productivity and sustainability, empowerment of the workforce, the development of environmentally friendly technologies and a broader corporate responsibility along the value chain (Ghobakhloo et al.,2024).

According to the European Commission (2021), three key drivers are central to the Industry 5.0 paradigm (European Commission,2021) which are:

- The human-centric driver emphasizes transitioning from purely technology-driven advancements to a focus on people and societal needs. It prioritizes addressing fundamental human interests in the production process. This includes empowering industrial workers with upskilling opportunities and continuous training for developing professional expectations and foster a harmonious equilibrium between the time and effort devoted to professional responsibilities and personal life (Khan, Haleem, & Javaid, 2023).
- Sustainability driver focuses on environmental conservation, which requires adopting a circular economy to boost resource efficiency through "reuse, repurposing, and recycling", while also minimizing pollution and natural impact.
- Resilience driver emphasizes resilience, aiming to strengthen industrial production to withstand disruptions and support critical infrastructure during emergencies (Youssef & Mejri, 2023).

## 3.1 The Human-Centric Driver

The global development of Industry 5.0 is marked by a human-centered approach that combines advanced technologies with sustainability and ethical considerations. It is transforming industrial production by creating workplaces where employees and machines can work harmoniously, leading to a more inclusive industrial landscape. Unlike Industry 4.0, which combines technology-driven, Ind 5.0 aims to remind the creative and skilled human resource of its place in the production process. Its worldwide development is driven by the need for a balance between advanced automation and the irreplaceable qualities that humans bring to production, such as creativity, ethical decision-making and adaptability. The concept of Industry 5.0 was born out of the need to emphasize the unique creativity of humans in the literature and to realize resource-efficient and socially responsible production by working together with powerful, intelligent and precise machines through collaborative robotics and artificial intelligence solutions (Maddikunta et al., 2022). This approach places a primary focus on the welfare of workers throughout the manufacturing process while emphasizing sustainability by optimizing resource use, minimizing waste, and enhancing resilience to strengthen the robustness of industrial production. Innovation lies at the core of this paradigm shift. The synergy between skilled human talent and advanced technologies is key to unlocking the full potential of I5.0 and elevating companies' innovation capabilities to new heights (Adel 2022; Djerdj Horvat, et al.,2024).

However, the rapid pace of technological change can lead to rapid outdate of employee skills, increasing the need for both external talent acquisition strategies and effective internal competency management. Organizations that invest in employee training and development not only strengthen their technological competencies, but also improve human-machine collaboration, which is crucial for fostering innovation under Ind 5.0 (Djerdj Horvat, et al.,2024).

Organizations that prioritize employee training and development not only strengthen their technological capabilities but also pave the way for improved human-machine collaboration in the innovation process (Sousa and Wilks, 2018). Company's that focus on fostering human-centricity—by investing in both emerging technologies and actively engaging employees in the innovation process—will have a positive impact on product innovation efforts.

## 3.2 Sustainability Driver

For industries to honor the planet's boundaries, they must embrace sustainable practices centered around circular processes. As we transition to Industry 5.0, the focus is on the collaboration between humans and robots in production, alongside the critical technologies required for nations and societies to align with sustainability goals. This approach will not only reduce waste and environmental impact but also enhance the efficiency and effectiveness of resource use, ultimately contributing to a healthier planet. This shift emphasizes sustainable practices, optimizing production processes while ensuring minimal environmental impact and fostering more responsible use of resources (Sharma & Gupta, 2024). Barata and Kayser stated that "Sustainability in Industry 5.0 is centered around circular processes that emphasize resource reuse, waste minimization, and reducing environmental impact". This approach supports a circular economy, improving resource efficiency and promoting environmental responsibility, while driving sustainable practices across industries (Barata & Kayser, 2024).

One of the major targets of Industry 4.0 is to shift production towards a system that emphasizes flexibility and efficiency, away from the extensive automation of the third industrial revolution. Industry 4.0 is regarded as a technological transformation focusing on the digitalization of industrial operations while aiming to increase automation. However, it is missing key elements such as sustainability and a human-centered approach, making it less suitable for addressing broader social and environmental concerns that are crucial for future industrial development (Sarkar, Shardeo, Dwivedi, & Pamucar, 2024). The environmental sustainability goals of the Industry 5.0 model are mainly supported by integrating value networks, promoting sustainable practices, utilizing smart automation, incorporating renewable energy, and creating smart products that are circular, resource-efficient, and operationally sustainable (Van Erp et al., 2024).

## 3.3 Resilience Driver

Resilience emphasizes the need for production systems that can easily adjust to different disruptions, while human-centricity plays a key role in enhancing resilience by utilizing the adaptability and flexibility of workers (Yasue, Mahmoodi, Zúñiga, & Fathi, 2025). Industry 5.0 emphasizes the synergy between human perception, intuition and creativity and the precision and efficiency of machines. It creates a collaborative partnership rather than an exchange. This cooperation is crucial for developing flexible, resilient resource management systems. It improves decision making speed and accuracy, while ensuring that technological progress aligns with human values and societal needs by prioritizing humans in the decision-making process (Ma, Yao, & Wang, 2024). Industry 5.0 emphasizes the ability of countries and employment to achieve their growth and sustainable goals. It aims to be a powerful source of prosperity, ensuring that production respects the resources and future of the planet while prioritizing the well-being of workers. This approach integrates sustainability and human-centered values at the heart of manufacturing processes (Huang, Wang, Li, Mourtzis, & Wang, 2022).

## 4. METHODOLOGY

Despite the growing popularity and prominence of Industry 5.0 as a research field, there is still a notable gap in comprehensive studies that examine the interconnections between its structure, development, and collaboration within the existing body of literature. This chapter addresses bridge these gaps by employing bibliometric analysis to broadly evaluate and understand the current state of research on Industry 5.0, with a specific focus on its applications in sustainability, human-centric approaches, and resilience.

The aim of this chapter is to explore articles related to Industry 5.0, determining influential resources, leading authors, and widely cited works, while shedding light on current research trends. Using specific selection criteria to documents that included the studied concepts in their titles, abstracts, or keywords, 1,489 publications indexed in the Web of Science (WOS) database from 2019 to 2024 were examined through VOSviewer.

Bibliometric maps are crucial in research focusing on similarity measures and mapping techniques. The graphical representation of these maps is often overlooked and most studies use basic software outputs. Simple representations work for small maps, but struggle with larger datasets that are becoming more common. For larger bibliometric maps, advanced graphical features such as zooming and labeling are needed. VOSViewer is introduced as a new tool for better visual display of bibliometric maps (Van Eck & Waltman, 2010). In bibliometric research, two main types of maps are used to examine how interest is shared and connected in academic literature. These maps help researchers visualize the relationships between different items such as articles, authors or journals. These two types of maps are called distance-based maps and graph-based maps. VosViewer creates clusters by focusing on the individuals being analyzed. In this context, each source is treated as a separate entity and is assigned to a single community, which is formed based on the relatedness of a particular variable (Mourao & Martinho, 2020).

The findings of this study are intended to help scientists, researchers, and decision-makers identify key research areas and emerging trends in the field of Industry 5.0, providing direction for future study efforts. Using data from Web of Science, this study seeks to examine the following mentioned research question using bibliographic data obtained from Web of Science "What are the publication trends, quantities, potential areas of Industry 5.0 between the years 2019 to 2024?"

While searching the studies; data were collected according to the following sequence; the titles, keywords and abstracts field "Industry 5.0" AND "Sustainability"; "Industry 5.0" AND "human-centric"; "Industry 5.0" AND "resilient" between the time period 2019-2024 from Web of Science database.

*Table 1. Data selection query and the total numbers between 2019-2024 years (Numbers are gathered from Web of Science database)*

| Title/Abstract/Author Keywords | Total Documents | Document Type Article | Publication Year 2019 | Publication Year 2020 | Publication Year 2021 | Publication Year 2022 | Publication Year 2023 | Publication Year 2024 |
|---|---|---|---|---|---|---|---|---|
| "Industry 5.0" | 1489 | 951 | 1 | 16 | 41 | 157 | 269 | 467 |
| "Industry 5.0" and "Sustainability" | 302 | 192 | | 2 | 6 | 21 | 49 | 114 |
| "Industry 5.0" and "Human-centric" | 265 | 157 | 1 | 1 | 5 | 23 | 47 | 80 |
| "Industry 5.0" and "Resilient" | 138 | 90 | | | 3 | 19 | 20 | 48 |

As illustrated in Figure 2, the data obtained from the Web of Science database indicates a steady increase in publications related to Industry 5.0 over time.

*Figure 2. Distribution of publication years of total documents "Industry 5.0" between 2019-2024 years (Numbers are gathered from Web of Science database)*

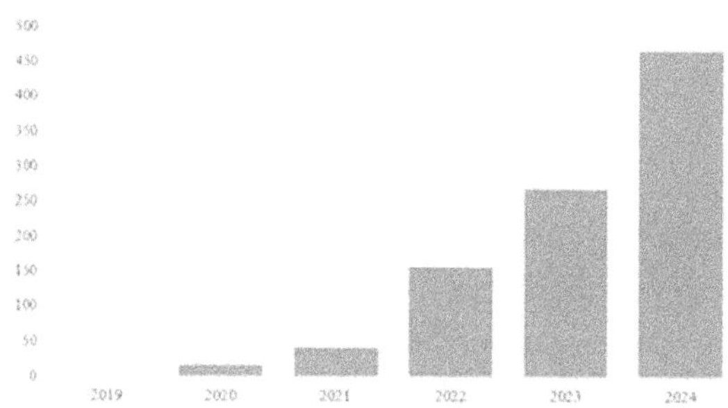


Figure 2 illustrates a steady rise in the number of studies published on Industry 5.0 over time, highlighting the growing academic interest in this emerging field. There is a remarkable upward trend in the volume of research, indicating that Industry 5.0 is becoming a more prominent topic of exploration and innovation. While research on Industry 5.0 experienced gradual growth in previous years, 2023 and 2024 marked a sharp rise, indicating a breakthrough in awareness and exploration of this field. The growing popularity of Industry 5.0 is reflected in the increasing volume of research focused on this area. As the concept gains traction, more studies are being published, exploring how human-centric and technology-integrated approaches can transform industries. Researchers are examining the incorporation of latest technologies, including artificial intelligence and robotics, with human creativity and problem-solving.

As it is shown in Figure 3 Industry 5.0 is a multidisciplinary area of study, with researchers from diverse fields such as engineering, robotics, artificial intelligence, and social sciences examining its potential effects on industry. To achieve a comprehensive understanding, it is essential to explore Industry 5.0 through perspectives like engineering, sustainability, and operations research. Engineering aims to develop and integrate advanced technologies, ensuring effective and safe human-machine interaction. Sustainability concentrates on reducing environmental impact, steering innovations toward eco-friendly practices and sustainable resource management. Operations research enhances decision-making and resource optimization, promoting efficiency and cost-effectiveness across various industries. By integrating technological innovation, environmental responsibility, and operational efficiency, these fields create a multi-faceted approach. This interdisciplinary framework ensures that advancements in Industry 5.0 are applied efficiently and sustainably, delivering benefits to both industry and society.

*Figure 3. Distribution of total documents "Industry 5.0" within Web of Science Categories between 2019-2024 years (Numbers are gathered from Web of Science database)*

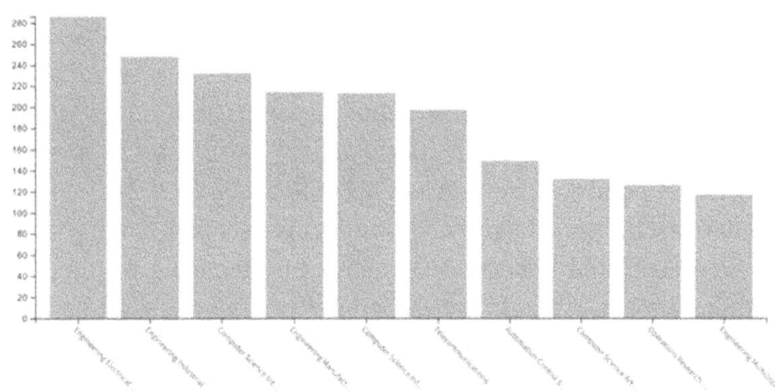


As it is shown in Figure 4 The top three publication titles are Sustainability (60 Articles), IEEE Transactions on Consumer Electronics (43 Articles), and Applied Sciences Basel (33 Articles).

*Figure 4. The publication titles of articles in "Industry 5.0" within Web of Science Categories between 2019-2024 years (Numbers are gathered from Web of Science database)*

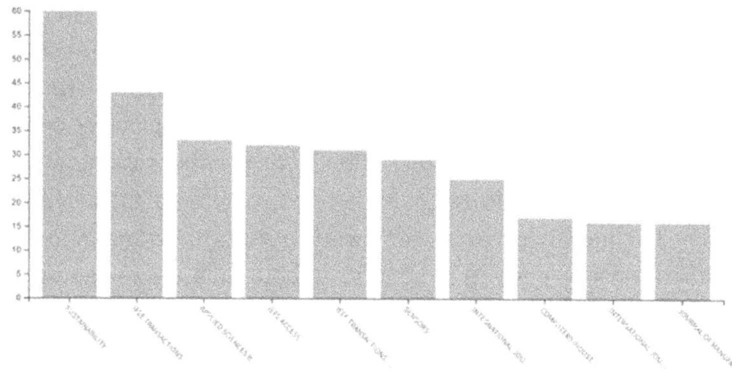

There are many studies conducted in different disciplines in the field of Industry 5.0. When these studies are analyzed, the most cited publications are given in Table 2. A general overview of the area can be drawn by exploring the most cited authors and articles, as well as co-citation analysis, co-authorship analysis etc. According to Table 2, "*Industry 4.0 and Industry 5.0-Inception, conception and reception*" is the most cited publication, published by Xun and his colleagues in 2021.

Xun et al. (2021) stated that Industry 4.0 provided intelligent decision-making for flexible, high-quality mass production, on the other hand Industry 5.0 emerged by focusing on social goals and employee welfare beyond economic growth. As can be understood from the goals set by the European Union in platforms such as the Paris Agreement, Sustainable Development Goals, OECD Better Life Index, the Industry 5.0 approach highlights sustainability and social justice as opposed to emphasizing technology, which is the focal point of the Industry 4.0 approach The authors describe Ind 5.0 as a worker-focused perspective, prioritizing the needs of employees and seeing them as a valuable investment than a cost. They agreed that technology should adapt to the different needs of employees by maintaining a happy, healthy and effective environment. Furthermore, Xun et al. (2021) argued that individualized human-machine interaction and bio-inspired materials are key technologies for Industry 5.0. Digital Twins and AI are crucial for system modeling and actionable intelligence. And also, they concluded by asking and answering 5 questions to encourage extensive discussions on the future of industry (Xun, Yuqian, Vogel-Heuser, & Lihui, 2021).

The second most cited study "*Industry 5.0: A survey on enabling technologies and potential applications*" was published by Maddikunta et al. in 2022. Maddikunta and his colleagues presented a discussion of the factors that led to the emergence of Industry 5.0. In this study, the developments leading up to Industry 5.0 are discussed from the first industrial revolution in 1780, which introduced mechanical power, to the fourth industrial revolution (Industry 4.0), which uses IoT and cloud technologies to create cyber-physical systems (CPS). They explained the different definitions and terms used by experts in the field and explained how the technologies used in Industry 4.0 can be adapted to Industry 5.0. This study identified edge computing, digital twins, collaborative robots (cobots), the Internet of Everything, blockchain, and advanced networking technologies like 6G that are crucial for the realization of Industry 5.0. Each of these technologies plays a significant role in enhancing human-machine collaboration and improving manufacturing processes. On the other hand, Maddikunta et al. discussed several practical applications of Industry 5.0, including intelligent healthcare, cloud manufacturing, and supply chain management with real life examples. These applications highlight the potential for Industry 5.0 to deliver customized products and improve overall production efficiency, thereby addressing the needs of modern consumers. This second most cited study serves as a foundational resource for understanding the emerging landscape of Industry 5.0, its technological underpinnings, and its potential impact on future manufacturing paradigms (Maddikunta, ve diğerleri, 2022).

The third most cited article in the ranking is Nahavandi's 2019 publication, *"Industry 5.0: A Human-Centric Solution."* It holds the distinction of being the most cited article featuring the keywords *Industry 5.0* and *Human-Centered.* Nahavandi emphasized that Industry 5.0 focuses on fostering collaboration between humans and machines, with robots serving as collaborators rather than competitors, thereby enhancing human creativity and productivity. The author highlights significant advancements in technologies like brain-machine interfaces, deep learning, and machine cognition, which are critical to the realization of Industry 5.0. These technologies empower robots to interpret human intentions and assist with tasks, thereby enhancing overall process efficiency. In addition, it is noted that environmental pollution has increased since the Second Industrial Revolution, and it is emphasized that environmentally conscious companies can gain a competitive advantage. Industry 5.0 is stated to have the potential to achieve this advantage by focusing on waste management and environmental sustainability. Nahavandi stated that the transformative role of robots in Industry 5.0, emphasizing their ability to learn from humans and adapt to working styles through advancements in sensing and machine cognition, fostering safer and more efficient workplaces. Contrary to concerns about job loss, Industry 5.0 is expected to generate more employment opportunities, with roles like Chief Robotics Officer (CRO) and increased demand for AI and robotics expertise driving economic growth. However, challenges remain, including resistance from senior stakeholders to adopt new technologies and ethical concerns surrounding autonomous systems, emphasizing the need for robust verification and validation processes in future research (Nahavandi, 2019).

*Table 2. Top 10 most cited articles in Industry 5.0 Research*

| *Rank* | *Author* | *Source Title* |
|---|---|---|
| *1* | (Xun, Yuqian, Vogel-Heuser, & Lihui, 2021) | Journal of Manufacturing Systems |
| *2* | (Maddikunta, ve diğerleri, 2022) | Journal of Industrial Information Integration |
| *3* | (Nahavandi, 2019) | Sustainability |
| *4* | (Leng, ve diğerleri, 2022) | Journal of Manufacturing Systems |
| *5* | (Choi, Kumar, Yue, & Chan, 2022; Lu, ve diğerleri, 2022) | Production and Operations Management |
| *6* | (Lu, ve diğerleri, 2022) | Journal of Manufacturing Systems |
| *7* | (Longo, Padovano, & Umbrello, 2020) | Applied Sciences-Basel |
| *8* | (Javed, ve diğerleri, 2022) | Cities |
| *9* | (Ivanov, 2023) | International Journal of Production Research |
| *10* | (Yan & Yu, 2022) | Journal of Cleaner Production |

Source: Citations are gathered from Web of Science database

VOSviewer software enables the visualization of co-authorship analysis, which examines the relationships and collaborations between researchers in a particular field. The insights gained from this analysis can support and encourage the development of new research collaborations and initiatives among (Donthu, Kumar, Mukherjee, & Pandey, 2021). A co-occurrence network was created to analyze the abstracts, titles and keywords of the sampled articles to identify the leading thematic clusters of Industry 5.0. Figure 5 shows this network created using VOSviewer. This network of co-occurrence highlights specific clusters that represent the major key aspects of Industry 5.0.

*Figure 5. Co-occurance network analysis of the keyword "Industry 5.0" between 2019-2024 years (Web of Science database and VOSviewer)*

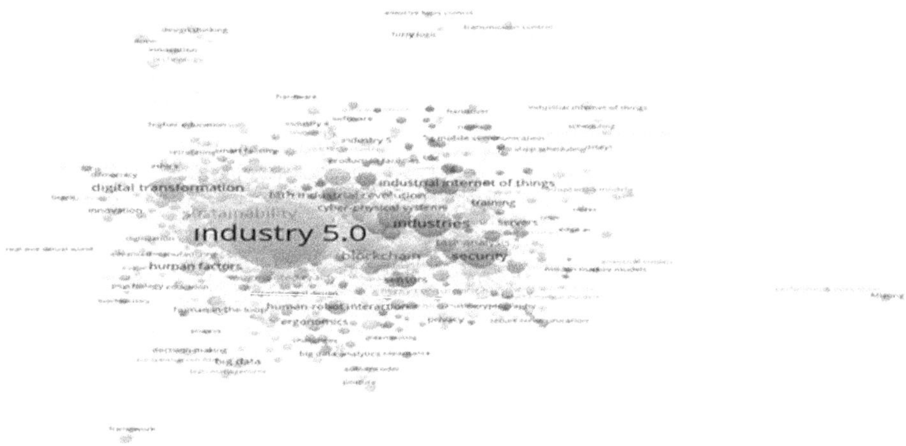


Keyword analysis plays an essential role in screening prior studies, as it emphasizes the themes covered in a specific research field. This technique allows a visual and quantitative display of main topics. These resulting networks are shown in different colors. They consist of circular nodes color-coded in blue, yellow, red or green and connected by links. Co-occurrence reveals the cross-connections among these layers. When a category arises, it is allocated to a certain color group and moves closer to the center if it has numerous shared connections. Strong linkages lead to clustering of categories together, indicating their frequent co-occurrence in the literature. Industry 5.0 is placed near the center, connecting with all categories, but this centrality may reflect its trend rather than its intrinsic importance for each category of study (Gartoumi, 2024).

Co-authorship analysis, showing the interaction between authors, highlights the cooperation of academic studies and the contribution from various countries and institutions. Collaboration between researchers constitutes an important element. This cooperation creates an important communication network where researchers share their intellectual assets and transfer new knowledge. This academic collaboration between researchers helps to improve research results and increase the quality and diversity of research. Analyzing co-authorship is valuable for gaining a thorough understanding of the distribution of research influence and the collaborative relationships among authors within a specific scientific field. It plays a important role in enhancing the production and cohesion of scientific research outcomes in that area (Li, Weng, Yue, Li, & Wang, 2021). Carrying out collaborative research in a given field plays a vital role in boosting scientific output. Analyzing co-authorship is very important in bibliometric study. The main purpose of co-authorship analysis is to identify the key cooperation and prominent research networks (Gartoumi, 2024).

Figure 6 shows the co-authorship analysis of the keywords "Industry 5.0" and "Resilient" within the titles, keywords and abstracts field and limiting the document type as articles from the Web of Science database.

*Figure 6. Co-authorship analysis of the keywords "Industry 5.0" and "Resilient" between 2019-2024 years (Web of Science database and VOSviewer)*

Within the field of Industry 5.0 and Resilient research the most cited publications among these studies are given in Table 3.

*Table 3. Top 10 most cited articles in Industry 5.0 and resilient research*

| Rank | Author | Source Title |
|---|---|---|
| 1 | (Leng, ve diğerleri, 2022) | Journal of Manufacturing Systems |
| 2 | (Ivanov, 2023) | International Journal of Production Research |
| 3 | (Huang, ve diğerleri, 2022) | Journal of Manufacturing Systems |
| 4 | (Sindhwani, ve diğerleri, 2022) | Technology in Society |
| 5 | (Saniuk, Grabowska, & Straka, 2022) | Sustainability |
| 6 | (Leng, ve diğerleri, 2023) | International Journal of Production Research |
| 7 | (Jan, ve diğerleri, 2021) | IEEE Transactions on Industrial Informatics |
| 8 | (Nourmohammadi, Fathi, & Ng, 2022) | Computers & Operations Research |
| 9 | (Xifan, ve diğerleri, 2024) | Journal of Intelligent Manufacturing |
| 10 | (Karmaker, ve diğerleri, 2023) | International Journal of Production Economics |

Source: Citations are gathered from Web of Science database

Leng et al. (2022) examined three essential features of Industry 5.0. These are human centericity, sustainability and resilient. The authors discuss key enablers, potential implementation pathways, future practices and difficulties associated with real implementation scenarios of Industry 5.0 approach. In this study, the authors propose a three-dimensional Industry 5.0 model. This three-dimensional model consists of a technical dimension, a reality dimension and an implementation dimension. The study aims to present the development processes of Industry 5.0 and outline the possible impacts and challenges of

Industry 5.0. In this comprehensive research, 3885 publications were examined and the insights obtained addressed the key enablers, technology system and potential implementation directions/pathways for value-driven Industry 5.0. In this research Leng et al. (2022) stated that Industry 5.0 is emerging to advance the sustainable development goals of building a highly intelligent society and promoting ecological values. Furthermore, Industry 5.0 is introduced to create a flexible and robust driver of prosperity within an interconnected industrial community.

Ivanov (2023) performed a study aiming to identify clusters related to the three pillars of Industry 5.0. These pillars are flexibility, sustainability and human-centericity. Using the SCOPUS database and VOS software, the author derived literature clusters and developed an inclusive view of the topics associated with these three pillars. Ivanov (2023) developed a conceptual model for Industry 5.0 and reviewed the existing literature on supply chain operations through cluster analysis with a focus on sustainability, resilience and human-centeredness. The related concepts associated with Industry 5.0 is built on several key technological pillars: "collaboration", "coordination", "communication", "automation", "data analysis" and "identification". Industry 5.0 also contains four main dimensions; "organization", "management", "technology" and "performance evaluation" - and functions at three hierarchical levels: societal level, network level and plant level (Ivanov, 2023). Ivanov stated that the impacts of Industry 5.0 are diverse and have broad implications spanning multiple dimensions and disciplines. This study focused on different perspectives on technology, organizational structure, performance evaluation and process management. It also offers opportunities for future research in other areas such as new product development and quality management etc.

Figure 7 shows the co-authorship analysis of the keywords "Industry 5.0" and "Sustainability" within the titles, keywords and abstracts field and limiting the document type as articles from the Web of Science database.

*Figure 7. Co-authorship analysis of the keywords "Industry 5.0" and "Sustainability" between 2019-2024 years (Web of Science database and VOSviewer)*

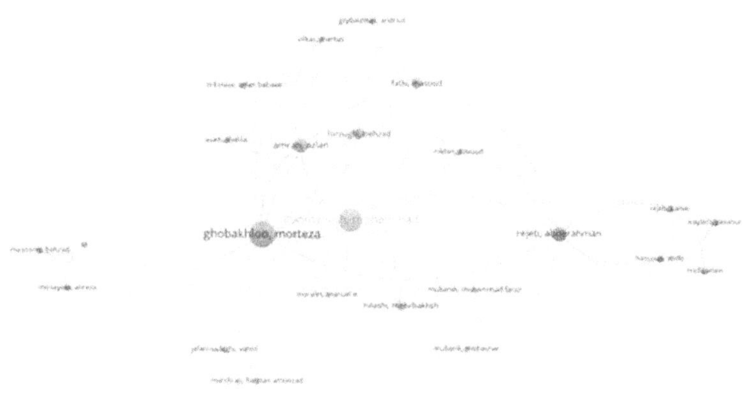


Within the field of Industry 5.0 and Sustainability research the most cited publications among these studies are given in Table 4.

*Table 4. Top 10 most cited articles in Industry 5.0 and sustainability research*

| *Rank* | *Author* | *Source Title* |
|---|---|---|
| *1* | (Leng, ve diğerleri, 2022) | Journal of Manufacturing Systems |
| *2* | (Lu, ve diğerleri, 2022) | Journal of Manufacturing Systems |
| *3* | (Ivanov, 2023) | International Journal of Production Research |
| *4* | (Bednar & Welch, 2020) | Information Systems Frontiers |
| *5* | (Carayannis & Morawska-Jancelewicz, 2022) | Journal of Knowledge Economy |
| *6* | (Fraga-Lamas, Lopes, & Fernandez-Carames, | Sensors |
| *7* | (Ghobakhloo, ve diğerleri, 2022) | Sustainable Production and Consumption |
| *8* | (Grabowska, Saniuk, & Gajdzik, 2022) | Scientometrics |
| *9* | (Broo, Okyay, & Sait, 2022) | Journal of Industrial Information Integration |
| *10* | (Sindhwani, ve diğerleri, 2022) | Technology in Society |

Source: Citations are gathered from Web of Science database

Figure 8 shows the co-authorship analysis of the keywords "Industry 5.0" and "human-centric" within the titles, keywords and abstracts field and limiting the document type as articles from the Web of Science database.

*Figure 8. Co-authorship analysis of the keywords "Industry 5.0" and "human-centric" between 2019-2024 years (Web of Science database and VOSviewer)*

Within the field of Industry 5.0 and Human-Centric research the most cited publications among these studies are given in Table 5.

*Table 5. Top 10 most cited articles in Industry 5.0 and human-centric research*

| *Rank* | *Author* | *Source Title* |
|---|---|---|
| *1* | (Nahavandi, 2019) | Sustainability |
| *2* | (Lu, ve diğerleri, 2022) | Journal of Manufacturing Systems |
| *3* | (Longo, Padovano, & Umbrello, 2020) | Applied Sciences-Basel |
| *4* | (Ivanov, 2023) | International Journal of Production Research |
| *5* | (Huang, ve diğerleri, 2022) | Journal of Manufacturing Systems |
| *6* | (Broo, Okyay, & Sait, 2022) | Journal of Industrial Information Integration |
| *7* | (Saniuk, Grabowska, & Straka, 2022) | Sustainability |
| *8* | (Cillo, Gregori, Daniele, Caputo, & Bitbol- | Journal of Knowledge Management |
| *9* | (Mourtzis, Panopoulos, Angelopoulos, Wang, | Journal of Manufacturing Systems |
| *10* | (Rozanec, ve diğerleri, 2023) | International Journal of Production Research |

Source: Citations are gathered from Web of Science database

Lu et al. (2022) stated that the shift towards well-being, sustainability and flexibility in Industry 5.0 has led to arguments emphasizing that production should be human-centered. This approach focuses on prioritizing the well-being of workers in production processes, rather than being system-centric, focusing primarily on efficiency, quality improvement and cost reduction. This paper aims to systematically establish a research agenda for human-centered production at the beginning of this potential industrial transformation and to catalyze important debates, discussions and advances in this emerging field. One of the key contributions of the study is the development of an industrial model of human needs (the Industrial Pyramid of Human Needs) that organizes human needs in the industrial context into five tiers, from basic security to self-actualization. Using this model, the authors describe human-centered production. In addition, we propose that the human-machine relationship follows the 5C journey "Co-existence", "Cooperation", "Collaboration", "Compassion" and "Co-evolution". To meet human needs at the highest level, human-centered production should give priority to fostering a conscious and co-evolving human-machine relationship.

The geographical distribution of publications reveals a wide range of studies originating from various regions ranging from Europe to Asia. As shown in Table 6, the countries with the highest frequency of research are China, Italy, India, and England.

*Table 6. Top ten countries industry 5.0*

| *Countries/Regions* | *Record Count* |
|---|---|
| *Peoples Republic of China* | 193 |
| *Italy* | 137 |
| *India* | 136 |
| *England* | 98 |
| *USA* | 74 |
| *Spain* | 64 |
| *Saudi Arabia* | 57 |
| *Germany* | 48 |
| *Australia* | 46 |
| *Pakistan* | 46 |

(Source: Numbers are gathered from Web of Science database)

## 5. CONCLUSION

The rapid transformation of business practices through new technologies in Industry 4.0 has led to the simultaneous emergence of Industry 5.0. While Industry 4.0 demonstrates humanity's progress in advancing the collaboration between humans and machines, Industry 5.0 appears as a complementary development that reinforces sustainability by placing humans at the center of this relationship. The aim of this paper is to offer an updated overview of the current state of Industry 5.0 research.

Bibliometric analysis has enabled us to identify key publication directions, overall trajectories, and significant topics within the scientific literature on Industry 5.0, with a particular focus on its human-centric, sustainability, and resilience aspects. We have pinpointed the most influential sources, authors, countries, and the connections between researchers contributing to Industry 5.0 studies. While the current literature on Industry 5.0 is still relatively limited, publication trends show that this field is expanding rapidly. A significant number of the most influential articles have been published recently, indicating that Industry 5.0 is still a vibrant and quickly advancing field. The main shortcoming of this chapter is that the Industry 5.0 concept has only been examined in the literature since 2019 and is a relatively new concept.

Additionally, for future studies, a more comprehensive examination can be made by investigating different data sources (such as Scopus, PubMed) and languages to understand Industry 5.0 from a broader perspective. In addition, Industry 5.0 is an emerging field and the inclusion of bibliographic mapping with the increase of studies in different disciplines such as engineering, medicine, sociology, psychology in future studies will benefit the in-depth understanding of the subject. In addition, examining the differentiation of Industry 5.0 practices according to industries will contribute to the literature.

As a result, this book chapter aims to enlighten the driving forces that contribute to a deeper exploration of the concept of Industry 5.0 in the context of scientific studies, academic literature, business world and organizations from Industry 1.0 to so far.

## REFERENCES

Adel, A. (2022). Future of Industry 5.0 in Society: HumanCentric Solutions, Challenges and Prospective Research Areas. *Journal of Cloud Computing (Heidelberg, Germany)*, 11(1), 1–15. DOI: 10.1186/s13677-022-00314-5 PMID: 36101900

Aslam, F., Aimin, W., Li, M., & Ur Rehman, K. (2020). Innovation in the era of IoT and industry 5.0: Absolute innovation management (AIM) framework. *Information (Basel)*, 11(2), 124. DOI: 10.3390/info11020124

Barata, J., & Kayser, I. (2024). How will the digital twin shape the future of industry 5.0? *Technovation*, 134, 103025. Advance online publication. DOI: 10.1016/j.technovation.2024.103025

Barata, J., & Kayser, I. (2024). How will the digital twin shape the future of industry 5.0? *Technovation*, 134, 103025. Advance online publication. DOI: 10.1016/j.technovation.2024.103025

Bayarçelik, E. B., & Bumin Doyduk, H. (2020). Digitalization of business logistics activities and future directions. Ü. Hacıoğlu içinde, . Digital Business Strategies in Blockchain Ecosystems: Transformational Design and Future of Global Business, (s. 201-238).

Bayarçelik, E. B., & Bumin Doyduk, H. (2020). Digitalization of business logistics activities and future directions. Ü. Hacıoğlu içinde, . *Digital Business Strategies in Blockchain Ecosystems: Transformational Design and Future of Global Business,* (s. 201-238).

Bednar, P. M., & Welch, C. (2020). Socio-Technical Perspectives on Smart Working: Creating Meaningful and Sustainable Systems. *Information Systems Frontiers*, 22(2), 281–298. DOI: 10.1007/s10796-019-09921-1

Broo, D. G., Okyay, K., & Sait, S. M. (2022). Rethinking engineering education at the age of industry 5.0. *Journal of Industrial Information Integration*, 25, 100311. Advance online publication. DOI: 10.1016/j.jii.2021.100311

Carayannis, E. G., & Morawska-Jancelewicz, J. (2022). The Futures of Europe: Society 5.0 and Industry 5.0 as Driving Forces of Future Universities. *Journal of the Knowledge Economy*, 13(4), 3445–3471. DOI: 10.1007/s13132-021-00854-2

Choi, T.-M., Kumar, S., Yue, X., & Chan, H.-L. (2022). Disruptive Technologies and Operations Management in the Industry 4.0 Era and Beyond. *Production and Operations Management*, 31(1), 9–31. DOI: 10.1111/poms.13622

Cillo, V., Gregori, G. L., Daniele, L. M., Caputo, F., & Bitbol-Saba, N. (2022). Rethinking companies' culture through knowledge management lens during Industry 5.0 transition. *Journal of Knowledge Management*, 26(10), 2485–2498. DOI: 10.1108/JKM-09-2021-0718

Ciucu-Durnoi, A., Delcea, C., Stănescu, A., Teodorescu, C., & Vargas, V. (2024). Beyond Industry 4.0: Tracing the Path to Industry 5.0 through Bibliometric Analysis. *Sustainability (Basel)*, 16(12), 5251. DOI: 10.3390/su16125251

Demir, K., Döven, G., & Sezen, B. (2019). Industry 5.0 and Human-Robot Co-working. *Procedia Computer Science*, 158, 688–695. DOI: 10.1016/j.procs.2019.09.104

Dmitry, I. (2023). The Industry 5.0 framework: Viability-based integration of the resilience, sustainability, and human-centricity perspectives. *International Journal of Production Research*, 61(5), 1683–1695. DOI: 10.1080/00207543.2022.2118892

Donthu, N., Kumar, S., Mukherjee, D., Pandey, N., & Lim, W. M. (2021). Donthu, N., Kumar, S., Mukherjee, D.How to conduct a bibliometric analysis: An overview and guidelines. *Journal of Business Research*, 133, 285–296. DOI: 10.1016/j.jbusres.2021.04.070

European Commission. (2016). *Factories of the Future PPP: Towards Competitive EU Manufacturing*. EU Commission.

Foundation, N. R. (2016). *Research, Innovation and Enterprise (RIE) 2015 Plan*. Prime Minister's Office of Singapore.

Fraga-Lamas, P., Lopes, S. I., & Fernandez-Carames, T. M. (2021). Green IoT and Edge AI as Key Technological Enablers for a Sustainable Digital Transition towards a Smart Circular Economy: An Industry 5.0 Use Case. *Sensors (Basel)*, 21(17), 5745. Advance online publication. DOI: 10.3390/s21175745 PMID: 34502637

Gartoumi, K. I. (2024). Five-Year Review of Blockchain in Construction Management: Scientometric and Thematic Analysis (2017-2023). *Automation in Construction*, 168, 105773. Advance online publication. DOI: 10.1016/j.autcon.2024.105773

Ghobakhloo, M., Iranmanesh, M., Mubarak, M. F., Mubarik, M., Rejeb, A., & Nilashi, M. (2022). Identifying industry 5.0 contributions to sustainable development: A strategy roadmap for delivering sustainability values. *Sustainable Production and Consumption*, 33, 716–737. DOI: 10.1016/j.spc.2022.08.003

Grabowska, S., Saniuk, S., & Gajdzik, B. (2022). Industry 5.0: Improving humanization and sustainability of Industry 4.0. *Scientometrics*, 127(6), 3117–3144. DOI: 10.1007/s11192-022-04370-1 PMID: 35502439

Hermann, M., Pentek, T., & Otto, B. (2016). Design principles for industrie 4.0 scenarios. *System Sciences (HICSS)49th Hawaii International Conference* (pp. 3928-3937). IEEE.

Horvat, D., Jäger, A., & Lerch, C. M. (2024). Fostering innovation by complementing human competences and emerging technologies: An industry 5.0 perspective. *International Journal of Production Research*, •••, 1–25. DOI: 10.1080/00207543.2024.2372009

Huang, S., Wang, B., Li, X., Zheng, P., Mourtzis, D., & Wang, L. (2022). Industry 5.0 and Society 5.0-Comparison, complementation and co-evolution. *Journal of Manufacturing Systems*, 64, 424–428. DOI: 10.1016/j.jmsy.2022.07.010

Ivanov, D. (2023). The Industry 5.0 framework: Viability-based integration of the resilience, sustainability, and human-centricity perspectives. *International Journal of Production Research*, 61(5), 1683–1695. DOI: 10.1080/00207543.2022.2118892

Jan, M. A., Khan, F., Khan, R., Mastorakis, S., Menon, V. G., Alazab, M., & Watters, P. (2021). Lightweight Mutual Authentication and Privacy-Preservation Scheme for Intelligent Wearable Devices in Industrial-CPS. *IEEE Transactions on Industrial Informatics*, 17(8), 5829–5839. DOI: 10.1109/TII.2020.3043802 PMID: 33981186

Javed, A., Shahzad, F., Rehman, S., Bin Zikria, Y., Razzak, I., Jalil, Z., & Xu, G. (2022). Future smart cities requirements, emerging technologies, applications, challenges, and future aspects. *Cities (London, England)*, 129, 103794. Advance online publication. DOI: 10.1016/j.cities.2022.103794

Kagermann, H., Wahlster, W., & Helbig, J. (2013). *Recommendations for implementing the strategic initiative INDUSTRIE 4.0 Final report of the Industrie 4.0 Working Group*. Forschungs Union.

Kagnicioglu, C. H., & Ozdemir, E. (2017). *Evaluation of SMEs in Eskişehir within the context of industry 4.0. Procedia*. PressAcademia.

Karmaker, C. L., Bari, A. M., Anam, M. Z., Ahmed, T., Ali, S. M., Pacheco, D. A., & Moktadir, M. A. (2023). Industry 5.0 challenges for post-pandemic supply chain sustainability in an emerging economy. *International Journal of Production Economics*, 258, 108806. Advance online publication. DOI: 10.1016/j.ijpe.2023.108806

Khan, M., Haleem, A., & Javaid, M. (2023). Changes and improvements in Industry 5.0: A strategic approach to overcome the challenges of Industry 4.0. *Green Technologies and Sustainability, 1*(2).

Kilavuz, F. (2023). A bibliometric analysis of multicultural education research. *Sosyal Bilimler ve Eğitim Dergisi, 6* (Education Special Issue), 216-238. DOI: 10.53047/josse.1359321

Leng, J., Sha, W., Lin, Z., Jing, J., Liu, Q., & Chen, X. (2023). Blockchained smart contract pyramid-driven multi-agent autonomous process control for resilient individualised manufacturing towards Industry 5.0. *International Journal of Production Research*, 61(13), 4302–4321. DOI: 10.1080/00207543.2022.2089929

Leng, J., Sha, W., Wang, B., Zheng, P., Zhuang, C., Liu, Q., Wuest, T., Mourtzis, D., & Wang, L. (2022). Industry 5.0: Prospect and retrospect. *Journal of Manufacturing Systems*, 65, 279–295. DOI: 10.1016/j.jmsy.2022.09.017

Li, J., Weng, G., Yue, P., Li, C., & Wang, N. (2021). A scientometric review of tourism carrying capacity research: Cooperation, hotspots, and prospect. *Journal of Cleaner Production*, 325, 129278. Advance online publication. DOI: 10.1016/j.jclepro.2021.129278

Longo, F., Padovano, A., & Umbrello, S. (2020). Value-Oriented and Ethical Technology Engineering in Industry 5.0: A Human-Centric Perspective for the Design of the Factory of the Future. *Applied Sciences (Basel, Switzerland)*, 10(12), 4182. Advance online publication. DOI: 10.3390/app10124182

Lu, Y., Zheng, H., Chand, S., Xia, W., Liu, Z., Xu, X., Wang, L., Qin, Z., & Bao, J. (2022). Outlook on human-centric manufacturing towards Industry 5.0. *Journal of Manufacturing Systems*, 62, 612–627. DOI: 10.1016/j.jmsy.2022.02.001

Ma, N., Yao, X., & Wang, K. (2024). A complex network-based approach for resilient and flexible design resource allocation in industry 5.0. *Computers in Industry*, 159-160, 104108. Advance online publication. DOI: 10.1016/j.compind.2024.104108

Maddikunta, P. K., Pham, Q.-V., B, P., Deepa, N., Dev, K., Gadekallu, T. R., Ruby, R., & Liyanage, M. (2022). Industry 5.0: A survey on enabling technologies and potential applications. *Journal of Industrial Information Integration*, 26, 100257. Advance online publication. DOI: 10.1016/j.jii.2021.100257

Mourao, P. R., & Martinho, V. D. (2020). Forest entrepreneurship: A bibliometric analysis and a discussion about the co-authorship networks of an emerging scientific field. *Journal of Cleaner Production*, 256, 120413. Advance online publication. DOI: 10.1016/j.jclepro.2020.120413

Mourtzis, D., Panopoulos, N., Angelopoulos, J., Wang, B., & Wang, L. (2022). Human centric platforms for personalized value creation in metaverse. *Journal of Manufacturing Systems*, 65, 653–659. DOI: 10.1016/j.jmsy.2022.11.004

Mrugalska, B., & Wyrwicka, M. K. (2017). Towards lean production in industry 4.0. *Procedia Engineering*, 182, 466–473. DOI: 10.1016/j.proeng.2017.03.135

Nahavandi, S. (2019). Industry 5.0-A Human-Centric Solution. *Sustainability (Basel)*, 11(16), 4371. Advance online publication. DOI: 10.3390/su11164371

Nourmohammadi, A., Fathi, M., & Ng, A. H. (2022). Balancing and scheduling assembly lines with human-robot collaboration tasks. *Computers & Operations Research*, 140, 105674. Advance online publication. DOI: 10.1016/j.cor.2021.105674

Office, C. (2015). *Report on The 5th Science and Technology Basic Plan*. Cabinet Office of Japan.

Ozdemir, V., & Hekim, N. (2018). Birth of industry 5.0: Making sense of big data with artificial intelligence, 'the Internet of things' and next-generation technology policy. *OMICS: A Journal of Integrative Biology*, 22(1), 65–76. DOI: 10.1089/omi.2017.0194 PMID: 29293405

Özkeser, B. (2018). *Lean Innovation Approach in Industry 5.0*. The Eurasia Proceedings of Science, Engineering & Mathematics.

Rafael, R., Shirley, A. J., & Liveris, A. (2014). *Rafael, R., Shirley, A. J., & Liveris, A. (2014). Report To The President Accelerating US Advanced Manufacturing. Report, US.* Washington DC: Report.

Rozanec, J. M., Novalija, I., Zajec, P., Kenda, K., Ghinani, H. T., Suh, S., & Soldatos, J. (2023). Human-centric artificial intelligence architecture for industry 5.0 applications. *International Journal of Production Research*, 20(20), 6847–6872. DOI: 10.1080/00207543.2022.2138611

Sachsenmeier, P. (2016). Industry 5.0—The relevance and implications of bionics and synthetic biology. *Engineering (Beijing)*, 2(2), 225–229. DOI: 10.1016/J.ENG.2016.02.015

Saniuk, S., Grabowska, S., & Straka, M. (2022). Identification of Social and Economic Expectations: Contextual Reasons for the Transformation Process of Industry 4.0 into the Industry 5.0 Concept. *Sustainability (Basel)*, 3(3), 1391. Advance online publication. DOI: 10.3390/su14031391

Santhi, A. R., & Muthuswamy, P. (2023). Industry 5.0 or industry 4.0S? Introduction to industry 4.0 and a peek into the prospective industry 5.0 technologies. *International Journal on Interactive Design and Manufacturing*, 17(2), 947–979. DOI: 10.1007/s12008-023-01217-8

Sarkar, B. D., Shardeo, V., Dwivedi, A., & Pamucar, D. (2024). Digital transition from industry 4.0 to industry 5.0 in smart manufacturing: A framework for sustainable future. *Technology in Society*, 78, 102649. Advance online publication. DOI: 10.1016/j.techsoc.2024.102649

Sharma, R., & Gupta, H. (2024). Harmonizing sustainability in industry 5.0 era: Transformative strategies for cleaner production and sustainable competitive advantage. *Journal of Cleaner Production*, 445, 141118. Advance online publication. DOI: 10.1016/j.jclepro.2024.141118

Sindhwani, R., Afridi, S., Kumar, A., Banaits, A., Luthra, S., & Singh, P. L. (2022). Can industry 5.0 revolutionize the wave of resilience and social value creation? A multi-criteria framework to analyze enablers. *Technology in Society*, 68, 101887. Advance online publication. DOI: 10.1016/j.techsoc.2022.101887

Sousa, M. J., & Rocha, Á. (2019). Skills for Disruptive Digital Business. *Journal of Business Research*, 94, 257–263. DOI: 10.1016/j.jbusres.2017.12.051

Van Eck, N., & Waltman, L. (2010). Software survey: VOSviewer, a computer program for bibliometric mapping. *Scientometrics*, 84(2), 523–538. DOI: 10.1007/s11192-009-0146-3 PMID: 20585380

Van Erp, T., Carvalho, N., Gerolamo, M., Gonçalves, R., Rytter, N., & Gladysz, B. (2024). Industry 5.0: A new strategy framework for sustainability management and beyond. *Journal of Cleaner Production*, 461, 142271. Advance online publication. DOI: 10.1016/j.jclepro.2024.142271

Xifan, Y., Ma, N., Zhang, J., Wang, K., Yang, E., & Faccio, M. (2024). Enhancing wisdom manufacturing as industrial metaverse for industry and society 5.0. *Journal of Intelligent Manufacturing*, 35(1), 235–255. DOI: 10.1007/s10845-022-02027-7

Xun, X., Yuqian, L., Vogel-Heuser, B., & Lihui, W. (2021). Industry 4.0 and Industry 5.0-Inception, conception and perception. *Journal of Manufacturing Systems*, 61, 530–535. DOI: 10.1016/j.jmsy.2021.10.006

Yasue, N., Mahmoodi, E., Zúñiga, E., & Fathi, M. (2025). Analyzing resilient performance of workers with multiple disturbances in production systems. *Applied Ergonomics*, 122, 104391. Advance online publication. DOI: 10.1016/j.apergo.2024.104391 PMID: 39342914

Yıldız, A. (2018). Endüstri 4.0 ve akıllı fabrikalar. *Sakarya University Journal of Science*, 548-558.

Yin, S., & Yu, Y. (2022). An adoption-implementation framework of digital green knowledge to improve the performance of digital green innovation practices for industry 5.0. *Journal of Cleaner Production*, 363, 132608. Advance online publication. DOI: 10.1016/j.jclepro.2022.132608

Youssef, A., & Mejri, I. (2023). Linking Digital Technologies to Sustainability through Industry 5.0: A bibliometric Analysis. *Sustainability*.

# Chapter 4
# Resilience and Human-Centric Perspectives for Organizations in Industry 5.0

**R. Ansrose**
https://orcid.org/0009-0000-4750-5848
*Christ University, India*

**Ila Anand**
https://orcid.org/0000-0001-8837-4450
*Christ University, India*

## ABSTRACT

*In the emerging world researchers put forward the idea of industry 5.0, focusing on the concept of human centricity, sustainability and resilience approaches in the organizations. Industry 5.0 includes technological advancement along with giving importance to the human capital. During the past, the industrial revolution emphasized the productivity, production quality and growth of business. There was less importance for the human capital and employees well being in the changing industrial style giving importance to the human capital, by integrating technological advancements. It is recognised for the societal values that are embedded, the whole industry 5.0 revolves around sustainability, human centric and resilience in the organization. In this book chapter we explore the concept and applicability of these topics. The book chapter used literature review method and case study analysis for thorough understanding of the subject.*

## 1. INTRODUCTION

Many organizations suffered significant losses during the pandemic, and numerous businesses saw declines because of the unstable market conditions. Although there are still obstacles to overcome, organizations are updating their plans to reduce the effects and rebuild effectively. The idea of industry 5.0 has been studied since 2007 but in 2021, the European Commission ultimately coined the term "Fifth revolution" after deliberating and assessing the situation. Industrial revolutions are the key turning

DOI: 10.4018/979-8-3693-8181-6.ch004

points in which the human capital, technology, industry culture, and other aspects of the economy all saw growth and advancement.

During the late 18th century, the first industrial revolution mainly focused on increasing productivity then it shifted to division of labors, economies of scale during the second industrial revolution. In the mid 20 century there was a drastic shift of industrial concept from traditional way of manufacturing and production to adapting and integrating technologies, automation of different technologies occurred. From the early 21st century, the 4.0 industry had a great impact and brought a huge change in the business environment and industry standards. During this revolution the integration of new technologies was much higher than the previous. The notable technological advancements were in big data, AI automations, IOT and many others. Due to the dynamic nature of the business environment here comes the need and importance of industry 5.0

"Industry 5.0 includes technological advancement along with giving importance to the human capital". During the past, the industrial revolution emphasized on the productivity, production quality and growth of business. There was a lack of importance for human capital and employee's wellbeing, but in the dynamic changing industrial style started giving importance to human capital, by integrating technological advancements. The main 3 pillars of industry 5.0 are sustainability, human centric and resilience. In this revolution they recognize the importance and ability of industry not only regarding the task completion but also the achievement of a new culture in the society wherein holistic and humanistic approach to uplift economic development. Due to the volatility of different factors which affects the business environment in order to reduce the hindrance and avoid unforeseeable loss and downfalls the organization is implementing the new ideology of resilience in the organizations. From a scientific point of view, the development and growth of the flexibility concept offer more impactful and in-depth methods to perceive the interconnectedness of society and the world's increasingly dynamic and challenging nature (Pinheiro et al., 2022). The actual meaning of resilience is "The ability of individuals to recover speedily following unpleasant events like shock, distress, etc" (Oxford University Press). According to the literature resilience is the ability to bounce back quickly with minimal efforts (Boin & Eeten, 2013).

The urgent need to solve some of the major issues affecting contemporary organizational landscapes is the foundation for the significance of studying Traditional industrial systems are insufficient to manage unexpected shocks including technology changes, economic uncertainties, and global crises because global markets are becoming more complex and unsure. (Wagner et al., 2024) The necessity to solve some of the most pressing issues facing modern organizational landscapes makes research on durability and employee focused perspectives in Industry 5.0 crucial. Global markets are becoming more intricate and volatile, and conventional industrial methods have not been able to handle hitherto unseen upheavals like technology advancements, unstable economies, and world crises (Wagner et al., 2024). This area of study is extremely important to comprehending how technical innovation and human creativity can complement one another and coexist to improve organizational performance in such a complicated global setting.

This chapter will critically examine the intricate relationship between human oriented perspectives and organizational ability to bounce back in Industry 5.0, which looks at how technological innovation and strategic integration of human potential can change organizational capabilities in a world that is becoming more complex by the day. This chapter's primary goal is to challenge established industrial paradigms. It highlights and demonstrates the new industry ecosystem wherein people focused adaptability is a fundamental force behind organizational transformation in the pursuit of innovation, sustainability, and societal impact. Through an overview of recent research, this chapter aims to compile a balanced perspective on organizational resilience, highlighting how human creativity, emotional intelligence, and adaptive capabilities within an organization may be important factors to cope with the complex technological and social environments of Industry 5.0.

In this book chapter we are going to discuss further the concept and different approaches in the organization in industry 5.0. The following section will go into depth regarding how we need to view growth and advancement in the context of Industry 5.0, which represents an important change in perspective. It involves rethinking the role of industry in society and placing a strong emphasis on creating value that encompasses human welfare and environmental stewardship in addition to fiscal success. The comprehensive strategy aspires to build a production era that will be more resilient, viable, and centered on individuals. With the help of a case study we will dive deeper into the potential various companies could employ similar strategies to capitalize on the principles of Industry 5.0. A multitude of firms that are making the shift to more resilient and human-centered operational frameworks can benefit greatly from the lessons we can take away from Haier's journey.

## 2. OBJECTIVES

This chapter will enable the reader to have a better understanding of sturdiness in organization and human centric organizational culture in the industry 5.0. In this chapter we will discuss the core concepts of industry 5.0 their impact and benefits in the society as well as in the organization. It also covers the importance of agility of the organization and human focused approach in individuals and also in the organizations. Further discussion about the technological aspect as an enabler of the new approaches. The chapter starts with a general and conceptual discussion about having a major stake in the industry 5.0, further will explore in depth the key terms and their potential advantages, challenges and opportunities. With the help of a case study (Haier Case study: Employee centric approach) we will debate the implementation of how these paradigms shift their objectives and business strategy. We will also explore the implications of this strategy and how it impacted the organizational growth and development of the organization and the advantages and disadvantages of the adaptation.

### 2.1 Key Learning Outcomes

- Describe the key concept of industry 5.0 and its conceptual framework, focusing on human resilience and human centric approach.
- Explaining the importance of human centric and adaptability to bounce back approaches in the organization for the further development of the industry and organization in the industry 5.0.
- Discuss the role of technologies as a key source of enabler in the efficient and effective implication and adaptation of the approaches in the dynamic organization environment.
- Discuss about the changes and threats that can be encountered in the shift of industry 4.0 to 5.0 and also the changes in the approach in organizations.

## 3. LITERATURE REVIEW

Industry 5.0 was put forward by the European Commission ten years after Industry 4.0 had been initially proposed. While it has been influenced by values in comparison to Industry 4.0, that is perceived to be driven by technology (Xu et al., 2021). The business climate is currently going through a paradigm transition from one focused on production and sales to one that integrates technologies and human-centered techniques to create a holistic working environment. According to current studies, in order to reduce and navigate the complexities of the new industrial era, it is necessary to take into account the application and need to embrace the proposal of industry 5.0 in contemporary society while taking into account the ethical concerns that can be encountered along with sustainable engagement and collaborative mentality among cross-sectoral (Barata & Kayser, 2023).

The crucial issue facing sector 4.0 was about the moral considerations that affected people in the community as well as those who worked in the economy, who were not receiving adequate consideration and who were lacking better working conditions in terms of work-life balance and physical structuring of the industry, The main factors focusing in the 5.0 industry are sustainability, human centric approach and elasticity. An exercise in looking forward produced Industry 5.0, a framework for describing how industry and new social demands and trends will coexist (Xu et al., 2021).

As "serving the requirements of this generation while preserving the capacity of future generations to continue to fulfill their own necessities," sustainability as per United Nations Brundtland Commission in 1987(The United Nations). Industry 5.0 represents a shift in organizational strategy from towards the conventional misuse of resources and in the direction of initiatives that are environmentally friendly, products that are environmentally conscious, and an environmentally conscious strategy. According to scholars, Industry 5.0 has the ability to advance goals for sustainable development including socio environmental responsibility, resilience, and human-centricity, as well as to surpass the profit-centered efficiency of Industry 4.0 (Ghobakhloo et al., 2022).

In the past few years, academics and professionals have concentrated primarily on disaster and crisis management (Boin & Eeten, 2013). The concept's significance is crucial during this instance since it addresses the organization's concern to create an environment in which uncertain events can be absorbed and recovered quickly with minimal impact on management. This ensures that business activities and responsibilities continue despite suffering significant consequences that would negatively affect the company's overall ability to operate (Abdullah et al., 2013).

Industry 4.0's primary goal was to increase productivity through the best possible use of available resources, organizational procedures, and technological interpretation. The literature study elucidates the rise of industry 5.0 and the elements that are propelling this new revolutionary movement. The three elements that form the foundation of the new revolution are explained in great detail by previous literary works. The literature research has clearly highlighted and understood the critical roles that sustainability, human centricity, and sturdiness play for industrial adaptation to new techniques and societal improvement.

## 4. METHODOLOGY

In order to determine the principles of industry 5.0, this study relies on the review of literature of previous research, emphasizing resilience and human-aligned methods contained within the organization and their ongoing development. The study is conducted with the support of research papers, journal articles, business reports, and case studies that are relevant to the subject, that are published in the last 10 years with the business and management context. There is a significant lack of resources in this area so the articles and resources used were irrespective of any national boundaries. The resources are selected through the applicability, relevance to the current market dynamics and alignments to the new approach, industry 5.0 in the business environment. There is an empirical literature gap in this context, the applicability and certain challenges that can be encountered in the implementation.

Theoretical frameworks for the contents that are relevant for the industry are available but there is a lack of addressing the potential drawbacks and hindrances that can be encountered. Also there is a lack of literature work in the applicability and adoption of industry 5.0. In this study we are using a dual approach using review of literature and also case study to understand the theoretical aspect as well as the real-world view of this new adaptation.

Since the subject is new and diversified, this study makes extensive use of previous research on the subject that was relevant to the content. A broad literature review was used to identify the conceptual framework, and data for the study was gathered. For the most part, journal articles and online articles are utilized for the literature review; however, certain industry reports, textbooks, and online articles are also employed for the in-depth analysis.

A real-world case study of Haier Group Corporation was employed to gain an in-depth knowledge of the concept, evaluate its applicability in real-life situations, analyze its effects, and determine how these approaches will affect the company's expansion and development. This analysis will also consider how other businesses might leverage similar strategies to capitalize on the principles of Industry 5.0. Also, with the help of another case study the application of Industry 5.0 principles was examined through a real-world case study of Siemens Corporation, emphasizing the incorporation of human-centered technology into manufacturing settings. In the era of Industry 5.0, this case study can assist any firm integrate technical advancement with human potential (Büchi et al., 2020).

## 5. DISCUSSION

### 5.1 Industry 5.0

#### 5.1.1 Brief overview of Industry 5.0

Due to low employee satisfaction and grievances in workplaces during the fourth industrial revolution, which is centered only on increasing productivity and production efficiency, new revolutions must be developed in order to keep up with changing market conditions. Industry 5.0 is the outcome of intensive research conducted during the industry 4.0 phase, which researched the gaps in the fourth revolution, how to close those gaps, and how to improve the industry environment in response to the dynamic changes taking place globally.

Industry 5.0 is based on three primary pillars: resilience, human centricity, and sustainability. In this revolution, they acknowledge the role and capacity of industry in achieving social and employee welfare, as well as in completing tasks and fostering a new, sustainable culture in society. This transformation that is more holistic driven embedded with the advancement of technologies embraces the workers empowerment and societal impact (Harbeke & Künlen, 2024)

According to Nahavandi, N. the shift of industry 5.0 it is a transformative approach to the organizational strategy refines different relationships that prevailed in the industry, emerges from a critical recognition that the real organizational resilience cannot be only achieve through the transformation of technologies alone it requires a holistic approach wherein human beings at the center of the strategic decision making (Nahavandi, 2019). In Industry 5.0, resilience is more than just an organization's ability to survive. It is a dynamic, adaptable capacity that combines technical innovation with human potential (Sommer et al., 2024).

Industry 5.0, according to Harbeke and Künlen (Harbeke & Künlen, 2024), is a more comprehensive societal shift in which industrial growth is inextricably related to social and human welfare. It forces us to reconsider how technology, employment, and human potential are related. In order to comprehend how this novel approach transforms our perception of organizational capacities in the age of Industry 5.0, this chapter thoroughly examines the deep connection between adaptability and workforce-oriented approaches. We will disentangle the intricate relationships that establish people as the real engine of organizational and technology innovation through state-of-the-art research, theoretical understanding, and real-world applications.

### 5.1.2 Evolution of Industry 5.0

Late 18th century was primarily concerned with raising productivity; in the second industrial era, it was more concerned with economies of scale and labor division majorly focused on the industrial enhancement of production and manufacturing. The industrial concept underwent a significant change in the middle of the 20th century, moving from the conventional methods of production and manufacturing to the automation of various technologies and the adaptation and integration of new technologies during this period many of the inventions of technologies occurred. The corporate environment and industry standards saw significant changes as a result of the 4.0 industry, which began to emerge in the early 21st century, the period in which technologies took a major stake in the efficiency and importance in the modern business world.

In a time of constant development, the concept of Industry 5.0 has emerged as a symbol of progress in the modern world. There are significant differences between the past phases of industrialization and this current phase, which is still under research and not fully implemented. At its core, Industry 5.0 envisions human workers happily collaborating with state-of-the-art technologies, like artificial intelligence-powered robotics. The most significant technology developments were in the areas of big data, IoT, AI automation, and many more. In the current era, the industry places greater emphasis on technologies than on human capital. However, in industry 5.0, the emerging industrial revolution, technological advancement was given equal weight with human capital (Carter & Wilkinson, 2023).

### 5.1.3 Importance of industry 5.0

Industry 5.0 is altering the paradigm and brings the resolution as it will lessen emphasis on the technology and assume that the potential for advancement is dependent on collaboration among the humans and robots. By using customized products, the industrial revolution is increasing client happiness. Industry 5.0 is necessary in today's business environment due to the recent technology advancements in order to provide the manufacturing industry with both competitive advantages and economic growth (Adel, 2022). The fifth industrial revolution enables the growth and development of society and organizations having strong societal values and ethical consideration for a better future. Industry 5.0 is substituting previous innovations, and due to its extreme precision and the reduction of human labor effort and time spent through mechanical work, it has proven a highly effective method (Adel, 2022).

## 5.2. Understanding Industry 5.0

### 5.2.1 Definition and Key Characteristics

Industry 5.0 is termed as the next stage in the industrial revolution. Industry 5.0 encompasses both technology innovation and prioritizing human capital. It is acknowledged for the deeply ingrained societal ideals, as is the entire industry. The main theme of industry 5.0 is prioritizing the wellbeing of the human capital as well as the societal wellbeing considering the development of the organization in order to achieve the strategic goals of the industry as well as organization, it is a future oriented process wherein integrating the present needs while not compromising the need the future. (Raiche & de Oliveira, 2023) It involves extensive human-robotic and digital system collaboration, with a focus on personalization, human creativity, and emotional intelligence in industrial processes. It also helps to lower employee workloads, improve work quality, and preserve a healthy work-life balance for workers. It does this by focusing on society values and goals rather than just economic ones (Barata & Kayser, 2023).

In contrast to previous revolutions, particularly industry 4.0, industry 5.0 places greater focus on a people focused approach. It emphasizes the value of the organization's human resource. For a more efficient workflow and higher caliber of output, human resources collaborate and integrate with technology. Because technology uses less labor and takes less time to complete tasks, it helps employees feel less stressed and overwhelmed about doing the tasks they are assigned. This promotes a healthy work-life balance (Barata & Kayser, 2023). Industry 5.0 aims to promote environmental sustainability and take into account the resource needs of future generations through circular economy models that reduce resource waste through production and other functions using the fewest resources possible. Its forerunner, Industry 4.0, aims to reduce environmental effect while increasing social value by integrating socio-environmental goals into its operating framework (Ghobakhloo et al., 2022). Industry 5.0's primary goal is to create a social culture and structure that can adapt to unforeseen circumstances and obstacles.

Resilience is one of industry 5.0's key features (Lengnick-Hall et al., 2011). One of the ideas that transcends the conventional definition of organizational adaptation. "The dynamic capacity of systems to anticipate, respond to, and learn from surprise disruptions while maintaining core functionality and capacity for transformation" is how Krings et al. (2024). According to this concept, it is not a passive state of survival but rather an active, adaptive process (Krings et al., 2024,). Industry 5.0 views it as a proactive, dynamic capability that is intricately woven into the technology and human ecosystems of the business rather than as a reactive mechanism. More than just a theoretical concept, Industry 5.0's more employee-oriented resilience model is a strategic necessity for businesses looking to prosper in a world that is becoming more complex and uncertain by the day. Organizations may create more inventive, flexible, and essentially sustainable approaches to organizational development by putting human potential back at the forefront of technical innovation.

### 5.2.2 Comparison of Industry 5.0 with Industry 4.0

The fifth industrial revolution, which emphasizes a more significant incorporation of technological advances and humans as interrelated components of the contemporary business environment, places more emphasis on digital collaboration between humans and machines than the fourth, which was focused on improving manufacturing and supply chain functions in the business circumstances. Integrating the aid of human critical thinking abilities, this transition will enable more precise and rapid industrial automation fulfillment with creativity, innovation, and successful products (*Industry 5.0: Adding the Human Edge to Industry 4.0*, n.d.).

Industry 5.0 is a socio-technical revolution where societal values are taken into consideration and integrated with technological breakthroughs, whereas industry 4.0 focused more on technical or digital transformation. Industry 5.0 is another name for a humanized vision of technical advancements in the industry that balances the requirements of society and workers now and in the future while optimizing energy use, material processing, and product life cycles in a sustainable manner (Barata & Kayser, 2023). Industry 4.0 is the intelligent networking of machines and processes for the industry based on the cyber physical system (CPS), technologies that achieve intelligent control using embedded networking systems. Industry 5.0 recognizes the power of industry to achieve societal goals beyond the production to the growth perspectives of individuals and society (Xu et al., 2021).

### 5.2.3 Core Pillars: Sustainability, Human-Centricity, and Resilience

The main 3 core pillars of industry 5.0 are resilience, human centricity and sustainability; they are the key drivers of the new industrial revolution. Sustainability is the new shift of mindset in the industry, people are concerned about the minimum utilization of resources. As per the oxford dictionary sustainability means the ability of the environment such as socio political, economic and cultural factors of human society aspects to continue while meeting the needs of the present while without compromising the need of the future to meet their needs and requirements (*Sustainability Noun - Definition, Pictures, Pronunciation and Usage Notes | Oxford Advanced Learner's Dictionary at OxfordLearnersDictionaries.com*, n.d.). Consumers are shifting their mentality towards sustainable products and production. The government encourages the industrial environment to be more sustainable so that smooth transition organizations are adapting several ways for sustainable development. Industrial Revolution 5.0 makes a way for this smooth transformation that is majorly sustainable and efficient for the industry as well as the society.

While during the Industrial Revolution 4.0 there was less consideration and importance for the human capital in the industry this caused low worker force satisfaction due to less incorporation of workers in the organization, fewer importance given for the human capital and some concerns with the trust, this is not only with employees but also stakeholders in the organization. Industry 5.0 mainly focuses on this factor so it can ease the work, along with a strong trust between the organizations and stakeholders. According to the World Economic Forum, the concept of human-centricity offers a fresh perspective on managing data as well as its potential uses. Focusing on anything that can be referred to as (self-)sovereignty, self-determination, self-governance, autonomy, agency, or the like, in terms of the individuals engaged in gathering information is known as human-centricity (*On the Importance of Human-Centricity and Data*, n.d.).

Resilience is very important in the contemporary condition of the economy, it is the capacity to regain happiness, success, etc. following a challenging or negative event (*RESILIENCE | English Meaning - Cambridge Dictionary*, 2024). Fernandez-Gonzalez defines resilience as a complex and interactive interaction between technology infrastructure, human potential, and organizational capacities from a systemic perspective. For them, it encompasses both generating places for ongoing learning and creativity as well as opposition (Fernandez-Gonzalez et al., 2024,). Resilient organizations thrive in spite of unanticipated, unpredictable, negative, and typically volatile circumstances. The main concern of Industry 5.0 is that an organization can enhance its strategic management of its human resources to cultivate competencies among its core employees. These competencies, when combined at the organizational level, enable organizations to respond to adversity in a resilient way (Lengnick-Hall et al., 2011).

## 5.3. The Concept of Organizational Resilience

### 5.3.1 Defining Organizational Resilience

Beyond the traditional idea of organizational adaptability, resilience has a more complex approach. Krings define resilience as a system's dynamic capacity to foresee, react to, and learn from the unexpected while preserving its essential functionality and adaptability. According to this concept, resilience is not a passive survival strategy but rather an active adaptive process (Krings et al., n.d.) . Fernandez-Gonzalez also considered the complicated interaction between technological foundation, individual potential, and capacity for organization (Fernandez-Gonzalez et al., 2024,). According to Duchek in ecological systems theory defines organizational resilience; “A dynamic, multilevel capability including Adaptive capacity, Learning mechanisms, Strategic foresight, Organizational agility, and Innovative potential Duchek (2020). According to Celik et al. (2022) from the perspective of management research can be articulated as comprehensive organizational competence, encompassing elements like technological adaptability, strategic flexibility, human resource management, innovative problem-solving, and a culture of continuous learning.

There are two different interpretations in the literature. According to a few, organizational capacity to bounce back after adversity and unanticipated adverse circumstances and restore regular operations. The capacity of an organization to rapidly and steadily restore the normal course of operations after experiencing adversity with little damage is known as organizational resilience. The expertise, abilities, and skills at the individual level as well as the internal procedures and techniques that a company employs to conceptually orient itself, take decisive action to move forward, and create an environment of different perspectives and adaptable incorporation which allows it to survive the possibly crippling effects of a disruptive shock are all components of the ability of an organization for resilience (Lengnick-Hall et al., 2011).The capacity to adjust, bounce back, and develop in the face of hardship, stress, or tragedy is a sign of resilience. It frequently entails becoming more powerful and competent when confronted with difficulties rather than just returning to one's pre-challenge position. Those that are resilient often possess traits like optimism, emotional control, problem-solving abilities, and the ability to keep a positive attitude in the face of adversity (Dreyer, 2024).

### 5.3.2 Types of Resilience

The idea of resilience can be applied to a wide range of business processes as well as to day-to-day living; it can be applied as a mindset that must be developed in order to develop the strength to overcome potentially disastrous situations. In both the management and psychological contexts, comes in various forms. Resilience is classified into four areas in the psychological context: mental/cognitive, social, emotional, and physical. Physical resilience is the body's capacity to bounce back from disease. The skill and capacity to control one's emotions and mental health in times of stress and strain is known as emotional resilience. The capability to fortify social networks and relationships in order to offer strength and support when needed during difficult times is known as social resilience. The last type of psychological resilience is cognitive or mental resilience, which is the capacity to maintain concentration, engage in critical analysis and evaluation, and make decisions under duress (Dreyer, 2024).

Financial, operational and organizational are the few forms of resilience from a management standpoint. The capacity of an organization to generate and possess the necessary cash to weather emergency conditions is known as financial resilience. The largest problems of the present are placing serious financial strain on people. These hurricanes can only be overcome by organizations that already have strong balance sheets (*6 Types of Resilience Companies Need Today*, 2021). Operational resilience is the ability to react constructively to misfortune that would endanger its capacity to function, where in organizational resilience focus on the overall plan, as well as its capacity to endure and operate following a disaster.

### 5.3.3 Importance of Resilience in the Face of Digital Disruption and Global Challenges

As we go deeper into this subject, it becomes clear that resilience to digital disruptions and challenges is not just a technological idea—given the potential for failure, but also an essential organizational and societal necessity in the increasingly interconnected world. Developing a strategic plan of action to follow in order to get out of the disruptive circumstance is beneficial to the organization. It facilitates the organization's ability to quickly adjust to changes with little disruption to its regular operations. It assists the company in developing a predictive model of the events or elements that disrupt and cause difficulty in the workplace following a thorough assessment and analysis of both internal and external factors.

## 5.4. Human-Centric Approaches in Industry 5.0

### 5.4.1 Defining Human-Centricity in Organizational Context

The industrial approach has undergone a significant change, with a focus presently shifted towards human capital instead of machinery and production. Industry 5.0's fundamental principle is a human-centric strategy, which places the welfare of the worker first and makes use of technical advancements to produce high-quality, cost-effective goods. An employee-oriented strategy is another way to describe this. By keeping employees in the center and giving them the proper pay, career growth, less work, a nice working environment, and various other kinds of implementation, this will be increasing employee satisfaction.

Employees or workers will have a strong sense of trust and commitment to the organization as a result. The main issue in the fourth industrial revolution was worker and employee dissatisfaction and grievances. A certain percentage of the human capital believed that technological advancements might result in instability and loss of employment, but in the fifth industrial revolution changing the mentality and making a strong base of trust to the employee that it is human capital oriented than technological, thus attention was paid to long-term strategies that would bridge the gap between industry 4.0 and human capital.

### 5.4.2 Balancing Human Skills With Technological Advancements

Technology aids in adapting to environmental changes and makes tasks less complicated for individuals. The market is dynamically growing in a collaborative culture where human skill and technology are interdependent. A lot of people are concerned about striking a balance between innovation in technology and human talents. Determining the necessary skill sets and what skills employees already possess can be problematic. It is crucial to bridge the gap between human talent and technology because integrating technologies, especially advancements in technology, may be simply deployed if the business has the suitable qualified worker or workers readily accessible.

A continuous learning environment and culture within the organization can help the organization maintain and balance human skill with technological advancement. The organization can invest a significant amount of money in employee training to help bridge the skills gap. By implementing the appropriate training and development initiatives after analyzing the organization's requirements and implementing the appropriate technologies. (*Integrating Technology and Human Skills for Future Workplaces*, 2024)

### 5.4.3 Siemens: A Case Study in Adaptive Workforce Transformation

Siemens is leading the way in the adoption of Industry 5.0, showcasing a creative method of integrating technology that is focused on people in digital manufacturing settings. The business has created a revolutionary approach that skillfully combines workforce empowerment and technology innovation because it understands the vital role that human potential plays (Büchi et al., 2020). Developing cooperative ecosystems where technology enhances rather than replaces human capabilities is at the heart of the organization's implementation strategy. The creation of collaborative robotics systems that support human workers and improve their operational effectiveness and decision-making skills is essential to this strategy. Siemens is notable for introducing "digital twin" technologies that provide workers extraordinary insights and control over complex manufacturing environments by allowing them to mimic and optimize production processes.

Siemens' adaptive workforce approach is based on continuous learning initiatives. The organization has proactively addressed possible skill obsolescence by implementing extensive reskilling activities that guarantee staff stay technologically relevant. These initiatives aim to establish a dynamic learning culture in which focused staff development is combined with technological advancements. The company's performance data demonstrate the impressive results of this strategy. Siemens demonstrated the significant potential of adaptive organizational approach technological integration by achieving a 27% improvement in staff productivity. A robust and creative organizational environment has been created by the strategy, which has also greatly increased employee engagement and technological adaptation in addition to numerical gains. Siemens is a prime example of the revolutionary potential of Industry 5.0 principles by emphasizing technology synergy and human potential. This makes Siemens an appealing model for businesses attempting to negotiate the challenging terrain of contemporary industrial innovation (Büchi et al., 2020).

### 5.4.4 Ethical Considerations in Human-Machine Collaboration

Every aspect has positive and negative consequences, which means it is important to evaluate them before implementation, especially when employing technologies. Organizations must give their staff the necessary training in order for the seamless adoption of new technologies, which will require a significant financial commitment and effort. The organization may suffer if new technologies are not successfully adopted and implemented, so it is important to examine the potential obstacles. Over the period of the fourth industrial revolution, the organization's primary concerns centered around employee and stakeholder acceptance and adaptability. However, the major obstacles they faced were related to ethical concerns. In this case of human-machine collaboration, the primary ethical issues that can come up at any point throughout the process.

The economic system is built on paying people for their contributions to the economy, which are typically measured in terms of hourly wages.

Data security, privacy, and safety are further important ethical considerations. In the current environment, there are many instances of hacking, data breaches, biases in artificial intelligence, and other issues. Organizations can mitigate these kinds of risky situations by adjusting procedures and carefully planning the adoption and modification of technologies after weighing the likelihood of success and failure.

## 5.5. Building Resilient Organizations in Industry 5.0

### 5.5.1 Strategies for Enhancing Organizational Resilience

The capacity of an organization to endure hardship is known as organizational resilience. In the context of organizations, it is a vital approach for guaranteeing long-term success and well-being. The economy is unpredictable and dynamic, so it's important to prepare strategically for potential outcomes and foresee potential outcomes in order to minimize their effects (How to Build Organizational Resilience: 6 Proven Steps, n.d.). An organization must have plans in place to lessen the effects of unforeseen circumstances. IBM undertook a research study in the real world and found that over 83% of organizations are dealing with ethical problems such as data breaches (Cost of a Data Breach 2024, n.d.). Organizations must devote time and money to creating methods that create a robust organizational culture in order to prevent ethical dilemmas.

Businesses can develop a resilient workforce by making investments in their people, especially in their employees. Human capital is the most significant asset of any firm. Investing in the individuals that comprise the business through methods of training and development that include coaching, mentoring, counseling, and many other approaches is the first step towards developing resilience. A company culture that fosters unity, motivates output, and supports it is said to be robust. Establishing a work atmosphere that fosters learning from mistakes, acknowledges accomplishments, and promotes cooperation across divisions and levels of experience is an excellent place to begin. Risk management, catastrophe preparedness, and business continuity must all be approached proactively in order to create a resilient firm. In order to do this, possible risks and dangers must be recognized in advance, and appropriate countermeasures must be put in place.

### 5.5.2 Role of Leadership in Fostering Resilience

The organization can gain significantly from the adoption of a resilient organizational culture. It has a favorable effect on the organization. In addition to developing tailored strategies, organizations also require leaders that possess the competence and ability to cultivate resilience and a resilient organizational culture. According to the human centric approach, an organization's ability to function and succeed depends on its human capital. Leaders are also necessary for the effective application in organizations (PAREKH, n.d.).

It takes time and a lot of work to develop a resilient team and apply the method, but it's a crucial step in the process of successfully implementing organizational change in their approach. Leaders have an impact; they serve as examples for others to follow and serve as motivators by modeling behavior and assisting others in adjusting to a changing environment. They are able to offer the peer group and other members the appropriate direction and assistance (PAREKH, n.d.). This approach not only closes the knowledge gap but also fosters personal growth and enhances staff adaptability. Having strong relationships within the organizational team is essential for motivating employees to collaborate and form connections with both internal and external parties. It improves understanding and communication between coworkers and lessens conflict (PAREKH, n.d.).

## 5.6. Human-Centric Practices for Organizations

### 5.6.1 Employee Well-Being and Work-Life Balance

The current workforce evaluates the company's initiatives in relation to every aspect of their endorsement and well-being, and this has grown into an important determinant for the firm's capacity to draw in, keep, and develop personnel (Kashyap et al., 2016). Employer branding and work force participants' satisfaction are being assessed by people in the contemporary organizational context, and employees are worried about the corporate culture and policies before considering an employment offer. Human capital at potential are assessing themselves based on their analysis of the organization's turnover rate.

Here lies the need and necessity of work-life balance rules and policies for workmen's welfare; these will improve the organization's reputation in the eyes of the public and expand its entire organizational views in the economy. According to reports, Richard Walton; The capability to balance work and life quality without sacrificing an individual's quality of life is known as work-life balance. Quality of work life (QWL) is another name for this idea. Preserving the equilibrium between work and personal life significantly influences the organization's overall expansion and advancement. Significant correlations between job happiness and employee satisfaction and the business can both benefit from it (Mirkamali & Thani, 2011).

Extended work hours are a prevalent adverse outcome that arises from an organization's inability to implement an efficient and effective strategy that addresses the well-being of employees and promotes work-life balance. According to recent studies, employees who work more than 55 hours a week are 1.66 times more likely to experience depression as a result of work pressure and an unhealthy work environment, a major organizational failure and are 1.74 times more likely to experience anxiety (*It's Time to Prioritize Your Work-Life Balance*, 2024). These results are caused by a lack of work-life balance and employee well-being policies, which can have a negative impact on the organization. Employers must maintain positive working conditions with integrated work-life balance and employee well-being policies for the benefit of both the workforce and the company in order to prevent situations (*It's Time to Prioritize Your Work-Life Balance*, 2024).

### 5.6.2 Inclusive and Diverse Workplace Cultures

Both staff and management work together to create the organization's culture, which is shaped by shared values and a mutual understanding among the members of the workforce. It is dependent upon various things. An effective and well-maintained work environment greatly depends on the company culture. Establishing a work environment that values inclusion and diversity is crucial (*Creating an Inclusive Workplace Culture Through Diversity*, 2024).

Individuals with varying backgrounds, norms, and thoughts have been welcomed and appreciated in the contemporary work environment, when a diverse workforce exists. It aids in attracting the greatest talent to the company, helps it achieve success by bringing in fresh ideas and viewpoints. As a result, stakeholders—particularly customers—view the business as having more value. It also brings fresh ideas and improvements to the company that support the achievement of long-term goals and accelerate growth. These factors improve employee loyalty since workers will feel appreciated and empowered.

### 5.6.3 Human-AI Collaboration Models

Human-AI collaboration is the union of people and AI-driven technologies to develop or generate things and information. Businesses can use artificial intelligence to communicate with consumers, workers, and other stakeholders through human-AI collaboration. Working in a variety of organizational environments and positions, people are increasingly turning to generative artificial intelligence, or GenAI (Pophal, n.d.). The primary benefits of human and artificial intelligence working together models will be increased productivity as monotonous and repetitive activities are eliminated. The employee's work-load is lessened, but technology—rather than labor—is used. It facilitates decision-making by offering a wide range of precise facts. It will assist the company in selecting the best course of action following data analysis and evaluation (Pophal, n.d.).

The primary disadvantage is the ethical and security risks. Accessing and analyzing sensitive data is necessary when working with AI systems, which creates privacy and security concerns. Sufficient surety must be implemented to safeguard data from unwanted access or possible breaches. Additionally, AI systems may inherit biases from algorithms or training data, which could produce biased results. To ensure that decisions are made fairly and ethically, humans must be watchful in observing and reducing these biases. Humans may become overly dependent on outputs produced by AI, which could impair their capacity for autonomous thought and judgment. It's critical to maintain oversight by humans and authority to make decisions while striking the right balance (Pophal, n.d.).

## 5.7. Technology as an Enabler of Resilience and Human-Centricity

### 5.7.1 Digital Tools for Enhancing Organizational Resilience

Digital technologies have been essential to the seamless operation and adoption of new methods and tactics within the company in the rapidly changing digital world. An organization's capacity to be human-centered and resilient is greatly enhanced by digital transformation, which also improves decision-making in the moment and increases adaptation to unforeseen events that may arise in the workplace. Artificial intelligence, the internet of things, automations, and other digital technologies present a substantial opportunity within the company.

Different technologies which can play a vital role are:

- **Virtual Reality Training Sessions:** Digital recreation of realistic situations for training purposes is known as virtual reality training. Trainees engage into a fully immersive, interactive learning environment where the boundaries between virtual and real reality are blurred by noises and visuals. Trainees can gaze, talk, and move independently in a 3D virtual space while interacting with replicated real-world equipment, machinery, other trainees, and instructors by using their virtual reality headsets and devices (*Understanding VR Training: A Comprehensive Guide*, n.d.).
- **Artificial Intelligence:** Artificial intelligence (AI) is a collection of technological advances that provide computers the capacity to carry out a wide range of sophisticated tasks, such as data analysis, suggestion creation, written and spoken comprehension, and vision (*What Is Artificial Intelligence (AI)?*, n.d.).
- **Cloud Computing:** The demand-based provision of computing resources (including storage and infrastructure) as internet-based services is known as cloud computing. It gets rid of the necessity for people and companies to pay for only the physical resources they utilize and oversee those resources properly (*What Is Cloud Computing?* n.d.).

These are some of the technologies which are crucial, currently popular and most effective in the real business environment. Technology aids the business in making the best possible use of its resources while achieving maximum efficacy and efficiency. The foundation of the contemporary period is technology, which improves the capacity to produce the intended results. By using machines and automation, it speeds up management's efforts to boost productivity and enhance performance. Industry 4.0 emphasizes the value and advantages of technology and helps the company to accomplish its goals and objectives in an effective way, however as was already noted, there are disadvantages to this fourth revolution.

### 5.7.2 Technologies Supporting Human-Centric Work Environments

The use of technologies made it easier to complete tasks and produced work that became of better quality. As a result, the industry saw significant growth in customer satisfaction and profitability, with technology playing a significant role in achieving these results. However, the employee-oriented strategy in the company, which led to an elevated level of employee discontent and turnover, was the main issue and disadvantage of industry 4.0. Technologies can be incorporated and used as a conduit to channelize work; they can also serve as an infrastructure for improved staff productivity and performance inside the company. According to technologists, technology has to be viewed as an aid or instrument that empowers workers to enhance their output and efficiency through cooperative efforts towards technical progress.

Organizations can successfully use the human-centric strategy in the work environment by properly integrating technology. Technology can assist a person in creating a work-life balance and coming with innovative solutions. It will improve the standard of job performance with fewer human input and reduce the possibility of mistakes being made while doing the task.

### 5.7.3 Ethical Considerations in Technology Adoption

In a rapidly evolving digital world, digital technology has been critical to the company's seamless operation and willingness to embrace novel approaches and techniques. In comparison with the fourth industrial revolution, which was concentrated on enhancing manufacturing and supply chain operations in the context of business, the fifth industrial revolution highlights a more essential incorporation of technological advancements and people as linked together elements of the modern business environment. It also builds a greater focus on digital interaction between humans and machines.

Major ethical concerns:

- **Privacy:** The majority elements that comprise the modern human lifestyle are incorporated with technology due to its quick expansion and development. Data-driven technologies, such as artificial intelligence, the internet of things, and data analytics, are growing more and more prevalent. These technologies entail gathering and using data from many sources. There is a good likelihood that this will cause ethical problems and raise concerns about the privacy of information. Data breaches and security issues may arise as a result of the data's accessibility and availability.
- **Data security:** Databases and information are easily accessible, and anyone can browse the data. The misuse of organizational and personal data is a significant concern in the current scenario. Questions exist regarding cybersecurity as well, raising the possibility of cyber attacks and cybersecurity issues like ransomware, phishing, malware, and injection attacks, among other concerns.
- **Algorithm biases:** Algorithms used in artificial intelligence and machine learning must be properly planned and implemented, as improper design can lead to biases and unfair outcomes. to lessen and stay clear of these kinds of worries. Businesses apply this algorithm at many stages of their management operations, and there's a good risk that stakeholders and employees may experience bias and injustice.

These are a few ethical difficulties that are previously identified and tried to solve. One of the main obstacles to industry 4.0 was the ethical challenges that businesses had to deal with. They needed to adopt new tactics and address these concerns in order to prevent and lessen the impact of any ethical issues that might arise. The adoption of technology in a human capital centered environment depends heavily on the consideration of ethical concerns; therefore, during the entire transformation process, the organization should take into account all potential implications of adaptation and implementation.

## 5.8. Measuring and Assessing Resilience and Human-Centricity

### 5.8.1 Key Performance Indicators for Resilience

Furthermore, there could be a variety of difficulties in building resilience within a company. One such question will be, "How well will the resilience plan function when a real event occurs?" Organizational resilience is the capacity of an organization to withstand adversity and gradually resume regular operations with little harm. Indicators of knowledge performance KPIs are a crucial measurement tool that, by assisting in the assessment of an organization's capacity for taking measured risks and carrying out its activities, guarantees that it is flexible and innovative.When making plans for future development that incorporate resilience and human centricity, KPI helps by giving an overview of the current state of the development process and the requirements for future development for the business.

Measuring the resilience and human centric approach can be measured using KPI which includes

- **Business continuity plan:** It gauges how well a plan is carried out in specific circumstances and how that results in the business. when creating the new business strategy. The frequency and outcome of these strategies will provide an accurate assessment of BCP's impact and effectiveness.
- **Time to recover from major disruptions:** If the business is taking considerable time to recover from a major environmental obstacle, it is indicating that they don't have a clear understanding of the issue that can be encountered and that it fails to implement adequate approaches to ensure continuation and smooth flow of organizational operations. This will give a clear idea of how effective the organization is at approaching a difficult situation that can occur.
- **Cost of resilience initiatives:** When implementing new rules and methods in a business, cost is a critical factor. Therefore, we must take the associated costs into account. We must evaluate all costs that may be incurred and that have an impact on the company as part of the entire process of determining the cost of resilience measures. The cost-benefit ratio must be determined. By helping with implementation costs and assessing profitability and return on investment for the cost of investing in resilience and human-centered approaches, we can determine the effectiveness of the initiatives that we can identify.

### 5.8.2 Metrics for Evaluating Human-Centric Practices

Evaluation is an important aspect of management. Understanding the report before and after the implementation of particular policies and approaches requires an assessment of the practices offered by the organization. This includes an assessment of the organization's human-centric approach, which entails determining how the environment is adapting to the new changes, how this new adaptability is affecting the workforce, how much the organization benefits from these human-centered methods, and how they prioritize employee engagement and satisfaction.

Evaluating human centric approaches are we can use some matrices that they are:

- Employee Engagement Score
- Employee Retention

- Turnover Rates
- Work-Life Balance
- Performance Level
- Inclusive Team Rates

These are a few of the matrices that the business utilizes to evaluate different chances for the human-centric methodology. For each and every component, the organization's residential and human-centered practices may be found and evaluated using this matrix.

**Employee engagement score:** Employee perceptions of the company's strategy and their own work are impacted by employee engagement, which makes it vital. Increased productivity, innovation, and brand loyalty are the results of a highly engaged workforce, which also boosts emotional and mental engagement in the firm. Strong employee engagement is directly correlated with each of these variables.

**Employee retention rates:** It is widely believed that organizations with strong employee retention rates also tend to have good hiring practices for both workers and job seekers. These modern scenarios evaluate the personnel retention rate of the organization. Their goal is to achieve retention rates that show how well the company can hang onto its employees. It clearly shows how content employees are with the business and vice versa. Thus, a high incidence of employee retention implies that the workers at that particular company are highly content with their working environment and organizational guidelines.

**Work life balance:** Work-life balance is crucial since industry 5.0 emphasizes sustainability, human centricity, and resilience. As a result, the success of the company's people focused strategy greatly depends on the welfare of its workforce. Industry 5.0 is focused on technology integration to reduce the pressure and stress on the workforce that was present in industry 4.0, as many industry 4.0 businesses lacked a work-life balance. This is due to the fact that a work-life balance matrix has been utilized in the past and is quite significant.

**Inclusive team rates:** In the modern world, inclusivity and diversity are essential. Therefore, having a highly dynamic inclusion and different rules for employees will enhance an organization's reputation with the public and with customers. Stakeholders in the business must also ensure that everyone working there is treated fairly and benefits from the same opportunities.

An organization's ability to succeed and develop depends critically on having a healthy workforce and productive staff. Thus, assessing the diversity and inclusivity of the team will improve the organization's acceptability, innovation, and flexibility. When people with diverse perspectives and ideas get together, they will produce enormously ambitious, creative, and productive plans that can support the organization's expansion and improvement.

## 5.9. Challenges and Opportunities

### 5.9.1 Potential Barriers to Implementing Resilient and Human-Centric Approaches

The application of cutting-edge strategies in the 5.0 sector greatly helped the company and the market. The company has a number of challenges in implementing human-centric practices and a resilient workforce. In terms of significance. It offers higher rates of employee engagement and retention coupled with better performance, quality, and the effective and efficient use of resources. But the different barriers that prevent strategies from being implemented effectively will also lead to issues with leadership, organizational culture, and constraints; improper use of technology; and a mismatch between organizational and technological aspects. A multitude of factors could impact and even act as a barrier to the implementation of these tactics.

The organization's new procedures will demand a large amount of funds for assessment, analysis and implementation. The organization's attempt to switch from outdated techniques to the new industry 5.0 resilience and human centric approaches is hampered by cost. First, we must ascertain the existing situation, which involves a substantial expense for the organization's personnel training and development. A further major obstacle is time-bound. It will take a while to meet the training and development requirements for the staff as well as to adjust. The organization will require a significant amount of time due to the extended procedure. They have to focus on the proper identification and assessment of application implementation.

### 5.9.2 Future Trends

Industry 5.0, a milestone in the history of the industrial revolution, aspires to collaborate between humans and technology through techniques that prioritize sustainability, human centricity, and organizational resilience. There will be a significant shift in the sector that combines technological advances and improvements with human capital. Industry 5.0 seeks to develop "smart hospitals," "smart cities," and "smart classrooms." (*Future of Industry 5.0 in Society: Human-Centric Solutions, Challenges and Prospective Research Areas - Journal of Cloud Computing*, 2022) This essentially means that technology will be integrated with many sectors to provide remote monitoring systems, which will facilitate the lives of those in the ideal professions. Medical imaging devices use machine learning.

Learning goes into effect for genetic data, natural language processing, various industries, and interests. This is especially for smart hospital plans and creative applications in the manufacturing sector, where industry 5.0 is revolving the manufacturing system globally and eliminating repetitive tasks from the human workforce for the goal of purpose and recycling of resources. (*Future of Industry 5.0 in Society: Human-Centric Solutions, Challenges and Prospective Research Areas - Journal of Cloud Computing*, 2022) As we observe the supply chain, we see the value of human-robot collaboration, cobot collaboration, and a reduction in the human labor force in industry.

Acquire hyper-personalization to various industries based on client requirements; additionally, offer eco-friendly and sustainable solutions that are highly customizable and less expensive than what the sector is now asking for. Other industries that use Industry 4.0 robots include blockchain analytics, internet of things, artificial intelligence, and big data integration. Cloud computing, which is used in a hybrid wave to meet the needs of computer service applications to store plus processing power and sixteen networks, is a key component of Industry 5.0, which aims to create a resilient, human-centered, and sustainable environment through the adoption of new strategies and objectives in tandem with organizational goals (*Future of Industry 5.0 in Society: Human-Centric Solutions, Challenges and Prospective Research Areas - Journal of Cloud Computing*, 2022).

## 5.10. Case Studies

### 5.10.1 Human Centric Approach by Haier Group in Industry 5.0

Established in Qingdao, China in 1984, Haier Group is a prominent global reader of home appliances and has grown to become a leader in both electronics and home appliances. The firm's transition from a traditional home appliance maker to industry 5.0 places a strong emphasis on the resilience and personnel focused sustainability strategy, which is industry 5.0's central tenet within the company (Zhao, 2024). The business uses cutting-edge technologies, such as big data, artificial intelligence, and the internet of things. In order to attract customers and maintain the health of their business, they are utilizing technical advancements and innovations in the production of electronics and household appliances while maintaining managerial, product, and quality standards. They are taking a people-first stance. We will examine how they are transforming the organization from traditional to human-centric and resilient in this case study, emphasizing workforce empowerment and adaptability in a constantly changing industry.

The company developed six key components that emphasize resilience and a workforce-oriented viewpoint in front of industry 5.0, and the RenDanHey system carries these out. The RenDanHey system, which emphasizes individual empowerment, innovation, and an entrepreneurial spirit, represents a significant shift from conventional corporate hierarchy. Haier has eliminated top-down management systems in favor of a network of tiny, autonomous units where staff members are empowered to take responsibility for their job and come up with creative solutions. This puts human potential as the main force behind organizational innovation and resilience, going beyond the simple incorporation of technology.

Its human-centric technological integration is one of its distinctive features. Modern technologies like artificial intelligence, big data, and the Internet of Things are used by Haier to enhance human potential rather than replace existing systems. Additionally, the business makes sure that the learning environment for employees is flexible enough to use technology rather than competing with human intelligence. An increased emphasis on people-centered tactics that highlights significant relevance to individual empowerment. They dispersed their organizational structures to encourage accountability, creativity, and ownership at several levels (Zhao, 2024).

The sustainability of a business is significantly impacted by the strategic change from a shareholder-focused to an employee-centric model. Workers are now value producers with the ability to spur organizational innovation rather than resources to be controlled. By using this strategy, Haier has been able to develop an organizational ecosystem that is more flexible and agile, allowing it to swiftly adjust to shifting market demands and technology advancements. The business changed its strategy from putting shareholders first to putting employees first, investing heavily in Ren. This is the place where workers build their own worth. They integrated workers, value, proposal, and employee satisfaction into their traditional hierarchical systems to create modern methods. Higher-ups' staff members found themselves in the little self-managed unit (Zhao, 2024).

Real-world applications of Haier's concept can be seen in a variety of organizational settings and industries. The RenDanHey system demonstrates how businesses can transform conventional workplace arrangements to create more inventive and resilient settings. Even the most conventional bureaucratic firms can benefit from Haier's decentralized management and employee empowerment strategy, which is applicable to the manufacturing, technology, and service sectors. The implementation of this concept in practice requires a number of crucial tactics. First and foremost, the organizational structure itself must be adaptable; it must facilitate individual innovations and speedier decision-making. Second, it becomes crucial to invest in ongoing education and skill development so that staff members can successfully take advantage of new technologies. Third, performance measures must move away from output-based measurements and toward more comprehensive evaluations of creativity, innovation, and teamwork.

This case study highlights the unambiguous fact that a business cannot function in isolation. The organization operates in a dynamic environment where employees' essential human-centric approach is highly necessary in the contemporary setting in the industry 5.0. The higher group demonstrates that for an industry revolution, sustainability, human centered approach, and resilience are the key pillars. The end of the fifth period is approaching. Therefore, we must all shift from the traditional method to a modern one that emphasizes people, society, and the organization while keeping in mind the business's desire to expand and improve all of these things.

## 6. CONCLUSION

As we transition into the era of Industry 5.0, organizations are faced with both challenges and opportunities in adapting to a new paradigm that emphasizes sustainability, human-centricity, and resilience. This chapter has explored the key concepts, strategies, and considerations for building resilient and people focused organizations in the context of Industry 5.0. The evolution from Industry 4.0 to 5.0 represents a significant shift in focus - from purely technological advancement to a more balanced approach that places equal importance on human capital and societal values.

Organizations striving to thrive in this new era must prioritize:

1. Building organizational resilience through strategic planning, risk management, and adaptive capabilities.
2. Fostering human capital focused practices that prioritize employee well-being, work-life balance, and inclusive workplace cultures.
3. Leveraging technology as an enabler of both resilience and human-centricity, while carefully navigating the ethical considerations of its adoption.

The case study of Haier Group demonstrates that successful implementation of Industry 5.0 principles is not only possible but can lead to significant competitive advantages. By empowering employees, fostering innovation, and maintaining adaptability, organizations can create sustainable value for all stakeholders.

As we look to the future, it is clear that the journey towards fully realizing the potential of Industry 5.0 is just beginning. Organizations will need to continually evolve their strategies, overcome barriers to change, and remain agile in the face of emerging trends and technologies. Those that successfully navigate this transition will be well-positioned to create value, drive innovation, and contribute positively to society in the years to come.

## 6.1. Research Limitations and Implication

There are still certain shortcomings even if this chapter is fully grounded in the analysis of industry 5.0 in every way, with a focus on the center of the topics and concepts. This is because the entire breadth of the study is based on secondary data from industry reports, journal papers, and case studies, all of which have biases because of interpretations from previous research. Second, the lack of empirical research and longitudinal data in this area limits the generalizability of findings and makes it difficult to draw firm conclusions regarding the implementation and long-term effects of Industry 5.0, as it is still a developing idea. Additionally, the analysis mostly concentrates on theoretical frameworks and one case study (Haier Group), which may not fully represent the range of Industry 5.0 applications across various organizational and cultural contexts, despite being illustrative. In order to fill in these gaps, future research should validate and expand on the conclusions in this chapter by undertaking empirical investigations in a variety of industries and geographical areas.

By outlining Industry 5.0's main pillars and how they alter organizational strategy, this chapter broadens our conceptual grasp of the notion. In order to close gaps in the literature, the book provides a fundamental framework for discussing the interaction between the technological and human elements that support industrial situations. Furthermore, this study paves the way for future theoretical investigations into adaptive frameworks that balance technology innovation with human creativity by utilizing ideas like organizational resilience and human-centered technological adoption. The chapter offers practical advice on how to apply Industry 5.0 concepts to improve organizational performance and flexibility. The strategies covered above can be used by managers and leaders to foster a human-centered workplace, ethical and sustainable technology use, and team resilience. For instance, the Haier Group case demonstrates how traditional organizational norms can be altered through decentralization, employee empowerment, and technology as an enabler. These insights will assist businesses in creating targeted plans to improve organizational sustainability, operational agility, and employee satisfaction.

## REFERENCES


Abdullah, N. A. S., Noor, N. L. M., & Ibrahim, E. N. M. (2013). Resilient Organization: Modelling The Capacity for Resilience. *International Conference on Research and Innovation in Information Systems.* DOI: 10.1109/ICRIIS.2013.6716729

Adel, A. (2022, September 08). Future of industry 5.0 in society: Human-centric solutions, challenges and prospective research areas. *Journal of Cloud Computing (Heidelberg, Germany)*, 11(40), 40. Advance online publication. DOI: 10.1186/s13677-022-00314-5 PMID: 36101900

Barata, J., & Kayser, I. (2023). Industry 5.0 – Past, Present, and Near Future. *Procedia Computer Science*, 219, 778–788. DOI: 10.1016/j.procs.2023.01.351

Boin, A., & Eeten, M. J. G. (2013). The Resilient Organization. *Public Management Review*, 15(3), 429–445. http://www.tandfonline.com/action/showCitFormats?doi=10.1080/14719037.2013.769856. DOI: 10.1080/14719037.2013.769856

Büchi, G., Cennamo, N., Mittal, A., & Weill, P. (2020). Digital transformation of industrial ecosystems: Organizational resilience, adaptive workforce strategies, and human-centric technological integration. *Strategic Management Journal*, 41(8), 1511–1536. DOI: 10.1002/smj.3193

Carter, N., & Wilkinson, F. (2023, October 19). *Industrialization, Labor, and Life*. National Geographic Education. Retrieved October 7, 2024, from https://education.nationalgeographic.org/resource/industrialization-labor-and-life/

Chabane, B., Komljenovic, D., & Abdul-Nour, G. (2023). Converging on human-centred industry, resilient processes, and sustainable outcomes in asset management frameworks. *Environment Systems & Decisions*, 43(4), 663–679. DOI: 10.1007/s10669-023-09943-w

*Cost of a data breach 2024*. (n.d.). IBM. Retrieved October 9, 2024, from https://www.ibm.com/reports/data-breach

*Creating an inclusive workplace culture through diversity*. (2024, March 28). LinkedIn. Retrieved October 9, 2024, from https://www.linkedin.com/pulse/creating-inclusive-workplace-culture-through-diversity-lakshmi-kaul-kof8c

Dreyer, J. (2024, August 07). *The 4 Types of Resilience in Action: Strengthening Your Mind and Body*. Jeanette Dreyer. https://www.jeanettedreyer.co.za/the-4-types-of-resilience-in-action/

Duchek, S. (2020). Organizational resilience: A capability-based conceptualization. *Business Research*, 13(1), 215–246. DOI: 10.1007/s40685-019-0085-7

Fernandez-Gonzalez, A., Rodriguez-Sanchez, M., & Martinez-Lopez, J. (2024). Systemic resilience in organizational transformation. *Journal of Organizational Change Management*, 37(1), 88–107.

Ghobakhloo, M., Iranmanesh, M., Mubarak, M. F., Mubarik, M., Rejeb, A., & Nilashi, M. (2022, September). Identifying industry 5.0 contributions to sustainable development: A strategy roadmap for delivering sustainability values. *Sustainable Production and Consumption*, 33, 716–737. DOI: 10.1016/j.spc.2022.08.003

Harbeke, E., & Künlen, L. (2024, November 19). *The dawn of Industry 5.0.* https://www.rothschildandco.com/en/newsroom/insights/2024/10/the-dawn-of-industry-5.0/#:~:text=Industry%205.0%20redefines%20the%20purpose,and%20societal%20impact%2C%20Chart%203

*How to build organizational resilience: 6 proven steps.* (n.d.). Everbridge. Retrieved October 9, 2024, from https://www.everbridge.com/blog/how-to-build-organizational-resilience-six-proven-steps/

*Industry 5.0: Adding the human edge to industry 4.0.* (n.d.). SAP. Retrieved October 8, 2024, from https://www.sap.com/mena/insights/industry-5-0.html

*Industry 5.0 - European Commission.* (2022, January 10). Research and innovation. Retrieved October 7, 2024, from https://research-and-innovation.ec.europa.eu/research-area/industrial-research-and-innovation/industry-50_en

*Industry 5.0 Market Trends and Growth Opportunities for 2024 - 2030.* (2024, August 23). LinkedIn. Retrieved October 12, 2024, from https://www.linkedin.com/pulse/industry-50-market-trends-growth-opportunities-2024-hiyof

*Integrating Technology and Human Skills for Future Workplaces.* (2024, June 24). LinkedIn. Retrieved October 9, 2024, from https://www.linkedin.com/pulse/integrating-technology-human-skills-future-workplaces-mcdermott-fvu5f

*It's Time to Prioritize Your Work-Life Balance.* (2024, March 13). Harvard Online. Retrieved October 9, 2024, from https://www.harvardonline.harvard.edu/blog/prioritize-work-life-balance

Kantur, D., & İşeri-Say, A. (2012). Organizational resilience: A conceptual integrative framework. *Journal of Management & Organization*, 18(6), 762–773. DOI: 10.5172/jmo.2012.18.6.762

Kashyap, S., Joseph, S., & Deshmukh, G. K. (2016). Employee Well-Being, Life Satisfaction and the need for Work-Life balance. *Journal of Ravishankar University*, 22, 11–23. https://www.researchgate.net/profile/Gopal-Deshmukh/publication/311322121_Employee_Well-Being_Life_Satisfaction_and_the_need_for_Work-Life_balance/links/58419b8608aeda6968138468/Employee-Well-Being-Life-Satisfaction-and-the-need-for-Work-Life-balance.pdf

Krings, D., Weber, K., & Schmidt, N. (n.d.). Dynamic resilience: Conceptual frameworks and empirical insights. *Strategic Management Journal*, 45(3), 212–235.

Lengnick-Hall, C. A., Beck, T. E., & Lengnick-Hall, M. L. (2011). Developing a capacity for organizational resilience through strategic human resource management. *Human Resource Management Review*, 21(3), 243–255. Advance online publication. DOI: 10.1016/j.hrmr.2010.07.001

Mirkamali, S. M., & Thani, F. N. (2011). A Study on the Quality of Work Life (QWL) among faculty members of University of Tehran(UT) and Sharif university of Technology (SUT). *Procedia: Social and Behavioral Sciences*, 29, 179–187. DOI: 10.1016/j.sbspro.2011.11.223

Nahavandi, S. (2019, August). Industry 5.0—A Human-Centric Solution. *Sustainability (Basel)*, 9(14), 2794. DOI: 10.3390/su11164371

*On the Importance of Human-Centricity and Data.* (n.d.). www3. weforum. org /docs /WE. Retrieved October 8, 2024, from https://www3.weforum.org/docs/WEF_On_the_Importance_of_Human_Centricity_2021.pdf

Oxford University Press. (n.d.). *resilience noun - Definition, pictures, pronunciation and usage notes | Oxford Advanced Learner's Dictionary at OxfordLearnersDictionaries.com.* Oxford Learner's Dictionaries. https://www.oxfordlearnersdictionaries.com/definition/english/resilience

Ozaki, A. (2022). Human-Machine Collaboration in Advanced Manufacturing: Strategic Integration and Workforce Development. *Journal of Technology and Innovation Management*, 45(3), 112–129.

PAREKH, M. (n.d.). *Role of Leadership in Fostering Workplace Resilience.* KNOLSKAPE EDITORAL TEAM. https://knolskape.com/blog/role-of-leadership-in-fostering-workplace-resilience/#:~:text=Resilient%20leaders%20possess%20self%2Dawareness,being%20of%20their%20team%20members

Pinheiro, R., Young, M., & Frigotto, M. L. (2022). *Towards Resilient Organizations and Societies.* Public Sector Organizations., DOI: 10.1007/978-3-030-82072-5

Pophal, L. (n.d.). *What Is Human AI Collaboration? | HR Glossary.* Visier. Retrieved October 9, 2024, from https://www.visier.com/blog/hr-glossary-what-is-human-ai-collaboration/

*RESILIENCE | English meaning - Cambridge Dictionary.* (2024, October 2). Cambridge Dictionary. Retrieved October 8, 2024, from https://dictionary.cambridge.org/dictionary/english/resilience#google_vignette

Sommer, A. F., Hedegaard, C., Dukovska-Popovska, I., & Steger-Jensen, K. (2024, August). Industry 5.0 in Manufacturing: Enhancing Resilience and Responsibility through AI-Driven Predictive Maintenance, Quality Control, and Supply Chain Optimization. *international. Journal of Multidisciplinary Research*, 6(4), 815–828. DOI: 10.36948/ijfmr.2024.v06i04.25733

*sustainability noun - Definition, pictures, pronunciation and usage notes | Oxford Advanced Learner's Dictionary at OxfordLearnersDictionaries.com.* (n.d.). Oxford Learner's Dictionaries. Retrieved October 8, 2024, from https://www.oxfordlearnersdictionaries.com/definition/english/sustainability

The United Nations. (n.d.). *Sustainability | United Nations.* The United Nations. https://www.un.org/en/academic-impact/sustainability

*Top 9 ethical issues in artificial intelligence | World Economic Forum.* (2016, October 21). The World Economic Forum. Retrieved October 9, 2024, from https://www.weforum.org/agenda/2016/10/top-10-ethical-issues-in-artificial-intelligence/

*6Types of Resilience Companies Need Today.* (2021, November 17). Harvard Business Review. Retrieved October 8, 2024, from https://hbr.org/2021/11/6-types-of-resilience-companies-need-today

*Understanding VR Training: A Comprehensive Guide.* (n.d.). PIXO VR. Retrieved October 12, 2024, from https://pixovr.com/what-is-virtual-reality-training/

Wagner, C., Bublitz, A., & Kaloudis, A. (2024). Organizational resilience in the age of digital disruption. *The Journal of Business Strategy*, 45(2), 78–95.

*What Is Artificial Intelligence (AI)?* (n.d.). Google Cloud. Retrieved October 11, 2024, from https://cloud.google.com/learn/what-is-artificial-intelligence

*What is Blockchain? - Blockchain Technology Explained.* (n.d.). AWS. Retrieved October 11, 2024, from https://aws.amazon.com/what-is/blockchain/?aws-products-all.sort-by=item.additionalFields.productNameLowercase&aws-products-all.sort-order=asc

*What is Cloud Computing?* (n.d.). Google Cloud. Retrieved October 11, 2024, from https://cloud.google.com/learn/what-is-cloud-computing

Xu, X., Lu, Y., Vogel-Heuser, B., & Wang, L. (2021, October). Industry 4.0 and Industry 5.0—Inception, conception and perception. *Journal of Manufacturing Systems*, 61, 530–535. DOI: 10.1016/j.jmsy.2021.10.006


Xu, X., Lu, Y., Vogel-Heuser, B., & Wang, L. (2021, October). Industry 4.0 and Industry 5.0—Inception, conception and perception. *Journal of Manufacturing Systems*, 61, 530–535. DOI: 10.1016/j.jmsy.2021.10.006

Zhao, S. (2024, May 7). *Employee-centered Industry 5.0 - Case analysis of Haier*. OAE Publishing Inc. Retrieved October 12, 2024, from https://www.oaepublish.com/articles/gmo.2023.122601

# Chapter 5
# Human-Centric Innovation: Building Sustainable Organizations for Industry 5.0

**K. Balaji**
https://orcid.org/0000-0002-3065-3294
*Christ University, Bengaluru, India*

## ABSTRACT

*Human -centric innovation is paramount in building sustainable organizations in the era of Industry 5.0. As businesses transition from purely technology-driven models to those that integrate human creativity and advanced technologies, a new paradigm emerges—one that places human well-being, ethical considerations, and sustainability at its core. This article delves into how organizations can leverage human-centric innovation to create more sustainable business practices, addressing environmental, social, and economic challenges. It discusses strategies such as empowering employees through inclusive decision-making, adopting design thinking to foster sustainable product development, and using digital tools that enhance both productivity and human health. By embracing a human-centered approach, organizations can achieve a balance between technological advancement and alignment with broader societal goals. This approach is crucial for navigating the complexities of Industry 5.0 and fostering sustainable growth in an increasingly interconnected world.*

## I. INTRODUCTION

Human-centric innovation is gradually becoming a key success factor in sustainable organization development in Industry 5.0. Industry 5.0 goes further and is unlike the former industrial revolutions, which were based only on technologies and productivity improvement but focused the work and management on the convergence of human beings with AI, robotics, and the Internet of Things. This evolution is a major transition in the way business is carried out, and having the potential to create not only greater economic value but also, crucially, greater social value.

Singly from the industrial revolution's major changes in technology and productivity have been seen in the history. Amid the First Industrial Revolution in the late 18th century, mechanized manufacture and movement changed by steam engines.: The Second Industrial Revolution that occurred during the late eighteen hundred and through the early nineteen hundred resulted from steam power, railroads,

DOI: 10.4018/979-8-3693-8181-6.ch005

electricity, mass production, and assembly lines, all of which contributed to even more industrial development. The third Industrial Revolution began in 1960s and was characterized by digitalization and automation of technology, appearance of information technology and computer systems, internet and connectivity all over the world.

These advances continued through Industry 3.0 that started in the early of the 21st century and Industry 4.0 that concentrated on the smart technologies, CPS, IoT and Big data analytics. This phase centred on the improvement of efficiency and flexibility within production lines through high mechanical and computerized automation systems. Still, at the same time, Industry 4.0 that spurred unprecedented technological advancement in all critical industries was criticized for overlooking human welfare and encouraging sustainability at the cost of people's jobs, privacy breaches, and environmental impacts.

Industry 5.0 is now emerging as a response to these challenges, offering a new framework that seeks to harmonize human creativity with digital technologies. The growth of Industry 5.0 represents a shift toward a more inclusive and sustainable industrial model. This paradigm integrates human intelligence and creativity with machine efficiency, emphasizing collaboration between humans and robots to achieve better outcomes. It encourages businesses to focus not only on financial performance but also on social and environmental impact, aligning corporate strategies with global sustainability goals, such as the United Nations' Sustainable Development Goals (SDGs).

The impact of Industry 5.0 on the world is profound and multifaceted. At its core, Industry 5.0 aims to make technology serve humanity, rather than replace it. This human-centric approach prioritizes ethical considerations, such as employee well-being, inclusivity, and social equity, alongside technological advancements. Organizations are encouraged to innovate with a focus on long-term sustainability, creating products and services that benefit both people and the planet. This shift is driving businesses to rethink their operational models, supply chains, and overall corporate missions, moving toward more responsible and resilient practices.

Moreover, the emphasis on human-centric innovation fosters a culture of continuous learning and adaptation, empowering employees to contribute creatively and meaningfully to organizational goals. By embracing new technologies, such as AI and robotics, alongside human intelligence, organizations can address complex global challenges—like climate change, resource scarcity, and social inequality—more effectively. This holistic approach is crucial for ensuring sustainable growth in an increasingly interconnected and rapidly changing world.

## Objectives of the Study

The study will seek to attain the following objectives to contribute to the development of an improved theoretical and practical understanding of sustainable organisational design in the context of Industry 5.0. First, it aims to understand and explore what measures firms around the globe consistently use, which are effectively managing to achieve their sustainability goals exemplified by companies implementing successful sustainability strategies. Through analysing these practices, the study seeks to understand where, how, and to what extent the mentioned companies create value from sustainability initiatives scrutinizing the financial value, brand value, and environmental outcomes. A further goal is to identify typical issues arising in the process of implementing sustainability and to state the measures applied to address these issues. The study also seeks to give best practices that other organizations too involved in sustainability can emulate. Lastly, it wants to look at new trends in sustainability and see how such trends may influence trends within organizations in the future.

## II. BACKROUND

The transition to Industry 5.0 has sparked a growing interest in how human-centric innovation can promote sustainable practices within organizations. Early studies laid the groundwork for these human-centric approaches in the workplace. Normann (1984) was among the pioneers to stress the significance of human factors in innovation, suggesting that companies should view employees not just as resources but as essential contributors to the innovation process. His research indicated that involving employees in decision-making boosts creativity and fosters a culture of ongoing improvement (Normann, 1984). Drucker (1985) built on this idea by underscoring the vital role of knowledge workers in innovation. He posited that organizations should cultivate environments that encourage knowledge sharing and learning to secure a sustainable competitive edge. Drucker's insights highlighted the necessity of recognizing human knowledge and creativity as key elements of organizational success (Drucker, 1985). In the 1990s, researchers began to delve deeper into the physical and psychological dimensions of human-centric innovation. Schneider and Bowen (1995) investigated how workplace design influences employee well-being and productivity. Their findings revealed that fostering a positive work environment—marked by safety, comfort, and opportunities for personal development—enhances employee engagement and innovation (Schneider & Bowen, 1995). Likewise, Laursen and Foss (2003) looked into the connection between human resource management practices and innovation outcomes.

Their study showed that organizations that adopt employee-friendly policies, such as flexible work options and professional development opportunities, are more likely to achieve effective and sustainable innovation (Laursen & Foss, 2003). The literature from the 2000s increasingly highlighted the significance of empowering employees as a catalyst for innovation. Amabile et al. (2004) conducted a thorough investigation. Hackman and Oldham (1980) developed the Job Characteristics Model, which suggested that job design could enhance employee motivation and satisfaction, leading to improved performance and innovation. Their research provided a framework for understanding how job characteristics, such as skill variety and task significance, contribute to both employee well-being and organizational sustainability (Hackman & Oldham, 1980). The integration of ethical considerations into human-centric innovation became more prominent in the literature by the early 2000s. Freeman (1984) introduced the stakeholder theory, which argues that organizations should consider the interests of all stakeholders, including employees, customers, suppliers, and the community, in their decision-making processes. This perspective laid the groundwork for sustainable business practices that align with social and ethical values (Freeman, 1984).

Carroll (1991) expanded on stakeholder theory by introducing the idea of corporate social responsibility (CSR). He highlighted those businesses should function in ways that are economically viable, legally compliant, ethically sound, and socially responsible. His research indicated that organizations that weave CSR into their fundamental strategies are more likely to achieve long-term sustainability (Carroll, 1991). As technology became increasingly integral to organizations, researchers began to explore how human-centred approaches could be harmonized with technological progress. Zuboff (1988) examined the dual nature of technology in organizations: automation and information. She posited that while technology can take over certain tasks, it can also enhance human abilities by offering new methods to access and analyse information, which can lead to innovative solutions (Zuboff, 1988).

Von Hippel (1986) investigated the idea of "user innovation," emphasizing the vital role that users or employees play in the creation of new products and services. His findings suggested that involving users in the innovation process can result in more sustainable and customer-focused solutions, underscoring the significance of merging human insights with technological advancements (Von Hippel, 1986). Research from the late 1990s to the early 2010s increasingly linked human-centred innovation with sustainability. Hart (1995) introduced the "natural-resource-based view" of the firm, which posits that sustainable competitive advantage stems from capabilities that foster environmental stewardship, such as pollution prevention and product stewardship. Hart's research highlighted the necessity for organizations to align their innovation strategies with sustainability objectives (Hart, 1995).

Porter and Kramer (2006) presented the idea of "shared value," contending that businesses can create economic value by tackling social and environmental issues. Their research illustrated that human-centred approaches, such as fostering inclusive work environments and actively engaging employees, are essential. Balaji, K. (2024) literature also promotes an understanding of the AI for Financial Innovations, driven with the human centric outlook: Changing the organization's ways and its offer in the future of finance and service" (P.24) Senge (1990) introduced the term learning organization, when such processes as lifetime education and its reorder for the sake of sustainability are considered as definite objectives. Also, based on Senge's work, it is stressed how essential it is for organizations to face up to challenges when employees are capable of self-organization and continuous innovation (Senge, 1990).

Cameron and Quinn (1999) looked into the relationship between organizational culture and innovation as well as organizational culture and the adaptation process. They showed that flexible approach to organizational culture, employee participation in the changes and free exchange of information lead to a better long-term capacity of renewal (Cameron & Quinn, 1999). By the 2010s, the sprawls started touching on human-centric innovation and its implications on a global industry. The "disruptive innovation" class was introduced by Christensen (1997), which suggested that human-centred approaches, where employees are empowered and think divergently, can lead to forms of innovation that disrupt industries (Christensen, 1997). Baldwin and Clark (2000) raised questions concerning the aesthetics of product structuring/development and interrelation with innovations. The study by K. Balaji, S. Karim and P. S. Rao (2023) argues about the human collaboration and cross functional varieties in scope of collaboration which allows the organization pour their creativity on modular design structures which are adaptable, modular and more sustainable (Baldwin & Clark, 2000).

On their part, Prahalad and Hamel (1990) argued and explained that core competencies are an important part of competitive advantage and emphasize organizations to focus more on the potential of people that is creativity building. Aligning human competencies for achievement of business goals is how sustainable competitive advantage is realised (Prahalad & Hamel, 1990). Human approaches combined with technology have been investigated as a way of delivering sustainable organizations by several scholars. For example, Smith (2022) examined the application of human-centred design principles along with AI and robotics with the aim of improving human satisfaction and productivity in manufacturing. Smith (2022) reported that job robots, which are chatbots, improved working conditions and job contentment by enabling humans to concentrate on the creative and managerial facets of the work in most cases while machines performed monotonous tasks. Also, within the framework of Industry 5.0, Davis and Johnson (2021) studied the absorption of human-centric innovation in digital transformation strategies and processes. In the course of their research, they stressed the need for the development of technology and the development of people to fully exploit the opportunities available for economic and social development. Davis and Johnson (2021) further concluded that organizations that emphasize on augmenting human effort with AI tend to perform better in terms of innovation and reach the competition goal. Thompson et al. (2019) provided valuable information on the usefulness of human-oriented approaches in intelligent factories which are designed to enhance the synergy between man and machine. Those who did so,

Thompson et al. (2019), explained, showed that employee involvement in decisions on the introduction of technologies in the initiatives concerning implementation of Industry 5.0 increased effectiveness significantly. Human-centric innovation is proposed in the literature not only to promote new markets, but also to propagate ethical business conduct and sustainability. Jones (2023) viewed Industry 5.0 not only as a technological revolution but also viewed it as an opportunity to embed ethics in technology development. According to his research, companies which follow ethical principles in AI implementation that includes responsible AI decision making and human-centric approaches, are more trusted and will join forces in achieving the development goals more effectively. In investigation of Kim and Park (2020), they noticed that human-centric innovations contribute to the environmental footprint reduction in the manufacturing sector as well. Their study established that businesses that adopted design thinking strategies to create green products had lowered their waste and energy output significantly, proving that human-centric innovations could transcend environmental barriers (Kim & Park, 2020). Miller and Smith (2018) were more interested in the consequences of AI technologies on the workplace. They argued for ethical considerations with human values rather than about technology for the sake of technology alone. Their evidences emphasized that enterprises with ethical changes management enable and build locational and their clientele faith (Miller & Smith, 2018).

Human-centric innovation has also shown to promote organizational resilience and adaptability towards various challenges. Garcia et al. (2024) inquired how organizations embed human-centred designs within their risk strategies to enhance resilience. They showed that such organizations that are active in employee engagement in the decision-making cycle tend to have a more dynamic orientation to respond to market and environmental changes (Garcia et al., 2024). Brown and Taylor (2017) explored how companies engage in human-centric innovation. They concluded that human-centred approaches, such as involving employees in supply chain innovation, can enhance flexibility and responsiveness to disruptions, thereby fostering long-term organizational sustainability (Brown & Taylor, 2017).

Williams (2016) also reported on how introducing human-centric innovation into corporate governance may lead to higher levels of agility and robustness. The research indicated that inclusive leadership practices that value employee input led to more innovative solutions to complex problems, particularly in fast-evolving industries (Williams, 2016). Literature also reveals an increasing awareness of the social consequences of human-centred innovations in Industry 5.0. K. K.Balaji (2023) investigated the potential of Industry 5.0 to address the Potential of Cryptocurrencies as An Asset Class-An Empirical Study in contributing to social sustainability through fostering inclusive work environments which are capable of serving a wider range of human needs and capabilities. Their research showed that companies implementing inclusive design features were more likely to recruit a more diverse workforce and retain employees better (Ahmed et al., 2022). Singh (2021) analysed the impact of human-centric innovation on workforce development and skills enhancement. His results revealed that organisations that are putting money into continuous learning and upskilling programmes create an environment of innovation and agility which are essential for continued success in the 5.0 era of industry (Singh, 2021). Martin and Cooper (2019) discussed the role of human-centric innovation in addressing social inequalities. K. Balaji (2023) proposed that through focus on Blockchain Based Banking Transaction Capability using Big Data, for the good of mankind and social justice, corporations could improve their corporate social responsibility (CSR) profiles and strengthen comm unity ties (Martin Cooper, 2019).

Discovery of the impact and potential of sustainable development with AI-enabled data analytics potentially lead to more insightful understanding of patterns of resource use that can empower organizations to be more strategic with sustainability efforts (Evans Green, 2018).

Lee et al. (2015) examined the potential of digital twin technology in monitoring and optimizing energy usage in industrial processes. Their results indicated that human-oriented digital twin applications might greatly help reduce national carbon emissions and enhance the general operational efficiency (Lee et al., 2015). Notwithstanding those commercial technologies are increasingly replacing traditional tools as the primary instruments in many uses, few scholars have addressed the fundamental impact of human-centric innovation on the entire industry. Peterson and Wallace (2023) described a strategic model for embedding human-centric innovation within corporate strategies. Balaji, K. (2024). emphasized aligning The Nexus of Smart Contracts and Digital Twins Transforming Green Finance with Automated Transactions in Investment Agreements through technological investments with human development goals to drive sustainable growth (Peterson Wallace, 2023). Rao (2017) analysed industry-wide trends in adopting human-centric innovation practices and found that sectors with higher levels of human-machine collaboration experienced faster innovation cycles and more sustainable growth rates (Rao, 2017). Nguyen and Hoang (2016) explained the contribution of industry partnerships to the creation of human-centred innovation. They contended that cross-industry collaboration is critical for knowledge sharing between industries, and for achieving systemic shifts towards more sustainable and inclusive business models (Nguyen Hoang 2016).

The analysed literature reveals that human-centric innovation plays a complex role in the creation of sustainable organizations in the context of Industry 5.0. Researchers have shown that combining human-centred design with cutting edge technologies can improve organisational resilience, sustainability and adaptability. In addition, ethical issues, social consequences, and the strategic integration of digital instruments play an important role in the design of the future of sustainable business actions. The synthesis of these studies shows that organizations that are adopting a human-centred innovation approach are well-suited to tackling the challenges ahead in Industry 5.0, to be sustainable long-term, and to be socially beneficial. Meanwhile, with the development of the concept of Industry 5.0 paradigm, future research is to concentrate on elaborating more holistic frameworks to direct organisations towards human-centric and sustainable practices in various environments.

## III. METHODOLOGY

To address these objectives, the study employs a multifaceted research methodology. It begins with a comprehensive literature review to establish a theoretical foundation on sustainable organizational design. This review includes an examination of academic books, peer-reviewed journals, and case studies to understand the current state of sustainability practices. The core of the study is a series of in-depth case studies of ten top companies recognized for their exemplary sustainability practices. This qualitative analysis draws on secondary data from company reports, sustainability disclosures, and industry publications. Additionally, interviews with industry experts and surveys of employees provide practical insights into the challenges and benefits of implementing sustainable practices. A comparative analysis of these companies helps identify patterns and best practices, offering a robust understanding of effective sustainability strategies.

## 3.1. Core Principles of Industry 5.0

*Human-Centric Design:* Human-centric design is a foundational principle of Industry 5.0, emphasizing the importance of placing human needs and well-being at the heart of technological and organizational development. This approach advocates for designing systems, processes, and work environments that enhance human capabilities, rather than merely optimizing efficiency or productivity. In Industry 5.0, this principle goes beyond traditional ergonomics and usability to include considerations of psychological well-being, job satisfaction, and meaningful work. By integrating human-centric design, organizations aim to create workspaces that foster collaboration, creativity, and innovation. This includes designing technology that complements human skills and provides tools that enhance, rather than replace, human effort. The focus is on developing environments where technology and human creativity work synergistically, leading to greater employee engagement and improved overall performance.

*Technological Integration:* Technological integration in Industry 5.0 involves the seamless incorporation of advanced technologies with human-centred approaches to drive organizational efficiency and innovation. Unlike previous industrial revolutions that often-prioritized automation and machine efficiency, Industry 5.0 seeks to balance technological advancements with human expertise. This integration includes leveraging technologies such as artificial intelligence (AI), robotics, and the Internet of Things (IoT) to augment human capabilities and support decision-making processes. For instance, collaborative robots (chat bots) are designed o work alongside humans, handling repetitive tasks while allowing employees to focus on more complex and creative work. The goal is to create a harmonious interaction between humans and machines, where technology supports and enhances human roles rather than replacing them. This approach not only boosts productivity but also ensures that technological developments contribute positively to the work environment and employee satisfaction.

*Ethical Considerations:* Ethical considerations are a critical component of Industry 5.0, reflecting a growing awareness of the social and moral implications of technological advancements. As organizations embrace new technologies and human-centric approaches, they must address ethical issues related to privacy, fairness, and the impact of automation on employment. Industry 5.0 emphasizes the need for responsible technology use, including the development of ethical AI systems that ensure transparency, accountability, and respect for human rights. This principle also involves creating policies that safeguard worker rights and promote equitable access to technology. Organizations are encouraged to adopt practices that align with corporate social responsibility (CSR) and sustainability goals, ensuring that technological innovations contribute positively to society and the environment. By integrating ethical considerations into their strategies, organizations in Industry 5.0 can build trust with stakeholders and foster a more inclusive and sustainable future.

## 3.2. Frameworks for Sustainable Design

Sustainable organizational design refers to creating structures, processes, and practices that promote long-term environmental, social, and economic sustainability. Frameworks for sustainable design provide structured approaches to integrating sustainability into organizational operations and strategy. These frameworks often include principles such as reducing resource consumption, minimizing waste, and ensuring that business practices contribute to broader societal goals. One widely recognized framework is the Triple Bottom Line (TBL) approach, which evaluates organizational performance based on three dimensions: people, planet, and profit. Another important framework is the Circular Economy, which emphasizes designing products and processes that enable the continual reuse of materials, reducing waste and promoting resource efficiency. By adopting these frameworks, organizations can systematically address sustainability challenges and align their operations with environmental and social goals, ultimately enhancing their resilience and long-term viability.

*Integrating Human-Centric Approaches:* Integrating human-centric approaches into organizational design involves creating environments and systems that prioritize the needs, well-being, and potential of employees. This approach recognizes that employees are central to achieving organizational goals and that their engagement and satisfaction significantly impact overall performance. Key aspects of integrating human-centric approaches include designing flexible workspaces that enhance collaboration and creativity, implementing policies that support work-life balance, and fostering a culture of continuous learning and development. Additionally, involving employees in decision-making processes and soliciting their feedback on organizational practices can lead to more innovative and effective solutions. By focusing on the human element, organizations can create a more motivated, productive, and innovative workforce, which is crucial for sustaining competitive advantage and achieving long-term success.

*Balancing Technological and Human Factors:* Balancing technological and human factors is essential in creating sustainable organizational designs that leverage the strengths of both elements. This balance involves ensuring that technological advancements complement and enhance human capabilities rather than overshadow them. In Industry 5.0, this means integrating technologies like artificial intelligence (AI) and automation in ways that support human decision-making and creativity. For example, while automation can handle routine tasks, human oversight is needed to manage complex and nuanced situations. Organizations must design systems that facilitate seamless interaction between humans and machines, ensuring that technology enhances rather than disrupts work processes. Additionally, it is important to consider the impact of technology on employee well-being and job satisfaction, ensuring that technological changes lead to positive outcomes for the workforce. By thoughtfully balancing technological and human factors, organizations can create efficient, innovative, and sustainable work environments that support both operational goals and employee needs.

## 3.3. The Global Industry 5.0 and Human Centric Innovation

The industry 5.0 market presents immense potential for businesses that are prepared to innovate and invest in the future of manufacturing advancements as shown in Figure 1.

*Figure 1. The global Industry 5.0 and human centric innovation (Market.us 2024)*

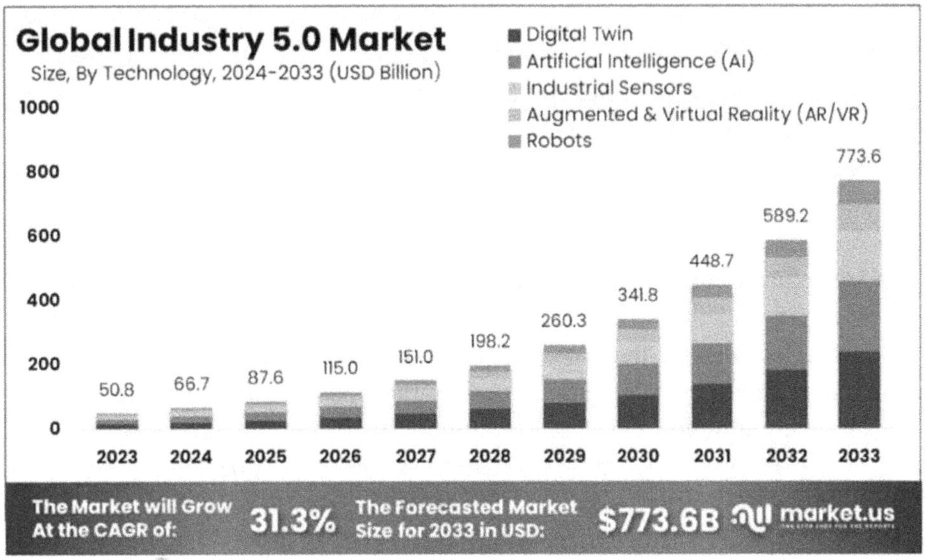


The above Figure 1 reveals that the global Industry 5.0 market is projected to grow from USD 50.8 billion in 2023 to USD 773.6 billion by 2033, at an impressive CAGR of 31.3%. In 2023, Digital Twin technology led the market with over 31% share, while the automotive sector dominated among industry verticals with a 27% share. Asia Pacific emerged as the regional leader, accounting for a 36% market share and generating USD 18.28 billion in revenue.

## 3.4. Role of Technology in Sustainable Organizations

*Advanced Technologies Supporting Sustainability*: Advanced technologies play a pivotal role in supporting sustainability within organizations by enabling more efficient resource use, reducing waste, and promoting eco-friendly practices. Innovations such as renewable energy systems, energy-efficient devices, and smart infrastructure contribute significantly to minimizing an organization's environmental footprint. For example, advanced energy management systems can optimize the use of renewable energy sources, while smart grids improve energy distribution efficiency. Additionally, technologies like blockchain facilitate transparency and traceability in supply chains, ensuring that products are sourced sustainably and ethically. Furthermore, sustainable technologies such as green computing and low-impact manufacturing processes reduce energy consumption and waste generation. By integrating these advanced technologies into their operations, organizations can achieve significant environmental benefits, enhance their sustainability credentials, and meet regulatory requirements more effectively.

*AI and Robotics in Enhancing Human-Machine Collaboration:* Artificial intelligence (AI) and robotics are transforming organizational practices by enhancing human-machine collaboration and improving overall efficiency. In the context of Industry 5.0, AI and robotics are designed to work alongside human employees, augmenting their capabilities rather than replacing them. AI systems can analyse vast amounts of data to provide actionable insights, support decision-making processes, and automate repetitive tasks. Robotics, particularly collaborative robots (chat bots), are used in manufacturing and other industries to handle mundane or physically demanding tasks, allowing human workers to focus on more complex and creative activities. This collaboration leads to increased productivity, reduced error rates, and enhanced innovation. By integrating AI and robotics into their workflows, organizations can improve operational efficiency while also fostering a more engaging and supportive work environment for their employees.

*Digital Twins and Real-Time Monitoring*: Digital twins and real-time monitoring technologies are revolutionizing how organizations manage their operations and optimize performance. A digital twin is a virtual replica of a physical asset, system, or process that simulates its real-world behaviour. This technology allows organizations to monitor and analyse the performance of their assets in real time, predict potential issues, and make data-driven decisions to enhance efficiency and sustainability. For example, digital twins can be used to optimize energy consumption in buildings or improve maintenance schedules for machinery, leading to reduced operational costs and minimized environmental impact. Real-time monitoring systems further enhance this capability by providing continuous feedback on various operational parameters, enabling organizations to respond swiftly to changes and address issues proactively. By leveraging digital twins and real-time monitoring, organizations can achieve greater operational efficiency, reduce waste, and support their sustainability goals more effectively.

## 3.5. Strategies for Fostering Innovation and Creativity

To foster innovation and creativity, organizations must implement strategies that encourage and support these qualities among employees. One effective approach is to create an environment that promotes psychological safety, where employees feel comfortable sharing ideas without fear of criticism or failure. Providing opportunities for continuous learning and development, such as training programs, workshops, and mentoring, can also stimulate creativity by exposing employees to new perspectives and skills. Additionally, organizations should encourage cross-functional collaboration, as diverse teams often generate more innovative solutions by combining different viewpoints and expertise. Implementing flexible workspaces and allowing employees autonomy in their projects can further enhance creativity by providing the freedom to explore new ideas and approaches. By adopting these strategies, organizations can cultivate a culture of innovation that drives progress and adaptability in a rapidly evolving business landscape.

### Aligning Organizational Culture with Sustainability Goals

Aligning organizational culture with sustainability goals is essential for driving human-centric innovation and ensuring long-term success. A culture that embraces sustainability integrates environmental, social, and economic considerations into its core values and practices. To achieve this alignment, organizations should embed sustainability principles into their mission, vision, and strategic objectives, ensuring that all employees understand and support these goals. Promoting a culture of transparency and accountability is also crucial, as it fosters trust and encourages employees to contribute to sustainability initiatives. Recognizing and rewarding efforts that advance sustainability objectives can further motivate employees and reinforce the importance of these goals. By aligning organizational culture with sustainability goals, organizations create a unified direction that supports both innovative practices and responsible environmental stewardship, ultimately leading to a more resilient and forward-thinking business model.

## 3.6. Models for Human-Centric Innovation in Designing Sustainable Organizations

The various models supporting the Human-Centric Innovation in Designing Sustainable Organizations have been discussed in Figure 2.

*Figure 2. Models supporting the human-centric innovation in designing sustainable organizations. (Review of Literature)*

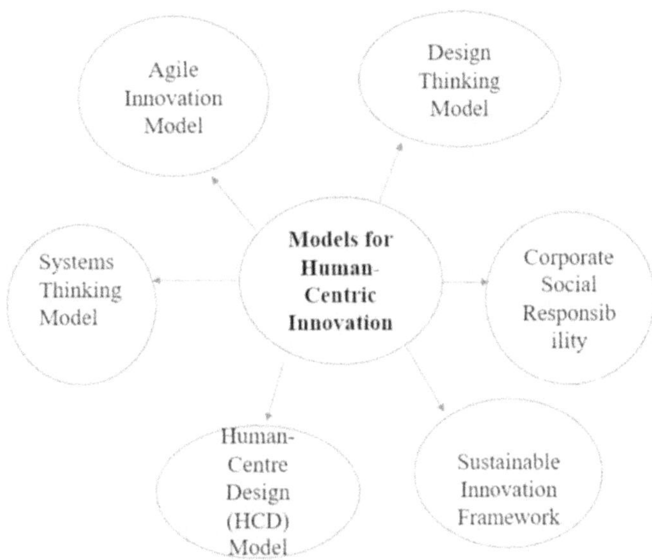


The detailed discussion on Models supporting the Human-Centric Innovation in Designing Sustainable Organizations (Figure 2) is as follows

*Design Thinking Model*: The Design Thinking model is a human-centric approach that emphasizes empathy, ideation, and iterative prototyping to solve complex problems and drive innovation. In the context of designing sustainable organizations, Design Thinking starts with understanding the needs and challenges of employees, customers, and other stakeholders. This model encourages deep empathy through user research and direct engagement, leading to insights that drive creative solutions. By involving diverse perspectives and continuously testing and refining ideas, organizations can develop innovative products, services, and processes that are both sustainable and aligned with human needs. The iterative nature of Design Thinking ensures that solutions are practical and responsive to evolving challenges, enhancing both sustainability and employee satisfaction.

*Human-Centred Design (HCD) Model:* This model focuses on creating systems, products, and services that prioritize the needs, preferences, and capabilities of users. In sustainable organizational design, HCD involves engaging employees and stakeholders throughout the design process to ensure that solutions are user-friendly and effective. This model emphasizes iterative design, where prototypes are tested and refined based on user feedback. HCD also considers the broader impact of design decisions on society and the environment, ensuring that innovations contribute positively to both. By integrating user insights and sustainability considerations, the HCD model helps organizations develop solutions that enhance employee well-being, operational efficiency, and environmental stewardship.

*Systems Thinking Model:* The Systems Thinking model approaches human-centric innovation by viewing organizations as interconnected systems rather than isolated entities. This model emphasizes understanding the relationships and dependencies between various components of an organization, including people, processes, technology, and the environment. In the context of designing sustainable organizations, Systems Thinking encourages holistic solutions that address the root causes of issues and promote long-term sustainability. By considering the entire system, organizations can identify opportunities for innovation that improve both human and environmental outcomes. This model also supports adaptive management practices, allowing organizations to respond effectively to changing conditions and continuously improve their sustainability performance.

*Corporate Social Responsibility (CSR) Framework:* The Corporate Social Responsibility (CSR) framework integrates human-centric innovation with broader social and environmental responsibilities. This model encourages organizations to align their business practices with ethical principles and sustainability goals. CSR involves engaging employees in sustainability initiatives, promoting fair labor practices, and supporting community development. By embedding CSR into organizational culture and operations, companies can foster a sense of purpose and commitment among employees, driving innovative solutions that address social and environmental challenges. The CSR framework also includes transparent reporting and accountability measures, ensuring that organizations are held responsible for their impact on society and the environment.

*Sustainable Innovation Framework:* The Sustainable Innovation Framework focuses on integrating sustainability into the innovation process from the outset. This model emphasizes the development of products, services, and processes that not only meet market needs but also contribute to environmental and social sustainability. The framework encourages organizations to set clear sustainability goals, such as reducing carbon emissions, minimizing waste, and promoting resource efficiency. It also involves stakeholder engagement to ensure that innovations align with societal expectations and address pressing challenges. By incorporating sustainability criteria into the innovation process, organizations can drive meaningful change and create solutions that benefit both people and the planet.

*Agile Innovation Model:* The Agile Innovation model applies principles of agility to the innovation process, emphasizing flexibility, collaboration, and rapid iteration. This model supports human-centric innovation by allowing organizations to quickly adapt to changing needs and feedback from employees and stakeholders. Agile methodologies, such as Scrum and Kanban, promote continuous improvement and iterative development, enabling organizations to address sustainability challenges in a responsive and effective manner. By fostering a culture of experimentation and collaboration, the Agile Innovation model helps organizations develop innovative solutions that enhance employee engagement, operational efficiency, and environmental performance.

Each of these models offers valuable approaches to integrating human-centric innovation into the design of sustainable organizations. By adopting and adapting these models, organizations can create environments that support employee well-being, drive creativity, and contribute to long-term sustainability goals.

## 3.7. Case Studies of Successful Applications in Designing Sustainable Organizations

*Patagonia*: Founded in 1973, Patagonia is renowned for its commitment to environmental sustainability and ethical business practices. The company has successfully integrated sustainability into its core operations, generating significant value both in terms of brand loyalty and environmental impact. Patagonia's initiatives include using recycled materials in its products, promoting fair labour practices, and investing in environmental activism. One notable application is the company's "Worn Wear" program, which encourages customers to repair and reuse their Patagonia gear, thus extending the life cycle of its products. This program has not only reduced waste but also strengthened Patagonia's brand as a leader in sustainability. The company's transparent approach to environmental impact reporting and its B Corp certification further reinforce its commitment, driving customer trust and loyalty while contributing to a circular economy.

*Unilever:* Established in 1929, Unilever has been a trailblazer in integrating sustainability into its business model. The company's "Sustainable Living Plan" is a comprehensive strategy aimed at reducing environmental impact while enhancing social value. Unilever focuses on sustainable sourcing of raw materials, reducing greenhouse gas emissions, and improving health and well-being through its products. One significant application of this approach is the company's shift to using 100% renewable energy across its global operations. This transition not only reduces the company's carbon footprint but also lowers energy costs, demonstrating a clear value proposition. Additionally, Unilever's commitment to reducing plastic waste through its "Zero Waste to Landfill" initiative exemplifies its dedication to environmental stewardship and operational efficiency.

*Tesla:* Founded in 2003, Tesla is a leader in sustainable energy solutions and electric vehicle technology. The company's mission to accelerate the world's transition to sustainable energy is evident in its innovative products and practices. Tesla's development of high-performance electric vehicles and energy storage solutions has revolutionized the automotive and energy sectors. One of Tesla's notable applications is its Gigafactory, which produces batteries and electric vehicles at scale while aiming for zero waste. The factory's use of renewable energy sources and advanced manufacturing processes highlights Tesla's commitment to sustainability and efficiency. The company's value generation extends beyond financial gains; Tesla has also significantly impacted global attitudes toward electric vehicles and clean energy.

*Google:* Founded in 1998, Google has made substantial strides in sustainability through its commitment to becoming a carbon-free company. Google's "Environmental Sustainability" initiatives include investing in renewable energy projects and improving the energy efficiency of its data centres. A key application of this commitment is the company's achievement of operating on 100% renewable energy since 2017. Google's use of advanced AI and machine learning to optimize energy consumption in its data centres has not only reduced its carbon footprint but also set a benchmark for other tech companies. The company's efforts in sustainability have bolstered its reputation as an industry leader in environmental responsibility and innovation.

*IKEA:* Established in 1943, IKEA has been at the forefront of sustainable business practices in the retail sector. The company's "People & Planet Positive" strategy focuses on sustainable product design, renewable energy, and social responsibility. A notable application is IKEA's use of sustainable materials, such as bamboo and recycled plastics, in its product lines. The company has also committed to using 100% renewable energy in its operations and supply chain by 2025. IKEA's investment in circular economy practices, including its "Circular Hub" initiative to refurbish and recycle used furniture, demonstrates its dedication to reducing waste and promoting sustainability. These efforts enhance IKEA's brand value while contributing to environmental and social sustainability.

*Starbucks:* Founded in 1971, Starbucks has integrated sustainability into its core operations through its "Starbucks Global Environmental Mission." The company focuses on ethical sourcing, reducing environmental impact, and supporting local communities. A significant application is Starbucks' commitment to sourcing 100% of its coffee through ethical sourcing programs such as C.A.F.E. Practices. The company has also invested in sustainable store design, including energy-efficient equipment and waste reduction strategies. Starbucks' commitment to reducing single-use plastic by offering reusable cups and straws further highlights its dedication to environmental responsibility. These initiatives have strengthened Starbucks' brand reputation and contributed to its overall value generation by appealing to environmentally conscious consumers.

*Microsoft:* Established in 1975, Microsoft has made significant strides in sustainability through its "Microsoft Sustainability" initiatives. The company aims to be carbon negative by 2030 and has set ambitious targets for reducing its environmental impact. One key application is Microsoft's investment in renewable energy projects and the development of energy-efficient technologies. The company's commitment to sustainability is evident in its data centres, which use advanced cooling technologies to reduce energy consumption. Microsoft's "AI for Earth" program leverages artificial intelligence to address environmental challenges such as climate change and biodiversity loss. These efforts not only enhance Microsoft's operational efficiency but also position the company as a leader in leveraging technology for environmental sustainability.

*Apple:* Founded in 1976, Apple has integrated sustainability into its business model through its "Apple Environmental Responsibility" initiatives. The company focuses on reducing its carbon footprint, using recycled materials, and improving energy efficiency. A notable application is Apple's commitment to making all of its products and supply chain carbon neutral by 2030. Apple has also invested in renewable energy projects and has achieved a significant milestone by powering its global facilities with 100% renewable energy. The company's use of recycled materials in its products, such as aluminium and rare earth elements, demonstrates its commitment to reducing environmental impact. These sustainability efforts have enhanced Apple's brand value and contributed to its leadership in the tech industry.

*Johnson & Johnson*: Established in 1886, Johnson & Johnson has implemented several sustainability initiatives as part of its "Health for Humanity" goals. The company focuses on reducing its environmental footprint, enhancing product sustainability, and supporting global health initiatives. A significant application is Johnson & Johnson's commitment to achieving zero waste to landfill across its global manufacturing sites. The company also invests in sustainable packaging and has made progress in reducing its carbon emissions. Johnson & Johnson's efforts in sustainability not only contribute to environmental conservation but also enhance its corporate reputation and align with its mission to improve global health and well-being.

*Siemens:* Founded in 1847, Siemens has been a pioneer in integrating sustainability into its operations and product offerings. The company's "Siemens Sustainability" strategy focuses on energy efficiency, reducing greenhouse gas emissions, and supporting sustainable urban development. A key application is Siemens' development of energy-efficient technologies, such as smart grids and renewable energy solutions. The company has also committed to achieving carbon neutrality in its operations by 2030. Siemens' investment in sustainable infrastructure projects, including green building solutions and intelligent transportation systems, demonstrates its commitment to advancing sustainability in various sectors. These initiatives enhance Siemens' value proposition by contributing to global environmental goals and supporting sustainable development.

Each of these companies demonstrates how integrating sustainability into business practices can generate significant value, enhance brand reputation, and contribute to global environmental and social goals. Their successful applications of sustainable practices provide valuable insights and models for other organizations striving to achieve similar outcomes.

## 3.8. Addressing Ethical Challenges in Industry 5.0

The ethical challenges that companies will face in the coming years are very clear. Thus Industry 5.0 is not only an opportunity but also a responsibility to reshape the modern business landscape. The main ethical issue is the risk of job displacement due to the use of robots and artificial intelligence (AI) which are the main driving forces of the future businesses. If machines start taking over the tasks of employees, there will be major changes in the workforce, which will, in turn, bring up the ethical issue of companies' accountability toward their employees. Companies need to deal with this by reskilling and upskilling the employees to new roles and through a fair and equitable transition process. The next ethical issue is about the responsibility of data and AI for the proper usage of AI. Due to the development of Industry 5.0, many companies now gather plenty of data, which arises privacy, security, and misuse doubts. A strict data protection policy along with ethical handling and responsible usage of data are the mandatory measures to be carried out in the course of safeguarding the privacy of a single individual. Experts argue that before building rapport and gaining the customer's trust, a company must first ensure that security measures, as well as the introduction and application of AI, are being followed.

In addition, the ethical implications of human-machine collaboration are important to be determined. On the other hand, the presence of robots and smart assistants that can interact with humans can indeed organize, monitor the workplace, and perform more tasks with high safety. The key to tackling these issues, therefore, is not to jump to conclusions. Yet, it is wise to ponder these questions because they provide the requisite driving forces for the organization's goal processes thus, making it feasible. Ethics of organizational design is primarily a human-related matter and therefore, it cannot be ignored. It is critical above all that these technologies should be used not as the only but rather as the main courtesy of human skills and that they should be implemented in such a way that human dignity and autonomy are honored.

## 3.9. Corporate Social Responsibility (CSR) and Sustainability

Industry 5.0 includes Corporate Social Responsibility (CSR) in the core of its ethical business practices. CSR refers to all the various activities that ensure a socially responsible, environmentally friendly but also economically viable practice of enterprises. Industry 5.0 is about bringing CSR, which entails bringing sustainable practice into core business strategies and operations for both environmental and social impacts. The sector is waking up to the full significance that CSR can bring in terms of strategy. This comes in the form of emissions reductions, waste reduction and a circular economy mentality. For example, Unilever and the likes have pledged to reach net-zero emissions as well as increase sustainability in all areas of its supply chains. It signals more and more that enduring success is inextricably tied to operating in a responsible fashion on the environment. Beyond environmental issues, CSR also touches on human rights, fair labor and community engagement. Enterprises are to Underwrite programmes that are social equality enhancing and culturally useful in their host communities. That means fair wages, safe jobs and corporate-social responsibility through philanthropy, community programs.

## 3.10. Inclusivity and Diversity in Organizational Design

Inclusivity and diversity are critical aspects of organizational design in the context of Industry 5.0. As the nature of work evolves, it is essential for organizations to foster diverse and inclusive workplaces that reflect a broad range of perspectives and experiences. Not only this approach increases creativity and innovation but also mirror through ethical and social purposes to increase. Inclusivity → Making sure all employees feel valued in a company and effectively have the same opportunities for growth. That means take binary measures such as gender equality, eliminate bias-hammer and remove the hurdles for diverse talent pipelines This is the journey where companies like Microsoft or IBM have already come, to prove how inclusive practices add to productivity and successfulness of an organization, in times like Now. Organisational Design diversity also includes the diverse organizational level cultural, social and demographic. It makes sure the products and services are available and engaging all types of customers hence market fit is better, less problems met for customers. Those companies that are inclusive and diverse are poised to serve global audiences both better and more efficiently, thereby gaining an advantage.

## 3.11. Measuring and Reporting Sustainability

Sustainability is a significant area of measurement and reporting for organizations that aim to demonstrate their environmental or social responsibility. Effective sustainability measurement and reporting promotes transparency, strengthens accountability, and enables organizations to monitor progress towards achieving sustainable goals. Creating relevant metrics and key performance indicators (KPIs), using appropriate reporting tools, and utilizing data analytics to improve performance are all part of this process.

The measurement and management of sustainability performance are framed by metrics and Key Performance Indicators (KPIs). They offer organizations with measurable and quantifiable data to monitor progress and establish targets. The measurement of sustainability includes carbon footprint, energy consumption, water usage, waste generation, and employee satisfaction and diversity ratios. Other metrics include BP, PPF, PMPI, etc.

The carbon footprint of an organization is a measure of the total greenhouse gas emissions it generates. The scope of this includes both direct emissions resulting from operations and indirect emissions that come from supply chains and product use. The measurement of energy usage involves analysing the amount of electricity consumed and the origin of that energy, including both renewable and non-renewable sources. Metrics are used to measure water usage and management practices, while measures are applied to waste generation and the impact of recycling/waste reduction initiatives.

## 3.12. Tools for Transparent Reporting

Accountability and transparency in sustainability performance are ensured through transparent reporting. Several frameworks and tools are available to help organizations report on their sustainability efforts in a comprehensive and transparent manner. Sustainability reporting is generally based on the Global Reporting Initiative (GRI). It provides guidelines and regulations for reporting economic, environmental, and social effects, assisting organizations to disclose information in a structured and standardized manner. GRI framework promotes transparency and comparability among different types of organizations and industries.

The SASB framework is a crucial instrument that establishes industry-specific guidelines for reporting sustainability outcomes. The main focus of SASB standards is on material sustainability issues that may impact financial performance, enabling organizations to convey information to investors and other stakeholders. Another useful tool is the Task Force on Climate-related Financial Disclosures (TCFD), which reports on climate- related risks and opportunities. The TCFD offers suggestions for sharing information on governance, strategy, risk management, and metrics related to climate change. The implementation of TCFD rules permits groups to give precise, uniform reporting on the financial consequences of climate change.

## 3.12. Leveraging Data Analytics for Continuous Improvement

Data analytics plays a pivotal role in driving continuous improvement in sustainability practices. By analysing data from various sustainability metrics and reporting tools, organizations can gain actionable insights into their performance and identify areas for enhancement. Advanced data analytics techniques, such as predictive analytics and machine learning, can be used to forecast future sustainability performance and identify potential risks. For example, predictive analytics can help organizations anticipate energy consumption patterns and optimize energy usage, while machine learning algorithms can identify patterns in waste generation and suggest more effective waste reduction strategies.

Real-time data analytics enables organizations to monitor sustainability metrics continuously and make timely adjustments. By integrating data from multiple sources, such as sensors, IoT devices, and operational systems, organizations can gain a comprehensive view of their sustainability performance and respond proactively to emerging issues. Additionally, data visualization tools can help communicate complex sustainability data in a clear and accessible manner. Interactive dashboards and reports allow stakeholders to explore data trends, compare performance against benchmarks, and track progress toward sustainability goals. By leveraging data analytics, organizations can drive continuous improvement in their sustainability efforts, enhance operational efficiency, and achieve better outcomes. Data-driven insights support informed decision-making and enable organizations to adapt their strategies to evolving sustainability challenges and opportunities.

## 3.13. Common Challenges in Designing Sustainable Organizations

Designing sustainable organizations presents several challenges that can impede progress. One significant obstacle is resistance to change, where employees and management may be reluctant to adopt new sustainability practices due to discomfort with disruption or entrenched habits. This resistance can delay or obstruct the implementation of innovative sustainability strategies. Another challenge is high initial costs; sustainable technologies and practices, such as renewable energy systems or green building materials, often require substantial upfront investments, which can deter organizations from pursuing these solutions. Additionally, a lack of expertise can hinder efforts to develop and manage sustainability initiatives. Many organizations may lack the specialized knowledge needed to effectively implement and sustain these practices. Integrating new sustainability practices with existing systems poses another difficulty, as aligning innovative strategies with current operations and technologies can be complex and resource-intensive. Finally, measuring the impact of sustainability efforts can be challenging without clear metrics, making it difficult to assess effectiveness and justify continued investment.

### 3.14. Regulatory Challenges for Human-Centric Innovation in Industry 5.0

Regulatory challenges for human-centric innovation in Industry 5.0 include balancing technological advancement with privacy, data security, and ethical AI use. Governments face difficulties in creating frameworks that protect workers' rights while promoting automation and human-AI collaboration. Ensuring job security and equitable access to reskilling programs is critical, as industries integrate advanced technologies. Furthermore, aligning regulations across borders is a challenge, given the global nature of digital transformation. Sustainable practices also require regulatory oversight to ensure industries adopt eco-friendly technologies without compromising efficiency or economic growth, adding complexity to policy development.

## IV. SOLUTIONS AND RECOMMENDATIONS

To address these challenges, several solutions can be implemented. To overcome resistance to change, organizations should foster a culture that embraces sustainability by engaging employees, providing education, and demonstrating leadership commitment. This approach helps to align employees with sustainability goals and encourages a collective effort towards change. For managing high initial costs, organizations can seek financial incentives such as government grants and subsidies, and form strategic partnerships to share resources and reduce financial burdens. Investing in training and development is crucial for overcoming the lack of expertise; providing employees with the necessary skills and knowledge through education and professional development can enhance the implementation of sustainability initiatives. Adopting incremental changes can help organizations integrate sustainability practices gradually, reducing the impact on existing systems and allowing for smoother transitions. Finally, developing and tracking metrics for sustainability efforts is essential for measuring impact and demonstrating progress. Establishing clear benchmarks and regularly reporting on these metrics helps organizations make data-driven decisions and justify continued investment in sustainable practices.

## V. FUTURE TRENDS AND DIRECTIONS

Future research could focus on several promising areas highlighted by the study. One potential direction is the exploration of how emerging technologies such as blockchain, advanced AI, and digital twins can further enhance sustainability practices. Longitudinal studies could also be conducted to assess the long-term impact of sustainability initiatives on organizational performance and resilience. Additionally, sector-specific analyses would provide a deeper understanding of the unique challenges and opportunities associated with sustainability practices in different industries.

Looking ahead, several trends are expected to shape the future of sustainable organizational design. The integration of AI and data analytics will play a pivotal role in enhancing sustainability efforts. Advanced technologies will enable organizations to monitor and optimize their sustainability practices with greater precision, providing valuable insights for decision-making. The growth of circular economy models is anticipated, emphasizing the importance of reusing, recycling, and minimizing waste. Organizations will increasingly adopt circular practices to reduce their environmental footprint and create value from waste materials. There will be a heightened focus on social sustainability, addressing issues such as diversity, equity, and community engagement. Organizations will be expected to contribute positively to societal well-being and address social impacts alongside environmental concerns. The advancement of green technologies will continue to drive progress, with innovations in renewable energy, green materials, and low-impact manufacturing enhancing sustainability. Lastly, there will be an increased emphasis on collaboration and partnerships. Organizations will work together with governments, NGOs, and other stakeholders to tackle complex sustainability challenges and drive systemic change. By staying attuned to these trends, organizations can advance their sustainability efforts and build more resilient and responsible business practices.

## VI.IMPLICATIONS OF THE STUDY

The study has significant implications for both academia and industry. Academically, it contributes to the theoretical understanding of sustainable organizational design by integrating insights from diverse industries and providing a comparative analysis of best practices. This theoretical contribution opens avenues for further research, particularly in exploring the impact of emerging technologies on sustainability and the role of social sustainability in organizational design. For industry professionals, the study offers practical recommendations for implementing or enhancing sustainability practices. These recommendations are grounded in real-world case studies and address common challenges faced by organizations. Companies can use these insights as benchmarks to evaluate their own sustainability practices and identify areas for improvement.

## VII.CONCLUSION

In conclusion, the study underscores the increasing importance of sustainable organizational design in the modern business landscape. By analysing successful case studies and identifying best practices, the research demonstrates how sustainability initiatives can drive value creation and enhance organizational performance. Despite the challenges inherent in implementing sustainable practices, companies that adopt effective strategies benefit from improved brand reputation, operational efficiencies, and alignment with environmental and social goals. The study highlights the need for ongoing research and innovation in sustainability, emphasizing the potential of emerging technologies and evolving trends. Integrating human-centric and technologically advanced approaches will be crucial for organizations aiming to build resilient and responsible business models that contribute positively to both the environment and society.

## REFERENCES


Ahmed, P. K., Shepherd, C. D., & Chen, J. (2022). Social sustainability and inclusive work environments in Industry 5.0. *Journal of Business Ethics*, 176(3), 423–439. DOI: 10.1007/s10551-022-05076-x

Amabile, T. M., Conti, R., Coon, H., Lazenby, J., & Herron, M. (2004). Assessing the work environment for creativity. *Academy of Management Journal*, 39(5), 1154–1184. DOI: 10.2307/256995

Balaji, K. (2023, June). Unlocking the Potential of BI-Enhancing Banking Transactions Through AI&ML Tools. In *2023 International Conference on Applied Intelligence and Sustainable Computing (ICAISC)* (pp. 1-6). IEEE.

Balaji, K. (2023, June). Blockchain Based Banking Transactions Enabled by Big Data. In 2023 5th International Conference on Energy, Power and Environment: Towards Flexible Green Energy Technologies (ICEPE) (pp. 1-6). IEEE.

Balaji, K. (2023, December). Exploring the Drivers and Effects on Supply Chain Resilience and Performance in an Emerging Market Using Artificial Intelligence. In 2023 3rd International Conference on Smart Generation Computing, Communication and Networking (SMART GENCON) (pp. 1-6). IEEE.

Balaji, K. (2024). Harnessing AI for Financial Innovations: Pioneering the Future of Financial Services. In Jermsittiparsert, K., Phongkraphan, N., & Lekhavichit, N. (Eds.), *Modern Management Science Practices in the Age of AI* (pp. 91–122). IGI Global., DOI: 10.4018/979-8-3693-6720-9.ch004

Balaji, K. (2024). Charting the Path to Global Prosperity: Unveiling the Impact and Promise of Sustainable Development. In Ordóñez de Pablos, P., Anshari, M., & Almunawar, M. (Eds.), *Harnessing Green and Circular Skills for Digital Transformation* (pp. 1–22). IGI Global., DOI: 10.4018/979-8-3693-2865-1.ch001

Balaji, K. (2024). The Nexus of Smart Contracts and Digital Twins Transforming Green Finance With Automated Transactions in Investment Agreements: Leveraging Smart Contracts for Green Investment Agreements and Automated Transactions. In Jafar, S., Rodriguez, R., Kannan, H., Akhtar, S., & Plugmann, P. (Eds.), *Harnessing Blockchain-Digital Twin Fusion for Sustainable Investments* (pp. 287–315). IGI Global., DOI: 10.4018/979-8-3693-1878-2.ch012

Balaji, K. (2024), "Artificial Intelligence for Enhanced Anti-Money Laundering and Asset Recovery: A New Frontier in Financial Crime Prevention," *2024 Second International Conference on Intelligent Cyber Physical Systems and Internet of Things (ICoICI)*, Coimbatore, India, 2024, pp. 1010-1016, DOI: 10.1109/ICoICI62503.2024.10696100

Balaji, K., & Babu, M. K. (2017). A study on the affect of technology on unplanned purchase behaviour among the customers across selected corporate retail chains of Andhrapradesh, India. *International Journal of Economic Research*, 14(4), 277–288.

Balaji, K., & Babu, M. K. (2017). A study on the role of the external and internal factors on consumer impulse buying behavior in selected retail outlets of Andhra Pradesh, India. *International Journal of Applied Business and Economic Research*, 15(4), 171–185.

Balaji, K., Karim, S., Naidu, N. G., Venkatesh, T., & Ranjitha, P. V., & ChandraSekhar, S. (2023, June). Examining the Potential of Cryptocurrencies as An Asset Class-An Empirical Study. In 2023 International Conference on Applied Intelligence and Sustainable Computing (ICAISC) (pp. 1-6). IEEE.

Balaji, K., Karim, S., & Rao, P. S. "Unleashing the Power of Smart Chatbots: Transforming Banking with Artificial Intelligence," *2024 International Conference on Advances in Computing, Communication and Applied Informatics (ACCAI)*, Chennai, India, 2024, pp. 1-7, DOI: 10.1109/ACCAI61061.2024.10602456

Balaji, K., & Kishore Babu, M. (2016). A study on consumer shopping patterns in current retail scenario across selected retail stores in Andhra Pradesh, India. *International Journal of Economic Research*, 13(4), 1629–1640.

Baldwin, C. Y., & Clark, K. B. (2000). *Design Rules: The Power of Modularity*. MIT Press. DOI: 10.7551/mitpress/2366.001.0001

Brown, A., & Taylor, K. (2017). Enhancing supply chain resilience through employee involvement. *The Journal of Supply Chain Management*, 53(2), 45–60. DOI: 10.1111/jscm.12110

Cameron, K. S., & Quinn, R. E. (1999). *Diagnosing and Changing Organizational Culture: Based on the Competing Values Framework*. Addison-Wesley.

Carroll, A. B. (1991). The pyramid of corporate social responsibility: Toward the moral management of organizational stakeholders. *Business Horizons*, 34(4), 39–48. DOI: 10.1016/0007-6813(91)90005-G

Christensen, C. M. (1997). *The Innovator's Dilemma: When New Technologies Cause Great Firms to Fail*. Harvard Business Review Press.

Davis, J., & Johnson, M. (2021). Human-AI collaboration and its impact on innovation performance. *Technology Management Review*, 34(1), 25–37. DOI: 10.1002/tmr.10435

Drucker, P. F. (1985). *Innovation and Entrepreneurship: Practice and Principles*. Harper & Row.

Evans, R., & Green, H. (2018). AI-driven data analytics for improved sustainability reporting. *Journal of Sustainable Development*, 11(4), 78–92. DOI: 10.5539/jsd.v11n4p78

Freeman, R. E. (1984). *Strategic Management: A Stakeholder Approach*. Pitman Publishing.

Garcia, A., Rodriguez, J., & Sanchez, L. (2024). Building resilience through human-centric risk management. *International Journal of Risk Management*, 29(1), 15–30. DOI: 10.1002/ijrm.12450

Hackman, J. R., & Oldham, G. R. (1980). *Work Redesign*. Addison-Wesley.

Hart, S. L. (1995). A natural-resource-based view of the firm. *Academy of Management Review*, 20(4), 986–1014. DOI: 10.2307/258963

Hernandez, P., Wong, H., & Patel, R. (2020). Leveraging digital tools for real-time sustainability reporting. *Journal of Environmental Management*, 269, 110810. DOI: 10.1016/j.jenvman.2020.110810

Jones, M. (2023). Ethical AI and sustainable business practices in Industry 5.0. *Journal of Business Ethics*, 188(2), 345–359. DOI: 10.1007/s10551-023-05045-x

Kim, Y., & Park, H. (2020). Design thinking and its impact on sustainability in manufacturing. *Sustainability Science*, 15(1), 101–118. DOI: 10.1007/s11625-019-00810-5

Laursen, K., & Foss, N. J. (2003). New human resource management practices, complementarities, and the impact on innovation performance. *Cambridge Journal of Economics*, 27(2), 243–263. DOI: 10.1093/cje/27.2.243

Lee, J., Park, S., & Kim, H. (2015). Energy optimization through digital twin technology in industrial processes. *Energy*, 85, 88–98. DOI: 10.5855/ENERGY.2015.24.1.088

Martin, G., & Cooper, S. (2019). Social equity and human-centric innovation: Implications for corporate social responsibility. *Business & Society*, 58(2), 348–369. DOI: 10.1177/0007650317734871

Miller, D., & Smith, K. (2018). Ethical frameworks for AI deployment in the workplace. *Journal of Business Ethics*, 152(4), 975–990. DOI: 10.1007/s10551-016-3340-1

Nguyen, T., & Hoang, M. (2016). Cross-industry collaborations and human-centric innovation. *Journal of Innovation Management*, 4(3), 56–73. DOI: 10.24840/2183-0606_004.003_0005

Nonaka, I., & Takeuchi, H. (1995). *The Knowledge-Creating Company: How Japanese Companies Create the Dynamics of Innovation*. Oxford University Press. DOI: 10.1093/oso/9780195092691.001.0001

Normann, R. (1984). *Service Management: Strategy and Leadership in Service Business*. Wiley.

Peterson, R., & Wallace, K. (2023). Strategic frameworks for human-centric innovation. *Strategic Management Journal*, 44(1), 123–142. DOI: 10.1002/smj.3404

Porter, M. E., & Kramer, M. R. (2006). Strategy and society: The link between competitive advantage and corporate social responsibility. *Harvard Business Review*, 84(12), 78–92. https://hbr.org/2006/12/strategy-and-society-the-link-between-competitive-advantage-and-corporate-social-responsibility PMID: 17183795

Prahalad, C. K., & Hamel, G. (1990). The core competence of the corporation. *Harvard Business Review*, 68(3), 79–91. https://hbr.org/1990/05/the-core-competence-of-the-corporation

Rao, P. S. (2017). Human-centric innovation and disruptive industry trends. *Journal of Technology Management*, 32(2), 142–158. DOI: 10.1016/j.jtm.2016.10.001

Schneider, B., & Bowen, D. E. (1995). *Winning the Service Game*. Harvard Business Review Press.

Senge, P. M. (1990). *The Fifth Discipline: The Art & Practice of The Learning Organization*. Doubleday.

Singh, R. (2021). Workforce development and continuous learning in Industry 5.0. *Journal of Vocational Behavior*, 89(1), 101–115. DOI: 10.1016/j.jvb.2021.103521

## ADDITIONAL READING

Smith, A. (2022). Integrating human-centred design principles with AI and robotics in manufacturing. *Journal of Advanced Manufacturing*, 12(3), 321–336. DOI: 10.1016/j.jam.2022.05.001

Thompson, R., Patel, N., & Davis, J. (2019). Optimizing human-machine interaction in smart factories. *International Journal of Production Economics*, 209, 56–68. DOI: 10.1016/j.ijpe.2018.12.001

Von Hippel, E. (1986). Lead Users: A Source of Novel Product Concepts. Management Science, 32*(7), 791-805. DOI: 10.1287/mnsc.32.7.791

Williams, S. (2016). Corporate governance and human-centric innovation: Enhancing adaptability and resilience. *Corporate Governance*, 16(2), 202–215. DOI: 10.1108/CG-04-2015-0055

Zuboff, S. (1988). *In the Age of the Smart Machine: The Future of Work and Power*. Basic Books.

# Chapter 6
# Human-Centric Digital Workplace:
## Designing for Employee Wellbeing and Productivity

**Sakshi**
https://orcid.org/0009-0007-8467-8079
*Lovely Professional University, India*

**Shivani Dhand**
https://orcid.org/0000-0002-4809-1365
*Lovely Professional University, India*

## ABSTRACT

*The swift transition of the workplace into the digital domain has engendered a problem of striking the right balance between employee wellness and technology innovation. Most traditional environments that place a lot of emphasis on active performance fail to consider an employee's mental, physical, and emotional well-being of employees. This chapter highlights the need for human-centered digital workplaces prioritizing well-being over productivity. It does this by explaining Self Determination Theory, which identifies three essential elements: autonomy, competence, and relatedness, which promotes healthier and more engaging populations. It continues to the forefront the use of other advances, especially AI and virtual realities, to make work more individualistic and enjoyable and address change management problems like digital exhaustion and diversity in digitization. Therefore, it presents practical ideas and suggestions to build sustainable employee-centric workplaces that improve quality of life and performance.*

## 1. INTRODUCTION

The last few decades have seen the adoption of human-centric workplaces as one of the critical elements of organizational design. In this case, the practice is no longer oriented towards profits and productivity but towards taking more balanced care of employees. This change has been brought about by the view that employee well-being goes beyond morality, as it is regarded as one of the most strategic events of the organization. The human-centric workplace model is oriented towards creating a workplace

DOI: 10.4018/979-8-3693-8181-6.ch006

that considers employees' psychological, emotional, and physical health, creating an environment where people feel appreciated and encouraged. This chapter discusses the significant aspects of the digital workplace from the human-centric perspective and how it relates to the well-being and productivity of employees in terms of technology, work design, and other organizational policies.

The human-centric workplace model is premised on the belief that an organization should always design and carry out its activities with its employees' needs, wants, and experiences integrated into that design or activity. Traditionally, workplaces were designed to support a hierarchy, a vector of power fully baked with more output focus than employee well-being. However, the human-centered model aims at environments where people can develop in all ways because there is an understanding that people who are happy, interested, and take care of their work will most likely be oriented to work rather than not. Examples of crucial elements of a human-centric workplace model are encouraging employee agency, psychological safety, opportunities for purposeful work, and organizational belongingness. Such psychological concepts as Self-Determination Theory assist with the understanding of these features. This theory, for instance, states that human beings are motivated by the need for autonomy, competence, and connection. The satisfaction of all or some of such needs increases the likelihood of higher motivation, satisfaction, and wellness among individuals. In a human-centered workplace, organizations are shaped so that processes, tools, and cultures are all designed to address these needs, resulting in a more productive and engaged workforce.

Furthermore, the approach they implemented is more human-centric in that, besides physical workplaces, technological tools, policies, and authority, employee wellness is considered in designing every organizational component. Such an approach indicates an increasing understanding that wellness not only entails an individual's physical aspect but encompasses the individual's emotional, mental, and social aspects in concern. Addressing these considerations enables better and more efficient working environments to be created, which is beneficial not only to the employees but also to the employing organization.

Changes in society, technology, and the economy during any given period have influenced the changing styles in work arrangements. In the early twentieth century, most workstations revolved around industries, and there was a high drive for effectiveness, uniformity, and vertical coordination. For instance, the scientific management principles espoused by Frederick Taylor sought to increase efficiency and productivity by employing division of labor with close supervision. In such models, managerial obligations focused on organizational goals and employee productivity. Thus, the well-being of individuals in the workplace was often secondary. With the change in the order of things coupled with the growth of knowledge-based economies, especially in the second half of the last century, organizations understood that employee engagement and creativity needed to be managed. The egalitarian and empowered forms of work marked a clear break from the traditional hierarchy, where the emphasis was on individual performance, employee training, and work-life balance.

Consequently, fundamental changes in the features and layout of workplaces have occurred in the 21st century with the invention of information technology and the everyday use of remote and hybrid work. That is, how work is conceptualized and carried out has changed with the arrival of digital technology. The use of technologies such as video conferencing, cloud computing, and artificial intelligence has made it possible for companies to implement more elastic work patterns. The need for this shift has been aggravated by the advent of COVID-19 when many companies were forced to implement a home policy and change their perception towards work from the office setting. Workplace strategies have been revised to include the physical transformation of offices and digital operations. As the digital workplace proliferates, so has the intermingling of work and personal lives, thereby bringing in its problems to the well-being of employees. Whereas digital resources make it seem like there is freedom of movement, they also create an environment known as the always-on culture, where employees are inclined to be reachable all the time, which has brought problems like digital exhaustion, excessive workloads, and a shift in work-life equilibrium. To mitigate these difficulties, the human-centric workplace model seeks to encompass technology to support employees' well-being instead of using technology that destroys it. Digital workplaces need to be designed by organizations in such a way as to enhance and protect the work-life balance, facilitate social engagement, and enable employees to self-manage their workload.

The relationship between employee well-being and productivity in the digital era has been reciprocal, as well-being has been prioritized as a critical driver of organizational performance. Research supporting this mutualism indicates that employees are engaged and productive when appreciated and cared for. In contrast, those companies with management systems that do not take care of the well-being of employees often report increased absenteeism, turnover, and disengagement, which threaten the overall output and profits of the firm. During the last few decades, the term productivity has been interpreted differently. No, it is not simply the amount of work done or the hours of engagement in particular activities. It is also essential to know those works' effectiveness and effects. Employees in an excellent mental and emotional state are more capable of creating ideas, tackling complicated issues, and interacting with fellow employees. This paradigm shift has made organizations view performance management from a broader and holistic perspective and avoid traditional metrics such as presentism, where employees report the number of hours worked or tasks finished.

Nonetheless, taking care of both aspects in the digital age is still challenging, and one must plan to do so. Organizations must go beyond equipping employees with the right tools and resources to enable them to perform their jobs effectively. They must also develop an environment that promotes the employees' mental, emotional, and physical well-being. Such working environment development should include providing work flexibility, ensuring inclusion, promoting psychological well-being, and providing opportunities for growth and development.

## 1.1 Purpose of the Chapter

Using the human-centric digital workplace model as a focal point, this chapter will explain how organizations can strategize and implement workplaces that cater to employee needs and, at the same time, increase output healthily. The chapter will address various issues, including core elements of the human-centered building, the effects of technological advancements on that structure and attitudes, and the ways of building a workplace for the modern man. The chapter is structured as follows: First, an extensive assessment of the human-centric workplace model will inform the reader of its efficiency and psychological justification. Subsequently, the chapter will focus on understanding the digital workplace from a technological point of view, clarifying the advantages and disadvantages of using such technologies. After that, the chapter will look at the possible measures that can be put in place to promote the digital workplace, focusing mainly on the employees' well-being, including work-life balance, mental health programs, and employee reshaping. There will be discussions on how organizations can create and implement productive workplaces that concur with the individuals' well-being. The last section will offer the trends in the modern workplace, which will touch on the digital workplace design and what is expected of the human workforce. At the end of this chapter, the reader will appreciate the principles governing the design of work environments, which consider both the welfare of the employees and the productivity of the organization, as well as how such principles could be used in their organizations.

## 2. THE ROLE OF TECHNOLOGY IN THE HUMAN-CENTRIC DIGITAL WORKPLACE

A human-centered digital workplace greatly emphasizes the technology that helps enhance employees' well-being, autonomy, flexibility, and productivity. Where technology has been carefully integrated, it is possible to create a workplace where employees feel engaged, appreciated, and included, instead of one where powerless tools exact maximum output and efficiency from an otherwise congested workplace. This section addresses the question of the possibilities available for pursuing the dual goals of employee well-being and productivity in the workplace, with the distinction between people-centered technologies and productivity-centered ones and specifics of such digital tools as artificial intelligence (AI), enterprise automation, and collaboration enablers.

### 2.1 Integration of Technology to Support Well-Being and Productivity

As industries start functioning in the digitally advanced world, technology has only been embraced in most cases for efficiency and productivity improvement. Nevertheless, with the recognition of employee wellness as an essential factor for driving performance in the long run, it becomes crucial to adopt a more severe attitude about integrating technology to focus on well-being and productivity. For example, including specific digital capabilities that help employees handle their workloads helps eliminate stress and burnout, improving employee engagement and mental health. Also, technologies that allow for communication and collaboration may help employees feel that they belong to the organization, which helps their social well-being. Organizations are employing different strategies to make digital workplaces more anthropocentric. For instance, infrastructure such as cloud-based tools, Slack, Microsoft Teams, Zoom, etc. Enables group work regardless of the geographical location of the employees.

Additionally, such applications enhance efficiency in the work environment as they often include team interaction, which minimizes the adverse effects of remote work, which is isolation. Likewise, there is a growing trend towards incorporating wellness programs within organizational cultures through apps and devices incorporating fitness activities, mindfulness, and mental wellness. Thus, thanks to these technological advancements, the organization can strike a healthy compromise between the two, and all employees will be able to perform well in all dimensions of their lives.

### 2.2 People-Centered vs. Productivity-Centered Technology

A distinction can be made in the digital workplace between people-oriented technology and those that lean towards productivity. Usually, technology seeks to design, above all else, the output and efficiency of its users. Such tools may help optimize a work process, mechanize specific duties, or monitor an employee's output, but they consider an employee's psychological state secondary. For instance, time management systems, performance management dashboards, or to-do list tools might create enabling conditions for employees regarding strict deadlines and an expectation of average performance, leading to heightened stress and burnout. Conversely, people-centric technology means the user's health, comfort, and pleasure come first. These technologies are meant to help employees perform their best work without impersonation of the management's micromanagement and still be able to cope with their work and personal schedules. Solutions like managed host services for employees, psychological well-being applications, furnished working environments, etc., are also included in the category. People-centered technology understands that employees are not robots and that their output is related to their physical, mental, and emotional health. When it comes to technology, emphasis on people also puts a premium on autonomy and the level of flexibility on the part of employees, which are very important for creating a conducive working environment. Research has established that employees who are permitted to control their work processes and work time to a greater extent are more considerable in terms of engagement, motivation, and job satisfaction (Ryan & Deci, 2000). Technology designed for human beings addresses such needs, enabling users to adjust their work experience according to their preferences and situations. For instance, flexible working hours software allows employees to select where they will be working and the timing, enabling them to juggle personal and work-related obligations.

## 2.3 Tools for Enhancing Employee Autonomy, Flexibility, and Collaboration

Employee freedom, flexibility, and teamwork are all emphasized in a human-centered digital workplace. Technology has made this possible since employees can now better control when and how they work. For instance, remote work tools such as video conferencing, file sharing, and VPN networks have enabled employees to work from almost any location without limiting efficiency. Also, project management tools, such as Trello, Asana, and Monday.com, allow employees to take ownership of their tasks and self-manage to a certain extent without losing sight of the bigger picture of the team. Teamwork, too, cuts across all human-centered digital workplaces. For instance, tools such as Slack and Microsoft Teams allow for location-agnostic teamwork among employees thanks to the features of these tools that allow for course communication even without face-to-face interaction. Office tools are intended to elicit causal relations in the workplace and alleviate distance in working environments. A review of the collation of various aged literature makes it evident that even automation of tasks through the advancement of AI technologies helps collaboration (Davenport & Ronanki, 2018). When utilized in the right way, technology can be of great use in improving employee satisfaction and well-being by promoting autonomy, flexibility, and collaboration. In other words, employees with some control over their working hours and tools for working collaboratively with colleagues will likely feel more engaged and empowered. Furthermore, flexible working policies have been found to alleviate stress and improve the work-life balance, which naturally enhances productivity and retention (Gajendran & Harrison, 2007).

## 2.4 The Impact of Technologies on Employee Experiences

Artificial Intelligence, technology, and online platforms have brought many changes in today's workplaces. This has altered how activities are done, including the interaction of employees with the firms they work for. AI-driven tools, for instance, can make decision processes faster, allow people to perform only tasks that are not repetitive, and give feedback and insights to employees. AI-based chatbots, for instance, can respond to basic customer queries, thus enabling employees to engage in more complex and value-adding activities. AI-based analytic platforms also allow an organization's employee performance to be monitored and the results to be analyzed to develop individual personnel training plans. Although beneficial in enhancing the effectiveness and efficiency of work processes, AI and automation come with the costs of unemployability, less human interaction, and more surveillance. There is a possibility of distress among employees regarding robotics in the workplace owing to the fear of dubiety of employment. Such causes hostile staff policies since their activities are supervised by machines performing functions human beings ought to do. Hence, it is foremost that businesses implement AI and automation in a way that is more conducive to work and that enhances existing work efforts instead of conceiving them as supplanting work. Concentrating on augmentation rather than full automation enables organizations to deploy AI to benefit their employees by giving them everything they require to thrive without losing the human touch of work (Marien, 2014). Digital solutions, such as cloud computing systems for teamwork and ERP systems, have also changed the working behaviors of employees. These solutions provide employees with information and the ability to work with other employees from anywhere and at any time. While these methods have allowed a higher degree of flexibility and collaboration, they also contribute to the digital fatigue phenomenon, where an individual becomes mentally fatigued due to prolonged use of digital screens and constant connectivity. To reduce such digital fatigue, organizations should encourage the responsible use of technologies by their employees where they are allowed to take or instead encouraged to take breaks, have work limits, and even switch off whenever it is necessary.

### 2.5 Overcoming Digital Overload

With the growth of technology in all aspects of work, digital weariness has become a prominent issue. This is the excessive usage of various tools in the workplace, from emails through video calls to short text messages, which can contribute to demoralization and the general kips' health. Studies have revealed that engaging in screen activities for an extensive period and the expectation of being connected with no respite leads to stress, anxiety, and even deterioration of one's mental state (Mark et al., 2008). In order to create fully human-centric solutions for the digital workplace, organizations must address and minimize the potential adverse impact of such technologies on employees' health. One of the preventive measures that can be adopted is the inclusion of time for digital detachments where employees do not engage in any screen activity and are kept away from work after official hours. There are also ways of encouraging them to observe such courtesy by asking them to silence their devices, for example, after a certain period of the day. Also, companies can organize wellness activities dealing with the issues of mindfulness, physical exercise, and other forms of mental assistance to counter the stress of digital working. Adjusting the balance between technology use and employee needs calls for a cross-cutting strategy that addresses physical, mental, and emotional well-being. Organizations can enhance employee well-being while promoting effective performance through people-centered technology, flexible work practices, and responsible engagement with technology at work.

## 3. DESIGNING FOR EMPLOYEE WELL-BEING

Employee well-being refers to individuals' mental, physical, and emotional state within an organization. In response to a more digital and hybrid working environment, employee well-being emerged as one of the focal points of businesses that strive to create a conducive working environment. Employee well-being in an organization means creating an environment where people are encouraged to work and are appreciated for their input without compromising their personal lives. This part will examine the components of employee well-being: mental, physical, and emotional, supplemented by measures aimed at improving well-being in the digital space; remote working, mindfulness, and mental health programs, work-life balance strategies; ergonomic sensitivity, among others, and how leadership can positively influence the wellbeing culture strategy.

## 3.1 Understanding Employee Well-Being

*Figure 1. Understanding employee wellbeing (https://haiilo.com/blog/employee-wellbeing-definition -importance-best-practice/)*

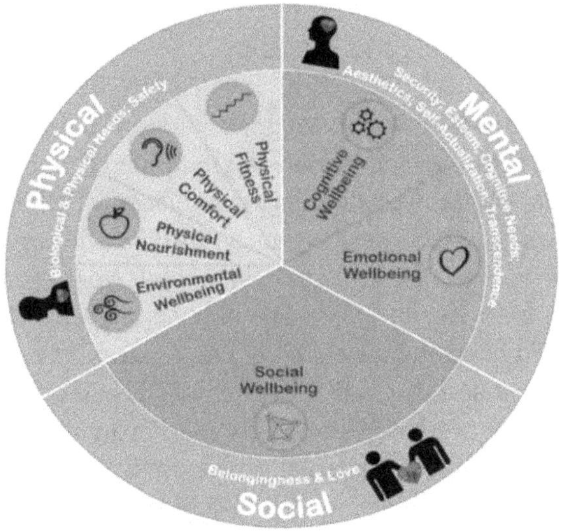


The well-being of employees is an all-encompassing concept that contains mental, physical, and emotional dimensions (Sudha et al., 2025). Cognitive, affective, and behavioral functioning in an integrated way, which leads to stability of mind and the resilience to cope with different organizational stresses and work management practices, are components of mental well-being. There are costs to the individual and the organization when there is poor mental workplace well-being. The adverse effects of mental well-being at work may include low productivity, increased absenteeism, and a tendency to burnout. Mental health is essential for employees as, according to the World Health Organization, depression and anxiety are the two mental health disorders that rank as the top ten causes of global disability (World Health Organization, 2020). Occupational health and physical well-being incorporate periodical sickness absence prevention and overall good health achieved through exercise, proper workplace design and policies, and other healthy lifestyle practices to avoid work injuries and illness. Many health concerns have been related to studying for long hours without proper movement, with some of them being related to the back, obesity, and even heart problems. Therefore, especially in a work setting with many information technology devices where employees must be seated most of the time, much emphasis should be put on one's physical health. Emotional well-being is the person's aptitude to control feelings, establish social connections, and withstand uncomfortable situations. This concept is closely related to mental and physical health. Those with high emotional equanimity are more prone to stay resilient, engaged, and happy at work. However, when emotional well-being is questioned, employees are more likely to be stressed, face conflict, and be alienated from work.

## 3.2 Strategies to Enhance Well-Being in the Digital Workplace

With increasing levels of digital and hybrid work models among organizations, there is a need for new strategies to support the well-being of employees. This section examines some of the most effective strategies to improve well-being practice in a digital workplace.

### 3.2.1 Flexible Work Hours and Hybrid Models

There is a shift in the attitude towards working regular hours and even structural work patterns. These facilities enable employees to organize their working hours around their commitments, enhancing their work balance and health. It has also been established that a relatively flexible environment leads to more satisfied employees who experience less stress as they easily cope with work and home roles (Bloom et al., 2015). Moreover, hybrid work models mix and match' home-working and office-working positions to yield the best of both scenarios. The office is not entirely discarded as the employees get the active work environment, when need be, thereby embracing the dexterity of an office and the comfort of a home office. It has been demonstrated that such hybrid employment lessens anxiety and fatigue because it enables individuals to delegate workplaces in a way that favors them, promoting their well-being (Gajendran & Harrison, 2007). Firms with alternative work policies tend to have a more engaged and productive workforce, which shows that such models benefit the employees' well-being.

### 3.2.2 Mindfulness and Mental Health Programs

Several organizations are launching mindfulness and mental health programs to enhance employees' mental health. Extensive research demonstrates that mindfulness elements, including meditation, focused breathing exercises, and even keeping a diary, can assist in managing stress and anxiety, enhance concentration, and regulate emotions (Kabat-Zinn, 2023). Moreover, beyond implementing mindfulness programs, companies are also spending their resources on mental health issues and services by providing EAPs that enable employees to access counselling therapy and other stress management mechanisms. It is also not uncommon anymore for institutions to have policies that encourage employees to take "mental health days" with pay. These interventions tend to help the employees' psychosocial well-being but also create a more accepting attitude towards mental health issues, thus encouraging those who may need it to go out and seek help (Greenhaus & Allen, 2011).

### 3.2.3 Work-Life Balance Initiatives

Achieving a healthy equilibrium between work and personal life is very important for employees' welfare, especially in present-day digital work environments where work and home are two spheres often intermingled. It gives the employees the power to work outside their formal offices at any given time, which helps in the emancipation of the employees; however, when this is not managed well, it creates issues such as overwork and even burnout. Therefore, employers should zealously encourage work-life balance by managing the expectations on work hours and discouraging employees from working beyond the set "office hours." Some organizations are now adopting restrictions on emails after work or mandating staff gloves during the day. For instance, in France, a law was passed that gives employees the right to disconnect, meaning they do not have to respond to work-related emails beyond their work hours

(Chiuffo, 2019). Such policies enhance and protect the employees' personal space from work invasion and vice versa, ensuring a stress-free and healthy working environment.

### 3.2.4 Promoting Physical Well-Being Through Ergonomic Design and Wellness Programs

However, physical well-being is often neglected in the workplace, while its contributions to an employee's health cannot be underrated. Ergonomics becomes even more critical in a digital workplace where most employees remain glued to their desks for long hours. The lack of proper ergonomics could result in several musculoskeletal complications like backaches, neck strain sprains, and other repetitive motion injuries, which would be detrimental to the productivity and well-being of employees. In this respect, to increase the well-being of employees, organizations ought to provide resources such as the purchase of ergonomic equipment like adjustable chairs, standing desks, and appropriate lighting, among other items (Antonaci et al., 2024). Allowing employees to sit or stand at will as is convenient for them during the workday will assist in equating the adverse effects of sitting for long periods.

Furthermore, wellness initiatives that promote such levels of movement, such as on-site gyms, online exercise lessons, and step count contests, can enhance the physical health of the employees and raise their spirits. Organizations also show that they include movement within the work… 'The workday has movement breaks every hour where people stretch for a few minutes or walk down the hall. Not only does this help keep physical discomfort at bay, but it also aids in clearing the mind and improving one's ability to focus, which translates to better overall health (Stringer, 2016).

### 3.2.5 The Role of Leadership and Culture in Prioritizing Well-Being

There is an interrelation between leadership and creating an organizational culture where the overriding concern for every employee is their wellness. Exhibiting such leadership commitment in words, actions, policies, or strategies will motivate employees to consider their health and well-being and reconcile personal and occupational obligations. A culture supportive of well-being is one in which the employees can speak openly about mental health without fear of judgment or punishment, look for help, or establish limitations. The convergence to a well-being culture can be enhanced through leaders' involvement in existing wellness activities, championing personal wellness, and work-life integration of subordinates (Sarioguz & Miser, 2024). Well-being is also a priority when leaders take mental health rest days, practicing mindfulness and etiquette after work communications. When it comes down to it, promoting such a culture entails a great deal of openness and effective channels of conveyance of information. Employees must know that their well-being is essential and that their organization is ready to meet all the needs and flexibility required to excel. Cultivating a well-being culture benefits organizations by increasing employee engagement, turnover control, and performance enhancement strategies (Schaufeli & Bakker, 2004).

## 4. ENHANCING PRODUCTIVITY THROUGH HUMAN-CENTRIC DESIGN

Furthermore, organizations are beginning to appreciate that employee well-being and productivity cannot be viewed in isolation. Therefore, the dilemma of enhancing productivity is solved by a new concept called human-centric design, which focuses on creating an enabling environment concerning the employees' physical, mental, and emotional needs. While this may sound like an optimization of the output of the workforce, it is creating an ecosystem in which people perform better, are more involved, and have a greater level of contentment in their jobs. In this paragraph, we will analyze the impact of well-being on one's productive capabilities, look at the workplace design as the 'verb' that helps maintain focus and concentration, and work experience customization, including people measuring tools with data analysis of productivity enhancement tactics, and finally the role development plays in projecting the humanity behind growth.

Any organization's productivity level greatly influences how healthy employees are cared for. Research has shown that employees in a work environment where they enjoy a high level of well-being tend to be more absorbed, passionate, and able to maintain their performance over a prolonged period (Schaufeli & Bakker, 2004). Conversely, when there is a threat to well-being, in this case, for example, due to mental illness, physical pain, or even exhaustion, work output suffers. Employees under pressure or anxiety are more prone to errors, delays, and even withdrawal from active engagement, which ultimately lowers their output. Implementing some health and wellness programs, onboarding flexible work schedules, and incorporating a general wellness approach can significantly boost productivity. The Harvard Business Review indicates that companies spending on employee well-being have a 21% productivity increase and 37% fewer absences (Mankins & Garton, 2017). Therefore, well-being becomes a strategic tool in organizations as it not only aids in improving the performance of individuals but also develops adaptable human resources for changing workplaces.

### 4.1 Designing Workplaces for Flow and Focus in a Digital Environment

A significant aspect of design geared towards its users is the provision of environments conducive to flow. Flow is a mental state of being wholly absorbed in an activity; hence, enhanced attentiveness, creativity, and productivity are achieved. However, the challenge of juggling attention in a rather attention-seeking digital environment makes the need to incorporate aspects that induce flow in workplaces even more paramount. Digital workplaces are flow-optimized. Work interruptions are minimized in these cases, and suitable apparatus is available to the employee to facilitate focus. For instance, many companies have embraced these applications to help employees handle notifications, eliminate disruptive interference, and organize their most urgent tasks. In addition, the physical space away from the office, even in the case of remote working, also aids in concentrating on work. Well-designed and positioned furniture, good lighting, and the availability of quiet rooms for intense work are some factors that make it possible for employees to get into the flow (Csikszentmihalyi, 1990). Apart from single workstations, collaboration spaces, both virtual and physical, need to be planned, to support interaction and collaboration between members. In a digital environment, tools such as Slack, Microsoft Teams, and Zoom enable employees to multitask and work simultaneously, alleviating the potential distractions from the group's physical presence. Still, those means of communication must play a very selective and essential role, maximizing productivity while preventing overstimulation of the information.

### 4.1.1 Personalized Work Experiences

Every employee has different strengths, and as much as desired, workplace designing strategies and management methods will be proven wrong in claiming to work for everybody. The emphasis on the person in the workplace design acknowledges that employees have different needs and preferences and hence seeks to provide different work experiences for every individual (Kim et al., 2024). Personalizations can also range from comprehensive concepts like providing different timetables for every employee to more personal approaches like providing specific training and management styles to different individuals. It is of utmost importance in personalized workplaces. While certain employees may flourish in office setups designed for teamwork, some may wish to work in still cubicles or enclosed spaces. Since individuals can modify or design their work surroundings to what pleases them, it becomes possible for the organization to create spaces where people actualize their abilities. For instance, previous studies have illustrated that employee with authority over their surroundings, such as changing the environment, lighting, and desk heights, tend to be more productive and satisfied. (Knight & Haslam, 2010). Apart from customizing the physical workplace, the individual experience can be enhanced using appropriate digital tools. For example, AI-powered productivity applications can assess employees' working patterns and propose unique improvement techniques. For instance, artificial intelligence can use the ultradian rhythms of a person to suggest the best times for deep work, resulting in increased output with people suffering from less cognitive load.

## 4.2 Leveraging Data and Feedback to Optimize Productivity Tools and Processes

Information and assessments are essential in pruning the work industry for efficiency. Data plays a critical role in human-centric entities as they work towards perfecting their employees' tools, processes, and even environments. This ensures that the employees are best equipped to carry out their duties. This helps an organization diagnose and resolve issues and make improvements that advance the organization's overall efficiency. Including employees' voices and opinions is essential in implementing and improving productivity-enhancing programs (Filippucci et al., 2024). Leadership can gauge issues and opportunities through regular or ad-hoc surveys, pulse checks, or direct conversations. This feedback can help inform decisions related to employee workplaces and processes so that changes are made that benefit employees. Data analytics tools can also achieve optimum productivity concerning the tools and processes provided. For instance, some organizations leverage management information by measuring e-mail users, meeting prevalence, and project deadlines to determine if staff are engaged in nonworthwhile efforts. In this regard, changes can be made to the organization by, for example, cutting down on unproductive meetings, improving communication systems, and incorporating technology in handling fewer essential duties rather than the core function of the employees (Labaye & Remes, 2015).

## 4.3 Importance of Training and Development in Maximizing Human Potential

Any human-centered design approach in the organization has to encompass the elements of training and development since these facilitate the employees to harness their skills, adjust to different situations, and even be their best. Exceptionally, in a digital workplace where there is constant change both in technology and processes, learning and development towards employees will be a significant determinant of their productivity. There are discernible benefits in performance management and employee engagement when the organization allocates resources toward employee development. LinkedIn research discovered that 94% of employees will stick to a company for a more extended period if their employer is committed to their growth (LinkedIn, 2019). Such changes, in particular, demand training programs emphasizing improving digital literacy, management of emotions, and leadership because most employees still work within a technology-oriented, complicated sphere. Organizations can also advance continuous learning through informal means such as sharing information, mentorship, and learning amongst colleagues. Ensuring employees have these kinds of tools and other forms like online courses, webinars, and attendance at conferences related to their field helps them learn current and widely accepted practices, which helps improve their productivity and input in the organization.

## 5. SELF-DETERMINATION THEORY AND WORKPLACE DESIGN

Self-Determination Theory (SDT) is a recognized psychological theory where increasing attention is paid to the human aspects of motivation, especially concerning work. Deci and Ryan (1985) developed SDT and explained that everyone needs autonomy, competence, and relatedness to maintain or enhance intrinsic motivation and well-being. This approach warrants practical propositions in designing work environments, more so in this age that provides for physiological organizations seeking more employee motivation and satisfaction within the digital workplace. This part of the chapter will define SDT, analyze how its fundamental principles can be dealt with in workplace design, and provide some examples of companies that have successfully implemented the concepts of SDT. The Self-Determination Theory focuses on motivation having two types: intrinsic - motivated by seeking activity where one finds satisfaction and interest - and extrinsic - motivated by seeking activity while expecting external rewards, perhaps in the form of abuse or pressure. As per SDT, when a person carries out an activity for the sake of that activity alone, he or she engages more effectively and shows a higher level of creativity and better performance. The theory defines three essential human nature components that must be fulfilled to maintain this intrinsic motivation:

- **Autonomy**: The need to feel in control of one's actions and decisions.
- **Competence**: The need to feel adequate and capable in achieving goals and handling tasks.
- **Relatedness**: The need to feel connected to others and experience a sense of belonging.

Once the requirements mentioned above are fulfilled within the work environment, it can be expected that the employees will be more intrinsically motivated, leading to more job satisfaction, commitment, and performance (Deci & Ryan, 2000). Conversely, if these needs are frustrated, employees may suffer from resignation, exhaustion, and lack of efficiency. Therefore, an appropriate workplace design following the principles of SDT can be a significant factor in improving an employee's motivation and well-being.

*Figure 2. Autonomy, competence, and relatedness (Author's Own)*

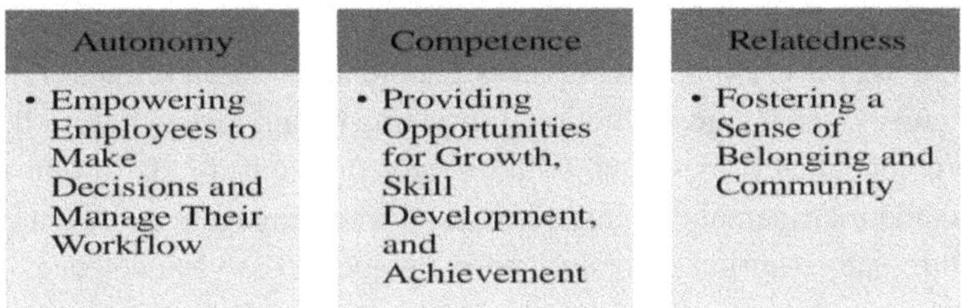


## 5.1 Case Studies of Organizations Successfully Applying SDT in Workplace Designs

Several organizations have come to appreciate the advantages of employing the SDT principles in designing their workplaces to enhance motivation, well-being, and productivity. The following case studies portray specific organizations' efforts towards applying SDT in fostering people-centered work environments.

5.1.1 Google: Considering the well-known 'people-first' approach adopted by Google, where employees are put before the twain and resources, this company has spearheaded the design of organizational amenities that encourage autonomy, competence, and relatedness. The organization offers its staff flexible working policies, encouraging them to determine their working hours and place. Google also provides countless options in the area of work enhancement through various courses and workshops aimed at increasing the competencies of the employees. In order to encourage relatedness, Google uses open office spaces, undertakings oriented to team building, and a high level of community integration to encourage employee interaction.

5.1.2 Atlassian: The Australian software organization has taken a unique approach to its workplace design by promoting employees' autonomy and competence (Pink et al., 2024). Employees are given substantial authority over their work, associated tasks, and time management, which explains why they do not exhaust themselves in operant conditioning. In addition, the organization is also known to provide much support for its employees' career advancement through training and other skill-enhancing activities. We can also fulfil relatedness needs at Atlassian as they embrace transparency and teamwork in the office and outside, where they use technology.

5.1.3 Zappos: An online shoe-selling portal, Zappos irrationally celebrates with its employees as it seeks to promote the relatedness aspect of employees. The workplace arrangement in the company focuses on encouraging teamwork, building communities, and promoting communication, all of which are essential to promoting bonding among employees. Zappos promotes acceptance and the appreciation of all employees through trust and inclusiveness and by recognizing employees' efforts. Moreover, the company endorses independence when carrying out one's work by allowing employees to make decisions and take responsibility.

# 6. CHALLENGES AND SOLUTIONS IN IMPLEMENTING HUMAN-CENTRIC DIGITAL WORKPLACES

The transition to a digital workplace that places people at its core presents tremendous chances to enhance human resources' satisfaction, emotional investment, and dispatch. On the flip side, an organization also has problems that it must deal with effectively to ensure that it embraces such a model. Such challenges include management of change, remote work engagement of employees, maintaining a collaborative culture, and ensuring diversity and inclusion in the virtual space. Thus, organizations must employ tactical measures to overcome such challenges, with human resources (HR) instrumental in facilitating change. This chapter addresses the main issues associated with **building** a modern digital workplace and presents how these issues can be resolved and what recommendations for best practices should be followed.

## 6.1 Challenges in Creating a Human-Centric Digital Workplace

### 6.1.1 Resistance to Change and Digital Transformation

One typical problem in building a human-centered digital workplace is change inertia. Change management makes work difficult as it usually alters the familiar way of doing things. Employees may become anxious about many changes, especially new technologies. For many, new technologies may be a source of distress. They would be worried that their knowledge will no longer be utilized or that they do not want to learn how to use the new equipment and systems (Ganz et al., 2010). This is especially true for those employees who tend to be technologically backward or have been accustomed to working in the old ways for a long time. There may also be factors like understanding why a human approach to a digital transformation is essential to the resistance to transformation processes. Employees are unaware of how coordination with colleagues using these platforms and AI-powered processes interlinks with their personal power, skills, and social connectedness. People do not entirely support these modifications without seeing their relevance from the top of the hierarchy (Herold et al., 2008).

### **6.1.2** Maintaining Employee Engagement in Remote and Hybrid Settings

The growing acceptance of remote and hybrid work patterns has altered the dynamics of employee relations, which is a positive change, but keeping employees engaged in their work has also become a problem. In most cases, office settings significantly promote employee engagement through personal interactions among colleagues, unplanned discussions, or simply a friendly working environment. However, such engagement is far more challenging in remote and hybrid models. For instance, employees may feel cut off and out of their teams' circle or avoid altogether participating in the company's way of life (Bailey & Kurland, 2002). Moreover, the issue of engagement can also be reduced by digital fatigue. Organizational practices have resulted in the growing utilization of virtual meetings; thus, employees suffer from the effects of excessive screen faces that worsen their work-life balance and their availability to be 'in the zone' (Wang et al., 2021). These and several other issues can result in inefficiency, loss of morale, and high turnover rates if left unattended.

### 6.1.3 Managing Diversity and Inclusion in Digital Workplaces

Creating a diverse and inclusive digital workplace is another challenge in implementing a human-centric workplace model. While digital tools have made it easier for organizations to connect with talent from diverse backgrounds across geographies, they have also introduced new complexities in ensuring that all employees feel included and supported. For example, communication barriers may arise when employees from different cultural or linguistic backgrounds work together in a virtual environment. Additionally, employees with varying access to technology or digital literacy may struggle to engage with digital platforms, leading to unequal participation and exclusion. Furthermore, in remote settings, unconscious bias can persist in hiring, promotions, and decision-making processes, as managers may rely more heavily on subjective impressions without the benefit of in-person interactions.

## 6.2 Practical Solutions and Best Practices for Overcoming These Challenges

### 6.2.1 Cultivating a Culture of Change and Learning

The most challenging resistance to change can be addressed by creating a culture that views digital transformation as a continuous evolution with learning at its core. This entails leadership walking the talk by disclosing the merits of the digital tools and how they are committed to the people-centered strategies of the organization. It also involves carrying out the necessary training and development to encourage the employees to work effectively in a digital space, as described (Kotter, 1996). When an organization creates a learning environment where employees can learn, ask questions, and even try working with new technology without the fear of making mistakes, it is more likely to lessen resistance time. Similarly, when new technologies are deployed, people in charge should allow employees to make some input. This way, the organization can implement justified tools across the different departments to solve existing problems and improve the employee experience. Involving employees in implementing change provides a sense of ownership and alleviates the sense of alienation.

### 6.2.2 Promoting Engagement Through Intentional Digital Design

In order to keep employees engaged during their remote or hybrid working hours, organizations need to emphasize creating deliberate digital experiences that capture some of the elements that enhance employee engagement in a typical work environment, which involves facilitating social interactions, teamwork, and team bonding using virtual means. For instance, organizations may conduct virtual team-building activities and provide spaces for casual socialization, such as informal catch-ups or a "water cooler" setting where employees are free to talk about anything other than work. Furthermore, digital well-being programs should be implemented to counteract the negative repercussions of concurrent media usage on employee performance. This will help to avoid setting an ambiguous standard that encourages employees to overexert themselves at work. It is beneficial to recommend rest, reduce the number of meetings to virtual ones, and set prohibited work hours for people to switch off devices physically. Also, social media messaging can provide adequate time frames for employees to respond, minimizing the 'always on' syndrome detrimental to productivity.

### 6.2.3 Building Inclusive Digital Workplaces

In order to address the issues related to the management of diversity and inclusion in virtual workplaces, organizations should take steps toward fostering environments that facilitate fair participation and representation. This can be accomplished in several ways:

- Inclusive Communication: Every communication channel must be available to every employee, including the language and location. Creating translation services or tools for people who are not native speakers, avoiding jargon in physical meetings, and ensuring that minority views are represented when making conclusions will help reduce this problem.
- Digital Accessibility: Employers must ensure that all employees, particularly those with disabilities or restricted access to technology, can access their digital systems (Bentley et al., 2024). This could mean purchasing assistive equipment, supplying online services training, or helping employees acquire suitable devices or internet facilities to work remotely.
- Bias Reduction: To combat the issue of unconscious bias in online systems, firms can adopt practices such as blind recruitment, homogenizing appraisal processes, and bias training for managers and other decision-makers, among others (Varsha, 2023). These practices help ensure that performance and competence, regardless of their perceived representations, are the primary considerations when judging employees.

## 7. ROLE OF HR IN SUPPORTING THE HUMAN-CENTRIC APPROACH

Human Resources is vital to establishing and maintaining a digital workplace that cares for employees. Since it is directly responsible for employee well-being, management, and development, HR is the only department in a position to spearhead the organizational changes needed to address the issues mentioned above. Some of the critical functions of HR in this context include the following:

- Change Management: The role of HR can assist in managing change by helping staff cope with the changes that come with the digital transformation processes. It encompasses communicating changes effectively, introducing training programs, and actively addressing the concerns of employees. HR also plays a crucial role during any organizational restructuring process in helping reduce the magnitude of resistance encountered and ensuring that employees' well-being is prioritized (Herold et al., 2008).
- Employee Well-Being: The HR department is tasked with the establishment and execution of well-being initiatives geared toward the physical, mental, and emotional health of the workforce. This could include providing resources for Mental health, physical rehab, and policy regulation on remote employees' engagement and work habits in an online workplace.
- Diversity and Inclusion Initiatives: The role of HR is vital in the Creation of Diversity inclusion within the organization. This entails carrying out recruitment processes that embrace diversity and inclusivity, sensitizing and providing training about unconscious bias, and ensuring that online mediums are accessible and friendly to every employee.
- Employee Feedback: The human resources department may collect and evaluate employee responses using digital tools and work practices. In organizations that practice regular employee

surveys and make data-based decisions, human resources can keep in step with the changing employee needs and wants.

## 8. EMERGING TRENDS

Technological innovations are on the rise not only in enhancing productivity but also in the aspect of employee well-being in ways that were previously not possible. Two key trends likely influencing the design of human-centric future workplaces are artificial intelligence well-being solutions and virtual reality work environments.

### 8.1 AI-Driven Well-Being Solutions

In managing employee well-being, AI will be significant as it will be able to provide personalized services based on the behaviours and activities of employees as well as mental health concerns. For instance, AI marketing strategies would be able to collect and analyze data from wearable technology, in which gamification engages users in tracking their physical activities, stress levels, and sleeping patterns and making health enhancement recommendations. AI could extend such services to offer virtual counselling, mood-tracking applications, and stress management before escalating stress (Mantello & Ho, 2024). These AI technologies for the employees' health will help move away from prescribed wellness programs and integrate such programs within the needs of every employee.

### 8.2 Virtual Reality Workplaces

The notion of a virtual reality workplace may appear ahead of time, but VR technologies are already being designed and utilized in specific sectors. VR workplaces in the future will create dynamic, engaging spaces with traditional office settings or go beyond them altogether. Zoom meetings, brainstorming sessions, or even joint work on a project can be done inside another reality, which imitates real life but is more flexible and creative (Adhyaru & Kemp, 2022). VR workplaces could also aid social interaction and bonding, thus lessening the effects of isolation and loneliness that remote working may bring.

### 8.3 Augmented Reality for Training and Skill Development

Besides VR, augmented reality (AR) technologies will significantly enhance coaching and skills. For example, gaining AR training can be practiced by employees in an environment that restricts on-the-job training. This kind of learning through experience is very beneficial for technical areas or industries where practical interaction is necessary. Therefore, adding AR to the organization's training programs makes it possible to provide more dynamic and exciting forms of learning that build employees' skills and morale (Blümel, 2013).

## 8.4 Personalization and Customization in Workplace Design

The rise of technology will further enhance and personalize the intricacy and effectiveness of designing workplaces. With this new approach to design, employees in the future will demand not just a particular-looking office or workstation but one that is tailor-made to suit their preferences, wants, and objectives. The notion of an office designed for maximum efficiency applicable to everyone will soon elapse as experiences catering to diverse work habits, inclinations towards learning, and even health become the norm.

- Personalized Workflows and Autonomy

The use of advanced technology will enhance the self-regulation of employees in the firm as applications that will customize workflows for users will become available. For instance, systems powered by artificial intelligence may examine an employee's productive hours and recommend to that individual a work schedule that is as strain-free as possible yet pushes for maximum output. Additionally, employees will have the willpower to decide the most preferred and practical tools and platforms to assist them in their duties, leading to a self-sustaining and productive environment (Ryan & Deci, 2017). Such a propensity will result in higher productivity and even more pleasure in one's job.

- Tailored Well-Being Programs

Similarly, well-being initiatives will be much more tailored as employees will have several mental, physical, and emotional health options. This will range from virtual fitness classes and ergonomics assessments to mindfulness apps and stress management programs, as employees will be given all the tools they need for their overall wellness. The program will also be advanced using wearable devices and technology-based health monitor systems to allow for better and more effective targeting of interventions (Mnatello & Ho, 2024).

## CONCLUSION

This chapter examined the human-centric digital workplace concept, emphasizing employee comfort, flexibility, and productivity. The transition from conventional workplaces to a paperless virtual workplace was accompanied by benefits and obstacles, with the advancement of technology being the most transforming aspect. We also looked at the impact of upcoming technologies like AI, VR, and AR in the current work geared towards optimizing teamwork, employee wellness, and efficiency. The central principle of the human-centric approach is that a workplace should serve the employee's individual needs by offering a structure that enables self-determination in three dimensions of SDT – autonomy, competence, and relatedness. Under such concepts, employees are empowered, as control over the working process is granted, growth prospects are given, and cosmopolitanism within the organizations is created. This chapter further expresses how technology can enhance organizational job satisfaction and efficiency when applied with a human touch.

Most importantly, the tools and platforms that AI drives enable us to customize work environments to fit employees' desires and objectives. In addition, expanding horizons of cooperation through so-called virtual reality and augmented reality collaboration technologies makes the so-called teamwork space less focused on the geographical positioning of the team in physical space. The development of the digital workplace has accelerated the need to promote factors such as work-life balance, flexibility, and the well-being of employees. These tendencies have emerged, especially after the COVID-19 virus, when most organizations embraced hybrid and fully remote work. Modern concepts such as flexible working hours, mental health initiatives, and ergonomicizing workplaces have been adopted as crucial components of employee retention and productivity remaining at optimum levels. Designing workplaces with a human-centric approach provides enormous advantages in the future. In the case of an individual employee, it results in enhanced well-being, increased job satisfaction, and improved levels of participation. Employees tend to be more creative and faithful to organizations that create conditions for autonomy, work-life balance, and growth. In this situation, turnover and absenteeism are less frequent, and better working relations and cooperation exist. In turn, for companies, a human-centered approach applied to the digital work environment results in increased productivity because supported employees generally perform better. Organizations that embrace AI-powered tools can fine-tune their systems and establish productive processes, even while ensuring the well-being of their employees. In addition, such flexible and customizable organizations are more appealing to young employees who wish to have a purpose and freedom at their places of work since they always attract the best talent. The increasing presence of technology and consideration for human adjustment can determine the direction in which the design of workplaces within strategic planning will take. Solutions propelled by artificial intelligence, virtual reality-based work environments, and individualized equipment will continue to transform the manner of working and cater to the various requirements of employees. Companies that incorporate the principles of this design into the workplace will be able to improve health and efficiency and guarantee that neither will be lost with healthy competition and digitalization once more sets in.

## REFERENCES

Adhyaru, J. S., & Kemp, C. (2022). Virtual reality as a tool to promote well-being in the workplace. *Digital Health*, 8, 20552076221084473. DOI: 10.1177/20552076221084473 PMID: 35284084

Antonaci, F. G., Olivetti, E. C., Marcolin, F., Castiblanco Jimenez, I. A., Eynard, B., Vezzetti, E., & Moos, S. (2024). Workplace Well-Being in Industry 5.0: A Worker-Centered Systematic Review. *Sensors (Basel)*, 24(17), 5473. DOI: 10.3390/s24175473 PMID: 39275383

Bailey, D. E., & Kurland, N. B. (2002). A review of telework research: Findings, new directions, and lessons for the study of modern work. Journal of Organizational Behavior: The International Journal of Industrial. *Journal of Organizational Behavior*, 23(4), 383–400. DOI: 10.1002/job.144

Bentley, S. V., Naughtin, C. K., McGrath, M. J., Irons, J. L., & Cooper, P. S. (2024). The digital divide in action: How experiences of digital technology shape future relationships with artificial intelligence. *AI and Ethics*, 4(4), 1–15. DOI: 10.1007/s43681-024-00452-3

Bloom, N., Liang, J., Roberts, J., & Ying, Z. J. (2015). Does working from home work? Evidence from a Chinese experiment. *The Quarterly Journal of Economics*, 130(1), 165–218. DOI: 10.1093/qje/qju032

Blümel, E. (2013). Global challenges and innovative technologies geared toward new markets: Prospects for virtual and augmented reality. *Procedia Computer Science*, 25, 4–13. DOI: 10.1016/j.procs.2013.11.002

Czikszentmihalyi, M. (1990). *Flow: The psychology of optimal experience*. Harper & Row.

Davenport, T. H., & Ronanki, R. (2018). Artificial intelligence for the real world. *Harvard Business Review*, 96(1), 108–116.

Deci, E. L., & Ryan, R. M. (2000). The" what" and" why" of goal pursuits: Human needs and the self-determination of behavior. *Psychological Inquiry*, 11(4), 227–268. DOI: 10.1207/S15327965PLI1104_01

Filippucci, F., Gal, P., Jona-Lasinio, C., Leandro, A., & Nicoletti, G. (2024). The impact of Artificial Intelligence on productivity, distribution and growth: Key mechanisms, initial evidence and policy challenges.

Gagné, M., & Deci, E. L. (2005). Self-determination theory and work motivation. *Journal of Organizational Behavior*, 26(4), 331–362. DOI: 10.1002/job.322

Gajendran, R. S., & Harrison, D. A. (2007). The good, the bad, and the unknown about telecommuting: Meta-analysis of psychological mediators and individual consequences. *The Journal of Applied Psychology*, 92(6), 1524–1541. DOI: 10.1037/0021-9010.92.6.1524 PMID: 18020794

Ganz, M., Nohria, N., & Khurana, R. (2010). Leading change. In *Handbook of leadership theory and practice: A Harvard Business School centennial colloquium* (pp. 527–568). Harvard Business Review Press.

Greenhaus, J. H., & Allen, T. D. (2011). Work–family balance: A review and extension of the literature.

Herold, D. M., Fedor, D. B., Caldwell, S., & Liu, Y. (2008). The effects of transformational and change leadership on employees' commitment to a change: A multilevel study. *The Journal of Applied Psychology*, 93(2), 346–357. DOI: 10.1037/0021-9010.93.2.346 PMID: 18361637

Kabat-Zinn, J. (2023). Wherever you go, there you are: Mindfulness meditation in everyday life. Hachette UK.

Kim, M., Kim, S., Kim, J., Song, T. J., & Kim, Y. (2024). Do stakeholder needs differ?-Designing stakeholder-tailored Explainable Artificial Intelligence (XAI) interfaces. *International Journal of Human-Computer Studies*, 181, 103160. DOI: 10.1016/j.ijhcs.2023.103160

Knight, C., & Haslam, S. A. (2010). The relative merits of lean, enriched, and empowered offices: An experimental examination of the impact of workspace management strategies on well-being and productivity. *Journal of Experimental Psychology. Applied*, 16(2), 158–172. DOI: 10.1037/a0019292 PMID: 20565201

Labaye, E., & Remes, J. (2015). Digital technologies and the global economy's productivity imperative. *Digiworld Economic Journal*, (100), 47.

Mankins, M. C., & Garton, E. (2017). *Time, Talent, Energy: Overcome Organizational Drag and Unleash Your Team s Productive Power*. Harvard Business Review Press.

Mantello, P., & Ho, M. T. (2024). Emotional AI and the future of wellbeing in the post-pandemic workplace. *AI & Society*, 39(4), 1883–1889. DOI: 10.1007/s00146-023-01639-8 PMID: 36776535

Marien, M. (2014). The second machine age: Work, progress, and prosperity in a time of brilliant technologies. *World Futures Review*, 2(2), 174. DOI: 10.1177/1946756714541404

Mark, G., Gudith, D., & Klocke, U. (2008, April). The cost of interrupted work: more speed and stress. In *Proceedings of the SIGCHI conference on Human Factors in Computing Systems* (pp. 107-110). DOI: 10.1145/1357054.1357072

Pink, S., Quilty, E., Grundy, J., & Hoda, R. (2024). Trust, artificial intelligence and software practitioners: An interdisciplinary agenda. *AI & Society*, •••, 1–14. DOI: 10.1007/s00146-024-01882-7

Sarioguz, O., & Miser, E. (2024). Artificial intelligence and participatory leadership: The role of technological transformation in business management and its impact on employee participation. *International Research Journal of Modernization in Engineering Technology and Science*, 6(2).

Schaufeli, W. B., & Bakker, A. B. (2004). Job demands, job resources, and their relationship with burnout and engagement: A multi-sample study. Journal of Organizational Behavior: The International Journal of Industrial. *Journal of Organizational Behavior*, 25(3), 293–315. DOI: 10.1002/job.248

Stringer, L. (2016). *The Healthy Workplace: How to Improve the Well-Being of Your Employees---and Boost Your Company's Bottom Line*. Amacom.

Sudha, M. R., Malini, G. B. H., Sankar, R., Mythily, M., Kumaresh, P. S., Varadarajan, M. N., & Sujatha, S. (2025). Predictive modeling for healthcare worker well-being with cloud computing and machine learning for stress management. International Journal of Electrical & Computer Engineering (2088-8708), 15(1).

Varsha, P. S. (2023). How can we manage biases in artificial intelligence systems–A systematic literature review. *International Journal of Information Management Data Insights*, 3(1), 100165. DOI: 10.1016/j.jjimei.2023.100165

Wang, B., Liu, Y., Qian, J., & Parker, S. K. (2021). Achieving effective remote working during the COVID-19 pandemic: A work design perspective. *Applied Psychology*, 70(1), 16–59. DOI: 10.1111/apps.12290 PMID: 33230359

# Chapter 7
# Leveraging Technology for Employee Well Being and Organizational Resilience

**Muhammad Nawaz Iqbal**
https://orcid.org/0009-0006-4266-4720
*Sir Syed University of Engineering and Technology, Pakistan*

## ABSTRACT

*New technologies available to organizations in the current world provide a great chance to achieve better results in terms of employees' welfare and level of tetrad factors at work. This chapter explores how organizations could use state-of-the-art IT solutions for employees' support and wellbeing enhancement without compromising human-centric design. It talks about how technology is used to design supportive networks to offer better stewardship as well as to introduce community feeling within working environments thus enhancing positive workplace flexibility that helps facilitate better work-life sustainability. The chapter also discusses the issues related to human sociality in the socially distanced world and presents the guidelines on how new technologies can be developed to fit in with such principles as sustainability and durability. However, organizations that concentrate on the persona of technology look forward to developing a more robust organizational resistance level to disruptions.*

## 1. INTRODUCTION

For organizations to better adapt to change they must possess certain attributes, and nowadays the buzzwords become: responsibility, innovation, reliability, and flexibility in terms of sustainability and digitization. In challenge of today's changing and globalized environment where organizations have to adapt as well as grow in conditions of crisis and change or extreme, planned or unplanned, beneficial or detrimental as well as be reversible or irreversible and might be accompanied by different frequently and to a high degree and often in various contexts and on various occasions. It only goes to illustrate how complex and challenging the activities and environment in which people work can be multidimensionality characteristics of change which impact on the creation of change (Ayres, 2000). It ensures that organizational development and implementation of business strategies and solutions is efficient. In addition to occasional change and small gradual changes, drastic changes, disturbances, break, a crisis

DOI: 10.4018/979-8-3693-8181-6.ch007

or meetings or "crashes" are growing essential and frequent, all of which have a great concerns organizations and its functioning (Burt, 2007).

The crisis which emerged internationally after the spread of the COVID-19 pandemic has significantly emphasized on the aspects of sustainability as being an important factor under the health consideration of view, the research analyses its social dimension, but also in the light of economic and environmental considerations (Hakovirta, 2020). Societal institutions such as companies and organizations have also demonstrated that are not ready for a obeyed the instruction of following the Public Health England guidelines to prevent this new identified infectious agent which is the COVID-19 coronavirus (Kraus et al., 2020). This criticality has called for the building of at least a first-line capability for responding to change, more rapidly, and thus require implementing proper actions for addressing the present conditions (Bartik et al., 2020).

It is quite apparent that the phenomenon of resilience has been widely discussed in relation to the emergence of the coronavirus emergency. Perhaps one of the most common assertions is that it is the resilient economies that better winners will appear from the crisis or that people need survival skills to begin a new undefined. When people and institutions use resilience as a term when they speak about it with the aim of constructing or preserving it, it is not. never quite sure exactly what the intended meaning of this term is (Takewaki, 2020) For the past twenty years, resilience has become an important subject, receiving more and more researchers' attention (Lv et al., 2018). Yet it was theorized so differently which led to many definitions, approaches, theories and interpretations (Linnenluecke, 2017). The researchers' interest has primarily focused on the conceptual meaning of resilience as an "absorptive" or "adaptive" capacity by adopting definitions mainly found in systems and evolutionary theory

This brings a question of what has been of the modern workplace owing to the advancement in technology and new trends in the global market. Working health has emerged as a major concern for organizations since they acknowledge the significance of maintaining employee health to support organizational performance, innovation and success. At the same time, the concept of organizational resilience has come into focus for describing how organizations can deal with disruptions especially in the aftermath of the global COVID 19 pandemic. Both of these areas are dependent on technology as many solutions for improvement of the situation with employees and making organizations ready for any surprises have been found here.

## 2. BACKGROUND

### 2.1 Evolution of Workplace Technology

IT has always played the key role in dictating organizational change since time immemorial. In this case, the change in the use of tools that has dominated business over the years starting with the industrial revolution through to the current digital revolution is the external factor of interest. As the developments in the technology front such as cloud computing, artificial intelligence, mobile computing gain depths, the organizational complexities too have shifted tremendously in recent years. These changes have gone a long way in improving productivity as well as creating other ways of improving the conditions of the employee.

The advancement in technology in the workplace has major impact to the way organization functions, communicates and succeeds. As from the industrial revolution whereby mechanical strategies began shifting industries as well as commerce, to the present technological revolution thru computer as well as the internet, technology has always been the leading reformist. In latest years, technology trends such as Cloud computing, Artificial Intelligence, Mobile technologies have proven to be the real game changers that provide efficiency and reliability to the businesses operating in the global market. The availability of data storage, data accessibility, and processing at the cloud platform level has dramatically changed the work environment by introducing geographic barriers. Thus, practice has adopted AI to be utilized in automation of processes, data analysis and even in decision making. As organizational elites seek flexibility, these technologies have not only improved efficiency but have made new opportunities to support employees' needs arising from work flexibility.

Today, the world of human resources is facing trends that can be viewed as a paradigm shift to the extent that Generative Artificial Intelligence (AI) technologies have become available. It is clear that several sectors have been revolutionized by AI, but possibly equally so is its ability to revolutionize all Human Resources (HR) functions (Ghosh et al., 2024). Even though AI and its branches such as machine learning have been used and applied for intelligence in many sectors, the ability to purely use written word also in expressing ideas, competencies, skills and even potential biases makes it the most favorable time to incorporate this technology into human intelligence. Still, it is very crucial to remember this duality. The requirements to build AI are not often complicated as they used to be in previous versions, however, is this advancement in applicability and usability a positive development? It is this function that was described in the famous paper 'Attention is All You Need' (Vaswani et al. 2017) and later implemented in the first large language model, ChatGPT (OpenAI), in 2022

Cloud computing has particularly transformed the way firms deal with information and communication in particular. Some of the key benefits include enabling employees' full access to only allowed tools and data by the cloud where remote work option has become very important in the workplace. This improvement brought a measure of flexibility in the general framework, whereby the personnel can perform their duties from any location that has internet connection. Such flexibility can mean increased high employee satisfaction and well-being as such people can balance work and personal life/ duties adequately. Others include energy cost likely to be incurred when operating physical office space is also likely to reduced thus making organizations more efficient and more capable to perform when faced with adversities.

As anticipated, there is increasing academic attention towards the application of AI in Human Resource Management. Developing evidence indicates that AI can greatly assist organizations in enhancing their HRM capabilities (Faliagka et al., 2014). Other researchers, however, claim that organizations are still unprepared for the implementation of AI in HRM because they lack the necessary skills and knowledge (Tambe et al., 2019). Most previous studies on AI applications have been conducted in other fields outside human resources and have mainly focused on information technology aspects (Faliagka et al., 2014). Although some work within management studies refers to the use of AI in an HRM context, they are fairly superficial, seeking to investigate how it can be successfully deployed in practice rather than its theorization (Ransbotham et al., 2017; Tambe et al., 2019). To put things in perspective, there is more awareness of AIs relevance to the future of HRM in the HRM industry than there is in academic research. Therefore, this research focuses on the features of employee recruitment using AI in different countries.

Resource managers have also not left employees' well-being out of the picture since artificial intelligence has taken up mundane routine practices. With the help of artificial intelligence, interfaces can forecast workload requirements, recommend software for effective working, and sometimes provide individual well-being assistance. For example, AI can choose employee interactions and indicate that they should take breaks or reduce productivity not to make stress levels increase. From the standpoint of business effectiveness AI generates valuable insights for better decision making, customers servicing by means of chatbots optimizing business processes. All of these contributions positively impact employee commitment since the workforce can instead dedicate effort towards other higher-order activities.

## 2.2 The Shift to Remote Work and Hybrid Models

The factor of socio-professional continuity, through distancing and organizing hybrid work contexts, became essential thanks to technology when the COVID-19 pandemic struck the world. Applications that include Zoom, Microsoft Teams, slack and among others became very crucial to functioning as the staff could effectively communicate and share ideas online. This shift has also exposed the opportunities that technology offers in addressing well-being issues as apps started to take central stage for handling stress, building social relations and achieving better work-life balance.

Mobile technologies have also been a key enabler of new ways of engagement of employees with work. With the advanced in communication technologies for example smart phones, tablets, and laptops, the employees can perform their duties while on the move. This has brought mobility which has proved to be a very important characteristic in the current complex working environment. It can also be used by a worker to ask work-related questions, to have a meeting, or to collaborate with other employees at different offices or incongruent with shift working hours at various parts of the globe. Therefore, the implementation of mobile technology has improved continuity among the employees and ensured team cohesion where working remotely and face to face.

more attention must be paid to proactive approaches for effective application and integration of remote and hybrid working arrangements. Nowadays, over-dependence on technology has been a predominant challenge as people use different tools and online platforms to communicate, access information and be entertained (Ahmed & Smith, 2023). There is no doubt that technology has changed the world for the better in every aspect of life, especially work-related. However, its misuse in the current world can significantly hinder the mental and physical health of a person. To illustrate, excessive screen use in, say, a computer or television for long hours can result in headache, eye strain as well as sleep disturbance among other health-related issues. Furthermore, being immersed in the world wide web and social networking sites all the time is a serious cause of social disconnection, stress and depression (Ahmed & Smith, 2023).

Hybrid working patterns are fundamentally different from the conventional understanding of work. For this reason, it calls for the restructuring of organizational practices in terms of provision for distributed teams, virtual work, and flexible working hours (Hasyim & Bakri, 2024). On the one hand, remote working enables one to balance between work and personal life more effectively, does not require commuting, and can be less stressful. On the other hand, it can pose challenges in communication, teamwork, management, and organizational control (Hasyim & Bakri, 2024).

The use of technology was made visible during the COVID-19 pandemic when workplace arrangements transitioned to remote work and new generation hybrid work solutions. Communities of practice such as Zoom, Microsoft teams, and slack were the essential necessity of working environment as they offered means for the interactions. One of the significant shifts in recent years was the widespread use of remote work as the new normal, for millions of employees around the globe. However, this shift initially presented some problems; through technology, organizations could readily respond. In addition to maintaining business continuity, the digital tools also ensured the reversing of the challenges within the care of the employees' welfare through social relations and mental health, as well as flexible working environments for the workplace to become more resistant to unknown disruptions.

With the changes in workplace dynamics and consent of the employees organizations have started adopting the concept of hybrid work. Also known as blended or flexible work, This is a modern arrangement that is different from the traditional office centered business models by combining telecommuting and office practices. As Derue & Ribeiro-da-Silva (2023) emphasizes, hybrid work means that employees will spend some of their working hours in a central office and may work at remote locations like home or branch offices. Indeed, recent studies reinforce the hybrid nature of work and its consequences on the organizational processes and the employee's wellbeing. Scholars have approached hybrid work from different perspectives discussing its advantages, its disadvantages, and most importantly how such a work structure can be brought into the organization. For example, Apergi et al. (2021) discussed technology as an enabling factor in processes of organization and hybrid work environments.

## 3. MAIN FOCUS OF THE CHAPTER

### 3.1 Technology and Employee Wellbeing

#### 3.1.1 Digital Tools for Mental Health Support

Besides, it important to consider the various well-being factors that defines an employee as they relate closely to health. Mental health support is available using technology from the provision of applications, workouts, training in mindfulness, and stress relief. Such applications as Headspace, Calm, Moodfit have recently become essential tools that help employees deal with stress and anxiety. These platforms create a path through which relaxation means become available on the click of a button and this boosts the psychological state of a worker without having to step out of work.

Studies have perpetually established the link between employees' well being and the performance of an organization. Employees who are engaged and satisfied perform better in terms of productivity, innovation, and overall organizational effectiveness. When it comes to organizational performance however, it is a complex issue affected by many internal and external factors (Ahmed & Smith, 2023).

The growing concern towards the wellness of the employees has caused people to recognize that health is not only the absence of diseases but also psychological also. To this, technology has stepped up to provide solutions for the different needs operating at these levels especially through innovative technology applications in mental health support systems. Applications to engage people with mental health support, including apps for meditation, mindfulness training, and managing stress has also grown to fit in organizations. These digital tools assist the employee by providing digital interfaces that support techniques in stress and anger engagement, general mood enhancement and focus.

These applications such as Headspace, Calm, and Moodfit have become repurposed tools for employees struggling with pressure and stressed workplaces. These applications provide three categories of mental health workouts: meditation, breathing, and cognitive behavioral workouts. The major benefit of these tools is the autonomy they present because employees can access it, interact with it at their convenience from any location. When starting from a break or after a difficult meeting, an employee can turn to these applications, helping in the direction of relaxation, and giving them the tools for controlling their mental states without having to interrupt their work.

Instead of having some individuals have to schedule their lives to have half hour chunks, or have to attend in-person sessions, applications like Headspace or Calm provide much more viable solutions that can be incorporated into the working day. This ease of access has a great impact on the reduction of the stigma of accessing a mental health help for the employees can access the help with ease in the comfort of their workplace. But, other equally time tested techniques have also been applied to enhance concentration and to decrease stress that enhances productivity for the benefit of the employer and the employee.

The choice of hybrid work models is influenced by the employee's preferences and their experiences. To this end, Mishra and Bharti (2023) explored the existing remote work literature in detail adding that the employees' needs and expectations differ along the age and sex spectrum, and across various job types. They stressed how there is a risk of ill-conceived hybrid work policies and practices whenever fundamental elements such as work style, personality, and situations of a given individual are ignored. Organizations that embrace employee voice, work flexibility, and work-life balance are more capable of winning the war for talents in hybrid workplaces. From a technology standpoint, creating sound communication systems and investing in shielding technologies for data resources are important for the advancement of hybrid working which entails a lot of remote working. Available technologies nowadays support teamwork, communication as well as information transfer among individuals located in different places at the same time (Modaresnezhad et al., 2021). Nevertheless, issues such as the protection of data, invasion of privacy, and burnout from the use of screens are still relevant and thus cyber security measures should still be taken seriously and financed (Allen et al., 2020).

Companies and other organizations have turned to acquiring digital mental health platforms as a way of fostering an organization full of healthy employees. Organizations provide these tools to illustrate their concern towards their employees' mental and emotion status through wellness programs. It is also beneficial to company morale as it rates staff positively, and improves attendance, staff retention, and motivation. To include mental health application in corporation wellness program signifies the view point towards mental health because it is significant component of general employee involvement and organizational development.

### 3.1.2 Employee Assistance Programs (EAPs) and Online Therapy

Technological advancement has modernized the old fashions Employee Assistance Programs through outreach services. Technology support options like Better Help and Talk space have also made it easier for the affected employees, to seek confidential psychological help. Such services can include online appointments plus assessment and also useful information about the mental health. Technology-based solutions for EAPs are viewed as an indication of occupational reserve for improved employees' psychological well-being and a more constructive working environment.

Tech advancement has enhanced the delivery of EAPs with the help of remote care services to offer help where such issues are mutually misunderstood and create solutions for a better state of mental health for employees. This has been the case because traditional EAPs have been modified to include online and remote treatments such as Better Help and Talk space. All such platforms offer several related services, including initial remote consultations with competent therapists, tests for mental disorders, and links to useful resources. This has helped eliminate many of the reasons why potential concern may not be able to present themselves for help – in terms of mobility, appointment time or privacy concerns.

In contrast, not growing at the same pace as development is the research base for the employee assistance Programme's (EAPs) efficacy. Most research on EAPs focused on those from external providers as well as those dealing with counseling services. The principal limitations involved were discrepancy between variable definitions and lack of a proper equivalent control group (Joseph et al., 2018). EAP emergence is absolutely outstripped as found in empirical research regarding its effectuality. EAP research has focused mainly on that which came from some outside providers and the counseling service with major limitation being inconsistent definitions of variables and absences of a similar control group (Joseph et al., 2018).

EAPs now expand their services to encompass all types of workforce especially with remote counseling services. The fact that employees are able to reach out to therapists from the comfort of their homes mostly via mobile devices or computer is a plus after the COVID 19 pandemic that has encouraged remote and hybrid working. Thus, options in terms of the time when individuals can have an appointment, as well as the ability to use text or video-communication make it possible to seek help and support without being afraid of losing working time. This kind of mental support has become necessary for the formation of a healthier and more robust worker population.

The fact that employers wishing to implement EAPs through technology-based approaches demonstrate considerable concern with regard to the psychological health of employees in the working environment can be viewed as a positive sign of a more sympathetic inclination toward them. Through offering employees opportunity to access sensitive mental health related services, employers play a major role in decreasing the perception that therapy is for the weak of heart and in the promotion of management of mental health conditions. In turn this not only increases employee morale/profit and productivity, but also lowers stress levels, absenteeism and improves job outcomes; that in the long run will be favorable to both employees and the organization.

### 3.1.3 Wearable Technology for Physical Health Monitoring

In systems that are used to monitor people's physical wellbeing, wearable technologies include, fitness trackers, smart watches, etc. Items like Fitbit and Apple Watch monitor primary health factors inclusive of pulse rate, physical movement, and rest. These technologies help the employees to accept healthier lifestyle by making it a sort of competition to get certain amount of daily physical activity. Employers can incorporate wearable technology in wellness incentives, where employees get rewarded for achieving health-related goals, and can improve on their general health.

Smart devices including health monitors and wrist watches have emerged as core equipment to monitor and enforce health standards of human beings. Among such devices, there are sensors that show heart rate, the number of steps, calories consumed, and sleep Cycle tracking devices such as the fit bit or apple watch. Such devices offer potential of near real time feedback on basic activity and health metrics - including steps taken during a day. This data can be employed by the employees to track their fitness data, individual health objectives, and therefore make suitable choices.

These technologies aim at making employees healthier by providing aspects of setting goals, sending reminders when you should be standing, and tracking your progress. Take for instance smart watches and other wearable technology that works on user's inactivity or encourages a certain amount of step count each day in a way reminding the user on the need to move frequently. Such reminders can be rather helpful in workplaces where people sit most of the time during the day and maybe even become physically inactive. With data sampled incorporated in smart phones or other devices, and trended over time, employees can make changes to their schedule to better support physical and mental fitness and wellbeing, thus increasing productivity.

This is, therefore, a relatively recent development for research, the use of such wearable devices for monitoring the health and safety of operators in the course of their work. Time can also be better managed as well as safety enhanced by the use of these devices in the workplaces. For instance, the explorative study on Khakurel et al (2018) expressed various functionalities associated with wearables in an occupational domicile. Stress minimization internal assignment monitoring systems, internal environmental awareness systems, and physical changes monitoring systems for treatment prevention are two such examples where wear wearables have been adopted. Heart rate data collected during a work period can be a measure of activity level demand, with elevated levels indicating higher physical fatigue cycles when more oxygenated blood is needed due to higher physiological activity requirements. In this way, it is argued that the use of wearable technologies at the workplace can yield benefits in the long run in the monitoring of the psychological and physiological conditions of the employees and ensuring their health and well-being (Mozgovoy, 2019).

Businesses should consider the use of wearable technologies as they boost employee wellness program and force conformity to healthy behavior among employees. Promotion can be achieved where employees are motivated to achieve the set goals in areas of health by for instance attaining a required number of steps in a week or an improvement in number of hours' sleep in a day. A notable fact is that in addition to increasing personal health, such programmes also have an overall positive effect on employees – fewer sickness and stress and more productivity. By incorporating wearable technology into wellness programs, organizations show a winning interest in working on the physical health of employees and a promotion of healthy lifestyles.

### 3.1.4 Promoting Work-Life Balance with Digital Tools

From the above scenario, the employers should make a point of attending to their employee needs for instance in the work-life balance as this is very healthy for the employees. This balance is helped by technology because it supplies the means for variable working conditions. Hence, it would be possible to use the calendar like Google or employ the platform like Trello to manage the working time; in any case, an employee will manage his working time; hence, the clear division exists between working and personal hours. Also, administrative work is minimized by automation tools, leaving more time for work that is valuable and critical for an employee; this strengthens its positive effect on the balance and the nonexistence of burnout cases.

Previously, it has been qualified as constructive criticism considering that the boundaries are what keeps work from intruding into one's private life. However, it is because of technology that boundaries have been defined to be more fluid therefore leading to 'work creep' or even burnout (Tochia, 2021). Burnout being contentious to both organizations and the government, this research paper seeks to examine technology in relation to work life balance (WLB) using the boundary theory framework. To enhance knowledge in this aspect, social media practitioners (SMPs) were chosen as the study sample because they could be said to be the heavy users of both technology and social media as well (Tochia, 2021).

Work-life balance is important to the well being of employees and technological tools have taken central stage in ensuring this balance. It also makes it possible for employees to set convenient working schedules given that the requirements of their employers' companies and the family and other responsibilities can all be well balanced. Applications such as Google Calendar enable employees to schedule their working days quite appropriately, foot or in the meeting, on different tasks, and during break time. Those are easily leveraged for working calendar and setting separate personal professional and working times to provide the workers with the needed time for rest, families, and leisure. This has overcome the problem of the fixed schedule which has a toll on a person's health hence minimizing stress.

Other than the planning and scheduling, the newer employee collaboration software like Trello and Asana can be used to organize employee work. The above platforms offer an outline of tasks, their due dates, and the overall project status thus enabling the employees to work smart and reduce incidences of working under immense pressure. COs can seem to partition large tasks and work into doable subtasks, assign duties and monitor progress in real-time thus assists to maintain organizational rhythm. These tools also allow team members work in an asynchronous manner which makes such employees to work at their convenient best time without always having to be in a meeting or attend to a task frequently.

Other benefits of work-life balance involve the function that these automated tools assist to conserve a lot of time that would have been spent on repetitive clerical tasks. Data encompasses automated functions, including data entry, report generation and other clerical functions, which releases a lot of time for employees, to engage in higher value activities, creative, ideas or planning. If the employees limit the areas they have to focus on trivial tasks, they may find more value in their responsibilities, and this will make them work without getting burnt out. Therefore, organizations should integrate the available digital technologies to improve flexibility in order to enhance work-life balance among its workers.

## 4. ORGANIZATIONAL RESILIENCE: A NEW PARADIGM

### 4.1 Defining Organizational Resilience

Business resiliency is actually the fact of organizational performance in conditions that are unfavorable and unstable. This encompasses and extends beyond what, and also how, an organization bounces back and effectively deals with negative occurrences, but also the capability of the organization to avoid, change for the better and implement ongoing improvements. Today, resilience is critical in the working environment because of the new reality of the existence of a pandemic.

Business continuity is the organizational ability to 'bounce back' and not only cope but thrive in the face of the firm's unpredicted adversities, shocks, or disasters. Resilience is not allowing a firm to just rise from the problematic incidences; it means that a firm should be able the seized the chances and make the firm to be changing in the ever changing world. This involves ability to identify threats within a short time and ability to examine the impacts of threats and plan on how to deal with threats. Continuity management is crucial to make an organization run effectively in spite of the drawbacks from the outside world or inside the organization.

Organizational resilience on the other hand comprises recovery, anticipation and preparation. Resilient organizations do not simple adapt to stakes, they prevent potential threats and prepare available strategies in order to avoid unfavorable consequences. Whether it be supply chain globalization or interfering with technological integration that comes from work from home, adaptable organizations are always evolving and improving. This freewheeling capability is a major reason why firms are able to anticipate long term success and functional in environment that is characterized by complexity and volatility.

Bearing all these considerations in mind, given the abundant theorists and researchers who have examined the strategic business-partnering function of human resource development within organizations, it is conceivable to also include an human resource development perspective in explaining organizational resilience (human resource development resilience) (Mitsakis, 2020). In this way, human resource development resilience may be regarded as a contemporary success factor for the organization that, together with other factors, can enhance or even increase the enhancement of the organization's resilience singularly and/or separately. So much more so in these complicated times that we live in today (for instance The global economic crisis, Brexit, globalization of the labor force etc.), change should be led by Human Resource Development within an organization and also human resource development should help in building organizational resilience through its policies and strategies. Nonetheless, human resource development resilience remains an undefined term and very little has been documented about it (Mitsakis, 2020).

In the new reality after the coronavirus, the question of organizational resilience is even more relevant. The COVID-19 pandemic showed that businesses have to be adaptive to significant macro level disruptions, including changes in demand, supply-chain disruptions and the emergence of new regulation. Those that had strong framework had the direction for change, embracing new techniques, shifting to operations from home and any necessary protective measures for employees and customers. This ability to operate during the period of the extant and uncertainty has cemented the importance of the survival not only for the resilience, the creation, innovation, as well maintenance of competitive advantage and faster growth in longer period in the business world.

## 4.2 The Interconnection Between Well-Being and Resilience

Both organizational resilience and employees' welfare are intertwined in one way or the other. Subjective well-being is important for the extent of participation and, therefore, for functioning which makes it an important component of resilience. Technology sustains this relationship through offering instruments that will guarantee the employees stay connected and are not alone during hardships. Here, showing that well-being through technology makes it possible for organizations to create an invulnerable generation of the workforce.

A comprehensive brief on the relationship between EE and OR is not possible without establishing that they are two faces of the same coin, Employee engagement, therefore, can be said to be central to organizational resilience. When employees have the physical, mental, and emotional capital they are in a position to cope with pressures, manage change and perform regardless of a crisis. Measures against burnout and stress as well as measures to promote work-life balance help to strengthen employees' resistance and can aid organizations in handling interferences. Consequently, this improves the organization's ability to cope with the existing ambiguity and adapt to failure or loss in the best way possible.

In resilience thinking, however, the ecology has dimensions itself much more into powerful and better theorizing, rather than its social dimensions. Recent syntheses of resilience, vulnerability, and political ecology (Nelson et al. 2007; Leach, 2008; Miller et al. 2010; Turner, 2010) emphasize more social aspects of resilience and partially help to offset such disproportions. These and other reviews speak to the significance of power as well as human agency (Davidson, 2010), the different actors' ways of constructing and framing tradeoffs that accompany specific strategies to sustain ecosystem services and meet livelihood needs (Campbell et al., 2010), and the challenge of articulating desirable pathways of change on account of determining the influence of complex relational networks (Crona & Bodin, 2010).

Technology therefore assumes a key function in maintaining this relationship through providing digital enablers that enhance employee engagement, most sufficiently in moments of change. For instance, mental health applications, wearable's and other devices in maintaining health, collaborative platforms mean that the workforce is productive, communicative and healthy while working remotely. These can go a long way in decreasing the stress overtime from practicing in volatile environments creating a stance in empowering workforce resilience. In this way, organizations continue supporting their employee through technologies during difficult situations encouraging them to remain as productive and vigilant as possible.

## 5. HOW TO BUILD ORGANIZATIONAL RESILIENCE THROUGH TECHNOLOGY

### 5.1 Automation and Workforce Agility

A selected few include robotic process automation (RPA) and artificial intelligence (AI) tools that can help minimize time spent on repetitive tasks thereby freeing up the staff to do what will add value. It is also important that organizations should be agile today, given that change is the only constant in business today. Automation is also effective in the reduction of operational intermittency that characterizes many tasks as they provide standard means and ways of performing critical tasks.

Successful digital transformation has much to do with changes in the organizational structure, processes, capabilities, and competencies. Most of the digital transformation research wings more towards what technology adaptation model addresses and, as such, the behavior and attitudes of people or their abilities on the whole. Recently, employee agility, in respect of technology adoption and Industry 4.0, has been gathering more focus (Muduli & Choudhury, 2024). Jacomo (2017) stated that worker agility is no longer a "nice-to-have", but has already become an acute reality for both companies and employees. Through new technology-enabled capabilities and critical expertise engagement, these strategic and tactical goals necessitate an agile workforce. Companies must initiate the process of developing the agile workforce to profit from such moving environments (Karpie 2018).

They include: Robotic Process Automation (RPA) and Artificial Intelligence (AI) are among the automation technologies that are fast revolutionize how any organization undertakes its daily operations by reducing reliance on routine and repetitive tasks. These technologies can deal with data input, communicating with customers, and even analysis, thereby, reducing important working time and allowing employees to work on more meaningful, innovative, and valuable tasks. One way is that organizations are able to offload the repetitive tasks that require heavy operational hours to automated systems hence enabling the employees to fund other important tasks such as innovation and development as well as identifying and solving problems that are crucial to the growth of organizations.

This kind of agility, which originates in automation, is especially important for organizational flexibility. Managing strategic change and learning is more challenging today because business environments are changing significantly faster, new competition can emerge suddenly in many industries, and companies are not always prepared for these kinds of changes. Automation makes this possible by reducing cycle time, reducing variance, and providing timely data that allow quick decisions to be made. When routine operation is done, human resources can always be rearranged so that there are appropriate measures taken to counter the new emerging changes or take advantage of the new emerging opportunities within the business market.

## 5.2 Cloud-Based Solutions for Operational Continuity

Cloud computing has become a critical element of organizational optimism. Business continuity is also achievable since the business can carry out operations from any other location, other than its physical site. This way cloud helps the organization to keep running without interruption of disruptions such as remote or multiple location employees. This flexibility strengthens the business because it minimizes dependency on tangible structures.

Flexibility becomes the outlined aspect, from which organizations can easily operate from any location through cloud computing application. The nature of cloud solutions enables the firm to place core information, business applications, and work processes on a single unified digital platform that is available to personnel regardless of their physical location. In physical disruption, therefore businesses can easily switch to operation from home without having to worry about lack of necessary input tools and materials.. This capability helps work to progress continuously and provides protection for productivity to be maintained and canceled work time to be reduced.

Mainly, business continuity makes certain that daily operations flow as usual even when adverse times may occur. Disaster recovery is about restoring the systems and technology quickly after any disruption takes place (Sahebjamnia, et al., 2015). Both ensure resilience so that the organization can face different challenges. In the modern context, cloud-based disaster recovery services have become one of the more important strategies in ensuring data protection and business continuity in any unexpected disaster or interruption. Therefore, the emphasis on planning and implementing cloud-based disaster recovery to secure critical data and applications should be heightened (Tatineni, 2023).

Another factor boosting resiliency is the application of cloud-based storage in the storage of data and neat and applications. Local disasters, such as power losses, equipment failures or natural disasters, put on-site traditional servers and data centers at risk. In contrast, cloud systems are usually provided by large suppliers who employ backup options and security measures affecting high availability. Such decentralization of data and resources, thus besides enhancing operational mobility also offers a safeguard against the concentrated focus of failure point which in turn helps organizational continuity in more stable and secure way.

Cloud makes it easy for organization to work in multiple locations since they can access and share documents, communicate, and work of projects in real time. Regardless of whether workers are in the same building or spread over different floors or cities or countries, the cloud platforms help keep everyone on the same page. It is highly important for today's workforce as new forms of work organization, such as remote and hybrid work, are emerging. Reliable cloud solutions create greater organizational ecosystem adaptability so businesses are prepared to change direction in response to the business environment proactively as well as uphold the dynamic operation in the course of their development process.

## 5.3 Data-Driven Decision Making and Risk Management

In particular, the use of predictive analytics and data driven decision making increases the ability of organizations to better 'see' threats and opportunities. Through the help of AI and machine learning, companies can evaluate large volume of data to predict events, look into identified risks, and determine ways by which to address these risks. This makes resilience stronger in organizations because it gets them ready for an event before it becomes a problem.

It would be useful for decision-makers in credit risk assessment to add some qualitative information in addition to the quantitative risk measures (Soares et al., 2011). Text mining will help fill this gap and enable the identification of patterns in large heterogeneous data (Agarwal & Dhar, 2014). Meaningful conclusions could be drawn from the data by appropriate analytical techniques. A fresh development is the immense speed at which economic and social transactions can now be captured, stored, and digitally made available (Agarwal & Dhar, 2014). Data are a challenge because so much is it diverse, structured, unstructured, and continuously being added to by new data types and sources.

Predictive analytics supported by big data and information technologies have now emerged as critical success tools for organizations that strive to deal with changing and unpredictable conditions of their environments. Every day, companies gather ample data and through the help of AI and machine learning, businesses are able to identify structures, patterns, as well as variations within the existing data. This capability lets the organization achieve a higher degree of accuracy in perceiving risks and opportunities while making decision consistent with its strategic plans. The reliance on data supports a preferential culture for timely and proper reactions as well as responses to the clients' actions.

Risk forecasting is one of the main areas where predictive analytics is valuable to prevent disruptions and come up with plans on how to approach it. Using historical data and understanding relationships, the organization is able to predict events and how they may affect its functionality. For instance, firms can assess sales patterns, consumer preference towards certain product, or variability of supply chain factors accurate enough to determine changes that may influence demand or supply. With this information, numerous organizations can develop contingency measures and resources that they can use to avoid possible problems before they become actual business crises. The proposed strategies also reduce the chances of negative impact towards performance making the organization more resilient.

## 6. TECHNOLOGY FOR ENHANCING EMPLOYEE ENGAGEMENT AND SATISFACTION

### 6.1 Gamification and Virtual Learning Platforms

Gamification is about incorporating gaming mechanisms into non-gaming environments for purposes of encouraging commitment: for example amongst employees during training and development processes. Bear in mind that virtual learning applications that implement gamification also improve the learning experience and increase employee motivation. Examples of such platforms include Coursera and Udemy and have incorporated factors such as badges, leader boards, and skill progress bar and have empowered employees to warm selves up in lifelong learning.

There are innumerable efforts pertaining to bringing gamification into education for an enhancement in student engagement. These entailed most often a platform or virtual learning environment in facilitating a common ground for students and at the same time documenting students' progression. However, some issues need to be solved before using gamification in learning environments (Tenório et al., 2018). Gamification has been mentioned increasingly as important in the context of environments for digital natives. Engagement can be created obtaining numerous gains benefiting the student in terms of his motivation on knowledge construction (Estevam & Kalinke, 2013).

At this present time, people embrace the use of gamification as a way of focusing on teaching and providing training to the employees since it employs games so that to influence the motivation levels of the learners. A number of the key features like the points, badges and rewards incorporated in the system are fun and can easily appeal to the competitive streak in people, and the need to learn in the organization. These practices break traditional training processes into fun, thereby better enabling the core memory and cognition of the human mind. When applied, this concept not only leads to greater engagement, but also to effective learning and growth of people within the company.

In their virtual learning platforms, Coursera and Udemy, masters of gamification have successfully integrated them into their main programs. These platforms will have some type of leader board that shows the employees' performance and activity level, which encourages the personnel to increase their competencies. Also, progress tracking systems allow learners to see their progress in colorful visual displays and motivate them to continue completing their course or reach their set learning goals. As these make the learning process more casual and simulate a game, employees are more likely to dedicate time into their personal improvement at the workplace.

## 6.2 AI-powered Personalization in Employee Experience

AI helps to deliver contextual, target end-to-end, and product-focused experiences to the employees with the help of resource, content, engagement mapping. The AI solutions such as Humu and Culture-Amp offer direction on the ways in which certain improvements can help increase employee satisfaction. This customization applies pressure on the depicted interests and needs of the employees and hence, increases the engagement degree.

This led to the establishment of e-learning technologies such as web-based learning, virtual classrooms, and digital collaboration tools among Sarabadani et al. (2017). The organization has generally updated all such technologies, which will serve as a new approach for the enhancement of skills and knowledge among employees. e-Learning refers to the use of computer and network technology, especially using an intranet or the Internet, to transfer information and deliver instruction to individuals (Lee et al., 2011). Like artificial intelligence, new technologies are also utilized for personalization of students according to their interests. AI, through machine learning, collects the individual user's data, processes data collected, and recommends courses for each learner based on their interest (Ashman et al., 2014). Just like how online companies such as amazon.com and netflix.com use recommender system technology to personalize and influence customer choices, LMS and e-learning systems exploit AI for interpreting and offering relevant courses to students (Klašnja-Milićević et al., 2011).

Self-learning or, more formally known as artificial intelligence or AI, has changed the way that people interact with their employers as well as employers with their employees, giving particularly tailored experiences and support mechanisms in today's modern work place. For example, using elements such as Humu and CultureAmp, companies can use information technology to analyze the employees' behaviors, their tendencies and their feedback to make recommendations that will suit them. Personalization in practice may take different operational forms such as bespoke learning activities, suitable wellness programs, or particular communication channels that fit employees' career ambitions. Businesses can therefore improve employee satisfaction, commitment and engagement by a great deal by making organizational support commensurate with individual goals.

The kind of personalization that AI inclusion delivers does not come at the expense of employee wellbeing or engagement, but rather improves it. Employees clearly appreciate receiving content and resources which are relevant to them which in turn increase their loyalty and commitment to the organization. For example, if an employee indicates that they would like to enhance their skills in a particular area, the AI can provide suggestions for courses or training programs that will assist in that area. This is why it is important for organizations to pay attention to the comprehensive individual needs of each and every employee; these care centers create an accessible avenue that encourages individual growth which in turn raises performance and satisfaction of the workforce.

## 6.3 Communication and Collaboration Tools

Communication helps in employee satisfaction and organization core strength. The use of advanced technologies, particularly software applications, such as Slack, Microsoft Teams, and Zoom, ensures that different departments across continents are connected with their employees. These applications are, however, important to keep the workers engaged and work together even in an environment where they are physically detached and it is a hybrid way of working.

Employee engagement and overall organizational productivity and durability depend on one important factor – communication. This is very true in the present scenarios where people are working remotely or in a hybrid work model. Communication applications like Slack, Microsoft Teams, and Zoom have redefined organizational range of communication by enabling communication crossing departmental boundaries and geographical distances. These applications enable real time interaction between individuals, instant exchange of information and cooperation on certain tasks irrespective of where the individuals are physically based at the moment. By eliminating communication barriers, organizations can guarantee that no employee is left out or in the dark further enhancing the engagement of the workforce.

Besides providing means for instantaneous interaction with other users, these systems enhance communication in other ways that promote team work and project execution. Team work is improved by capabilities such as sharing documents, video conferencing, and task lists integrated into the system. This creates room for better ideas and work quality. Team members have no problems in calling for discussions, attending video conferences to work on a project or giving opinions on the ongoing work which increases output and also contributes to bonding. Such a feeling of togetherness is key for keeping workers happy especially in situations where physical interaction is not possible due to factors such as distance.

At the same time, they can integrate communication and collaboration applications which will ensure that there is transparency and sharing of information in the organization. Availability of crucial information and resources enables employees to make decisions and play their roles within the teams more efficiently. Such transparency acts as a catalyst strengthening the bonding of trust between employees and employers leading to enhancement of their job satisfaction levels. As the organizations still grapple with the effects of the evolution of the work structure, the temptation of equipping the effects of communication and collaboration will be critical in ensuring the employees' well-being and the ability of the organization to withstand the shocks presented by such a situation.

## 7. ROLE OF ARTIFICIAL INTELLIGENCE IN PREDICTIVE WELL BEING ANALYTICS

### 7.1 Predictive Analytics for Proactive Health Measures

Real-time employee monitoring through Ai and predictive analytics can also be used to prevent health risks of concerned parties before it gets out of hand. As per an AI study, there are systems that incorporate several elements such as wearables, normative, and even productivity industries which can flag certain signs such as stress, burnout, or even the physical health decline. This allows organizations to avoid any issues in advance and for example change the work structure or introduce particular wellness interventions.

Machine learning and predictive analytics have transformed and ushered a golden future in the field of health when it comes to preventing diseases and have changed the concept of how diseases are identified, diagnosed, and treated. These technologies could potentially redefine the whole landscape of healthcare, by helping early preventive measures that would save millions of lives (Ibrahim & Saber, 2023). Today, accessing and leveraging huge amounts of data, machine learning, and predictive analytics empower healthcare professionals to provide insights for, and direct actions in making informed decisions. Accordingly, several facets of healthcare have received, and will continue to receive; some of the most profound impacts by these technologies in the shape of, today, and in the future, defining a new experience in health (Ibrahim & Saber, 2023).

On account of Artificial Intelligence (AI) predictive analytics is changing the traditional way organizations think about Employee Experience. They can monitor employees' health trends and take preventive measures about productivity management by integrating data from wearable's, employee engagement systems and even work tools. Such preventive strategies are even more effective as they externalize patterns For example, the Organization can prevent non-fatal health problems such as burnout, stress or even lack of physical engagement that might lead to other complex issues that require acute care.

The application of predictive analytics enables organizations to roll out wellness programs that are more specific to the needs of employees. For instance, if data shows a high number of employees reporting high-stress levels, the HR department may start stress relieving programs like offers of mindfulness workshops, stress relief tools and even redistribution of work. This approach mitigates adverse effects of such risks on employees and also boosts productivity and engagement of employees because they are cared for in their health endeavors. An employee responding to certain assessed risks through such interventions increases the likelihood of the organization achieving a more positive outcome with regards to health

### 7.2 AI-Powered Mental Health Support Systems

AI-based chatbots and virtual mental health assistants allow on-demand help for each employee irrespective of the time of day or night according to their mental health needs. Introduced systems engage users immediately by offering methods of supervising oneself, tools for assessing mental illness, and materials to be used. Woebot and Wysa, and tools designed similarly are now infiltrating the HR wellness programs, aiding toward user friendly, high scale employee mental health management service solutions which do not take in many people.

Due to the extensive rise in mental illnesses all around the globe, there has arisen an urgent need for innovations to bridge the gap between the material and emotional resource deficits in support provision of those in need. The situation worsened with the advent of COVID-19, which further isolates people and erects blocks to most services, including mental health ones (Pierce et al., 2020). Besides the limitations of care because of geographic barriers and scope of a country, AI has emerged as a possible new remedy, developing and applying models in situations where AI can provide mental health services on digital and scalable platforms (Lakho et al., 2024).

AI-based solutions for mental health problems help companies to meet the needs of the employees in the area of their mental health to a completely new level; they now become reachable; and moreover - always available, which is rather a distinct advantage. Chatbots and virtual mental health assistants like Woebot and Wysa offer help to employees who are likely experiencing stress, anxiety and other forms of mental disorder. Such systems can talk back user, offer tennis strategies and even evaluate users' mental health status by way of guided assessment. This makes it easy for people to get help without feeling ashamed and they are able to help themselves and stay healthy without being afraid of others' judgment.

The inclusion of platforms for mental health powered by the use of artificial intelligence in human resource wellness therapy programs are meant to enable organizations to offer solutions that are scalable according to the changing demographics of the workforce. The standard practice of psychiatric care, though beneficial, implements barriers that is expensive and time-consuming in their endeavor to face the huge demand for mental health care services by employees. For such large entities, the human resources in provision of mental health services may not be sufficient to meet the services demand; hence AI systems come into play facilitating such services. By availing such tools to their employees, organizations can improve the inclusivity of the culture as the employees would not feel left out on the efforts of enhancing their mental well-being.

## 8. SOLUTIONS AND RECOMMENDATIONS

In order to use technology for the wellness of employees and for organizational resilience, the first thing that companies must do is that they must focus on AI powered applications and tools. Such solutions may offer a fully incorporated application and resources depending on the specifications of the employee in real time. With the acquisition of AI based mental health platforms, organizations can assure that their employees get instant relief, strategies and evaluation. Such model not only helps in dealing mental health issues in individuals, but also encourages healthy work environment by removing the stigma associated with help seeking.

Second, and more importantly, organizations should reallocate a part of their budget to train and up skill their employees so that they can fully take digital tools and technologies. Employees will be equipped to make full use of these capabilities by providing training on how to use the communication and collaboration tools and data reporting and analysis and devices such as wearable. Such a course should focus on the necessity of mental and physical wellness and motivate workers to adopt these tools in their daily lives. By improving employees' digital skills, companies tend to create a more active and resistant workforce ready to deal with the peculiarities of the changing work environment.

Furthermore, there is a need for the organizations to put in place measures that encourage a healthy work-life balance and also takes care of their staffs. The introduction of technology-enabled flexible working conditions has been shown to greatly improve staff contentment and minimize the incidences of stress and exhaustion. It is important for organizations to promote the use of such productivity enhancing tools that allow the employees to control how much work they do without encroaching into their personal lives. And more importantly, it is important to promote a workplace atmosphere that encourages mental wellness and allows for discussions about challenges that can be faced by employees.

For continued effectiveness, wellness programs should be routinely evaluated and changed if necessary, taking into consideration the views of the employees, and facts and statistics derived from research. Predictive analytics needs to be implemented in organizations to forecast the occurrence of incidences that may endanger the health of the employees and revise plans accordingly. This approach will assist in the temporal improvement of wellness programs by the organizations to ensure that they meet the current wants of their employees. In this way, by keeping an eye on health indicators and the level of worker engagement, organizations will be able to take preventative measures instead of dealing with the situation when it is too late and build a healthy and strong organization.

## 9. FUTURE RESEARCH DIRECTION

On the other hand, it will be important to study the effects of AI incorporated mental health productivity enhancing solutions on employee productivity and engagement over long periods of time. And while some studies have been put forward on the effects of these systems and tools after their immediate use, not in all cases such studies are sufficient to explain the changes in mental health caused by these tools in the dynamics. Their durability will help organizations understand the rationale for use and maintenance of such technologies.

It is important to also consider the effect of using data-guided interventions for personalized wellness programs. For instance, the research has the potential to analyze the impact of specific wellbeing strategies on employee effectiveness and wellbeing based on individual employee characteristics. This may involve reviewing the effectiveness of various personalization approaches and examining the way they could be incorporated in the existing wellness systems. As industries continue to emphasize evidence based management, the ability to appreciate the importance of individualization will be key to effective designing of campaigns.

Moreover, as a point for consideration in future research; it would be important to evaluate the impact that the culture of the organization has on the success of the implementation of the digital wellbeing tool. Different cultural dimensions could affect the degree to which employees will interact with such technology-based wellness programs. Sometimes their aim may be a technology adoption barrier and/or a cultural change to one that is more supportive and open around such initiatives.

Another important direction for future explorations is technology and well-being in connection with diversity, equity, and inclusion (DEI). This is essential as research also indicates the need to examine how well-being in the digital age can cater to the employees of different types of organizations. Meeting this challenge is imperative as it allows organizations to create an equal opportunity environment for all its employees. Each group has unique challenges, especially among the minorities, in finding and maximizing the available well-being resources and any activities targeting them.

## 9.1 Emerging Concept of Industry 5.0

Industry 5.0 is paradigm shift compared to the fourth industrial revolution, I4.0, where objects and tools are powered by technology; not only considering the technological perspective but also involving human aspect, creativity and development and environmental perspective with technology. It aims at the combined integration of humans and robots with the aim of having collaborative robots align with people in a way that optimizes productivity, customer experience and creativity. This approach places a human worker back at the core of manufacturing processes, concentrating on how best to apply self-organization, creativity, problem-solving, and empathy, with the help of AI, IoT, and robotics as a means of automating routine data processing and data collection.

It also emphasis es on the way in which industries have been required to embrace sustainable practices conforming to environmental and social standards. Industry 5.0 promotes the use of circular economy models, minimized resource intake, & technologies that are factors of sustainability. It enshrines the principle of survivability by building structures that maintain capability in the face of breaks in continuity in economy, ecology, or technology. This human-oriented and environmentally friendly strategy corrects the Industry 4.0 drawbacks, making the industrial environment more flexible and diverse. Besides, Industry 5.0 is concomitant with societal goals and objectives of technology development as these are meant to be on the advantage of people and societies and not just entities. It targets firstly the quality of working life, secondly, genuine work principle, and thirdly, digital inclusion. This kind of conceptual approach reshapes the productivity new to include both the profit, sustainability, and with societal benefit components. Therefore, Industry 5.0 is not just the next phase of manufacturing renaissance but a he whole concept incorporating visions for the future of industries as well as human beings and the world.

## 10. CONCLUSION

The incorporation of technology in employees' well-being programs is crucial, especially in building a resilient workforce, which is necessary, given the current business environment. Such complexities of remote and hybrid working have called for a very high engagement of digital tools in organizations in a bid to keep employees engaged as well as enhance mental and physical wellbeing. The introduction of technologies such as AI-based therapists, health monitoring gadgets, effective communication tools among others, is transforming the way organizations meet the demands of employees. In addition to these individual well-being solutions, with the help of these organizations also foster an environment which encourages discussing mental health issues and work-life balance without stigma.

There are other approaches such as using predictive analytics that can readily help organizations improve managing health workforce and health resilience in the workplace. This is especially critical as it would help in preventing potential problems by identifying possible problems early on and customizing wellness strategies around them. It allows them to cushion themselves from risks that aggressive borderline behavior trends pose. It is easier for them to incorporate new threats into the existing frameworks and modify the action plan. Hence the workers know that they are respected and their contribution is not in vain. As a result, the firms can increase their efficiency and enhance statistical measures of the organization, and this can be beneficial for both the employees and the employers.

In emphasizing the deployment of technology-enhanced wellness programs, the multi-disciplinary approach that brings together the Human Resources, Information Technologies, and health services unit cannot be overlooked. This enables the departments to formulate all-encompassing wellness programs appropriate for every section of the workforce. This cross-functional method helps organizations to design specific solutions that enhance both physical and mental wellbeing of individuals thus ensuring that the organization remains strong even in turbulent times. And given that more and more societies and companies become aware of the inseparable link between organizational success and the wellbeing of the employees, it will be paramount to nurturing this cooperation.

There should be a need for organizations to facilitate research and innovations in their well-being practices. Research will be needed to understand the effects of the new technologies on peoples' health over long periods of time, how cultures will influence the practices and finally why ethics should be the priority of workplace wellbeing interventions. Organizations should strive to embrace these values so that they can raise an active workforce that can respond to various changes over time, maintaining high standards of job satisfaction and performance for the organization for several years.

## REFERENCES


Agarwal, R., & Dhar, V. (2014). Big data, data science, and analytics: The opportunity and challenge for IS research. *Information Systems Research*, 25(3), 443–448. DOI: 10.1287/isre.2014.0546

Ahmed, S., & Smith, E. (2023). The Future of Work: Adapting to Remote and Hybrid Models. *Abbottabad University Journal of Business and Management Sciences*, 1(01), 1–12.

Allen, T. D., French, K. A., Dumani, S., & Shockley, K. M. (2020). A cross-national meta-analytic examination of predictors and outcomes associated with work–family conflict. *The Journal of Applied Psychology*, 105(6), 539–576. https://doi.org/https://doi.org/10.1037/apl0000442. DOI: 10.1037/apl0000442 PMID: 31535873

Apergi, L. A., Bjarnadottir, M. V., Baras, J. S., Golden, B. L., Anderson, K. M., Chou, J., & Shara, N. (2021). Voice interface technology adoption by patients with heart failure: Pilot comparison study. *JMIR mHealth and uHealth*, 9(4), e24646. https://doi.org/https://doi.org/10.2196/24646. DOI: 10.2196/24646 PMID: 33792556

Ashman, H., Brailsford, T., Cristea, A. I., Sheng, Q. Z., Stewart, C., Toms, E. G., & Wade, V. (2014). The ethical and social implications of personalization technologies for E-lEarning. *Information & Management*, 51(6), 819–832. DOI: 10.1016/j.im.2014.04.003

Ayres, R. U. (2000). On forecasting discontinuities. *Technological Forecasting and Social Change*, 65(1), 81–97. DOI: 10.1016/S0040-1625(99)00101-8

Bartik, A. W., Bertrand, M., Cullen, Z. B., Glaeser, E. L., Luca, M., & Stanton, C. T. (2020). *How Are Small Businesses Adjusting to Covid-19? Early Evidence from a Survey No. w26989*. National Bureau of Economic Research. DOI: 10.3386/w26989

Burt, G. (2007). Why are we surprised at surprises? Integrating disruption theory and system analysis with the scenario methodology to help identify disruptions and discontinuities. *Technological Forecasting and Social Change*, 74(6), 731–749. DOI: 10.1016/j.techfore.2006.08.010

Campbell, B. M., Sayer, J. A., & Walker, B. B., (2010). Navigating trade-offs: working for conservation and development outcomes. *Ecology and Society, 15*(2):16. [online] URL: http:// www.ecologyandsociety .org/vol15/iss2/art16/

Crona, B., & Bodin, Ö. (2010). Power asymmetries in small scale fisheries: a barrier to governance transformability? *Ecology and Society, 15*(4):32. [online] URL: http://www. ecologyandsociety.org/vol15/iss4/art32/

Davidson, D. J. (2010). The applicability of the concept of resilience to social systems: Some sources of optimism and nagging doubts. *Society & Natural Resources*, 23(12), 1135–1149. DOI: 10.1080/08941921003652940

Derue, H., & Ribeiro-da-Silva, A. (2023). Therapeutic exercise interventions in rat models of arthritis. *Neurobiology of Pain*, 13, 100130. DOI: 10.1016/j.ynpai.2023.100130 PMID: 37179770

Estevam, E. J. G., & Kalinke, M. A. (2013). Recursos Tecnológicos e Ensino de Estatística na Educação Básica: um cenário de pesquisas brasileiras. *Rev. Bra. de Informática Na Educação, 21*(02).

Faliagka, E., Iliadis, L., Karydis, I., Rigou, M., Sioutas, S., Tsakalidis, A., & Tzimas, G. (2014). On-line consistent ranking on e-recruitment: Seeking the truth behind a well-formed CV. *Artificial Intelligence Review*, 42(3), 515–528. DOI: 10.1007/s10462-013-9414-y

Ghosh, R., Nachmias, S., Murdoch, D., & McGuire, D. (2024). Prioritizing humans: HRD's vital role in AI adoption for workplace success. *Human Resource Development International*, 27(3), 319–323. DOI: 10.1080/13678868.2024.2354627

Hakovirta, M., & Denuwara, N. (2020). Denuwara, N. How COVID-19 Redefines the Concept of Sustainability. *Sustainability (Basel)*, 12(9), 3727. DOI: 10.3390/su12093727

Hasyim, H., & Bakri, M. (2024). Organizational Transformation in Adopting Hybrid Work Models: A Literature Review on Organizational Changes and Employee Readiness. *Jurnal Manajemen Bisnis*, 11(2), 1170–1182. DOI: 10.33096/jmb.v11i2.806

Ibrahim, M. S., & Saber, S. (2023). Machine learning and predictive analytics: Advancing disease prevention in healthcare. *Journal of Contemporary Healthcare Analytics*, 7(1), 53–71.

Jacomo, P. (2017). Workforce Agility: Are you ready now? Future of work. [Online] [Cited 4.02.19] Available from the World Wide Web: URLhttps://www.digitalistmag.com/future-of-work/2017/01/09/workforce-agilityare-you-ready-now-04828683/

Joseph, B., Walker, A., & Fuller-Tyszkiewicz, M. (2018). Evaluating the effectiveness of employee assistance programmes: A systematic review. *European Journal of Work and Organizational Psychology*, 27(1), 1–15. DOI: 10.1080/1359432X.2017.1374245

Karpie, A. (2018). Beyond Contingent Workforce Management: Embracing an Agile Workforce. [Online][Cited 3.02.19] Available from the World Wide Web: URL< http://spendmatters.com/2018/06/14/beyond-contingent-workforce managementembracing-an-agile-workforce/>

Khakurel, J., Melkas, H., & Porras, J. (2018). Tapping into the wearable device revolution in the work environment: A systematic review. *Information Technology & People*, 31(3), 791–818. DOI: 10.1108/ITP-03-2017-0076

Klašnja-Milićević, A., Vesin, B., Ivanović, M., & Budimac, Z. (2011). E-learning personalization based on hybrid recommendation strategy and learning style identification. *Computers & Education*, 56(3), 885–899. DOI: 10.1016/j.compedu.2010.11.001

Kraus, S., Clauss, T., Breier, M., Gast, J., Zardini, A., & Tiberius, V. (2020). The economics of COVID-19: Initial empirical evidence on how family firms in five European countries cope with the corona crisis. *International Journal of Entrepreneurial Behaviour & Research*, 214(5), 26. DOI: 10.1108/IJEBR-04-2020-0214

Lakho, S., Farooqi, S. A., Zafar, F., & Siraj, S. (2024). Developing AI-Powered Chatbots for Mental Health Support. *Spectrum of engineering sciences, 2*(3), 179-199.

Leach, M. (Ed.). (2008). Re-framing resilience: a symposium report. STEPS Working Paper 13, STEPS Centre, Brighton, UK.

Lee, Y., Hsieh, Y., & Ma, C. (2011). A model of organizational employees' E-lEarning systems acceptance. *Knowledge-Based Systems*, 24(3), 355–366. DOI: 10.1016/j.knosys.2010.09.005

Linnenluecke, M. K. (2017). Resilience in business and management research: A review of influential publications and a research agenda. *International Journal of Management Reviews*, 19(1), 4–30. DOI: 10.1111/ijmr.12076

Lv, W. D., Tian, D., Wei, Y., & Xi, R. X. (2018). Innovation Resilience: A New Approach for Managing Uncertainties Concerned with Sustainable Innovation. *Sustainability (Basel)*, 10(10), 3641. DOI: 10.3390/su10103641

Miller, F., Osbahr, H., Boyd, E., Thomalla, F., Bharwani, S., Ziervogel, G., Walker, B., Birkmann, J., Van der Leeuw, S., Rockström, J., Hinkel, J., Downing, T., Folke, C., & Nelson, D. (2010). Resilience and vulnerability: complementary or conflicting concepts? Ecology and Society 15(3):11. [online] URL: https://www.ecologyandsociety.org/vol15/iss3/art11/

Mishra, N., & Bharti, T. (2023). Exploring the nexus of social support, work–life balance and life satisfaction in hybrid work scenario in learning organizations. The Learning Organization, ahead-of-print. https://doi.org/https://doi.org/10.1108/tlo-08-2022-0099

Mitsakis, F. V. (2020). Human resource development (HRD) resilience: A new 'success element'of organizational resilience? *Human Resource Development International*, 23(3), 321–328. DOI: 10.1080/13678868.2019.1669385

Modaresnezhad, M., Andrews, M. C., Mesmer-Magnus, J., Viswesvaran, C., & Deshpande, S. (2021). Anxiety, job satisfaction, supervisor support and turnover intentions of mid-career nurses: A structural equation model analysis. *Journal of Nursing Management*, 29(5), 931–942. https://doi.org/https://doi.org/10.1111/jonm.13229. DOI: 10.1111/jonm.13229 PMID: 33617110

Mozgovoy, V. (2019). Stress Pattern Recognition Through Wearable Biosensors in the Workplace: Experimental Longitudinal Study on the Role of Motion Intensity. *Proceedings - 6th Swiss Conference on Data Science, SDS 2019, 172740*, 37–45.

Nelson, D. R., N. Adger, & K. Brown. (2007). Adaptation to environmental change: contributions of a resilience framework. *Annual Review of Environment and Resources, 32*:395–419. http://dx.doi.org/. energy.32.051807.090348.DOI: 10.1146/annurev

Pierce, M., Hope, H., Ford, T., Hatch, S., Hotopf, M., John, A., & Abel, K. M. (2020). Mental health before and during the COVID-19 pandemic: A longitudinal probability sample survey of the UK population. *The Lancet. Psychiatry*, 7(10), 883–892. DOI: 10.1016/S2215-0366(20)30308-4 PMID: 32707037

Ransbotham, S., Kiron, D., Gerbert, P., & Reeves, M. (2017). Reshaping business with artificial intelligence: Closing the gap between ambition and action. *MIT Sloan Management Review*, 59(1), 1–17.

Sahebjamnia, N., Torabi, S. A., & Mansouri, S. A. (2015). Integrated business continuity and disaster recovery planning: Towards organizational resilience. *European Journal of Operational Research*, 242(1), 261–273. DOI: 10.1016/j.ejor.2014.09.055

Sarabadani, J., Jafarzadeh, H., & ShamiZanjani, M. (2017). Towards understanding the determinants of employees' E -learning adoption in workplace. *International Journal of Enterprise Information Systems*, 13(1), 38–49. DOI: 10.4018/IJEIS.2017010103

Soares, J. O., Pina, J., Ribeiro, M., & Lopes, M. C. (2011). Quantitative vs. qualitative criteria for credit risk assessment. *Front. Finance Econ.*, 8(1), 69–87.

Takewaki, I. (2020). New Architectural Viewpoint for Enhancing Society's Resilience for Multiple Risks Including Emerging COVID-19. *Frontiers in Built Environment*, 6, 143. DOI: 10.3389/fbuil.2020.00143

Tambe, P., Cappelli, P., & Yakubovich, V. (2019). Artificial intelligence in human resources management: Challenges and a path forward. *California Management Review*, 61(4), 1542. DOI: 10.1177/0008125619867910

Tatineni, S. (2023). Cloud-Based Business Continuity and Disaster Recovery Strategies. *International Research Journal of Modernization in Engineering Technology and Science*, 5(11), 1389–1397.

Tenório, M. M., Reinaldo, F. A. F., Góis, L. A., Lopes, R. P., & dos Santos, G., Junior. (2018). Elements of gamification in virtual learning environments: A systematic review. In *Teaching and Learning in a Digital World:Proceedings of the 20th International Conference on Interactive Collaborative Learning–Volume 2* (pp. 86-96). Springer International Publishing.

Tochia, C. (2021). How the digital workforce has re-defined boundary management and perceptions of technological tools on maintaining work-life balance (Doctoral dissertation, University of Southampton).

Turner, B. L.II. (2010). Vulnerability and resilience: Coalescing or paralleling approaches for sustainability science? *Global Environmental Change*, 20(4), 570–576. DOI: 10.1016/j.gloenvcha.2010.07.003

Vaswani, A., Shazeer, N., Parmar, N., Uszkoreit, J., Jones, L., Gomez, A. N., & Polosukhin, I. (2017). Attention Is All You Need. Advances in neural information processing systems, *31st Conference on Neural Information Processing Systems (NIPS 2017)*, Long Beach, CA, USA.

## KEY TERMS AND DEFINITION

**Durability in Workplace:** The durability in the workplace is the capability of systems, processes and structures to endure challenges and remain operational over the years. It encompasses more than simply physical properties such, as buildings and machinery, for more so, it includes systems and processes which structure's management is able recalibrate in the event of changing situations. A durable organization is an organization that is able still uphold its day to day activities and core values despite interruptions and in this case, stability is preserved. This approach however encourages growth and helps to build resilience in periods of turbulence as it enables the organizations to perform optimally under uncertainty.

**Employee Assistant Program (EAP) or Counseling Services:** Employee Assistant Programs (EAP) are programs that are set in particular organizations that help in maintaining the wellbeing of employees and their productivity by offering them service that deals with both their personal issues and their job related issues. These services include counseling, which may provide for mental well health, legal and financial assistance as well as crisis management. With such resources available to employees in a work place, there is a clear sign that such organizations are committed to the health of their employees, creating a conducive working environment and therefore increasing productivity.

**Employee Well-Being:** Employee well-being in a workplace context refers to the health, happiness, and contentment of an individual's life within the work environment. It is comprised of the physical, mental, emotional, and social health of an individual and combines to make up the quality of life of an employee. In organizations that foster employee well-being, there are conducive environments created that enhance positive experiences, job satisfaction, and therefore productivity and the rate of retention. This model understands that people work better and are willing to give their best in an organization when their efforts and commitment to the organization are appreciated.

**Organizational Adaptability:** This expresses an organization's capability to adjust its workforce rapidly to the changing environment, market demands and other challenges. These include the force to change resource allocation, redeploy human resources and even change work processes and their designs. Agile workforces are those which are flexible, cooperate with each other and are always dynamic in nature learning all the time which makes the organization competitive and able to respond to changes. Optimizing workforce agility is a working strategy that improves the organization's resilience and enhances its problem- solving factors and its ability to act on threats and opportunities in the organization's environment.

**Organizational Resilience:** It is defined as an organization's ability to prepare for any threatening occurrences, recover from the actual disruptions and troubleshoot the internal as well as external challenges. This concept goes beyond recovery from a crisis to being proactive and adjusting to the new reality. Such organizations devise plans which include risk mitigation, optimization of resources, and promotion of a creative and risk taking attitude. In this way, resilience encourages survival of operations in business but also prosperity in unfriendly environments, thereby promoting the growth and success of the businesses in the long run.

**Sustainability:** Sustainability in the workplace entails workplace practices which are environmentally, socially, and economically responsible. It means engaging in activities that do not cause adverse impact on the environment and seek social fairness and economic gain at the same time. Sustainable practices include conserving resources and minimizing waste and encourage sourcing materials in a socially responsible manner and developing a working environment where workers practice sustainability. Integrating sustainability in business operations not only helps in making the world a better place but also improve the image of the business and attract like-minded customers and workers.

**Work Life Balance:** It is known to be the proportion of time and energy that an individual devotes to his or her specific occupation as opposed to the other activities available to him or her such as family, health and nutrition. This entails dealing with the various demands of working in such a way that employees can attend to their personal and family responsibilities while at the same time safeguarding their health and work performance. Work-life balance has health benefits as it fosters employee wellbeing, lowers the risk of burnout and enhances job satisfaction. Organizations that advocate for the adoption of such policies and practices as work-life balance, are at a better position to create a sense of belonging among the employees, thus increasing their engagement and reducing turnover.

**Workplace Flexibility:** Workplace flexibility implies the freedom of workers to decide over the work arrangements, such as place, time, and the manner in which work is done. Such options may entail working from home, having flexible hours, working on some days and for longer hours than usual, or working for short hours and days. Flexible workplace policies are sensitive to the varying needs and lifestyles of employees and therefore help improve employee satisfaction and the work life balance. Most importantly, Companies that allow such flexibility can entice and retain talent, boost employee responsiveness, and improve overall productivity.

# Chapter 8
# Towards Sustainable and Human-Centered Organizations Through the Prevention of Compulsory Citizenship Behaviors:
## A Bibliometric Analysis

**Zeynep Kaptan**
https://orcid.org/0000-0002-4877-430X
*Istanbul University, Turkey*

**Bora Yildiz**
https://orcid.org/0000-0002-0373-6457
*Istanbul University, Turkey*

**Halit Basbuga**
https://orcid.org/0000-0001-9286-8912
*Gebze Technical University, Turkey*

## ABSTRACT

*The existence of sustainable organizations relies on human-centered approaches that prioritize employee well-being while avoiding compulsory citizenship behaviors (CCB). This study presents a bibliometric analysis of CCB research using data from the Web of Science database. Results reveal key trends: most articles are authored collaboratively, with contributors like Hongdan Zhao, Huai-Liang Liang, Zhenglong Peng, and Bora Yildiz making notable impacts. "Frontiers in Psychology" is the most relevant journal, and institutions such as Tongji University, Da-Yeh University, Huaqiao University, and Istanbul University are highly influential. Thematic analysis highlights "citizenship pressure," "interpersonal deviance," and "employee silence" as motor themes, while basic themes include work-family conflict, turnover intention, job stress, and burnout. Issues like "facades of conformity" and "impression management" are classified as niche or emerging themes. This study enriches the understanding of CCB research and offers insights for future studies.*

DOI: 10.4018/979-8-3693-8181-6.ch008

## INTRODUCTION

Employees are of vital importance for the sustainable organizations (Barney & Arikan, 2005; Casey & Sieber, 2016). The optimal utilization of organizational resources relies on recognizing skilled human resources as valuable assets. Accordingly, managing these sources strategically is important in terms of the organizational success and sustainability. In this context, the presence of organizations that are human-centric, care about the well-being of their employees and understand them is inevitable in terms of sustainability. Therefore, ensuring the psychosocial and physiological well-being of employees and paying attention to their economic welfare is important for the human-centered and sustainable organizations (Kobayashi et al., 2018; Mariappanadar & Hochwarter, 2022; Stan, 2018).

From the perspective of human resource management and organizational behavior literature, the concept of human-centric has a very comprehensive nature. Although there is no clear definition yet for human-centered organizations, according to a systematic review study conducted on this concept, these types of organizations include the following four interrelated characteristics: *common good purpose* (purpose beyond profit, stakeholders beyond shareholders, fill a need, address an issue, contribute to human thriving), *positive human experiences* (employees as capable, problem solving learners, cultures in which employees are connected, respected, and values, opportunities to learn and grow, meaningful work), *humanistic values* (dignity and well-being, care and kindness, justice and fairness, whole person), *team structure* (semi-autonomous, self-managed teams, team ownership of work, connective mechanisms between teams), and *participatory practices and tools* (participatory research, innovation and ideation, experimentation, feedback, healthy conflict)) (Townsend & Romme, 2024). This title encompasses a wide range of factors, including human relations, employee experience, talent management, organizational culture, organizational success, human resources management, and strategic human resource management (Hector & Cameron, 2023).

We predict that employees in people-oriented organizations will exhibit organizational citizenship behaviors, which are voluntary extra-role behaviors, based on the assumption that these employees will be happy, satisfied, and have high organizational commitment (Hamzah et al., 2020; Huang et al., 2012; Huang et al., 2021; Shin, 2012). Organizational citizenship behaviors (OCB) refer to volunteer employee behaviors that are not explicitly recognized by formal reward systems but still contribute to the effective functioning of the organization (Organ, 1988). These behaviors are an important concept that emphasizes voluntary actions and behaviors of employees that go beyond their prescribed roles (Muthuraman & Al-Haziazi, 2017; Ucok & Erbay, 2022). OCB encompasses discretionary behaviors that are not explicitly rewarded or required by the organization but significantly contribute to its effectiveness and functioning (Anderson, 2017; Organ, 1988). However, since citizenship behaviors are often informally encouraged and rewarded, employees may feel pressure to engage in organizational citizenship behaviors (Bolino et al., 2010). Vigoda-Gadot (2006), proposed that when external pressure is applied, organizational citizenship behaviors lose their voluntary nature and referred to these behaviors as compulsory citizenship behaviors (CCB). CCB includes behaviors that employees feel pressure to perform due to external pressures, formal obligations, or expectations set by the organization or leaders (Liang et al., 2022). In this context, citizenship behavior becomes a matter of obligation rather than voluntary choice and transforms into CCB (Bolino et al., 2013; Vigoda-Gadot, 2006; Zhang et al., 2011). Compulsory citizenship behaviors can have detrimental effects on organizational factors, leading to undesirable outcomes (Vigoda-Gadot, 2006; Yildiz et al., 2023).

Comprehensive and frontier studies provide a broad explanation of CCB (Vigoda-Gadot, 2006; Yildiz et al., 2023). The literature still lacks a comprehensive bibliometric analysis that summarizes the key findings, research trends, emerging, declining, motor, niche, and basic research themes in the literature.

Evidence collectively suggests that CCB has detrimental effects on both organizations and individuals (Yildiz et al., 2023). Despite its growing importance, the scientific interest in this topic is still in its infant stage. To fill this gap, a recent meta-analysis investigated the theoretical correlates of CCB (Yildiz et al., 2023). However, given that the meta-analysis only synthesized the quantitative papers in the literature, its efforts to fill this gap remain insufficient. To go beyond that meta-analysis, by combining quantitative and qualitative studies, this study aims to investigate the CCB by using bibliometric analysis. Thus, by means of this study, we could identify critical themes (e.g. basic, niche, emerging/declining, and motor themes) that either facilitate or hinder the development of sustainable and human-centered organizations. By identifying the obstacles and enabler factors that fall under these four themes, organizations, managers, or HRM professionals can develop strategies that contribute to employee well-being and organizational sustainability. The linkage between understanding the nature of CCB and developing strategies to hinder them both will facilitate more human-centered approaches and organizational sustainability in the long run.

Using the bibliometric analysis method, this study aims to examine compulsory citizenship behaviors. By determining the emerging/declining, basic, niche, and motor themes, this study seeks to illuminate how CCB is harmful for individuals and organizations, how it affects employee well-being, and, in turn, individual and organizational sustainability. Moreover, by establishing a solid linkage between the CCB and human-centered sustainable organizations, this study will draw the attention of managers, organizations, policymakers, and HRM professionals to how sustainable and huma-centered organizations can be possible by minimizing or hindering CCB.

Bibliometrics is a significant research method that provides quantitative analysis of data such as articles, citations, journals, and research areas in scientific literature, offering insights into a specific subject or field (Kilavuz, 2023; Tutar et al., 2023). The bibliometric analysis of CCB will help researchers to understand the current state of research in the literature, identify trends, thematic map, and obtain important findings that will guide future research. In this context, this article presents a bibliometric analysis of academic studies on CCB. Specifically, it will explore and evaluate key trends, significant topics, most cited articles, and commonly used concepts in the literature related to CCB. This study also will guide future researchers by providing important clues on which areas to focus more on in the study of CCB. The research questions formulated based on the aforementioned explanations are as follows:

$RQ_1$- Which countries or institutions stand out in the field of CCB, and which countries contribute more significantly?

$RQ_2$- Which researchers, publications, and institutions receive the most citations and which researchers, publications, and institutions the most productive in studies on CCB?

$RQ_3$- Which researchers, institutions, or countries collaborate in studies on CCB, and which relationships (researchers, institutions, or countries) are more common?

$RQ_4$- What publications are considered foundational or transformative in the field of CCB?

$RQ_5$- What are the emerging/declining, niche, basic, and motor themes in the extant literature?

## THEORETICAL BACKGROUND

From the strategic management perspective, according to the resource-based view (Barney & Arikan, 2005; Barney, 2001), it can be said that human resources of organizations are rare, inimitable and valuable core competencies of organizations (Prahalad & Hamel, 2009). Therefore, protecting such a resource, realizing its value and ensuring its sustainability are important in terms of providing sustainable competitive advantage over competitors. Managing human resources strategically is also important to achieve firms long-term aims and overall strategies. According to the human capital (Becker, 1992, 2009) and strategic human capital theories (Wright et al., 2001), to achieve long-term organizational goals, employees are viewed as valuable and strategic assets that leverages organizations' competitive advantage. Moreover, training and education can enhance their expertise and proficiency, which significantly contribute to the achievement of organizational goals (Becker, 2009; Wright et al., 2001). Providing these factors, on the one hand, can cause employees to achieve the tasks determined in the formal job descriptions, and on the other hand, it can also cause employees to go beyond their job descriptions that are labeled as extra role behaviors (Becker & Kernan, 2003; Caillier, 2016).

## CONCEPTUAL FRAMEWORK

One of the extra role behaviors is organizational citizenship behaviors (OCB) (Morrison, 1994; Organ, 2014). Organizational citizenship behaviors (OCB) refer to volunteer employee behaviors that are not explicitly recognized by formal reward systems but still contribute to the effective functioning of the organization (Organ, 1988). However, since citizenship behaviors are often informally encouraged and rewarded, employees may feel pressure to engage in organizational citizenship behaviors (Bolino et al., 2010). Vigoda-Gadot (2006), proposed that when external pressure is applied, organizational citizenship behaviors lose their voluntary nature and referred to these behaviors as compulsory citizenship behaviors (CCB).

A recent comprehensive meta-analysis on the topic of CCB (Kaptan, 2024; Yildiz et al., 2023) highlighted its prevalence and increasing importance. That study indicates that the majority of researchers use the social exchange theory, abusive theory, and conservation of resources theory to explain the potential antecedents and consequences of CCB. The same study also highlighted Turkey, China, and Taiwan as countries where CCB research accounts for a significant proportion of total literature publication. As it can be seen from these countries, it is easy to say that CCB is a common set of behaviors in the eastern culture. Therefore, while bibliometric nature of the literature on this topic is important, it is also important to discuss this behavior from the Hofstede's national culture dimension (Hofstede, 1984). Further, while gender and number of children are the demographic characteristics that significantly related to CCB, there are also significant dispositional, perceptional, and behavioral correlates. Specifically, careerism, moral disengagement and turnover intentions were the most prominent dispositional outcomes of CCB. In the perceptional variables felt obligation and work-family conflict are strongly and significantly correlated variables. Organizational cynicism and burnout are stand out consequences as important attitudes. In the behavioral outcomes of CCB facades of conformity and counterproductive workplace behaviors have the highest effect sizes. Work alienation and anger toward the organizations were identified as the most dominant emotional reactions to CCB. Yildiz et al. (2023) also found that job autonomy, with its reducing effect, significantly inhibits the harmful effects of CCB. Similarly, they found a positive and significant correlation between CCB and leader-member exchange, organizational identification, psychological safety, interactional justice, distributive justice, job satisfaction, and organizational commitment.

As can be understood from the above explanations, CCB has been associated with many concepts in the organizational behavior literature. The relevant meta-analysis's synthesis suggests that these behaviors are prevalent in organizations, particularly in countries with Eastern cultures, and that cultural factors also play a role. Additionally, the fact that CCB are usually linked to negative or undesirable predictors and outcomes suggests that more study should be done on this topic.

## METHODOLOGY

In this study to explore the intellectual structure of the CCB research in the literature, we employed a bibliometric analysis. Bibliometric analysis was conducted on 51 publications retrieved from WoS. The research aims to understand the knowledge in the field of CCB, track the improvement of the area, and provide further researches directions.

The data screening of studies focusing on CCB was conducted using the Web of Science (WoS) database. To identify publications related to CCB, the phrase "compulsory citizenship" was searched within English language studies published in the WoS database between 2006 and 2024. In this bibliometric analysis, a total of 51 publications containing the terms "compulsory citizenship behavior" OR "compulsory citizenship behavior" AND "compulsory citizenship" in the WoS database were examined using Bibliometrix package (Aria & Cuccurullo, 2017) in the R statistical language (Team, 2023). Additionally, some scientific maps were created using the VOSviewer program (van Eck & Waltman, 2009).

### Inclusion and Exclusion Criteria

The specific of criteria must be fulfilled by the 51 studies included in the analysis.:

1. Relevant publications should address the topic of compulsory citizenship behaviors.
2. Publications should represent scholarly studies such as journal articles, conference papers, or book chapters.
3. The studies included in the analysis must have been published between 2006 and 2024.
4. Relevant publications should be written in English and included in the WoS database.
5. Selected studies must include national or international publications and focus on research in the field of management.

Exclusion criteria for the bibliometric analysis of studies on compulsory citizenship behaviors include:

1. Studies that do not pertain to compulsory citizenship behaviors or address related topics.
2. Studies that fall outside the predetermined types of publications designated for analysis.
3. Studies published outside the specified years, such as those published before 2006 or after 2024.
4. Studies published in other languages except English.
5. Studies indexed from databases outside of Web of Science.
6. Studies that fail to meet sufficient scientific standards or lack peer review processes.

## Study Selection

An analysis of the database resulted in the identification of 60 studies in the Web of Science. Upon evaluating the eligibility of the 60 records, 9 articles did not meet the inclusion criteria and were excluded from the analysis. Consequently, 51 studies were selected for inclusion in the bibliometric review (See Figure 1).

*Figure 1. PRISMA flow diagram*

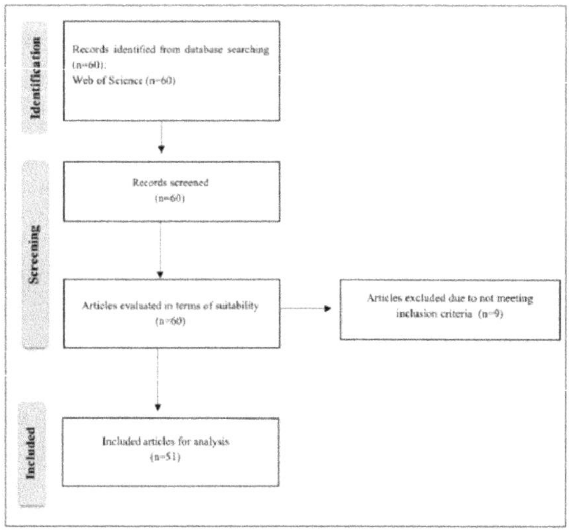


## RESULTS

After reviewing Table 1, it is clear that the majority of the 51 publications published between 2006 and 2024 were co-authored. The yearly growth rate in compulsory citizenship behavior (CCB) research is 11.42%, and the average citations per publication are 15.92. The cumulative count of writers for 51 articles is 132, with 6 of these articles authored by a single individual.

*Table 1. Descriptive statistics*

| Description | Results |
|---|---|
| Timespan | 2006-2024 |
| Documents | 51 |
| Sources (journals, books etc) | 32 |
| Annual growth rate (%) | %11.42 |
| Average citations per doc | 15.92 |

continued on following page

*Table 1. Continued*

| Description | Results |
|---|---|
| Authors | 132 |
| International co-authorships (%) | %29.41 |
| Single-authored docs | 6 |
| Co-authors per doc (%) | 3.18 |
| Keywords | 110 |
| References | 2677 |

## Annual Scientific Production of CCB

The number of articles published by year in the Figure 2 reveals the development and level of interest in the concept of compulsory citizenship behaviors in the scientific literature. First, one article was published on this subject in 2006 and 2007, but there was a stagnation in the following years (2008-2011). A steady increase has been observed since 2012.

A significant increase was experienced especially in the 2018-2023 period. While 2022 reached the highest number with 11 articles, this increase continued in 2023 and 2024, but a slight decrease (7 articles) was observed in 2024. These data show that academic interest in the concept of compulsory citizenship behaviors has increased rapidly, especially in the last five years, and more research has been conducted in this period. This increase shows that the concept has started to attract more attention and has gained an important place in the literature. However, the decrease in 2024 may indicate that more research should be done on the sustainability of this interest.

*Figure 2. Annual scientific production*

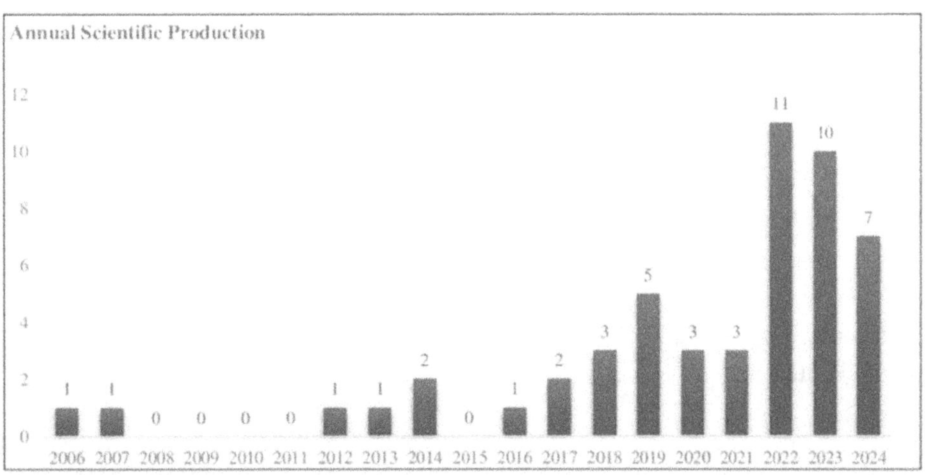

## Information about Researchers, Countries and Institutions

This research involved an analysis encompassing contributions from 85 institutions across 16 countries, reviewing 51 papers authored by 132 individuals in the domain of CCB research. An analysis of author distribution by country reveals that China is the most prolific nation, with a total of 28 papers in this domain. Türkiye follows with 4 articles, while Pakistan and the United States each offer 3 articles. Table 2 provides a detailed account of the distribution statistics for each nation. Table 2 shows that the most prolific institutions in the domain of compulsory citizenship behaviors, with publishing rates of 4.71%, are Tongji University, Da-Yeh University, Huaqiao University, Istanbul University, and Shanghai University. These universities have made significant progress in the field. In terms of international collaboration, Egypt, France, the United Kingdom, the United States, Pakistan, and China exhibit the greatest rates of cooperation. Nevertheless, since many countries tend to collaborate domestically, the level of cross-country collaboration may be lower than within-country collaborations. Moreover, China has made substantial contributions to the discipline via extensive cooperation at both national and international levels. since many countries tend to collaborate domestically, the level of cross-country collaboration may be lower than within-country collaborations. This underscores China's significance as a leading nation in the realm of compulsory citizenship behaviors.

*Table 2. The top 10 countries and institutions contributing to CCB research [n(%)]*

| | Country | A | Freq. | SCP | MCP | MCP (%) | Institutions | N (85, %) |
|---|---|---|---|---|---|---|---|---|
| 1 | China | 28 | 54.9 | 19 | 9 | 32.1 | Tongj University | 4 (%4.71) |
| 2 | Türkiye | 4 | 7.8 | 4 | 0 | 0.0 | Da-Yeh University | 4 (%4.71) |
| 3 | Pakistan | 3 | 5.9 | 2 | 1 | 33.3 | Huaqiao University | 4 (%4.71) |
| 4 | USA | 3 | 5.9 | 2 | 1 | 33.3 | Istanbul University | 4 (%4.71) |
| 5 | Israel | 2 | 3.9 | 2 | 0 | 0.0 | Shanghai University | 4 (%4.71) |
| 6 | United Kingdom | 2 | 3.9 | 1 | 1 | 50.0 | University of Haifa | 3 (%3.53) |
| 7 | Cyprus | 1 | 2.0 | 1 | 0 | 0.0 | Bandırma Onyedi Eylul University | 2 (%2.35) |
| 8 | Egypt | 1 | 2.0 | 0 | 1 | 100.0 | Birkbeck University London | 2 (%2.35) |
| 9 | France | 1 | 2.0 | 0 | 1 | 100.0 | Brunel University | 2 (%2.35) |
| 10 | Ghana | 1 | 2.0 | 1 | 0 | 0.0 | Indian Institute of Management Tiruchirappalli | 2 (%2.35) |
| | **Total** | 46 | 90.3 | 32 | 14 | 348.7 | | 31 (%36.47) |

**Notes:** A: Number of articles; SCP: Single country publications; MCP: Multiple country publication

Figure 3 compares the cultural dimensions (Hofstede, 1984) of four countries (China, Pakistan, Türkiye, and the United States).

*Figure 3. Comparison of cultural dimensions of countries*

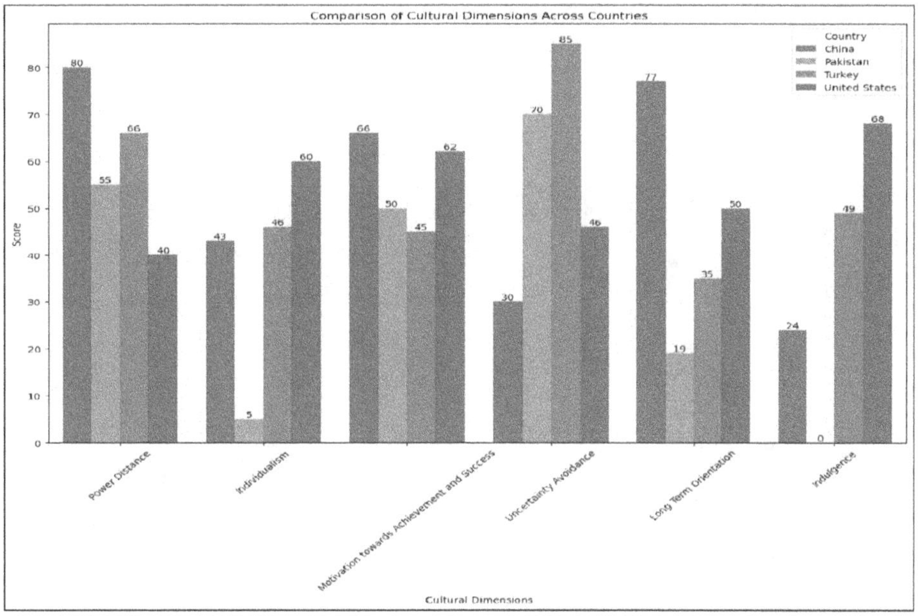


Figure 4 illustrates the collaboration network with 50 distinct universities organised into 7 discrete clusters. Graphic vividly depicts relationships and clustering among various institutions within collaboration network. Figure 4 highlights the two clusters exhibiting the most robust cooperative network. The foremost cluster exhibiting the most robust collaboration network comprises prominent institutions, including Huaqiao University, Tongji University, Shanghai University, Kedge Business School, University Oxford, Beijing Normal University, Dayeh University and Shanghai Normal University, which have forged a significant collaborative alliance. The second cluster with the most intense collaboration network comprises Istanbul University, Bandirma Onyedi Eylul University, Birkbeck College-University of London, Brunel University, Istanbul Bilgi University, University of London, and Ardahan University, which have formed a robust collaborative network. These institutions have established a robust collaborative network in the study of compulsory citizenship behaviors.

Figure 5's three-field plot analysis provides a significant perspective on CCB examination. This research's comprehensive assessment of the top 15 authors, nations, and keywords enhances understanding of the subject's breadth. This study highlights a significant focus on China in CCB research. China assumes a leading position in the field, representing around 34.48% of the performed research. After analyzing the contributions from the top 15 writers, it appears that Zhao H. stands out with a 16% contribution. Additional writers, including Wang H. (13%), He P. (12%), Peng Z. (10%), and Yildiz B. (9%), have also rendered substantial contributions.

The analysis of keyword use by writers based on their countries provides a compelling viewpoint. In their research, Chinese academics have used a methodology that emphasizes topics such as "burnout," "turnover intention," "felt obligation," "anger towards the organization," and "abusive supervision." Moreover, subjects such as "organisational citizenship behaviours," "work-family conflict," "employee silence," "job stress," and "job performance" are notable terms in the study.

Some authors' involvement in international collaboration is a notable characteristic. Zhao H. has collaborated with the USA, United Kingdom, and France in his research, in addition to China. Consequently, the keywords used exhibit commonalities across these nations. This global partnership highlights the universal aspects of compulsory citizenship behaviors.

*Figure 4. The collaboration network among institutions*

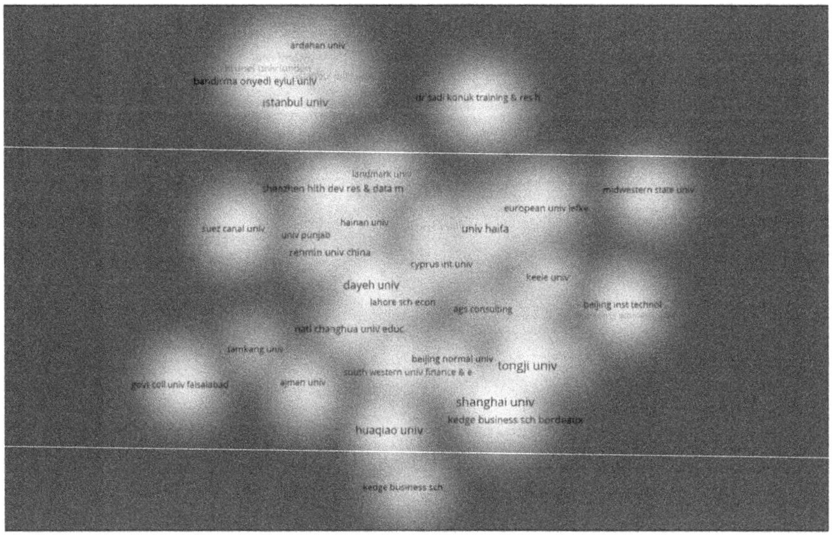


*Figure 5. Three-field plot of CCB literature*

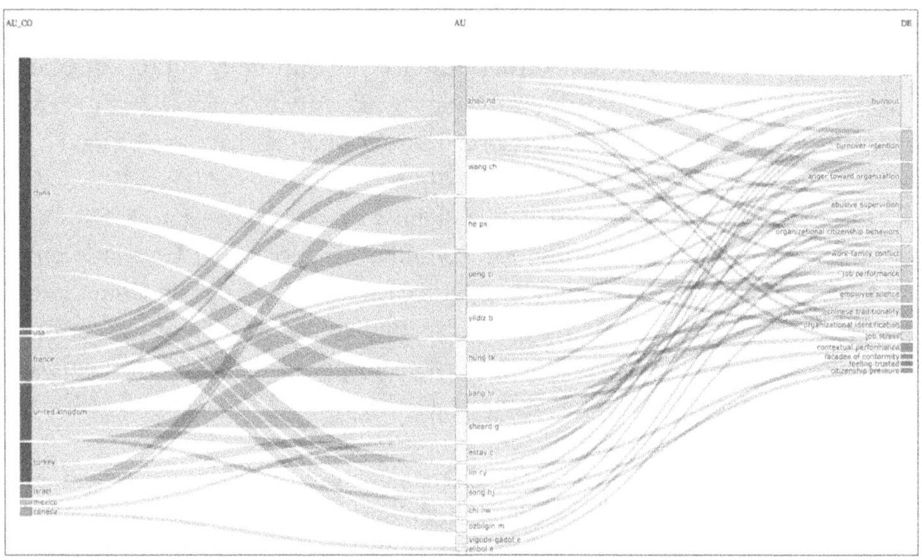

## Compulsory Citizenship Behaviors Studying Authors and Publishing Journals

32 different periodicals published a total of 51 distinct papers authored by 132 individuals. Reviewing the first 10 of these 32 journals reveals that 28 out of 51 papers appeared in them. Table 3 provides a detailed presentation of the first ten writers. The prominent writers authored 33 publications, representing 64.71% of the CCB literature. Hongdan Zhao is the most prolific author, having contributed significantly to the CCB field with six works (11.76%). The contributions of various writers in the CCB literature are as follows: Huai-Liang Liang (7.84%), Zhenglong Peng (7.84%), Bora Yildiz (7.84%), Peixu He (5.88%), Eran Vigoda-Gadot (5.88%), Chia-Hsuan Wang (5.88%), Nai-Wen Chi (3.92%), Esengül Elibol (3.92%), and Christophe Estay (3.92%). When examining the top 10 journals publishing research on CCB, it is evident that Frontiers in Psychology has the highest number of publications, contributing a total of 8 articles (15.69%). Further details regarding contributions from other journals can be reviewed in Table 3.

*Table 3. Leading authors and journals in the field of CCB [n(%)]*

| | Authors | N | Articles Frac. | Journals | N (51, %) |
|---|---|---|---|---|---|
| 1 | Zhao H. | 6 | 1.82 | Frontiers in Psychology | 8 (%15.69) |
| 2 | Liang H. | 4 | 2.67 | Current Psychology | 5 (%9.80) |
| 3 | Peng Z. | 4 | 1.28 | Psychology Research and Behavior Management | 3 (%5.88) |
| 4 | Yildiz B. | 4 | 2.00 | Social Behavior and Personality | 3 (%5.88) |
| 5 | He P. | 3 | 0.65 | International Journal of Hospitality Management | 2 (%3.92) |
| 6 | Vigoda-Gadot E. | 3 | 2.25 | Journal for the Theory of Social Behavior | |
| 7 | Wang C. | 3 | 0.87 | Journal of Nursing Management | 2 (%3.92) |
| 8 | Chi N. | 2 | 0.75 | Journal of Psychology | 2 (%3.92) |
| 9 | Elibol E. | 2 | 0.67 | 2019 AIB Southeast Asia regional conference: Us-China trade war deglobalization and international business (AIBSEAR) | 1 (%1.96) |
| 10 | Estay C. | 2 | 0.45 | Asia Pacific Business Review | 1 (%1.96) |
| | **Total** | 33 | 13.41 | **Total** | 28 (%54.90) |

**Notes:** N, number of publications; Articles Frac., fractionalized article count

Furthermore, when evaluating Table 4, we can examine the authors' scientific impact and productivity through various metrics (h-index, g-index, m-index, total number of citations (TC), number of articles (NP), and first publication year (PY_start)). Zhao H., Peng Z., and He P. stand out as the authors with the highest h-index in this field. The h-index indicates that an author has at least "h" number of publications and at least "h" number of citations (Gann, 2024). This indicates that these authors have done important and frequently cited research on the topics they work on (Mondal et al., 2023).

Also, Zhao H. and Peng Z. are the authors with the highest g-index values. The g-index complements the h-index by taking into account the total number of citations by the author (Ali, 2021). It provides information about the number and impact of the authors' most cited works (Egghe, 2006).

Yildiz B and Liang H have the highest m-index values. The m-index indicates the productivity rate, considering the duration of the author's research career (Hirsch, 2005). A high m-index indicates that the author has made influential publications in a short time (Stellenbosch, 2017).

Zhao H. and Vigoda-Gadot E. stand out as the researchers with the highest citation rate. This indicates that their publications are followed and referenced by a wide audience.

Zhao H and Peng Z are among the authors who have published the most articles. This shows that their contributions to the research topic are also numerically strong. Also, Vigoda-Gadot E is the earliest author to start working in this field. This shows that the author has been researching this topic for a long time and made one of the first contributions in this field. When the citation counts, index values and publication counts are evaluated together, Table 4 shows that both experienced and new researchers actively contribute to the field of compulsory citizenship behaviors.

*Table 4. First 10 authors impact studying on CCB*

| | Authors | h_index | g_index | m_index | TC | NP | PY_start |
|---|---|---|---|---|---|---|---|
| 1 | Zhao H. | 6 | 6 | 0.462 | 274 | 6 | 2012 |
| 2 | Peng Z. | 4 | 4 | 0.308 | 209 | 4 | 2012 |
| 3 | He P. | 3 | 3 | 0.429 | 158 | 3 | 2018 |
| 4 | Yildiz B. | 3 | 4 | 0.750 | 31 | 4 | 2021 |
| 5 | Elibol E. | 2 | 2 | 0.500 | 24 | 2 | 2021 |
| 6 | Estay C. | 2 | 2 | 0.286 | 116 | 2 | 2018 |
| 7 | Liang H. | 2 | 3 | 0.667 | 9 | 4 | 2022 |
| 8 | Ozbilgin M. | 2 | 2 | 0.667 | 6 | 2 | 2022 |
| 9 | Sheard G. | 2 | 2 | 0.167 | 67 | 2 | 2013 |
| 10 | Vigoda-Gadot E. | 2 | 3 | 0.105 | 283 | 3 | 2006 |

**Notes:** TC, overall citations; NP, total number of articles; PY-start, year of first publications

## Global and Local Citations of CCB Studies

Table 5 shows in which journals the studies of specific authors on compulsory citizenship behaviors were published, the total number of citations (TC) to these studies, and the average number of citations per year (TCPY). When analyzing the table, the following points stand out: The article published by Vigoda-Gadot E. (2007) in the *Journal of Business and Psychology* has the highest total number of citations, with 144 citations. This shows that the article is quite influential in the literature on compulsory citizenship behaviors. The article published by Vigoda-Gadot E. (2006) in the *Journal for the Theory of Social Behavior* is another highly influential study, receiving 139 citations. The article published by He P. (2019) in the *Journal of Business Ethics* has the highest TCPY value, with an average of 13.67 citations per year. This indicates that the article has been heavily referenced in a short time and is closely followed by researchers in the field. The article published by He P. (2020) in *Frontiers in Psychology* also has a high TCPY value of 8.40, indicating that the study is up-to-date and important.

Vigoda-Gadot E. and He P. have published their most influential studies in the field of compulsory citizenship behaviors in prestigious and widely followed journals. *Journal of Business and Psychology* and *Journal of Business Ethics* are among the important platforms in this regard. Zhao H. and He P. have contributed to this field with their articles published in journals in the area of psychology and social behavior, especially the *Journal of Psychology and Social Behavior and Personality.*

This table presents the authors and research that have the greatest impact on CCB, as well as the publications in which these studies are published. Studies with high citations and high TCPY values in particular make significant contributions to the literature in this field.

*Table 5. Total global citations count for leading 10 researchers and journals*

| | Authors | Journals | TC | TCPY |
|---|---|---|---|---|
| 1 | Vigoda-Gadot E. (2007) | Journal Business and Psychology | 144 | 8.00 |
| 2 | Vigoda-Gadot E. (2006) | Journal for the Theory of Social Behavior | 139 | 7.32 |
| 3 | He P. (2019) | Journal of Business Ethics | 82 | 13.67 |
| 4 | Zhao H. (2014) | Journal of Psychology | 63 | 5.73 |
| 5 | Zhao H. (2013) | Journal of Psychology | 44 | 3.67 |
| 6 | He P. (2020) | Frontiers in Psychology | 42 | 8.40 |
| 7 | He P. (2018) | Social Behavior and Personality | 34 | 4.86 |
| 8 | Wang H. (2019) | International Journal of Hospitality Management | 26 | 4.33 |
| 9 | Liu Y. (2017) | Social Behavior and Personality | 23 | 2.88 |
| 10 | Yildiz B. (2021) | Journal of Nursing Management | 22 | 5.50 |

Table 6 presents information on the number of local citations (LC), the number of global citations (GC), and the percentage of local citations to global citations (LC/GC) of articles on compulsory citizenship behaviors by specific authors. According to Table 6, Vigoda-Gadot E.'s articles in the *Journal for the Theory of Social Behavior* (2006) and the *Journal of Business and Psychology* (2007) are the studies with the highest number of local citations, with 41 local citations each. This indicates that the articles have an important place in the community or regional literature in which they are located. The articles by Vigoda-Gadot E. are also considerably higher in total citation count (139 and 144 citations) compared to other studies, indicating that the articles have attracted great interest and are widely referenced both locally and internationally. Also, He P.'s *Journal of Business Ethics* (2019) article also attracts attention with 82 general citations, indicating that the article is a source recognized and used in a wide academic circle.

Ahmadian S. (2017) has a very high LC/GC ratio of 92.86% with his article published in the journal *Business and Economic Horizons*. This shows that the vast majority of the citations received by the article come from local sources. The article is extremely influential in the local literature, but has a more limited impact in terms of the number of global citations.

Peng Z. (2012) received 60.00% local citation rate for his article in *Nankai Business Review International*. This shows that the article has a significant impact in the local area but has received relatively less citations internationally.

He P. (2018)'s article in the journal *Social Behavior and Personality* shows that local citations are higher than general citations with a 41.18% LC/GC ratio, indicating that the study is noteworthy in both local and general academic circles.

Table 6 provides important information for understanding the place of authors' work in the literature on CCB and the impact of these works both locally and internationally. Studies with a high LC/GC ratio have a significant impact, particularly in the local literature, but lower global citation counts may indicate that these studies are less well-known internationally or are more recent.

*Table 6. Total local citations count for leading 10 researchers and journals*

| | Authors | Journals | LC | GC | LC/GC Ratio (%) |
|---|---|---|---|---|---|
| 1 | Vigoda-Gadot E. (2006) | Journal for the Theory of Social Behavior | 41 | 139 | 29.50 |
| 2 | Vigoda-Gadot (2007) | Journal Business and Psychology | 41 | 144 | 28.47 |
| 3 | Zhao H. (2014) | Journal of Psychology | 24 | 63 | 38.10 |
| 4 | He P. (2019) | Journal of Business Ethics | 20 | 82 | 24.39 |
| 5 | Zhao H. (2013) | Journal of Psychology | 17 | 44 | 38.64 |
| 6 | He P. (2018) | Social Behavior and Personality | 14 | 34 | 41.18 |
| 7 | He P. (2020) | Frontiers in Psychology | 14 | 42 | 33.33 |
| 8 | Ahmadian S. (2017) | Business and economic horizons | 13 | 14 | 92.86 |
| 9 | Peng Z. (2012) | Nankai Business Review International | 12 | 20 | 60.00 |
| 10 | Liu Y. (2017) | Social Behavior and Personality | 10 | 23 | 43.48 |

**Notes:** LC, Local citation; GC, Global citation

The collaboration map provides various metrics to analyze the authors' positions and relationships within the academic collaboration network (Agbo et al., 2021). In the map, authors are divided into different clusters and evaluated with various network centrality metrics (betweenness, closeness, PageRank) (Shao et al., 2018). In Figure 6 illustrates the network framework of 132 researchers engaged in domain of CCB. Figure 6 illustrates the collaborative network of the first 50 authors for a clearer understanding.

Authors are divided into 6 different clusters. These clusters represent the density of collaboration among authors and the groups in which these authors collaborate more frequently (Zwack et al., 2023). For example, Liang HL, Wang CH, and Hung TK are in the same cluster, indicating that these authors collaborate more frequently with each other.

Zhao H has the highest betweenness centrality score of 3,300. This indicates that Zhao has an important role in facilitating the flow of information among other authors and bridging various groups (O' Daniel & Rosenstein, 2008). Peng Z is second with a betweenness centrality score of 1,700. This indicates that Peng also plays a similarly important mediating role, but is not as central as Zhao.

Zhao H stands out as the author with the highest impact on the collaboration map with a PageRank score of 0.048. PageRank measures an author's influence in the network and the importance of their connections to other authors (Yan & Ding, 2011).

Wang C and Peng Z also stand out with their PageRank scores of 0.039, indicating that they are also important nodes in the network. Other authors typically have PageRank scores around 0.027, indicating that their influence in the network is more limited.

This analysis provides important information for understanding the positions and roles of authors in the academic collaboration network. Authors such as Zhao H and Wang C are important authors who are at the center of the network, directing the flow of knowledge and building bridges between other authors.

*Figure 6. The network of collaboration among the leading 50 researchers*

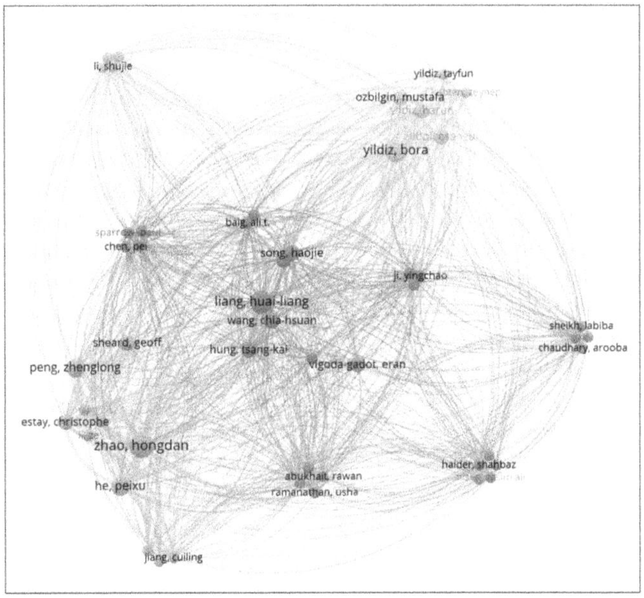


## Co-Citation Relationships Among Researchers and Journals in CCB Research

Figure 7 displays the co-citation relationships of researchers in the field of compulsory citizenship behaviors, organized into six clusters. The primary cluster highlights the most frequently cited author, Vigoda-Gadot. Vigoda-Gadot's articles, entitled "Redrawing the Boundaries of OCB?" This cluster is led by "An empirical examination of compulsory extra-role behaviour in the workplace," published in 2007, and "Compulsory citizenship behaviour: Theorising some dark sides of the good soldier syndrome in organisations," published in 2006. Authors citing these papers are shown in the red cluster, exemplified by Bolino M., Peng Z., Bandura A., and Spector P. Of the 50 writers, 14 (28%) have referenced Vigoda-Gadot.

Transitioning to the second cluster, Tepper B.J.'s 2000 essay, "Consequences of Abusive Supervision," is notable. Sixteen out of fifty writers (24%) from the blue cluster reference Tepper's essay. These six separate clusters elucidate the citation links within the domain of CCB more clearly.

*Figure 7. The network of collaboration among the leading 50 researchers*

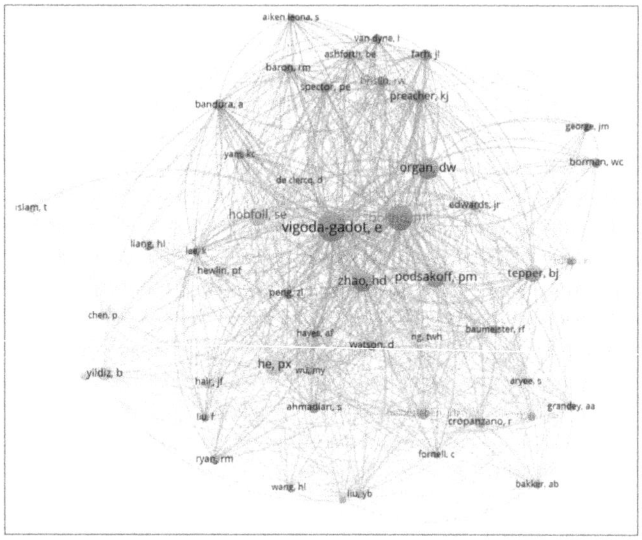


In Figure 8, a co-citation relationship among journals is illustrated, constructed by identifying and linking documents that cite each other. This network reveals the relationships and connections between various studies within a specific research area. To simplify visual complexity, this study focuses on the first 50 journals with the highest number of publications.

Figure 8 shows that the co-citation relationships of journals is organized into three primary clusters. The first cluster is centered around the *Journal of Applied Psychology* plays a central role and forms a co-citation relationship along with journals like *the Academy of Management Journal, Journal of Organizational Behavior*, and *Journal of Management*. In the second cluster, the *Frontiers in Psychology,* which establishes a co-citation relationship with journals such as journals *such as Journal of Personality and Social Psychology, Journal of Business Ethics and Journal of Business Economics and Management Research.* In the third cluster, the *Academy of Management Journal* plays a central role and forms a co-citation relationship along with journals like *Journal of Occupational Psychology, Journal of Psychology* and *Journal for the Theory of Social Behaviour.*

Of the 50 journals, 17 (34%) are categorised in the green cluster, 17 (34%) are categorised blue cluster, while 16 (32%) are classified in the blue cluster. This clarifies the common citation connections and grouping across journals in a more clear and understandable way.

Figure 8 illustrates a co-citation network among academic publications. We establish this network by recognising and linking publications that cite one another. This network elucidates the relationships among various research within a certain discipline. This study examined the first 50 published publications focused on reducing visual complexity.

Figure 8 categorises the co-citation networks of journals into two primary classifications. The Journal of Applied Psychology is a fundamental element of the first cluster. This journal establishes a co-citation relationship with the Academy of Management Journal, Journal of Organizational Behavior, and Journal of Management. The Frontiers in Psychology is essential in the second cluster, establishing a co-citation relationship with Journal of Personality and Social Psychology, Journal of Business Ethics.

Of the 50 journals, 17 (34%) are categorised in the green cluster, 17 (34%) are categorised blue cluster, while 16 (32%) are classified in the blue cluster. This elucidates prevalent citation relationships and classifications across journals in a more coherent and comprehensible manner.

*Figure 8. The network of co-citation among the leading 50 journals*

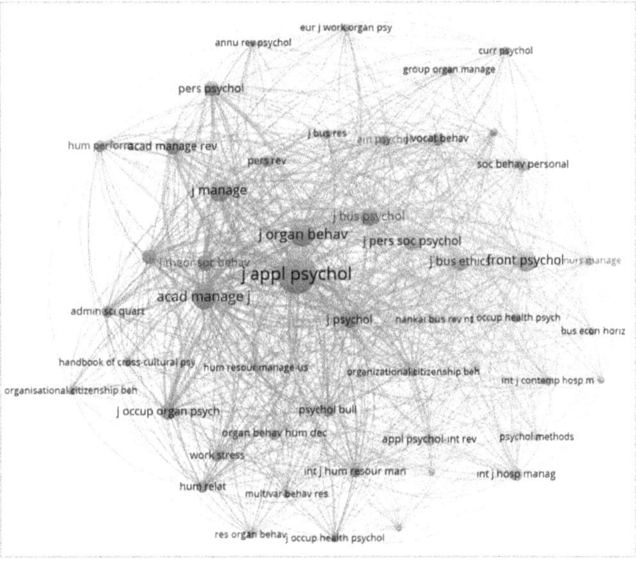


## Keywords Analysis in CCB Research

TreeMap analysis provides a visual understanding of the main concepts of a specific research field and their prevalence in the literature (Long et al., 2017). This analysis can help you identify which topics have been studied more and which topics have been studied less (Walker, 2018). This information can be useful in identifying research gaps and areas where you can focus future studies (Chand, 2023). Figure 9 illustrates the frequency of terms used in CCB research. This analysis examines the 20 most frequently used terms across the 51 studies reviewed. This study reveals that, out of 109 keywords, the terms with the greatest frequencies are "burnout," "organisational citizenship behaviours," "job stress," "work-family conflict," "abusive supervision," "job performance," and "turnover intention."

*Figure 9. TreeMap overview of the 20 leading keywords in CCB research*

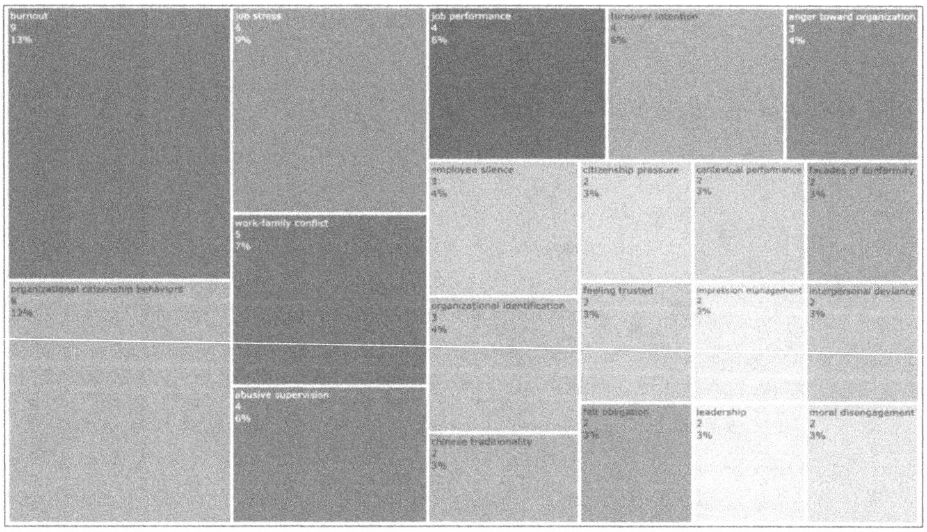


Figure 10 reflects the frequency of various terms associated with studies on compulsory citizenship behaviors. High-frequency terms such as burnout (9), organizational citizenship behaviors (8), job stress (6), and work-family conflict (5) point to central themes in the literature on compulsory citizenship behaviors, suggesting that compulsory citizenship behaviors are often linked to negative outcomes such as burnout, stress, and work-life imbalance. Terms such as abusive supervision (4), job performance (4), and turnover intentions (4) are also prominent in the analysis. These focus on how compulsory citizenship behaviors can lead to a toxic work environment, impact performance, and increase turnover intentions. Also, the variety of terms, such as interpersonal deviance (2), negative affect (2), abusive behavior (1), and counterproductive work behavior (1), suggests that the literature has examined a wide range of negative behaviors and emotional reactions associated with CCB. Keywords related to leadership (abusive supervision, leadership, charismatic leadership) and management (human resource management) may reflect the role of organizational structure and leadership styles in promoting or discouraging CCB.

*Figure 10. WordCloud representation of the top 20 keywords in CCB research*

Figure 11 presents the trend topic analysis of the words across time. According to the figure, terms such as Chinese traditionality gained popularity and gained traction relatively early in 2012. The term appears to have been influential until the third quarter (Q3) of 2013, but interest in the word may have waned thereafter. The term organizational citizenship behaviors became popular in 2014 and maintained its relevance until 2020. This term continued to attract the attention of researchers for a long time. Terms such as contextual performance and organizational identification began to attract attention in 2014-2016 and continued to be influential until 2020-2021. The terms employee silence and job stress came to the fore in 2018 and received ongoing interest until 2022. Terms like burnout and work-family conflict became popular in 2021 and remained in the spotlight until 2023. Burnout, in particular, had become a much-discussed topic due to the pandemic and increased workloads. Anger toward organization is one of the newest trending topics and has begun to gain traction in the 2022-2024 period. This term could be the subject of further research in the future. In addition, terms such as impression management, abusive supervision, and citizenship pressure began to attract attention in the post-2020 period and peaked in 2021-2022. These terms can be considered current issues and maintain their importance in the literature on CCB.

In general, trend topics analysis shows how topics related to compulsory citizenship behavior studies have evolved over the years and which topics are popular in which periods. It is understood that topics such as burnout, anger toward organization, work-family conflict and job performance have gained importance in recent years and that these topics may be focused on more in the future.

*Figure 11. Trend topics analysis in CCB studies*

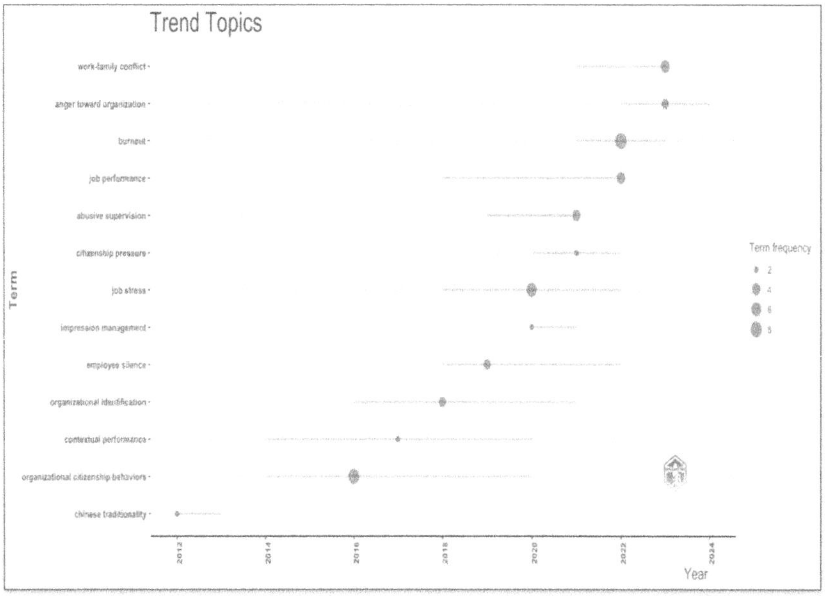


A comprehensive study of the thematic map derived from 51 papers from the Web of Science database spanning from 2006 to 2024 has been undertaken to elucidate advancements in CCB research. The study employed bibliometric approaches to focus on keywords, including those that appeared at least three times in the thematic analysis. The objective was to identify the key themes and keywords within the field of CCB research.

The acquired data reveals that the provided topics include four primary divisions. We categorised and examined the keywords for each subject based on their centrality and impact density. Figure 12 illustrates this classification into four quadrants. The quadrants include niche themes, motor themes, emerging or decreasing themes, and basic themes, respectively (Alkhammash, 2023). We have selected and meticulously analyzed the principal concepts in CCB research using these topics, and provided graphic representations for examination.

The thematic map analysis shows that niche subjects like "Chinese traditionality" and "contextual performance," which exhibit high density but low interest levels, are the focus of a cluster of keywords among the 51 studies on CCB.

A cluster of terms, including "citizenship pressure" and "interpersonal deviance," which are characterized by significant attention and density, demonstrates a pronounced trend within the study domain of CCB in motor themes.

The grouping of words found in main themes, like "organisational citizenship behaviours," "job stress," "job performance," "burnout," "abusive supervision," "turnover intention," and "attitude towards organisation," shows a high level of interest but a low level of density in the thematic analysis.

We can classify the notions of employee silence and moral disengagement as motor themes when their density and centrality increase, and as fundamental themes when these factors decrease. Similarly, we can include the notions of conformance facades and impression control as niche themes or topics that are developing or waning over time, based on their density and centrality.

*Figure 12. Thematic map of keywords*

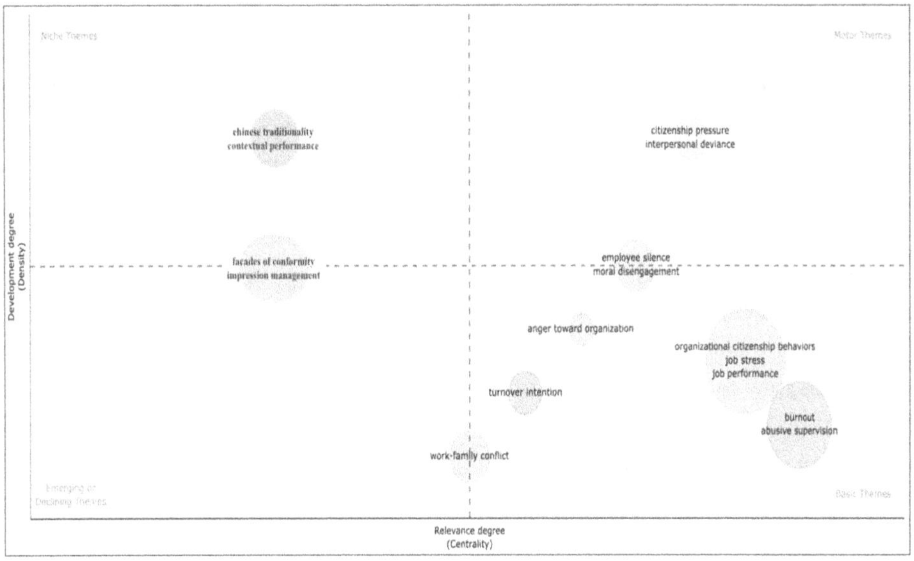


## DISCUSSION

The results of this study provide a detailed overview of trends and developments in the literature on compulsory citizenship behaviors. The number of articles published in 2006-2007 was quite low. However, a continuous increase has been observed since 2012. There was a significant increase in the 2018-2023 period, with the highest number in 2022. There is a slight decrease in 2024. This shows that the subject has received increasing academic interest in recent years, but there are question marks about the sustainability of this interest in 2024. In particular, the dramatic increase in the concept in the following years can be explained by the increase in the number of studies in the literature with the recognition of the concept of CCB and the fact that the concept has become a phenomenon that can be seen all over the world as a result of the excessive workload brought by COVID-19, which started in early 2020 (Kaptan, 2024; Yildiz et al., 2023; Yildiz et al., 2022). Therefore, it can be said that the CCB phenomenon, which is mostly common in eastern culture countries, has spread to different parts of the world.

The studies consist of 51 articles and were written by 132 different authors. The top ten authors published 64.71% of the total articles. Hongdan Zhao stands out as the most productive author. These data reveal the significant impact and contributions of certain authors in this field. Zhao H. and Peng Z. have high h-index and g-index values, indicating that these authors have produced frequently cited and influential research. Yildiz B. and Liang H. have high m-index values, indicating that they have produced important publications in a short time. This highlights their significant impact and productivity in the field.

The works of Vigoda-Gadot E. are notable for their high total citation counts and high annual citation averages, indicating that these works are important sources in the field. One of the potential reasons for this finding is that Vigoda-Gadot E.'s works are the frontiers of the CCB field. Therefore, most CCB research cites these sources to define the construct and explain the theoretical arguments behind it. The collaboration network among authors reveals that Zhao H. and Peng Z. played important connecting roles, indicating that these authors guided the flow of knowledge and collaborations.

The analysis of the journals identified two significant clusters. *The Journal of Applied Psychology* is central to the first cluster, the *Frontiers in Psychology* stands out in the second cluster. This helps to identify co-citation networks and important sources among journals.

China is the leading nation in article production. While Türkiye and other nations contribute, China's preeminence in research is clearly evident. These results may be elucidated using Schooler and Hofstede's (1983) national cultural aspects. Power distance is high in China, Pakistan and Türkiye, where hierarchical structures are accepted. This may indicate that employees are more inclined to comply with demands from their superiors, and therefore compulsory citizenship behaviors may be more common in these countries. Power distance levels are lower in the United States when we compare with the other three countries. This may indicate that employees are less authority-oriented and may be more likely to question requests (in US). This may indicate that compulsory citizenship behaviors may be less common in Western countries. The United States has the highest level of individualism, while Türkiye, Pakistan, and China have a more collectivistic structure. In countries with low levels of individualism, employees may be more prone to display compulsory citizenship behaviors in order to maintain group harmony (Smith et al., 1998). In the United States, employees may be more resistant to such compulsory citizenship behaviors because individual rights are more prominent. There are no significant differences between countries in the dimension of motivation towards achievement and success. However, high motivation towards success in general may trigger employees to take on extra tasks for the success of the organization (Osabiya, 2015; Riyanto et al., 2021). In this case, compulsory citizenship behaviors may be observed in countries where the motivation towards achievement and success is high. In addition, uncertainty avoidance is high in Türkiye and Pakistan, as shown in Figure 3. In these countries, uncertainty avoidance may lead employees to faced in compulsory citizenship behaviors because uncertainty avoidance may increase the tendency to obey rules and perform extra tasks requested by managers (Altuncu et al., 2012; Goodwin et al., 2022). This rate is decreased in China and the United States, indicating that workers may be less inclined to engage in compulsory citizenship behavior under uncertain circumstances. Figure 3 indicates that China exhibits the greatest degree of long-term orientation, while Pakistan has the lowest degree. In countries that focus on long-term goals, employees may more easily accept compulsory citizenship behaviors considering the long-term interests of the organization. In countries with a short-term orientation, such behaviors may be less acceptable when they are contrary to the individual interests of the employees (Demirkiran & Yonet, 2023). Finally, the United States and Pakistan have higher rates of indulgence, suggesting that individuals prioritize their own happiness and personal fulfillment (Sommer, 2014). In such cultures, compulsory citizenship behaviors may be less acceptable when they are contrary to employees' personal interests. China and Türkiye have lower rates of indulgence, suggesting that individuals tend to conform more to social norms and rules (Pryor & Howe, 2018) and may more readily accept compulsory citizenship behaviors.

In the analysis of keywords, keywords such as "burnout", "organizational citizenship behaviors", and "job stress" stand out as the most frequently used terms in the field. These findings are consistent with the findings of a recent comprehensive meta-analytic systematic review (Yildiz et al., 2023). Such that burnout was found as the significant attitudinal correlate of CCBs (He et al., 2018; Jin & Hahm, 2019; Liang et al., 2022). Organizational citizenship behaviours was found as negative behavioral correlate of CCB (Lin & Chi, 2022; Wang & Huang, 2019). Also, job stress as an undesirable emotional variable positively correlated with CCB (Chen et al., 2021; Unaldi Baydin et al., 2020). As can be understood from these findings, CCB is positively related to negative constructs while it is negatively related to positive constructs. Therefore, it can be said that CCBs are a set of behaviors that have destructive effects for both individuals and organizations.

The thematic map shows the evolution and main trends in the research literature of the subject by grouping various keywords into four main themes: basic, niche, emerging/declining, and motor themes. Accordingly, issues of "facades of conformity" and "impression management" are located at the intersection of niche and "emerging/declining" themes. It can be said that there is not enough researcher interest in these concepts or that these topics are studied by very few researchers. Therefore, considering that the centrality and density values of these papers which were conducted by past research are low, it can be said that the impact of these publications may not be very high in the short term, but they may have a high potential in the long term.

The "motor" themes include "citizenship pressure," "interpersonal deviance," and "employee silence." Motor themes are the themes with the highest centralization and concentration. As can be seen, when the topics in these themes are examined, it is seen that citizenship pressure comes to the fore. In recent years, it can be said that the increasing workload of businesses, the excessive workload that emerged with the pandemic the desire of businesses to show more performance to cover the losses that occurred after the pandemic, and the competitive pressure in the business world where competition is high, have created the necessity for employees to do extra work (Barpanda & Saraswathy, 2023; Na'imah & Nur, 2021). Therefore, the theme of citizenship pressure has started to be examined by researchers in recent years (Liang, 2022; Liu et al., 2017). On the other hand, it can also be said that employees give more passive reactions as a response to the compulsory citizenship behaviors they are exposed to. For example, due to reasons such as the lack of alternative jobs in the labor market, continuance commitments in their current workplaces (Che, 2015; Peng & Zhao, 2012; Telli Danismaz, 2021), and the lack of job alternatives, employees can exhibit "employee silence" (He et al., 2018; Su et al., 2021), and " counterproductive work behaviors" (Guarino, 2016; Su et al., 2021; Zuo, 2022). When considered in the context of social exchange theory (Blau, 1964), it can be said that employees react negatively to the compulsory citizenship pressures that organizations apply to their employees.

The basic themes include work-family conflict (Yildiz et al., 2023), turnover intention (Yildiz et al., 2023), anger towards the organisation (Yildiz et al., 2023), organisational citizenship behaviours (Yildiz et al., 2023), job stress (Yildiz et al., 2023), job performance (Yildiz et al., 2023), burnout (Yildiz et al., 2023) and abusive supervision (Yildiz et al., 2023). Furthermore, employ silence (Yildiz et al., 2023) and moral disengagement (Yildiz et al., 2023) are situated at the intersection of the basic and motor themes. As can be understood from here, it can be said that the basic studies focus especially on the negative effects of compulsory citizenship on the individual (individual), the negative effects on performance (organization), and the role of managers in the emergence of these behaviors (leadership). Therefore, it can be said that the fact that compulsory citizenship behaviors have a structure that is addressed at different unit of analysis indicates the need to address the issue from different perspectives. These research topics that located in the basic themes are with high centrality and low density. The study issues under this area have mostly been examined in previous studies. Consequently, we advise that anyone doing CCB research start their literature evaluation by examining studies on these topics. By doing so, one may swiftly grasp the theoretical perspectives from which contemporary research addresses these subjects and the nature of the findings they reveal. We believe this will diminish the prevalence of non-original research in the literature.

The results of this study comprehensively outline the growing academic interest in compulsory citizenship behaviors, key authors, and major themes in the literature. These trends and key sources in the literature provide valuable insights for future research.

## CONCLUSION

This study employed bibliometric analysis to summarize the existing literature on CCB. With this study we identified several key findings that shed light on the negative aspects of CCB and paved the way for future research. Firstly, policy makers and managers, who aim to minimize these behaviors and their undesirable outcomes, find significance in the majority of publications conducted in eastern cultures. Therefore, managers in these cultures should use more humanistic and understandable approaches when developing work expectations for their employees. They should also implement clearer and more specific job descriptions, along with limitations on time, location, and job units, to prevent Compulsory Citizenship Behaviors (CCB), such as restricting internet usage or blocking work systems during non-work hours. CCB negatively impacts both employees and organizations. They negatively impact psychological well-being and social relationships. Also, they hinder organizational performance and foster sabotage and anger toward the organization. For organizations to be sustainable and human-centric, managers and powerful individuals who are eligible for policy-making should implement realistic performance expectations, foster an environment where employees can be themselves, listen to employee voices, specify ethical codes and moral standards that prioritize employee rights and well-being, facilitate Organizational Citizenship Behavior (OCB), prioritize relaxing activities and work-life balance, and employ effective leadership styles such as transformational leadership, servant leadership, and authentic leadership. They should also prioritize the quality of relationships between employees and themselves to ensure the success of human-centric organizations. Achieving and utilizing these strategies and tools will serve as a preventive measure for CCB, thereby supporting a sustainable and human-centric organization.

### Limitations

This research focused on the bibliometric profile of academic researches on compulsory citizenship behaviors. However, the study has some limitations. The research exclusively utilized the Web of Science (WoS) database. The omission of research conducted in different disciplines and languages may lead to an incomplete perspective. Also, only English articles were examined in the study. Disregarding research conducted in other languages and contributions from local publications may result in an incomplete global analysis. There may be limitations to the bibliometric methods employed in the study. For instance, relying solely on a specific dataset carries the risk of overlooking some important publications or research.

## Recommendations for Future Researchers

Future studies could conduct a more comprehensive examination by exploring different data sources (such as Scopus, PubMed) and languages. This could assist in understanding the topic from a broader perspective. Compulsory citizenship behaviors could also be examined in disciplines beyond business. For instance, insights from fields like psychology, sociology, and education could contribute to a more multifaceted understanding of the subject. The study covers a specific period. Future researchers could better understand the topic's evolution over time by examining a wider timeframe or changes in specific periods. Research on compulsory citizenship behaviors could focus on how it contributes to practical applications. For example, the effects of these studies could be explored in areas such as leadership practices, workplace productivity, or workplace relationships within businesses.

## REFERENCES


Abukhait, R., Khattak, M. N., Shaya, N., & Ramanathan, U. (2023). The underlying mechanism between compulsory citizenship behaviors and employee innovative work behaviors and knowledge sharing: A moderated mediation model. *Frontiers in Psychology*, 14, 1128499. Advance online publication. DOI: 10.3389/fpsyg.2023.1128499 PMID: 36865361

Agbo, F., Oyelere, S., Suhonen, J., & Tukiainen, M. (2021). Scientific production and thematic breakthroughs in smart learning environments: A bibliometric analysis. *Smart Learning Environments*, 8(1), 1. Advance online publication. DOI: 10.1186/s40561-020-00145-4

Ahmadian, S., Sesen, H., & Soran, S. (2017). Expanding the boundaries of compulsory citizenship behavior: Its impact on some organizational outputs. *Business and Economic Horizons*, 13(1), 110–118. DOI: 10.15208/beh.2017.08

Ali, M. J. (2021). Understanding the 'g-index' and the 'e-index'. *Seminars in Ophthalmology*, 36(4), 139–139. DOI: 10.1080/08820538.2021.1922975 PMID: 33952018

Ali Nisar, Q., Haider, S., Waqas, A., Khan, W. A., & Selem, K. M. (2024). Cost of organizational citizenship behaviors: Serial mediation model of citizenship fatigue. *Management Research Review*, 47(6), 904–927. DOI: 10.1108/MRR-08-2023-0540

Altuncu, Y., Oz Aktepe, S., & Islamoglu, G. (2012). Preliminary study for the development of uncertainty acoidance instrument in Turkey. *Journal of Business, Economics & Finance, 1*(4).

Anderson, H. J. (2017). Organizational-citizenship behavior. In Zeigler-Hill, V., & Shackelford, T. K. (Eds.), *Encyclopedia of Personality and Individual Differences* (pp. 1–3). Springer International Publishing., DOI: 10.1007/978-3-319-28099-8_788-1

Aria, M., & Cuccurullo, C. (2017). bibliometrix: An R-tool for comprehensive science mapping analysis. *Journal of Informetrics*, 11(4), 959–975. https://doi.org/https://doi.org/10.1016/j.joi.2017.08.007. DOI: 10.1016/j.joi.2017.08.007

Azila-Gbettor, E. M., Mensah, C., & Abiemo, M. K. (2023). Compulsory citizenship behaviour and job outcome among unpaid interns: The buffering role of perceived co-worker support. *Higher Education. Skills and Work-Based Learning*, 14(1), 55–75. DOI: 10.1108/HESWBL-01-2023-0006

Baig, A. T., & Riaz, Z. (2021). Tracing an unyielding work compulsion: A moderated mediation model of abusive supervision and compulsory citizenship behavior. *Frontiers in Psychology*, 12, 746823. Advance online publication. DOI: 10.3389/fpsyg.2021.746823 PMID: 34912271

Barney, J., & Arikan, A. (2005). The resource-based view: Origins and implications. In (pp. 123-182). https://doi.org/DOI: 10.1111/b.9780631218616.2006.00006.x

Barney, J. B. (2001). Resource-based theories of competitive advantage: A ten-year retrospective on the resource-based view. *Journal of Management*, 27(6), 643–650. DOI: 10.1177/014920630102700602

Barpanda, S., & Saraswathy, G. (2023). The impact of excessive workload on job performance of health-care workers during pandemic: A conceptual mediation-moderation model. *IJMAR*, 10(1), 24–39. DOI: 10.18646/2056.101.23-002

Bashir, M., Shaheen, K., Saleem, S., Bhutta, M. K., Abrar, M., & Jun, Z. (2019). The mediating role of psychological need thwarting in the relationship between compulsory citizenship behavior and psychological withdrawal. *Frontiers in Psychology*, 10, 2595. Advance online publication. DOI: 10.3389/fpsyg.2019.02595 PMID: 31849742

Becker, G. S. (1992). Human capital and the economy. *Proceedings of the American Philosophical Society*, 136(1), 85–92.

Becker, G. S. (2009). *Human capital: A theoretical and empirical analysis, with special reference to education*. University of Chicago press.

Becker, T. E., & Kernan, M. C. (2003). Matching commitment to supervisors and organizations to in-role and extra-role performance. *Human Performance*, 16(4), 327–348. DOI: 10.1207/S15327043HUP1604_1

Blau, P. M. (1964). Exchange and power in social life. *Sociological Inquiry*, 34(2). Advance online publication. DOI: 10.1111/j.1475-682X.1964.tb00583.x

Bolino, M., Turnley, C., Gilstrap, W. H., & Suazo, J. B. (2010). Citizenship under pressure: What's a "Good Soldier" to do? *Journal of Organizational Behavior*, 31(6), 835–855. DOI: 10.1002/job.635

Bolino, M. C., Klotz, A. C., Turnley, W. H., & Harvey, J. (2013). Exploring the dark side of organizational citizenship behavior. *Journal of Organizational Behavior*, 34(4), 542–559. DOI: 10.1002/job.1847

Caillier, J. G. (2016). Does public service motivation mediate the relationship between goal clarity and both organizational commitment and extra-role behaviours? *Public Management Review*, 18(2), 300–318. DOI: 10.1080/14719037.2014.984625

Casey, D., & Sieber, S. (2016). Employees, sustainability and motivation: Increasing employee engagement by addressing sustainability and corporate social responsibility. *Research in Hospitality Management*, 6(1), 69–76. DOI: 10.2989/RHM.2016.6.1.9.1297

Chand, R. (2023). Framework for identifying research gaps for future academic research. *IRA International Journal of Education and Multidisciplinary Studies*, 19(2), 160. DOI: 10.21013/jems.v19.n2.p12

Chaudhary, A., Cheema, A. U., Sheikh, L., & Islam, T. (2023). How does compulsory citizenship behavior disturb police employees' psychological health? The roles of work–family conflict and putting family first. *International Journal of Public Sector Management*, 36(4/5), 420–439. DOI: 10.1108/IJPSM-03-2023-0073

Che, X. (2015). *Effects of occupational stressors on nurses' safety performance and well-being: A within-individual study* [Doctoral dissertation, University of South Florida].

Chen, P., Xu, Y., Sparrow, P., & Cooper, C. (2021). Compulsory citizenship behaviour and work-family conflict: A moderated mediation model. *Current Psychology (New Brunswick, N.J.)*, 42(8), 6641–6652. DOI: 10.1007/s12144-021-01973-4

Chen, P., Xu, Y., Sparrow, P., & Cooper, C. (2023). Compulsory citizenship behaviour and work-family conflict: A moderated mediation model. *Current Psychology (New Brunswick, N.J.)*, 42(8), 6641–6652. DOI: 10.1007/s12144-021-01973-4

Cheng, L. Z. (2019). Compulsory citizenship behavior and facades of conformity with the mediating effect of work stress: A social exchange theory perspective. *[2019 aib southeast Asia regional conference: Us-China trade war, deglobalization, and international business (aibsear)].* AIB Southeast Asia Regional Conference - US-China Trade War, Deglobalization, and International Business, Cebu, PHILIPPINES.

Chi, N.-W., Lin, C.-Y., Bruning, P. F., & Hung, Y. (2024). Forced to be a good citizen: Exploring the bright-and dark-side effects of daily compulsory citizenship behaviours on subsequent proactive helping and interpersonal deviance. *Journal of Occupational and Organizational Psychology*, 97(2), 647–671. DOI: 10.1111/joop.12486

Chou, S. Y., Ramser, C., Chang, T., & Han, B. (2020). Emergence of interpersonal helping in times of crises: A theoretical model of prosperity and eradication of interpersonal helping in organizations. *Management Decision*, 58(10), 2257–2273. DOI: 10.1108/MD-08-2020-1041

Coldwell, D. A. L., & Callaghan, C. W. (2014). Specific organizational citizenship behaviours and organizational effectiveness: The development of a conceptual heuristic device. *Journal for the Theory of Social Behaviour*, 44(3), 347–367. DOI: 10.1111/jtsb.12046

Demirkiran, E., & Yonet, O. (2023). Are geert Hofstede's cultural dimensions correlated with pandemic statistics worldwide? *Gumushane University e-Journal of Faculty of Communication, 11*. https://dergipark .org.tr/en/download/article-file/3174748

Duan, W.-Y., Wu, T.-J., Wei, A.-P., & Huang, Y.-T. (2024). Reducing the adverse effects of compulsory citizenship behaviour on employee innovative behaviour via AI usage in China. *Asia Pacific Business Review*, •••, 1–21. DOI: 10.1080/13602381.2024.2332731

Egghe, L. (2006). Theory and practice of the g-index. *Scientometrics*, 69(1), 131–152. Advance online publication. DOI: 10.1007/s11192-006-0144-7

Eivazzadeh, N., & Nadiri, H. (2022). An empirical study to investigate the coercive management behavior: Evidence from academia. *E+M. Ekonomie a Management*, 25(1), 42–59. DOI: 10.15240/tul/001/2022-1-003

Ergul, A.S. & Kerse, G. (2024). The mediating role of organizational identification in the effect of compulsory citizenship behavior on employee silence: The case of Turkish (Konya Province) manufacturing industry. *Ekonomski vjesnik/Econviews, 37*(1), 127–138. https://doi.org/DOI: 10.51680/ev.37.1.9

Gann, L. (2024). *What is an h-index? How do I find the h-index for a particular author?* The University of Texas, MD Anderson Cancer Center. https://mdanderson.libanswers.com/faq/26221#:~:text=The%20h%2Dindex%20is%20calculated,cited%20at%20least%2017%20times

Goodwin, J., Rob, P., Freeston, M., Garland, D., Grahame, V., Kernohan, A., Labus, M., Osborne, M., Parr, J. R., Wright, C., & Rodgers, J. (2022). Caregiver perspectives on the impact of uncertainty on the everyday lives of autistic children and their families. *Autism*, 26(4), 827–838. DOI: 10.1177/13623613211033757 PMID: 34291688

Guarino, S. N. (2016). *"It's more unfair for me": The moderating role of equity sensitivity on the relationship between compulsory citizenship behavior and distributive justice* [Doctoral dissertation, Saint Louis University]. ProQuest Dissertations and Thesis Global.

Hamzah, H., Hubeis, M., & Hendri, I. (2020). The effect of career development, justice organization and quality of work life to organizational commitment andiImplications to organizational citizenship behavior of employees at PT. *Perkebunan Nusantara XIII.International Review of Management and Marketing*, 10(3), 101–109. https://econjournals.com/index.php/irmm/article/view/10002. DOI: 10.32479/irmm.10002

He, P., Peng, Z., Zhao, H., & Estay, C. (2019). How and when compulsory citizenship behavior leads to employee silence: A moderated mediation model based on moral disengagement and supervisor-subordinate guanxi views. *Journal of Business Ethics*, 155(1), 259–274. DOI: 10.1007/s10551-017-3550-2

He, P., Wang, X., Wu, M., & Estay, C. (2018). Compulsory citizenship behavior and employee silence: The roles of emotional exhaustion and organizational identification. *Social Behavior and Personality*, 46(12), 2025–2047. DOI: 10.2224/sbp.7452

He, P., Zhou, Q., Zhao, H., Jiang, C., & Wu, Y. J. (2020). Compulsory citizenship behavior and employee creativity: Creative self-efficacy as a mediator and negative affect as a moderator. *Frontiers in Psychology*, 11, 1640. Advance online publication. DOI: 10.3389/fpsyg.2020.01640 PMID: 32793046

He, P. X., Wang, X. L., Li, Z., Wu, M. Y., & Estay, C. (2018). Compulsory citizenship behavior and employee silence: The roles of emotional exhaustion and organizational identification. *Social Behavior and Personality*, 46(12), 2025–2048. DOI: 10.2224/sbp.7452

He, Q., Fu, J., Wu, W., & Pervaiz, S. (2022). Does compulsory citizenship behavior necessarily reduce employee? Work well-being? The role of relative deprivation and resource compensation based on compulsory citizenship behavior. *Psychology Research and Behavior Management*, 15, 1105–1119. DOI: 10.2147/PRBM.S321689 PMID: 35535130

Hector, O., & Cameron, R. (2023). Human-centric management: Nurturing talent, building culture, and driving organizational success. *The International Journal of Science in Society*, 5(4), 511–525. DOI: 10.54783/ijsoc.v5i4.809

Hirsch, J. E. (2005). An index to quantify an individual's scientific research output. *Proceedings of the National Academy of Sciences of the United States of America*, 102(46), 16569–16572. DOI: 10.1073/pnas.0507655102 PMID: 16275915

Hofstede, G. (1984). *Culture's consequences: International differences in work-related values*. Sage.

Huang, C. C., You, C. S., & Tsai, M. T. (2012). A multidimensional analysis of ethical climate, job satisfaction, organizational commitment, and organizational citizenship behaviors. *Nursing Ethics*, 19(4), 513–529. DOI: 10.1177/0969733011433923 PMID: 22753457

Huang, N., Qiu, S., Yang, S., & Deng, R. (2021). Ethical leadership and organizationaş citizenship behavior: Mediation of trust and psychological well-being. *Psychology Research and Behavior Management*, 14, 655–664. DOI: 10.2147/PRBM.S311856 PMID: 34104011

Hung, T.-K., Lee, S.-C., Wu, Y.-S., & Hsieh, H.-M. (2022). Compulsory citizenship behavior and employees' contextual performance: Roles of perceived psychological safety and political skill. *Social Behavior and Personality*, 50(11), 1–13. DOI: 10.2224/sbp.11918

Hung, T.-K., Wang, C.-H., Tian, M., Lin, M., & Liu, W.-H. (2022). How to prevent stress in the workplace by emotional regulation? The relationship between compulsory citizen behavior, job engagement, and job performance. *SAGE Open*, 12(2), 21582440221105483. Advance online publication. DOI: 10.1177/21582440221105483

Jin, X., & Hahm, S. (2019). The influence of high-power distance on turnover intention and emotional exhaustion among information technology workers in Korea: The mediating effects of compulsory citizenship behavior. *International Journal of Innovation. Creativity and Change*, 7(4), 262–278.

Kaptan, Z. (2024). *A systematic literature review of compulsory citizenship behaviors: A bibliometric and meta-analysis study* [Master dissertation, Istanbul University]. Council of Higher Education Thesis Center.

Kilavuz, F. (2023). A bibliometric analysis of multicultural education research. *Journal of Social Sciences And Education, 6*(Education Special Issue), 216-238. https://doi.org/DOI: 10.53047/josse.1359321

Kobayashi, K., Eweje, G., & Tappin, D. (2018). Employee wellbeing and human sustainability: Perspectives of managers in large Japanese corporations. *Business Strategy and the Environment*, 27(7), 801–810. DOI: 10.1002/bse.2032

Liang, H. L. (2022). Compulsory citizenship behavior and facades of conformity: A moderated mediation model of neuroticism and citizenship pressure. *Psychological Reports*, 125(6), 1–21. DOI: 10.1177/00332941211031794 PMID: 34325551

Liang, H.-L. (2022). Compulsory citizenship behavior and facades of conformity: A moderated mediation model of neuroticism and citizenship pressure. *Psychological Reports*, 125(6), 3141–3161. DOI: 10.1177/00332941211031794 PMID: 34325551

Liang, H.-L. (2024). How and when authoritarian leadership affects compulsory citizenship behavior? A moderated mediation model of façade creation and leader-member exchange. *Current Psychology (New Brunswick, N.J.)*, 43(24), 1–13. DOI: 10.1007/s12144-024-05909-6

Liang, H. L., Yeh, T. K., & Wang, C. H. (2022). Compulsory citizenship behavior and its outcomes: Two mediation models. *Frontiers in Psychology*, 13, 869744. Advance online publication. DOI: 10.3389/fpsyg.2022.869744 PMID: 35300160

Liang, H.-L., Yeh, T.-K., & Wang, C.-H. (2022). Corrigendum: Compulsory citizenship behavior and its outcomes: Two mediation models. *Frontiers in Psychology*, 13, 869744. Advance online publication. DOI: 10.3389/fpsyg.2022.869744 PMID: 35300160

Lin, C.-Y., & Chi, N.-W. (2022). Understanding why and when compulsory citizenship behaviors lead to subsequent destructive voice and citizenship behaviors: The retributive justice and impression management perspectives. *Human Performance*, 35(5), 303–322. DOI: 10.1080/08959285.2022.2121964

Lin, C.-Y., & Chi, N.-W. (2022). Understanding why and when compulsory citizenship behaviors lead to subsequent destructive voice and citizenship behaviors: The retributive justice and impression management perspectives. *Human Performance*, 35(5), 303–322. DOI: 10.1080/08959285.2022.2121964

Liu, F., Chow, I. H., & Huang, M. (2019). Increasing compulsory citizenship behavior and workload: Does impression management matter? *Frontiers in Psychology*, 10, 1726. Advance online publication. DOI: 10.3389/fpsyg.2019.01726 PMID: 31402890

Liu, Y., Zhao, H., & Sheard, A. (2017). Organizational citizenship pressure, compulsory citizenship behavior, and work–family conflict. *Social Behavior and Personality*, 45(4), 695–704. DOI: 10.2224/sbp.6064

Liu, Y., Zhao, H., & Sheard, G. (2017). Organizational citizenship pressure, compulsory citizenship behavior, and work-family conflict. *Social Behavior and Personality*, 45(4), 695–704. DOI: 10.2224/sbp.6064

Long, L., Hui, L., Fook, G., & Zainon, W. M. N. (2017). A study on the effectiveness of tree-maps as tree visualization techniques. *Procedia Computer Science*, 124, 108–115. DOI: 10.1016/j.procs.2017.12.136

Mariappanadar, S., & Hochwarter, W. A. (2022). A three-way synergistic effect of work on employee well-being: Human sustainability perspective. *International Journal of Environmental Research and Public Health*, 19(22), 14842. DOI: 10.3390/ijerph192214842 PMID: 36429568

Mondal, H., Deepak, K. K., Gupta, M., & Kumar, R. (2023). The h-Index: Understanding its predictors, significance, and criticism. *Journal of Family Medicine and Primary Care*, 12(11), 2531–2537. DOI: 10.4103/jfmpc.jfmpc_1613_23 PMID: 38186773

Morrison, E. W. (1994). Role definitions and organizational citizenship behavior: The importance of the employee's perspective. *Academy of Management Journal*, 37(6), 1543–1567. DOI: 10.2307/256798

Muthuraman, S., & Al-Haziazi, M. (2017). Examining the factors of organizational citizenship behavior with reference to corporate sectors in Sultanate of Oman. *International Review of Management and Marketing*, 7(1), 413–422.

Na'imah, T., & Nur, S. A. (2021). Job stress on teachers during the Covid-19 pandemic: The role of workload and organizational climate. *International Journal of Social Science and Human Research*, 4(10), 2763–2768.

Norris, S. E. (2018). The business education of charismatic leaders and good soldiers. *International Journal of Adult Vocational Education and Technology*, 9(2), 11–29. DOI: 10.4018/IJAVET.2018040102

O' Daniel, M., & Rosenstein, A. H. (2008). *Professional communication and team collaboration* (Rg, H., Ed.). Agency for Healthcare Research and Quality (US)., https://www.ncbi.nlm.nih.gov/books/NBK2637/

Organ, D. W. (1988). *Organizational citizenship behavior: The good soldier syndrome*. Lexington Books/D. C. Heath and Com.

Organ, D. W. (2014). *Organizational citizenship behavior: It's construct clean-up time*. Psychology Press.

Osabiya, B. (2015). The effect of employees motivation on organizational performance. *Journal of Public Administration and Policy Research*, 7(4), 62–75. DOI: 10.5897/JPAPR2014.0300

Peng, Z., & Zhao, H. (2012). Does organization citizenship behavior really benefit the organization? Study on the compulsory citizenship behavior in China. *Nankai Business Review International*, 3(1), 75–92. DOI: 10.1108/20408741211201935

Peng, Z. L., & Zhao, H. D. (2012). Does organization citizenship behavior really benefit the organization? Study on the compulsory citizenship behavior in China. *Nankai Business Review International*, 3(1), 75–92. DOI: 10.1108/20408741211201935

Pradhan, S., & Gupta, P. (2021). Abusive supervision and work-family conflict: An empirical investigation of Indian professionals. *International Journal of Conflict Management*, 32(3), 493–513. DOI: 10.1108/IJCMA-07-2020-0130

Prahalad, C. K., & Hamel, G. (2009). *The core competence of the corporation*. Routledge.

Pryor, C., & Howe, P. (2018). *Conform to the social norm: Why people follow what other people do*. The University of Melbourne. https://findanexpert.unimelb.edu.au/news/2944-conform-to-the-social-norm--why-people-follow-what-other-people-do

Qin, G., & Zhang, L. (2024). How compulsory citizenship behavior depletes individual resources -a moderated mediation model. *Current Psychology (New Brunswick, N.J.)*, 43(2), 969–983. DOI: 10.1007/s12144-023-04386-7

Riyanto, S., Endri, E., & Herlissha, N. (2021). Effect of work motivation and job satisfaction on employee performance: Mediating role of employee engagement. *Problems and Perspectives in Management*, 19(3), 162–174. DOI: 10.21511/ppm.19(3).2021.14

Sajuyigbe, A. S., Inegbedion, H. E., Ayeni, A. W., & Ighomereho, S. O. (2022). Compulsory citizenship behavior, work-life balance, and turnover intention in academia: Mediating effects of emotional intelligence. *Journal of Behavioral Science*, 17(2), 58–72.

Shao, C., Cui, P., Xun, P., Peng, Y., & Jiang, X. (2018). Rank correlation between centrality metrics in complex networks: An empirical study. *Open Physics*, 16(1), 1009–1023. https://doi.org/doi:10.1515/phys-2018-0122. DOI: 10.1515/phys-2018-0122

Shin, Y. (2012). CEO ethical leadership, ethical climate, climate strength, and collective organizational citizenship behavior. *Journal of Business Ethics*, 108(3), 299–312. Advance online publication. DOI: 10.1007/s10551-011-1091-7

Shu, C.-Y., Chiang, Y.-H., & Lu, C.-H. (2018). Authoritarian leadership supervisor support and workers' compulsory citizenship behavior. *International Journal of Manpower*, 39(3), 468–485. DOI: 10.1108/IJM-10-2016-0191

Smith, P. B., Dugan, S., Peterson, A. F., & Leung, W. (1998). Individualism: Collectivism and the handling of disagreement. A 23 country study. *International Journal of Intercultural Relations*, 22(3), 351–367. https://doi.org/https://doi.org/10.1016/S0147-1767(98)00012-1. DOI: 10.1016/S0147-1767(98)00012-1

Sommer, R. M. (2014). *Relationship goals: Prioritizing personal fulfillment for lasting love.* TherapyIdeas. https://www.therapyideas.net/details/relationship-goals-prioritizing-personal-fulfillment-for-lasting-love/

Song, H., Li, Y., Zhang, Q., & Cheng, Y. (2023). The moderating effects of trust and felt trust on the nonlinear relationship between compulsory citizenship behavior and counterproductive work behavior. *Psychology Research and Behavior Management,* 15(16), 2517–2531. DOI: 10.2147/PRBM.S413674 PMID: 37431432

Song, H., Yin, Q., Zhang, Q., & Li, Y. (2023). The impact of compulsory citizenship behavior on job performance of new-generation knowledge workers: The roles of ego depletion and relational energy. *Psychology Research and Behavior Management,* 28(16), 2367–2381. DOI: 10.2147/PRBM.S413932 PMID: 37404575

Spector, P. E. (2016). When more can become less high performance work systems as a source of occupational stress. In N. M. Ashkanasy, R. J. Bennett, & M. J. Martinko (Eds.), *Understanding the high performance workplace: The line between motivation and abuse,* 148–169. Routledge/Taylor & Francis Group.

Stan, O. M. (2018). Steps towards sustainability–human resource capital and employee wellbeing–benchmarking evidence. *Economics, Management, and Financial Markets,* 13(3), 290–300.

Stellenbosch. (2017). *How to measure your impact.* Stellenbosch University Library and Informantion Service. https://libguides.sun.ac.za/c.php?g=1199094&p=8770045

Su, L., Chen, Y., & Li, Y. (2021). *Compulsory citizenship behavior leads to counterproductive work behavior: A multiple mediation path.* The 2021 12th International Conference on E-business, Management and Economics (ICEME 2021), July 17-19, 2021, Beijing, China (New York, NY: ACM) DOI: 10.1145/3481127.3481191

Suhail, A., Haq, I. U., Azeem, M. U., & Vigoda-Gadot, E. (2024). Compulsory citizenship behavior, role overload, creativity and service-oriented voluntary behavior: Does generational difference have an impact? *Personnel Review,* 53(8), 2126–2146. Advance online publication. DOI: 10.1108/PR-12-2022-0894

Team, R. C. (2023). _*R: A Language and Environment for Statistical Computing*_. Vienna, Austria. <https://www.R-project.org/>

Telli Danismaz, A. (2021). *Examination the role of the need to succeed and presenteeism in the relationship between compulsory citizenship behavior and organizational commitment* [Doctoral dissertation, The Council of Higher Education Thesis Center, Yildiz Technical University, Türkiye].

Townsend, M., & Romme, A. G. L. (2024). The emerging concept of the human-centered organization: A review and synthesis of the literature. *Humanistic Management Journal,* 9(1), 53–74. DOI: 10.1007/s41463-024-00168-w

Tutar, H., Nam, S., & Cagiltay, C. G. (2023). Bibliometric analysis and visual mapping of the articles published in the ILEF Journal from the beginning to the present [Başlangıcından Bugüne İLEF Dergisinde Yayınlanan Makalelerin Bibliyometrik Analizi ve Görsel Haritalandırılması]. *Kastamonu İletişim Araştırmaları Dergisi,* (10), 87–105. DOI: 10.56676/kiad.1163603

Ucok, D. I., & Erbay, E. O. (2022). Organizational citizenship behavior: The other side of the coin. *Marmara Üniversitesi İktisadi ve İdari Bilimler Dergisi*, 44(1), 162–182. DOI: 10.14780/muiibd.1135558

Unaldi Baydin, N., Tiryaki Sen, H., Kartoglu Gurler, S., Dalli, B., & Harmanci Seren, A. K. (2020). A study on the relationship between nurses' compulsory citizenship behaviours and job stress. *Journal of Nursing Management*, 28(4), 851–859. DOI: 10.1111/jonm.13009 PMID: 32187768

Unaldi Baydin, N., Tiryaki Sen, H., Kartoglu Gurler, S., Dalli, B., & Harmanci Seren, A. K. (2020). A study on the relationship between nurses' compulsory citizenship behaviours and job stress. *Journal of Nursing Management*, 28(4), 851–859. DOI: 10.1111/jonm.13009 PMID: 32187768

Vigoda-Gadot, E. (2006). Compulsory citizenship behavior: Theorizing some dark sides of the good soldier syndrome in organizations. *Journal for the Theory of Social Behaviour*, 36(1), 77–93. Advance online publication. DOI: 10.1111/j.1468-5914.2006.00297.x

Vigoda-Gadot, E. (2006). Compulsory citizenship behavior: Theorizing some dark sides of the good soldier syndrome in organizations. *Journal for the Theory of Social Behaviour*, 36(1), 77–93. DOI: 10.1111/j.1468-5914.2006.00297.x

Vigoda-Gadot, E. (2007). Redrawing the boundaries of OCB? An empirical examination of compulsory extra-role behavior in the workplace. *Journal of Business and Psychology*, 21(3), 377–405. DOI: 10.1007/s10869-006-9034-5

Walker, D. J. (2018). Visualisation with treemaps and sunbursts in many-objective optimisation. *Genetic Programming and Evolvable Machines*, 19(3), 421–452. DOI: 10.1007/s10710-018-9329-0 PMID: 30956541

Wang, C.-H., Liang, H.-L., & Yu, Y.-C. (2024). How does workplace bullying lead to employee compulsory citizenship behavior and affect spouse well-being? Anger as the mediating role. *Current Psychology (New Brunswick, N.J.)*, 43(8), 7131–7143. DOI: 10.1007/s12144-023-04923-4

Wang, H., & Huang, Q. (2019). The dark side of feeling trusted for hospitality employees: An investigation in two service contexts. *International Journal of Hospitality Management, 76 (Part A)*, 122-131. https://doi.org/DOI: 10.1016/j.ijhm.2018.04.001

Wang, H., & Huang, Q. (2019). The dark side of feeling trusted for hospitality employees: An investigation in two service contexts. *International Journal of Hospitality Management*, 76, 122–131. DOI: 10.1016/j.ijhm.2018.04.001

Wang, S., Liu, Y., Zhang, J., & Li, S. (2023). Why, how and when the double-edged sword of workplace friendship impacts differentiated organizational citizenship behavior: A relationship motivation theory approach. *Current Psychology (New Brunswick, N.J.)*, 42(16), 13838–13855. DOI: 10.1007/s12144-022-03818-0

Wright, P. M., Dunford, B. B., & Snell, S. A. (2001). Human resources and the resource based view of the firm. *Journal of Management*, 27(6), 701–721. DOI: 10.1177/014920630102700607

Yan, E., & Ding, Y. (2011). Discovering author impact: A PageRank perspective. *Information Processing & Management*, 47(1), 125–134. https://doi.org/https://doi.org/10.1016/j.ipm.2010.05.002. DOI: 10.1016/j.ipm.2010.05.002

Yildiz, B. (2022). The reliability and validity of the compulsory citizenship behaviors (CCBs) scale: Six-step R-based psychometrics protocol among nurses in Turkey. *Perspectives in Psychiatric Care*, 58(1), 395–403. DOI: 10.1111/ppc.12805 PMID: 33908632

Yildiz, B., & Elibol, E. (2021). Turnover intention linking compulsory citizenship behaviours to social loafing in nurses: A mediation analysis. *Journal of Nursing Management*, 29(4), 653–663. DOI: 10.1111/jonm.13200 PMID: 33128815

Yildiz, B., Kaptan, Z., Yildiz, T., Elibol, E., Yildiz, H., & Ozbilgin, M. (2023). A systematic review and meta-analytic synthesis of the relationship between compulsory citizenship behaviors and its theoretical correlates [Systematic Review]. *Frontiers in Psychology*, 14, 1120209. Advance online publication. DOI: 10.3389/fpsyg.2023.1120209 PMID: 37213371

Yildiz, B., Kaptan, Z., Yildiz, T., Elibol, E., Yildiz, H., & Ozbilgin, M. (2023). A systematic review and meta-analytic synthesis of the relationship between compulsory citizenship behaviors and its theoretical correlates. *Frontiers in Psychology*, 14, 1120209. Advance online publication. DOI: 10.3389/fpsyg.2023.1120209 PMID: 37213371

Yildiz, B., Yildiz, H., & Ozbilgin, M. (2022). How do compulsory citizenship behaviors affect moral disengagement in organizations? Significance of anger toward the organization during the COVID-19 pandemic [Original Research]. *Frontiers in Psychology*, 13, 1038860. Advance online publication. DOI: 10.3389/fpsyg.2022.1038860 PMID: 36506970

Yildiz, B., Yildiz, H., & Ozbilgin, M. (2022). How do compulsory citizenship behaviors affect moral disengagement in organizations? Significance of anger toward the organization during the COVID-19 pandemic. *Frontiers in Psychology*, 13, 1038860. Advance online publication. DOI: 10.3389/fpsyg.2022.1038860 PMID: 36506970

Yin, J., Ji, Y., & Ni, Y. (2023). Does "Nei Juan" affect "Tang Ping" for hotel employees? The moderating effect of effort-reward imbalance. *International Journal of Hospitality Management*, 109, 103421. DOI: 10.1016/j.ijhm.2022.103421

Zhang, W., Liu, W., Wu, Y., Ma, C., Xiao, X., & Zhang, X. (2022). How fear of external threats plays roles: An examination of supervisors' trait anger, abusive supervision, subordinate burnout and CCB. *International Journal of Environmental Research and Public Health*, 19(24), 16810. DOI: 10.3390/ijerph192416810 PMID: 36554690

Zhang, Y., Liao, J., & Zhao, J. (2011). Research on the organizational citizenship behavior continuum and its consequences. *Frontiers of Business Research in China*, 5(3), 364. DOI: 10.1007/s11782-011-0135-2

Zhao, H., Peng, Z., & Chen, H.-K. (2014). Compulsory citizenship behavior and organizational citizenship behavior: The role of organizational identification and perceived interactional justice. *The Journal of Psychology*, 148(2), 177–196. DOI: 10.1080/00223980.2013.768591 PMID: 24684078

Zhao, H., Peng, Z., Han, Y., Sheard, G., & Hudson, A. (2013). Psychological mechanism linking abusive supervision and compulsory citizenship behavior: A moderated mediation study. *The Journal of Psychology*, 147(2), 177–195. DOI: 10.1080/00223980.2012.680522 PMID: 23469477

Zuo, W. (2022). *The relationship between compulsory citizenship behavior and job involvement*. National Research TOMSK State University.

Zwack, C., Haghani, M., Hollings, M., Zhang, L., Gauci, S., Gallagher, R., & Redfern, J. (2023). The evolution of digital health technologies in cardiovascular disease research. *npj. Digital Medicine*, 6(1), 1. DOI: 10.1038/s41746-022-00734-2 PMID: 36596833

# Chapter 9
# Exploring the Interplay Between Technostress, Digital Leadership, and Innovative Work Behavior

**Elif Bilginoglu**
https://orcid.org/0000-0003-1481-0170
*Independent Researcher, Turkey*

**Uğur Yozgat**
https://orcid.org/0000-0001-9893-3551
*İstanbul Nişantaşı Üniversitesi, Turkey*

## ABSTRACT

*Within the framework of digital transformation, this chapter examines the relationship between innovative work behavior, technostress, and digital leadership. It examines how innovation is encouraged by digital leadership while tackling issues like technostress, brought on by the usage of new digital technologies. According to the study, effective digital leadership reduces the negative consequences of technostress while simultaneously fostering innovative work behaviors of employees. Additionally, it explores the mediating role of technostress, which, depending on how employees handle the demands of the digital workplace, can either impede or strengthen the beneficial role of digital leadership in fostering innovation.*

## 1. INTRODUCTION

Leadership has long captivated the attention of philosophers and historians, who have consistently explored its significance. Over time, both human society and scholars have delved deeper into the subject, examining its complexities across various eras (Awan & Mahmood, 2010). Over the last few years, the concept of digital leadership has increased in significance, emerging as a critical determinant in driving successful organizational digital transformation. This concept has been recognized as vital for steering

DOI: 10.4018/979-8-3693-8181-6.ch009

firms through digital reforms, ensuring their adaptability and long-term sustainability in an increasingly digital environment (Karakose et al., 2022).

The transition to a digital organization has created significant leadership gaps, as the skills required for high-performing leaders today differ greatly from those of past generations. Digitalization, a global megatrend, is transforming both the internal operations and external value-adding initiatives of organizations. To stay competitive, organizations must adapt their processes and offerings in response to the ongoing digital technological advancements. In this fast-paced environment, leaders need specific skills and characteristics to effectively guide their organizations through digital transformation (Philpot & Roy, 2017; Tagscherer & Carbon, 2023). Essential skills and traits for digital leaders are; ***Visionary thinking***: Digital leaders should have the ability to foresee the future and identify opportunities for leveraging digital technologies to create value. This encompasses acknowledging advancing trends and integrating them into the organization's strategy (Kreutzer et al., 2017; McKinney, 2023; Sposato: 79). ***Adaptability***: The accelerated speed of technological evolution calls for leaders to be flexible and open to new ideas. Digital leaders must be receptive to adjust strategies and approaches as new information and technologies emerge (Bennis, 2013; Brett, 2019; Johnson, 2023; Pillay, 2024). ***Technical proficiency***: While digital leaders do not need to be experts, they should have a solid understanding of digital tools and technologies to make informed decisions and effectively communicate with technical teams (Awad, 2024: 36). ***Strong communication skills***: Effective communication is crucial for leading digital transformation. Digital leaders must articulate their vision and strategy clearly, inspire their teams, and foster open communication across the organization (Ahlquist, 2023; Sheninger, 2019; Young, 2022). ***Collaboration and team building***: Digital transformation often involves cross-functional teams working together towards common goals. Digital leaders need to build and lead collaborative teams, fostering a culture of cooperation and shared purpose (Gilli et al., 2023; Salih, 2024; Young, 2022). ***Innovation mindset***: An innovation mindset is essential for digital leaders. They ought to promote experimentation, treat failure as a valuable learning experience, and constantly explore improvements in processes and offerings through technology (Salih, 2024; Johnson, 2023). ***Customer-centric approach***: Recognizing and giving priority to customer demands is crucial in the digital era. Digital leaders must focus on creating value for customers through personalized, seamless experiences enabled by digital technologies (Cavus & Aghamiri, 2023: 244; Morgan, 2024; Ravichandran et al., 2016; Udofia, 2024). ***Change management skills***: Leading digital transformation involves managing change effectively. Digital leaders should be skilled in change management techniques, helping employees navigate the transition and addressing any resistance or challenges that arise (Busulwa, 2023; Kupiek, 2021). ***Data-driven decision-making***: Leveraging data to inform decisions is a key characteristic of digital leaders. They should be competent in interpreting data and using insights to drive strategic initiatives and measure the success of digital projects (Cavus & Aghamiri, 2023: 244; Johnson, 2023; Udofia, 2024; Unhelkar & Gonsalves, 2021). ***Resilience and persistence***: Digital transformation can be a long and challenging process. Digital leaders need to demonstrate resilience and persistence, staying committed to the vision and goals despite obstacles and setbacks (Sinclair, 2024; Udofia, 2024; Young, 2022). By embodying these skills and traits, digital leaders can efficiently address the complexities of digital transformation, ensuring their organizations stay ahead amid a fast-evolving digital world.

Digital leaders must be adept at leveraging technological advancements to enhance efficiency and drive innovation. This involves staying current with the latest digital trends and tools and understanding how to integrate them into organizational processes to streamline operations and improve productivity (Cavus & Aghamiri, 2023: 244). For instance, a digital leader might implement advanced data analytics to gain insights into customer behavior, leading to more personalized marketing strategies and improved customer satisfaction.

Furthermore, digital leaders cultivate an environment of ongoing learning and adaptability. As digital technologies evolve rapidly, it is crucial for leaders to encourage their teams to embrace new tools and methodologies. This can be achieved through regular training sessions, workshops, and promoting a growth mindset among employees. By doing so, leaders ensure that their workforce remains agile and capable of responding to technological changes (Johnson, 2023).

Effective digital leaders also need proficient interpersonal capabilities to direct diverse groups and handle complex stakeholder connections. This includes the ability to outline a distinct vision for the future, motivate and enthuse employees, and build a sense of trust and collaboration within the team (Alanazi, 2022; Dueholm Müller et al., 2024). For example, a leader who diligently considers employees' worries and delivers constructive criticism can foster a more engaged and harmonious team, which is better equipped to tackle the digital transformation challenges.

In addition to technical proficiency and strategic vision, effective digital leaders also require exceptional relational competencies to manage diverse teams and engage with complex stakeholder relationships. These skills are essential for fostering a collaborative and creative work setting, essential for successful digital transformation. By fostering open communication, inspiring and motivating employees, and building trust, digital leaders can create a team that is well equipped to tackle the challenges of digital transformation. This approach not only enhances the team's overall performance but also further contributes to a positive and innovative organizational culture (Dondi et al., 2021; Klus & Müller, 2021; Kupiek, 2021).

In addition to these skills, digital leaders must be strategic thinkers capable of envisioning and executing long-term plans that align with the digital landscape. This involves identifying opportunities for digital innovation, assessing potential risks, and making informed decisions that drive organizational growth (Brett, 2019; Sheninger, 2019). For example, a digital leader might spearhead the development of a new digital product or service that meets emerging market needs, positioning the organization as a leader in its industry.

Moreover, digital leaders should be adept at change management, as digital transformation often involves significant shifts in organizational structure, culture, and processes. Leaders need to guide their teams through these changes, addressing any resistance and ensuring a smooth transition. This requires clear communication, empathy, and the ability to manage conflicts effectively (Merlano, 2024).

By cultivating these qualities, leaders can effectively address the challenges of digital transformation and position their organizations for ongoing success. They play an essential role in merging traditional and digital business practices, ensuring that their organizations remain competitive in an increasingly digital world. Their ability to bridge this gap is crucial for maintaining relevance and obtaining continuous success in today's quick-paced, technology-led setting.

Thus, the importance of effective digital leadership is extensively highlighted in the literature, emphasizing its indispensable role in fostering organizational success. Previous research demonstrates that effective digital leadership is not only desirable but also necessary for businesses dealing with the digital age challenges, as it fosters innovation and adaptation (Brett, 2019; Kreutzer et al., 2017; Wagner, 2018).

However, as organizations embrace digital transformation under the guidance of effective digital leadership, they also face new challenges. Among these is the emergence of technostress, a phenomenon that arises from the constant integration of new digital tools and technologies into the workplace. While digital leadership fosters innovation and adaptability, it must also address the growing tension employees experience as they navigate an increasingly digital work environment (Berger et al., 2023; Marsh et al., 2022). Consequently, it becomes crucial to explore how digital leadership not only fosters innovation within organizations but also influences the psychological and operational challenges, such as technostress, that employees encounter. Understanding the balance between driving innovative work behavior and mitigating the negative impacts of technostress is essential for achieving sustainable digital transformation. Hence, this study aims to examine the dual influence of digital leadership on both innovative work behavior and technostress. It seeks to provide valuable insights into the evolving demands placed on leadership in the digital age. Understanding how digital leadership can simultaneously promote innovation and alleviate technostress will help organizations effectively confront the digital transformation challenges.

## 2. THEORETICAL BACKGROUND

### 2.1. Digital Leadership

Digital transformation is defined as the organizational changes initiated and influenced by the widespread adoption and integration of digital technologies (Hanelt et al., 2021). This process significantly influences various aspects of an organization, including its operations, value creation activities, and overall strategic direction, necessitating leaders to adapt and acquire new skills to effectively navigate this evolving landscape. This transformation has a significant impact on leadership dynamics and goes beyond technological advancements. More than merely a shift in technology, digital transformation is fueling the emergence of new leadership capabilities necessary to successfully steer through the complexity of the contemporary corporate ecosystem (Brunner et al., 2021; Imran et al., 2020; Larson & DeChurch, 2020). Executives must cultivate a trifecta of technical proficiency, adaptability, and emotional intelligence as companies increasingly employ digital tools and strategies. These abilities are crucial for encouraging innovation, guiding groups through transitions, and making informed decisions based on data-driven insights. Traditional managerial skills, including as mastery of fundamental digital tools like PowerPoint, Excel, and email, are no longer enough for leadership success in the rapidly changing digital landscape. Rather, modern leaders must be flexible in the digital realm, combining hard and soft talents to successfully lead their teams and negotiate challenging situations. This shift is driven by the increasing reliance on digital communication, remote work environments, and the need for data-driven decision-making, which demands a more nuanced approach to leadership. Consequently, the leadership mindset must adapt to align with the evolving expectations of a digitally empowered workforce (EHL Insights, 2023). In a time of intense competition and fast change, effective leaders will be those who can embrace and leverage digital technologies (Dueholm Müller et al., 2024; Katanic, 2021; Munsamy et al., 2023; Ongena et al., 2024). Accordingly, the concept of digital leadership has arisen as an essential aspect in guiding organizations through this transformation.

Digital leadership includes guiding an organization through digital transformation to uphold competitiveness and agility in a quickly transforming digital and social media realm (Digital Marketing Institute, 2024). This definition emphasizes the importance of leading an organization in adapting to digital changes to stay relevant and competitive. Digital leaders are tasked with navigating the intricacies of digital transformation, ensuring that their organizations harness new technologies effectively. This involves not only integrating cutting-edge tools and systems but also fostering a culture that embraces change, innovation, and continuous improvement. By guiding their teams through the obstacles and possibilities of the digital era, digital leaders are key players in driving organizational success and maintaining a competitive edge.

Digital leadership is a comprehensive framework aimed at developing a customer-centric, tech-enabled advanced business model by ***transforming leadership roles, skills, and styles*** (involves redefining leadership responsibilities, enhancing digital expertise, and adopting innovative leadership approaches that support digital initiatives and drive organizational innovation), ***establishing a digital organization*** (includes creating effective governance structures, articulating a clear vision, establishing core values, designing a flexible organizational structure, fostering a digital culture, and refining decision-making processes to support digital transformation) and ***optimizing people management and collaboration*** (entails improving strategies for managing a diverse and digitally proficient workforce, enhancing the effectiveness of virtual teams, facilitating knowledge sharing, and improving communication and collaboration to align with digital objectives) (Eberl & Drews, 2021).

## 2.2. Technostress

Technostress is a specific form of stress that arises from the increasing use of information and communication technologies in the workplace. As organizations adopt new digital tools to keep up with dynamic markets and gain competitive advantage, employees are required to continuously adapt to evolving work demands. While these technologies enable constant connectivity (Tarafdar et al., 2014), they also introduce stress for individuals, particularly as they struggle to meet the pressures of an ever-changing digital work environment. This phenomenon has been well documented in the literature (Ayyagari et al., 2011; Tarafdar et al., 2007). The concept of technostress is often used interchangeably with *"digital stress"*, highlighting the pervasive impact of digitalization on workplace well-being (Wrede et al., 2023). Given the continuous growth of digitalization across various sectors such as business, public administration, and society, it is anticipated that this issue will remain a significant area of interest for both research and practical implementation (Calderon-Monge & Ribeiro-Soriano, 2024).

The term technostress was conceived originally by Brod (1984: 16) to denote *"a modern disease caused by one's inability to cope or deal with technology in a healthy manner"*. This concept has become increasingly significant as technology continues to develop and penetrate various aspects of life. Since its initial mention in practitioner writings during the 1980s and 1990s (Nastjuk et al., 2024: 361), in recent years, technostress has become increasingly significant across various fields (Torres, 2021). The growing relevance of technostress highlights its widespread impact on both organizational performance and individual well-being. In the field of information systems management, technostress is a critical concern, as employees are frequently required to use various digital tools and platforms to perform their job functions. The rapid pace of technological change can overwhelm employees, reducing their productivity and job satisfaction. Organizations must implement strategies to mitigate technostress, such as providing ongoing training, promoting a balanced approach to technology use, and creating a supportive work environment. Within organizational behavior, technostress is examined in terms of its impact on employee performance and well-being. High levels of technostress can negatively affect job performance, reduce job satisfaction, and increase turnover intentions. Understanding the factors that contribute to technostress and developing effective interventions is crucial for maintaining a healthy and productive workforce. Organizations can benefit from fostering a culture that supports continuous learning and adaptability, helping employees manage the demands of technological change. In the realm of occupational health psychology, technostress is explored as a factor influencing overall employee health and well-being. This field examines how the demands of technology use can lead to stress-related health problems and investigates strategies to promote healthier interactions with technology. For instance, encouraging regular breaks, setting boundaries for technology use, and promoting physical activity can help alleviate the adverse effects of technostress. Overall, technostress has emerged as a significant issue in recent years, affecting various aspects of work and personal life. As technology continues to evolve and integrate more deeply into our daily routines, it is essential to address the challenges associated with technostress. By understanding its sources and impacts, both organizations and individuals can develop strategies to mitigate its effects and promote overall well-being.

Technostress, a concept introduced by Weil and Rosen (1997), is understood in two significant ways. Firstly, it refers to any negative impact on human attitudes, thoughts, behaviors, and psychology that results directly or indirectly from technology. Secondly, as described by Tarafdar et al. (2007), it concerns the stress experienced by individuals because of using information systems, originating from the demands these systems impose on them.

Technostress is a multifaceted phenomenon that encompasses various dimensions of human interaction with technology. As technology becomes an integral part of daily life, both in personal and professional spheres, the implications of technostress become more pronounced.

Technostress, like to general stress, is a process contingent upon an individual's experience and evaluation (Califf et al., 2020; Tarafdar et al., 2017); yet, it is frequently characterized as the *"dark side"* of technology (Bondanini et al., 2020; Delpechitre et al., 2019; Salanova et al., 2013; Tarafdar et al., 2020). In this context, technostress creators are identified as the key drivers behind the onset of technostress. The term *"technostress creators"* refers to factors that cause stress due to integration of ICT in the work environment (Torres, 2021), including techno-overload, -invasion, -insecurity, -complexity, and -uncertainty (Ragu-Nathan et al., 2008; Tarafdar et al (2007). Molino et al. (2020) proposed a brief version of these technostress creators, focusing on three key dimensions: techno-overload, -invasion, and -complexity. These three dimensions were specifically highlighted, as they are particularly relevant in today's context, where the integration of technologies for work-related purposes is forecasted to increase, partly due to the rise of remote working. Given these conditions, the impression of technology overload, the hazard of work and technology penetrating personal life, and the complexities of navigating technology can be significant stress sources. Information and communication technologies induce stress due to their complexity, frequent changes, steep learning curves, increased workload, the demand for excessive multitasking, and the technical issues and errors that often accompany those (Ragu-Nathan et al., 2008: 422).

Leaders play an essential role in the digital transformation process by guiding and supporting their followers as they navigate challenges such as the constant need to acquire new technological skills (Cortellazzo et al., 2019). To mitigate the effects of technostress on employees, strong leadership is required (Nastjuk et al., 2024). Leaders' ability to help employees adapt to new organizational realities and continuous sociotechnical changes is crucial to the success of digital transformation initiatives (Karimi & Walter, 2015).

With the increasing integration of digital technologies in the workplace, employees are facing greater challenges. Consequently, leadership must evolve to address these demands, offering the necessary support to help employees manage the pressures of digital work, thereby ensuring that their capacity and motivation to perform are maintained (Rademaker et al., 2023).

Based on the reviewed literature, the following hypothesis is proposed:

$H_1$: Digital leadership alleviates technostress.

This hypothesis suggests that effective digital leadership can reduce the stress employees experience due to the demands and changes associated with technology. In other words, when leaders adeptly manage digital tools and guide their teams through technological transitions, they can help mitigate the negative impacts of technostress, thereby fostering a more supportive and productive work environment.

## 2.3. Innovative Work Behavior

In today's digital landscape, an organization's ability to innovate is critical for maintaining a competitive edge. Leveraging employees' creative ideas to improve products, services, and workflows is one way to address the growing demand for innovation (Curzi et al., 2019; Kmieciak, 2021). Organizational innovation is driven by creative work behaviors demonstrated by its staff (Hock-Doepgen et al., 2024). Thus, fostering individual innovation becomes a key skill employees need to possess, which directly affects how managers inspire and evaluate their teams (Curzi et al., 2019).

In this scenario, grasping the influences that promote personal innovative conduct is vital for enhancing an organization's innovation capacity (Gao and Gao, 2024; Hermundsdottir & Aspelund, 2021; Kor et al., 2022).

Innovative work behavior refers to the origination, adoption, and utilization of new concepts for products, technological advancements, and work methodologies used by employees (Yuan & Woodman, 2010). Various scholars as follows (i) it involves the actions of staff members who bring forth new and beneficial ideas in their workplace activities and services (Xu and Suntrayuth, 2022) describe employee innovation behavior, (ii) it is characterized as a purposeful strategy by employees aimed at achieving organizational goals and objectives through the generation, management, and implementation of novel ideas. This approach helps the organization gain a competitive edge and ensures sustainability (Bawuro et al., 2019), (iii) It encompasses the combination of physical and mental work activities performed by employees, whether individually or in groups, to complete tasks necessary for developing innovations (Messmann (2012), (iv) innovation behavior is viewed as the set of activities through which employees generate and implement new ideas, products, or processes to benefit the organization. It involves both the creation and application of knowledge to achieve organizational improvement and adaptation (Mumford and Gustafson, 1988). These definitions collectively emphasize that employee innovation behavior is not just about having new ideas but also about effectively implementing these ideas to drive organizational success. It is anticipated that innovative work behavior will result in creative and advantageous outcomes for people, teams, or organizations (Bos-Nehles & Veenendaal, 2017). The development of new manufacturing techniques and management systems, as well as the extension and renewal of existing goods, services, protocols, and processes, are examples of these innovative outputs (Crossan & Apaydin, 2010).

Innovative work behavior is recognized as one of the most critical characteristics that organizations require in today's competitive landscape (Anderson et al., 2014). According to Anderson et al. (2004), innovative behaviors by employees, which were once viewed as inappropriate, disrespectful, or even subversive, are now highly sought after by organizations striving to compete in a fast-paced and ever-changing global business landscape. These behaviors, when exercised appropriately, can drive significant improvements in adaptability, creativity, and overall organizational success, underscoring the necessity of nurturing a culture that supports and prizes innovation. This emphasizes how such behaviors, when aligned with the organization's goals and values can greatly benefit the workplace.

The studies (e.g., Ayoub et al., 2023; Parnitvitidkun, 2021; Parnitvitidkun et al., 2024) further supports this, revealing that employees' innovative work behavior is a crucial source of competitive advantage.

Previous research consistently highlights the strong link between leadership and innovative work behavior, showing a positive relationship between these variables (Mumford et al., 2002; Judge & Piccolo, 2004; Jaskyte, 2004; Khan et al., 2012; Deprez & Euwema, 2017; Contreras et al., 2017; Alheeta et al., 2021;). However, Erhan et al. (2022) noted a critical gap in the literature regarding the influence of digital leadership on innovative work behavior. Despite the increasing integration of digital technologies in the workplace, either research exploring how digital leaders foster or hinder innovation among employees remains limited. This gap in understanding poses challenges for organizations seeking to leverage digital leadership to enhance their innovative capabilities. The lack of studies on this topic underscores the need for further research to better comprehend the dynamics between digital leadership and innovation in today's work environment.

It is undeniable that employees are the driving force behind organizations, and their innovative actions are vital to the organization's innovation performance. Therefore, organizations must implement strategies that promote employees' willingness to innovate and foster their innovative behaviors (Li & Zheng, 2014).

A successful digital workplace that fosters employee innovation is largely driven by effective digital leadership (Zulu & Khosrowshahi, 2021), crucial for promoting innovation within organizations (Adair, 2009; Oke et al., 2009; Yuan & Khan, 2024), facilitates rapid decision-making, manages digital transformation change (Kohli & Johnson, 2011). Effective digital leaders not only need to stay ahead of the latest technological advancements and set an example for continuous learning but also cultivate an environment that encourages innovation within their teams (Malakyan, 2019). Furthermore, recent research demonstrates that digital leadership significantly enhances a company's innovative performance by leveraging digital tools, thereby contributing to long-term sustainability (Benitez et al., 2022).

Based on the reviewed literature, the following hypothesis is proposed:

$H_2$: Digital leadership increases employees' innovative work behavior.

This hypothesis suggests that leadership styles and strategies that effectively leverage digital tools and technologies can enhance the innovative behaviors of employees. Essentially, it posits that when leaders effectively incorporate digital solutions and demonstrate digital competency, they are likely to inspire and motivate their employees to engage in innovative activities and contribute creatively to the organization's goals.

As digital transformation advances, employees are not only expected to continuously innovate, but also to adapt to rapidly evolving digital environments. However, this can lead to technostress, which may interfere with their ability to engage in innovative work behavior. While digital leadership is typically seen as a positive force that encourages innovation, technostress can act as a counterbalancing factor, potentially mediating this relationship. Specifically, technostress could either amplify or reduce the impact of digital leadership on innovative work behavior, depending on how well employees manage the stress associated with digital tools and environments (Califf et al., 2020; Tarafdar et al., 2017).

This mediating effect is crucial in understanding the dynamics between leadership and innovation within a digital context. If employees experience high levels of technostress, it may impede their capacity to innovate, even under strong digital leadership. Conversely, with effective stress management strategies in place, the negative impact of technostress might be mitigated, allowing digital leadership to have a more pronounced positive effect on innovation.

Based on the reviewed literature, the following hypothesis is proposed:

$H_3$: Technostress mediates the relationship between digital leadership and employees' innovative work behavior.

This hypothesis suggests that the stress experienced by employees due to technological changes and demands (technostress) plays a crucial role in influencing how digital leadership affects their innovative behaviors at work.

## 3. METHOD

### 3.1. Proposed Model

The proposed research model can be found below (Figure 1).

*Figure 1. Proposed research model*

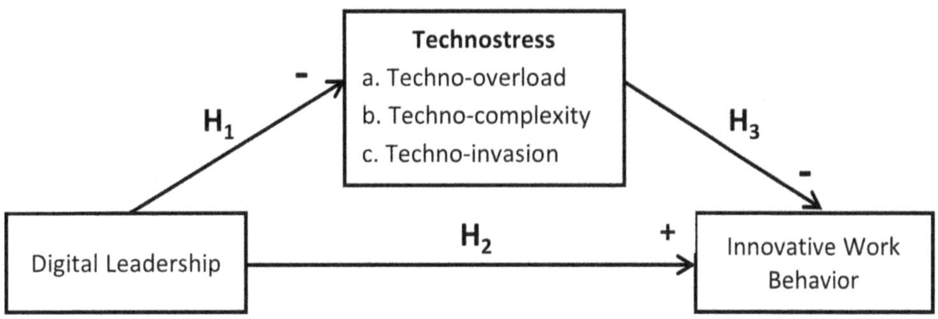


### 3.2. Participants and Procedure

As noted by KPMG (2022: 5), digital leaders are sitting everywhere in the organization, a single Chief Digital Officer etc. is no longer responsible for enterprise-wide transformation like in older days. Drawing from this perspective, we identified all employees within the organization as the target sample for this study. By involving a broad cross-section of the workforce, we aim to capture a comprehensive understanding of how digital leadership, irrespective of hierarchical position, influences both innovative work behavior and the experience of technostress. This approach aligns with the view that digital transformation is no longer the sole responsibility of top leadership but a shared organizational endeavor.

### 3.3. Hypotheses

Based on a review of the literature, the following hypotheses are proposed:

$H_1$: Digital leadership alleviates technostress.
$H_{1a}$: Digital leadership alleviates techno-overload.
$H_{1b}$: Digital leadership alleviates techno-complexity.

$H_{1c}$: Digital leadership alleviates techno-invasion.
$H_2$: Digital leadership increases employees' innovative work behavior.
$H_3$: Technostress alleviates employees' innovative work behavior.
$H_{2a}$: Techno-overload alleviates employees' innovative work behavior.
$H_{2b}$: Techno-complexity alleviates employees' innovative work behavior.
$H_{2c}$: Techno-invasion alleviates employees' innovative work behavior.
$H_4$: Technostress mediates the relationship between digital leadership and employees' innovative work behavior.
$H_{4a}$: Techno-overload mediates the relationship between digital leadership and employees' innovative work behavior.
$H_{4b}$: Techno-complexity mediates the relationship between digital leadership and employees' innovative work behavior.
$H_{4c}$: Techno-invasion mediates the relationship between digital leadership and employees' innovative work behavior.

## 3.4. Measures

Measuring digital leadership, the-6-item Digital Leadership scale developed by Zeike et al (2019) was used.

To measure technostress levels, we employed the 11-item Technostress Creators Scale developed by Molino et al. (2020). This scale is well-recognized in academic literature and addresses three key dimensions of technostress; ***techno-overload*** (captures the stress caused by the excessive demands of technology, leading employees to work faster and longer hours), ***techno-invasion*** (highlights how technology blurs the boundaries between work and personal life, causing employees to feel constantly connected and unable to disconnect from work) and ***techno-complexity*** (deals with the stress and frustration arising from the complexity of new technologies, which can make employees feel overwhelmed and incompetent).

By utilizing this scale, we aim to gain a comprehensive understanding of the specific stressors faced by employees due to technology use. This helps provide a reliable and valid assessment of technostress in the context of digital leadership and innovation.

To measure employees' innovative work behavior, we used the 9-item scale developed by Janssen (2000, 2001) and later adapted into Turkish by Önhon (2016). This scale assesses various aspects of innovative behavior, including idea-generation, -promotion, and -realization.

## 3.5. Results

Demographics, hypothesis tests and results are below.

### 3.5.1. Demographics

426 volunteers working in different sectors in İstanbul participated; age ranging 18 to 55 years old (M = 31.43, Std.Dev.= 8.07), tenure 8.52 years (Std.Dev. = 6.77), were married (55.2%), mostly male (58.0%), and have a university degree (49.1%)

### 3.5.2. Hypothesis Testing

The correlations between the studied variables were analyzed using SPSS Statistics software, version 21.0. This software is well regarded for its robust statistical analysis capabilities, making it an ideal choice for examining the relationships between the variables in our study.

To assess the effects of the hypothesized variables, we employed Structural Equation Modeling (SEM). Following the methodology suggested by Preacher and Hayes (2004), we used LISREL 9.1 for our SEM analysis. LISREL (Linear Structural Relations) is a specialized software package designed for structural equation modeling. We incorporated 5,000 bootstrap samples into our analysis. Bootstrapping is a resampling method that allows for more accurate estimation of the sampling distribution of a statistic, providing confidence intervals that are more reliable. This approach helps to address potential biases in the estimates, ensuring that the confidence intervals are more accurate and reflective of the true population parameters. By using this comprehensive and rigorous approach, we were able to obtain robust and reliable results, validating the proposed hypotheses and providing a deeper understanding of the relationships among the variables in our study.

None of the items were deleted because all of the loading are greater than 0.50. According to items' factor loadings (≥ .50) and construct reliability values (≥ .70) of the scales shown in Figure 1 necessary conditions were fulfilled (Hair et al., 2005).

*Table 1. Cronbachs' alpha, average value extracted (AVE), composite reliability (CR) values and factor loadings*

| | Items' Factor Loadings (r>0.5) | AVE (AVE>0.5) | CR (CR>0.7) | Cronbach's Alpha |
|---|---|---|---|---|
| *Digital Leadership (DL)* | | *.618* | *.907* | *.903* |
| DL6 | .843 | | | |
| DL5 | .818 | | | |
| DL3 | .775 | | | |
| DL4 | .762 | | | |
| DL1 | .760 | | | |
| DL2 | .756 | | | |
| ***Technostress*** | | | | |
| ***Techno-overload (TO)*** | | ***.659*** | ***.884*** | ***.845*** |
| TO4 | .918 | | | |
| TO2 | .883 | | | |
| TO3 | .716 | | | |
| TO1 | .707 | | | |
| ***Techno-complexity (TC)*** | | ***.597*** | ***.856*** | ***.819*** |
| TC2 | .814 | | | |
| TC1 | .774 | | | |
| TC3 | .759 | | | |
| TC4 | .742 | | | |

continued on following page

*Table 1. Continued*

| | Items' Factor Loadings (r>0.5) | AVE (AVE>0.5) | CR (CR>0.7) | Cronbach's Alpha |
|---|---|---|---|---|
| *Digital Leadership (DL)* | | *.618* | *.907* | *.903* |
| ***Techno-invasion (TI)*** | | ***.513*** | ***.867*** | ***.804*** |
| TI2 | .847 | | | |
| TI1 | .848 | | | |
| TI3 | .785 | | | |
| ***Innovative Work Behavior (IWB)*** | | ***.572*** | ***.923*** | ***.928*** |
| IWB2 | .827 | | | |
| IWB4 | .794 | | | |
| IWB7 | .773 | | | |
| IWB3 | .773 | | | |
| IWB5 | .755 | | | |
| IWB1 | .731 | | | |
| IWB6 | .729 | | | |
| IWB9 | .710 | | | |
| IWB8 | .704 | | | |

When the square root of the Average Variance Extracted (AVE) values for all latent constructs surpasses the correlation coefficients between each focal construct and other constructs, it demonstrates that the constructs are distinct from one another. This finding not only highlights the discriminant validity of the constructs but also reinforces the credibility and soundness of the constructs used in the study. This validation process not only ensures the robustness of the study's findings but also lays a strong foundation for future research.

*Table 2. Constructs' correlation matrix*

| | Mean | Std.Dev. | 1 | 2 | 3 | 4 | 5 |
|---|---|---|---|---|---|---|---|
| ***Digital Leadership*** | 3.623 | 1.140 | *(.786)* | | | | |
| ***Techno-overload*** | 4.107 | 1.195 | -.280*** | *(.812)* | | | |
| ***Techno-complexity*** | 3.713 | 1.016 | -.206*** | .164*** | *(.773)* | | |
| ***Techno-invasion*** | 3.400 | 1.161 | -.228*** | .164*** | .358*** | *(.716)* | |
| ***Innovative Work Behavior*** | 3.290 | 1.176 | .472*** | -.440*** | -.293*** | -.302*** | *(.756)* |

*** $p < 0.001$.

Note: The diagonal values in brackets are the squared root of AVE of each construct

The best fitting fit indices were chosen (Hooper et al., 2008). According to the structural models' fit indices, here indices' values (CFI = .91, IFI = .91, and NNFI = .90) exceeding .90 and $\mathcal{X}^2$/df) = 2.93, RMSEA = .065 proves a good and acceptable model fit for proposed structural model (Schumacker & Lomax, 2010).

Table 3 illustrates that digital leadership significantly influenced by techno-overload, complexity and invasion (β = -.280***/-.206***/-.228***) - $H_1$ ($H_{1a}$/$H_{1b}$/$H_{1c}$) was supported and innovative employees' work behavior (β = .472***) - $H_2$ was supported. $H_3$ ($H_{3a}$/$H_{3b}$/$H_{3c}$) was also supported where the results indicated that employees' by techno-overload, complexity and invasion affect their innovative work behavior (β = -.440***/-.293***/-.302***).

Rules suggested by Baron and Kenny (1986) were strictly followed by the determination of employees' technostress mediation effect in the relationships between digital leadership and employees' innovative work behavior. To test the mediating effect of employees' technostress between digital leadership and employees' innovative work behavior, where the hypotheses $H_1$ ($H_{1a}$/$H_{1b}$/$H_{1c}$) (DL → TO/TC/TI), $H_2$ (DL → IWB) and $H_3$ ($H_{3a}$/$H_{3b}$/$H_{3c}$) (TO/TC/TI → IWB) were supported, at the last step DL and TO/TC/TI were simultaneously fed into the model. Recorded growth in $R^2$ and decline in standardized beta values with improved input constructs the partially mediating effects of TO/TC/TI between DL and IWB (Baron & Kenny, 1986). In addition, the hypothesis $H_4$ ($H_{4a}$/$H_{4b}$/$H_{4c}$) has been supported.

*Table 3. Direct hypothesized and mediated models' regression weights*

| Hypothesis | β (beta) | t-value | F-value | $R^2$ | $R^2$ | Tol. | VIF | Sobel | |
|---|---|---|---|---|---|---|---|---|---|
| DL → TO | -.206*** | -4.327 | 18.727 | .042 | | | | | $H_{1a}$✓ |
| DL → TC | -.281*** | -6.026 | 36.314 | .079 | | | | | $H_{1b}$✓ |
| DL → TI | -.228*** | -4.832 | 23.350 | .052 | | | | | $H_{1c}$✓ |
| DL → IWB | .472*** | 11.026 | 121.580 | .223 | | | | | $H_2$✓ |
| TO → IWB | -.293*** | -6.308 | 39.789 | .086 | | | | | $H_{3a}$✓ |
| TC → IWB | -.439*** | -10.075 | 101.500 | .193 | | | | | $H_{3b}$✓ |
| TI → IWB | -.302*** | -6.525 | 42.574 | .091 | | | | | $H_{3c}$✓ |
| DL → IWB<br>TO → IWB | .430***<br>-.204*** | 10.081<br>-4.793 | 75.428 | .263 | .040 | .958 | 1.044 | 3.579** | $H_{4a}$✓ |
| DL → IWB<br>TC → IWB | .378***<br>-.333*** | 9.094<br>-8.005 | 101.879 | .325 | .102 | .921 | 1.086 | 5.230** | $H_{4b}$✓ |
| DL → IWB<br>TI → IWB | .425***<br>-.205*** | 9.916<br>-4.778 | 75.336 | .263 | .040 | .948 | 1.055 | 4.232** | $H_{4c}$✓ |

SPSS macro PROCESS Model 4 of PROCESS (Hayes, 2013) with digital leadership as a predictor and innovative work behavior as an outcome with technostress as mediator was used to calculate the following estimates (10,000 bootstrap samples, 95% bias-corrected confidence intervals for the indirect effect): (a) standardized paths from DL to IWB (before and after controlling for the coping variables (CV) TO/TI/TC), (b) standardized path from DL to the CV (TO/TC/TI), (c) standardized path from the CV (TO/TC/TI) to IWB, (d) the indirect effects (the pathways from DL to IWB through TO/TC/TI). Indirect effects emerged for proposed mediator. Heightened technostress reduced through digital leadership fostered interest in innovative work behavior, completely indirect effect -.0443, 95% CI [.0170, .0744] / .0965, 95% CI [.0576, .1395] / .0438, 95% CI [.0203, .0839]. See Figures 2, 3, and 4.

*Figure 2. Mediational pathways of digital leadership on innovative work behavior with techno-overload as mediator*

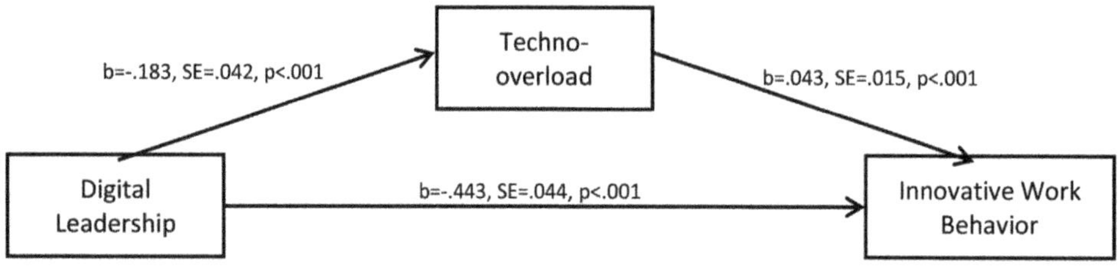


*Figure 3. Mediational pathways of digital leadership on innovative work behavior with techno-complexity as mediator*

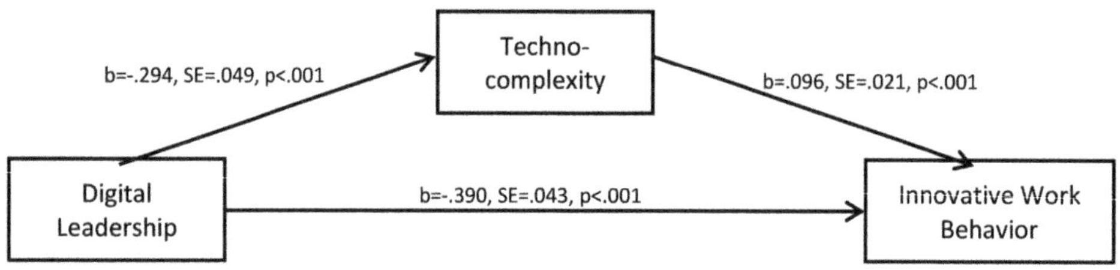


*Figure 4. Mediational pathways of digital leadership on innovative work behavior with techno-invasion as mediator*

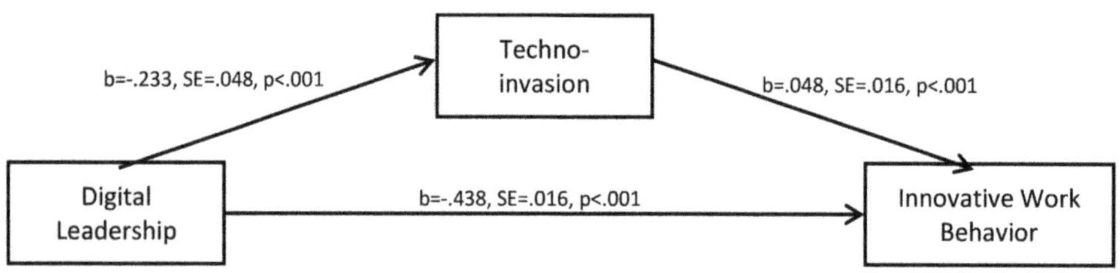


## 4. CONCLUSION

Leadership has gained significant research focus due to its profound effect on organizational achievement (Spagnoli et al., 2020). Leaders are essential in designing organizational atmospheres where challenges are transformed into opportunities for remarkable achievements (Kouzes & Posner, 2017). This impact of leaders on organizational success has become even more evident with the dynamics of change created by digitalization (Tagscherer & Carbon, 2023)

Although leaders face difficulties because of digital transformation (Bartsch et al., 2021), digital leadership facilitates organizations in dealing with risks and recurring uncertainties (Fenwick et al., 2021). In this process, digital leadership stands out as a concept that allows organizations to respond swiftly to evolving environmental circumstances. Digital leadership is a new topic that has gained interest from several different areas (Cortellazzo et al., 2019; Tigre et al., 2023: 40). This study explores the complex interplay between digital leadership, technostress, and innovative work behavior in the context of digital transformation. The findings indicate that effective digital leadership is crucial for promoting innovation and easing the detrimental effects of technostress on personnel. Digital leaders foster innovation by creating environments that are both creative and adaptable. They also alleviate technostress by offering the necessary guidance and resources to help employees manage the challenges associated with digital tools and work settings.

The three features of technostress indicators; techno-overload/-invasion /–complexity emerge as significant factors in this relationship. Techno-overload refers to the excessive workload created by technology, while techno-invasion highlights the intrusion of work into personal time through constant connectivity. Techno-complexity, on the other hand, deals with the challenge of learning and using new technologies effectively. This study demonstrates that digital leadership plays a crucial role in mitigating these stressors, allowing employees to engage more effectively in innovative work behavior.

The mediating role of technostress emerges as a crucial factor influencing the overall effectiveness of digital leadership in enhancing innovative work behavior. While digital leadership generally promotes innovation, high levels of technostress can hinder its positive effects. However, with appropriate leadership strategies and interventions to manage stress, organizations can optimize the benefits of digital leadership while minimizing the challenges technostress imposes.

Additionally, this study aligns with existing research that emphasizes the fundamental significance of leadership in managing technostress and fostering innovation within organizations. For instance, Ly and Ly (2024) demonstrated that various leadership styles significantly influence technostress levels among employees. Their research suggests that leadership approaches can either exacerbate or alleviate the stress caused by technological demands. Supportive leadership, for example, helps employees navigate technology-related stress more effectively.

Rademaker et al. (2023) further support this by showing that effective leadership can reduce technostress among employees. Leaders who engage with their teams, provide emotional support, and encourage open communication can help employees manage technology-related stressors, ultimately improving job satisfaction and productivity.

Similarly, Sary et al. (2023) discovered that digital competency in leaders positively impacts innovative work behavior. Leaders proficient in digital tools inspire their employees to engage in creative and innovative activities, motivating them to think imaginatively and develop original solutions.

Research conducted by Turel and Gaudioso (2018) underscores the crucial role of a constructive leadership atmosphere in preventing employees from seeing technology as a source of stress. Leaders who establish a supportive work environment can help employees view technology as an empowering tool rather than a source of stress. This supportive approach encourages greater adoption of innovative practices by creating an atmosphere where employees feel confident and capable in their use of technology. A positive leadership climate can include several elements; ***open communication*** (Leaders who foster open and transparent communication can address employees' concerns and provide clarity on how to effectively use technology), ***training and development*** (Offering continuous training and development opportunities is key for furnishing employees with the skills they need to master new technologies.), ***recognition and support*** (Acknowledging employees' efforts and providing support when they encounter challenges can reduce the stress associated with technological change), and ***encouraging Innovation*** (Leaders who encourage experimentation and reward innovative ideas create a culture where employees feel safe to explore and adopt new technologies). By cultivating a positive leadership climate, organizations can significantly reduce technostress and enhance the overall well-being and productivity of their workforce.

Moreover, Tigre et al. (2023) noted that digital leadership goes beyond managing technology; it represents a mindset and practice-based approach crucial in challenging times. Addressing aspects of technostress such as techno-overload/-invasion/-complexity is essential for balancing digital tool management and fostering a culture of innovation.

Studies by Ahmed et al. (2024), Erhan et al. (2022), Salam (2023), and Gao and Gao (2024) reveal that ability to adeptly navigate digital transformation and provide the necessary resources and guidance encourages employees to take initiative and engage in innovative practices, ultimately benefiting the organization. Effective digital leadership directly and beneficially influences the cultivation of an innovative organizational culture, supporting the argument that such leadership enhances employee innovation.

Additionally, Benitez et al. (2022) found that digital leadership boosts an organization's innovation outcomes. Leaders who embrace digital tools and strategies can significantly boost their organization's innovative capabilities. Abbas et al. (2024) reinforced this by highlighting that digital leadership drives innovative work by fostering creativity and progress within the organization.

Integrating these findings, it is clear that digital leadership not only helps manage technostress but also plays a crucial role in promoting and sustaining innovation within organizations. This underscores the importance of developing digital leadership skills to handle the complexities of the current workplace and drive continuous improvement and innovation.

Future research should focus on measuring and evaluating the technostress experienced by leaders themselves, broadening the current understanding beyond employee experiences. Leaders, who are responsible for managing teams and navigating complex digital transformations, often face significant pressures that can exacerbate technostress. Assessing how these stressors affect leadership abilities, decision-making processes, and overall effectiveness would provide valuable insights into leadership performance and organizational outcomes (Madden, 2024). Additionally, future research should investigate how the three dimensions of technostress (techno-overload/-invasion/-complexity) evolve as new digital technologies are introduced in the workplace. Understanding how leadership can adapt to these evolving stressors is crucial for sustaining innovation in digitally transforming organizations.

In conclusion, as the interest in digital leadership grows, its profound influence on both innovation and technostress becomes clearer. Future studies should explore leadership strategies that can effectively manage technostress and enhance innovative work behavior in rapidly evolving digital environments. These insights will be instrumental in developing leadership programs that equip leaders with the resilience and skills needed to thrive in the digital age.

## REFERENCES


Abbas, S. M., Latif, M., & Sarwar, F. (2024). Digital Leadership and Innovative Work Behavior in IT Sector: The Mediating Role of Digital Entrepreneurial Orientation and Digital Organizational Culture. *Employee Responsibilities and Rights Journal*. Advance online publication. DOI: 10.1007/s10672-024-09503-7

Adair, J. (2009). *Leadership for Innovation: How to Organize Team Creativity and Harvest Ideas*. Kogan Page.

Ahlquist, J. (2023). *Digital Leadership in Higher Education: Purposeful Social Media in a Connected World*. Routledge. DOI: 10.4324/9781003444244

Ahmed, F., Naqshbandi, M. M., Waheed, M., & Ain, N. U. (2024). Digital Leadership and Innovative Work Behavior: impact of LMX, Learning Orientation and Innovation Capabilities, Management Decision, Vol. ahead-of-print No. ahead-of-print. https://doi.org/DOI: 10.1108/MD-04-2023-0654

Alanazi, A. T. (2022). Digital Leadership: Attributes of Modern Healthcare Leaders. *Cureus*, 14(2), e21969. DOI: 10.7759/cureus.21969 PMID: 35282530

Alheeta, A. F., Al Adwanb, A., Areiqatc, A. Y., Zamild, A. M. A., & Saleh, M. A. (2021). The Effect of Leadership Styles on Employees' Innovative Work Behavior. *Management Science Letters*, 11, 239–246. DOI: 10.5267/j.msl.2020.8.010

Anderson, N., De Dreu, C. K. W., & Nijstad, B. A. (2004). The Routinization of Innovation Research: A Constructively Critical Review of the State-of-the- Science. *Journal of Organizational Behavior*, 25(2), 147–173. DOI: 10.1002/job.236

Anderson, N., Potočnik, K., & Zhou, J. (2014). Innovation and Creativity in Organizations: A State-of-the- science Review, Prospective Commentary, and Guiding Framework. *Journal of Management*, 40(5), 1297–1333. DOI: 10.1177/0149206314527128

Awad, E. M. (2024). *Managing Corporate Knowledge in the Digital Age: The Hidden Power*. International Technology Group Ltd.

Awan, M. R., & Mahmood, K. (2010). Relationship among Leadership Style, Organizational Culture and Employee Commitment in University Libraries. *Library Management*, 31(4/5), 253–266. DOI: 10.1108/01435121011046326

Ayoub, A. E. H., Almahamid, S. M., & Al Salah, L. F. (2023). Innovative Work Behavior Scale: Development and Validation of Psychometric Properties in Higher Education in the GCC Countries. *European Journal of Innovation Management*, 26(1), 119–133. DOI: 10.1108/EJIM-04-2021-0176

Ayyagari, R., Grover, V., & Purvis, R. (2011). Technostress: Technological Antecedents and Implications. *Management Information Systems Quarterly*, 35(4), 831–858. DOI: 10.2307/41409963

Baron, R. M., & Kenny, D. A. (1986). The Moderator-Mediator Variable Distinction in Social Psychological Research: Conceptual, Strategic, and Statistical Considerations. *Journal of Personality and Social Psychology*, 51(6), 1173–1182. DOI: 10.1037/0022-3514.51.6.1173 PMID: 3806354

Bartsch, S., Weber, E., Büttgen, M., & Huber, A. (2021). Leadership Matters in Crisis-induced Digital Transformation: How to Lead Service Employees Effectively during the COVID-19 Pandemic. *Journal of Service Management*, 32(1), 71–85. DOI: 10.1108/JOSM-05-2020-0160

Bawuro, F., Shamsuddin, A., Wahab, E., & Chodozie, C. (2019). Prosocial Motivation and Innovative Behavior: An Empirical Analysis of Selected Public University Lecturers in Nigeria. *International Journal of Scientific & Technology Research*, 8(9), 1187–1194.

Benitez, J., Arenas, A., Castillo, A., & Esteves, J. (2022). Impact of Digital Leadership Capability on Innovation Performance: The Role of Platform Digitization Capability. *Information & Management*, 59(2), 103590. DOI: 10.1016/j.im.2022.103590

Bennis, W. (2013). Leadership in a Digital World: Embracing Transparency and Adaptive Capacity. *Management Information Systems Quarterly*, 37(2), 635–636.

Berger, M., Schäfer, R., Schmidt, M., Regal, C., & Gimpel, H. (2023). How to Prevent Technostress at the Digital Workplace: A Delphi Study. *Journal of Business Economics*. Advance online publication. DOI: 10.1007/s11573-023-01159-3 PMID: 38625156

Bondanini, G., Giorgi, G., Ariza-Montes, A., Vega-Muñoz, A., & Andreucci-Annunziata, P. (2020). Technostress Dark Side of Technology in the Workplace: A Scientometric Analysis. *International Journal of Environmental Research and Public Health*, 17(21), 8013. DOI: 10.3390/ijerph17218013 PMID: 33143270

Bos-Nehles, A. C., & Veenendaal, A. A. R. (2017). Perceptions of HR Practices and Innovative Work Behavior: The Moderating Effect of an Innovative Climate. *International Journal of Human Resource Management*, 30(18), 2661–2683. DOI: 10.1080/09585192.2017.1380680

Brett, J. (2019). *Evolving Digital Leadership: How to Be a Digital Leader in Tomorrow's Disruptive World*. Apress. DOI: 10.1007/978-1-4842-3606-2

Brod, C. (1984). *Technostress: The Human Cost of the Computer Revolution*. Addison-Wesley.

Brunner, M., Gonzalez-Castañé, G., & Ravesteijn, P. (2021). How Digital Leadership Competences and IT Capabilities Affect an Organization's Ability to Digitally Transform and Adopt New Technologies. *Journal of International Technology and Information Management*, 30(4), 7. Advance online publication. DOI: 10.58729/1941-6679.1526

Busulwa, R. (2023). *Navigating Digital Transformation in Management*. Routledge.

Calderon-Monge, E., & Ribeiro-Soriano, D. (2024). *The Role of Digitalization in Business and Management: A Systematic Literature Review,* Review of Managerial Science. *Review of Managerial Science*, 18(2), 449–491. DOI: 10.1007/s11846-023-00647-8

Califf, C. B., Sarker, S., & Sarker, S. (2020). The Bright and Dark Sides of Technostress: A Mixed-Methods Study Involving Healthcare IT. *Management Information Systems Quarterly*, 44(2), 809–856. DOI: 10.25300/MISQ/2020/14818

Cavus, N., & Aghamiri, S. (2023). Conceptual Intelligence, Digital Transformation, and Leadership Skills: Key Concepts for Modern Business Success. In Daimi, K., Alsadoon, A., & Coelho, L. (Eds.), *Cutting Edge Applications of Computational Intelligence Tools and Techniques* (pp. 231–253). Springer Nature. DOI: 10.1007/978-3-031-44127-1_11

Contreras, F., Espinosa, J. C., Dornberger, U., & Acosta, Y. A. C. (2017). Leadership and Employees' Innovative Work Behavior: Test of a Mediation and Moderation Model. *Asian Social Science*, 13(9), 9–25. DOI: 10.5539/ass.v13n9p9

Cortellazzo, L., Bruni, E., & Zampieri, R. (2019). The Role of Leadership in a Digitalized World: A Review. *Frontiers in Psychology*, 10, 1938. DOI: 10.3389/fpsyg.2019.01938 PMID: 31507494

Crossan, M. M., & Apaydin, M. (2010). A Multi-dimensional Framework of Organizational Innovation: A Systematic Review of the Literature. *Journal of Management Studies*, 47(6), 1154–1191. DOI: 10.1111/j.1467-6486.2009.00880.x

Curzi, Y., Fabbri, T., Scapolan, A. C., & Boscolo, S. (2019). Performance Appraisal and Innovative Behavior in the Digital Era. *Frontiers in Psychology*, 10, 1659. DOI: 10.3389/fpsyg.2019.01659 PMID: 31379682

Delpechitre, D., Black, H. G., & Farrish, J. (2019). The Dark Side of Technology: Examining the Impact of Technology Overload on Salespeople. *Journal of Business and Industrial Marketing*, 34(2), 317–337. DOI: 10.1108/JBIM-03-2017-0057

Deprez, J., & Euwema, M. (2017). You Can't Always Get What You Want? Leadership Expectations of Intrapreneurs. *Journal of Managerial Psychology*, 32(6), 430–444. DOI: 10.1108/JMP-04-2016-0107

Digital Marketing Institute. (2024). *Characteristics of Digital Leadership.* Retrieved at https://digitalmarketinginstitute.com/resources/lessons/digital-leadership_characteristics-of-digital-leadership_lxig#:~:text=What%20is%20Digital%20leadership%3F,part%20of%20your%20organizational%20culture

Dondi, M., Klier, J., Panier, F., & Schubert, J. (2021). *Defining the Skills Citizens Will Need in the Future World of Work.* Retrieved at https://www.mckinsey.com/industries/public-sector/our-insights/defining-the-skills-citizens-will-need-in-the-future-world-of-work#/

Dueholm Müller, S., Konzag, H., Agger Nielsen, J., & Bergsdóttir Sandholt, H. (2024). Digital Transformation Leadership Competencies: A Contingency Approach. *International Journal of Information Management*, 75, 102734. DOI: 10.1016/j.ijinfomgt.2023.102734

Eberl, J. K., & Drews, P. (2021). *Digital Leadership – Mountain or Molehill? A Literature Review,* International Conference on Wirtschaftsinformatik 223–237. DOI: 10.1007/978-3-030-86800-0_17

Erhan, T., Uzunbacak, H. H., & Aydin, E. (2022). From Conventional to Digital Leadership: Exploring Digitalization of Leadership and Innovative Work Behavior. *Management Research Review*, 45(11), 1524–1543. DOI: 10.1108/MRR-05-2021-0338

Fenwick, M., McCahery, J. A., & Vermeulen, E. P. M. (2021). Will the World Ever Be the Same After COVID-19? Two Lessons from the First Global Crisis of a Digital Age. *European Business Organization Law Review*, 22(1), 125–145. DOI: 10.1007/s40804-020-00194-9

Gao, P., & Gao, Y. (2024). How Does Digital Leadership Foster Employee Innovative Behavior: A Cognitive–Affective Processing System Perspective. *Behavioral Sciences (Basel, Switzerland)*, 14(5), 362. DOI: 10.3390/bs14050362 PMID: 38785853

Gilli, K., Nippa, M., & Knappstein, M. (2023). Leadership Competencies for Digital Transformation: An Exploratory Content Analysis of Job Advertisements. *German Journal of Human Resource Management*, 37(1), 50–75. DOI: 10.1177/23970022221087252

Hair, J. F., Black, W. C., Babin, B. J., Anderson, R. E., & Tatham, R. L. (2005). *Multivariate Data Analysis* (6th ed.). Pearson Education, Inc.

Hanelt, A., Bohnsack, R., Marz, D., & Antunes Marante, C. (2021). A Systematic Review of the Literature on Digital Transformation: Insights and Implications for Strategy and Organizational Change. *Journal of Management Studies*, 58(5), 1159–1197. DOI: 10.1111/joms.12639

Hayes, A. F. (2013). *Introduction to Mediation, Moderation, and Conditional Process Analysis: A Regression-based Approach*. Guilford Publications.

Hermundsdottir, F., & Aspelund, A. (2021). Sustainability Innovations and Firm Competitiveness: A Review. *Journal of Cleaner Production*, 280, 124715. DOI: 10.1016/j.jclepro.2020.124715

Hock-Doepgen, M., Montasser, J. S., Klein, S., Clauss, T., & Maalaoui, A. (2024). The Role of Innovative Work Behavior and Organizational Support for Business Model Innovation. *R & D Management*. Advance online publication. DOI: 10.1111/radm.12671

Hooper, D., Coughlan, J., & Mullen, M. (2008). *Structural Equation Modelling: Guidelines for Determining Model Fit*, Electronic Journal of Business Research Methods, 6(1), 53-60. Retrieved at http://arrow.dit.ie/cgi/viewcontent.cgi?article=1001&context= buschmanart.

Imran, F., Shahzad, K., Butt, A., & Kantola, J. (2020). Leadership Competencies for Digital Transformation: Evidence from Multiple Cases. In: Kantola, J., Nazir, S. & Salminen, V. (Eds.) *Advances in Human Factors, Business Management and Leadership:Proceedings of the AHFE 2020 Virtual Conferences on Human Factors, Business Management and Society, and Human Factors in Management and Leadership*, July 16-20, 2020, USA, 81-87. Advances in Intelligent Systems and Computing, Vol 1209. Cham: Springer. DOI: 10.1007/978-3-030-50791-6_11

Insights, E. H. L. (2023, July 27). *Why Digital Leadership Is A Non-negotiable for Future Success*. Retrieved at https://hospitalityinsights.ehl.edu/digital-leadership-for-future-success

Janssen, O. (2000). Job Demands, Perceptions of Effort-Reward Fairness and Innovative Work Behaviour. *Journal of Occupational and Organizational Psychology*, 73(3), 287–302. DOI: 10.1348/096317900167038

Janssen, O. (2001). Fairness Perceptions as a Moderator in the Curvilinear Relationships between Job Demands, and Job Performance and Job Satisfaction. *Academy of Management Journal*, 44(5), 1039–1050. DOI: 10.2307/3069447

Jaskyte, K. (2004). Transformational Leadership, Organizational Culture, and Innovativeness in Nonprofit Organizations. *Nonprofit Management & Leadership*, 15(2), 153–168. DOI: 10.1002/nml.59

Johnson, J. (2023). *Leadership in the Digital Age: Thriving in an Era of Constant Change*. Jeffrey Johnson.

Judge, T. A., & Piccolo, R. F. (2004). Transformational and Transactional Leadership: A Meta-analytic Test of Their Relative Validity. *The Journal of Applied Psychology*, 89(5), 755–768. DOI: 10.1037/0021-9010.89.5.755 PMID: 15506858

Karakose, T., Kocabas, I., Yirci, R., Papadakis, S., Ozdemir, T. Y., & Demirkol, M. (2022). The Development and Evolution of Digital Leadership: A Bibliometric Mapping Approach-Based Study. *Sustainability (Basel)*, 14(23), 16171. DOI: 10.3390/su142316171

Karimi, J., & Walter, Z. (2015). The Role of Dynamic Capabilities in Responding to Digital Disruption: A Factor-based Study of the Newspaper Industry. *Journal of Management Information Systems*, 32(1), 39–81. DOI: 10.1080/07421222.2015.1029380

Katanic, S. (2021, July 21). *Effective Digital Leadership Is Key to Digital Transformation.* Retrieved at https://www.forbes.com/councils/forbesagencycouncil/2021/07/21/effective-digital-leadership-is-key-to-digital-transformation/

Khan, M. J., Aslam, N., & Riaz, M. N. (2012). Leadership Styles as Predictors of Innovative Work Behavior. *Pakistan Journal of Social and Clinical Psychology*, 9(2), 17–22.

Klus, M. F., & Müller, J. (2021). The Digital Leader: What One Needs to Master Today's Organisational Challenges. *Journal of Business Economics*, 91(8), 1189–1223. DOI: 10.1007/s11573-021-01040-1

Kmieciak, R. (2021). Critical Reflection and Innovative Work Behavior: The Mediating Role of Individual Unlearning. *Personnel Review*, 50(2), 439–459. DOI: 10.1108/PR-10-2018-0406

Kohli, R., & Johnson, S. (2011). Digital Transformation in Latecomer Industries: CIO and CEO Leadership Lessons from Encana Oil & Gas (USA) Inc. *MIS Quarterly Executive*, 10(4), 141–156.

Kor, B., Rodriguez Fernandez, D., & Acarturk, E. (2022). Antecedents of Individual Innovative Behavior in the Digital Era. *Proceedings - Academy of Management*, 2022(1), 16865. Advance online publication. DOI: 10.5465/AMBPP.2022.16865abstract

Kouzes, J. M., & Posner, B. Z. (2017). *The Leadership Challenge: How to Make Extraordinary Things Happen in Organizations*. John Wiley & Sons.

KPMG. (2022). *KPMG Guide to Digital Leadership: Developing Inspiring and Effective Digital Leaders at Every Level.* Retrieved at https://assets.kpmg.com/content/dam/kpmg/sa/pdf/2021/digital-leadership-guide.pdf

Kreutzer, R. T., Neugebauer, T., & Pattloch, A. (2017). *Digital Business Leadership: Digitale Transformation – Geschäftsmodell - Innovation – Agile Organisation – Change-Management.* Springer Gabler. DOI: 10.1007/978-3-658-11914-0

Kupiek, M. (2021). *Digital Leadership, Agile Change and the Emotional Organization: Emotion as a Success Factor for Digital Transformation Projects*. Springer Nature. DOI: 10.1007/978-3-658-33489-5

Larson, L., & DeChurch, L. A. (2020). Leading Teams in the Digital Age: Four Perspectives on Technology and What They Mean for Leading Teams. *The Leadership Quarterly*, 31(1), 101377. DOI: 10.1016/j.leaqua.2019.101377 PMID: 32863679

Li, X., & Zheng, Y. (2014). The Influential Factors of Employees' Innovative Behavior and the Management Advices. *Journal of Service Science and Management*, 7(6), 446–450. DOI: 10.4236/jssm.2014.76042

Ly, B., & Ly, R. (2024). Technostress in Times of Change: Unveiling the Impact of Leadership Styles in Cambodia's Public Organizations in the Wake of COVID-19. *Cogent Business & Management*, 11(1), 2331645. Advance online publication. DOI: 10.1080/23311975.2024.2331645

Madden, K. (2024, April 12). *The Tech-Savvy Executive: Overcoming Digital Anxiety in Leadership.* Retrieved at https://www.forbes.com/councils/forbescoachescouncil/2024/04/12/the-tech-savvy-executive-overcoming-digital-anxiety-in-leadership/

Malakyan, P. G. (2019). Digital Leader-followership for the Digital Age: A North American Perspective. In Franco, M. (Ed.), *Digital Leadership—A New Leadership Style for the 21st Century*. IntechOpen., DOI: 10.5772/intechopen.89820

Marsh, E., Perez Vallejos, E., & Spence, A. (2022). The Digital Workplace and Its Dark Side: An Integrative Review. *Computers in Human Behavior*, 128, 107118. DOI: 10.1016/j.chb.2021.107118

McKinney, P. (2023, August 24). *Visionary Thinking: How Leaders Shape the Future*. Retrieved at https://www.philmckinney.com/visionary-thinking-how-leaders-shape-the-future/

Merlano, C. A. (2024). Digital Leadership and Transformation in Contemporary Times. *International Journal of Digital Strategy, Governance, and Business Transformation*, 13(1), 1–20. Advance online publication. DOI: 10.4018/IJDSGBT.352047

Messmann, G. (2012). *Innovative Work Behaviour Investigating the Nature and Facilitation of Vocational Teachers' Contributions to Innovation Development.* Universität Regensburg, Unpublished Doctoral Dissertation.

Molino, M., Ingusci, E., Signore, F., Manuti, A., Giancaspro, M. L., Russo, V., & Cortese, C. G. (2020). Wellbeing Costs of Technology Use during Covid-19 Remote Working: An Investigation Using the Italian Translation of the Technostress Creators Scale. *Sustainability (Basel)*, 12(15), 5911. Advance online publication. DOI: 10.3390/su12155911

Morgan, B. (2024). *The 8 Laws of Customer-focused Leadership: New Rules for Building a Business Around Today's Customer*. Harpers Collins Publishers.

Mumford, M. D., & Gustafson, S. B. (1988). Creativity Syndrome: Integration, Application, and Innovation. *Psychological Bulletin*, 103(1), 27–43. DOI: 10.1037/0033-2909.103.1.27

Mumford, M. D., Scott, G. M., Gaddis, B., & Strange, J. M. (2002). Leading Creative People: Orchestrating Expertise and Relationships. *The Leadership Quarterly*, 13(6), 705–750. DOI: 10.1016/S1048-9843(02)00158-3

Munsamy, M., Dhanpat, N., & Barkhuizen, E. N. (2023). The Development and Validation of a Digital Leadership Competency Scale. *Acta Commercii*, 23(1), a1057. DOI: 10.4102/ac.v23i1.1057

Nastjuk, I., Trang, S., Grummeck-Braamt, J. V., Adam, M. T. P., & Tarafdar, M. (2024). Integrating and Synthesising Technostress Research: A Meta-analysis on Technostress Creators, Outcomes, and IS Usage Contexts. *European Journal of Information Systems*, 33(3), 361–382. DOI: 10.1080/0960085X.2022.2154712

Oke, A., Munshi, N., & Walumbwa, F. O. (2009). The Influence of Leadership on Innovation Processes and Activities. *Organizational Dynamics*, 38(1), 64–72. DOI: 10.1016/j.orgdyn.2008.10.005

Ongena, G., Morsch, P., & Ravesteijn, P. (2024). *Digital Leadership Competency to Enhance Digital Transformation.* International Journal of Innovation and Technology Management., DOI: 10.1142/S0219877024500421

Önhon, Ö. (2016). *The Relationship Between Organizational Climate for Innovation and Employees' Innovative Work Behavior; The Moderating Effects of Leadership Behavior; ICT Sector in Turkey.* T.C. Marmara Üniversitesi, Unpublished Doctoral Dissertation.

Parnitvitidkun, P. (2021). *Dimensions of Innovative Work Behavior in Digital Transformation,* KKBS Journal of Business Administration and Accountancy, 5(3), 69–96. Retrieved at https://so04.tci-thaijo.org/index.php/kkbsjournal/article/view/248992

Parnitvitidkun, P., Ponchaitiwat, K., Chancharat, N., & Thoumrungroje, A. (2024). Understanding IT Professional Innovative Work Behavior in the Workplace: A Sequential Mixed-methods Design. *Journal of Open Innovation*, 10(1), 100231. DOI: 10.1016/j.joitmc.2024.100231

Philpot, S., & Roy, I. (2017, February 28). *Leadership Disrupted: Pushing the Boundaries- 2017 Global Human Capital Trends.* Retrieved at https://www2.deloitte.com/us/en/insights/focus/human-capital-trends/2017/developing-digital-leaders.html

Pillay, N. (2024, November 11). Becoming a Digital Leader: Cultivating a Mindset for the Future. Retrieved at https://www.acumenmagazine.co.za/articles/becoming-a-digital-leader-cultivating-a-mindset-for-the-future-12750.html

Preacher, K. J., & Hayes, A. F. (2004). SPSS and SAS Procedures for Estimating Indirect Effects in Simple Mediation Models. *Behavior Research Methods, Instruments, & Computers*, 36(4), 717–731. DOI: 10.3758/BF03206553 PMID: 15641418

Rademaker, T., Klingenberg, I., & Süß, S. (2023). *Leadership and Technostress: A Systematic Literature Review.* Management Review Quarterly., DOI: 10.1007/s11301-023-00385-x

Ragu-Nathan, T. S., Tarafdar, M., Ragu-Nathan, B. S., & Tu, Q. (2008). The Consequences of Technostress for End Users in Organizations: Conceptual Development and Empirical Validation. *Information Systems Research*, 19(4), 417–433. DOI: 10.1287/isre.1070.0165

Ravichandran, A., Taylor, K., & Waterhouse, P. (2016). DevOps for Digital Leaders: Reignite Business with a Modern DevOps-Enabled Software Factory. New York: Springer. Science+Business Media. DOI: 10.1007/978-1-4842-1842-6

Salam, A. (2023). Navigating the Digital Landscape: Exploring the Interplay of Digital Leadership, E-Learning Anxiety, and Innovative Behavior. *Journal of Digitovation and Information System*, 3(1), 32–46. DOI: 10.54433/JDIIS.2023100020

Salanova, M., Llorens, S., & Cifre, E. (2013). The Dark Side of Technologies: Technostress Among Users of Information and Communication Technologies. *International Journal of Psychology*, 48(3), 422–436. DOI: 10.1080/00207594.2012.680460 PMID: 22731610

Salih, A. M. (2024). *Digital Leadership: Evidence from Theory and Practice*. Routledge.

Sary, F. P., Dudija, N., & Moslem, M. (2023). Do Digital Competency and Self-leadership Influence Teachers' Innovative Work Behavior? *European Journal of Educational Research*, 12(3), 1449–1463. DOI: 10.12973/eu-jer.12.3.1449

Schumacker, R. E., & Lomax, R. G. (2010). *A Beginner's Guide to Structural Equation Modeling*. Routledge.

Sheninger, E. (2019). *Digital Leadership: Changing Paradigms for Changing Times*. Corwin Press.

Sinclair, H. (2024). *Digital Dawn: The Rise of New Business Realities*. Lars Meiertoberens.

Spagnoli, P., Molino, M., Molinaro, D., Giancaspro, M. L., Manuti, A., & Ghislieri, C. (2020). Workaholism and Technostress During the COVID-19 Emergency: The Crucial Role of the Leaders on Remote Working. *Frontiers in Psychology*, 11, 620310. Advance online publication. DOI: 10.3389/fpsyg.2020.620310 PMID: 33424730

Sposato, M. (2024). Digital Leadership in Organizations for Digital Transformation. In Espinosa, C., & Oliver, E. (Eds.), *Multidisciplinary Organizational Training of Human Capital in the Digital Age* (pp. 77–96). IGI Global Scientific Publishing.

Tagscherer, F., & Carbon, C.-C. (2023). Leadership for Successful Digitalization: A Literature Review on Companies' Internal and External Aspects of Digitalization. *Sustainable Technology and Entrepreneurship*, 2(2), 100039. DOI: 10.1016/j.stae.2023.100039

Tarafdar, M., Cooper, C. L., & Stich, J. (2017). The Technostress Trifecta - Techno Eustress, Techno Distress and Design: Theoretical Directions and An Agenda for Research. *Information Systems Journal*, 29(1), 6–42. DOI: 10.1111/isj.12169

Tarafdar, M., Pirkkalainen, H., Salo, M., & Makkonen, M. (2020). Taking on the "Dark Side" - Coping with Technostress. *IT Professional*, 22(6), 82–89. DOI: 10.1109/MITP.2020.2977343

Tarafdar, M., Pullins, E. B., & Ragu-Nathan, T. S. (2014). Technostress: Negative Effect on Performance and Possible Mitigations. *Information Systems Journal*, 25(2), 103–132. DOI: 10.1111/isj.12042

Tarafdar, M., Tu, Q., Ragu-Nathan, B. S., & Ragu-Nathan, T. S. (2007). The Impact of Technostress on Role Stress and Productivity. *Journal of Management Information Systems*, 24(1), 301–328. DOI: 10.2753/MIS0742-1222240109

Tigre, F. B., Curado, C., & Henriques, P. L. (2023). Digital Leadership: A Bibliometric Analysis. *Journal of Leadership & Organizational Studies*, 30(1), 40–70. DOI: 10.1177/15480518221123132

Torres, C. C. (2021). Adaptation and Validation of Technostress Creators and Technostress Inhibitors Inventories in a Spanish-Speaking Latin American Country. *Technology in Society*, 66, 101660. DOI: 10.1016/j.techsoc.2021.101660

Turel, O., & Gaudioso, F. (2018). Techno-stressors, Distress and Strain: The Roles of Leadership and Competitive Climates. *Cognition Technology and Work*, 20(2), 309–324. DOI: 10.1007/s10111-018-0461-7

Udofia, E. (2024). *The Digital Leader: Demystifying Leadership in the Digital Transformation Era*. Xlibris.

Unhelkar, B., & Gonsalves, T. (2021). *Artificial Intelligence for Business Optimization: Research and Applications*. CRC Press. DOI: 10.1201/9781003120926

Wagner, D. J. (2018). *Digital Leadership: Kompetenzen – Führungsverhalten - Umsetzungsempfehlungen*. Springer Fachmedien Wiesbaden GmbH. DOI: 10.1007/978-3-658-20127-2

Weil, M. M., & Rosen, L. D. (1997). *TechnoStress: Coping with Technology @Work @Home @Play*. John Wiley & Sons.

Wrede, S. J. S., Claassen, K., Rodil Dos Anjos, D., Kettschau, J. P., & Broding, H. C. (2023). Impact of Digital Stress on Negative Emotions and Physical Complaints in the Home Office: A Follow Up Study. *Health Psychology and Behavioral Medicine*, 11(1), 2263068. DOI: 10.1080/21642850.2023.2263068 PMID: 37818414

Xu, Z., & Suntrayuth, S. (2022). Innovative Work Behavior in High-tech Enterprises: Chain Intermediary Effect of Psychological Safety and Knowledge Sharing. *Frontiers in Psychology*, 13, 1017121. DOI: 10.3389/fpsyg.2022.1017121 PMID: 36353082

Young, J. (2022). *Leadership Resilience in a Digital Age*. Routledge.

Yuan, F., & Khan, M. S. (2024). *Investigating the Impact of Digital Leadership on Innovation Performance of Public Universities in Yunnan, China,* Journal of Infrastructure. *Policy and Development*, 8(9), 7663. DOI: 10.24294/jipd.v8i9.7663

Yuan, F., & Woodman, R. (2010). The Role of Performance and Image Outcome Expectations. *Academy of Management Journal*, 53(2), 323–342. DOI: 10.5465/amj.2010.49388995

Zeike, S., Bradbury, K., Lindert, L., & Pfaff, H. (2019). Digital Leadership Skills and Associations with Psychological Well-Being. *International Journal of Environmental Research and Public Health*, 16(14), 2628. DOI: 10.3390/ijerph16142628 PMID: 31340579

Zulu, S. L., & Khosrowshahi, F. (2021). A Taxonomy of Digital Leadership in the Construction Industry. *Construction Management and Economics*, 39(7), 565–578. DOI: 10.1080/01446193.2021.1930080

# Chapter 10
# Evaluating Corporate Reputation in the Digital Environment:
## Insights From a Systematic Literature Review

**Jelena Krstić**
*Institute of Economic Sciences, Belgrade, Serbia*

## ABSTRACT

*Intensification of the use of digital technologies and communication channels in business practice significantly influences corporate reputation building and maintaining, by enabling more efficient reaching of target audiences and greater interactivity in communication. In the digital age, the practice of managing corporate reputation implies the continuous monitoring of various digital channels such as social media, and data analysis based on advanced analytics and artificial intelligence. As the increasing number of corporate communication and relation building practices takes on digital forms, with the intensification of this field in practice, the volume of research is also increasing. Therefore, the focus of this chapter is on providing a comprehensive overview of this topic, by conducting a systematic review of the relevant literature and by indicating the dominant areas of research, methodological frameworks that are applied for data collection and analysis and existing findings related to it.*

## INTRODUCTION

Corporate reputation represents the sum of opinions, impressions and attitudes that a certain public (customers, suppliers, business partners, employees etc.) has built about the organization during a longer period of time. It represents the ultimate outcome of corporate activities aimed at creating and establishing appropriate communication relationships with various stakeholder groups from its environment, but is also created under the impact of factors such as media publicity, personal experience etc. Communication through different digital channels, such as websites and social networks, has become an indispensable means of contacting target groups, exchanging information, influencing public attitudes and building

DOI: 10.4018/979-8-3693-8181-6.ch010

long-term relationships (Krstić & Ćorić, 2021; Skočajić et al., 2024). Corporate presence on websites, social networks and blogs allows companies to interact directly with stakeholders, which can positively affect reputation if the communication is conducted transparently and responsibly (Marinović et al., 2022). However, the digital environment also brings many challenges and risks, as negative information, such as negative comments and online reviews can quickly go viral and harm company's reputation. Thus, effective reputation management in the digital world involves creating quality and authentic content to be shared on digital platforms, as well as proactive monitoring of online content and quick reactions to potential crises (Aureli & Supino, 2017).

Modern organizations, wanting to stay relevant in the digital age have to be human-centric, resilient and dedicated to sustainability. Measuring online corporate reputation plays a central role in achieving these characteristics because it represents how the public, consumers, and employees perceive the organization's values and behavior in the digital space. Reputation directly affects the perception of the organization as human-centric, meaning it is focused on people, through the analysis of feedback on how the company treats its customers and employees. Also, sustainability is reflected through public discourse on environmental and social initiatives undertaken by the organization, while resilience becomes visible through reactions to crises and changes in the online environment. Therefore, measuring reputation across digital channels, through social network analysis, reviews and comments allows organizations to identify opportunities to improve their strategies and ensure alignment with contemporary values. Industry 5.0, focused on personalization and collaboration between people and technology, directly encourages more accurate measurement of digital corporate reputation through advanced analytical tools and greater responsiveness to user needs.

Within the digital environment, building and maintaining corporate reputation has undergone significant changes due to the accelerated speed of communication, accessibility to information and global connectivity (Ramos & Casado-Molina, 2021). In accordance with that, the significance of building and managing the favorable online reputation of a company as a strategic element of its competitiveness (Rodríguez-Díaz et al., 2018) and business sustainability (von Berlepsch et al., 2024) is well recognized in the literature. Effective management of the corporate reputation in the digital environment demands continuous tracking, measurement and evaluation of the reputation on all digital channels. Certain tools, such as social media monitoring tools, represent valuable means to keep track of public opinion and identify trends in real time. However, this represents only one dimension of the reputation measurement, and wider view of this construct is often necessary so the company management can get real insight into the public perception and attitudes. Some of the authors in this field have proposed unique frameworks and scales for online reputation measurement (e.g. Dutot & Castellano, 2015; Puma Flores & Rosa-Díaz, 2023). These measurement instruments contain different dimensions and different evaluation criteria in order to assess corporate reputation in the digital environment from different angles. However, although digital reputation represents a field with a wide range of investigation, in the academic context, there has not yet been implemented enough empirical studies related to reputation assessment. Nevertheless, identifying existing instruments and methods for measuring online reputation, which are currently available in the literature, represents a significant step in identifying research directions in this context. There are few systematic reviews related to online reputation concept available in the literature (e.g. Cioppi et al., 2019; Al-Yazidi et al., 2020). In this context, the purpose of this chapter is to provide a comprehensive theoretical framework on the basis of collection, analysis and synthesis of previous research results, focusing on the topic of online corporate reputation assessment and evaluation.

## 1. LITERATURE REVIEW

As explained by Dutot and Castellano (2015), reputation "represents the aggregate perception of all of a firm's constituents". It includes the formed perception of both, stakeholders from internal and external environment, regarding company's overall reputation. Walker (2010) defined corporate reputation as specific representation of previous actions and future prospects of a company which is built over time and remains stable over time. Lange et al. (2011) observe corporate reputation as a construct which is subjectively created by external subjects, but represents organization's objective reality. As per El Marrakchi et al. (2015a), reputation represents the way community estimates certain business entity based on the acquired information and gathered experience. Reputation can be seen as the collective sum of different images held by various stakeholder groups. This understanding of reputation is valuable because it distinguishes reputation from the concept of image while establishing it as a broader, collective construct (Westermann & Forthmann, 2020). Loke and Reitter (2021) defined corporate reputation as "a sociocognitive construct consisting of the organization's perception that a stakeholder has, that is built through past impressions". According to one of the most recent explanations of this concept, it can be defined as stakeholders' perception of company overall attractiveness (Nuortimo et al., 2024).

Corporate reputation of an organization represents the ultimate outcome of that organization's activities aimed at creating and establishing appropriate communication links with individuals and groups from its environment. It is the result of establishing direct contact with the organization and forming opinions about it based on the entire collection of impressions, created over a period of time. It is basically regarded as a concept which reflects the collective perception of the company in public and, if it is positive, it can bring many benefits for the company and thus contribute to overall corporate performance (Hojdik & Majtán, 2017; Caputo et al., 2023). Reputation represents an intangible asset which provides companies with competitive advantage in the marketplace (Ponzi et al. 2011; Wepener & Boshoff, 2015; Rodríguez-Díaz et al. 2018; Loke & Lam-Lion, 2021; Özhan et al., 2023) and which is closely related to organization's overall business success (Loke & Reitter, 2021). Since it is considered to be an asset, unfavorable reputation might severely damage the organization (Loke & Lam-Lion, 2021). Corporate reputation is something that represents the added value of an organization, in addition to the specifications and performance of its products. Reputation is built continuously and over time, which requires a long-term orientation of the organization demanding "a conscious, company-wide, strategic focus on building and maintaining a positive corporate reputation among key stakeholders" (Goldring, 2015).

However, with intensification of digital technologies, the significance of the concept of reputation in digital environment has risen. Many companies are investing efforts to manage their image and reputation on internet and within virtual communities. Social media are used as efficient channels for attracting attention, building relationships with public, sharing experiences, establish interactive communication with consumers (Ferreira & Zambaldi, 2019). In accordance with that, in recent times, more and more attention is given to the concept of digital reputation which is also available in the literature under other terms such as web reputation, online reputation and e- reputation (Puma Flores & Rosa-Díaz, 2023). The concept of e-reputation mainly includes the traditional concept of reputation widened with digital insights, however, there is no unique definition of this term among researchers. E-reputation is often regarded as "an extension" of reputation acquired in the offline environment to an online environment (Chun & Davies, 2001). One of the simplest definitions of the concept explains it as a transfer of reputational issues to the Internet environment (Pollák & Markovič, 2022). As noted by Rodríguez-Díaz et al. (2018), it represents "a set of opinions, experiences, and evaluations of customers shared on websites about a product, service, or brand". Reuber and Fischer (2011) pointed out visibility and quality as two dimensions of an online reputation. Visibility indicates the importance of being visible online, while quality relates to providing products and services of high quality through online channels. As stated by Dutot and Castellano (2015), "e-reputation refers to the elements of reputation that are specifically derived from electronic contacts". Same authors emphasized that online reputation does not depend solely on corporate activities but it is co-created and co-managed by stakeholder groups. This concept is, thus, characterized by interactivity and credibility, as well as trust, security and confidentiality in a virtual world. In case of completely online businesses, that sell projects online, a favorable digital reputation act as a factor which decreases the perceived risk by consumers, which may represent main barrier for online purchasing (Youness & Valette-Florence, 2017). Just as corporate reputation in a general sense, an online reputation represents a strategic resource, which significantly affects financial performance by generating benefits on a short- and long-term, and contributes the overall prosperity of the organization (Oncioiu et al., 2020). The monitoring of online reputation represents one of the keys success factors of the implementation of digital communication strategy, since it enables the adaptation of the communication plan to achieved results and making proper decisions to make certain corrections or more drastic changes (Onciou et al., 2020).

Rosamond (2020) pointed out to the existence of two predominant online reputation paradigms – an incremental paradigm of reputation capital and a volatile paradigm of reputation warfare. The first framework views capital linked to online reputation as an intangible asset, and second presents an incremental approach to understanding how online reputational value accumulates, assuming it can seamlessly "add up" across different platforms. However, the widespread measurement of online reputation has given rise to a second, more volatile paradigm—reputation warfare. This paradigm focuses on the inevitable conflicts that arise from the continuous calculation of reputational capital. Reputation warfare highlights unpredictable and indirect methods of assessing online reputation value. This author defined reputational volatility as the distribution of reputational risk (expressing the potential to achieve both gains and losses in reputation capital), which is made visible through platform metrics (e.g. ratings and 'Likes') and the interactions they generate.

The importance of corporate reputation as an area in corporate management has grown over the last two decades (Melewar et al., 2022), which has simultaneously led to the development of various techniques for its assessment. Considering that corporate reputation represents valuable asset of the company, the ways it can be accurately measured has been gaining increasing interest of researchers and practitioners (Money & Hillenbrand, 2006; Klein et al., 2019). There are some widely known measures of corporate reputation, such as Reputation quotient (RQ), defined by Fombrun et al. (2000), Customer-based reputation (CBR) proposed by Walsh and Beatty (2007) and well-known RepTrak, defined Fombrun et al. (2015). Those measurement techniques and instruments include various constructs that make up reputation, and there is no single measure of corporate reputation in the literature and practice. Given that corporate reputation includes the perception of various aspects of the company's operations, it is clear that it is a multidisciplinary phenomenon, which can therefore be defined from different perspectives. Thus, the proper measurement of corporate reputation has always been challenging as reputation depends on multiple factors and stakeholders (Klein et al., 2019; Loke & Reitter, 2021). Thus, accurately measuring corporate reputation has proven difficult, limiting managers' ability to assess this valuable intangible asset effectively (Wepener & Boshoff, 2015; Ramos & Casado-Molina, 2021). Many of these measurement instruments have been criticized for not being reliable enough or not being able to capture all aspects of reputation, particularly aspects related to the digital environment (Khan & Digout, 2018; Al-Yazidi et al., 2020; Xie & Lui, 2020).

In the contemporary business environment, managing an online corporate reputation is strategically important for improving the company's overall performances (Ramos & Casado-Molina, 2021). Companies need to continuously monitor and analyze ways their online reputation is being built through a variety of different channels such as social media (Rodríguez-Díaz et al., 2018; Pollák & Markovič, 2022). Accordingly, measures related to reputation deal with website and social media analytics. The importance of monitoring online traffic, reviews, ratings, comments etc. has become an imperative in relation to monitoring of online reputation (Aureli & Supino, 2017). In addition to that type of analytics, it has become necessary to continuously collect, analyze and qualitatively interpret data from digital channels in order to determine the reputation in the digital environment (Ramos & Casado-Molina, 2021). Reputation evaluation based on the "listening" of social media data has become essential element of the management process (Kotras, 2020). As social media have become crucial means for the assessment of opinions and feelings shared among internet users, they are also essential for managing corporate reputation (El Marrakchi et al., 2015a; Shad Manaman et al. 2016; Youness & Valette-Florence, 2017). In social media context, when information is rapidly spread among numerous users, it has become crucial to continuously monitor users' conversations and comments and effectively assess the way they perceive the company and, thus, prevent any negative consequences on the corporative image and reputation (Peng & Wan, 2023).

Some platforms which rely on user reviews act as reputation systems which represent an important means for helping users evaluate the company and its products/services and make decisions whether to trust it (Fu et al., 2016). Online reviews provided by online users represent one of the constituents of online reputation since they possess a significant influence on other users' perception and attitudes (Mellinas & Martin-Fuentes, 2024; Oh et al., 2020; Thompson & Haynes, 2017). In case when online reputation is observed as a measure of ratings provided by customers, it affects the expectations of future users and other stakeholders (Rodríguez-Díaz et al., 2018).

In addition to the measures mentioned above, many others are taken into account in business practice, and the number of items included in the measure of online reputation is increasing. In this sense, the techniques and methods of measuring reputation are also changing, the application of which reputation is assessed in a qualitative or quantitative sense.

## 2. METHODOLOGY

This research is based on the systematic literature analysis, as a key method which enables thorough reviewing of the current body of knowledge and identifying knowledge gaps. It includes identification, evaluation and integration of the findings of relevant high-quality studies guided by set research questions (Al-Yazidi et al., 2020). Literature review represents a key part of the research process which allows researchers to look at current knowledge in a certain area and identify gaps in knowledge and represent the basis for conducting further empirical research (Krstić et al., 2019). For this purpose, a specific framework PRISMA 2020, developed by Page et al. (2021) is applied to conduct an analysis. PRISMA (Preferred Reporting Items for Systematic Reviews and Meta-Analyses) is chosen as it represents one of the well-known frameworks which was previously used in various qualitative studies related to different business fields (e.g. Peixoto et al., 2021; Abelha et al., 2020; Galletta et al., 2024; Albhirat et al., 2024).

This framework might be slightly adapted to fit the current research task, as was the case in some of the previous studies (e.g. Moher et al., 2015; Abelha et al., 2020). Main components of the PRISMA framework, which were applied as different stages of this study include:

- Formulation of the research question and research objectives – In the first stage of the research, a clearly formulated research question(s) and objective(s) were defined, and they acted as guides of literature search and analysis in the next phases.
- Defining of research protocol - A detailed research protocol included the list of relevant databases, keywords used for searching, defined inclusion/exclusion criteria, literature time range etc.
- Searching the literature basis – In this phase, a comprehensive search of relevant database by using carefully constructed keywords, was conducted.
- Selection of sources – In this phase, selection and evaluation of the quality of the identified literature sources (including articles, book chapters and conference papers) was performed according to pre-defined criteria. After this phase, only the sources which meet the inclusion criteria underwent further, more detailed analysis.
- Data extraction – Each of the selected sources was analyzed and relevant data related to previous study results were extracted.
- Data synthesis – In this phase, a qualitative synthesis of findings was performed.
- Reporting and interpretation of findings – In this, last phase, the results of the systematic literature review are presented in the chapter, both in narrative and graphic form. The findings, as well as research implications are discussed and possible directions for future research are highlighted at the end of the chapter.

In the first phase, research questions, which function as guidelines for analysis in the following phases were formulated. Those research questions are:

RQ1: What is the current scope of research on online reputation measurement/assessment?
RQ2: Is there a change in the course of research topics in the field of online reputation measurement/assessment over time?
RQ3: What measurement metrics and methodologies are most represented in the research in the field of online corporate reputation?

This research aims to provide an overview of the existing literature and point to the methodological directions guided by those research questions. In the second stage, a research protocol that describes the methods and criteria for inclusion and exclusion of literature sources, and search strategies was defined. The basic criteria for the inclusion of scientific articles are the keywords "digital corporate reputation", "e-reputation" or "online reputation" as well as phrases like: "management" and "evaluation/assessment/measurement". Also, only articles published in journals and conference proceedings that could be accessed in their entirety via the Internet were selected. Defined inclusion and exclusion criteria are given in Table 1.

*Table 1. Criteria for inclusion and exclusion of literature sources*

| Criteria for inclusion | Criteria for exclusion |
|---|---|
| Focus on measuring online reputation | Focus on another topic |
| Full text availability | Full article not available |
| Text written in English | Text not written in English language |
| Date range between 2014 and 2024. | Outdated from the defined range |
| Relation to set research questions | Not related to research questions |
| Published in selected digital database | Not published in the selected database |

As the third step, a comprehensive literature search in the relevant database was conducted guided with previously defined keywords. In this case, the academic database Web of Science was chosen, as one of the most credible databases of scientific publications. The selected keywords were searched among paper titles. Eventually, the matching of the keywords with the literature sources was done by using a mix of terms related to online reputation and its measurement with different frameworks/scales/indices. Applying the keywords in the database initially yielded 538 results including journal articles, chapters and conference papers published within the defined date range of ten years, that is a period 2014-2024. Then, the selection and evaluation of the quality of the identified sources was carried out according to pre-defined criteria. Editorial materials, book reviews and other publications that could not be accessed in their entirety, as well as to meet other criteria were excluded. All articles in which online corporate reputation and its evaluation are not the main focus of research were excluded. For example, articles related to the assessment of corporate reputation in general were excluded, and only publications related to the measurement of the online corporate reputation were retained. Also, all studies published in languages other than English were excluded. Finally, the author reviewed the titles and abstracts of the studies initially identified as relevant and made a definite decision on which studies met all inclusion criteria and eliminated articles with content which did not fit the study topic. As a result of this phase, a set of 30 publications that met all the inclusion criteria were obtained in order to enter the next, more detailed analysis (Table 2).

In the following phase, data extraction was performed. It includes collection of relevant data from selected publications, including research subjects and study objectives, applied research methods and outcomes. In the next step, the integration and qualitative synthesis of the results was carried out. The obtained results are presented in textual and tabular form, followed by a discussion of implications, limitations and possible directions for future research.

## 3. RESULTS

On the basis of the analysis of the selected literature sources, online reputation assessment methods applied by different authors, have emerged as main differentiation criteria. Therefore, based on the type of methodology, studies were systematized into two main groups. The first group included studies containing scales/models/indices calculated on the basis of the analysis of empirically collected data. This research mainly included surveys as means for data collection. The second group used secondary data collected from online platforms such as social media and applied methods of machine learning for content analysis. Authors of studies from this group pointed out that corporate reputation assessment methodologies based on surveys of different public groups are basically too expensive and time-consuming, and the results could quickly become outdated (e.g. Klein et al., 2019; Rantanen et al., 2020; Loke & Reitter, 2021). In accordance with that, they recommend using available online information gathered from various digital channels to measure companies' reputation as accurate and time-efficient means (e.g. Peng & Wan, 2023). The largest number of sources from this group dates from the period 2020 to 2024, which indicates the intensification of research in this area during the last years.

*Table 2. The results of the exploration of the literature (in chronological order)*

| Author(s) | Scale | Measured items | Methods |
|---|---|---|---|
| Syed Alwi & Da Silva (2007) | 'Corporate Character Scale' by Davies et al. (2004) applied in an online context | Emotional brand attributes | Survey on a convenience sample of respondents<br>Statisitical analysis (first- and second-order confirmatory factor analysis) |
| Dutot & Castellano (2015) | E-reputation scale | Four dimensions (brand characteristic, website quality, service quality and social media) | Survey of a sample of respondents and students of digital business<br>Focus group of professionals<br>Statistical analysis (Principal Component Analysis) |
| El Marrakchi et al. (2015a) | Reputation Measuring System (RMS) | Five dimensions:"what" (indicators taken as input),"How"(evaluating techniques), "who" (Actors participating in the process),"where" And "when" (spatial and temporal dimensions) | A vector model for representing reputation in online social networks by using the Bayesian ststistics |
| El Marrakchi et al. (2015b) | Intelligent Reputation Measuring System (IRMS) | The reputation score measured and comparison with existing social media metrics | Measuring reputation by applying the Bayesian Model using data from online social network |
| El Marrakchi et al. (2016) | Intelligent Reputation Measuring System (IRMS) | The reputation score measured and comparison with existing social media metrics | Measuring reputation by applying the Bayesian Model using real-time data from social media |
| Pollák et al. (2016) | Online reputation of tourist companies | Ratings on websites and comparison against the widespread sentiment analysis | Advanced sentiment analysis<br>Statistical testing |
| Steenkamp & Rensburg (2016) | A conceptual framework for reputation management on SNSs | Data from social media sites | Computer-aided qualitative data analysis<br>Sentiment analysis |
| Shad Manaman et al. (2016) | A reputation management system | Positive, negative, neutral, and irrelevant corporate profiles | Sentiment analysis methods using social media data<br>N-gram learning approach |
| Whiting et al. (2017) | A tool for measuring SMEs' reputation, engagement and goodwill (REG) | Six indicators: "captured" customer opinions, contact with customer database, website traffic, Google Search ranking, customer database size and social media following | A discrete choice experiment (DCE) based on PAPRIKA method via an online survey<br>Cluster analysis |

continued on following page

*Table 2. Continued*

| Author(s) | Scale | Measured items | Methods |
|---|---|---|---|
| Youness & Valette-Florence (2017) | Customer-based online reputation | Eight dimensions: customer orientation, good employer, reliable and financially strong company, reliable delivery, innovativeness and singularity, high standard offerings, and social and environmental responsibility | Interviews of clients of top e-commerce websites, the collage projective technique and album online method<br>Two surveys<br>Statistical analysis (exploratory and confirmatory factor analyses) |
| Pollák et al. (2018) | Total online reputation (TOR) | Factors of online reputation (Google ratings and number of Facebook fans) | Nonautomated multifactor sentiment analysis<br>Statistical analysis |
| Klein et al. (2019) | An information retrieval approach | A reputation based on comments on social media | Collection and machine learning-based sentiment analysis of reputation-related textual content from online media |
| Pollák et al. (2019) | Modified TOR | Multlti-factor analysis of online reputation | Multifactor sentiment analysis<br>Statistical analysis |
| Rantanen et al. (2020) | A multi-dimensional classification framework | Six dimensions: quality, reliability, responsibility, successfulness, pleasantness and innovativeness | Retrieval of social media comments<br>and applying a convolutional neural network (CNN) to automatically classify the comments |
| Vaccaro et al. (2020) | A Comparison Matrix Geometric Index (CMGI) | Modelling consumer preference between groups of competitors | Qualitative data (emotions expressed in communications on social media)<br>Comparisons in natural language |
| Oncioiu et al. (2020) | Online reputation measurement model for optimizing corporate sustainability | Dimensions: online visibility, employee satisfaction, increased sales, return on assets, corporate social responsibility disclosure level | Data collected from companies, equilibrium analysis model (short- and long-term)<br>An econometric approach |
| Westermann & Forthmann (2020) | Adapted Fombrun et al.'s reputation model | Six dimensions of companies' Reputation Quotient | Social listening method by using AI tools (Natural Language Processing) |
| Zaki Ahmed & Rodríguez-Díaz (2020) | The scale containing reputation variables used on web | The perceived quality of service across seven variables used by TripAdvisor | Factorial analysis<br>Multiple regression analysis |
| Loke & Reitter (2021) | Overall online reputation | Corporate reputation demensions as defined by Fombrum et al. (2015) | Machine-learning aspect based sentiment analysis (ABSA) of online reviews<br>Natural Language Processing |
| Rust et al., (2021) | Social media-based brand reputation tracker using value-brand-relationship framework | Stakeholders' overall impression | Data mining of Twitter comments |

continued on following page

*Table 2. Continued*

| Author(s) | Scale | Measured items | Methods |
|---|---|---|---|
| Yu & Han (2021) | Multidimensional reputation scale | Four factors: reliability, technical skills, customer service, and accessibility | A Delphi study involving a group of professionals<br>Exploratory and confirmatory factor analysis<br>Structural equation modeling |
| Ramos & Casado-Molina (2021) | Online Corporate Reputation Index (OCRI) | Tangible and intangible business assets | Modelling and evaluating online reputation by using panel data methods |
| Orrego et al. (2021) | Automated online reputation measurement | Data from online news sources and social media sites | Sentiment Analysis<br>Natural language processing |
| Loke & Lam-Lion (2021) | Tool for assessment of employees' perception of organization | The content of online reviews | Sentiment analysis<br>Natural language processing and semantic search |
| Luoma-aho et al. (2021) | The Public Sector Net Promoter Score (PSNPS) | The perception which stakeholders have of organizations in public sector | Survey of stakeholder groups<br>Statistical analysis |
| Al-Yazidi et al. (2022) | A hybrid model for reputation measuring in online social networks | Qualitative (content) and quanitattive data (number of tweets/followers) extracted from Twitter | Multi Criteria Decision Making (MCDM) methods<br>Sentiment analysis (Natural language processing and machine learning techniques) |
| Shamma et al. (2023) | The scale of e-reputation developed by Dutot and Castellano (2015) | Four dimensions (brand characteristic, website quality, service quality and social media) | An online survey<br>Structural equation modelling approach |
| Puma Flores & Rosa-Díaz (2023) | Total Online Reputation Index (TOR) in B2B markets | Thirten variables of online reputation | Interviews with experts and managers<br>Advanced sentiment analysis |
| Peng & Wan (2023) | A corporate image evaluation index system | Content from digital channels | An automatic text analysis by applying a topic classification and sentiment analysis |
| Youness et al. (2024) | Online corporate reputation scale from customer perspective | Seven items: avant-garde, singularity, exclusivity, savings, return policy, freedom and speed | (AOL) technique and individual-difference multidimensional scaling approach (INDSCAL) |

## 3.1. Studies Based on Stakeholder Surveying

This group of articles is based on empirical research conducted on samples of stakeholders through specially designed questionnaires. In their research, Syed Alwi and Da Silva (2007) compared the corporate brand images of two retail companies, one operating exclusively online and the other solely offline. The measurement was carried out using the existing 'Corporate Character Scale', which was developed by Davies et al. (2004) and which contained almost fifty items related to seven emotional brand attributes, namely "agreeableness, enterprise, competence, chic, ruthlessness, informality and machismo". The results showed that survey respondents (customers of both companies) saw the online company as less formal and more innovative compared to the other one that operates exclusively offline. Dutot and Castellano (2015) constructed the first and one of the most well-known scales designed especially for measuring e-reputation. The scale was based on existing literature and insights provided by students in the field of digital business, a focus group of professionals and an online survey of a sample of respondents. As a result, they obtained a scale containing 15 items grouped into four major dimensions, namely "brand characteristic, website quality, service quality and social media". In one of the recent studies, Shamma et al. (2023) used and tested the applicability of Dutot and Castellano (2015)'s scale of e-reputation, in a new context and they confirmed the validity of three of the four dimensions from the original model.

Whiting et al. (2017) developed a tool to be used for the purpose of rating and scoring of SMEs' reputation, engagement and goodwill (REG), which included SMEs' presence on the Internet and social media following. They conducted a discrete choice experiment by applying the PAPRIKA method via an online survey in order to determine weights indicating the significance of six indicators linked to reputation, engagement and goodwill of enterprises. Those indicators were: "captured" customer opinions of the organization, contact with customer database, website traffic, Google Search ranking, customer database size, and social media following.

Starting from the identified lack of measures of the online reputation from the perspective of customers, Youness and Valette-Florence (2017) developed and validated a scale which included more than forty items related to the reputation of e-commerce websites together with eight online reputation dimensions, precisely "customer orientation, good employer, reliable and financially strong company, reliable delivery, innovativeness and singularity, high standard offerings, and social and environmental responsibility". In order to collect data to test and validate the scale, they conducted three qualitative and two quantitative studies (surveys). In one recent study, Youness et al. (2024) also investigated which specific items are relevant for evaluating corporate reputation from the perspective of customers. They based their research on the qualitative projective "Album on Line" (AOL) technique, which was applied in order to better understand the thoughts of customers which were stored and collected as images. The procedure included a sample of respondents who were distributed between affective and cognitive scenarios in an equal manner. Then, the application of an individual-difference multidimensional scaling approach (INDSCAL) was performed aiming to display the overall semantic space among items that were generated. Using the AOL technique, a group of sixty items related to affective and cognitive scenarios in the context of online and offline reputation was generated. Based on further analysis, six clusters were obtained for each of the scenarios. The author concluded that the following seven items could be included in the scales for measuring corporate reputation, namely: "avant-garde, singularity, exclusivity, savings, return policy, freedom and speed".

Authors Oncioiu et al. (2020) developed a model of online reputation that includes the following dimensions: "online visibility, employee satisfaction, increased sales to customers who improve the company's image, return on assets and level of corporate social responsibility disclosure". Their reputation measurement model was based not only on assessment of reputation from the perspective of customers, with the aim of increasing the company's sales, but also on the assessment from the perspective of employees as one of the key groups whose perception is often neglected in the reputation building context.

In their study, Yu and Han (2021) aimed to develop and validate multidimensional reputation criteria for assessing online shopping malls, which have experienced rapid growth since the onset of the COVID-19 pandemic. Based on the results of a Delphi study which involved a group of professionals, items determining the reputation of online shopping malls were further used to construct a questionnaire distributed to consumers. The results indicated that four basic factors of online shopping mall reputation – "reliability, technical skills, customer service and accessibility".

Luoma-aho et al. (2021) tried to determine to what extent it is possible to use the Net Promoter Score (NPS), a popular Word of Mouth measurement tool, as a measure of the reputation of organizations in the public sector. They examined how effectively NPS reflects public sector reputation and explore the characteristics of the various stakeholder groups categorized by NPS within the public sector. They conducted a stakeholder survey of an institution from the public sector and concluded that the NPS framework requires adaptation to the characteristics public sector, and consequently suggested "The Public Sector Net Promoter Score (PSNPS)" as an adequate WOM measure in the context of public sector.

The aim of the research by Puma Flores and Rosa-Díaz (2023) was to define an adequate method for evaluating online corporate reputation in B2B markets. In order to realize this, the authors conducted quantitative and qualitative study containing three stages, which was based on in-depth interviews of managers and experts. In the next phase, they applied advanced sentiment analysis of the online content (websites, social media), and in the final, constructed the Total Online Reputation Index (TOR). The study resulted in 13 variables which significantly shape online reputation: "the quality of the website, detailed information about the products and the company, the presence of the brand in the digital press, and the presence in social networks, storytelling on the website, e-commerce channels, available B2B marketplaces for purchasing or closing deals, number of visitors to the website, frequency of content updates, correct translation of the website into other languages, ease of finding the website, SEO positioning on Google, and quick response to communications".

## 3.2. Studies Based on Social Media Content Analysis

This, second group of research is based exclusively on the analysis of secondary data, primarily data collected from internet sites and social media. El Marrakchi et al. (2015a) proposed a Reputation System, used for the measurement of corporate brand reputation on social networks, based on a vector model that could be used for representing reputation in social networks. This system provides a reputation score of a product or company, which is measured on the basis of community opinions without asking any rating from community members. Starting from the existing social media monitoring tools (SMM), which are necessary source because they provide companies with insight into what people think about their brand, what they are talking about and in what way, El Marrakchi et al. (2015b) introduced the Intelligent Reputation Measuring System (IRMS) intended to be used for measuring the reputation scores. In their subsequent study, El Marrakchi et al. (2016) pointed out the shortcomings of existing SMM tools which, even though they provide important insight for managers, only in a number of few can be used to calculate an overall reputation score. Applying their Intelligent Reputation Measuring System (IRMS), which scores reputation in a social network by applying a multi-context and people-oriented model, using real data from Twitter, these authors pointed out the advantages of this tool compared to other available tools.

In their research, Pollák et al. (2016) considered the online reputation of tourism organizations as one element of sustainable e-marketing. They emphasized the available ways and methods for evaluating online reputation in this sector. They conducted an analysis of the reputation that exists in the digital environment, taking into account the rating of organizations on internet platforms such as Booking and TripAdvisor, and then comparing these ratings against the widespread sentiment analysis. By applying statistical testing, between-factors relationships (online reputation scores on the basis of advanced sentiment analysis in comparison with the reputation indices on rating sites) that influence online reputation in a hyper competitive digital environment were examined. Pollák et al. (2018) sought to present the most effective ways to measure online reputation, as a very sensitive intangible asset, of companies operating in the field of transport and logistics. They used multi-factor sentiment analysis to test their model for measuring Total online reputation (TOR). They took into account ratings from Google, which are reflected in numerically expressed user reviews and Facebook Competive Score (number of fans). The control measurements conducted in the analysis aimed to identify and describe key relationships and variables to support the development and presentation of an accessible and practical tool for measuring online reputation in the dynamic digital environment. In their subsequent work, Pollák et al. (2019) applied their multi-factor analysis of reputation gained online - in this case the modified Total online reputation (TOR) methodology to assess the online reputation of entities operating in the field of tourism. In the first step, the online ratings were converted into percentages, and then compared with the ratings in the offline sphere. Then, with the application of statistical testing, the relationship between the factors that influence online reputation was established.

Shad Manaman et al. (2016) proposed a Reputation Management System which can be used for the purpose of measuring the company's reputation based on data collected from social media, primarily from Twitter. This reputation measurement method was based on the N-gram learning approach, which includes training and testing steps. First, the name of the company and the tweets related to it were taken into account, and it was determined whether the tweets had a positive or negative effect on the reputation. In the step related to training, the authors took into account four corporate profile types (positive, negative, neutral, and irrelevant) for each company, and used major percentage of tweets to build corporate profiles. In a second step, by testing the remaining tweets, they were also assigned to profiles to determine how they affect corporate reputation. Starting from the fact that stakeholders, as users of social media, are increasingly engaged in communication with companies, Steenkamp and Rensburg (2016) took into the account that they can also be considered co-creators of communication content. In this sense, the authors developed a conceptual framework for reputation management on SNSs (social networking sites). This concept was based on the monitoring and collection of data that stakeholders publish on these sites and their analysis. The authors conducted the analysis using computer-aided qualitative data analysis software (CAQDAS). This way, they performed an analysis of stakeholder sentiment, identified key communication discourses on social networks and determined risks and threats to corporate reputation.

Criticizing traditional ways of measuring corporate reputation based on public surveys, which is a demanding and expensive undertaking, Klein et al. (2019) proposed the use of social media as the primary sources of information for measuring reputation. In this sense, the authors proposed an information retrieval approach that can be used for the automatic collection of textual content related to the company's reputation, and then sentiment analysis of that content, which is based on machine learning. In this way, companies can assess their online reputation in an efficient and cost-effective manner. Similarly, Rantanen et al. (2020) developed a corporate reputation classification framework based on multiple dimensions, which is specific for the online content. The basis for reputation assessment is user content on social media. The authors pointed out that manual analysis and classification of this content is ineffective considering the amount of data and its heterogeneity, so the classification supported by machine learning is an adequate substitute for it. The classification framework of online reputation developed by those authors contains six basic dimensions formulated on the basis of previous literature – "quality, reliability, responsibility, successfulness, pleasantness and innovativeness". After retrieval of content from social media, they used a convolutional neural network (CNN) for automatic classification of comments based on manually annotated training data. In the same manner, in order to indicate an alternative to public survey, which is a time-consuming and costly measure, Loke and Reitter (2021) proposed an aspect-based sentiment analysis for the purpose of collection and analysis of user content available on the Internet, driven by machine learning. This type of analysis is useful because it saves costs, time and human effort to assess corporate reputation and provides the ability to break down the overall reputation into several dimensions. This provides companies with a more detailed insight into the constituents of their reputation and provides an informational basis for further courses of action, whether it is a question of supporting an established positive reputation or improving a negative one.

Vaccaro et al. (2020) stated that previously developed indices for measuring online reputation, although they represent important information for the development of marketing campaigns, are usually tailored to a specific company or brand and are not useful for comparing the reputations of two or more competitors. Therefore, the authors proposed a Comparison Matrix Geometric Index (CMGI), which represents a novel qualitative online reputation metric, which includes an assessment of the emotional reactions of users but also a direct comparison expressed in communication via social media, which indicates relative preferences between several alternatives. Ramos and Casado-Molina (2021) developed an Online Corporate Reputation Index (OCRI) as a measure of a company's economic performance in the digital environment and tested it on corporations in banking sector. Grounded on collected data from economic and financial sources, websites, media, social media sources etc., this index was developed with the application of business intelligence tools in combination with panel econometric models. The online reputation model evaluates both intangible assets (like emotions, attitudes, experiences) expressed by stakeholders regarding these key companies, and tangible business assets (like stock market value). Data for the analysis was drawn from various digital sources, including economic and financial platforms, hypertextual sources (such as mass media, online publications, websites), multimedia platforms (like YouTube), and social networks (like Twitter and Facebook).

Starting from the challenge of determining how stakeholders perceive a brand over time, Rust et al. (2021) pointed out that measures of reputation must include the "voice" of stakeholders, and not simply ratings on the Internet, as well as be related to the financial value of the brand. In this context, the authors developed a brand reputation tracker related to social media. The reputation tracker is based on the technique of mining Twitter comments for the world's top 100 brands, on a weekly, monthly and quarterly basis. As a result, authors demonstrated that it is possible to monitor reputation in real time and longitudinally. The positive characteristic of the tracker is that it is highly responsive to time and context, enabling companies to swiftly react to market dynamics. This way of measuring reputation makes brand reputation both financially measurable and actionable for managers in real time and over a period of time. Al-Yazidi et al. (2022) proposed a corporate reputation measurement model in online social networks (OSNs) that is based on multi criteria decision making techniques by means of which different features are integrated into one comprehensive reputation metric. They built their model based on a huge data set that includes posts on Twitter which was used to measure the reputation of a group of well-known worldwide companies. This model is based on a combination of quantitative (number of tweets/followers) and qualitative features and analysis of posts extracted from Twitter, interactions and user sentiments, and provides a valuable insight on how the company is actually perceived on social media.

By grounding their method on an adapted Fombrun et al.'s Reputation Quotient, Westermann and Forthmann (2020) conducted an evaluation of the reputation of 500 companies based on data from a large number of Internet data sources. They measured six dimensions of companies' Reputation Quotient: products and services, employer 's performance, economic performance, performance of the management, performance through sustainability and emotional appeal. The analysis was based on the social listening method, which enables automated recording and an algorithm-based analysis of online conversations which were considered to be major drivers of reputation by the authors. In this way, managers are given insight into how different groups of stakeholders experience the company, taking into account different dimensions.

Orrego et al. (2021) developed three literature-based methodologies that allow for the assessment of online reputation based on the analysis of data from online sources. All three methodologies were based on automated analysis procedures. Without an automated Online Reputation Management (ORM) system, this task must be handled manually by a designated person within the company, which can lead to operational errors, process delays, and limitations on scalability as the volume of items (such as news and comments) to review increases. Automating the procedure of measurement of corporate online reputation can address these challenges. With this regard, these authors presented the development of three methodologies, based on existing literature, to explore online reputation measurement using information sources like Twitter and Google News. Similarly, Peng and Wan (2023) formulated a method of assessment of corporate image based on the available literature. In the next phase, an automatic text analysis of available information on online channels was carried out through a topic classification and sentiment analysis algorithm.

Loke and Lam-Lion (2021) investigated the best way to examine the ways in which employees, as one of the key stakeholder groups, perceive the company. They concluded that sentiment analysis, in combination with semantic search, represents a suitable method for evaluating the company's reputation. They analyzed the content of online reviews posted by employees which indicate their attitudes towards the company. Stakeholder' reviews were also taken as a measure of online reputation by Zaki Ahmed and Rodríguez-Díaz (2020). They tended to measure the online reputation of airline companies by using variables used by TripAdvisor and customer online reviews were taken as the proper information signaling service quality and perceived value. The insight into customer-related information was used for further calculation of online reputation and recommendations for strategic positioning of airline companies in the digital environment.

## CONCLUSION

Since this chapter contains a qualitative approach to literature analysis, it results in comprehensive literature review on the topic of evaluation and assessment of corporate reputation in the digital environment. The research presented in this chapter is grounded in a systematic literature review, which represents a structured process that allows researchers to identify, evaluate, and synthesize all relevant studies on a particular topic. The focus of the chapter is on providing a general overview of the topic, by pointing out to relevant studies and existing research findings with this regard. By putting accent on frameworks for online reputation management and scales and tools for online reputation measurement, it contributes to the body of the knowledge within this specific topic. The findings could serve as a theoretical background for further research in this field and a source of references to other researchers, providing them with useful informational basis for empirical studies.

As for the first research question (RQ1), which refers to the current scope of research on online reputation measurement/assessment, the conclusion is that the number of researches on this topic is increasing, which is expected considering the importance of communication and interaction with stakeholders through digital channels. In this way, there is a need to identify and assess the constituents of corporate reputation that are specific to the digital environment. The identification and assessment of the constituents of online reputation allow a better understanding of factors that influence the perception of a corporate brand built by individuals and organizations in the digital space. This is critical for proactive reputation management, building trust and minimizing negative image impacts. A marked heterogeneity was found regarding the variables (dimensions of reputation) that different authors take into account in their research (RQ2). Over time, more and more parameters related to social media have been included, whether they are quantitative indicators (e.g. number of followers, fluctuation of followers, numerically expressed ratings/reviews) or qualitative (character of the content placed on social media). In the end, a distinct dominance of methodological frameworks grounded in the analysis of secondary data available through various internet platforms, primarily social media and rating platforms, was established. As these datasets are quite extensive, in most cases they are analyzed using sentiment analysis based on some of the machine learning techniques. The number of studies that are based on surveying a certain target group is decreasing, taking into account that this type of data is more difficult to obtain and more time and financial resources are required (RQ3). The increase in research measuring online reputation using social media data is understandable due to its availability, scope, and realistic insight into actual user opinions and interactions. Unlike surveys, social media provide dynamic and immediate information, which is often less subject to respondent bias which eenables faster and more accurate analysis of perception in a wider context.

The research results provide valuable insights for organizations that strive to become human-centric, sustainable, and resilient in the digital age. Measuring and managing corporate reputation in the digital environment is not just a technical process, but a strategic activity that helps organizations respond to the demands of key stakeholders, build trust and ensure long-term sustainability. Understanding online reputation is key to designing organizations that put people at the center of attention, adapt to the challenges of modern society through sustainable practices, and develop resilience to dynamic changes in the digital ecosystem. In this way, the results of this literature-based research contribute to the wider discourse on the transformation of organizations in accordance with the core values of the contemporary business environment.

As common for review papers, the presented research possesses certain limitations, mainly related to the complexity of data integration and potential author bias. Differences in study designs, populations, interventions, and outcomes can make it difficult to systematically combine results from different studies, and heterogeneity in this context can limit the comparability and potential for generalization of results. Additionally, predefined inclusion/exclusion criteria may limit the scope of analyzed sources which might lead to overlooking some relevant findings outside the strict framework of research questions and keywords used for searching. Finally, systematic literature reviews may be a subject to a certain degree of author bias, given that researchers make certain subjective decisions when selecting studies, extracting data and conduct qualitative analysis, which may affect the quality of final results. Therefore, in the context of future research directions, it is suggested to include related search parameters and define different criteria for classification and grouping of studies in the field of digital corporate reputation.

## REFERENCES

Abelha, M., Fernandes, S., Mesquita, D., Seabra, F., & Ferreira-Oliveira, A. T. (2020). Graduate employability and competence development in higher education—A systematic literature review using PRISMA. *Sustainability (Basel)*, 12(15), 5900. DOI: 10.3390/su12155900

Al-Yazidi, A. S., Berri, J., & Mehedi Hassan, M. (2022). Novel hybrid model for organizations' reputation in online social networks. *Journal of King Saud University. Computer and Information Sciences*, 34(8), 5305–5317. DOI: 10.1016/j.jksuci.2022.01.006

Al-Yazidi, S., Berri, J., Al-Qurishi, M., & Al-Alrubaian, M. (2020). Measuring reputation and influence in online social networks: A systematic literature review. *IEEE Access : Practical Innovations, Open Solutions*, 8, 105824–105851. DOI: 10.1109/ACCESS.2020.2999033

Albhirat, M. M., Rashid, A., Rasheed, R., Rasool, S., Zulkiffli, S. N. A., Zia-ul-Haq, H. M., & Mohammad, A. M. (2024). The PRISMA statement in enviropreneurship study: A systematic literature and a research agenda. *Cleaner Engineering and Technology*, 18, 100721. DOI: 10.1016/j.clet.2024.100721

Aureli, S., & Supino, E. (2017). Online reputation monitoring: An exploratory study on Italian hotel managers' practices. *International Journal of Hospitality & Tourism Administration*, 18(1), 84–109. DOI: 10.1080/15256480.2016.1264903

Caputo, A., Molino, M., Cerato, B., & Cortese, C. G. (2023). Employer attractiveness: Two instruments to measure employer branding and reputation. *SAGE Open*, 13(3), 21582440231192188. Advance online publication. DOI: 10.1177/21582440231192188

Chun, R., & Davies, G. (2001). E-reputation: The role of mission and vision statements in positioning strategy. *Journal of Brand Management*, 8(4), 315–333. DOI: 10.1057/palgrave.bm.2540031

Cioppi, M., Curina, I., Forlani, F., & Pencarelli, T. (2019). Online presence, visibility and reputation: A systematic literature review in management studies. *Journal of Research in Interactive Marketing*, 13(4), 547–577. DOI: 10.1108/JRIM-11-2018-0139

Davies, G., Chun, R., da Silva, R., & Ropert, S. (2004). A Corporate Character Scale to assess employee and customer views of organization reputation. *Corporate Reputation Review*, 7(2), 125–146. DOI: 10.1057/palgrave.crr.1540216

Dutot, V., & Castellano, S. (2015). Designing a measurement scale for E-Reputation. *Corporate Reputation Review*, 18(4), 294–313. DOI: 10.1057/crr.2015.15

El Marrakchi, M., Bellafkih, M., & Bensaid, H. (2015a). *Towards reputation measurement in online social networks. 2015 Intelligent Systems and Computer Vision.* ISCV., DOI: 10.1109/ISACV.2015.7105540

El Marrakchi, M., Bensaid, H., & Bellafkih, M. (2015b). Scoring reputation in online social networks. *10$^{th}$ International Conference on Intelligent Systems - Theories and Applications (SITA)*, 20-21 October 2015, Rabat, Morocco, pp. 1-6. https://DOI: 10.1109/SITA.2015.7358420

El Marrakchi, M., Bensaid, H., Bellafkih, M., & Bensaid, H. (2016). Intelligent reputation scoring in social networks: Use case of brands of smartphones. *11th International Conference on Intelligent Systems: Theories and Applications (SITA)*, 19-20 October 2016, Mohammedia, Morocco, pp. 1-6, https://DOI: 10.1109/SITA.2016.7772261

Ferreira, M., & Zambaldi, F. (2019). The mediating role of consumer engagement with the brand community and its effect on corporate reputation. *International Journal on Media Management*, 21(1), 45–64. DOI: 10.1080/14241277.2019.1585354

Fombrun, C., Ponzi, L., & Newburry, W. (2015). Stakeholder Tracking and Analysis: The RepTrak® System for Measuring Corporate Reputation. *Corporate Reputation Review*, 18(1), 3–24. DOI: 10.1057/crr.2014.21

Fombrun, C. J., Gardberg, N. A., & Sever, J. M. (2000). The Reputation QuotientSM: A multi-stakeholder measure of corporate reputation. *Journal of Brand Management*, 7(4), 241–255. DOI: 10.1057/bm.2000.10

Fu, X., Yue, K., Liu, L., & Liu, L. (2016). Aggregating ordinal user preferences for effective reputation computation of online services. *2016 IEEE International Conference on Web Services (ICWS)*, San Francisco, CA, USA, 2016, pp. 554-561, DOI: 10.1109/ICWS.2016.77

Galletta, S., Mazzù, S., Naciti, V., & Paltrinieri, A. (2024). A PRISMA systematic review of greenwashing in the banking industry: A call for action. *Research in International Business and Finance*, 69, 102262. DOI: 10.1016/j.ribaf.2024.102262

Goldring, D. (2015). Reputation orientation. *Marketing Intelligence & Planning*, 33(5), 784–803. DOI: 10.1108/MIP-11-2013-0183

Hojdik, V., & Majtán, S. (2017). Online reputation management as an integral part of company business management. *Proceedings of the 2nd Annual International Scientific Conference of Business Economics, Management and Marketing (ISCOBEMM)*, Zajeci, Czech Republic, May 25-26, pp.76-83.

Khan, S., & Digout, J. (2017). The Corporate Reputation Reporting Framework (CRRF). *Corporate Reputation Review*, 21(1), 22–36. DOI: 10.1057/s41299-017-0041-4

Klein, A., Riekert, M., & Dinev, V. (2019). Accurate retrieval of corporate reputation from online media using machine learning. *Annals of Computer Science and Information Systems*, 43-46, 43–46. Advance online publication. DOI: 10.15439/2019F169

Kotras, B. (2020). Opinions that matter: The hybridization of opinion and reputation measurement in social media listening software. *Media Culture & Society*, 42(7-8), 1495–1511. DOI: 10.1177/0163443720939427

Krstić, J., & Ćorić, N. (2021). Public health communication: Skin cancer prevention implications. *Management: Journal of Sustainable Business and Management Solutions in Emerging Economies*, 29(1), 63–85. DOI: 10.7595/management.fon.2021.0036

Krstić, J., Reljić, M., & Filipović, S. (2019). Factors influencing electricity consumption: A review of research methods. *Management: Journal of Sustainable Business and Management Solutions in Emerging Economies*, 24(2), 13–22. DOI: 10.7595/management.fon.2018.0021

Lange, D., Lee, P. M., & Dai, Y. (2011). Organizational reputation: A Review. *Journal of Management*, 37(1), 153–184. DOI: 10.1177/0149206310390963

Loke, R., & Lam-Lion, R. (2021). A company's corporate reputation through the eyes of employees measured with sentiment analysis of online reviews. *Proceedings of the 10th International Conference on Data Science, Technology and Applications*, 378-385. DOI: 10.5220/0010620600002993

Loke, R., & Reitter, W. (2021). Aspect based sentiment analysis on online review data to predict corporate reputation. *Proceedings of the 10th International Conference on Data Science, Technology and Applications (DATA)*, 343-352. DOI: 10.5220/0010607200002993

Luoma-aho, V., Canel, M., & Hakola, J. (2021). Public sector reputation and netpromoter score. *International Review on Public and Nonprofit Marketing*, 18(3), 419–446. DOI: 10.1007/s12208-021-00280-9

Marinović, N., Vlastelica, T., & Krstić, J. (2022). Evaluating digital corporate identity: Application of AHP method in website quality analysis. *Industrija*, 3/4(50), 55–74. DOI: 10.5937/industrija50-44052

Melewar, T. C., Dennis, C., & Foroudi, P. (2022). *Building corporate identity, image and reputation in the digital era*. Routledge.

Mellinas, J. P., & Martin-Fuentes, E. (2024). The Complex World of Online Reviews: Criteria for Establishing a Global Index for Accommodation. In Berezina, K., Nixon, L., & Tuomi, A. (Eds.), *Information and Communication Technologies in Tourism 2024. ENTER 2024. Springer Proceedings in Business and Economics*. Springer., DOI: 10.1007/978-3-031-58839-6_44

Moher, D., Shamseer, L., Clarke, M., Ghersi, D., Liberati, A., Petticrew, M., Shekelle, P., & Stewart, L. A. (2015). Preferred Reporting Items for Systematic Review and meta-analysis Protocols (PRISMA-P) 2015 Statement. *Systematic Reviews*, 4(1), 1–9. DOI: 10.1186/2046-4053-4-1 PMID: 25554246

Money, K., & Hillenbrand, C. (2006). Using Reputation Measurement to Create Value: An Analysis and Integration of Existing Measures. *Journal of General Management*, 32(1), 1–12. DOI: 10.1177/030630700603200101

Nuortimo, K., Harkonen, J. & Breznik, K. (2024). Exploring corporate reputation and crisis communication. *Journal of Marketing Analitics*. DOI: 10.1057/s41270-024-00353-8

Oh, H. K., Jung, J., Park, S., & Kim, S. W. (2020). A robust reputation system using online reviews. *Computer Science and Information Systems*, 17(2), 487–507. DOI: 10.2298/CSIS191122007O

Oncioiu, I., Popescu, D.-M., Anghel, E., Petrescu, A.-G., Bîlcan, F.-R., & Petrescu, M. (2020). Online company reputation—A thorny problem for optimizing corporate sustainability. *Sustainability (Basel)*, 12(14), 5547. DOI: 10.3390/su12145547

Orrego, C., Villa, L. F., Sepúlveda-Cano, L. M., & Giraldo, M. L. M. (2021). Organizational online reputation measurement through natural language processing and sentiment analysis techniques. In Applied Computer Sciences in Engineering: 8th Workshop on Engineering Applications, WEA 2021, Medellín, Colombia, October 6–8, 2021 [Springer International Publishing.]. *Proceedings*, 8, 60–71.

Özhan, Ş., Ozhan, E., & Habiboglu, O. (2023). The analysis of brand reputation and willingness to pay price premium with regression analysis and classification algorithms. *Kybernetes*, Vol. ahead-of-print No. ahead-of-print. DOI: 10.1108/K-02-2023-0231

Page, M. J., McKenzie, J. E., Bossuyt, P. M., Boutron, I., Hoffmann, T. C., Mulrow, C. D., Shamseer, L., Tetzlaff, J. M., Akl, E. A., Brennan, S. E., Chou, R., Glanville, J., Grimshaw, J. M., Hróbjartsson, A., Lalu, M. M., Li, T., Loder, E. W., Mayo-Wilson, E., McDonald, S., & Moher, D. (2021). The PRISMA 2020 statement: An updated guideline for reporting systematic reviews. *Systematic Reviews*, 10(1), 105906. DOI: 10.1186/s13643-021-01626-4 PMID: 33781348

Peixoto, B., Pinto, R., Melo, M., Cabral, L., & Bessa, M. (2021). Immersive virtual reality for foreign language education: A PRISMA Systematic Review. *IEEE Access : Practical Innovations, Open Solutions*, 9, 48952–48962. DOI: 10.1109/ACCESS.2021.3068858

Peng, Z., & Wan, Y. (2023). Generating business intelligence through automated textual analysis: Measuring corporate image with online information. *Chinese Management Studies*, 17(3), 545–572. DOI: 10.1108/CMS-07-2021-0318

Pollák, F., Dorcák, P., Markovič, P., & Soviar, J. (2019). Innovative approaches to the reputation management in the tourism sector. Innovation and transformation in a digital world (IDIMT-2019), September 4–6, Kutná Hora, Czech Republic, pp.285-292.

Pollák, F., Dorčák, P., Račeta, N., & Svetozarovová, N. (2016). Sustainable E-marketing of selected tourism subjects from the Mediterranean through active online reputation management. In *Leon-Garcia, A., et al. Smart City 360°. Lecture Notes of the Institute for Computer Sciences, Social Informatics and Telecommunications Engineering* (Vol. 166). Springer., DOI: 10.1007/978-3-319-33681-7_60

Pollák, F., & Markovič, P. (2022). Challenges for Corporate Reputation—Online Reputation Management in Times of Global Pandemic. *Journal of Risk and Financial Management*, 15(6), 250. DOI: 10.3390/jrfm15060250

Pollák, F., Soviar, J., & Svetozarovová, N. (2018). Selected approaches to sustainable development of corporate reputation - empirical study of online reputation management of subjects from the field of supply chain management. *8th Carpathian Logistics Congress on Logistics, Distribution, Transport and Management (CLC)*, 3-5 December, Prague, Czech Republic, pp. 324-329.

Ponzi, L. J., Fombrun, C. J., & Gardberg, N. A. (2011). RepTrak™ Pulse: Conceptualizing and validating a short-form measure of corporate reputation. *Corporate Reputation Review*, 14(1), 15–35. DOI: 10.1057/crr.2011.5

Puma Flores, M. J., & Rosa-Díaz, I. M. (2023). Online reputation for food sector exporters in the B2B context: The importance of sustainability. *Foods*, 12(20), 3862. DOI: 10.3390/foods12203862 PMID: 37893755

Ramos, C. M. Q., & Casado-Molina, A.-M. (2021). Online corporate reputation: A panel data approach and a reputation index proposal applied to the banking sector. *Journal of Business Research*, 122, 121–130. DOI: 10.1016/j.jbusres.2020.08.061

Rantanen, A., Salminen, J., Ginter, F., & Jansen, B. J. (2020). Classifying online corporate reputation with machine learning: A study in the banking domain. *Internet Research*, 30(1), 45–66. DOI: 10.1108/INTR-07-2018-0318

Reuber, A. R., & Fischer, E. (2011). International entrepreneurship in internet-enabled markets. *Journal of Business Venturing*, 26(6), 660–679. DOI: 10.1016/j.jbusvent.2011.05.002

Rodríguez-Díaz, M., Alonso-González, R., Rodríguez-Voltes, C. I., & Rodríguez-Voltes, A. C. (2019). A rating of the online reputation balance in lodgings. *Administrative Sciences*, 9(3), 58. DOI: 10.3390/admsci9030058

Rodríguez-Díaz, M., Rodríguez-Díaz, R., Rodríguez-Voltes, A. C., & Rodríguez-Voltes, C. I. (2018). Analysing the relationship between price and online reputation by lodging category. *Sustainability (Basel)*, 10(12), 4474. DOI: 10.3390/su10124474

Rodríguez-Díaz, M., Rodríguez-Voltes, C. I., & Rodríguez-Voltes, A. C. (2018). Gap analysis of the online reputation. *Sustainability (Basel)*, 10(5), 1603. DOI: 10.3390/su10051603

Rosamond, E. (2020). From reputation capital to reputation warfare: Online Ratings, trolling, and the logic of volatility. *Theory, Culture & Society*, 37(2), 105–129. DOI: 10.1177/0263276419872530

Rust, R. T., Rand, W., Huang, M.-H., Stephen, A. T., Brooks, G., & Chabuk, T. (2021). Real-time brand reputation tracking using social media. *Journal of Marketing*, 85(4), 21–43. DOI: 10.1177/0022242921995173

Shad Manaman, H., Jamali, S., & AleAhmad, A. (2016). Online reputation measurement of companies based on user-generated content in online social networks. *Computers in Human Behavior*, 54, 94–100. DOI: 10.1016/j.chb.2015.07.061

Shamma, H. M., El Masry, R., & Dutot, V. (2023). When online reputation drives consumers' online repurchase intentions: An Egyptian story. *Global Business Review*, 0(0), 09721509231155276. Advance online publication. DOI: 10.1177/09721509231155276

Skočajić, I., Pavković, V., Krstić, J., Kostić-Stanković, M., Vlastelica, T., & Rajić, T. (2024). Urban tourism appeal: The effectiveness of communication channels and multimedia formats in creating tourists' expectations. *Sustainability (Basel)*, 16(11), 4552. DOI: 10.3390/su16114552

Steenkamp, H., & Rensburg, R. (2016). Harnessing stakeholder sentiment on social networking sites: A new conceptual framework for online reputation management. *Communicare*, 35(2), 55–84. DOI: 10.36615/jcsa.v35i2.1597

Syed Alwi, S. F., & Da Silva, R. V. (2007). Online and offline corporate brand images: Do they differ? *Corporate Reputation Review*, 10(4), 217–244. DOI: 10.1057/palgrave.crr.1550056

Thompson, S., & Haynes, M. (2017). The value of online seller reputation: Evidence from a price comparison site. *MDE. Managerial and Decision Economics*, 38(3), 302–313. DOI: 10.1002/mde.2777

Vaccaro, G., Cabrera, F., Pelaez, J. I., & Vargas, L. G. (2020). Comparison matrix geometric index: A qualitative online reputation metric. *Applied Soft Computing*, 96, 106687. DOI: 10.1016/j.asoc.2020.106687 von Berlepsch, D., Lemke, F., & Gorton, M. (2024). The importance of corporate reputation for sustainable supply chains: A systematic literature review, bibliometric mapping, and research agenda. *Journal of Business Ethics*, 189(1), 9–34. DOI: 10.1007/s10551-022-05268-x PMID: 36259069

Walker, K. (2010). A systematic review of the corporate reputation literature: Definition, measurement, and theory. *Corporate Reputation Review*, 12(4), 357–387. DOI: 10.1057/crr.2009.26

Walsh, G., & Beatty, S. E. (2007). Customer-based corporate reputation of a service firm: Scale development and validation. *Journal of the Academy of Marketing Science*, 35(1), 127–143. DOI: 10.1007/s11747-007-0015-7

Wepener, M., & Boshoff, C. (2015). An instrument to measure the customer-based corporate reputation of large service organizations. *Journal of Services Marketing*, 29(3), 163–172. DOI: 10.1108/JSM-01-2014-0026

Westermann, A., & Forthmann, J. (2020). Social listening: A potential game changer in reputation management. How big data analysis can contribute to understanding stakeholders' views on organisations. *Corporate Communications*, 26(1), 2–22. DOI: 10.1108/CCIJ-01-2020-0028

Whiting, R. H., Hansen, P., & Sen, A. (2017). A tool for measuring SMEs' reputation, engagement and goodwill: A New Zealand exploratory study. *Journal of Intellectual Capital*, 18(1), 170–188. DOI: 10.1108/JIC-02-2016-0028

Xie, H., & Lui, J. C. S. (2020). Mining deficiencies of online reputation systems: Methodologies, experiments and implications. *IEEE Transactions on Services Computing*, 13(5), 887–900. DOI: 10.1109/TSC.2017.2730206

Youness, C., & Valette-Florence, P. (2017). Online reputation scale development: A customer perspective. *Developments in Marketing Science:Proceedings of the Academy of Marketing Science*, 569–579. DOI: 10.1007/978-3-319-47331-4_109

Youness, C., Valette-Florence, P., & Assaf, C. (2024). Global corporate reputation: A projective qualitative approach from a customer perspective. *Qualitative Market Research*, 27(1), 108–128. DOI: 10.1108/QMR-04-2023-0052

Yu, H., & Han, E. (2021). Developing a measure for online shopping mall reputation (OSMR). *Sustainability (Basel)*, 13(7), 3818. DOI: 10.3390/su13073818

Zaki Ahmed, A., & Rodríguez-Díaz, M. (2020). Analyzing the online reputation and positioning of airlines. *Sustainability (Basel)*, 12(3), 1184. DOI: 10.3390/su12031184

# Chapter 11
# Board Structure and Sustainability Performance:
## A Study on Turkish Manufacturing Companies

**Ayfer Aksu**
*Başkent University, Turkey*

**İrge Şener**
https://orcid.org/0000-0002-1876-9411
*Çankaya University, Turkey*

**A. Kadir Varoğlu**
https://orcid.org/0000-0001-7857-5013
*Başkent University, Turkey*

## ABSTRACT

*The adoption of the innovative perspective of Industry 5.0 at the highest level in organizations is important for ensuring sustainability in every field and the board of directors' role becomes increasingly important in improving companies' sustainability performance. This chapter first presents the theoretical and conceptual background of Industry 5.0 and sustainability, the role of boards of directors in sustainability, and corporate sustainability reporting. Then, the findings of an empirical study that examine the impact of board structure on companies' sustainability performance are presented. The study aims to contribute by revealing which characteristics of companies' boards of directors positively impact sustainability performances of the companies. The data from 166 manufacturing firms listed on Borsa Istanbul have been used in the research. Findings suggest that both the size of the board and the presence of women on the board have a positive impact on sustainability performance.*

DOI: 10.4018/979-8-3693-8181-6.ch011

## INTRODUCTION

Throughout history, the Industrial Revolutions, driven by scientific and technological paradigm shifts, have led to transformative developments across all systems of society (Leng et al., 2022, p. 279; Pinheiro et al., 2019, p. 831). The process of transformation accelerated with the initiation of Industry 4.0 technologies and has continued with Industry 5.0, a new paradigm shift that complements Industry 4.0 (Ghobakhloo et al. 2022; Xu et al., 2021), by prioritizing human safety and well-being.

The First Industrial Revolution (Industry 1.0), which emerged in the eighteenth century, heralded the onset of mechanization in manufacturing through the utilization of steam-driven power. The defining characteristic of the Industry 1.0 was the replacement of manpower with steam power, leading to profound changes in industries such as textiles, shipbuilding, and railroads, ultimately resulting in increased productivity and output. This increase in productivity and production volume facilitated the evolution of companies into large, multi-partner enterprises (Sharma and Singh, 2020, pp. 66-67). This period can be considered as the starting point of corporate governance.

The Second Industrial Revolution (Industry 2.0), spanning from the late nineteenth century to 1980s, was characterized by significant technological advancements in electricity and mechanics (Aslam et al., 2020, p. 2). During this period, production of inexpensive steel led to the expansion of transportation networks, enabling access to diverse sources of raw materials. The most important technological innovations of this era were the use of electricity in industry and the advent of assembly lines, which marked the transition to serial production (Özsoylu, 2017, p. 42).

The Third Industrial Revolution (Industry 3.0), which prevailed from 1980 to 2000, was characterized by the transition from analog production systems to digital systems, ushered in the era of modular products (Yin et al., 2017, p. 848). Technological advancements during this period led to reduced costs, increased average labor productivity, and the emergence of overcapacity, necessitating downsizing and market exits. However, corporate internal control systems during this period struggled to effectively address issues related to slow growth and the need for market exits. For example, General Motors' board of directors only dismissed a CEO who had resisted strategic change, for a decade after the firm lost around $6.5 billion in 1990-1991 (Jensen, 1993, p. 853).

The Fourth Industrial Revolution, which was launched at the Hannover Fair in Germany in 2011 and continues till present time, has facilitated autonomous decision-making processes, real-time and continuous monitoring of corporate processes, and the creation of value through strong networks with early stakeholder involvement. The execution of business model shift strategies aligned with Industry 4.0 has required companies to invest in areas such as digitization, artificial intelligence, smart manufacturing, autonomous robots, Internet of Things, horizontal and vertical system integration, cyber-physical systems, and cybersecurity (Hussainey et. al., 2022, p. 458). However, technological investments in Industry 4.0 have generally focused on the cost-effective dimension of sustainability, with insufficient emphasis on technologies aimed at environmental protection and enhancing the Earth's environmental sustainability (Nahavandi, 2019, p. 13). During industrial revolutions that have prioritized the economic aspects of sustainability, production systems have struggled to adapt to innovative societal demands for "sustainability", "human-centeredness", and "carbon emissions" (Leng et al., 2022, p. 279).

The Fifth Industrial Revolution initiated in 2016 with Japanese government's introduction of "Society 5.0" initiative, which aimed to generate a "Super Smart Society." Built on a foundation of digital technology and aimed at delivering superior well-being to all members of society (Shiroishi et al., 2018), Industry 5.0 seeks to establish a human-centered, sustainable, and resilient industrial paradigm (Ghobakhloo et al., 2022; Karmaker et al., 2023). The enhanced human-machine communication introduced by Industry 5.0 enables individuals to express themselves and access personalized products and services (Ozkeser, 2018).

Throughout the world's industrial development process, the manufacturing sector has consistently been a key driver of economic growth. However, it is also well-known that the production process, along with increasing and diversifying consumption, causes destructive effects on both the environment and human well-being (Gutowski et al., 2013). Accordingly, the pressure from society on manufacturing companies to adopt sustainable practices is intensifying.

It is expected that Industry 5.0, with its focus on human-centeredness and societal needs, will help resolve the misalignment between production and societal needs (Leng et al., 2022, p. 279). On the other hand, it is evident that the adoption of the regenerative vision of Industry 5.0 at the organizational level will require corporate boards to play a central role. Boards will fulfill this role by advising management, providing direction, making strategic decisions, overseeing management activities, and facilitating access to resources. Furthermore, sustainability reporting, which has been practiced for many years, should be considered a valuable tool in the governance context on the path to achieving the industry characterized by "sustainability," "human-centeredness," and "resilience," as envisioned by Industry 5.0.

Sustainability reports provide disclosures on companies' sustainability-related goals and strategies, environmental management, stakeholder engagement, responsibilities to its personnel, shareholders, and society, adopted international standards, and social responsibility practices. It is suggested that investigating the relationships between the boards' characteristic and sustainability compliance level using companies' sustainability reports could offer insights into the governance structures that will prepare companies for Industry 5.0. Some studies concerning corporate governance suggest that institutional investors believe board members are in position to remarkably influence the company performance (Westphal and Bednar, 2005; Sonnenfeld, 2002).

Hence, taking into account the value of the Industry 5.0 contribution to sustainability and human-centeredness, this chapter focuses on the relationship between the board structure and the sustainability performance of manufacturing firms. In this context, the research question addressed is:

> Is there a relationship between the board structure (board size, gender diversity, ratio of independent members, educational level of board members, and CEO duality) and the sustainability performance of manufacturing companies listed on Borsa Istanbul?

In line with this question, after this introductory part, theoretical and conceptual background is summarized in second heading. Third part covers research goal, methodology and findings; and the chapter concludes with findings and limitations.

## THEORETICAL AND CONCEPTUAL BACKGROUND

### Sustainability

Sustainability can be defined in general terms as "maintaining well-being over a long, perhaps even an indefinite period" (Kuhlman & Farrington, 2010). Today, negative phenomena that have become significant global issues, such as natural disasters, carbon emissions, water and air pollution, and social inequalities (Manning et al., 2019), are thought to be the result of weak sustainability activities linked to economic development driven by industrialization (Ansong, 2017; Zainal, 2013). In this context, sustainability holds a central position at both global and corporate levels. The 'United Nations World Commission on Environment and Development' (WCED) released a report titled "Our Common Future" in 1987. Since G. H. Brundtland chaired the Commission, the report is also known as "The Brundtland Report". The Report emphasizes that the critical global environmental issues are particularly the result of extreme poverty in some regions of the world and unsustainable consumption and production patterns in others. By calling for a strategy that integrates development and the environment, it established guiding principles for "sustainable development" which is defined by WCED as "development that meets the needs of the present without compromising the ability of future generations to meet their own needs" (WCED, 1987, p. 24). Similarly, Dyllick & Hockerts (2002) also defined corporate sustainability as "meeting the needs of a firm's direct and indirect stakeholders without compromising its ability to meet the needs of future stakeholders" (cited by; Şener et. al, 2016, p. 85).

In the 2000s, corporate social responsibility and sustainability approaches began to converge towards shared objectives centered on society, the environment, and stakeholders (Dragu, 2019). In 2015, the United Nations introduced the Sustainable Development Goals (SDGs) as a component of the 2030 Agenda for Sustainable Development (Martínez-Ferrero & García-Meca, 2020; Yamane and Kaneko, 2022). Adopted by 193 United Nations member states, these 17 goals seek to eliminate poverty, safeguard the planet, and guarantee that all individuals live in peace and prosperity by 2030. The United Nations SDGs officially came into effect in January 2016. The integration of these goals into corporate governance principles and organizational policies of nations is imperative. Furthermore, achieving these targets, which are closely related to environmental, social, and governance (ESG) criteria, necessitates the support of innovation and technology offered by Industry 5.0 (Rehman et al., 2023). Industry 5.0 has the capacity to positively impact all facets of ESG by placing humans in the heart of industrial processes and utilizing technology to enhance the conditions for workers and take advantage of new opportunities (Leng et al., 2022).

Moreover, for the purpose of reducing environmental degradation and pollution, the European Union (EU) encourages companies to align with SDGs. In 2021, the European Union introduced the Extended Producer Responsibility (EPR) initiative to motivate producers, such as manufacturers, to prioritize the reuse, recycling, and recovery of materials before disposing of them in landfills and to enhance the existing Waste Framework Directive. The Directive mandates businesses to safeguard human health and the environment by reducing waste and its harmful effects through efficient management.

Apart from development of institutions initiatives, achieving sustainability on a global scale is contingent upon the active participation of organizations in related initiatives. It is imperative that sustainability is integrated into organizational culture, missions, visions, and corporate governance codes. The manufacturing sector plays a pivotal role in realizing SDGs, as it is responsible for product design and consumption of natural resources throughout production processes. By optimizing the utilization of resources and minimizing waste, this industry can make significant contributions to sustainability. Furthermore, the adoption of innovative technologies and green practices, enhancement of energy efficiency, and promotion of a circular economy are essential strategies for mitigating environmental impact.

## Industry 5.0 and Sustainability

As previously mentioned, Industry 5.0 comprehensively encompasses the elements of sustainability, along with resilience, and human-centeredness. With the emergence of Industry 5.0, there has been an increasing emphasis on sustainability endeavors, especially within the framework of The United Nations SDGs (Singh, 2022). According to Ghobakhloo et. al. (2022), Industry 5.0;

- Does not focus solely on efficiency-driven competition, but also prioritizes sustainable development,
- Empowers humans and sets technological development goals through a human-centered approach,
- Contributes to environmental sustainability through smart, renewable systems,
- Utilizes appropriate technologies and operational methods to expand the range of corporate responsibility at every stage of the value chain,
- Promotes stakeholder prioritization in governance of technology, innovation, and management of sustainability performance.

The adoption of Industry 5.0 technologies can offer a wide range of advantages to organizations and society (Rehman, 2023). Considering that a significant portion of non-renewable resources is consumed by the manufacturing sector (Malek & Desai, 2020), it can be argued that the manufacturing sector has the greatest potential to benefit from the advantages of Industry 5.0. These benefits are not limited to waste minimization, material and resource efficiency.

Some of the obvious benefits associated with sustainability are outlined below.

- increased effectiveness through task automation processes
- improved quality and security through timely identification of errors and vulnerabilities and mitigation of hazards (Hermann, 2019; Chen, 2023)
- cost reduction through process optimization
- optimized resource utilization, minimized waste and reduced environmental load (Almusaed et al., 2023),
- enhanced work environment, employee well-being, satisfaction, and growth opportunities (Doyle Kent & Kopacek, 2021)
- mitigated the legal and credibility risks linked to non-sustainable practices (Asif et al., 2023),
- protected employee health via automation of high risky duties, and lessening occupational disease
- data-based good corporate governance (Maddikunta et al., 2021),
- facilitated investment in skills and education related to ESG (Xu et al., 2021)
- reduced irregularities and fraud providing timely insights and predictive capabilities (Rupa et al., 2021).

Despite the many advantages listed above, companies may encounter sustainability-related risks while trying to ensure sustainability. For example, when a manufacturing company complies with the sustainability rules of regulatory authorities during the supply process, supplier options may decrease. As the Volkswagen Dieselgate example exposes, companies may issue false documents stating that they are compliant even though they are apparently not congruent with sustainability principles. Supply risks, reputational risks, and similar problems can lead to cost increases and legal sanctions (Göçer et al., 2018). In this regard, the role of boards of directors is crucial for companies to manage risks with appropriate strategies and leverage external resources by capitalizing on opportunities.

## Boards of Directors Role in Sustainability

Sustainability has emerged as a critical concept at the organizational level, largely due to companies prioritizing short-term profitability over long-term objectives that account for the interests of all stakeholders, while neglecting the risks and opportunities related to ESG factors. Today, increasing demands from regulatory authorities and stakeholders necessitate a more comprehensive and in-depth incorporation of sustainability considerations within governance procedures (Rehman, 2021). Governance at the organizational level must not only create value for firms themselves and their stakeholders today, but also ensure the ability to pass value on to future generations (World Business Council for Sustainable Development, 2020). These considerations further underscore the heightened importance of the boards' role, a crucial component of governance.

Boards of directors, which act as the bridge between a company's shareholders and the management responsible for daily operations (Stiles & Taylor, 2001, p. 4), provide ongoing support to management in strategic processes (Åberg et al., 2019; McNulty & Pettigrew, 1999; Ravasi & Zattoni, 2006). However, the responsibilities of boards are not limited to approving strategies and budgets. They also have significant impacts on important strategic decisions. Ultimately, boards are accountable for the competency of the organizations to withstand challenges and accomplish their aims and goals. Additionally, boards contribute to sustainability by overseeing risk management systems and mechanisms designed to ensure compliance with current laws, including human rights, environmental protection, equal opportunity, digital security, data privacy, health and safety, and the safeguarding of personal data (Organization for Economic Co-Operation and Development [OECD], 2023). In the context of Industry 5.0, where governance and technology must be addressed together (Ghobakhloo et al., 2024, p. 2), the role of the board becomes even more critical. The effectiveness of a board depends on how well it fulfills its functions (Van den Berghe & Levrau, 2013, p. 153). By performing their core functions effectively, boards can provide strong leadership and oversight to help organizations adapt to the industry 5.0 environment and ensure their sustainability (Goh, 2024).

In research on board roles, frequently the 'control', 'service', 'strategy' and 'resource selection' roles are discussed (Inglis and Weaver, 2000; Huse and Rindova, 2001, pp. 153-158; Aguilera, 2005). The significance attributed to each of the functions is shaped by different theoretical perspectives (Huse & Rindova, 2001; Jonsson, 2013). The most referenced theories are "Agency Theory", "Stewardship Theory", and "Resource Dependency Theory" (Huse & Rindova, 2001; Zahra & Pearce, 1989; Van den Heuvel, 2006).

The **Agency Theory** suggests governance frameworks that enforce strict monitoring processes on managers to prevent behavior contrary to shareholders' interests (Sundaramurthy & Lewis, 2003; Eisenhardt, 1989; Zahra & Pearce, 1989). Agency theorists believe that fundamental role of the board is "monitoring" (Dalton et al., 2003; Elson, 1995; Jensen, 1993). According to the Agency Theory, board members are not there to assist the CEO and their team in managing the company, but rather to safeguard the shareholders' interests (Carver, 2000, p. 79). As a result, Agency Theory fundamentally views board members as the final "internal auditors" overseeing the decisions of the company's top management (Fama, 1980, p. 294). External directors are considered an integral part of this process and often serve on audit committees. According to the agency approach, a high ratio of external board members and, consequently, the independence of the board are vital for effective governance (McIntyre et al., 2007). Several studies focusing on the links between boards and company performance have shown that a higher ratio of independent directors improves efficiency and helps enhance organizational performance (Aksoy et al., 2020; Aguilera et al., 2008; Jackling & Johl, 2009; Rhoades et al., 2000). Perry & Shivdasani (2005) concluded that boards composed primarily of external directors improve operational performance in restructured firms. Moreover, according to Agency Theory, when CEO also serves as the board chair (defined as CEO duality), conflicts with stakeholders may arise due to the blurred line between management and oversight (Hussain, et al., 2018). Indeed, some studies have found that CEO duality affects companies' sustainability performance negatively (Giannarakis, 2014; Allegrini & Greco, 2013).

On the other hand, there are several studies in literature that determine negative relationships or no relationship between independent board members and firm performance. Dalton et al. (1998) found no systematic relationship between board independence and firm performance in their meta-analysis. Several recent empirical studies have also found that the presence of independent or external directors on the board is either unrelated to financial performance or negatively affects financial performance. The results contradict Agency Theory's argument that managers should independently monitor management's actions to maximize shareholder benefits (Hsu, 2010; Dulewicz and Herbert, 2004).

The argument of Agency Theory that managers prioritize their own interests, therefore must be closely monitored by the board, contradicts the Stewardship Theory. Drawing from sociology and psychology, **Stewardship Theory** highlights the strategic role of the board by emphasizing its potential to provide qualified advice to management and actively contribute to the formation of strategy (Sundaramurthy & Lewis, 2003). The Theory suggests that the board's role is to give guidance management and help the organization achieve its mission and goals (Hillman & Dalziel, 2003). Stewardship Theory, presented as an alternative perspective to the Agency Theory by Donaldson and Davis (1991), emphasizes co-operation and alignment rather than control and conflict (Sundaramurthy & Lewis, 2003; Pastoriza & Arinio, 2008). It argues that managers, acting as stewards, will act in the firm's best interests rather than individual economic interests. (Donaldson & Davis, 1991; Hernandez, 2012; Schillemans & Basuioc, 2015). Instead of being strictly controlled, stewards should be granted autonomy to take administrative actions. This suggests that combining CEO and board chair roles (CEO duality) could be beneficial. Some studies support Stewardship Theory's arguments concerning sustainability (Jizi et al., 2014; Janggu et al., 2014). However, some other studies have found no significant relationship between CEO duality and sustainability performance (Aksoy et al., 2020; Cheng & Courtenay, 2006; Said et al., 2009). Furthermore, it has been argued that Stewardship Theory overlooks the fact that the relationship between boards of directors and management is generally characterized by conflicts and disagreements (Zahra & Pearce, 1989).

On the other hand, from the perspective of Resource Dependence Theory, the role of a board of directors extends beyond merely overseeing management. **Resource Dependency Theory** highlights the board of directors' role to provide resources to the organization, which may include financial, human, or knowledge resources (Hillman et al., 2009; Hillman & Dalziel, 2003). According to Pfeffer and Salancik (1978), who developed theory, boards enhance corporate performance by facilitating access to external resources and improving the company's reputation (Christopher, 2010). The theory's core principle is that resources are key to organizational success, and control over these resources is the central tenet of power (Muth & Donaldson, 1998). Boards have garnered the most attention in testing the theory (Hillman et al., 2009), as their ability to form connections, collaborate, and legitimize is expected to contribute corporate performance positively (Huse & Rindova, 2001). Pfeffer (1987) and Hillman et al.

(2000) argue that boards improve company performance by facilitating access to resources. The board's resource-providing function may be influenced by factors such as board size, gender diversity, and the educational level of its members, which could in turn affect sustainability performance.

In some studies, it has been found that board size positively affects sustainability related firm performance (Daniel-Vasconcelos et al., 2022; Aksoy et al., 2020; Chams & García-Blandón, 2019; Arena et al., 2014; Janggu et al., 2014; Jizi et al., 2014; Rao et al., 2012). However, other studies have found a negative effect (De Andres et al., 2005; Prado-Lorenzo & Garcia-Sanchez, 2010), or no significant relationship between board size and sustainability performance (Collevecchio & Gionfriddo, 2023; Saha & Akter, 2013; Ienciu et al., 2012; Galbreath, 2011; Jo & Harjoto, 2011). Setó-Pamies (2015) suggests that women's skills can play a strategic role in managing firms' social responsibilities and sustainability practices, which is a view supported by numerous empirical studies (Collevecchio & Gionfriddo, 2023; Noureldin & Basuony, 2021:288; Arayssi et al., 2016:376; Fernandez-Feijoo, 2014; Galbreath, 2011). However, some studies have found no impact of women representation on board about sustainability reporting and performance (Aksoy et al., 2020; Giannarakis, 2014). Additionally, studies have found that the presence of highly educated board members has a positive impact on sustainability performance (Colakoglu et al., 2020; Chams & García-Blandón, 2019; Kagzi & Guha, 2018; Post et al., 2011). In accordance with previous literature, board size, ratio of female board members, ratio of independent board members, educational level of board members and CEO duality are included in the present study as independent variables.

## Corporate Sustainability Reporting

Sustainability reporting practices involves addressing stakeholders' informational needs regarding the "economic", "environmental", and "social" impacts of companies' activities (WCED, 1987). The idea of corporate sustainability reporting (CSR) is based on the principle of "corporate social responsibility," which gained prominence in the 1970s as businesses' environmental and social impacts drew increased attention. In its early stages, CSR reporting involved companies issuing standalone environmental or social reports. The establishment of the Global Reporting Initiative (GRI) in 1997, an independent, international organization, marked a significant acceleration in this field. The GRI Standards, established by the Global Sustainability Standards Board (GSSB), are now the most used sustainability reporting standards worldwide, aiming to help businesses and organizations be transparent and accountable for their impacts (Klynveld Peat Marwick Goerdeler [KPMG], 2020).

The Global Reporting Initiative defines sustainability reporting as "reporting on how an organization contributes or intends to contribute in the future to the improvement or deterioration of economic, environmental, and social conditions, developments, and trends at the local, regional, or global level" (The Global Reporting Initiative [GRI], 2015; Moses et al., 2020, p. 5). In recent years, efforts to integrate sustainability reporting into corporate financial reporting have intensified. In 2021, the IFRS Foundation announced the establishment of the International Sustainability Standards Board (ISSB). In 2023, the IFRS Foundation released "IFRS-S1 General Requirements for Disclosure of Sustainability-related Financial Information" and "IFRS-S2 Climate-related Disclosures" (International Financial Reporting Standards (IFRS), 2023).

Significant regulatory developments have also taken place in Europe. On January 5, 2023, the European Commission (EC) issued the Corporate Sustainability Reporting Directive (CSRD), mandating that companies operating within the European Union of a certain size must identify, prevent, mitigate, and report on the social and environmental impacts of their operations. In line with this directive, the European Commission adopted the "European Sustainability Reporting Standards (ESRS)" on July 31, 2023, which are to be used by all companies subject to the CSRD (EC, 2023). The U.S. Securities and Exchange Commission (SEC), responsible for regulating and overseeing capital markets, requires companies and investment funds to provide clearer disclosures on the criteria they use related to sustainability. As part of these regulations, companies are also expected to disclose how their boards assess sustainability-related risks and how these risks are managed.

In summary, today, corporate sustainability reporting practices have transformed from a voluntary initiative into a core component of corporate governance and is now subject to independent auditing in many countries. The objectives and metrics of sustainability reporting, along with the results of assurance audits, serve as essential tools for evaluating an organization's sustainability performance. Additionally, stakeholders, particularly institutional investors, are increasingly seeking data from companies regarding environmental, social, and governance risks and the implications of uncertainties on corporate performance. The prevailing perception is that stakeholders are more likely to favor companies prioritizing sustainability (Mahoney et al., 2013).

## Corporate Sustainability Reporting in Türkiye

The first regulations regarding sustainability reporting in Türkiye were established by the Capital Markets Board. In this context "Sustainability Principles Compliance Framework" has been prepared to determine the compliance of publicly traded companies with Environmental, Social, and Corporate Governance (ESG) principles. Even though the application of the principles outlined in this Compliance Framework is voluntary, companies are required to disclose whether they comply with the principles according to the "comply or explain" rule. For companies specified in paragraph 5 of article 1 of the Capital Markets Board's Communiqué on Corporate Governance No. II-17.1, the inclusion of the sustainability principles compliance framework in their annual reports is mandatory starting from the 2021 reports, which cover data from 2020 onwards. For companies that are applying for an initial public offering and/or listing on the stock exchange, this requirement applies starting from the year following their listing on the stock exchange (Capital Markets Board, 2020).

In Türkiye, currently the sustainability compliance level of publicly traded companies is disclosed to public through 'Public Disclosure Platform'. Using 56 compliance criteria outlined in the 'Sustainability Principles Compliance Framework', companies disclose their compliance level for each criterion. For a company to comply with a principle included in the Sustainability Principles Compliance Report, it must have either carried out activities or taken measures that ensure compliance in the relevant area and disclose these to the public. For example, related to principle *"The committees and/or units responsible for the implementation of ESG policies, the highest-level executives responsible for ESG issues in the company and their duties have been determined."*; a company may state that responsible committees have been established, senior executives responsible for ESG issues have been determined, the roles and responsibilities have been distributed, and all these issues have been announced to the public in the company's 2022 Annual Activity Report.

The "Sustainability Principles Compliance Report" consists of four sections, as shown in Table 1 (Capital Markets Board, 2020).

*Table 1. Sustainability principles compliance framework*

| | Number of Principles |
|---|---|
| **1. General Principles** | **12** |
| 1.1. Strategies, Policies, and Targets | 3 |
| 1.2. Implementation and Monitoring | 5 |
| 1.3. Reporting | 3 |
| 1.4. Verification | 1 |
| **2. Environmental Principles** | **24** |
| **3. Social Principles** | **18** |
| 3.1. Human and Employee Rights | 13 |
| 3.2. Stakeholders, International Standards, and Initiatives | 5 |
| **4. Corporate Governance Principles** | **2** |

In the "General Principles" section of the Sustainability Principles Compliance Report, the company's statements regarding compliance with 12 principles are provided. "General Principles" pertain to the identification and reporting of the company's priorities, policies, goals and performance, and the public disclosure of results.

The compliance topics that are salient in relation to the objectives of this study are listed below:

- Priority issues, risks and opportunities related to ESG
- ESG policies (e.g. environmental, human rights and employee policies)
- Short-term and long-term ESG goals
- Committees and units responsible for ESG and their duties
- Report to the Board of Directors
- Implementation and action plans related to ESG targets
- ESG Key Performance Indicators and performance measurement results
- Lawsuits filed against the company regarding ESG issues
- Independent third-party verification of ESG performance measurements

The "Environmental Principles" section includes the company's statements on compliance with 24 principles. These principles relate to environmental reporting, performance incentive systems and targets on environmental issues, the integration of environmental concerns into business aims and targets and corporate strategies, relationships with non-governmental organizations, environmental indicators such as greenhouse gas emissions, environmental impacts and goals, renewable energy production and usage, energy consumption, energy efficiency, strategies for combating the climate crisis, and carbon pricing. The compliance topics that are significant in relation to the objectives of this study are listed below:

- Reporting on environmental management systems
- Performance incentive systems for stakeholders
- Integration of priority environmental issues into business goals and strategies
- Partnerships with stakeholders
- Greenhouse gas emissions

- Standards, protocols, methodologies used in data collection and calculation
- Progress towards reducing environmental impacts
- Climate crisis strategy and action plan
- Data on production and use of renewable energy
- Carbon pricing

In the "Social Principles" section, the company's statements on compliance with 18 principles are presented. The criteria in this section are of key importance for Industry 5.0 goals. These principles involve the company's Corporate Human Rights and Employee Rights Policy and practices, the improvement of working conditions, diversity and inclusivity, consideration of groups sensitive to specific economic, environmental, and social factors, occupational health and safety policies, data protection, ethical policies, community investment, social responsibility, financial inclusion, and access to finance, relations with stakeholders, adopted sustainability principles, and memberships or affiliations with international organizations and principles. The compliance topics that are salient in relation to the objectives of this study are listed below:

- The company's Corporate Human Rights and Employee Rights Policy covering the Universal Declaration of Human Rights, ILO Conventions and other relevant legislation.
- Provisions on fair labor, labor standards, women's employment, and inclusiveness
- Protection of the rights of vulnerable groups, ensuring equal opportunities for minorities
- Practices that prevent and correct discrimination, inequality, child labor, human rights violations
- Investment in workers, talent management, union rights, compensation, benefits, work-life balance
- Employee satisfaction, handling employee complaints and resolving disputes
- Health and safety policies, preventing workplace accidents, accident statistics
- Personal data protection and data security
- Ethics policy
- Community investment, social responsibility, financial inclusiveness
- Employee participation in decisions on ESG policies and practices
- The global reporting standards adopted by the company

The "Corporate Governance Principles" section includes the company's statements regarding compliance with two principles. These principles relate to social responsibility activities, training, the importance of sustainability, and obtaining stakeholder engagement on sustainability measures and strategies.

On the other hand, with the amendment to the Turkish Commercial Code in 2022, the Public Oversight Accounting and Auditing Standards Authority (POAASA) was authorized to establish the Türkiye Sustainability Reporting Standards in alignment with international standards. POAASA adopted the International Sustainability Reporting Standards issued by the International Sustainability Standards Board (ISSB) and has established the internal regulations. In this context, "TSRS 1: General Provisions Regarding Disclosure of Sustainability-Related Financial Information" and "TSRS 2: Climate-Related Disclosures" have been released. In addition, "Guidance on Sector-Based Application" of TSRS 2 has been issued. The guidance assists companies by providing "sustainability disclosure topics" and "metrics" for the implementation of some of the disclosure provisions in TSRS 2. Within the scope of the guidance, 68 sector-specific implementation recommendations have been published to date, most of which are specific to the manufacturing sector (POAASA, 2024a).

Companies meeting specific criteria are required to prepare corporate sustainability reports. For example, if manufacturing company XYZ exceeds the thresholds determined by POAASA in at least two of the criteria "total assets", "annual net sales revenue" and "number of employees" for two consecutive years, it will be required to submit sustainability reporting. Companies must begin reporting on corporate sustainability as of January 1, 2024. It is also anticipated that in 2025, sustainability audits will be conducted by auditors authorized by the POAASA. The authority to perform sustainability assurance audits is granted to those who pass the sustainability auditing exam conducted by POAASA Board. (POAASA, 2024b).

Since the reporting and auditing mandated by the POAASA regulations have not yet been implemented, the Sustainability Principles Compliance Framework developed by the Capital Markets Board has been used in this study to analyze the sustainability performance of the manufacturing companies.

## METHODOLOGY

### Research Goal and Sample

The manufacturing sector can make significant contributions to the process of adopting the circular economy and achieving sustainability goals through good governance, as well as reducing, reusing, and recycling. Furthermore, boards of directors are expected to contribute to sustainability by overseeing risk management and control mechanisms designed to achieve compliance with sustainability policies and rules, as well as by contributing to corporate strategies. Besides, boards of directors are expected to contribute to sustainability by overseeing risk management and control mechanisms designed to ensure compliance with sustainability regulations, as well as by contributing to corporate strategies. Therefore, in this chapter, empirical research conducted by the authors is included. In this research, publicly traded manufacturing companies have been taken as study samples. The study aimed to evaluate the impact of certain structural characteristics of the board members on corporate sustainability performance. In accordance with this aim, the independent variables of the study are size of the board, ratio of female member, ratio of independent member, educational level of board members and CEO duality.

The sample of the research consists of data from 166 manufacturing companies listed on Borsa Istanbul in Türkiye in 2022, as well as data from 1,120 board members serving on the boards of these companies. As shown in Table 2, the companies included in the sample have manufacturing in 9 different sub-industries and the first three industries that most of companies in the sample operates in, are "Chemicals, Pharmaceuticals, Petroleum, Rubber and Plastic Products" (23,5%), "Food, Beverages and Tobacco" (18,1%) and "Metal Goods, Machinery, Electrical Equipment and Transportation Vehicles" (17,5%).

*Table 2. Descriptive statistics of the sample*

| Industry | n | % |
|---|---|---|
| Basic Metal | 17 | 10,2 |
| Food, Beverages and Tobacco | 30 | 18,1 |
| Paper and Printing of Paper Products | 11 | 6,6 |
| Chemicals, Pharmaceuticals, Petroleum, Rubber and Plastic Products | 39 | 23,5 |
| Metal Goods, Machinery, Electrical Equipment and Transportation Vehicles | 29 | 17,5 |
| Forest Products and Furniture | 3 | 1,8 |
| Stone and Soil Based Manufacturing | 17 | 10,2 |
| Textile, Clothing and Leather Manufacturing | 19 | 11,4 |
| Other Manufacturing | 1 | 0,6 |

The assessment of the dependent variable, sustainability performance, in this study is based on the statements provided in the "Sustainability Principles Compliance Report" for 2022, disclosed to the public on the Public Disclosure Platform. Responses to relevant sustainability criteria were evaluated as follows: a "yes" response was assigned a value of "2", a "partially" response was assigned a value of "1", and a "no" response was assigned a value of "0". Responses marked as "not applicable" were excluded from the analysis. The average value of responses across all criteria was used as the basis for analysis. Among the samples, 8 companies achieved a perfect score for sustainability performance, and only one company lacked a sustainability performance score.

Regarding the independent variables of the study, board size was measured as the number of board members; gender diversity on the board of directors was measured by the ratio of the number of female board members to the total number of board members and the ratio of independent board members to the total number of board members. Data were obtained from the Public Disclosure Platform. The educational background of board members was categorized as "primary education," "secondary education," "associate degree," "bachelor's degree," "master's degree," and "doctorate," with data gathered from the board members' biographies available in the companies' annual reports and official disclosures. Information not available on the Public Disclosure Platform was obtained from board members' social media profiles (i.e. LinkedIn). Information regarding the other variable in the study, the dual role of the CEO also serving as the chairman of the board (CEO duality), was obtained from the Public Disclosure Platform.

## Analysis and Findings

Table 3. shows information about the board structure of the companies within research samples. Accordingly, the minimum number of board of directors only for one company is 4 (n=1); whereas 2 companies have 14 board members which is represented as the maximum number of board of directors within the sample. The companies have an average of 7 board members, and most of the companies (36.1%; n=60) have 5 board members. On the other hand, there are still companies with boards that do not have female members. The representation of female members on boards is quite low, with one member on the average. Besides, 27.1% (n=45) of companies do not have female board members; most of the companies appointed only one female board member (37.3%; n=62). Moreover, 8 companies (4.8%) have 4 female members on their boards, which is the highest representation rate. The presence of independent board members is better than female representation. Most companies in the sample appointed 2 independent board members (74.7%; n=124) on the average. While only 2 companies (1,2%) have 5 independent board members, there are 3 companies that do not have any independent board members. Most companies' boards consist of members who are university or master's graduates (76%; n=126). It is also inferred that most companies separated their Board Chairman and CEO positions, with only 15,1% (n=25) of companies having CEO duality.

*Table 3. Board structure of the sample*

| | Min | Max | Mean | б |
|---|---|---|---|---|
| Board Size | 4 | 14 | 6,75 | 2,038 |
| Number of Female Board Members | 0 | 4 | 1,26 | 1,096 |
| Number of Independent Board Members | 0 | 5 | 2,28 | 0,697 |

It is found that there exist significant relations between variables. Board size, ratio of female board members and ratio of independent board members are correlated positively with the dependent variable sustainability performance. However, significant relations with sustainability performance exist only for board size and ratio of female board members. On the other hand, correlations of board educational level and CEO duality with sustainability performance are negative and also these relations are not significant (Table 4).

*Table 4. Correlation analysis of research variables*

| | Board Size | Female Member % | Independent Member % | Board Educational Level | CEO Duality | Sustainability Performance |
|---|---|---|---|---|---|---|
| Board Size | 1 | | | | | |
| Ratio of Female Board Members | -0,045 | 1 | | | | |
| Ratio of Independent Board Members | -0,314** | 0,026 | 1 | | | |
| Board Members Educational Level | 0,013 | 0,228* | -0,007 | 1 | | |
| CEO Duality | -0,221** | 0,074 | -0,075 | -0,156 | 1 | |
| Sustainability Performance | 0,390** | 0,126* | 0,031 | -0,057 | -0,192 | 1 |

* Correlation is significant at the 0,05 level.

** Correlation is significant at the 0,01 level.

The results of the regression analysis indicate that board size ($\beta=0,418$; $p<0,05$), percentage of female board members ($\beta=0,150$; $p<0,05$) have a significant positive effect on sustainability performance of companies (Table 5). It is also noteworthy that, although there is not a significant effect, the educational level of board members and CEO duality has a negative effect on companies' sustainability performance.

*Table 5. Linear regression analysis of research variables (dependent variable: sustainability performance)*

| Variables | Standardized β Coefficient | T | p |
|---|---|---|---|
| Board Size | 0,418 | 5,311 | ,000 |
| Female Board Members (%) | 0,150 | 2,104 | ,037 |
| Independent Board Members (%) | 0,088 | 1,157 | ,249 |
| Board Members Educational Level | -0,093 | -1,286 | ,200 |
| CEO Duality | -0,095 | -1,278 | ,203 |
| F = 7,883, p<0,05 Adjusted $R^2$ = 0,173 | | | |

## CONCLUSION

Sustainability is becoming an increasingly important agenda across all industries in the context of Society 5.0. Industry 5.0, which focuses on human-centeredness and societal needs, is expected to help address the misalignment between production and societal demands by placing greater emphasis on sustainability (Leng et al. 2022, p. 279). In this context, the role of boards of directors, the most critical component of governance in overseeing, shaping strategies, and providing resources, becomes increasingly important in improving firms' sustainability performance. Although academic studies on sustainability have increased in recent years, research examining the relationship between the boards of directors and sustainability performance for Turkish companies remains limited (i.e. Aksoy et al. 2020). Furthermore, to our knowledge, this study is the first to examine the impact of board characteristics on sustainability performance based on a detailed review of the disclosures in companies' Sustainability Principles Compliance Reports.

The study presented in this chapter analyzes data from the Sustainability Principles Compliance Reports of 166 manufacturing companies listed on Borsa Istanbul for the year 2022. Variables include the number of board members, the ratio of independent directors, the ratio of female board members, CEO duality, and the education levels of board members.

The results reveal that board size, as measured by the number of board members, has the most significant impact on the sustainability performance of the companies in the sample. Based on the results, it can be concluded that the competence of boards of directors, which are expected to simultaneously fulfill diverse roles such as monitoring, service, strategy, and resource selection, improves with an increase in the number of members. This finding aligns with recent studies in the literature (Daniel-Vasconcelos et al. 2022; Aksoy et al. 2020; Arena et al. 2014; Janggu et al., 2014; Jizi et al. 2014; Rao et al., 2012). Additionally, the ratio of female members on the board was found to positively influence sustainability performance. This result facilitates the implication that gender diversity on boards may enhance a company's sustainability performance by fostering creativity, qualified negotiation, and sound decision-making, and that women can be more sensitive about sustainability. In parallel with the results reached by Adams and Ferreira (2009), it can also be inferred that the higher level of participation by women in board meetings compared to men has an impact on these outcomes. Similar findings have been reported in studies by Collevecchio & Gionfriddo (2023), Noureldin & Basuony (2021), Arayssi et al. (2016), Fernandez-Feijoo (2014), Galbreath (2011), Boulouta (2013), and Harjoto et al. (2015). On the other hand, no significant relationship was found between the ratio of independent board members, the education levels of board members, CEO duality, and sustainability performance.

With these findings, this study contributes to both sustainability and governance literature. The results suggest that having a larger board positively influences sustainability performance. Although the ratio of female members on boards remains low, the presence of women appears to lead boards to place higher emphasis on and invest more in sustainability issues. This result recommends that regulatory authorities and practitioners increase the number of board members to bring more diverse experiences to the boardroom and ensure a higher representation of women on corporate boards.

## FUTURE RESEARCH DIRECTIONS

This study has its limitations. The findings are limited to the data from 166 manufacturing companies. Further, the data are cross-sectional for the year 2022. Future studies may include panel data from companies in other sectors in Türkiye and cover multiple years. That should yield more advanced results. Specific factors, such as national policies, cultural influences, and sector-specific issues that shape the behavior of companies in Türkiye and affect sustainability and corporate governance, may be included and examined in greater depth within such datasets. Additionally, the measurement of sustainability performance of the firms in this study is based on their own disclosures. Future research may employ different methods to measure sustainability performance. The fact that mandatory sustainability assurance audits will be launched in Türkiye in 2025 offers new opportunities for future research. Panel dataset studies, based on data from the mandatory sustainability assurance audits, should reveal better insights and more depth in the future. Further, it is hoped that the findings may be an input into the evidence set of regulatory initiatives and processes. The research framework developed and proposed in this chapter may also be extended into an international context. That extension requires future research that will unify the measurement of firm-specific sustainability performance across borders.

In conclusion, it must be acknowledged that studies utilizing the visible structural characteristics of boards and their members can only provide limited insights into the impact of boards on corporate performance. However, the challenges of obtaining insider information on board operations lead researchers, as in the study presented here, to rely on proxy indicators such as board composition, size, educational background, and diversity. The authors believe that as the number of such studies increases, the cumulative knowledge generated will undoubtedly make more significant contributions to the corporate governance and sustainability fields.

## REFERENCES


Åberg, C., Bankewitz, M., & Knockaert, M. (2019). Service tasks of board of directors: A literature review and research agenda in an era of new governance practices. *European Management Journal*, 37(5), 648–663. DOI: 10.1016/j.emj.2019.04.006

Adams, R. B., & Ferreira, D. (2009). Women in the boardroom and their impact on governance and performance. *Journal of Financial Economics*, 94(2), 291–309. DOI: 10.1016/j.jfineco.2008.10.007

Aguilera, R. V. (2005). Corporate governance and director accountability: An institutional comparative perspective. *British Journal of Management*, 16(1), 39–53. DOI: 10.1111/j.1467-8551.2005.00446.x

Aguilera, R. V., Filatotchev, I., Gospel, H., & Jackson, G. (2008). An organizational approach to comparative corporate governance: Costs, contingencies, and complementarities. *Organization Science*, 19(3), 475–492. DOI: 10.1287/orsc.1070.0322

Aksoy, M., Yilmaz, M. K., Tatoglu, E., & Basar, M. (2020). Antecedents of corporate sustainability performance in Turkey: The effects of ownership structure and board attributes on non-financial companies. *Journal of Cleaner Production*, 276, 1–11. DOI: 10.1016/j.jclepro.2020.124284

Allegrini, M., & Greco, G. (2013). Corporate boards, audit committees and voluntary disclosure: Evidence from Italian Listed Companies. *The Journal of Management and Governance*, 17(1), 187–216. DOI: 10.1007/s10997-011-9168-3

Ansong, A. (2017). Corporate social responsibility and access to finance among Ghanaian SMEs: The role of stakeholder engagement. *Cogent Business & Management*, 4(1), 1385165. DOI: 10.1080/23311975.2017.1385165

Arayssi, M., Dah, M., & Jizi, M. (2016). Women on boards, sustainability reporting and firm performance. *Sustainability Accounting. Management and Policy Journal*, 7(3), 376–401.

Arena, C., Bozzolan, S., & Michelon, G. (2014). Environmental reporting: Transparency to stakeholders or stakeholder manipulation? An analysis of disclosure tone and the role of the board of directors. *Corporate Social Responsibility and Environmental Management*. Advance online publication. DOI: 10.1002/csr.1350

Aslam, F., Aimin, W., Li, M., & Rehman, K. U. (2020). Innovation in the era of IoT and industry 5.0: Absolute innovation management (AIM) framework. *Information (Basel)*, 11(2), 1–24. DOI: 10.3390/info11020124

Boulouta, I. (2013). Hidden connections: The link between board gender diversity and corporate social performance. *Journal of Business Ethics*, 113(2), 185–197. DOI: 10.1007/s10551-012-1293-7

Capital Markets Board. (2020). Sürdürülebilirlik İlkeleri Uyum Çerçevesi https://spk.gov.tr/data/63a17b1a8f95db0fa40e3309/s%C3%BCrd%C3%BCr%C3%BClebilirlik%20ilkeleri%20uyum%20cercevesi.pdf

Carver, J. (2000). The opportunity for re-inventing corporate governance in joint venture companies. *Corporate Governance*, 8(1), 75–80. DOI: 10.1111/1467-8683.00182

Chams, N., & García-Blandón, J. (2019). Sustainable or not sustainable? The role of the board of directors. *Journal of Cleaner Production*, 226, 1067–1081. DOI: 10.1016/j.jclepro.2019.04.118

Cheng, E. C. M., & Courtenay, S. M. (2006). Board composition, regulatory regime and voluntary disclosure. *The International Journal of Accounting*, 41(3), 262–289. DOI: 10.1016/j.intacc.2006.07.001

Christopher, J. (2010). Corporate governance—A multi-theoretical approach to recognizing the wider influencing forces impacting on organizations. *Critical Perspectives on Accounting*, 21(8), 683–695. DOI: 10.1016/j.cpa.2010.05.002

Collevecchio, F., & Gionfriddo, G. (2023). Adopting a social purpose in for-profit firms: The role of the board of directors. *The International Entrepreneurship and Management Journal*, 19(3), 1467–1499. DOI: 10.1007/s11365-023-00879-w

Daily, C. M., & Dalton, D. R. (1994). Corporate governance and the bankrupt firm: An empirical assessment. *Strategic Management Journal*, 15(8), 643–654. DOI: 10.1002/smj.4250150806

Dalton, D. R., Daily, C. M., Certo, S. T., & Roengpitya, R. (2003). Meta-analyses of financial performance and equity: Fusion or confusion? *Academy of Management Journal*, 46(1), 13–26. DOI: 10.2307/30040673

Dalton, D. R., Daily, C. M., Ellstrand, A. E., & Johnson, J. L. (1998). Meta-analytic reviews of board composition, leadership structure, and financial performance. *Strategic Management Journal*, 19(3), 269–290. DOI: 10.1002/(SICI)1097-0266(199803)19:3<269::AID-SMJ950>3.0.CO;2-K

Daniel-Vasconcelos, V., Ribeiro, M., & Crisostomo, V. L. (2022). Does gender diversity moderate the relationship between CSR committees and sustainable development goals disclosure? Evidence from Latin American companies. *RAUSP Management Journal*, 57(4), 434–456. DOI: 10.1108/RAUSP-02-2022-0063

De Andres, P., Azofra, V., & Lopez, F. (2005). Corporate boards in OECD countries: Size, composition, functioning and effectiveness. *Corporate Governance*, 13(2), 197–210. DOI: 10.1111/j.1467-8683.2005.00418.x

Donaldson, L., & Davis, J. H. (1991). Stewardship theory or agency theory: CEO governance and shareholder returns. *Australian Journal of Management*, 16(1), 49–64. DOI: 10.1177/031289629101600103

Dragu, I. (2019). The evolution of corporate sustainability and corporate social responsibility towards the common goal of integrated reporting: Antecedents and perspectives for organizations and stakeholders. In Idowu, S. O., & Del Baldo, M. (Eds.), *Integrated Reporting, CSR, Sustainability, Ethics & Governance* (pp. 77–93). Springer., DOI: 10.1007/978-3-030-01719-4_4

Dulewicz, V., & Herbert, P. (2004). Does the composition and practice of boards of directors bear any relationship to the performance of their companies? *Corporate Governance*, 12(3), 263–280. DOI: 10.1111/j.1467-8683.2004.00368.x

Dyllick, T., & Hockerts, K. (2002). Beyond the business case for corporate sustainability. *Business Strategy and the Environment*, 11(2), 130–141. DOI: 10.1002/bse.323

EC. (2023). https://finance.ec.europa.eu/news/commission-adopts-european-sustainability-reporting-standards-2023-07-31_en

Eisenhardt, K. M. (1989). Building theories from case study research. *Academy of Management Review*, 14(4), 532–550. DOI: 10.2307/258557

Elson, C. (1995). Director compensation and the management captured board-the history of a symptom and a cure. *Southern Methodist Law Review*, 50, 127–174.

Fama, E. F. (1980). Agency problems and the theory of the firm. *Journal of Political Economy*, 88(21), 288–307. DOI: 10.1086/260866

Fernandez-Feijoo, B., Romero, S., & Ruiz-Blanco, S. (2014). Women on boards: Do they affect sustainability reporting? *Corporate Social Responsibility and Environmental Management*, 21(6), 351–364. DOI: 10.1002/csr.1329

Galbreath, J. (2011). Are there gender-related influences on corporate sustainability? A study of women on boards of directors. *Journal of Management & Organization*, 17(1), 17–38. DOI: 10.5172/jmo.2011.17.1.17

Ghobakhloo, M., Iranmanesh, M., Mubarak, M. F., Mubarik, M., Rejeb, A., & Nilashi, M. (2022). Identifying industry 5.0 contributions to sustainable development: A strategy roadmap for delivering sustainability values. *Sustainable Production and Consumption*, 33, 716–737. DOI: 10.1016/j.spc.2022.08.003

Ghobakhloo, M., Mahdiraji, H. A., Iranmanesh, M., & Sadeghi, V. J. (2024). From Industry 4.0 digital manufacturing to industry 5.0 digital society: A roadmap toward human-centric, sustainable, and resilient production. *Information Systems Frontiers*. Advance online publication. DOI: 10.1007/s10796-024-10476-z

Giannarakis, G. (2014). The determinants influencing the extent of CSR disclosure. *International Journal of Law and Management*, 56(5), 393–416. DOI: 10.1108/IJLMA-05-2013-0021

Göçer, A., Fawcett, S. E., & Tuna, O. (2018). what does the sustainability-risk interaction look like? Exploring nuanced relationships in emerging economy sustainability initiatives. *Sustainability (Basel)*, 10(8), 2716. DOI: 10.3390/su10082716

Goh, M. H. (2024). https://blog.bcm-institute.org/operational-resilience/roles-and-responsibilities-for-board-of-directors-in-operational-resilience?hsCtaTracking=fdbeddea-0d0f-4f52-9a10-b6960c807070%7C04c707ba-642d-42b0-829c-0a73213e36d4

Gutowski, T. G., Allwood, J. M., Herrmann, C., & Sahni, S. A. (2013). Global assessment of manufacturing: Economic development, energy use, carbon emissions, and the potential for energy efficiency and materials recycling, *Annual Review of Environment and Resources, 38* (81)-106.

Harjoto, M., Laksmana, I., & Lee, R. (2015). Board diversity and corporate social responsibility. *Journal of Business Ethics*, 132(4), 641–660. DOI: 10.1007/s10551-014-2343-0

Hernandez, M. (2012). Toward an understanding of the psychology of stewardship. *Academy of Management Review*, 37(2), 172–193. DOI: 10.5465/amr.2010.0363

Hillman, A. J., Cannella, A. A., & Paetzold, R. L. (2000). The resource dependence role of corporate directors: Strategic adaptation of board composition in response to environmental change. *Journal of Management Studies*, 37(2), 235–256. DOI: 10.1111/1467-6486.00179

Hillman, A. J., & Dalziel, T. (2003). Boards of directors and firm performance: Integrating agency and resource dependence perspectives. *Academy of Management Review*, 28(3), 383–396. DOI: 10.5465/amr.2003.10196729

Hillman, A. J., Withers, M. C., & Collins, B. J. (2009). Resource dependence theory: A review. *Journal of Management*, 55, 27–47.

Hsu, H. E. (2010). The relationship between board characteristics and financial performance: An empirical study of United States initial public offerings. *International Journal of Management*, 27(2), 332–341.

Huse, M., & Rindova, V. (2001). Stakeholders' expectations of board roles: The case of subsidiary boards. *The Journal of Management and Governance*, 5(2), 153–178. DOI: 10.1023/A:1013017909067

Hussainey, K., Albitar, K., & Alkaraan, F. (2022). Corporate narrative reporting on industry 4.0 technologies: Does governance matter? *International Journal of Accounting and Information Management*, 30(4), 457–476. https://www.emerald.com/insight/1834-7649.htm. DOI: 10.1108/IJAIM-02-2022-0024

Ienciu, I. A., Popa, I. E., & Ienciu, N. M. (2012). Environmental reporting and good practice of corporate governance: Petroleum industry case study. *Procedia Economics and Finance*, 3, 961–967. DOI: 10.1016/S2212-5671(12)00258-4

Inglis, S., & Weaver, L. (2000). Designing agendas to reflect board roles and responsibilities: Results of a study. *Nonprofit Management & Leadership*, 11(1), 65–77. DOI: 10.1002/nml.11106

International Financial Reporting Standards (IFRS). (2023). https://www.ifrs.org/issued-standards/ifrs-sustainability-standards-navigator/

Jackling, B., & Johl, S. (2009). Board structure and firm performance: Evidence from India's top companies. *Corporate Governance*, 17(4), 492–509. DOI: 10.1111/j.1467-8683.2009.00760.x

Janggu, T., Darus, F., Zain, M. M., & Sawani, Y. (2014). Does good corporate governance lead to better sustainability reporting? An analysis using structural equation modeling. *Procedia: Social and Behavioral Sciences*, 145, 138–145. DOI: 10.1016/j.sbspro.2014.06.020

Jensen, M. C. (1993). The modern industrial revolution, exit, and the failure of internal control systems. *The Journal of Finance*, 48(3), 831–880. DOI: 10.1111/j.1540-6261.1993.tb04022.x

Jizi, M., Salama, A., Dixon, R., & Stratling, R. (2014). Corporate governance and corporate social responsibility disclosure: Evidence from the US banking sector. *Journal of Business Ethics*, 125(4), 601–615. DOI: 10.1007/s10551-013-1929-2

Jo, H., & Harjoto, M. (2011). Corporate governance and firm value: The impact of corporate social responsibility. *Journal of Business Ethics*, 103(3), 351–383. DOI: 10.1007/s10551-011-0869-y

Jonsson, E. I. (2013). One role is not big enough: A multi-theoretical study of board roles in SMEs. *International Journal of Business Governance and Ethics*, 8(1), 50–68. DOI: 10.1504/IJBGE.2013.052741

Kagzi, M., & Guha, M. (2018). Does board demographic diversity influence firm performance? Evidence from Indian-knowledge intensive firms. *Benchmarking*, 25(3), 1028–1058. DOI: 10.1108/BIJ-07-2017-0203

Karmaker, C. L., Bari, A. M., Anam, M. Z., Ahmed, T., Ali, S. M., de Jesus Pacheco, D. A., & Moktadir, M. A. (2023). Industry 5.0 challenges for post-pandemic supply chain sustainability in an emerging economy. *International Journal of Production Economics*, 258, 258. DOI: 10.1016/j.ijpe.2023.108806

Khitiri, B. (2017). Theories of corporate governance: Legal analysis *[TSU]*. *Journal of Law*, 2, 117–148.

Klynveld Peat Marwick Goerdeler. (2020). *The time has come: The KPMG survey of sustainability reporting*. KPMG International.

L'Huillier, B. (2014). What does "corporate governance" actually mean? *Corporate Governance (Bradford)*, 14(3), 300–319. DOI: 10.1108/CG-10-2012-0073

Leng, J., Sha, W., Wuest, T., Wang, B., Zheng, P., Zhuang, C., Liu, Q., Wuest, T., Mourtzis, D., & Wang, L. (2022). Industry 5.0: Prospect and retrospect. *Journal of Manufacturing Systems*, 65, 279–295. DOI: 10.1016/j.jmsy.2022.09.017

Malek, J. & Desai, T. N. (2020). A systematic literature review to map literature focus of sustainable manufacturing. *Journal of Cleaner Production, 256,* 1-20 120345

Manning, B., Braam, G., & Reimsbach, D. (2019). Corporate governance and sustainable business conduct-effects of board monitoring effectiveness and stakeholder engagement on corporate sustainability performance and disclosure choices. *Corporate Social Responsibility and Environmental Management*, 26(2), 351–366. DOI: 10.1002/csr.1687

McIntyre, M. L., Murphy, S. A., & Mitchell, P. (2007). The top team: Examining board composition and firm performance. *Corporate Governance (Bradford)*, 7(5), 547–561. DOI: 10.1108/14720700710827149

McNulty, T., & Pettigrew, A. (1999). Strategists on the board. *Organization Studies*, 20(1), 47–74. DOI: 10.1177/0170840699201003

Moses, E., Che-Ahmad, A., & Abdulmalik, S. O. (2020). Board governance mechanisms and sustainability reporting quality: A theoretical framework. *Cogent Business & Management*, 7(1), 1–23. DOI: 10.1080/23311975.2020.1771075

Muth, M. M., & Donaldson, L. (1998). Stewardship theory and board structure: A contingency approach. *Corporate Governance*, 6(1), 5–28. DOI: 10.1111/1467-8683.00076

Nahavandi, S. (2019). Industry 5.0 - A human-centric solution. *Sustainability (Basel)*, 11(16), 4371. Advance online publication. DOI: 10.3390/su11164371

Noureldin, N., & Basuony, M. A. K. (2021). Females on board and sustainability performance in a developing country: Evidence from Egypt [Special issue]. *Corporate Ownership & Control*, 19(1), 288–298. DOI: 10.22495/cocv19i1siart6

Organisation for Economic Co-Operation and Development. (2023). *G20/OECD Principles of Corporate Governance 2023*. OECD Publishing., DOI: 10.1787/ed750b30-

Ozkeser, B. (2018). Lean innovation approach in industry 5.0. *The Eurasia Proceedings of Science, Technology* [EPSTEM]. *Engineering & Mathematics*, 2, 422–428.

Özsoylu, A. F. (2017). Industry 4.0. *Journal of Çukurova University Faculty of Economics and Administrative Sciences*, 1, 41–64.

Pastoriza, D., & Ariño, M. A. (2008). When agents become stewards: Introducing learning in the stewardship theory. *1st IESE Conference on "Humanizing The Firm And The Management Profession" Barcelona, IESE Business School*, 1-17.

Perry, T., & Shivdasani, A. (2005). Do Boards Affect Performance? Evidence from Corporate Restructuring. *The Journal of Business*, 4(78), 1403–1432. DOI: 10.1086/430864

Pfeffer, J. (1987). A resource dependence perspective on intercorporate relations. *Intercorporate Relations: The Structural Analysis of Business*, 25-55.

Pfeffer, J., & Salancik, G. R. (1978). *The external control of organizations: A resource dependence perspective*. Harper & Row.

Pinheiro, P., Putnik, G. D., Castro, A., Castro, H., Dal, B. F. R., & Romero, F. (2019). Industry 4.0 and industrial revolutions: An assessment based on complexity. *FME Transactions*, 47(4), 831–840. DOI: 10.5937/fmet1904831P

POAASA. (2024a). Kamu Gözetimi, Muhasebe ve Denetim Standartları Kurumu. https://www.kgk.gov.tr/SustainabilityDetailForm/11455/Raporlama%20Standartlar%C4%B1

POAASA. (2024b). Kamu Gözetimi, Muhasebe ve Denetim Standartları Kurumu. https://www.kgk.gov.tr/surdurulebilirlik

Post, C., Rahman, N., & Rubow, E. (2011). Green governance: Boards of directors' composition and environmental corporate social responsibility. *Business & Society*, 50(1), 189–223. DOI: 10.1177/0007650310394642

Prado-Lorenzo, J. M., & Garcia-Sanchez, I. M. (2010). The role of the board of directors in disseminating relevant information on greenhouse gases. *Journal of Business Ethics*, 97(3), 391–424. DOI: 10.1007/s10551-010-0515-0

Rao, K. K., Tilt, C. A., & Lester, L. H. (2012). Corporate governance and environmental reporting: An Australian study. *Corporate Governance (Bradford)*, 12(2), 143–163. DOI: 10.1108/14720701211214052

Ravasi, D., & Zattoni, A. (2006). Exploring the political side of board involvement in strategy: A study of mixed-ownership institutions. *Journal of Management Studies*, 43(8), 1671–1702. DOI: 10.1111/j.1467-6486.2006.00659.x

Rehman, A., Ganesan, Y., & Haron, H. (2023). What is priority for organization: environmental, social and governance or sustainable corporate governance: literature review. In Çalıyurt, K. (Ed.), *History of Accounting, Management, Business and Economics, Accounting, Finance, Sustainability, Governance& Fraud: Theory and Application* (pp. 167–191). Springer. DOI: 10.1007/978-981-99-3346-4_8

Rhoades, D. L., Rechner, P. L., & Sundaramurthy, C. (2000). Board composition and financial performance: A meta-analysis of the influence of outside directors. *Journal of Managerial Issues*, 12(1), 76–91.

Saha, A. K., & Akter, S. (2013). Corporate governance and voluntary disclosure practices of financial non-financial sector companies in Bangladesh. *Journal of Applied Management Accounting Research*, 11(2), 45–61.

Said, R., Zainuddin, Y. H., & Haron, H. (2009). The relationship between corporate social responsibility disclosure and corporate governance characteristics in Malaysian public listed companies. *Social Responsibility Journal*, 5(2), 212–226. DOI: 10.1108/17471110910964496

Schillemans, T., & Busuioc, M. (2015). Predicting public sector accountability: From agency drift to forum drift. *Journal of Public Administration: Research and Theory*, 25(1), 191–215. DOI: 10.1093/jopart/muu024

Şener, İ., Varoğlu, A., & Karapolatgil, A. A. (2016). Sustainability reports disclosures: Who are the most salient stakeholders? *Procedia: Social and Behavioral Sciences*, 235, 84–92. DOI: 10.1016/j.sbspro.2016.11.028

Setó-Pamies, D. (2015). The relationship between women directors and corporate social responsibility. *Corporate Social Responsibility and Environmental Management*, 22(6), 334–345. DOI: 10.1002/csr.1349

Sharma, A., & Singh, B. J. (2020). Evolution of Industrial Revolutions: A review [IJITEE]. *International Journal of Innovative Technology and Exploring Engineering*, 9(11), 66–73. DOI: 10.35940/ijitee.I7144.0991120

Shiroishi, Y., Uchiyama, K., & Suzuki, N. (2018). Society 5.0: For human security and well-being. *Computer*, 51(7), 91–95. DOI: 10.1109/MC.2018.3011041

Singh, P. (2022). *Using ICT and energy technologies for improving global engineering education*. Intech Open., DOI: 10.5772/intechopen.100097

Sonnenfeld, J. A. (2002). What makes great boards great? *Harvard Business Review*, 80(9), 106–113. PMID: 12227143

Stiles, P., & Taylor, B. (2001). *Boards at Work: How Directors View their Roles and Responsibilities*. Oxford University Press.

Sundaramuthy, C., & Lewis, M. (2003). Control and collaboration: Paradoxes of governance. *Academy of Management Review*, 28(3), 397–415. DOI: 10.2307/30040729

United Nations. (2015). The 17 goals. *United Nations Department of Economic and Social Affairs*. https://sdgs.un.org/goals

Van den Berghe, L., & Levrau, A. (2013). *Fine-Tuning Board Effectiveness is Not Enough*. In: Kakabadse and Van den Berghe. Chapter 6. *How to Make Boards Work: An International Review, London: Palgrave Macmillan.*

Van den Heuvel, J., Van Gils, A., & Voordeckers, W. (2006). Board roles in small and medium-sized family businesses: Performance and importance. *Corporate Governance: An International Review, 14*(5), 467-485. https://doi.org/. 1467-8683.2006.00519.x.DOI: 10.1111/j

Westphal, J. D., & Bednar, M. K. (2005). Pluralistic ignorance in corporate boards and firms' strategic persistence in response to low firm performance. *Administrative Science Quarterly*, 50(2), 262–298. DOI: 10.2189/asqu.2005.50.2.262

World Business Council for Sustainable Development. (2020). *The state of corporate governance in the era of sustainability risks and opportunities*. World Business Council for Sustainable Development.

World Commission on Environment and Development. (1987). Our common future. *World Commission on Environment and Development, 383.*

Xu, X., Lu, Y., Vogel-Heuser, B., & Wang, L. (2021). Industry 4.0 and industry 5.0-inception, conception and perception. *Journal of Manufacturing Systems*, 61, 530–535. DOI: 10.1016/j.jmsy.2021.10.006

Yin, Y., Stecke, K. E., & Li, D. (2017). The evolution of production systems from Industry 2.0 through Industry 4.0. *International Journal of Production Research*, 56(1–2), 848–861. DOI: 10.1080/00207543.2017.1403664

Zahra, S., & Pearce, J. A.II. (1989). Boards of directors and corporate financial performance: A review and integrative model. *Journal of Management*, 15(2), 291–334. DOI: 10.1177/014920638901500208

Zainal, D. (2013). A longitudinal analysis of Corporate Social Responsibility Reporting (CSRR) in Malaysia public listed firms: Pre- and post-mandatory CSRR requirement. *International Journal of Advanced Research in Management and Social Sciences*, 2(1), 245–262.

## KEY TERMS AND DEFINITIONS

**CEO Duality:** Refers to a situation where the Chief Executive Officer (CEO), who is responsible for the company's daily operations, also leads the board of directors, which is responsible for monitoring and guiding the company's strategies and governance.

**Comply or Explain:** Refers to a principle that explains that institutions are required to comply with the principles and rules determined by regulatory authorities or specified in other legal texts, or to provide explanations regarding the reasons for non-compliance if they fail to comply. It is a concept frequently used in the field of corporate governance and ESG.

**Corporate Sustainability Reporting:** It refers to the disclosure by an organization about how it manages sustainability-related risks and opportunities, its environmental, social, and governance performance and impacts. As an important tool in ensuring participation, transparency and accountability, sustainability reports can be published under different names and in different formats (e.g. ESG reporting, non-financial reporting, social reporting, CSR reporting and socio-economic and socio-environmental reporting) or presented as an integrated report.

**Corporate Governance:** Corporate governance is the combination of systems, processes and structures implemented by boards of directors to ensure that corporate objectives are achieved. Boards of directors, which are the most important component of governance, inform, direct, manage, and monitor the activities of the organization.

**Good Governance:** It refers to exercises of the entrusted authority in an accountable, transparent and honest manner. Good governance ensures that the organization complies with ethical rules and legal and administrative regulations and that risks are effectively managed.

**Human-Centeredness:** In the context of Industry 5.0, human-centeredness refers to placing the fulfillment of human needs and the protection of their interests at the core of the production process, while simultaneously leveraging new and advanced technologies.

**Independent Board Members:** The directors who are independent of the management and commercial activities of the company. By providing an objective and diverse perspective, independent directors are expected to play a significant role in ensuring that the organization adheres to the principles of transparency, accountability, and good governance.

**Industry 5.0 (I5.0):** This can be defined as a paradigm that aims to facilitate creating industrial value by integrating advanced technology with sustainability, human-centeredness and resilience.

**Resilience:** It refers to creating and maintaining infrastructure that provides a higher degree of robustness against extraordinary circumstances in industrial production, such as natural disasters, epidemics, geopolitical crises, etc.

**Sustainability:** Respecting the boundaries of the planet, reducing energy consumption and greenhouse gas emissions, preventing depletion and degradation of natural resources via reusing, reducing and recycling, and ultimately meeting today's needs without endangering the needs of future generations.

# Chapter 12 The Effect of Servant Leadership on Organizational Citizenship Behavior in NGOs: Psychological Capital as a Mediator

**Hiba Ali Baroudi**
https://orcid.org/0000-0003-0253-9491
*Istanbul University, Turkey*

**Ayşe Güven Ergüney**
*Yeditepe University, Turkey*

## ABSTRACT

*The main research objective is to investigate the relationship between Psychological Capital (PsyCap), and Servant Leadership (SL) with Organizational Citizenship Behavior (OCB) in NGOs operating in Turkey. The research is quantitative research conducted by a survey distributed to people working in NGOs in Turkey. The collected sample was 201 valid responses. The research hypotheses were tested using Smart PLS (v. 3.2.8), adopting a significant level of 95% two-tailed. It has been found that SL is positively related to OCB in NGOs and PsyCap mediates this relationship. The research finding suggests that to maintain a high level of OCB, NGOs are mainly required to enhance SL among their leaders and to maintain a high level of positive PsyCap among their employees. To overcome the research limitations, it is recommended that future studies develop and examine special scales for organizational behavior concepts prepared specially for NGOs and test the current research model in different regions and within a longitudinal study.*

## 1. INTRODUCTION

Turkey has been the destination of many refugees in recent years leading Turkish humanitarian agencies to be under a great deal of pressure due to the enormous number of refugees. Therefore, many international non-profit humanitarian organizations had to exist and operate intensively in Turkey. In addition, many new NGOs were established to deal with the needs of the growing number of refugees

DOI: 10.4018/979-8-3693-8181-6.ch012

(World Bank, 2021). The increased number of non-governmental organizations (NGOs) urges a better understanding of how to enhance employees' productivity and encourage them to adopt extra work. Although organizational behavior and its related terms have long been studied in for-profit organizations, we still know little about organizational citizenship behavior (OCB) in non-profit organizations (McMurray, 2009). This research tries to fill this gap in the literature and highlight several problems related to employees' behavior in NGOs. The first highlighted problem is the influence of leadership style on workers' attitudes toward extra work. Then the research tries to find out whether employees' positive psychological status explains the effect of leadership on employees' intention to perform more than formally required.

NGOs are essential to promoting sustainable community development because they address issues of social justice, healthcare, and education. They usually cover the gaps created by government projects that are inefficient and resource-constrained. However, NGOs themselves could face similar challenges, such a lack of funding and poor administration, in their efforts to make a bigger impact (Abiddin, Ibrahim, & Aziz, 2022). Nonprofits are essential in supplying basic essentials and allowing access to government services during emergencies, such as the Syrian refugee crisis in Turkey. These organizations often face challenges such as internal dispute and a lack of funding, which can diminish their effectiveness despite their tremendous contributions (Atar, Hossain, & Ullah, 2022).

NGOs have a broad definition and different scopes that make it challenging to specify a particular definition. However, Alan and Flower (2013) distinguished NGOs from other organizations in that they cannot distribute surplus coming from profits and their existence is not related to law. NGOs are formed by volunteers' initiatives for a specific shared goal; they are independent and self-governed. Therefore, NGOs have been defined by different researchers in multiple ways. One of the latest definitions of NGOs is Damon's (2020) definition that an NGO is an organization with a non-commercial mission that focuses on the prosperity of education, culture, society, and the environment and operates independently of government. NGOs are usually task-oriented organizations that bring people with the same interests to work together for a specific target (Singh, 2014). Weiss and Gordenker (1996) mentioned that the term NGO could include social movement organizations, private voluntary organizations, independent sector, civic society, and non-state actors. Damon (2020) added donor agencies, coordinating organizations, and international organizations.

NGOs have many unique features that differentiate them from regular governmental or for-profit organizations. One of the most valued features of NGOs is their neutrality and independence (Damon, 2020). Moreover, for-profit organizations differ from non-profit organizations in terms of vision and mission with different reasons for existence and organizational motivations; For-profit organizations work on making profits, and NGOs work on social missions (Quarter & Richmond, 2001). Another unique feature of NGOs is that NGOs' most common financial resource is donations and fundraising (Damon, 2020). In addition, rewarding employees is usually related to the numerical and financial base in profit organizations like sales. In non-profit organizations, it is mainly associated with accomplishing a social mission (McMurray, 2009). Therefore, NGOs' performance evaluation and accountability are different from other types of organizations and need to be adjusted to increase the effectiveness of the related operations (Edwards & Hulme, 2014). NGOs are task-oriented, decentralized, and present a high level of commitment (Damon, 2020). In terms of challenges, NGOs face different challenges than other types of organizations. In profit organizations, managers need to meet external market forces, maintain capital access, maintain good relations with investors, and handle ownership transitions, recruitment, and governance challenges (Hoekstra & Peterson, 2005). On the other hand, managers in NGOs face different types of challenges trying to balance mission, passion, efficiency, and effectiveness (Bear & Fitzgibbon, 2005).

Good governance is necessary for NGOs to function effectively because it ensures moral behavior and accountability, both of which are vital for maintaining corporate goals and building trust. Numerous internal mechanisms and international third-party initiatives assist NGOs in upholding the highest standards of ethics and integrity (Ortega-Rodríguez, Martín-Montes, Licerán-Gutiérrez, & Moreno-Albarracín, 2023). According to Mitchell (2015) leadership styles that emphasize resemblance, diversity, commitment, professionalism, and decentralized structures, are characteristics of effective non-governmental organizations. Accordingly, effective management and leadership differ as well. In other words, NGO challenges are related to the spiritualization of employees who monitor their behavior and performance (McMurray, 2009).

And as we live in a digital Era, Servant leadership is essential in the context of digital transformation. It has been shown to have a major impact on the adoption of digital transformation methods, especially when it comes to employee empowerment and trust-building (Hamyeme, Belagra, Bouzidi, 2024). This leadership approach fosters a culture of cooperation and candid communication, which aids in navigating the challenges of digital transformation (Musaigwa & Kalitanyi, 2024).

Despite the differences between profit organizations and NGOs, generally available literature extends research results conducted regarding for-profit organizations to NGOs. It is not possible to consider NGOs as regular organizations, and it is not appropriate to extend the research findings related to regular organizations to NGOs (Dandridge, 1979; Westhead, & Cowling, 1998). However, there is a lack of documentation of the impact of NGOs' accomplishments as a sector (Edwards & Hulme, 2014). One of these terms is organizational behavior. Although organizational behavior and its related terms have long been studied in for-profit organizations, we still know little about OCB in non-profit organizations (McMurray, 2009).

The main objective of the conducted research is to scrutinize the relationship between Servant Leadership with OCB in non-profit organizations operating in Turkey. Also, the paper aims to understand the relationship and what are the reasons for this potential relationship by studying the mediation effect of PsyCap on the relationship between SL and OCB. To reach the research objective, the following questions were asked and aimed to be answered by the research results: Does servant style of leadership affect OCB in NGOs? Does the association between Servant Leadership and the level of OCB depend on the existence of perceived PsyCap of the non-profit organization?

## 2. LITERATURE REVIEW

### Influence of Leadership on Organizational Citizenship Behavior

OCB was defined by Organ (2005) as a discretionary personal behavior that fosters the adequate functioning of an organization, although it is not explicitly identified by the formal compensation policies. According to Organ, et al. (2006) OCB constitutes voluntary social behavior of an employee that differs from what is formally required and not mentioned in the job description and positively influences both others in the organization and the organization itself. Moreover, (OCB) indicates that an employee's behavior is consistent with an organization's purposes and procedures. However, Habeeb (2019) stated that although (OCB) concept has matured and its definition has been assorted, its core, dimensions, and antecedents have remained relatively unchanged. OCB has been an interesting topic for researchers to find out its relations with other organizational concepts like psychological capital (Psycap) (Pradhan, Jena, & Bhattacharya, 2016; Luthans et al., 2007; Subramaniam & Janadari, 2020), and Servant Leadership (Dierendonck, 2011; Kiker, Callahan, & Kiker,2019).

OCB could participate in increasing the level of productivity of both managers and employees by enhancing good practices, sharing knowledge, exchanging suggestions, offering help when needed, and feedback to managers (Podsakoff & MacKenzie, 1994). OCB increases the level and quality of performance by reducing the effort required to resolve conflicts, handle complaints, and generate sharing resources that allow managers to manage activities and engage in planning (Organ, 1988). Also, OCB enhances organizational performance by attracting and retaining promising employees and decreasing turnover (Organ, 1988). OCB could maintain a balanced level of performance among employees (Podsakoff & MacKenzie, 1994) when all employees are willing to handle tasks of other absent or overloaded team members creating a unified level of performance among all group members. OCB increases employees' adaptation to unstable environments (Schmidt, 2012). When there is a changing environment, employees who are used to handling extra-role duties can adapt and deal with changes.

One of the critical factors that affect employees' behavior is leadership style (Mi, et al., 2019; Ritz,, Giauque, Varone, & Anderfuhren, 2014; McMurray, 2009; Adil & Kamal, 2018). Singh (2014) concluded that within NGOs, the dominant leadership style is Servant Leadership. Servant Leadership is exhibited when directors merge their inducement to direct with their need to aid (Dierendonck, 2011; Greenleaf, 1977). Servant Leadership is achieved when people are empowered and developed by expressing "humility, authenticity, interpersonal acceptance, and stewardship; and by providing direction" (Dierendonck, 2011). Moreover, NGOs' Servant Leadership style could enhance leadership capabilities and development programs (Singh, 2014).

## Servant Leadership

Servant Leadership influences both employees and organizations positively. Servant Leadership emphasizes providing increased service to followers and encourages all types of growth for followers, such as personal, professional, and spiritual (Greenleaf, 1977). By spreading learning and growth opportunities to followers, servant leaders develop people (Laub, 1999). Greenleaf (1977) defined the role of a servant leader as the leader who functions for the maturation of people and society. Moreover, the main determinants of servant Leadership are that it conceives and treasures people, exhibits authenticity, builds community, and provides and shares leadership (Laub, 1999). In addition, Spears & Lawrence (2004) distinguished the servant leader from other types of superiors in that he practices listening, compassion, healing, cognition, persuading, conceptualization, focus, stewardship, dedication to the growth of people, and constructing community.

The increasing body of empirical research on Servant Leadership identifies numerous established research avenues and areas within the literature that require further investigation. Servant Leadership has been shown to improve employee outcomes through numerous antecedents and mediating and moderating processes at the individual level such as OCB and proactive behavior (Chiniara & Bentein, 2016; Newman et al., 2017; Walumbwa et al., 2010). The impact of Servant Leadership on employees' OCB was investigated by Ozyilmaz and Cicek (2015), who discovered that OCB is significantly improved by Servant Leadership. The study underscores the importance of Servant Leadership and highlights when employees perceived their leaders as servant leaders, they were more likely to exhibit OCB. In addition, Servant Leadership has been shown to be a useful way to understand small differences in these organizationally essential criterion measures, above and beyond transformational, ethical, and authentic leadership (Hoch et al., 2018).

In Turkish Cultural Context servant leadership is perceived to have a high correlation with paternalistic leadership styles, highlighting that leadership practices are strongly influenced by cultural dynamics[REMOVED HYPERLINK FIELD] (Öner, 2014). Accordingly, several researchers tackled Servant leadership in different Turkish sectors for a deeper understanding of the outcomes of such a style of leadership. In Turkish hospitality sector, Servant Leadership has been found affecting Service Quality that a higher levels of perceived servant leadership among supervisors leads to a better service quality provided by hotel's front-line employees (Koyuncu et. al. 2014; Burke,2014). Moreover, compared to authentic leadership in Turkish hospitality sector, Servant leadership has a stronger indirect impact on career satisfaction and adaptive performance through work engagement (Kaya & Karatepe, 2020). Relatedly, in Turkish public sector, servant leadership has been found enhancing work engagement among employees, mediated by motivating language and perceived organizational support (Uluturk, 2023). Servant leadership positively affects the psychological capacities of employees, which in turn enhances their productivity (Baykal, 2020).

Overall, the positive relationship between Servant Leadership and outcomes such as job performance, OCB, job satisfaction, organizational commitment, and follower trust has been proven (Kiker, Callahan, & Kiker, 2019). This leads to the following hypothesis:

H1: Servant Leadership has a positive relationship with OCB.

## Psychological Capital

Psychological capital (PsyCap) is defined as "what you can become in terms of positive development" (Avolio & Luthans, 2006). PsyCap is a higher-order need for human capital as it aids in handling various behavioral issues of an association (Pradhan, Jena, & Bhattacharya, 2016). Avolio & Luthans (2006) distinguished PsyCap from other forms of capital since what you have reflects financial capital, what you know constitutes human capital, and who you know represents social capital. PsyCap contains four different dimensions. The first dimension is self-efficacy which means being confident to handle a challenging task. The second dimension is optimism which means to anticipate current and future success. The third dimension is hope which means heading to goals and adjusting paths to reach goals. The last dimension is resilience which means sustainability when facing challenges and problems in order to succeed (Luthans, Avolio, Avey, & Norman, 2007). The processes required for the focus, interpretation, and retention of constructive and good memories that promote wellbeing can be facilitated by PsyCap. PsyCap can have a broadening and developing effect on positive emotional states, making it a positive psychological resource that can be used when faced with challenges (Fredrickson 2001, 2009). Lastly, PsyCap can support long-term well-being by reducing the common negativity bias and hedonic adaption (Cameron 2008).

It has been discovered that Psycap has anticipated a number of organizational behaviors since its founding. In a meta-analysis by Avey et al. (2011) of 51 independent samples which contains over 12,000 employees including diverse organizational contexts as well as NGOs, the researchers conclude that PsyCap is a powerful predictor for many job-related positive outcomes including employee attitudes such as job satisfaction, organizational commitment and psychological well-being and constructive behaviors like OCBs. On the contrary, PsyCap negatively relates to undesirable attitudes like cynicism, turnover intentions, and stress, and behaviors like deviance. Hongbo et al. (2021) highlighted that PsyCap mitigates the link between OCB and ego depletion, thereby reducing service sabotage behavior. Many studies present the positive effect of PsyCap on OCB. Luthans et al. (2007) indicated a significant positive relationship between the four dimensions of PsyCap with performance and satisfaction. Later on, Avey, Luthans, and Youssef (2010) found that PsyCap is positively related to extra role OCBs. Gupta, Shaheen, and Reddy (2017) found that PsyCap positively affects OCB. Similarly, Kataria, Rashmi, and Rastogi (2022) demonstrated that PsyCap enhances change-oriented OCBs. Lastly, in their study, Parent-Rocheleau, Bentein, and Simard (2020) observed that similarity in PsyCap between leaders and followers enhances OCB, whereas dissimilarity diminishes it. Furthermore, Subramaniam & Janadari (2020) found that the relationship between authentic leadership and OCB is partially mediated by PsyCap. In addition, the relationship between PsyCap and OCB has been studied by several researchers. Pradhan, Jena, & Bhattacharya (2016) found that PsyCap is positively related to OCB, similar to Subramaniam & Janadari (2020) findings, which also supported the relationship between PsyCap and OCB. This leads to the formation of the research's first hypothesis:

H2: PsyCap has a positive relationship with OCB.

The importance of PsyCap can be understood better within the context of an organization's overall assets. Each organization has both tangible and intangible assets. Tangible assets are the traditional economic assets and were mainly discussed and considered rather than the tangible ones. However, there is an increase in the consideration of the importance of intangible assets. Human capital is one of the essential intangible assets that drew the attention of enlightened managers recently. Human refers to employees of the organization and capital refers to resources invested for the anticipated future (Luthans, Luthans, & Luthans, 2004).

The Conservation of Resources (COR) theory, which was developed by Hobfoll (1989), is a recognized theoretical framework in the examination of organizational behavior, motivation, and stress. According to COR theory, individuals aim to acquire, preserve, cultivate, and preserve resources that are essential for their well-being. Resources are either tangible such as physical assets or intangible such as personal qualities, and social support and include objects, personal characteristics, conditions, and energies, according to Hobfoll. Hobfoll and Lilly (1993) elaborated on this by proposing that the motive of protecting resources is derived from the intention to prevent resource loss, recover from losses, and acquire new resources. This framework is particularly important in organizational contexts for understanding job burnout and work engagement, as it emphasizes the impact of resource availability on employees' capacity to manage stress and perform positive behaviors. As a result, employees with a high-level of PsyCap frequently demonstrate behavior that is indicative of voluntary actions that improve organizational efficiency (Youssef, Luthans, & Avey, 2010).

Servant Leadership, which emphasizes serving and empowering employees, creates a supportive environment fostering the development of personal resources such as PsyCap which equips employees with the mental and emotional resources needed to thrive and engage in positive organizational behaviors. According to COR theory, individuals who have adequate assets are more willing to exceed their official job responsibilities and participate in OCB due to their increased sense of competence and support in their roles. This highlights the significance of leadership styles that cultivate and maintain people's personal resources, resulting in enhanced organizational outcomes. Servant Leadership, characterized by prioritizing the needs of employees and fostering a supportive environment enhances PsyCap and leads employees to engage in OCB, going beyond their formal job duties to benefit the organization. Studies support job characteristics, personality traits, supportive organizational climate, and leadership styles as antecedents of PsyCap and variables to be accounted for in PsyCap models (Avey 2014).

Karatepe and Talebzadeh (2016) found that PsyCap mediates the relationship between Servant Leadership and work engagement among flight attendants, leading to improved work engagement, service recovery performance, and life satisfaction. Similarly, Clarence et.al (2020) found that Servant Leadership positively influences teachers' affective commitment and psychological well-being through the mediation of PsyCap. Bouzari and Karatepe (2017) found that PsyCap fully mediates the impact of Servant Leadership on several positive work behaviors in the hospitality industry. These behaviors include lateness attitude, intention to stay with the organization, service-sales ambidexterity, and service-oriented OCB (Bouzari & Karatepe, 2017).

The relationship between leadership and OCB with the mediation effect of PsyCap is supported by recent empirical research. Qamar and Soomro (2023) found that PsyCap significantly mediates the relationship between Servant Leadership and service excellence, indicating that leaders who support and develop their employees' PsyCap can enhance performance outcomes. Howladar and Rahman (2021) revealed that organizational commitment partially mediates the relationship between Servant Leadership and OCB, highlighting the role of supportive leadership in enhancing employee commitment and citizenship behaviors. Elche, Ruiz-Palomino, and Linuesa-Langreo (2020) demonstrated that Servant Leadership positively influences OCB through the mediating roles of employee empathy and group service climate, supporting the notion that servant leaders enhance employees' psychological and emotional resources, fostering a climate that encourages OCB Walumbwa, Hartnell, and Oke (2010) showed that Servant Leadership positively affects OCB through the mediating roles of commitment to the supervisor, self-efficacy, procedural justice climate, and service climate, highlighting the multifaceted ways in which Servant Leadership fosters an environment conducive to OCB. These studies collectively indicate that by enhancing employees' PsyCap, leaders provide them with the necessary psychological resources to engage in discretionary behaviors that benefit the organization.

Hence we build our third and fourth hypotheses;

H3: Servant Leadership has a positive relationship with PsyCap.

H4: PsyCap mediates the relationship between Servant Leadership and OCB..

## 3. RESEARCH METHODOLOGY

This research is quantitative research conducted by a questionnaire developed by existing literature measurements containing several instruments to measure each variable. Quantitative research is based on several structured questions that form a questionnaire later translated into numerical data (Sekaran & Roger, 2016). The adopted instruments were measured by a Likert five-point scale. The survey has been distributed to employees working in NGOs in Turkey. The collected sample is 202 responses from employees working for NGOs that operate in Turkey. The survey started by asking a question whether the respondent works for an NGO or not to ensure that all the respondents are actual NGO's employees. Accordingly, one of the received responses has been deleted.

The research-dependent variable is OCB, measured by adopting nine instruments representing three dimensions (Help, civic virtue, and sportsmanship). OCB measurement is a shorter version of the Podsakoff & MacKenzie (1994) scale developed by Raineri, Paille, & Morin (2012). The research independent variable is Servant Leadership. The adopted scale to measure Servant Leadership contains seven instruments and has been developed by Liden R., et al. (2015) which is a shorter form of Liden, Wayne, Zhao, and Henderson's (2008) 28-item Servant Leadership measurement scale. The mediator variable is PsyCap which has been measured by adopting Lorenz, et al. (2016) scale that contains four dimensions, i.e., hope, resilience, optimism, and efficacy, with 12 questions. Figure 1 presents the research conceptual framework.

*Figure 1. Research conceptual model*

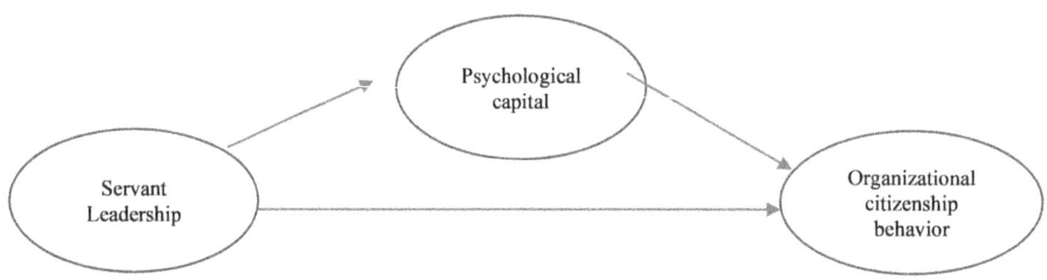


To analyze research data, Smart PLS (v. 3.2.8) and Excel were used. First, Excel is used to calculate percentages of demographics and to scan data. Then a structural equation model was conducted using Smart PLS (v. 3.2.8). To evaluate the research model, measurement and structural model were assessed. The assessment is conducted using Smart PLS (v. 3.2.8), adopting a significant level of 95% two-tailed. The assessment of the measurement model includes assessing Cronbach's alpha, factor outer loading, composite reliability, and discriminant validity. The structural model assessment included evaluating r squared and r squared adjusted, and collinearity assessment.

After evaluating the measurement and structural model, the research model was accepted to test the research hypotheses. Thus, t-test and p-value calculations, along with an evaluation of the path coefficient were calculated.

## 5. RESULTS

### 5.1 Demographics

Table 1 presents the demographics of the research sample. Most of the sample were males with 175 responses that form 87.06% of the sample. Accordingly, females were presented with only 26 responses which is 12.94%of the sample. The majority of the sample was between 30-39 years old with 116 respondents which forms 57.71% of the sample. The second biggest age group is 20-29 with 42 responses which forms 20.9% of the sample. Then comes the 40-49 age group with 30 responses and a percentage of 14.93% of the sample. Finally, the last age group is more than 50 with 13 responses that form 6.47% of the sample.

Respondent educational levels are High school or less (42 responses, 20.4% of the sample); Diploma (31 respondents, 15.42% of the sample); Bachelor (93 respondents, 46.27% of the sample) and finally, higher education (36 respondents, 17.91% of the sample).

*Table 1. Respondents' demographics*

| Gender | Count of Gender | Percentage |
|---|---|---|
| Female | 26 | 12.94% |
| Male | 175 | 87.06% |
| Grand Total | 201 | 100.00% |
| Age Group | Count of Age | Percentage |
| 20-29 | 42 | 20.90% |
| 30-39 | 116 | 57.71% |
| 40-49 | 30 | 14.93% |
| More than 50 | 13 | 6.47% |
| Grand Total | 201 | 100.00% |
| Educational level | Count of Educational level | Percentage |
| High school or less | 41 | 20.40% |
| Diploma | 31 | 15.42% |
| Bachelor | 93 | 46.27% |
| Higher education | 36 | 17.91% |
| Grand Total | 201 | 100.00% |

## 5.2 Measurement Model Assessment

### 5.2.1 Reliability Assessment

In order to evaluate the reliability of the research model, two main values, Cronbach's Alpha and Composite Reliability were assessed. Cronbach's Alpha forms an indicator to measure the model's internal consistency. The accepted value of Cronbach's Alpha is above 0.7, and any value below 0.6 indicates a lack of reliability (Hair, Hult, & Sarstedt, 2017). As shown in Table 2, all the Cronbach's alpha values of research variables exceed 0.7.

Another critical assessment needed to assess the measurement model regarding the internal model consistency is composite reliability, and it has been calculated as shown in Table 2. The accepted value of composite reliability is bigger than 0.7, and it is achieved within all the variables of the proposed model.

*Table 2. Reliability assessment*

| | Cronbach's alpha | Composite reliability (rho_a) | Composite reliability (rho_c) |
|---|---|---|---|
| OCB | 0.737 | 0.778 | 0.811 |
| PsyCap | 0.767 | 0.819 | 0.824 |
| Servant Leadership | 0.866 | 0.885 | 0.897 |

### 5.2.2 Discriminant Validity

Discriminant validity is conducted to evaluate the uniqueness of each variable from other variables. If the correlation between two different variables is higher than the correlation within the same variable, that means the discriminant validity is not acceptable (Moore, Mccabe, & Bruce, 2013). As shown in Table 3, the correlation within the same variable is higher than the correlation with other discriminant variables. According to the discriminant validity results, the research model is valid.

*Table 3. Discriminant validity*

| | Civic | Efficacy | Help | Hope | OCB | Optimism | PsyCap | Resilience | SLeadership | Sportsmanship |
|---|---|---|---|---|---|---|---|---|---|---|
| **Civic** | 1 | 0.352 | 0.38 | 0.334 | 0.865 | 0.368 | 0.434 | 0.181 | 0.362 | 0.342 |
| **Efficacy** | 0.352 | 1 | 0.251 | 0.368 | 0.321 | 0.424 | 0.732 | 0.389 | 0.123 | 0.042 |
| **Help** | 0.38 | 0.251 | 1 | 0.181 | 0.676 | 0.194 | 0.273 | 0.203 | 0.134 | 0.197 |
| **Hope** | 0.334 | 0.368 | 0.181 | 1 | 0.304 | 0.579 | 0.774 | 0.319 | 0.194 | 0.101 |
| **OCB** | 0.865 | 0.321 | 0.676 | 0.304 | 1 | 0.366 | 0.411 | 0.168 | 0.38 | 0.635 |
| **Optimism** | 0.368 | 0.424 | 0.194 | 0.579 | 0.366 | 1 | 0.855 | 0.337 | 0.268 | 0.2 |
| **PsyCap** | 0.434 | 0.732 | 0.273 | 0.774 | 0.411 | 0.855 | 1 | 0.571 | 0.233 | 0.133 |
| **Resilience** | 0.181 | 0.389 | 0.203 | 0.319 | 0.168 | 0.337 | 0.571 | 1 | 0.021 | -0.05 |
| **SLeadership** | 0.362 | 0.123 | 0.134 | 0.194 | 0.38 | 0.268 | 0.233 | 0.021 | 1 | 0.312 |
| **Sportsmanship** | 0.342 | 0.042 | 0.197 | 0.101 | 0.635 | 0.2 | 0.133 | -0.05 | 0.312 | 1 |

## 5.3 Structural Model Assessment

An essential value to evaluate the structural model is the measure of collinearity which is necessary to prove that all independent variables in the regression model are genuinely independent (Hair, Hult, & Sarstedt, 2017). To measure collinearity, the VIF value is calculated for all independent variables. As shown in Table 4, all VIF values for the independent variables are less than the value of 5 which is accepted since collinearity should not exceed 5 (Kock & Lynn, 2012). The value of VIF for independent variables is accepted and is ideal (less than 2) for all variables.

*Table 4. Collinearity statistics VIF*

| | VIF |
|---|---|
| OCB -> Civic | 1.000 |
| OCB -> Help | 1.000 |
| OCB -> Sportsmanship | 1.000 |
| PsyCap -> efficacy | 1.000 |
| PsyCap -> Hope | 1.000 |
| PsyCap -> OCB | 1.057 |

continued on following page

*Table 4. Continued*

| | VIF |
|---|---|
| PsyCap -> Optimism | 1.000 |
| PsyCap -> Resilience | 1.000 |
| SLeadership -> OCB | 1.057 |
| SLeadership -> PsyCap | 1.000 |

## 5.4 Evaluation of the Effect Size

F square presents the effect size of each variable on the dependent variable, thus values of $f^2 \geq 0.02$ mean that the variable has a small effect on the dependent variable while $f^2 \geq 0.15$ means that the effect is medium and $f^2 \geq 0.35$ means the effect is large (Moore, Mccabe, & Bruce, 2013). According to effect size analysis, Servant Leadership ($f^2 = 0.115$) and PsyCap ($f^2 = 0.148$) have a small effect on OCB ($0.02 \geq f^2 < 0.15$). Also, Servant Leadership has a small effect ($0.02 \geq f^2 < 0.15$) on PsyCap ($f^2 = 0.057$).

*Table 5. The effect sizes*

| | f-square |
|---|---|
| PsyCap -> OCB | 0.148 |
| SLeadership -> OCB | 0.115 |
| SLeadership -> PsyCap | 0.057 |

## 5.5 Testing the Research Hypotheses

The research proposed four hypotheses which have been tested by evaluating path coefficients and conducting a t-test to find out the t-value and p-value. For a two-tailed significant level of 95%, the hypothesis should score a p-value less than .05 and a t-value bigger than 1.96 to be accepted (Moore, Mccabe, & Bruce, 2013). Accordingly, the research results in Table 5 supported all the proposed research hypotheses (H1, H2, H3, and H4).

The first research hypothesis scored values are ($t= 5.667$, $p= 0$, $\beta = 0.380$) which means p-value < 0.05 and t-value > 1.96 which leads to accepting the first research hypothesis. Accordingly, the positive relationship between Servant Leadership and OCB in NGOs operating in Turkey has been proven.

The second research hypothesis demonstrated values of ($t= 5.962$, $p= 0$, $\beta =0.341$). The results support the proposed hypothesis which means that there is a proven positive relationship between PsyCap and OCB.

The third research hypothesis scored values are ($t= 2.772$, $p= 0.006$, $\beta =0.233$). This result leads to accepting the second research hypothesis and proving the positive relationship between Servant Leadership and PsyCap.

The fourth research hypothesis results are ($t=2.269$, $p= 0.023$, $\beta =0.079$). These results indicate that PsyCap fully mediates the relationship between Servant Leadership and OCB.

Overall, the results confirm the proposed theoretical framework and demonstrate the relationship and interplay between the proposed constructs.

*Table 6. Hypothesis testing*

| | Original sample (O) | Sample mean (M) | Standard deviation (STDEV) | T statistics (\|O/ STDEV\|) | P values |
|---|---|---|---|---|---|
| SLeadership-> OCB | 0.380 | 0.389 | 0.067 | 5.667 | 0.000 |
| PsyCap -> OCB | 0.341 | 0.345 | 0.057 | 5.962 | 0.000 |
| SLeadership -> PsyCap | 0.233 | 0.243 | 0.084 | 2.772 | 0.006 |
| SLeadership -> PsyCap -> OCB | 0.079 | 0.085 | 0.035 | 2.269 | 0.023 |

## 6. DISCUSSION

The research findings supplement the available body of literature in multiple ways and are consistent with it, as well as with other studies that have been published. The first study's conclusion that Servant Leadership and OCB have a positive relationship is consistent with earlier studies' findings, such as those of Ozyilmaz and Cicek (2015) and Kiker, Callahan, & Kiker (2019), which also show this relationship. Also, it supports the available literature that concluded with the finding that Servant Leadership has been shown to improve employee outcomes such as OCB and proactive behavior (Chiniara & Bentein, 2016; Newman et al., 2017; Walumbwa et al., 2010).

The results of this study contribute to the body of literature by reinforcing the theory that Servant Leadership is one of the critical antecedents of OCB. By showing the strong path coefficient demonstrating the direct positive relationship of Servant Leadership with OCB, the importance of leaders focusing on the needs of followers, setting up a supportive climate, and fostering altruistic behaviors is evidenced. These findings are aligned with past studies but extend the domain under study to the NGO sector in Turkey, which has been underexplored in existing literature. The current research extends the established relationship which includes varying types of organizations, by analyzing this relationship in a different context, that of NGOs.

According to the research results regarding employees working in NGOs, the positive relationship between their PsyCap within its four dimensions and OCB is significantly proven. This finding enhances the findings of Subramaniam & Janadari (2020) and Radhan, Jena, & Bhattacharya (2016) who found that PsyCap is positively related to OCB. This finding could be added to Luthans et al. (2007) which indicated a significant positive relationship between the four dimensions of PsyCap with performance and satisfaction since they also present positive organizational behavior.

In accordance with COR theory that individuals aim to acquire, preserve, cultivate, and preserve resources that are essential for their well-being, the third and fourth research findings were aligned with the same context. As intangible assets, employees with a high level of PsyCap frequently demonstrate behavior that is indicative of voluntary actions that improve organizational efficiency (Youssef, Luthans, & Avey, 2010). Some previous studies collectively indicate that by enhancing employees' PsyCap, leaders provide them with the necessary psychological resources to engage in discretionary behaviors that benefit the organization (Walumbwa, Hartnell, and Oke, 2010; Elche, Ruiz-Palomino, and Linuesa-Langreo, 2020). In accordance with that, this study confimed the positive relationship between Servant Leadership and PsyCap which aligns with Karatepe and Talebzadeh's (2016) findings while highlighting the significant role of PsyCap in enhancing OCB serves as a vital resource that empowers employees to go beyond their formal job responsibilities.

Regarding Psycap as a full mediator of the association between Servant Leadership and OCB, the research finding supplements the available literature of Psycap as a mediator between Servant leadership and other positive organizational behaviors and attitudes like Karatepe and Talebzadeh (2016) finding that PsyCap mediates the relationship between Servant Leadership and work engagement. Similarly, the current research finding of the mediation adds to Clarence et.al (2020) conclusion that Servant Leadership positively influences teachers' affective commitment and psychological well-being through the mediation of PsyCap. In addition to that the research result supports Bouzari and Karatepe's (2017) finding that PsyCap fully mediates the impact of Servant Leadership on several positive work behaviors in the hospitality industry. This finding is particularly noteworthy demonstating the correlation between Servant Leadership and increased OCB. The Servant Leaders create a nurturing and empowering climate that boosts the workers' PsyCap, leading them to actively participate in OCB. The inclusion of PsyCap as a mediator is a valuable contribution to the existing research on how leadership style affects voluntary behavioral outcomes.

The study provides practical insights for NGO administrators and leaders. Considering the influence established between Servant Leadership and OCB, NGOs can prioritize the implementation of leadership development programs focused on Servant Leadership principles in light of the proven impact of Servant Leadership on OCB. These programs may encompass mentoring schemes, seminars, and training sessions that are intended to foster leaders who prioritize the development and well-being of their team members. Additionally, the significance of PsyCap in improving OCB implies that NGOs should allocate resources to interventions that are designed to increase the psychological resources of their employees. Initiatives to foster a supportive and optimistic work environment, resilience training, and positive psychology interventions are viable strategies. Organizations can ultimately improve their efficacy and sustainability by fostering a more engaged and proactive workforce by enhancing employees' PsyCap.

The cultural context of Turkey provides an additional layer of understanding to these findings. Turkish culture is collectivist and high-power distance in nature (Hofstede, 2001). The concept of a supportive and empowering leader may be particularly effective in high power distance cultures in bridging hierarchical levels to foster OCB. Additionally, the communal and altruistic elements of OCB are particularly well-suited for the collectivist nature of Turkish society which may even strengthen the observed relationships.

## 7. CONCLUSION

The research's main objective was to investigate the relationship between Servant Leadership and OCB in NGOs operating in Turkey by investigating the possible mediation of PsyCap. The results indicated a positive relationship between servant leadership and OCB in NGOs operating in Turkey. In addition, the relationship between positive PsyCap and OCB of employees in non-profit organizations was proven. Finally, the research found that PsyCap mediates the effect of Servant Leadership on OCB. These research findings have several practical implications.

The research findings could be helpful for NGOs and might participate in their development. To maintain a high level of OCB, NGOs should work on enhancing servant leadership among their leaders this will lead NGOs to maintain a high level of PsyCap among their employees. Thus, NGO leaders should invest in maintaining a high level of servant leadership and enhancing positive PsyCap with its four dimensions to increase OCB with its three dimensions that lead to an increase in the level of productivity of both managers and employees (Podsakoff & MacKenzie, 1994; Organ, 1988).

This study has limitations that necessitate additional investigation, despite its contributions. One of the main drivers for this research is the anticipated differences between regular for-profit organizations and NGOs; however, the study adopted scales designed and tested for regular organizations without considering the differences between the two types of organizations. This forms the first research limitation and to overcome that, it is recommended that future studies develop and examine special scales for organizational behavior concepts prepared specially for NGOs. The second research limitation is that the capacity to make causal inferences is restricted by the cross-sectional design (Stone-Romero & Rosopa, 2008). Longitudinal studies could offer more robust evidence of the causal relationships between Servant Leadership, PsyCap, and OCB. This study could be replicated in various cultural and organizational contexts in order to improve the external validity of the results in future research. Furthermore, the investigation of the mediating role of PsyCap was conducted; however, potential moderators, including organizational culture, job satisfaction, and employee engagement, could be investigated to gain a more comprehensive understanding of the dynamics of these relationships.

## REFERENCES


Abiddin, N., Ibrahim, I., & Aziz, S. (2022). Non-Governmental Organisations (NGOs) and Their Part towards Sustainable Community Development. *Sustainability (Basel)*, 14(8), 4386. Advance online publication. DOI: 10.3390/su14084386

Adil, A., & Kamal, A. (2018). Impact of Perceived Authentic Leadership and Psychological Capital on Burnout: Mediating Role of Psychological Ownership. *Psychological Studies*, 63(3), 243–252. DOI: 10.1007/s12646-018-0446-x

Ainsworth, J. (2020). Feelings of ownership and volunteering: Examining psychological ownership as a volunteering motivation for nonprofit service organizations. *Journal of Retailing and Consumer Services*, 52, 101931. DOI: 10.1016/j.jretconser.2019.101931

Atar, E., Hossain, F., & Ullah, A. (2022). Syrian refugees in Turkey: exploring the role of I/ NGOs in refugee crisis. Third World Quarterly(44, 231 - 245.), 231 - 245, https://doi.org/.DOI: 10.1080/01436597.2022.2144208

Avey, J., Luthans, F., & Youssef, C. M. (2010). The Additive Value of Positive Psychological Capital in Predicting Work Attitudes and Behaviors. *Journal of Management*, 36(2), 430–452. DOI: 10.1177/0149206308329961

Avey, J. B., Luthans, F., & Youssef, C. M. (2014). The additive value of positive psychological capital in predicting work attitudes and behaviors. *Journal of Management*, 36(2), 430–452. DOI: 10.1177/0149206308329961

Avolio, B., & Luthans, F. (2006). *The high-impact leader Authentic, resilient leadership that gets results and sustains growth*. McGraw-Hill.

Baykal, E. (2020). Effects of Servant Leadership on Psychological Capitals and Productivities of Employees. *Effects of Servant Leadership on Psychological Capitals and Productivities of Employees.*, 34, 273–291. DOI: 10.16951/atauniiibd.533275

Bear, A., & Fitzgibbon, M. (2005). Leadership in a not-for-profit world: a mixed toolbox. In Sims, R. R., & Quatro, S. A. (Eds.), *Leadership: Succeeding in the Private, Public, and Not-for-profit Sectors* (pp. 87–104). M.E. Sharpe.

Bouzari, M., & Karatepe, O. M. (2017). Test of a mediation model of psychological capital among hotel salespeople. *International Journal of Contemporary Hospitality Management*, 29(7), 2178–2197. DOI: 10.1108/IJCHM-01-2016-0022

Burke, R., Koyuncu, M., Ashtakova, M., Eren, D., & Cetin, H. (2014). Hotel Star Ratings And Perceptions Of Servant Leadership And Service Quality Provided By Front-Line Service Workers In Four- And Five-Star Hotels In Turkey. An Exploratory Study. *Isguc The Journal of Industrial Relations and Human Resources*, 16(3), 3–9. DOI: 10.4026/1303-2860.2014.0251.x

Chiniara, M., & Bentein, K. (2016). Linking servant leadership to individual performance: Differentiating the mediating role of autonomy, competence and relatedness need satisfaction. *The Leadership Quarterly*, 27(1), 124–141. DOI: 10.1016/j.leaqua.2015.08.004

Clarence, M., Devassy, V. P., Jena, L. K., & George, T. S. (2020). The effect of servant leadership on ad hoc schoolteachers' affective commitment and psychological well-being: The mediating role of psychological capital. *International Review of Education*, 67(3), 305–331. DOI: 10.1007/s11159-020-09856-9

Damon, P. (2020). *Participants: nongovernmental organizations, including the private sector and academia* (4th ed.). Introduction to International Disaster Management.

Dandridge, T. (1979). Children are not little grown-ups: Small business needs its own organization theory. *Journal of Small Business Management*, •••, 17.

Dierendonck, D. (2011). Servant Leadership: A Review and Synthesis. *Journal of Management*, 37(4), 1228–1261. DOI: 10.1177/0149206310380462

Edwards, M., & Hulme, D. (2014). *Non-governmental organisations-performance and accountability: Beyond the magic bullet*. Routledge. DOI: 10.4324/9781315070704

Elche, D., Ruiz-Palomino, P., & Linuesa-Langreo, J. (2020). Servant leadership and organizational citizenship behavior: The mediating role of empathy and service climate. *Journal of Business Research*, 110, 110–122.

Fowler, A. (2013). *Striking a balance: A guide to enhancing the effectiveness of non-governmental organisations in international development*. Routledge. DOI: 10.4324/9781315070735

Greenleaf, R. (1977). *Servant leadership: a journey into the nature of legitimate power and greatness*. Poulist Press.

Gupta, M., Shaheen, M., & Reddy, P. K. (2017). Impact of psychological capital on organizational citizenship behavior. *Journal of Management Development*, 36(7), 973–983. DOI: 10.1108/JMD-06-2016-0084

Habeeb, S. (2019). A proposed instrument for assessing organizational citizenship behavior in BFSI companies in India. *Cogent Business & Management*, 6(1), 1–20. DOI: 10.1080/23311975.2019.1625702

Hair, J., Hult, G., & Sarstedt, M. (2017). *A premium on partial least squares structural equation modelling (PLS-SEM)*. SAGE.

Hamyeme, S., Belagra, F., & Bouzidi, F. (2024). The Effect of Implementing Servant Leadership Practices on the Adoption of Digital Transformation for Companies in the Telecommunications Sector. *Business Ethics and Leadership*. https://doi.org/.DOI: 10.61093/bel.8(3).26-42.2024

Hobfoll, S. E. (1989). Conservation of resources: A new attempt at conceptualizing stress. *The American Psychologist*, 44(3), 513–524. DOI: 10.1037/0003-066X.44.3.513 PMID: 2648906

Hobfoll, S. E., & Lilly, R. S. (1993). Resource conservation as a strategy for community psychology. *Journal of Community Psychology*, 21(2), 128–148. DOI: 10.1002/1520-6629(199304)21:2<128::AID-JCOP2290210206>3.0.CO;2-5

Hoch, J. E., Bommer, W. H., Dulebohn, J. H., & Wu, D. (2018). Do ethical, authentic, and servant leadership explain variance above and beyond transformational leadership? A meta-analysis. *Journal of Management*, 44(2), 501–552. DOI: 10.1177/0149206316665461

Hoekstra, E., & Peterson, S. (2005). Beyond Wall Street: leadership challenges unique to small private companies and entrepreneurial firms. Sims, R.R. and Quatro, S.A. (Eds), Leadership: Succeeding in the Private, Public, and Not-for-profit Sectors, M.E Sharpe, 46-64.

Hosftede, G. (2001). *Culture's Consequences: Comparing Values, Behaviors, Institutions, and Organizations Across Nations* (2nd ed.). Sage Publications.

Howladar, M. H. R., & Rahman, M. M. (2021). Influence of servant leadership on organizational citizenship behavior: The role of organizational commitment. *International Journal of Research in Business and Social Science*, 10(1), 39–50.

Karatepe, O. M., & Talebzadeh, N. (2016). An empirical investigation of psychological capital among flight attendants. *Journal of Air Transport Management*, 55, 193–202. DOI: 10.1016/j.jairtraman.2016.06.001

Kataria, A., Rashmi, K., & Rastogi, M. (2022). Fostering change-oriented OCBS: An analysis of India's IT talent. *Journal of Asia Business Studies*.

Kaya, B., & Karatepe, O. (2020). Does servant leadership better explain work engagement, career satisfaction and adaptive performance than authentic leadership? *International Journal of Contemporary Hospitality Management*, 32(6), 2075–2095. Advance online publication. DOI: 10.1108/IJCHM-05-2019-0438

Kiker, D., Callahan, J., & Kiker, M. (2019). Exploring the boundaries of servant leadership: A meta-analysis of the main and moderating effects of servant leadership on behavioural and effective outcomes. *Journal of Managerial Issues*.

Kock, M., & Lynn, G. (2012). Lateral collinearity and misleading results in variance-based SEM: An illustration and recommendation. *Journal of the Association for Information Systems*, 13(7), 546–580. DOI: 10.17705/1jais.00302

Koyuncu, M., Burke, R., Astakhova, M., Eren, D., & Çetin, H. (2014). Servant leadership and perceptions of service quality provided by front-line service workers in hotels in Turkey: Achieving competitive advantage. *International Journal of Contemporary Hospitality Management*, 26, 1083–1099. DOI: 10.1108/IJCHM-06-2013-0238

Laub, J. (1999). Assessing the servant organization: Development of the servant leadership. *Review of General Psychology*, •••, 326–341.

Liden, R., Wayne, S., Meuser, J., Hu, J., Wu, J., & Liao, C. (2015). Servant leadership: Validation of a short form of the SL-28. *The Leadership Quarterly*, 26(2), 254–269. DOI: 10.1016/j.leaqua.2014.12.002

Liden, R., Wayne, S., Zhao, H., & Henderson, D. (2008). Servant leadership: Development of a multidimensional measure and multilevel assessment. *The Leadership Quarterly*, 19(2), 161–177. DOI: 10.1016/j.leaqua.2008.01.006

Luthans, F., Avolio, B., Avey, J., & Norman, S. (2007). Positive psychological capital: Measurement and relationship with performance and satisfaction. *Personnel Psychology*, 60(3), 541–572. DOI: 10.1111/j.1744-6570.2007.00083.x

Luthans, F., Luthans, K., & Luthans, B. (2004). Positive psychological capital: Beyond human and social capital.

Luthans, F., Luthans, K. W., & Luthans, B. C. (2004). Positive psychological capital: Beyond human and social capital. *Business Horizons*, 47(1), 45–50. DOI: 10.1016/j.bushor.2003.11.007

McMurray, A. (2009). Leadership, climate, psychological capital, commitment, and wellbeing in a non-profit organization. *Leadership and Organization Development Journal*, •••, 436–457.

Mi, L., Gan, X., Xu, T., Long, R., Qiao, L., & Zhu, H. (2019). A new perspective to promote organizational citizenship behaviour for the environment: The role of transformational leadership. *Journal of Cleaner Production*, 239, 118002. DOI: 10.1016/j.jclepro.2019.118002

Mitchell, G. (2015). The Attributes of Effective NGOs and the Leadership Values Associated with a Reputation for Organizational Effectiveness. *Nonprofit Management & Leadership*, 26(1), 39–57. DOI: 10.1002/nml.21143

Moore, D., Mccabe, G., & Bruce, G. (2013). *The basic practice of statistics* (6th ed.). W.H Freeman and Company.

Musaigwa, M., & Kalitanyi, V. (2024). Effective leadership in the digital era: an exploration of change management. *Technology audit and production reserves*. https://doi.org/.DOI: 10.15587/2706-5448.2024.297374

Newman, A., Schwarz, G., Cooper, B., & Sendjaya, S. (2017). How servant leadership influences organizational citizenship behavior: The roles of LMX, empowerment, and proactive personality: JBE JBE. *Journal of Business Ethics*, 145(1), 49–62. DOI: 10.1007/s10551-015-2827-6

Öner, Z. (2012). Servant leadership and paternalistic leadership styles in the Turkish business context: A comparative empirical study. *Leadership and Organization Development Journal*, 33(3), 300–316. DOI: 10.1108/01437731211216489

Organ, D., Podsakoff, P., & MacKenzie, S. (2006). *Organizational citizenship behavior: Its nature, antecedents, and consequences*. Sage. DOI: 10.4135/9781452231082

Organ, D. W. (1988). Organizational citizenship behavior: The good soldier syndrome. Lexington books/ DC heath and com.

Ortega-Rodríguez, C., Martín-Montes, L., Licerán-Gutiérrez, A., & Moreno-Albarracín, A. (2023). Nonprofit good governance mechanisms: A systematic literature review. *Nonprofit Management & Leadership*. Advance online publication. DOI: 10.1002/nml.21598

Ozyilmaz, A., & Cicek, S. S. (2015). How does servant leadership affect employee attitudes, behaviors, and psychological climates in a for-profit organizational context? *Journal of Management & Organization*, 21(3), 263–290. DOI: 10.1017/jmo.2014.80

Parent-Rocheleau, X., Bentein, K., & Simard, G. (2020). Positive together? The effects of leader-follower (dis)similarity in psychological capital. *Journal of Business Research*, 110, 435–444. DOI: 10.1016/j.jbusres.2020.02.016

Podsakoff, P. M., & MacKenzie, S. B. (1994). An examination of the psychometric properties and nomological validity of some revised and reduced substitutes for leadership scales. *The Journal of Applied Psychology*, 79(5), 702–713. DOI: 10.1037/0021-9010.79.5.702

Pradhan, R., Jena, L., & Bhattacharya, P. (2016). Impact of psychological capital on organizational citizenship behavior: Moderating role of emotional intelligence. *Cogent Business & Management*, 3(1), 3. DOI: 10.1080/23311975.2016.1194174

Qamar, F., & Soomro, S. A. (2023). Investigating the impact of servant leadership on service excellence: The mediating role of PsyCap as a personal resource and buffering role of conscientiousness. *Global Knowledge, Memory and Communication.*

Quarter, J., & Richmond, B. (2001). Accounting for social value in nonprofits and for-profits. *Nonprofit Management & Leadership*, 12(1), 75–85. DOI: 10.1002/nml.12106

Raineri, N., Paille, P., & Morin, D. (2012). Organizational citizenship behavior: An intergenerational study.

Ritz, A., Giauque, D., Varone, F., & Anderfuhren, S. (2014). From Leadership to Citizenship Behavior in Public Organizations: When Values Matter. *Review of Public Personnel Administration*, 34(2), 128–152. DOI: 10.1177/0734371X14521456

Schmidt, J. (2012). Do people in NGOs perform civic behavior? Organizational citizenship behavior in Polish NGOs – results of an empirical study. Tenth International Conference of the International Society for Third Sector Research (ISTR) Fondazione ForTeS - Fondazione Scuola di alta Formazione per il Terzo Settore. Italy.

Sekaran, U., & Roger, B. (2016). *Research methods for business* (7th ed.). John Wiley & Sons.

Singh, K. (2014). Non- Governmental Organizations (NGOs) have become influential development agents in the developing world in recent decades through their so-called "sustainable" activities. *The Journal of American Science*, 11(1), 1–11.

Spears, L., & Lawrence, M. (2004). *Practicing Servant Leadership: Succeeding through trust, bravery, and forgiveness. San Francisco*. Jossey-Bass.

Stone-Romero, E. F., & Rosopa, P. J. (2008). The relative validity of inferences about mediation as a function of research design characteristics. *Organizational Research Methods*, 11(2), 326–352. DOI: 10.1177/1094428107300342

Subramaniam, S., & Janadari, N. (2020). Authentic leadership and organizational citizenship behaviour: The role of psychological capital. *International Journal of Productivity and Performance Management.*

Uluturk, B. (2023). How Servant Leadership Influences Street-Level Bureaucrats' Work Engagement: The Mediating Roles of Motivating Language and Perceived Organizational Support. *Management Communication Quarterly*. Advance online publication. DOI: 10.1177/08933189231219708

Walumbwa, F. O., Hartnell, C. A., & Oke, A. (2010). Servant leadership, procedural justice climate, service climate, employee attitudes, and organizational citizenship behavior: A cross-level investigation. *The Journal of Applied Psychology*, 95(3), 517–529. DOI: 10.1037/a0018867 PMID: 20476830

Weiss, T., & Gordenker, L. (1996). *NGOs, the UN, and global governance*. Lynne Rienner. DOI: 10.1515/9781685855987

Westhead, P., & Cowling, M. (1998). Family firm research: The need for a methodological rethink. *Entrepreneurship Theory and Practice*, 23(1), 31–56. DOI: 10.1177/104225879802300102

World Bank. (2021, Jun. 22). 10 Years On, Turkey Continues Its Support for an Ever-Growing Number of Syrian Refugees. Retrieved Nov. 18, 2021, from https://www.worldbank.org/: https://www.worldbank.org/en/news/feature/2021/06/22/10-years-on-turkey-continues-its-support-for-an-ever-growing-number-of-syrian-refugees

Youssef, C. M., Luthans, F., & Avey, J. B. (2010). The additive value of positive psychological capital in predicting work attitudes and behaviors. *Journal of Management*, 36(2), 430–452. DOI: 10.1177/0149206308329961

## KEY TERMS AND DEFINITIONS

**Hope:** Heading to goals and adjusting paths to reach goals.

**Non Governmental Organization (NGO):** Distinguished from other organizations in that they cannot distribute surplus coming from profits and their existence is not related to law. NGOs are formed by volunteers' initiatives for a specific shared goal; they are independent and self-governed.

**Optimism:** To anticipate current and future success.

**Organizational Citizenship Behavior:** Extra role behavior and defined as a discretionary personal behavior that fosters the adequate functioning of an organization, although it is not explicitly identified by the formal compensation policies.

**Psychological Capital:** it Is what you can become in terms of positive development and forms a higher-order need for human capital as it aids in handling various behavioral issues of an association.

**Resilience:** Sustainability when facing challenges and problems in order to succeed.

**Self-Efficacy:** Being confident to handle a challenging task.

**Servant Leadership:** A leadership style that emphasizes providing increased service to followers and encourages all types of growth for followers, such as personal, professional, and spiritual.

**The Role of a Servant Leader:** Defined as the leader who functions for the maturation of people and society.

# Chapter 13
# A Thematic Analysis of Literature on the Startup Assessment Criteria: Startup Success Factors Revisited

**Nihan Yildirim**
https://orcid.org/0000-0002-6279-3849
*Istanbul Technical University, Turkey*

**Yusuf Maz**
https://orcid.org/0000-0001-5730-2454
*Istanbul Technical University, Turkey*

## ABSTRACT

*Assessing early-stage startups is inherently subjective due to limited data and unpredictability, complicating the accurate prediction of their success and suitability for investment. Despite previous research highlighting the influence of entrepreneurial team characteristics, managerial capabilities, and financials on investment decisions, the factors driving startup success are multifaceted requiring a more nuanced understanding. This paper revisits existing literature through a thematic review, synthesizing key success determinants to provide a comprehensive framework for evaluating startups. Findings emphasize the critical role of the entrepreneurial team, market conditions, innovation potential, financials, and strategic readiness in investment decisions. The study proposes a practical classification system to aid funders, incubators, and accelerators in systematically evaluating startups to make more informed investment decisions, and inspire startups in self-assessment and improvement.*

## 1. INTRODUCTION

There is still a need for advanced approaches in start-up assessment, especially for early-stage start-ups, which is a process that has subjectivity due to the lack of sufficient data, leading to unpredictability of future success or failure, especially in developing economies context. Venture capital and investors can also expect customized assessment and evaluation schemes for various geographical regions or by the

DOI: 10.4018/979-8-3693-8181-6.ch013

start-up development stages that increase the difficulty of developing effective evaluation frameworks. Therefore, for startups' success factors, it is necessary to provide a multi-dimensional and inclusive criteria set to be adapted in the evaluation and assessment process during the investment and funding phases. The current state of knowledge in literature, many characteristics such as team composition, leadership abilities, financial performance or potential, market fit or innovativeness of the products, or the risk management approach have ben listed as factors to be considered in startup evaluation (Jáki et al., 2022), the success factors of these ventures extend to an extensive and multi-dimensional list that requires in-depth understanding. As well, the uncertainty of startup success and the necessity for more precise assessment approaches to enhance startup selection and funding results (Csaszar et al., 2006) keeps the startup success factors on the agenda of entrepreneurship research. The success factors that can be considered for startups vary from team characteristics to reputation, or from strategic vision to partnerships (Erdogan & Koohborfardhaghighi, 2019). Consequently, investors may weigh various quantitative and qualitative factors when evaluating an early-stage startup (Bai & Zhao, 2021). The nonlinear nature of different success factors of startups, such as the dilemma of business success despite negative financial performance (Ceausu et al., 2018), makes it more challenging to elaborate on the success enablers of startups clearly. Investors may look for the ability to stay in the safe zone through careful long-term growth planning and proactiveness for future problems through strong financial planning, but they may also consider significant competition in the market as a crucial factor when evaluating ventures (Milkova et al., 2018). This complex landscape of early-stage startup assessment underscores the importance of a comprehensive, multifactor approach to evaluating startup potential, addressing both immediate viability and long-term sustainability.

Therefore, identifying the characteristics of successful startups is highly valuable in terms of both economic and social impact, as it enables the effective allocation of funding to the most promising projects (Hudakova et al., 2019). For example, the assessment of a startup team's qualifications significantly influences the decision-making process; however, there is a lack of detailed understanding regarding the specific criteria used to evaluate teams. This gap in knowledge arises primarily from the fact that previous research has primarily focused on evaluating entire proposals, resulting in broad criteria rankings (Franke et al., 2008). Selection criteria or the importance ratings of the criteria change during the evaluation stages. Yin and Luo (2018) looked at the different stages of the accelerator selection process. Their research showed that accelerator managers use a small set of implicit decision criteria. Using these key criteria to guess what will happen with more startups, they show early signs that the criteria in the first stage are more important for understanding "rejection" decisions, while the criteria in the last stage are more helpful for understanding "selection" decisions (Yin & Luo, 2018). In addition, evaluation processes vary from country to region. For instance, the primary distinction between the incubator policies of the USA and Europe appears to be the emphasis placed on financial factors in the United States, as opposed to the "soft" criteria, such as the management team and market fit, in Europe (Lin et al., 2021). Therefore, it is important to consider regional conditions when creating a success factor inventory.

Through revisiting the existing literature and synthesizing the accumulated knowledge on the startups, success determinant factors, the study adopts a thematic comprehensive literature review merging the multi-dimensional discussions in the previous decades to help funders, support mechanisms such as incubator or accelerators in startup selection and evaluation in a developing economy context of Turkey. Moreover, the study proposes a classification of success factors that can inspire startup selection practices of funders and supporters, or it can aid new ventures in their self-assessment processes and locating their improvement areas. The review encompasses factors across diverse categories such as team dynamics, market conditions, innovativeness, financial health, and strategic orientation, capturing the complexity of startup ecosystems.

The following sections will present the methodology, findings from the thematic literature review on the major categories of startup success factors that can be used as evaluation criteria. Finally, the paper presents the conclusion of the findings with future research options.

## 2. LITERATURE REVIEW

Identifying the characteristics of a successful startup is highly valuable in terms of both economic and social impact, as it enables the effective allocation of funding to the most promising projects (Hudakova et al., 2019). Nevertheless, the existing standards for choosing projects demonstrate a significant rate of failure, for example, as a considerable proportion of startups financed by venture capital cease operations within five years. These figures emphasize the uncertainty of startup success and emphasize the necessity for more precise assessment approaches to enhance startup selection and funding results. (Csaszar et al., 2006). Assessment of startups, especially in their early stages, is inherently subjective due to the limited data and higher unpredictability. Moreover, investor interest tends to be concentrated both in specific regions and stages of development, making it challenging to accurately predict a start-up's success, let alone determine its fit within an investor's investment strategy. Consequently, investors may weigh various factors, both quantitative and qualitative, when evaluating an early-stage startup (Bai & Zhao, 2021). For example, the assessment of a startup team's qualifications significantly influences the decision-making process. However, there is a lack of detailed understanding regarding the specific criteria that are in use to evaluate teams. This gap in knowledge arises primarily from the fact that previous research has primarily focused on evaluating entire proposals, resulting in broad criteria rankings (Franke et al., 2008).

Previous literature focused on startup evaluation and assessment criteria from various perspectives and contexts. Most initial studies, such as MacMillan et al. (1985) focused on Venture Capitalists' criteria for evaluating new ventures, through expert opinions revealing the importance of leadership and reputation. Franke et el. (2008) investigated the venture capitalists' evaluations of start-up teams focusing on trade-offs, knock-out criteria. Hudakova et al. (2019) explored the key criteria and competences to define the sustainability of start-up teams and projects in the incubation and acceleration phases. Bondarenko et al. (2019) also revisited the multi-criteria mechanisms for selecting projects in fintech acceleration programs. Systematic literature review of Ferrati and Muffatto (2019) also provided a vast list of startup assessment criteria adopted by equity investors. Pramana et al. (2020) explored these criteria in high-flyer technology startup investments in Indonesia, while Skalicka et al. (2023) revisited the early-stage decision making on startup selection by business angels in an emerging market. However, there is still a research opportunity in exploring the startup evaluation criteria from the view of corporate incubators, and in developing economy contexts. In the developing economy context.

Selection criteria or the importance ratings of the criteria changes during the stages of evaluation. Yin and Luo (2018) underlined that the accelerators use a small set of key implicit decision and that criteria regarding early signs in the first stage are more important for understanding "rejection" decisions, while the criteria in the last stage are more helpful for understanding "selection" decisions (Yin & Luo, 2018). In addition, evaluation processes vary from country to region. For instance, the primary distinction between the incubator policies of the United States and Europe appears to be the emphasis placed on financial factors in the United States, as opposed to the "soft" criteria, such as the management team and market fit, in Europe (Lin et al., 2021), Therefore it is important to consider regional conditions when creating an evaluation framework. The details of the literature that focused on the criteria regarding early-stage startup evaluation frameworks that can be utilized by corporate incubators are presented in the Analysis and Findings Section.

Corporate incubators are examples of organized programs to improve companies' ability to deal with innovation, making working together with startups easier (Möllmann, 2023). Both corporate incubators and accelerators help startups in important ways, but in different times of their development and for different lengths of time. Incubators help new businesses grow from an idea to a prototype over a longer period of time, while accelerators, on the other hand, use funding and partnerships to help startups that already have goods that can be sold quickly grow their markets (Denysiuk, 2021). Whether a startup should go with a corporate incubator, or a corporate accelerator relies on its needs, the resources and networks it has access to, and the strategic goals of the corporate body that is supporting it. Corporate incubators are specialized, for-profit organizations set up by parent companies to help new businesses grow and develop, mostly by using the parent company's existing technology base with a major goal of facilitating the technological progress within the company by either providing non-financial support to outside startups that have new business ideas or technologies (Becker and Gassmann, 2006). As part of the incubation process, new businesses that show promise are chosen and given full support, such as teaching, feedback, and management advice (Guttman, 2023). Corporate incubators provide many benefits, such as financial support, office space, necessary equipment, and connections with many experts in the field and possible investors with a main goal of creating revenues by quickly starting new businesses, incorporating successful projects into the main business of the company, or creating new technologies that make more people want to buy the parent company's goods (Kötting, 2020).

## 3. METHODOLOGY AND ANALYSIS

The comprehensive literature review on startup evaluation criteria was conducted by systematically sourcing articles from Web of Science and SCOPUS, focusing on scientific publications indexed up to March 2023. The search query used targeted terms related to startup selection, assessment, and evaluation, filtered by business subject area, publication type, and language. This search yielded 206 articles in Scopus and 199 in Web of Science. To refine the selection, abstracts were screened to identify relevant articles for an in-depth thematic analysis. The search query used was as follows:

TITLE-ABS-KEY (("start*up") AND ("selection" OR "assessment" OR "evaluation")) AND PUBYEAR > 1999 AND PUBYEAR < 2024 AND (LIMIT-TO (DOCTYPE, "ar")) AND (LIMIT-TO (LANGUAGE, "English")) AND (LIMIT-TO (SUBJARE, "BUSI"))

In the thematic analysis phase, both researchers classified the text corpus provided from the 206 indexed articles retrieved from the Scopus by the codes occurred on the clustered conceptual maps. These codes represented the themes **Team**, **Market**, **Idea**, **Financials**, and **Strategy as high-level factors for** startup success that included the detailed selection criteria. Researchers independently conducted this coding. To ensure the consistency of the coding and to eliminate the redundancy, coders conducted two rounds of review for refining the overlaps. In the end of this process a final list of 36 criteria were identified. Moreover, the intercoder reliability checks were done in each round. When the intercoder reliability rate remained below 80%, the codes were reviewed in a consensus discussion. Non-consensus themes were excluded from the study. Through this systematic approach the thematic literature review resulted in solid criteria set that can be used in the practices of startup evaluation and selection by corporate incubators.

## 4. FINDINGS

From the thematic literature review, the startup evaluation criteria revealed in the literature are summarized in the following sections.

### 4.1. Entrepreneurial Team as a Startup Criteria

As to evaluation of startups, VCs emphasize criteria on entrepreneurs, manager backgrounds, and management team experience over market and product criteria, indicating that the human factor is more critical than the definite market or product characteristics (Pintado et al., 2007). Bai and Zhao (2021) by machine learning algorithms predicted the factors that would significantly influence startup investment decisions, concluding on the paramount importance of team management as a key criterion. Since the team management is found within the top five criteria deemed crucial for effective investment decisions, incubators and investors should prioritize assessing the quality and dynamics of a startup team (Bai & Zhao, 2021). Franke et al. (2008) highlighted that, for German VCs, heterogeneous teams with different industry experience, education, and leadership experience are the top three factors influencing startup investment decisions. The diversity and collective expertise within a team of startup owners, recognition and knowledge of these team-related criteria may prove helpful in optimizing startup selection (Franke et al., 2008).

#### The Team's Experience in the Relevant Industry

Erdogan and Koohborfardhaghighi (2019) emphasize two critical factors, team experience and the startup's position within its network, are significantly linked to the startup's future success. Also, a seasoned and skilled team plays a major role in shaping a startup's trajectory. There is a significant positive effect of the industry experience of the team on startups' likelihood of securing investment (Muñoz-Bullon et al., 2015)

#### The Entrepreneurial Experience of the Team

From the case of solo, nascent entrepreneurs, confidence in forthcoming opportunities positively influences the emergence of a venture, while the impacts of entrepreneurial experience and early planning on initiating a venture are more indirect (Dimov, 2010). Conversely, industry experience is a strong deterrent against quitting, making it much less likely that a business would fail when challenged (Dimov, 2010). Pierrakis and Owen (2018), looking at the investment criteria of angel investors and accelerators, pointed out that angel investors are more likely to invest in a team or entrepreneur with a proven track record in entrepreneurship than accelerators do. However, for both parties, past experience in venture building positively affects investment. Taweesangrungroj (2015) also emphasized the importance of entrepreneurial experience. Government organizations prefer projects led by people with a track record of successful entrepreneurship.

## Work Experience of the Team

Hashai and Zahra (2022) noted that while experience within the same firm or industry can benefit early growth of startups, it may negatively impact later growth as startups accumulate experiential knowledge. A diverse mix of experiences—both within the same company and across different industries—generally enhances growth at all stages, highlighting that varied prior experiences among founders positively affect the growth trajectory of startups (Hashai & Zahra, 2022).

Onetti et al. (2015) examined the impact of founders' job experiences on startup growth, categorizing them based on the specificity and international nature of their experiences. Their findings indicate that diverse experiences contribute positively to growth in both early and later stages. Furthermore, a stronger international orientation significantly enhances the ability to access resources, adapt to entrepreneurial roles, and secure funding, supporting the view that founders' capabilities and knowledge are crucial success factors for startups (Onetti et al., 2015).

## Personal Characteristics of the Leading Entrepreneur (Leadership, Dedication, Coaching, etc.)

Kubickova et al. (2013) identified founders' management capabilities and problem-solving skills as essential to assessing startup success, showing that founders' leadership and strategic skills are critical. A founder's management skills and ability to deal with problems determines the overall success of a startup (Kubickova et al., 2013). Cesausu (2018) studied the accelerators in Romania and found that the qualitative attributes of the founder, as well as education, prior experience, age, and expertise, play a pivotal role in the performance of a new venture. These qualities translate into strategic assets for the business, guiding the development of strategies and effectively coordinating resources. Conversely, excessive proactiveness, defined as the ability to identify opportunities and take initiative, may have a limited impact on performance and can potentially divert the entrepreneur's focus and unnecessarily prolong the time-to-market (Cesausu, 2018).

For fintech accelerators, Bondarenko et al. (2019) emphasized the importance of a leader with charismatic qualities and solid entrepreneurial acumen. This underlines the dual role expected from the leader, highlighting the importance of inspirational leadership qualities and practical business skills (Bondarenko et al., 2019). When evaluating the early stages of a company, the due diligence conducted can be primarily limited to verifying the founder's competency and integrity (Pramana et al., 2020).

## References, Network, and Reputation

Entrepreneurs' reputations have long been recognized as significant in startup assessments (MacMillan et al., 1985). The size of an entrepreneur's business network is crucial in startup's survival, emphasizing the relational aspect of entrepreneurship, where the scale and depth of an entrepreneur's network significantly impact the sustainability and viability of new businesses (Raz & Gloor, 2007).

Yin and Luo (2018) highlighted the importance of strong references as a key assessment criterion for evaluating startups, where positive endorsements from influential people enhance a startup's perceived credibility. External references and the founder's reputation are also considered by equity investors, underscoring the value placed on external validation (Ferrati et al., 2021). Simões et al. (2020) also mentioned startup reputation as a key indicator of growth potential, suggesting that a positive public image within the business community can attract potential investors, serving as a valuable signal for future growth (Simões et al., 2020). Additionally, Erdogan and Koohborfardhaghighi (2019) noted that the reputation of the startup's partners also can positively influence assessments.

### Diversity of Talent Within the Team

Among the dynamics of team composition, a heterogeneous team, combining technical and management skills, is highly valued in startup evaluation (Franke, 2006). The teams focused solely on management are often unviable, especially in technical fields, and that teams of only engineers can also be disadvantageous (Franke, 2006), pointing out the necessity for a balance of technical and managerial skills to achieve favorable evaluations (Franke, 2006). Similarly, investors prioritize heterogeneous teams with diverse industry experience and varied team backgrounds, ranking this issue among the top criteria influencing investment decisions (Majumdar & Mittal, 2023). Additionally, the diversity among team members contributes more to success than individual ability levels, emphasizing the importance of collective dynamics and diverse perspectives within a startup team since varied skills and expertise significantly enhance the overall effectiveness and success of the venture (Hoogendoorn et al., 2017).

### Educational and Academic Background of the Team

Venture capitalists view a startup team's educational background as necessary, while the presence of university graduates across the team does not significantly affect their evaluation. A mixed team can provide valuable diversity, whereas an all-graduate team may offer a higher average level of human capital (Franke et al., 2006).

### Ages of Team Members

Franke et al. (2008) highlight that founder and employee age significantly influence investment decisions, with the 35–45 age range being particularly advantageous. Similarly, Pierrakis and Owen (2019) found a positive, statistically significant correlation between founders' age and investment backing for both accelerator and angel-funded startups.

### Number of Members of the Team

While four members are often cited as the typical size for startup teams (Franke et al., 2006), some studies suggest that increasing the number of members can enhance a startup's success as it adds talent diversity (Ceausu et al., 2018). However, Esen et al. (2023) found that larger top management teams negatively affect the likelihood of securing investment. Ceausu et al. (2018) noted that team size is considered for accelerators. Pasayat et al. (2023) also identified the number of employees and co-founders as key factors influencing investor decisions.

### Qualitative Characteristics of the Team Members

Franke et al. (2006) emphasize the importance of qualitative traits like perseverance and stress resistance in startup evaluations, though assessing these attributes is challenging, particularly within the short evaluation periods. It is a difficult and complex task to integrate such qualitative factors into the immediate investment criteria. Similarly, Jaki et al. (2022) stress the significant role of managerial capabilities in investors' decisions addressing key traits such as commitment, background, risk assessment ability, and financial knowledge.

## 4.2. Market

Market conditions are key factors for startup evaluation as they define the startups' potential to succeed in the market (Salomon, 2018). These conditions provide a comprehensive understanding of the business and competition environment in startups operate. They also refer to the competitive landscape, regulatory frameworks, scalability potential, and current and future demand for the products startups offer. Favorable market conditions enhance the success chance of startups, making them favorable to accelerators and incubators (Fiorentino et al., 2021). Understanding market conditions is also essential in early-stage technology startups assessments (Spender et al., 2017).

### Market and Target Market Size

The market size reflects the potential customer base which is critical for a startup's success. A larger market offers more opportunities for growth and profitability, allowing startups to scale their businesses and reach a wider audience (Csaszar et al., 2006). However, these markets can also bear intense competition challenging startups to differentiate and maintain profitability. On the other hand, smaller markets have disadvantages such as limiting expansion and hindering hinder long-term success. Hence, it is essential to evaluate the market size, competition levels, and the startup's ability to stand out in the market (Sato et al., 2012).

### Market Risk / Ease of Market Entry

The ease of market entry refers to the relative simplicity a new startup can be established in a market by overcoming barriers regarding information, skills, regulations, networks, and social norms (Scillitoe and Birasnav 2022). Factors such as culture and regulations influence this concept. Entrepreneurs must systematically gather and analyze information about potential markets to develop effective market entry strategies. Startups that successfully identify different market opportunities can gain an advantage by entering markets with fewer competitive barriers (Gruber et al., 2013).

### Market Growth Rate

The **market growth rate** is a key indicator of a market's profitability level. Strong demand and a large customer base signal a high market growth rate (Smith et al., 2010). As a result, this metric is frequently employed in evaluating startups (Mohammadi & Shafiee, 2022; Aerts et al., 2007).

**Competition conditions in the market** are also considered since startups in competitive markets having successful late-stage ventures often and established companies' threats, face challenges due to their limited resources (Eisenmann, 2020). In this condition, startups can still maintain competitiveness through agility and innovation. Milkova et al. (2018) categorized competition into new entrants and substitute products, underlining the importance of competition when evaluating starups.

**Globalization potential** allows startups access to larger markets and reach to global customers (Bartlett, Mroczkowski, et al., 2020). Globalization offers entrepreneurs opportunities for considerable growth (Kusio et al., 2023). However, globalization has challenges of increased competition, complex regulations, and cultural differences. To succeed globally, startups must early adopt a global approach and value, form strong networks and alliances, and also develop customization based on localized experiences. Agility also enables adaptation to the evolving global environment (Neubert, 2018; Pasayat et al.). Globalization also offers valuable opportunities for learning from strong competitors. International startups must monitor changes in the constantly evolving global markets and adjust their response strategies. While it poses significant challenges,

## 4.3. Idea

A startup concept is crucial, but it may differ by business (Scott et al., 2015). The original concept is essential for startups in industries that largely depend on research and development (R&D) and in which the concept is often associated with intellectual property rights without being flexible for modification. Hence, the startup's commercial potential can be evaluated more accurately at an early stage since in these industries they do not undergo significant changes frequently. Startups in less R&D intensive industries typically revolve around the entrepreneurial teams' characteristics and experience, allowing the modification of the business idea when required. In such situations, the entrepreneur's ability to implement and adjust ideas becomes more important than the original idea (Scott et al., 2015).

### Innovation

Innovation is required for success, but it is also risky for startups due to its uncertainty and dependence on resources such as capital. By employing an ex-ante measure of innovativeness, Hyytinen et al. (2015) revealed a negative correlation between innovation and survival. Founders having high-risk tolerance, focus on the long-term rewards of innovation, but they also must consider the obstacles innovation causes in the early stages (Hyytinen et al., 2015). In less innovative industries having lower demand for improvement, a slightly original concept can distinguish the startup from the less original rivals. In less competitive industries, startup's product has more potential to fulfil a market need resulting in a rapid acceptance and considerable expansion potential (Aminova & Marchi, 2021).

## Importance of the Problem Solved

The need can be defined as the problem to be solved for a customer (Beverly, 2017). Finding a "burning need" is essential for the startups' success. Startups focusing on these needs may acquire market validation faster, since customers will be willing to pay for their products bringing solution. A strong alignment between the problem and the product can result in faster product adoption and increased customer loyalty over time (Beverly, 2017). Startups must understand the difference between a critical need (painkiller) and a secondary need (vitamin). This approach ensures a solid product-market fit (Finger & Samwer, 2013).

## Scalability

Scalability is startups' ability to expand and increase operations without facing restrictions or limitations (Rasmussen and Tanev, 2016). Startups having a business strategy that can be expanded or increased in size are more likely to achieve long-term success as they can adjust to changing market conditions. Entrepreneurs must prioritize the validation of their business model to ensure its scalability. Startups can achieve sustainable growth and long-term success by scalability through embracing a lean startup approach (Rasmussen & Tanev, 2016).

## Ease of Imitation or Substitute

Startups' success and growth potential are significantly impacted by the difficulty of the imitation of their idea and model. These characteristics offer competitiveness by creating barriers for new entrants, sustaining a solid market presence. The distinctiveness of startup's product can set it apart from competitors and attract customers and investors, boosting bargaining power and contributing to the long-term success and profitability (Rastkhiz et al., 2018; Paradkar et al., 2015).

## Intellectual Property Rights

Intellectual property as tangible assets is crucial for startup success, offering a competitive advantage by securing exclusivity over their innovations and inventions. IP also safeguards the market share and revenue by preventing imitation. Moreover, it enhances the startup's attractiveness to investors as it proves the uniqueness and profitability potential. Intellectual property can secure funding and partnerships and foster further innovation and investment in R&D (Graham & Sichelman, 2016). Successful IP management is needed to attract investment, promote innovation, and protect the startup's competitive position (Pena, 2002).

## Idea/Solution Verification and Validation

Product validation, especially during the ideation phase, is important since it is a foundational step of transforming a concept into a viable business. It ensures that the product-market demand fit which is crucial for the product's success (Pramana et al., 2020). Validation process helps startups navigate the uncertainties in early stages, allowing them to adjust their business models and product offerings, or pivot their strategies based on the feedback from potential customers. By a proactive approach, the risk of investing in products without market demand is minimized, maximizing the success potential through ensuring that product meets target market's expectations (Seppänen et al., 2017). By utilizing minimum viable products (MVPs) and actionable metrics, startups can validate their assumptions and respond to feedback in a Lean Startup approach conserving their limited resources and identifying potential opportunities. Idea validation provides startups with the necessary insights to make well-informed decisions, pivot quickly, and pursue the most feasible business opportunities timely and effectively (Terho et al., 2016).

## The Current Stage of the Product (Idea, Prototype, Final Product, etc.)

The product's maturity, showing whether the product is equipped with the essential functionality and features to meet customer needs, must also be considered as it indicates progress and readiness for the market. A product that has reached maturity guarantees its reliability and stability, enhancing startup's competitiveness in the market. A mature product is one of the most important signals for time-to-market prediction, which affects the selection of startups in accelerators (Beyhan et al., 2021).

## Sustainability of Competitive Advantage

Evaluating startup teams for incubation requires a complete understanding of their competitive advantage which plays a crucial role in differentiating the startup from its competitors and creating a distinctive value proposition. Competitive advantages can be rooted in the technology, intellectual property rights, business models, or partnerships, positioning the startup more favorably for investors, enhancing the market success potential (Mohammadi & Shafiee, 2022).

## Technology Readiness Level

Developed by NASA, the Technology Readiness Level (TRL) used across sectors to assess technology development (Héder, 2017). TRL can be a strong indicator of the potential success of the startups (Tritoasmoro et al., 2024). Startups often include technologies within the TRL range from 5 to 7. TRL 5 signifies that a technology has undergone validation in a pertinent industrial setting, indicating a certain degree of assurance in its practical implementation, while TRL6 showcases technology in a relevant industrial environment, demonstrating greater advancement and preparation for real-world application, and TRL 7 is a technological prototype effectively showcased in a functional setting, presenting preparedness for implementation (Gbadegeshin et al., 2022). Startups that can pass the "Valley of Death," a phase characterized by difficult transitions from concept to marketable product, generally achieve (TRL) 7 during their establishment.

## Technical Feasibility

Technical feasibility determines the ability of a startup to solve a technical issue within specific limitations, assessing the ability of solving a technical challenge and the feasibility of solution, considering the objectives and constraints. This assessment is an essential part of the early stages in the product development process before economic feasibility (Bause et al., 2014). Failing to validate technical feasibility increases the startup's risk of failure (Cantamesa et al., 2018).

## 4.4. Financials

In startup assessment and evaluation, after 1970, there was a shift from short term financial success towards incorporating non-financial measurements, such as operational and strategic indicators, to examine all aspects of the business holistically (Hudaková et al., 2019). This shift recognizes the limitations of traditional financial assessments and raises a need for more advanced and various methods in evaluating early-stage startups (Skalicka et al., 2023). Financial assessments of startups are still highly important for the selection phase and often serve as a key criterion for decision-making (Ferrati & Muffatto, 2019). Nevertheless, assessing the financial aspects of early-stage startups can be challenging due to the lack and inaccuracy data (Majumdar & Mittal, 2023). The future financial performance of startups depends heavily on firm resources, external relations, and market opportunities, which are inherently uncertain and hard to forecast. Hence, adopting alternative approaches that consider these dynamic and unpredictable factors in startup evaluation is crucial.

### Key Financial Indicators

Financial metrics like Return on Investment (RoI), Internal Rate of Return (IRR), and Net Present Value (NPV) are important financial signs that should be closely monitored and analysed (Mohammadi & Shafiee, 2022). Although the financial performance of early-stage startups may be relatively thin (Arshi et al., 2021), previous studies have suggested these metrics as essential performance measures (Mohammadi & Shafiee, 2022; Rastkhiz et al., 2018; Shafi, 2021). Assessing regular cash flow as a measure of profitability and managerial achievements of startups (Csaszar et al., 2006; Hashai & Zahra, 2022; Sari et al., 2022), can be difficult due to the absence of historical data (Montani et al., 2020).

**Profitability** significantly has impact on the startups' success; hence, it is an inherent selection criterion favorable for incubators and investors (Ceausu et al., 2018). Startups generating profits in early stages are more likely to achieve long-term success. However, the correlation between profitability and the success of a business may not be linear, as certain startups may initially have negative financial performance (Pasayat et al., 2022).

### Realism of Financial Forecasts

Due to startups limited financial history, startups' financial valuation is primarily based on their projected expectations. Many start-ups have failed against financial pressures due to inadequate financial preparation (Arshi et al., 2021). Hence, the realism and accuracy of startups' financial forecasts and plans are crucial in the evaluation process (Sari et al., 2022).

## 4.5. Strategy

Since startup assessment based on historical performance is challenging due to the lack of data on past financial benefits, or market responses and validation, evaluation must include a forward-thinking framework considering the future plans with past achievements (Bai & Zhao, 2021).

## Vision

The strategic vision of founders is essential for selecting successful startups (Erdogan & Koohborfardhaghighi, 2019). Strategic vision is a guide for decision-making, fostering resilience, allowing startup management to transform challenges into opportunities (Hudakova et al., 2019). Various researchers considered the vision essential for startup success (Ferrati et al., 2021; Salomon, 2018; Shafi, 2021).

## Business Plan

Making a strong business plan is important when launching new goods or starting up new businesses, and it is one of the best ways to ensure business success (Rasmussen & Tanev, 2016). This concept is so widely accepted that competition is based on just startup business plans (Demirhan et al., 2019). A well-written business plan is an indicator of successful startups in terms of market opportunity exploration (Csaszar et al., 2006; Shafi, 2021; Yin & Luo, 2018; Bondarenko et al., 2019).

## Realistic Risk Analysis

Risk is one of the most important dimensions to be considered for startup evaluation. Risk management involves finding and devising ways to lower risks (Arshi et al., 2021). By managing risk effectively, startups can be more resilient and can maintain their long-term success (Skare et al., 2023; Hudakova et al., 2019).

## Marketing Strategy

A well-planned marketing strategy can enable startups achieve growth and sustainability (Bai & Zhao, 2021; Taweesangrungroj et al., 2022). For long-term success, startups must establish a strong brand presence and a brand identity through effective marketing strategies underlining their unique value offerings. Additionally, marketing strategy elaborates on the ways to connect with potential customers, target specific market segments, generate leads and sales, cultivate customer loyalty, and gather valuable consumer data.

## Financial Strategy

The financial strategy and plans are most important for predicting the startups' future financial performance. Startups can prepare themselves for potential funding and cost challenges and position themselves for long-term growth by preparing effective financial plans (Sreenivasan & Suresh, 2023). Startups must achieve financial stability with a well-crafted financial plan to adapt to changes and shocks. In the financial strategy, especially liquidity planning is essential to manage and understand the cash flows and adjust them in challenging times (Sreenivasan & Suresh, 2023).

### Operational Strategy

Startups' operational plan facilitates optimized resource allocation, enhanced efficiency and productivity, scalability, improved customer satisfaction, competitive advantage, and higher financial performance (Rompho, 2018). Moreover, a clearly defined operational strategy allows a company to optimize its procedures, anticipate future expansion, differentiate itself in the market, adapt to changes, and mitigate risks. The operational strategy is the foundation for effective operations helping startups achieve their strategic objectives (Naumov, 2017).

### Current and Planned Strategic Partnerships

Startup strategic alliances involve a complex network of suppliers and partners operationalizing their business strategies (de Mello et al., 2022). These partnerships shape the startup's trajectory, foster synergies, and boost their competitiveness. Startups gain resources, experience, and market reach through strategic alliances, propelling them to lasting success (Al Sahaf & Al Tahoo, 2021). Many researchers adopted partnerships as an indicator of successful startups (Erdogan & Koohborfardhaghighi, 2019; Ceausu et al., 2018).

### Sensitivity to Political and Economic Fluctuations

The economic and political environment shaping market circumstances directly affects startup success (Kozubikova et al., 2019). Politics involve governmental incentives, regulations, support, the legislative environment, bureaucracy, and education. As well, supportive policies, efficient administrative processes, accessible funding, and skilled labor facilitate startup success (Kozubikova et al., 2019). Sensitivity of startups to these political or economic factors results in a lack of resilience in causing higher risks (Nikoloudis et al., 2017). Therefore, several studies have identified sensitivity as a critical risk factor that must be considered in startup assessments (Gerhardt et al., 2021; Gbadegeshin et al., 2022; Mohammadi & Shafiee, 2022).

### Strategic Compatibility

A strategic fit for incubators and accelerators means their goals, objectives, and capabilities align with the startups' they select and accept to their programs. Incubators and accelerators seek strategic fit to improve program effectiveness, create value for both parties, foster synergistic partnerships, differentiation in the market, and ensure long-term success. They also can customize assistance, coaching, and resources to entrepreneurs with strategic fit, building a mutually beneficial ecosystem (Shankar & Shepherd, 2019).

## 4.6 Analysis of Findings: Proposed Startup Evaluation Criteria

For corporate incubators, a practical classification system can be structured around five primary categories of team, market, concept and innovation, financial health and forecasting and strategy. Table 1 presents the criteria within these categories, and the literature sources of them in details:

*Table 1. Analysis of findings*

| Criteria Category | Criteria | Sources |
|---|---|---|
| Team Factor | Experience of the Team | (Dimov, 2010) (Pierrakis and Owen, 2018), (Taweesangrungroj, 2015) (Hashai and Zahra, 2022) (Onetti et al., 2015) (Erdogan and Koohborfardhaghighi, 2019) (Muñoz-Bullon et al., 2015) (Bai and Zhao, 2021) (Pintado et al., 2007) |
| | Personal Characteristics of the Leading Entrepreneur | (Kubickova et al., 2013) (Kubickova et al., 2013). (Cesausu, 2018). (Bondarenko et al., 2019) (Pramana et al., 2020) (Bai and Zhao, 2021) (Pintado et al., 2007) |
| | Reputation and network | (MacMillan et al., 1985) (Raz & Gloor, 2007). (Yin and Luo, 2018) (Ferrati et al., 2021) (Simões et al., 2020) (Simões et al., 2020) (Koohborfardhaghighi, 2019) (Bai and Zhao, 2021) (Pintado et al., 2007) |
| | Diversity and Composition of the Team | (Franke, 2006) (Majumdar & Mittal, 2023). (Hoogendoorn et al., 2017) (Bai and Zhao, 2021) (Pintado et al., 2007) |
| | Quantitative Characteristics – Size and age - of the Team | (Franke et al., 2006), (Ceausu et al., 2018) (Esen et al., 2023) (Pasayat et al., 2023) Franke et al. (2008) (Pierrakis and Owen, 2019) (Bai and Zhao, 2021) (Pintado et al., 2007) |
| | Qualitative Characteristics of the Team Members | (Franke et al., 2006) (Jaki et al., 2022) |
| Market | Target Market Size and Growth Rate | (Smith et al., 2010) (Mohammadi & Shafiee, 2022) (Aerts et al., 2007) (Salomon, 2018) (Fiorentino et al., 2021) |
| | Market Risk / Ease of Market Entry | (Scillitoe and Birasnav 2022) (Gruber et al., 2013) (Salomon, 2018) (Fiorentino et al., 2021) |
| | Competition Conditions in the Market | (Eisenmann, 2020) (Milkova et al., 2018) (Spender et al., 2017) (Salomon, 2018) (Fiorentino et al., 2021) |
| | Globalization Potential | (Bartlett, Mroczkowski, et al., 2020) Neubert, 2018; Pasayat et al., 2022) (Kusio et al., 2023) (Salomon, 2018) (Fiorentino et al., 2021) |
| Idea - Concept and Innovation | Originality of Idea | (Scott et al., 2015) |
| | Problem-Solving Potential | (Beverly, 2017) (Finger & Samwer, 2013) |
| | Innovation Degree | (Hyytinen et al., 2015) (Aminova & Marchi, 2021) |
| | Ease of Imitation | (Rastkhiz et al., 2018) (Paradkar et al., 2015). |
| | Scalability | (Rasmussen and Tanev, 2016) |
| | Market Validation (Product-Market Fit) | (Pramana et al., 2020) (Seppänen et al., 2017) (Terho et al., 2016) |
| | Current Stage of the Product and TRL | (Beyhan et al., 2021) (Tritoasmoro et al., 2024) (Gbadegeshin et al., 2022) (Héder, 2017) |
| | Competitive Advantage | (Mohammadi & Shafiee, 2022) |
| | Intellectual Property Rights (IPRs) | (Pena, 2002) (Graham & Sichelman, 2016) |
| Financial Health and Forecasting | Key Financial Indicators (ROI, IRR, NPV) | (Skalicka et al., 2023) (Ceausu et al., 2018) (Pasayat et al., 2022) (Majumdar & Mittal, 2023) (Ferrati & Muffatto, 2019) (Hudaková et al., 2019) (Hashai & Zahra, 2022; Sari et al., 2022) (Montani et al., 2020) (Csaszar et al., 2006) (Mohammadi & Shafiee, 2022) (Rastkhiz et al., 2018) (Shafi, 2021) (Arshi et al., 2021) |
| | Financial Forecasts | (Arshi et al., 2021) (Sari et al., 2022) |

continued on following page

*Table 1. Continued*

| Criteria Category | Criteria | Sources |
|---|---|---|
| Strategic and Operational Readiness | Vision and Business Plan Robustness | (Bai & Zhao, 2021) (Hudakova et al., 2019) (Ferrati et al., 2021) (Salomon, 2018) (Csaszar et al., 2006) (Erdogan & Koohborfardhaghighi, 2019) (Shafi, 2021) (Yin & Luo, 2018) (Bondarenko et al., 2019) (Demirhan et al., 2019) (Rasmussen & Tanev, 2016) |
| | Risk Management | (Arshi et al., 2021) (Skare et al., 2023) (Hudakova et al., 2019) |
| | Functional Strategies | (Naumov, 2017) (Rompho, 2018) (Sreenivasan & Suresh, 2023) (Bai & Zhao, 2021) (Taweesangrungroj et al., 2022) |
| | Sensitivity to political and economic fluctuations | (Kozubikova et al., 2019) (Gerhardt et al., 2021) (Gbadegeshin et al., 2022) (Mohammadi & Shafiee, 2022) (Nikoloudis et al., 2017) |
| | Strategic Partnerships | (Erdogan & Koohborfardhaghighi, 2019) (Ceausu et al., 2018) (Al Sahaf & Al Tahoo, 2021) (de Mello et al., 2022) |
| | Strategic Compatibility | (Shankar & Shepherd, 2019) |

## 5. CONCLUSION AND DISCUSSION

This research delves into the complex factors that can be used for the evaluation and assessment of early-stage startups by thematically analyzing the current literature and by proposing a holistic view on the categorized criteria framework that can be utilized by the corporate incubators. Such research is needed in practice, as identifying the characteristics of successful startups enables the effective allocation of resources resulted in valuable economic and social impact (Hudakova et al., 2019). Due to the significant rate of failure of the startups selected by the investors in recent years, there is a need for precise assessment approaches to enhance startup selection (Csaszar et al., 2006). However, the previous literature focused on primarily on the evaluation by broad criteria rankings (Franke et al., 2008) mostly from investors' view (Ferrati and Muffatto, 2019; Pramana et al., 2020; Bai & Zhao, 2021; Skalicka et al., 2023). Moreover, despite the fact that startup selection criteria or their relative importance vary by the stages of startups (Yin and Luo; 2018), there is still limited research on the startup evaluation and assessment criteria in the context of early-stages, which tend to be subjective due to data shortages and high uncertainty (Bai & Zhao, 2021), especially from developing economy context though the evaluation schemes vary by country or region (Lin et al., 2021).

During the evaluation of startups, especially regarding early-stage startups, there is a need for forward-thinking approach, considering various factors that vary from organizational patterns to market characteristics and the product/service concept or strategic competency.

Key findings from the literature highlight the importance of several factors:

• Across multiple studies, the startup teams' and managers/founders' characteristics, experience, and networks occurred as top criteria in startup selection, where the assessment of a startup team's qualifications significantly influences the decision-making process (Bai & Zhao, 2021). This study contributes by providing a detailed understanding regarding the specific criteria for evaluating the startup teams. Team category often surpasses other factors related to the market, product, strategy and financials, since the team enhances the potential of the startups for growth and resilience. However, evaluating the teams of startups is a complex process considering various factors regarding team characteristics and leadership patterns. A combination of competencies and skills of the members contribute to the building of a balanced and effective management team. Among these factors, team members' and leaders' personal characteristics bear importance such as the entrepreneurial, professional and work background, the education, age, reputation and external linkages/networks. Also, the team dynamics regarding the diversity, team size play a role in startup success. Networks and reputation represent the teams' potential to build partnerships for securing resources and overcoming market and business barriers. They also shape the startup's credibility in funding rounds. A team with diverse skills, backgrounds, and perspectives enhances creativity, problem-solving, and adaptability. Optimal team size is a variable that depends on the type of the startup: Too large or small teams may be disadvantageous in growth and progress phases. Also, the importance of the team-related factor varies by the context such as the industry, life cycle phase of the startup or the product characteristics and value proposed by the startup. Still, a well-structured team having the above-mentioned characteristics offers higher potential for being selected by incubators and for investment. The findings consistently underscore the role of the entrepreneurial team as a decision factor.

- Market with its size, growth rate, competitive dynamics and the globalization potential of the startup, have significant place in the startup assessment. Favorable market conditions empower startups towards survival and growth. An evaluation on the market factors elaborates on the current and potential of the startups' scalability and sustainability. Competitors from successful late-stage ventures and enterprises also increase competition towards early-stage startups, posing significant challenges. A successful evaluation framework must carefully deal with the market position and the competitive advantage of the startups.
- A startup idea must be unique and innovative, especially in R&D-intensive sectors. In more conventional and less innovation-oriented industries, the implementation success of the product or service idea gains more importance. Startup ideas addressing urgent and critical needs - the "painkiller" issues- have a higher potential for market success. Hence, while a strong initial concept is the main driver of startup success in R&D oriented markets, the implementation ability is more important in the other traditional markets linked to the advantages of owning intellectual property. However, startup evaluators must keep in mind that radical innovation embedded in the business idea can increase the risks for early-stage startups. Here scalability gains importance for long-term success to be leveraged in overcoming operational bottlenecks. Moreover, a sustainable competitive advantage, whether through intellectual property or unique business models, is essential for standing out in the market. Additionally, difficult-to-imitate products provide competitive edges. Validating the product-market fit early through customer feedback, ensuring technical feasibility, and achieving advanced stages in the Technology Readiness Level (TRL) indicating market readiness to support a holistic evaluation framework for startups.
- Assessing the financial health of a startup, represented through financial metrics is a challenging task especially in early stages. Realistic financial forecasts and the robustness of financial strategies are essential for securing confidence between the incubator and its incubees. Additionally, a mature business plan reflects the potential of long-term success. The future financial performance of startups is dependent on many non-deterministic variables such as future firm resources, to-be established external relationships, and expected market opportunities. Hence, conventional financial metrics remain insufficient to act as only predictors of success. Still, profitability must be taken as a critical success factor, that can be traced through early profits that signal survival potential. However, profitability's indication on the long-term success is not always certain, as the historical data on startups showed that some successful startups initially showed low financial performance in early stages. Another limitation is that startup evaluations rely on projections, because the financial historical data of these ventures are

limited. This challenge underlines the high importance of forecast accuracy of startup financial metrics to mitigate financial risks.

• Strategical readiness must also be considered during startup evaluation. The startups are expected to have an operational strategy to ensure operational efficiency and optimized resource allocation with scalability. Having strategic alliances also offers startups wider access to critical resources and to market reach, thereby strengthening their competitiveness. Strategic readiness also refers to the resilience of a venture through demonstrating an adaptability to political and economic shifts. Moreover, the incubators look for strategic compatibility between their corporation and the startups they incubate to foster mutual relationships.

Through constructing categories of criteria, this classification framework presents a holistic and flexible approach, enabling incubators to evaluate startups in a structured way effectively. Based on the differing priorities of the corporate incubator regarding their industry, the evaluation framework can be customized through assigning weights on the criteria categories.

In conclusion, previous literature on startup evaluation criteria presents a multifaceted structure on the potential success of early-stage startups. The evaluation criteria of startups have a variety reflecting different dimensions regarding the potential for growth, scalability, and long-term success. This study's collection on startup evaluation criteria serves the literature, as Scott et al. (2015) and Rasmussen and Tanev (2016) underlined that the evaluation process of startups must be grounded in structured research.

Further research can explore the relative importance of the proposed success factors and their categories through applying quantitative methods. As well, cross-national or regional comparative studies can provide insights on the impact of cultural, economic, and regulatory contexts in startup funding choices of incubators. Moreover, the technological advancement in Artificial Intelligence and blockchain, can transform startup evaluation practices through utilizing predictive analytics and monitoring of their financial or organizational transactions. Examining psychological factors that influence incubator decisions also offers a valuable research venue. Last but not least, exploration on the effects of government policies and regulations on startup growth can offer valuable insights to decision makers in corporate incubators encouraging their contribution to innovation and economic development.

## ACKNOWLEDGEMENT

We would like to express our sincere gratitude to the Istanbul Technical University Scientific Research Unit (ITU BAP) for their generous support through Grant Nr. SYL-2023-44746.

## REFERENCES

Aerts, K., Matthyssens, P., & Vandenbempt, K. (2007). Critical role and screening practices of European business incubators. *Technovation*, 27(5), 254–267. DOI: 10.1016/j.technovation.2006.12.002

Al Sahaf, M. & Al Tahoo, L. (2021). Examining the key success factors for startups in the Kingdom of Bahrain, International Journal of Business Ethics and Governance, 9–49.

Aminova, M. and Marchi, E. (2021). The role of innovation on start-up failure vs. its success, International Journal of Business Ethics and Governance, 41–72.

Arshi, T. A., Rao, V., Islam, S., & Morande, S. (2021). SECURE–a new business model framework for measuring start-up performance. *Journal of Entrepreneurship in Emerging Economies*, 13(3), 459–485. DOI: 10.1108/JEEE-02-2020-0043

Bai, S., & Zhao, Y. (2021). Startup investment decision support: Application of venture capital scorecards using machine learning approaches. *Systems*, 9(3), 55. DOI: 10.3390/systems9030055

Bartlett, D., Mroczkowski, T. et al. (2020). Globalizing startups: Business development organizations in the Bay Area, Diversity, Innovation, and Clusters: Spatial Perspectives, 157.

Bause, K., Radimersky, A., Iwanicki, M., & Albers, A. (2014). Feasibility studies in the product development process. *Procedia CIRP*, 21, 473–478. DOI: 10.1016/j.procir.2014.03.128

Becker, B., & Gassmann, O. (2006). Corporate incubators: Industrial R&D and what universities can learn from them. *The Journal of Technology Transfer*, 31(4), 469–483. DOI: 10.1007/s10961-006-0008-6

Beverly, H. (2017). *Navigating your way to startup success*. Walter de Gruyter GmbH & Co KG. DOI: 10.1515/9781501507083

Beyhan, B., Akcomak, S., & Cetindamar, D. (2021). The Startup Selection Process in Accelerators: Qualitative Evidence from Turkey. *Entrepreneurship Research Journal*, 14(1), 27–51. DOI: 10.1515/erj-2021-0122

Bondarenko, T., Zhdanova, O., & Klimova, N. (2019). Multi-Criteria Mechanism for Selecting Projects by Fintech Accelerators, International Science and Technology Conference" FarEaston"(ISCFEC 2019), Atlantis Press, pp.6–10.

Cantamessa, M., Gatteschi, V., Perboli, G., & Rosano, M. (2018). Startups' roads to failure. *Sustainability (Basel)*, 10(7), 2346. DOI: 10.3390/su10072346

Ceausu, I., Olaru, M., Ionescu, R., & Tohanean, D. (2018). Case study: Romanian startup accelerators—Startup selection and evaluation, 4th BASIQ International Conference on New Trends in Sustainable Business and Consumption Proceedings, pg, Volume 714.

Csaszar, F., Nussbaum, M., & Sepulveda, M. (2006). Strategic and cognitive criteria for the selection of startups. *Technovation*, 26(2), 151–161. DOI: 10.1016/j.technovation.2005.01.010

de Mello, V. G., Kovaleski, J. L., Zola, F. C., Lima, F. R.Junior, Aragao, F. V., & De Genaro Chiroli, D. M. (2022). Proposal of a Fuzzy-QFD model for startup selection. *Technology Analysis and Strategic Management*, 52(3), 1395–1415.

Demirhan, D., Temel, S., & Durst, S. (2019). *The role of public entrepreneurship programs in fostering technology-based entrepreneurship: a Turkish case study, Societal Entrepreneurship and Competitiveness*. Emerald Publishing Limited.

Denysiuk, L. (2021). Success factors for corporate-startup collaboration, Technical Report, LBS Working Paper

Dimov, D. (2010). Nascent entrepreneurs and venture emergence: Opportunity confidence, human capital, and early planning. *Journal of Management Studies*, 47(6), 1123–1153. DOI: 10.1111/j.1467-6486.2009.00874.x

Eisenmann, T. R. (2020). Determinants of early-stage startup performance: Survey results, Harvard Business School Entrepreneurial Management Working Paper, (21-057).

Erdogan, E., & Koohborfardhaghighi, S. (2019). Delivering a Systematic Framework for the Selection and Evaluation of Startups: *15th International Conference, GECON 2018*, Pisa, Italy, September 18–20, 2018, Proceedings, pp.151–159. DOI: 10.1007/978-3-030-13342-9_13

Esen, T., Dahl, M. S., & Sorenson, O. (2023). Jockeys, horses or teams? The selection of startups by venture capitalists. *Journal of Business Venturing Insights*, 19, e00383. DOI: 10.1016/j.jbvi.2023.e00383

Ferrati, F., Chen, H., & Muffatto, M. (2021). A Deep Learning Model for Startups Evaluation Using Time Series Analysis, F. Matos, M. Ferreiro, Rosa, and I. Salavisa, editors, Proceedings of 16th European Conference On Innovation & Entrepreneurship (Ecie, 2021), Vol 1, pp.311–320, Electr Network, Sep 16-17, 2021.

Ferrati, F. and Muffatto, M. (2019). A systematic literature review of the assessment criteria applied by equity investors, volume 1, pp.304–312.

Finger, M., & Samwer, O. (2013). *America's most successful startups: Lessons for entrepreneurs*. Springer Science & Business Media.

Fiorentino, R., Longobardi, S., & Scaletti, A. (2021). The early growth of start-ups: Innovation matters. Evidence from Italy. *European Journal of Innovation Management*, 24(5), 1525–1546. DOI: 10.1108/EJIM-02-2020-0057

Franke, N., Gruber, M., Harhoff, D., & Henkel, J. (2006). What you are is what you like - similarity biases in venture capitalists' evaluations of start-up teams. *Journal of Business Venturing*, 21(6), 802–826. DOI: 10.1016/j.jbusvent.2005.07.001

Franke, N., Gruber, M., Harhoff, D., & Henkel, J. (2008). Venture capitalists' evaluations of start-up teams: Trade-offs, knock-out criteria, and the impact of VC experience. *Entrepreneurship Theory and Practice*, 32(3), 459–483. DOI: 10.1111/j.1540-6520.2008.00236.x

Fuertes-Callén, Y., Cuellar-Fernández, B., & Serrano-Cinca, C. (2022). Predicting startup survival using first years financial statements. *Journal of Small Business Management*, 60(6), 1314–1350. DOI: 10.1080/00472778.2020.1750302

Gbadegeshin, S. A., Al Natsheh, A., Ghafel, K., Mohammed, O., Koskela, A., Rimpiläinen, A., Tikkanen, J., & Kuoppala, A. (2022). Overcoming the valley of death: A new model for high technology startups. *Sustainable Futures : An Applied Journal of Technology, Environment and Society*, 4, 100077. DOI: 10.1016/j.sftr.2022.100077

Gerhardt, V., Dos Santos, J., Rubin, E., Neuenfeldt, A., & Siluk, J. (2021). Stakeholders' perception to characterize the start-ups' success. *Journal of Technology Management & Innovation*, 16(1), 38–50. DOI: 10.4067/S0718-27242021000100038

Graham, S. J., & Sichelman, T. S. (2016). *Intellectual property and technology startups: what entrepreneurs tell us, Technological Innovation: Generating Economic Results* (Vol. 26). Emerald Group Publishing Limited.

Gruber, M., MacMillan, I. C., & Thompson, J. D. (2013). Escaping the prior knowledge corridor: What shapes the number and variety of market opportunities identified before market entry of technology start-ups? *Organization Science*, 24(1), 280–300. DOI: 10.1287/orsc.1110.0721

Gutmann, T. (2023). Organizational design choices for corporate incubators. *IEEE Transactions on Engineering Management*, (99), 1–15. DOI: 10.1109/TEM.2023.3265511

Hashai, N., & Zahra, S. (2022). Founder team prior work experience: An asset or a liability for startup growth? *Strategic Entrepreneurship Journal*, 16(1), 155–184. DOI: 10.1002/sej.1406

Héder, M. (2017). From NASA to EU: The evolution of the TRL scale in Public Sector Innovation. *The Innovation Journal*, 22(2), 1–23.

Hoogendoorn, S., Parker, S. C., & Van Praag, M. (2017). Smart or diverse start-up teams? Evidence from a field experiment. *Organization Science*, 28(6), 1010–1028. DOI: 10.1287/orsc.2017.1158

Hudakova, M., Urbancova, H., & Vnouckova, L. (2019). Key Criteria and Competences Defining the Sustainability of Start-Up Teams and Projects in the Incubation and Acceleration Phase. *Sustainability (Basel)*, 11(23), 6720. DOI: 10.3390/su11236720

Hyytinen, A., Pajarinen, M., & Rouvinen, P. (2015). Does innovativeness reduce startup survival rates? *Journal of Business Venturing*, 30(4), 564–581. DOI: 10.1016/j.jbusvent.2014.10.001

Jáki, E., Major, F., & Molnár, E. (2022). *Key Competencies of Startup Teams Sought After by Investors*. DOI: 10.1007/978-3-030-81663-6_5

Kötting, M. (2020). Corporate incubators as knowledge brokers between business units and ventures: A systematic review and avenues for future research. *European Journal of Innovation Management*, 23(3), 474–499. DOI: 10.1108/EJIM-12-2017-0201

Kozubikova, L., Kotaskova, A., Dvorsky', J., & Kljucnikov, A. (2019). The impact of political factors' perception on the suitability of international business environment: The case of startups. *Economics & Sociology (Ternopil)*, 12(1), 61–79. DOI: 10.14254/2071-789X.2019/12-1/3

Kubickova, A., Dohnal, M., & Doubravsky', K. (2013). Qualitative decision–making a model of an investment into start-up companies. *International Journal of Technology Intelligence and Planning*, 9(3), 165–180. DOI: 10.1504/IJTIP.2013.059656

Kusio, T., Miskiewicz, R., Borowiecki, R., Fijałkowska, J., Rzepka, A., Gross-Gołacka, E., & Ristvej, J. (2023). Startups: The Global Context of Functioning and the Need for Innovation Openness. *Journal of Intercultural Management*, 15(3), 50–77. DOI: 10.2478/joim-2023-0011

Lin, M., Chen, Z., Chen, R., & Fujita, H. (2021). Evaluation of startup companies using multicriteria decision making based on hesitant fuzzy linguistic information envelopment analysis models. *International Journal of Intelligent Systems*, 36(5), 2292–2322. DOI: 10.1002/int.22379

MacMillan, I. C., Siegel, R., & Narasimha, P. S. (1985). Criteria used by venture capitalists to evaluate new venture proposals. *Journal of Business Venturing*, 1(1), 119–128. DOI: 10.1016/0883-9026(85)90011-4

Majumdar, R., & Mittal, A. (2023). *Startup Financing: Some Evidence from the Indian Venture Capital Industry*. FIIB Business Review.

Milkova, M., Andreichikova, O., & Andreichikov, A. (2018). Venture Capitalists decision making: Applying analytic network process to the startups' evaluation. *International Journal of the Analytic Hierarchy Process*, 10(1), 1–18. DOI: 10.13033/ijahp.v10i1.511

Mohammadi, N., & Shafiee, M. (2022). How design thinking help us to select startups for the acceleration period? *Journal of Entrepreneurship in Emerging Economies*, 14(6), 1353–1368. DOI: 10.1108/JEEE-07-2021-0274

Mohammadi, N., & Shafiee, M. (2022). Predicting the success of seed-stage startups to enter the acceleration program and receive seed money. *International Journal of Entrepreneurial Venturing*, 14(2), 168–201. DOI: 10.1504/IJEV.2022.122654

Möllmann, J. (2023). More than a handshake–knowledge transfer in structured corporate–startup collaboration programs. *Journal of Knowledge Management*, 27(10), 2604–2624. DOI: 10.1108/JKM-03-2022-0222

Montani, D., Gervasio, D., & Pulcini, A. (2020). Startup company valuation: The state of art and future trends. *International Business Research*, 13(9), 31–45. DOI: 10.5539/ibr.v13n9p31

Muñoz-Bullon, F., Sanchez-Bueno, M. J., & Vos-Saz, A. (2015). Startup team contributions and new firm creation: The role of founding team experience. *Entrepreneurship and Regional Development*, 27(1-2), 80–105. DOI: 10.1080/08985626.2014.999719

Naumov, S. A. (2017). *Managing operational capabilities in startup companies*. Massachusetts Institute of Technology.

Neubert, M. (2018). The impact of digitalization on the speed of internationalization of lean global startups. *Technology Innovation Management Review*, 8(5), 44–54. DOI: 10.22215/timreview/1158

Nikoloudis, C., Strantzali, E., & Aravossis, K. (2017). Applying the multi-criteria method Promethee II for the startup ranking during a business ideas competition, Proceedings of the 6th International Symposium on Operational Research "OR in the digital era—ICT challenges" Thessaloniki, Greece.

Onetti, A., Pepponi, F., & Pisoni, A. (2015, August). How the founding team impacts the growth process of early-stage innovative startups. *Sinergie Italian Journal of Management*, 33(May), 37–53.

Paradkar, A., Knight, J., & Hansen, P. (2015). Innovation in start-ups: Ideas filling the void or ideas devoid of resources and capabilities? *Technovation*, 41, 1–10. DOI: 10.1016/j.technovation.2015.03.004

Pasayat, A. K., Mitra, A., & Bhowmick, B. (2022). Determination of essential features for predicting start-up success: An empirical approach using machine learning. *Technology Analysis and Strategic Management*, 36(1), 1–19.

Pena, I. (2002). Intellectual capital and business start-up success. *Journal of Intellectual Capital*, 3(2), 180–198. DOI: 10.1108/14691930210424761

Pierrakis, Y., & Owen, R. (2022). Startup ventures and equity finance: How do Business Accelerators and Business Angels' assess the human capital of socio-environmental mission-led entrepreneurs? Innovation. *Innovation (North Sydney, N.S.W.)*, 25(4), 371–395. DOI: 10.1080/14479338.2022.2029706

Pintado, T. R., De Lema, D. G. P., & Van Auken, H. (2007). Venture capital in Spain by stage of development. *Journal of Small Business Management*, 45(1), 68–88. DOI: 10.1111/j.1540-627X.2007.00199.x

Pramana, A., Dalimunthe, Z., Gandakusuma, I., & Rizkianto, E. (2020). Evaluation Criteria of High-Flyer Tech Startup Investments by Venture Capital Firms in Indonesia, K. Soliman, editor, Education Excellence and Innovation Management: A 2025 Vision To Sustain Economic Development During Global Challenges, Int Business Informat Management Assoc, pp.4054–4062, 35th International-Business-Information-Management-Association Conference (IBIMA), Seville, SPAIN, APR 01-02, 2020.

Rasmussen, E. S., & Tanev, S. (2016). *Lean start-up: Making the start-up more successful, Start-up creation*. Elsevier. DOI: 10.1016/B978-0-08-100546-0.00003-0

Rastkhiz, S. E. A., Dehkordi, A. M., Farsi, J. Y., & Azar, A. (2018). A new approach to evaluating entrepreneurial opportunities. *Journal of Small Business and Enterprise Development*, 26(1), 67–84. DOI: 10.1108/JSBED-01-2018-0013

Raz, O., & Gloor, P. A. (2007). Size really matters—New insights for start-ups' survival. *Management Science*, 53(2), 169–177. DOI: 10.1287/mnsc.1060.0609

Rompho, N. (2018). Operational performance measures for startups. *Measuring Business Excellence*, 22(1), 31–41. DOI: 10.1108/MBE-06-2017-0028

Salomon, V. (2018). Strategies of startup evaluation on crowd investing platforms: The case of Switzerland. *Journal Of Innovation Economics & Management*, (26), 63–88. DOI: 10.3917/jie.pr1.0029

Sari, R., Dewanti, P., Fajar, M., Priantinah, D., & Pranesti, A. (2022). Development of Early Startup Companies' Valuation Model Based on Android Mobile Application: The Angel Investor's Perspective. *JOIV: International Journal on Informatics Visualization*, 6(2), 382–389. DOI: 10.30630/joiv.6.2.992

Sato, Y., Tabuchi, T., & Yamamoto, K. (2012). Market size and entrepreneurship. *Journal of Economic Geography*, 12(6), 1139–1166. DOI: 10.1093/jeg/lbr035

Scillitoe, J. L., & Birasnav, M. (2022). Ease of market entry of Indian startups: Formal and informal institutional influences. *South Asian Journal of Business Studies*, 11(2), 195–215. DOI: 10.1108/SAJBS-07-2019-0131

Scott, E. L., Shu, P., & Lubynsky, R. M.. (2015). *Are'better'Ideas More Likely to Succeed?: An Empirical Analysis of Startup Evaluation, Technical Report*. Harvard Business School.

Seppänen, P., Tripathi, N., Oivo, M., & Liukkunen, K. (2017). How Are Product Ideas Validated? The Process from Innovation to Requirements Engineering in Software Startups, Software Business: 8th International Conference, ICSOB 2017, Essen, Germany, June 12-13, 2017, Proceedings 8, Springer, pp.3-17.

Shafi, K. (2021). Investors' evaluation criteria in equity crowdfunding. *Small Business Economics*, 56(1), 3–37. DOI: 10.1007/s11187-019-00227-9

Shankar, R. K., & Shepherd, D. A. (2019). Accelerating strategic fit or venture emergence: Different paths adopted by corporate accelerators. *Journal of Business Venturing*, 34(5), 105886. DOI: 10.1016/j.jbusvent.2018.06.004

Simões, J., Ferreira, F., Peris-Ortiz, M., & Ferreira, J. (2020). A cognition-driven framework for the evaluation of startups in the digital economy: Adding value with cognitive mapping and rule-based expert systems. *Management Decision*, 58(11), 2327–2347. DOI: 10.1108/MD-09-2019-1253

Skalicka, M., Zinecker, M., Balcerzak, A. P., & Pietrzak, M. B. (2023). Business angels and early stage decision-making criteria: Empirical evidence from an emerging market, Economic research-. *Ekonomska Istrazivanja*, 36(1), 25–50. DOI: 10.1080/1331677X.2022.2063920

Skare, M., Gavurova, B., & Polishchuk, V. (2023). A decision-making support model for financing start-up projects by venture capital funds on a crowdfunding platform. *Journal of Business Research*, 158, 113719. DOI: 10.1016/j.jbusres.2023.113719

Smith, B. R., Kickul, J. R., & Wilson, F. (2010). *Entrepreneurial opportunity evaluation: a discrete choice analysis of financial and social entrepreneurial opportunity attributes, Values and Opportunities in Social Entrepreneurship*. Springer.

Spender, J. C., Corvello, V., Grimaldi, M., & Rippa, P. (2017). Startups and open innovation: A literature. *European Journal of Innovation Management*, 20(1), 4–30. DOI: 10.1108/EJIM-12-2015-0131

Sreenivasan, A., & Suresh, M. (2023). Readiness of financial resilience in start-ups. *Journal of Safety Science and Resilience = An Quan Ke Xue Yu Ren Xing (Ying Wen)*, 4(3), 241–252.

Taweesangrungroj, A., Rattanabanchuen, R., & Sinthupinyo, S. (2022). A Decision-Making Model of Technological-Focused Government Agency Selection of Technological Start-Up Businesses. *Trends in Sciences*, 19(1), 1749–1749. DOI: 10.48048/tis.2022.1749

Terho, H., Suonsyrjä, S., & Systä, K. (2016). The developers' dilemma: Perfect product development or fast business validation? Product-Focused Software Process Improvement: 17th International Conference, PROFES 2016, Trondheim, Norway, November 22-24, 2016, Proceedings 17, Springer, pp.571–579.

Tritoasmoro, I. I., Ciptomulyono, U., Dhewanto, W., & Taufik, T. A. (2024). Determinant factors of lean start-up-based incubation metrics on post-incubation start-up viability: Case-based study. *Journal of Science and Technology Policy Management*, 15(1), 178–199. DOI: 10.1108/JSTPM-12-2021-0187

Yin, B., & Luo, J. (2018). How Do Accelerators Select Startups? Shifting Decision Criteria Across Stages. *IEEE Transactions on Engineering Management*, 65(4), 574–589. DOI: 10.1109/TEM.2018.2791501

# Chapter 14
# Organizational Research in the Western Balkans: A Comprehensive Bibliometric Review


**Gentjan Ulaj**
https://orcid.org/0009-0004-8543-7152
*Istanbul University, Turkey*

**Mahmut Hızıroğlu**
*Istanbul University, Turkey*

**Gentian Hoxhalli**
*Luarasi University, Albania*

**Vehap Kola**
https://orcid.org/0000-0001-7107-3563
*University of New York, Tirana, Albania*

**Enrik Sejdinaj**
https://orcid.org/0009-0005-9388-091X
*Mediterranean University of Albania, Albania*


## ABSTRACT


*Research on organizations in the Western Balkans has grown significantly over the past 30 years, highlighting the need for a comprehensive review. This bibliometric study examines the state of organizational research by performing bibliometric analysis, identifying research clusters through co-word analysis, and conducting trend topic analysis to uncover emerging themes. Using VOSviewer and Biblioshiny, the study analyzes 1,037 papers from the Scopus database. Findings reveal consistent growth in publications, especially after 2015. Co-word analysis identifies five major research clusters: SMEs, Kosovo, Serbia, entrepreneurship, and innovation. Future research is recommended to explore how businesses prepare for potential EU integration, the role of institutional support or voids in entrepreneurship rates, the effects of brain drain on organizations in the Western Balkans, and the dynamics of returnee entrepreneurs. This study provides valuable insights into the intellectual structure and trends in organizational research in the region and offers a foundation for future studies.*


DOI: 10.4018/979-8-3693-8181-6.ch014

## 1. INTRODUCTION

Management and organizational researchers have recently shown significant interest in the Western Balkans (WB6). This region is in Europe and is formed by six independent countries: Albania, Kosovo, Montenegro, North Macedonia, Serbia, Bosnia, and Hercegovina (Jano, 2023). The concept of the "Western Balkans" came into use as a geographical and geopolitical term at the beginning of the 21st century. Its significance grew as the European Union advanced its regional strategies and introduced a renewed focus on developing the EU and its peripheral regions, including the Balkans (Popovic *et al.*, 2020).

These countries share a similar and conflicting history. While most of them lived under the Ottoman Empire for many years, in the last century, five lived under Yugoslavia, except Albania. The breakup of Yugoslavia established new countries, resulting in new and ongoing conflicts (Bartlett, 2007). Despite it being an independent state, the context of the region is similar. All countries are undergoing dynamic transformations driven by economic reforms, integration into European Union efforts, and political stabilization (Belloni, 2009).

In recent decades, the region has seen major shifts in economic structures pushed by post-communist reforms, increased foreign direct investment (FDI), and a growing number of small and medium-sized firms (SMEs). Despite substantial improvements, some difficulties remain, including higher corruption, institutional voids, and limited access to global markets (Bartlett, 2009). These characteristics create a complex environment for enterprises and present various managerial issues (Sanfey & Milatovic, 2018).

Despite the growing body of academic research, there remains a significant need for a comprehensive overview of organizational studies within the Western Balkans (WB6) context. Several bibliometric studies have been conducted at the country level, such as Albania (Lis *et al.*, 2021), Serbia (Ivanović *et al.*, 2015), and the region as a whole (Jano, 2023), and this study addresses this gap by focusing specifically on organizational research. Our bibliometric study aims to present a comprehensive analysis of management and organizational studies in the WB6 region by utilizing various bibliometric methods, such as performance analysis, co-word analysis, thematic analysis, and trend analysis. These methods allow us to extensively investigate the most influential authors, key papers, dominant countries, and researched topics in the region. Furthermore, we explore how the focus of organizational research in WB6 has evolved over time, identifying trends and key areas that have shaped the field.

The remainder of this study is structured as follows. In the next section, we describe our proposed methodology. In the third section, we present the results of the performance analysis. The fourth part shows the results of the co-word analysis and trend topics in organizational research in Western Balkans. In the fifth part, we discuss our findings and offer future research directions for scholars. The final part of this article concludes with recommendations for future research.

## 2. METHODOLOGY

Applying quantitative methods, such as citation analysis (Ramos-Rodríguez & Ruíz-Navarro, 2004), to bibliometric data, such as citation and author counts, is known as bibliometric analysis (Broadus, 1987). Scholars may confuse meta-analysis and bibliometric analysis because of their quantitative nature; however, the primary distinction between the two is that bibliometric analysis maps intellectual structure (Guerra Fernandes *et al.*, 2022), whereas meta-analysis summarizes the findings in a specific field (Combs *et al.*, 2011). There are two primary reasons for the increasing popularity of bibliometric publications (Mukherjee et al., 2022; Öztürk et al., 2024). First, the exponential expansion of available data makes a thorough mapping of academic subjects possible (Zupic & Čater, 2015). Second, a range of software tools improves the accessibility and efficiency of the analysis process (Aria & Cuccurullo, 2017; Donthu et al., 2021).

The two primary streams of bibliometric approaches include science mapping and performance analysis (Marzi et al., 2024). Science mapping is a popular tool for learning about the dynamics and social structure of a research stream (Van Eck & Waltman, 2010; Zupic & Čater, 2015), whereas the primary goal of performance analysis is to assess the performance of nations, organizations, and authors on a particular topic (Öztürk *et al.*, 2024). Bibliometric analysis is frequently applied in management research. Scholars have conducted extensive research in the management field (Mas-Tur *et al.*, 2020), focusing on subtopics such as strategic management (Barca & Hızıroğlu, 2009; Ramos-Rodríguez & Ruíz-Navarro, 2004), internationalization (Dabić et al., 2020; Ulaj & Hızıroğlu, 2024), and immigrant entrepreneurship (Hoxhalli *et al.*, 2024). In addition, bibliometric analyses have been undertaken in certain regions, including Europe (Bilir *et al.*, 2020), Latin America (Diaz Tautiva *et al.*, 2024), and the Arab World (Jamali *et al.*, 2023), to provide a more nuanced understanding of these topics within specific geographical contexts.

To conduct a bibliometric analysis, we followed the recommendations of Donthu *et al.* (2021), Marzi et al. (2024) and Öztürk *et al.* (2024). First, we define the aim of our research. Our main objective is to assess research in the organizational field in the Western Balkans and map the field's intellectual and conceptual framework. In line with our aim, the research questions were as follows:

1- What is the yearly trend in publications and citations related to organizational research in WB6, and how has it evolved over time?
2- Who are the most influential authors, and which countries contribute the most to organizational research in WB6, based on citation impact and academic output?
3- Which papers from WB6 have had the greatest influence on organizational research, as measured by citations and scholarly recognition?
4- What are the key conceptual building blocks of organizational research in WB6?
5- What are the emerging trends in organizational research in the WB6?

The second stage involved selecting the methods used in our research (Donthu *et al.*, 2021). Starting with the most relevant publication trends, citation trends, authors, influential countries, and comparable metrics from other studies (Apriliyanti & Alon, 2017; Donthu et al., 2021; García-Lillo et al., 2017), we performed a performance analysis of the area. Performance analysis itself is not sufficient to conduct a bibliometric analysis (Marzi et al., 2024; Öztürk et al., 2024). After identifying trend subjects in the field, we mapped the structure of the research undertaken by Western Balkan researchers using co-word analysis (Dabić *et al.*, 2020; Nerur *et al.*, 2008). Co-word analysis, or keyword co-occurrence, is a method that directly analyzes the content of a publication (Castriotta et al., 2021). In this analysis, the inputs, which are words, are generally extracted from the keywords of the authors in publications (Bretas & Alon, 2021). Scholars use this technique to examine how many repeated words underlie the main research themes in a specific field. Additionally, the co-occurrence or co-absence of keywords can be used to identify research clusters in a specific field of study (Donthu *et al.*, 2021).

The next stage was to choose articles and gather data from the Scopus database. The two primary databases utilized in social science bibliometric research are Scopus and the Web of Science (Aria & Cuccurullo, 2017; Marzi et al., 2024). However, we chose to use the Scopus database because we believe it is better suited for mapping smaller study areas, in line with previous studies (Bilir *et al.*, 2020; Bretas & Alon, 2021). Building upon existing literature (Diaz Tautiva *et al.*, 2024), we used nine keywords ("firm*" or "business*" or "corporate*" or "compan*" or "enterprise*" or "venture*" or "organization*" or "organization*" or "sme*") to identify research related to organizations. Furthermore, we included the names of each country within the Western Balkan region (e.g., Albania, Montenegro, Kosovo, Serbia, North Macedonia, and Bosnia and Hercegovina). Using these research criteria in the Article Title, Abstract, or Keywords search section, we were able to identify 8126 documents. We also filtered publications between 1990 and 2023 to further narrow our scope, resulting in 7650 documents. Additionally, we rely only on publications in Business, Management, and Accounting and analyze only Articles that are in the English language, resulting in a final sample of 1074 articles, a number that is optimal for bibliometric analysis (Donthu *et al.*, 2021). This process culminates in the analysis and presentation of results. We use various analysis-facilitating tools, such as Bibliometrix with the R package (Aria & Cuccurullo, 2017) and VOSviewer (Van Eck & Waltman, 2010).

Additionally, we must add some comments to the procedure, which are the characteristics of the region. Kosovo, situated in the Western Balkans, is not recognized as an independent state in the Scopus database. As a result, city names such as Pristina, Peja, or Gilan often appear instead of country names in the dataset. To address this issue, the authors meticulously analyzed and standardized the data by clustering all relevant cities in the corresponding country, Kosovo. The authors identified three papers in which the country name was recorded as Yugoslavia. Upon closer examination, these papers were found to have been published in 2006, 2014, and 2015.

To ensure data accuracy, the country designation "Yugoslavia" was replaced with the current country name corresponding to the location of affiliated universities: two papers were associated with the University of Niš and one with the University of Belgrade. Consequently, all instances of "Yugoslavia" were updated to "Serbia" in the dataset. Aswell analysis revealed an anomalous situation regarding the journal Textiles Eastern Europe, which is represented in our database with 37 publications, yet has received no citations. Several irregularities were identified on careful examination. The publications in our database span from 2003 to 2011, with a notable concentration between 2006 and 2008. However, cross-referencing with the Scopus database revealed a significantly higher volume of publications for the same period, with 86, 102, and 60 documents published annually. Moreover, 34 of the 37 articles listed in our database lacked attributed authorship, raising further concerns about the journal's reliability. Given these discrepancies, the authors unanimously decided to exclude Textiles Eastern Europe journal from the final dataset to ensure the integrity and accuracy of the analysis. Finally, the data cleaning and modifications described, including adjustments for inconsistencies related to Kosovo and Yugoslavia, reduced the final dataset size from 1,074 to 1,037 published papers.

## 3. PERFORMANCE ANALYSIS

In this section, we analyse the yearly and total number of publications and citations in the Western Balkan context. In addition, we present a summary of the most influential papers and the most cited authors in the field. We conclude our performance analysis by identifying the most productive countries and journals with the highest number of publications.

### 3.1 Yearly and Total Publications

*Figure 1. Yearly and total publications*

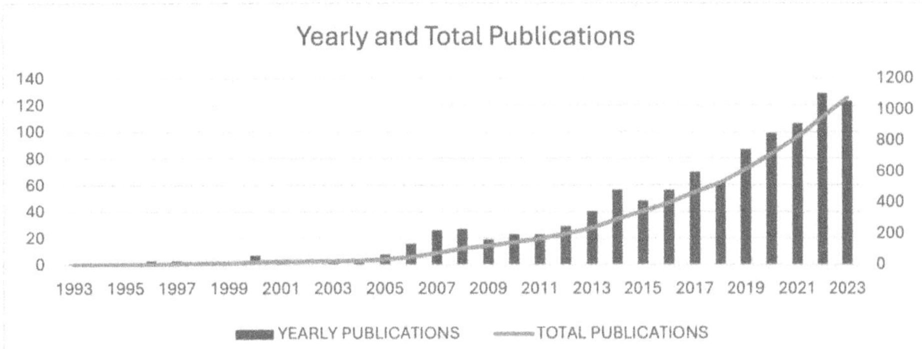


The data indicate a consistent increase in organizational studies from the Western Balkans, with a moderate expansion from 1993 to 2005 when the total number of articles reached only 32. Nevertheless, starting in 2006, there was a notable increase in the annual number of publications, reaching a substantial peak in 2015. As of 2020, the number of annual publications has exceeded 99, and by 2023, the total number of publications has reached 1,037. The accelerated increase, especially in the past ten years, indicates a significantly expanding scholarly interest and institutional support for organizational studies in the region, positioning the Western Balkans as an increasingly significant contributor to global study in this area. The annual growth rate of published papers is 17,4%, which demonstrates the significance of organizational studies in the Western Balkans.

## 3.2 Yearly and Total Citations

*Figure 2. Yearly and total citations*

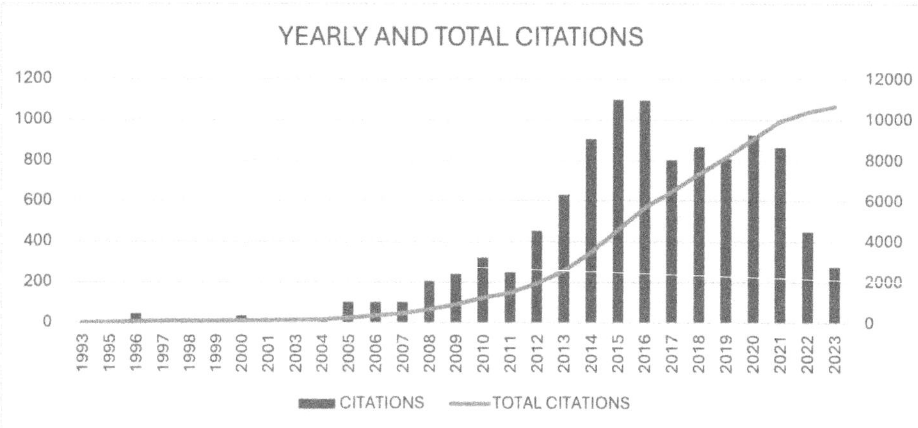


The citation data in the above table indicate a consistent rise in the impact of organizational research originating from the Western Balkans, with few citations being recorded prior to 2005. Starting in 2005, there was a substantial increase in the number of citations received each year, reaching over 100 by 2006, and experiencing strong growth that persisted until the late 2000s. An exceptionally significant surge occurred from 2008 to 2015, with annual citations more than tripling, reaching a peak of 1,100 in 2015. Despite a consistent yearly citation rate of approximately 800–900, starting in 2016, the overall number of citations steadily increased and reached 10,656 by 2023.

## 3.3 Most Influential Papers

*Table 1. Most influential papers*

| Rank | Authors | Title | Year | Citations |
|---|---|---|---|---|
| 1 | **Ramadani V.; Gërguri S.; Dana L.-P.; Tašaminova T.** | Women entrepreneurs in the Republic of Macedonia: Waiting for directions | 2013 | 265 |
| 2 | **Todorović M.L.; Petrović D.T.; Mihić M.M.; Obradović V.L.; Bushuyev S.D.** | Project success analysis framework: A knowledge-based approach in project management | 2015 | 187 |
| 3 | **Ramadani V.; Hisrich R.D.; Gërguri-Rashiti S.** | Female entrepreneurs in transition economies: Insights from Albania, Macedonia and Kosovo | 2015 | 186 |
| 4 | **Cabrilo S.; Dahms S.** | How strategic knowledge management drives intellectual capital to superior innovation and market performance | 2018 | 185 |
| 5 | **Dženopoljac V.; Janoševic S.; Bontis N.** | Intellectual capital and financial performance in the Serbian ICT industry | 2016 | 169 |

continued on following page

*Table 1. Continued*

| Rank | Authors | Title | Year | Citations |
|---|---|---|---|---|
| 6 | **Demirović Bajrami D.; Terzić A.; Petrović M.D.; Radovanović M.; Tretiakova T.N.; Hadoud A.** | Will we have the same employees in hospitality after all? The impact of COVID-19 on employees' work attitudes and turnover intentions | 2021 | 163 |
| 7 | **Sadiku-Dushi N.; Dana L.-P.; Ramadani V.** | Entrepreneurial marketing dimensions and SMEs performance | 2019 | 140 |
| 8 | **Bontis N.; Janošević S.; Dženopoljac V.** | Intellectual capital in serbia's hotel industry | 2015 | 139 |
| 9 | **Herrera-Echeverri H.; Haar J.; Estévez-Bretón J.B.** | Foreign direct investment, institutional quality, economic freedom and entrepreneurship in emerging markets | 2014 | 124 |
| 10 | **Hashi I.; Krasniqi B.A.** | Entrepreneurship and SME growth: Evidence from advanced and laggard transition economies | 2011 | 122 |

The table above presents the most frequently cited papers from our Scopus data. Although highly cited publications are normally regarded as the most impactful in their research field, older articles often receive more citations than new ones because of their longer presence in academic debates (Block *et al.*, 2020).

The most cited article is "Women entrepreneurs in the Republic of Macedonia: Waiting for directions" with 265 citations. In their study Ramadani *et al.* (2013) evaluated the circumstances and challenges of female entrepreneurs in North Macedonia and offered future recommendations for the government to enhance their efforts to establish and sustain successful businesses. Second most cited article is "Project success analysis framework: A knowledge-based approach in project management" from Todorović *et al.* (2015) with 187 citations. This study was conducted with 103 project managers in Serbia and confirmed that project success analysis significantly affects knowledge transfer and acquisition. Another study focusing on female entrepreneurship, titled "Female entrepreneurs in transition economies: insights from Albania, Macedonia and Kosovo" is ranked the third most cited publication with 186 citations. In their study, Ramadani *et al.* (2015) investigated the characteristics of female entrepreneurs' motives to start a business, their family status, and the management problems that they face in Albania, Kosovo, and North Macedonia. This is the most influential work in terms of region in organizational research.

## 3.4 Most Important Authors

*Table 2. Most important authors*

| RANK | AUTHOR | PUBLICATIONS | CITATIONS |
|---|---|---|---|
| 1 | Veland Ramadani | 17 | 1014 |
| 2 | Léo-paul Dana | 5 | 542 |
| 3 | Shqipe Gërguri-Rashiti | 3 | 534 |
| 4 | Besnik A. Krasniqi | 16 | 461 |
| 5 | Nick Bontis | 3 | 361 |
| 6 | Vladimir Dženopoljac | 3 | 361 |
| 7 | Robert d. Hisrich | 3 | 295 |

continued on following page

*Table 2. Continued*

| RANK | AUTHOR | PUBLICATIONS | CITATIONS |
|---|---|---|---|
| 8 | Marina Dabić | 6 | 272 |
| 9 | Tatjana Tašaminova | 1 | 265 |
| 10 | Gadaf Rexhepi | 9 | 257 |

Based on their publishing output and citation impact, the table above quantifies the leading authors who have made significant contributions to organizational research in the WB6. In total, 2189 different authors appear in our database; while most studies are conducted with more than one author, the average number of authors per paper is 2,84. Almost 30% of papers with co-authors were conducted through international cooperation. Veland Ramadani is on top of the list with 17 articles and an impressive 1,014 citations, indicating his substantial impact on the discipline. Despite having only five publications, Léo-Paul Dana has achieved a remarkable citation total of 542, which demonstrates the significant influence of his work. Shqipe Gërguri-Rashiti, although having only three papers, received 534 citations, highlighting the significance of her scientific contributions. Besnik A. Krasniqi is notable for his 16 publications and 461 citations, indicating high output and prestige. Additional noteworthy writers include Nick Bontis and Vladimir Dōenopoljac, each of which has authored three papers and received 361 citations. Robert D. Hisrich, Marina Dabić, Tatjana Tašaminova, and Gadaf Rexhepi complete the list, each reporting different numbers of publications but consistently achieving high citation counts, indicating the extensive influence of their research. It is important to note that some authors (for example, Léo-paul Dana) appear in our database as co-authors with researchers from Western Balkans.

## 3.5 Country Ranking

*Table 3. Most cited countries in Western Balkan*

| Rank | Country | Documents | Citations |
|---|---|---|---|
| 1 | Serbia | 461 | 4666 |
| 2 | North Macedonia | 131 | 1648 |
| 3 | Albania | 106 | 619 |
| 4 | Montenegro | 46 | 367 |
| 5 | Kosovo | 82 | 321 |
| 6 | Bosnia and Herzegovina | 19 | 196 |

In our study, we also ranked WB6 countries based on their contributions to organizational research, which were measured by the number of documents published and total citations. Serbia has 461 publications and 4,666 citations, highlighting its dominant role in the region's research output and impact. North Macedonia has 131 publications and 1,648 citations, indicating significant academic activity and recognition. Albania ranks third, with 106 documents and 619 citations, while Montenegro and Kosovo produced 46 and 82 publications, respectively, with relatively lower citation counts. Bosnia and Herzegovina have 19 documents and 196 citations, respectively. This ranking highlights the varying levels of research productivity and influences on organizational research across WB6. In addition, we identified the conditions necessary for clarification in this part of the study. Kosovo is not acknowledged as an independent state in the Scopus database. We manually examined all country names in multiple forms (for example, the University of Pristine, Gjilan) and categorized them under the name Kosovo if they were situated within its territory.

### 3.6 Most Publishing Journals

*Table 4. Most publishing journals*

| Rank | Source | Documents | Citations |
|---|---|---|---|
| 1 | Quality - Access To Success | 52 | 122 |
| 2 | Journal Of East European Management Studies | 43 | 205 |
| 3 | Serbian Journal Of Management | 30 | 120 |
| 4 | Custos E Agronegocio | 22 | 113 |
| 5 | Engineering Economics | 20 | 167 |
| 6 | Wseas Transactions On Business And Economics | 18 | 25 |
| 7 | Academic Journal Of Interdisciplinary Studies | 16 | 49 |
| 8 | Journal Of Governance And Regulation | 16 | 55 |
| 9 | Journal Of Cleaner Production | 14 | 513 |
| 10 | South East European Journal of Economics and Business | 14 | 115 |

The analysis of important journals publishing research on organizational subjects in the Western Balkans indicates significant contributions and various degrees of influence. Quality: Access to Success leads to productivity with 52 publications and 122 citations, while the Journal of East European Management Studies has significant production (43 publications) and an outstanding citation impact (205 citations). Serbian Journal of Management (30 articles, 120 citations) and Engineering Economics (20 publications, 167 citations) are other important journals. While publishing just 14 papers, the Journal of Cleaner Production has the highest citation count (513), indicating its international standing in sustainability research. The South-East European Journal of Economics and Business contributed 14 papers and 115 citations.

## 4. SCIENTIFIC MAPPING

This section uses scientific mapping techniques to summaries Western Balkan's conceptual framework. Co-word analysis was employed to identify the links among the significant concepts and terms used in the literature. This method illustrates the conceptual framework of the study area by outlining the co-occurrence of the keywords. We identified the most significant themes by analyzing the frequency and network of co-occurring keywords. Additionally, a trend topic analysis was performed to determine the evolution of the study domain over time. This analysis identifies the most significant and rising fields of study and offers insights into the evolving focus of research on WB6. Visualizing these trends makes it possible to recognize how specific topics have changed in significance and to identify future research paths.

## 4.1 Co-Word Analysis

*Figure 3. Co-word analysis*

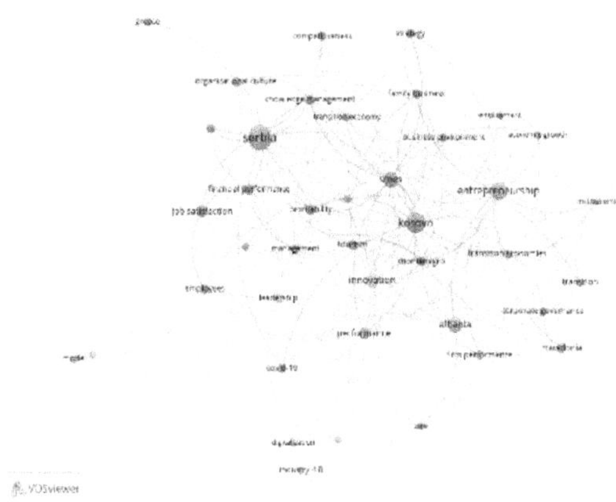

*Table 5. Most frequent keywords*

| Ranking | Keyword | Occurrences |
|---|---|---|
| 1 | Serbia | 102 |
| 2 | Kosovo | 67 |
| 3 | Entrepreneurship | 51 |
| 4 | Albania | 39 |
| 5 | Smes | 39 |
| 6 | Innovation | 33 |
| 7 | Job Satisfaction | 22 |
| 8 | Performance | 20 |
| 9 | Profitability | 19 |
| 10 | Financial Performance | 18 |

The figure above illustrates the co-word analysis and density distribution of the keywords across the network. A minimum occurrence threshold of 10 was established. Out of 3,086 author keywords, only those with at least 10 occurrences were included in this analysis. This resulted in 41 keywords that met the inclusion threshold. The analysis was conducted using VOSviewer software (Van Eck & Waltman, 2010), allowing for visualization and examination of the relationships among the keywords.

Additionally, we compiled a list of the top ten keywords within the Western Balkan context. Notably, three countries were prominently represented: Serbia (102 occurrences), Kosovo (67 occurrences), and Albania (39 occurrences). Other frequently occurring keywords include "entrepreneurship", "SMEs", "innovation", "performance", and "job satisfaction", indicating their significant presence and importance within the dataset.

*Table 6. Co-word analysis clusters*

| Cluster | Main Topic | Keywords |
|---|---|---|
| **Cluster 1- Red** | Smes | Family Business, Financial Performance, Intellectual Capital, Knowledge Management, Management, Montenegro, Profitability, Smes, Strategy, Tourism, Transition Economy |
| **Cluster 2- Green** | Entrepreneruship | Albania, Corporate Governance, Entrepreneruship, Firm Performance, Institutions, Macedonia, Sme, Transition, Transition Economies |
| **Cluster 3-Blue** | Kosovo | Corporate Social Responsibility, Covid-19, Developing Countries, Economic Growth, Employees, Employment, Job Satisfaction, Kosovo, Performance |
| **Cluster 4- Purple** | Serbia | Competitiveness, Greece, Organizational Culture, Serbia |
| **Cluster 5- Yellow** | Innovation | Digitalization, Industry 4.0, Innovation, Leadership, Model, Quality System, Sustainability, |

The first cluster (red), labelled as SMEs, is concentrated on research on small and medium-sized businesses and family businesses as one form of them. Jahmurataj *et al.* (2023) investigated the factors that are important for family businesses to live long and concluded that quality relationships, family culture, and knowledge transfer have a positive impact on the longevity of companies while surprising founders' educations do not significantly have any effect. Additionally, Toska *et al.* (2022) argue that family businesses prepare their generation of successors from childhood by engaging them in business and helping them build an entrepreneurial mindset.

The second cluster is labelled the entrepreneurship (green) cluster. In this cluster in terms of countries, we observe that country names such as Albania and Macedonia (North Macedonia) have emerged, suggesting that these countries' publications are focused on entrepreneurship issues(Kraja & Berberi, 2023; Ramadani *et al.*, 2014). In their study conducted in Albania with 393 businesses in Albania, Çera *et al.* (2021) found that trust in institutions is essential for entrepreneurs to find an attractive business climate in an emerging context. Additionally Williams and Kosta (2020) found that businesses that start as unregistered start-ups have higher annual sales growth compared to others, primarily due to institutional weakness that Albanian experience. Moreover, Ramadani *et al.* (2014) argue that Albanian ethnic entrepreneurs in North Macedonia start their businesses for primary economic reasons and use their informal networks and relationships to support their entrepreneurial journey. Beyond these studies, Albanian research extends to a variety of related topics including job performance (Çopani & Kola, 2023), strategy (Yener *et al.*, 2014), and various aspects of entrepreneurship (Drishti *et al.*, 2016).

We name Kosovo the third cluster (blue) because this keyword appears at the center of our cluster. Elezaj and Ramaj (2023) conducted a wide study with 300 CEOs in Kosovo and found that innovation and branding activities of the firm have a positive significant impact in companies' sales growth. Moreover, Murati-Leka (2023) states that digital marketing and digitalization of processes help firms in Kosovo promote their brand better. Moreover, there has been a notable increase in recent publications by authors associated with Kosovo. This surge reflects the growing academic interest in entrepreneurship (Krasniqi, 2007; Mustafa *et al.*, 2023) and the role of institutions (Bağış *et al.*, 2024). Additionally, there has been an increase in the number of studies focusing on the effects of COVID-19 on entrepreneurship within this cluster (Kryeziu et al., 2022). These studies explore how the pandemic reshaped entrepreneurial activities, strategies, and resilience in the WB6.

The fourth cluster is Innovation (Yellow). Our data show that innovation topics are connected to all countries in the Western Balkans. In their study Emini *et al.* (2023) stated that innovation leads to an increase in financial performance in firms located in North Macedonia. Mahmutaj and Krasniqi (2020) argue that not all innovations positively affect performance. In a study of 278 companies from Kosovo, they found that marketing innovation leads companies to sales growth, but new product innovations have the opposite effect. Kajtazi *et al.* (2023) conducted a study with 168 big companies in Albania, Kosovo, and North Macedonia and found that corporate sustainability is highly impacted by business model innovations. Paunović *et al.* (2022) compared family and non-family businesses in Serbia and found no differences in their performance in business process innovation. Moreover, they concluded that business process innovation helps family and non-family companies increase consumer satisfaction and retention in the Serbian context.

The final cluster was labelled Serbia (purple). This is because most studies in this cluster were conducted by Serbian researchers or in the Serbian context. Rajković *et al.* (2020) highlighted the effects of national culture on entrepreneurship. In their study conducted in Serbia, they found that national culture positively impacts entrepreneurship, especially that of young people, to overcome unfavorable circumstances and become independent. Additionally, Popović-Pantić *et al.* (2020) studied Serbian female entrepreneurs and highlighted the adverse effects of COVID-19 on their businesses, while on the other hand, it also had a positive impact on spending time with family.

## 4.2 Thematic Map

*Figure 4. Research trends: Static strategic diagram source*

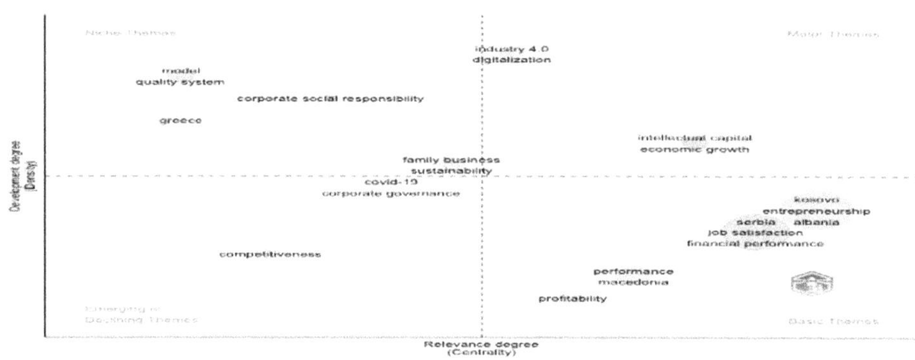


The examination of the research topics was finalized with a strategic diagram illustrating the significance of the topics based on their density and centrality, facilitating their positioning in various quadrants. Figure 5 illustrates that the research themes were categorized into six specialized themes in the lower quadrants, while an additional six were identified as the main streams in the upper quadrants. The 12 research themes were grouped into four different clusters regarding centrality and density.

In the emerging themes cluster, we observe that studies related to COVID-19, corporate governance, and competitiveness have taken place. These themes are highly influenced by studies that investigate the impact of COVID-19 on Western Balkan companies. Kryeziu *et al.* (2022) studied the impact of the pandemic on SMEs in Kosovo. They conclude that in all businesses included in their study, income has decreased, and family firms are among the most affected by this decrease. In a study conducted in North Macedonia, Mucha (2020) found that female entrepreneurs predominantly employed defensive strategies during a crisis, whereas their male counterparts favored offensive approaches. Women-owned enterprises, particularly in the textile sector and beauty salons, have noticed substantial declines in revenue, workforce, and customers. Businesses managed by men in the high-end jewelers and restaurant sectors also experienced difficulties in maintaining personnel at minimum pay levels. Nonetheless, pharmacies, supermarkets, and detergent manufacturers are profitable. All enterprises, including profitable ones, faced issues with raw material supply due to the pandemic.

Quadrant 2 lists the topics that have the potential to become major themes. Consistent with the results obtained in the co-word analysis, the most prominent topics were those related to Entrepreneurship, Serbia, Kosovo, Albania, performance, job satisfaction, profitability, and Macedonia. Most studies in Albania and Kosovo are related to entrepreneurship (Ramadani *et al.*, 2014). Furthermore, we identified an association between research conducted in Serbia and job satisfaction and the financial performance of companies. In their study of 813 employees in Serbia, Lepojevic *et al.* (2018) found that job satisfaction is affected by different job characteristics at different career phases. Connections and communication are important during the initial stages. Promotions influence satisfaction in the advancement stage, additional advantages in the subsequent phase, and contingent rewards in the decline phase. Compensation and employment characteristics continuously influenced job satisfaction at all levels. Terek *et al.* (2015) gathered data from 394 middle managers across 123 Serbian enterprises. Their findings suggest that, to enhance financial performance, companies should priorities contemporary media and focus on the organization's media presence over that of the CEO. Integrating both new and old media is essential for improving corporate success, with a particular focus on company exposure.

In the third quadrant, the consolidated themes are economic growth, intellectual capital, digitalization, and Industry 4.0. Cabrilo and Dahms (2018) studied the relationship between intellectual capital and innovation by collecting data from 101 Serbian companies. They conclude that structural and relational capital have a direct impact on innovation performance, while human capital alone does not show a significant effect. Komnenic and Pokrajčić (2012) found that human capital is positively associated with corporate performance, as measured by return on assets (ROA), return on equity (ROE), and productivity in a sample of 37 multinational companies (MNCs) operating in Serbia between 2006 and 2008. However, structural capital is only significantly linked to return on equity (ROE), with no significant effect on the other performance measures. Another motor theme in organizational studies on WB6 is digitalization. Voza *et al.* (2022) concluded that digitalization has a considerable positive impact on environmental issues and sustainability. Furthermore, Rashiti *et al.* (2023) argue that digital transformation is important in the banking sector to improve performance and increase market share.

The fourth quadrant encompasses specialized topics, or those that are becoming obsolete. These topics include quality systems, Greece, corporate social responsibility, sustainability, and family businesses. Tafolli and Grabner-Kräuter (2020) presented evidence that employees' perceptions of corporate social responsibility (CSR) correlate positively with perceived ethical leadership and satisfaction at work, while showing an adverse relationship with perceived organizational corruption. Berber *et al.* (2022) studied 73 private firms in Serbia and found that corporate social responsibility (CSR), has a positive relationship with corporate reputation, with each CSR dimension (responsibility to employees, customers, local community, environment, and suppliers) contributing to this effect.

## 4.3 Thematic Evolution

*Figure 5. Thematic evolution source: Biblioshiny report*

The evolution of the main topic from 1993 to 2023 and the connections between them are illustrated in the Sankey Diagram (Figure 5). The themes from 1993 to 2016 are displayed on the left, whereas those from 2017 to 2020 are positioned in the middle. The themes for 2021 and the end of 2023 are also on the left.

It is clear that some topics remained prominent across all periods. For example, Serbia appears centrally in the first period and continues to be significant in the second and third periods, though not always in the same position. In the first period, the analysis identified eight keywords that appear frequently: quality management, entrepreneurship, Serbia, job satisfaction, developing countries, globalization, corporate governance, and profitability.

During the second period, we observe an increased focus on studies related to Kosovo, while entrepreneurship, profitability, and Serbia continue to be the central themes. Additionally, several new topics emerged in this period, such as management, brand, family business, efficiency, financial reporting, risk, competitiveness, development, intellectual capital, the hotel industry, and quality systems.

Although the third period was shorter in duration, the number of topics was relatively small. However, there is continuity with recurring keywords, such as Kosovo, Serbia, management, and efficiency. The remaining key topics in the final period included marketing, strategy, corporate performance, financial performance, organizational culture, and firm performance.

## 4.4 Trend Topics

To enrich our study, we aim to identify topics that have significantly increased in recent years. We analyzed our data using the R Bibliography package (Aria & Cuccurullo, 2017) and listed the trends in WB6 organizational research.

In the early period, especially before the 2000s, there was a significant scarcity of subjects in the dataset, mostly because of the limited number of publications during that era. The technique employed in the research exclusively accounts for terms that occur a minimum of 10 times in the dataset, thus highlighting the limited number of themes in earlier years. As we approached the first decade of the 2000s, a distinct change occurred, with subjects such as investments, institutions, exports, international trade, and the textile industry prevailing in the research domain. These regions reflected the economic conditions of the era, as the Western Balkans moved through post-transition economies and increasingly participated in international trade as well as investment initiatives.

Post-2010, the scope of the study expanded. The growing focus on decision making, female entrepreneurship, and project management indicates a transition towards contemporary problems in business and organizational studies. These themes reflect worldwide trends toward inclusive entrepreneurship, the rise of women in leadership roles, and the growing complexity of decision-making in a progressively global business environment.

Recently, we noted that the predominant themes in Western Balkan organizational research are marketing, e-commerce, corporate development, and innovation. These subjects reflect the region's growing digitisation, implementation of innovative business models, and increase in entrepreneurship within the digital economy. As businesses adopt new technologies and strategies to maintain competitiveness, these subjects have become critical focal points for scholars aiming to understand and navigate the changing business environment.

Furthermore, a significant trend in the last decade has been the introduction of COVID-19 as the primary focus of study. The epidemic has significantly affected the world economy, and the Western Balkans have also seen its consecuences. Research has increasingly focused on comprehending the problems presented by the pandemic, especially its effects on corporate operations, supply networks, digital transformation, and organizational resilience. The pandemic has highlighted the necessity for businesses to adjust swiftly to evolving conditions, likely fuelling the increase in studies on crisis management, company continuity, and organizational digital transformation.

Our study indicates a distinct evolution in the research themes of organizational studies in the Western Balkans. The research environment is evolving in response to local and global trends, transitioning from early subjects to economic transition and trade to contemporary issues of innovation, digitisation, and pandemic-related difficulties. The increasing significance of subjects such as marketing, e-commerce, and COVID-19 illustrates the evolving characteristics of the region's economic landscape and the changing focus of academics, as they address new possibilities and difficulties.

During the COVID-19 pandemic, other significant topics have emerged in recent years, such as financial performance, profitability, small and medium-sized companies (SMEs), and tourism. These sectors underscore the increasing significance of financial sustainability and profitability as essential determinants of company performance, especially for SMEs, which are pivotal to the economy of the Western Balkans. The tourist industry in the area has garnered heightened study focus, possibly owing to its pivotal function in economic recovery and growth, especially in the post-pandemic context, alongside the growing necessity to comprehend sustainable tourism practices and the sector's adaptability to emerging difficulties.

*Figure 6. Trend topics source: Biblioshiny report*

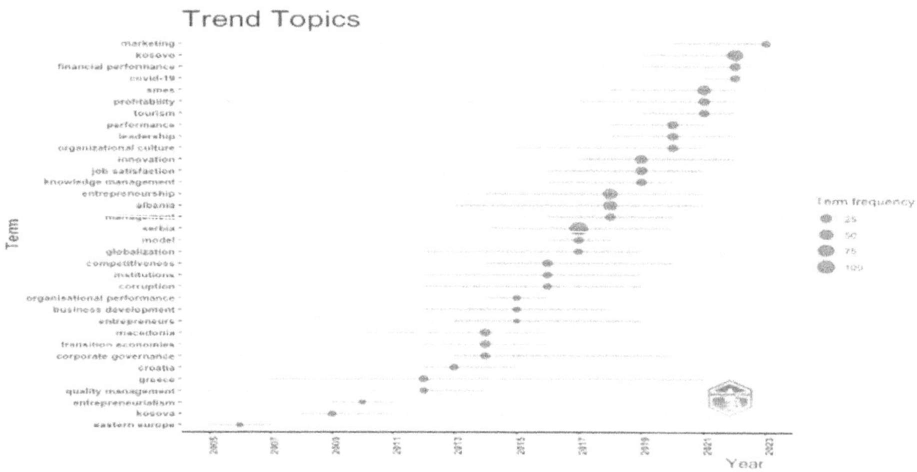


## 5. DISCUSSION AND FUTURE RESEARCH

This study provides a comprehensive overview of organizational studies conducted in the WB6. Our research provides important insights into the progress and influence of organizational studies in the Western Balkans. Initially, we see a gradual increase in research production, characterized by significant exponential growth starting in 2015, indicating an upward trend in research participation in the region, similar to the trend identified previously in the literature from Jano (2023) in his bibliometric study of all studies published in the region. Veland Ramadani has emerged as the leading academic, with his study, "Women Entrepreneurs in the Republic of Macedonia: Waiting for Directions," recognized as the most significant publication in the discipline. This highlights the increasing emphasis on entrepreneurship and gender in organizational studies.

The country ranking in our study is similar to that in previous work (Kovac *et al.*, 2024). Serbia is the most productive and influential nation in WB6, excelling in both publication quantity and total citations, thus underscoring its substantial contribution to the advancement of academic discussion in organizational studies. Other nations in the area, such as Kosovo, North Macedonia, and Albania, also influence the development of research, although to differing extents. Additionally, our co-word analysis identified five principal research clusters: SME, Entrepreneurship, Kosovo, Innovation, and Serbia. These clusters not only represent the thematic goals of the region's study but also highlight the multidisciplinary character of organizational studies, encompassing subjects such as small- and medium-sized firms, innovation, and regional emphasis, including Kosovo and Serbia.

These clusters indicate the primary thematic avenues of study in WB6. The "SME" cluster highlights the significance of small and medium-sized firms as a primary focus, demonstrating their essential contribution to the area economy (Jano, 2023). Future studies in this cluster can further investigate how small and medium-sized companies from WB6 navigate structural barriers such as lack of finance and institutional voids and support from the government. Additionally, we recommend that scholars research the effect of digital transformation in these companies, and how family and non-family businesses prepare to compete with EU businesses in the future. Also, how SMEs from WB6 transit to more green economy practices it present a good avenue for research. Lastly scholars should comparatively research between SMEs located in different countries to better understand commonalities and differences between them.

The "Entrepreneurship" cluster highlights the increasing focus on cultivating new enterprises and entrepreneurial ecosystems, crucial for economic advancement. Regarding to entreprenurship, future research can be oriented in better understanding the role entrepreurial ecosystems, focusing on the role of incubators, accelerators and government or EU support programs in increasing the likelyhood of success. Considering the high number of diasporas that these countries have, it would be very important to study the entreprenurial journey of returnee immigrants, how they use the network, and the knowledge gained in other countries. Finally, we call for more studies to understand the challenges and opportunities that females or young entrepreneurs face in the region.

The "Kosovo" and "Serbia" clusters demonstrate a regional focus, indicating that these nations have an important role to study topics, perhaps owing to their unique economic and managerial challenges. Future studies could examine the institutional differences between countries, entrepreneurship rates, and paths. Scholars should investigate the role of the tourism sector in both economies.

Finally, the "Innovation" cluster underlines the crucial function of innovation in enhancing competitiveness and shaping business strategies within the region. Future studies could examine existing and emerging innovation clusters by focusing on key industries and core competencies. Similarly, researchers must focus on investigating the drivers of innovation in WB6. In addition, an identified gap is the relationship between innovation and social entrepreneurship to address the problems faced by the region. Lastly, more studies should be conducting in understanding the role of intellectual and social capital of workers and founders on innovations in companies.

We further analyze the centrality and density of research topics in WB6. The analysis indicates a significant change in research objectives across several vital issues. Topics such as COVID-19, corporate governance, and competitiveness are gaining popularity as vital fields of focus and are likely to evolve into essential issues in future research. Themes pertaining to entrepreneurship, with regional emphases on Serbia, Kosovo, Albania, and Macedonia, along with performance, work satisfaction, and profitability, are growing and expected to attain greater significance. Established research domains, such as economic development, intellectual capital, digitization, and Industry 4.0, remain highly relevant. Conversely, specialised or declining subjects, such as quality systems, corporate social responsibility, sustainability, and family business, seem to be fading in prominence, indicating a shift in the focus of the study. These changes highlight the shifting dynamics of academic research and changing objectives within the field. In this vein, we highly recommend more research on corporate governance practices in WB6. Additionally, more research is needed in green and social entrepreneurship, since are clearly missing as research topics.

Additionally, we analyzed the evolution of research topics in the WB6 region. The major research subjects from 1993 to 2023 demonstrate both continuity and change. Key topics, including Serbia, entrepreneurship, profitability, and quality management, have always been essential across every period.

Nevertheless, a significant shift in emphasis occurred over time. During the second phase (2017-2020), emerging subjects such as Kosovo, brand management, family businesses, and intellectual capital were prominent, while issues such as corporate governance and globalisation continued to be significant. The third phase (2021-2023) exhibited a more focused range of subjects, with persistent themes such as Kosovo, Serbia, management, and efficiency, as well as a growing interest in marketing, strategy, and organizational performance.

Trend topics in WB6 organizational research have focused on numerous critical areas, including the effects of COVID-19, financial performance, profitability, small and medium-sized firms (SMEs), marketing, e-commerce, innovation, and tourism. These growing subjects signify the region's adjustment to the digital revolution, economic difficulties, and the necessity for company resilience and sustainability in a swiftly changing global environment.

Our analysis reveals a notable absence of research on organization and management theory within the scientific landscape of the WB6 region. The predominant emphasis on quantitative methodologies, coupled with the secondary and supplementary application of qualitative approaches, has constrained the exploration of topics central to organizational theory. Addressing this gap necessitates future research that foregrounds organization and management theory within the unique context of post-communist and developing regions. Employing innovative methodologies and prioritizing qualitative approaches could enrich theoretical perspectives on organization and management studies, thereby contributing to a more comprehensive understanding of these fields in the WB6 context.

We recommend conducting further research on the internationalization of SMEs from the region. The anticipated integration of the region into the European Union is expected to encourage companies to expand into multiple markets. Therefore, analyzing the challenges and opportunities associated with internationalization is considered a significant area of focus by the authors.

Additionally, continuous emigration of highly qualified individuals from the Balkans presents significant obstacles to the region's job market and economic growth. Research in this field may quantitatively evaluate the effects of brain drain on innovation, productivity, and economic growth.

Further study subjects could include the influence of diaspora networks in promoting economic growth and enabling knowledge transfer to the region. Investigating the potential of digital nomad policies or possibilities for remote employment to enhance professional retention may prove useful. Ultimately, research on the alignment of educational reforms with labor market needs will reveal ways to more effectively prepare the workforce with the necessary skills in a rapidly evolving global economy.

Mitigating brain drain is essential for maintaining sustained economic development, promoting innovation, and ensuring the region's competitiveness in the international market.

## 6. CONCLUSION

The volume of publications on organizations in the WB6 region has grown significantly over time, highlighting the need for a comprehensive overview of the field. This study analyzes the current state of organizational research in WB6 by examining the most influential authors, journals, countries, and key papers. Additionally, through co-word analysis, we identified five main research clusters (SME, entrepreneurship, Kosovo, innovation, and Serbia), with emerging trends in topics such as marketing, financial performance, entrepreneurship, and organizational culture. These areas have gained increasing attention in the region's academic landscape. The study also offers directions for future research, emphasizing the need for further exploration of these topics to better understand their evolving role in organizational development in WB6.

## 7. LIMITATIONS

This study has certain limitations which must be noted. First, we concentrated our work on only on articles published in English related to WB6, ignoring books and other publication formats. Future research must integrate various type of documents including books to overcome this limitation.

Second, our study is limited by the geopolitical complexities of the region. For instance, the Scopus database does not acknowledge Kosovo as an independent nation and, throughout the period from which we obtained our data, Yugoslavia was still documented as a single country. We recommend that researchers conduct bibliometric studies focusing on specific countries such as Albania and Serbia.

Third, we only utilized the Scopus database because of its extensive coverage of journals and publications. Future research should use additional datasets, such as the Web of Science or Pro-Quest, to expand the analytical reach.

Fourth, the co-word analysis method we employed is highly dependent on the use of specific keywords, which may sometimes carry different meanings and thus may be clustered together inaccurately.

## REFERENCES


Apriliyanti, I. D., & Alon, I. (2017). Bibliometric analysis of absorptive capacity. *International Business Review*, 26(5), 896–907. DOI: 10.1016/j.ibusrev.2017.02.007

Aria, M., & Cuccurullo, C. (2017). bibliometrix: An R-tool for comprehensive science mapping analysis. *Journal of Informetrics*, 11(4), 959–975. DOI: 10.1016/j.joi.2017.08.007

Bağış, M., Altınay, L., Kryeziu, L., Kurutkan, M. N., & Karaca, V. (2024). Institutional and individual determinants of entrepreneurial intentions: Evidence from developing and transition economies. *Review of Managerial Science*, 18(3), 883–912. DOI: 10.1007/s11846-023-00626-z

Barca, M., & Hızıroğlu, M. (2009). 2000'li Yıllarda Türkiye'de Stratejik Yönetim Alanının Entellektüel Yapısı. *Eskişehir Osmangazi Üniversitesi İktisadi ve İdari Bilimler Dergisi*, 4(1), 113–148.

Bartlett, W. (2007). The Western Balkans. In *Varieties of capitalism in post-communist countries* (pp. 201–218). Springer. DOI: 10.1057/9780230627574_11

Bartlett, W. (2009). Economic development in the European super-periphery: Evidence from the Western Balkans. *Economic annals, 54*(181), 21-44.

Belloni, R. (2009). European integration and the Western Balkans: Lessons, prospects and obstacles. *Journal of Balkan & Near Eastern Studies*, 11(3), 313–331. DOI: 10.1080/19448950903152177

Berber, N., Aleksić, M., Slavić, A., & Jelača, M. S. (2022). The relationship between corporate social responsibility and corporate reputation in Serbia. *The Engineering Economist*, 33(3), 232–245. DOI: 10.5755/j01.ee.33.3.29316

Bilir, C., Güngör, C., & Kökalan, Ö. (2020). Operations research/management science research in Europe: A bibliometric overview. *Advances in Operations Research*, 2020, 1–14. DOI: 10.1155/2020/1607637

Block, J., Fisch, C., & Rehan, F. (2020). Religion and entrepreneurship: A map of the field and a bibliometric analysis. *Management Review Quarterly*, 70(4), 591–627. DOI: 10.1007/s11301-019-00177-2

Bretas, V. P., & Alon, I. (2021). Franchising research on emerging markets: Bibliometric and content analyses. *Journal of Business Research*, 133, 51–65. DOI: 10.1016/j.jbusres.2021.04.067

Broadus, R. N. (1987). Toward a definition of "bibliometrics". *Scientometrics*, 12(5-6), 373–379. DOI: 10.1007/BF02016680

Cabrilo, S., & Dahms, S. (2018). How strategic knowledge management drives intellectual capital to superior innovation and market performance. *Journal of Knowledge Management*, 22(3), 621–648. DOI: 10.1108/JKM-07-2017-0309

Castriotta, M., Loi, M., Marku, E., & Moi, L. (2021). Disentangling the corporate entrepreneurship construct: Conceptualizing through co-words. *Scientometrics*, 126(4), 2821–2863. DOI: 10.1007/s11192-020-03846-2

Çera, G., Çera, E., Ribeiro, H. N. R., & Maloku, S. (2021). The role of trust in government and institutional environment in future business climate. *International Journal of Entrepreneurial Venturing*, 13(5), 425–442. DOI: 10.1504/IJEV.2021.119143

Combs, J. G., Ketchen, J., David, J., Crook, T. R., & Roth, P. L. (2011). Assessing cumulative evidence within 'macro'research: Why meta-analysis should be preferred over vote counting. *Journal of Management Studies*, 48(1), 178–197. DOI: 10.1111/j.1467-6486.2009.00899.x

Çopani, D., & Kola, V. (2023). The Impact of Transformational Leadership in Relation to Job Performance in the Aviation Industry of Albania. *Proceedings of the 1st Bengkulu International Conference on Economics, Management, Business and Accounting (BICEMBA 2023)*

Dabić, M., Maley, J., Dana, L.-P., Novak, I., Pellegrini, M. M., & Caputo, A. (2020). Pathways of SME internationalization: A bibliometric and systematic review. [</jrn>]. *Small Business Economics*, 55, 705–725.

Diaz Tautiva, J. A., Rifo Rivera, F. I., Barros Celume, S. A., & Rifo Rivera, S. A. (2024). Mapping the research about organisations in the latin american context: A bibliometric analysis. *Management Review Quarterly*, 74(1), 121–169. DOI: 10.1007/s11301-022-00296-3

Donthu, N., Kumar, S., Mukherjee, D., Pandey, N., & Lim, W. M. (2021). How to conduct a bibliometric analysis: An overview and guidelines. *Journal of Business Research*, 133, 285–296. DOI: 10.1016/j.jbusres.2021.04.070

Drishti, E., Kruja, D., & Curcija, M. (2016). An evaluation of the impact of entrepreneurship education on the entrepreneurship intentions in the Albanian late transition context. In *Routledge Handbook of Entrepreneurship in Developing Economies* (pp. 463–486). Routledge.

Elezaj, S., & Ramaj, V. (2023). The Role of Innovation and Branding on Enterprise Sales Growth in Transition Countries. *Academic Journal of Interdisciplinary Studies, 12.*

Emini, E., Ibraimi, S., & Rexhepi, G. (2023). The role of democratic leadership style and organisational learning in innovations and financial performance of enterprises. *International Journal of Environment. Workplace and Employment*, 7(3), 260–273. DOI: 10.1504/IJEWE.2023.135481

García-Lillo, F., Claver-Cortés, E., Úbeda-García, M., & Marco-Lajara, B. (2017). Exploring the intellectual structure of research on 'born globals' and INVs: A literature review using bibliometric methods. *Journal of International Entrepreneurship*, •••, 1–29.

Guerra Fernandes, J. A., Marques, C. S., Silva, R., & Martins, H. (2022). Ethnic entrepreneurship: A bibliometric review and future research agenda. *Strategic Change*, 31(4), 397–413. DOI: 10.1002/jsc.2516

Hoxhalli, G., Ulaj, G., & Kola, V. (2024). Immigrant Entrepreneurship in Europe: Insights from a Bibliometric Analysis. *International Journal of Management Science and Business Administration, 10*(6), 7-18. https://doi.org/. 2014.106.1001DOI: 10.18775/ijmsba.1849-5664-5419

Ivanović, D., Fu, H.-Z., & Ho, Y.-S. (2015). Publications from Serbia in the Science Citation Index Expanded: A bibliometric analysis. *Scientometrics*, 105(1), 145–160. DOI: 10.1007/s11192-015-1664-9

Jahmurataj, V., Ramadani, V., Bexheti, A., Rexhepi, G., Abazi-Alili, H., & Krasniqi, B. A. (2023). Unveiling the determining factors of family business longevity: Evidence from Kosovo. *Journal of Business Research*, 159, 113745. DOI: 10.1016/j.jbusres.2023.113745

Jamali, D., Samara, G., & Meho, L. I. (2023). Determinants of research productivity and efficiency among the Arab world's accredited business schools. *Management Review Quarterly*, 1-33.

Jano, D. (2023). Mapping Balkan–Southeast European studies. *Southeast European and Black Sea Studies*, 23(4), 801–817. DOI: 10.1080/14683857.2022.2153400

Kajtazi, K., Rexhepi, G., Sharif, A., & Ozturk, I. (2023). Business model innovation and its impact on corporate sustainability. *Journal of Business Research*, 166, 114082. DOI: 10.1016/j.jbusres.2023.114082

Komnenic, B., & Pokrajčić, D. (2012). Intellectual capital and corporate performance of MNCs in Serbia. *Journal of Intellectual Capital*, 13(1), 106–119. DOI: 10.1108/14691931211196231

Kovac, N., Żmija, K., Roy, J. K., Kusa, R., & Duda, J. (2024). Digital divide and digitalization in Europe: A bibliometric analysis. *Equilibrium.Quarterly Journal of Economics and Economic Policy*, 19(2), 463–520. DOI: 10.24136/eq.2899

Kraja, Y. B., & Berberi, A. (2023). Female Entrepreneurs and Motivational Factors. *International Journal of Professional Business Review: Int.J. Prof. Bus. Rev.*, 8(5), 10.

Krasniqi, B. A. (2007). Barriers to entrepreneurship and SME growth in transition: The case of Kosova. *Journal of Developmental Entrepreneurship*, 12(01), 71–94. DOI: 10.1142/S1084946707000563

Kryeziu, L., Bağiş, M., Kurutkan, M. N., Krasniqi, B. A., & Haziri, A. (2022). COVID-19 impact and firm reactions towards crisis: Evidence from a transition economy. *Journal of Entrepreneurship. Management and Innovation*, 18(1), 169–196.

Lepojevic, V., Djordjevic, B., & Ivanovic-Djukic, M. (2018). Mediating effects of career stage on job-related characteristics-job satisfaction relationship. *The Engineering Economist*, 29(2), 215–225.

Lis, A., Bello, K., & Górka, J. (2021). Albania as an object and a context of research in economic sciences: Bibliometric analysis. *Ekonomia i Prawo.Economics and Law*, 20(1), 139–154.

Mahmutaj, L. R., & Krasniqi, B. (2020). Innovation types and sales growth in small firms: Evidence from Kosovo. *South East European Journal of Economics and Business*, 15(1), 27–43. DOI: 10.2478/jeb-2020-0003

Marzi, G., Balzano, M., Caputo, A., & Pellegrini, M. M. (2024). Guidelines for Bibliometric-Systematic Literature Reviews: 10 steps to combine analysis, synthesis and theory development. *International Journal of Management Reviews*.

Mas-Tur, A., Kraus, S., Brandtner, M., Ewert, R., & Kürsten, W. (2020). Advances in management research: A bibliometric overview of the Review of Managerial Science. *Review of Managerial Science*, 14(5), 933–958. DOI: 10.1007/s11846-020-00406-z

Mucha, S. (2020). Ethnic Albanian family businesses and COVID-19 pandemic: A gender-based comparison. *Journal of Family Business Management*, 12(1), 170–182. DOI: 10.1108/JFBM-07-2020-0074

Mukherjee, D., Lim, W. M., Kumar, S., & Donthu, N. (2022). Guidelines for advancing theory and practice through bibliometric research. *Journal of Business Research*, 148, 101–115. DOI: 10.1016/j.jbusres.2022.04.042

Murati-Leka, H. (2023). Kosovo's initial-stage venture capital market: Challenges and perspectives. *International Journal of Entrepreneurship and Small Business*, 50(1), 23–34. DOI: 10.1504/IJESB.2023.10058944

Mustafa, I., Pula-Shiroka, J., Krasniqi, B. A., Ramadani, V., & Kryeziu, L. (2023). Informal Entrepreneurship in Kosovo: An Institutionalist Approach. In *Entrepreneurship Development in the Balkans: Perspective from Diverse Contexts* (pp. 151-169). Emerald Publishing Limited.

Nerur, S. P., Rasheed, A. A., & Natarajan, V. (2008). The intellectual structure of the strategic management field: An author co-citation analysis. *Strategic Management Journal*, 29(3), 319–336. DOI: 10.1002/smj.659

Öztürk, O., Kocaman, R., & Kanbach, D. K. (2024). How to design bibliometric research: An overview and a framework proposal. *Review of Managerial Science*, •••, 1–29.

Paunović, M., Ružičić, M. M., & Moravčević, M. L. (2022). Business process innovations in family firms: Evidence from Serbia. *Journal of Family Business Management*, 13(1), 166–184. DOI: 10.1108/JFBM-03-2022-0044

Popovic, G., Eric, O., & Stanic, S. (2020). Trade openness, institutions and economic growth of the western Balkans countries. *Montenegrin Journal of Economics*, 16(3), 173–184. DOI: 10.14254/1800-5845/2020.16-3.14

Popović-Pantić, S., Semenčenko, D., & Vasilić, N. (2020). Women Entrepreneurship in the Time of COVID-19 Pandemic: The case of Serbia. *Journal of Women's Entrepreneurship & Education*.

Rajković, J., Nikolić, M., Ćoćkalo, D., Stojanović, E. T., & Kovačić, S. (2020). National culture and the entrepreneurial intentions of students in Serbia. *Journal for East European Management Studies*, 25(1), 105–141. DOI: 10.5771/0949-6181-2020-1-105

Ramadani, V., Gërguri, S., Dana, L.-P., & Tašaminova, T. (2013). Women entrepreneurs in the Republic of Macedonia: Waiting for directions. *International Journal of Entrepreneurship and Small Business*, 19(1), 95–121. DOI: 10.1504/IJESB.2013.054330

Ramadani, V., Hisrich, R. D., & Gërguri-Rashiti, S. (2015). Female entrepreneurs in transition economies: Insights from Albania, Macedonia and Kosovo. *World Review of Entrepreneurship, Management and Sustainable Development*, 11(4), 391–413. DOI: 10.1504/WREMSD.2015.072066

Ramadani, V., Rexhepi, G., Gërguri-Rashiti, S., Ibraimi, S., & Dana, L.-P. (2014). Ethnic entrepreneurship in Macedonia: The case of Albanian entrepreneurs. *International Journal of Entrepreneurship and Small Business*, 23(3), 313–335. DOI: 10.1504/IJESB.2014.065525

Ramos-Rodríguez, A. R., & Ruíz-Navarro, J. (2004). Changes in the intellectual structure of strategic management research: A bibliometric study of the Strategic Management Journal, 1980–2000. *Strategic Management Journal*, 25(10), 981–1004. DOI: 10.1002/smj.397

Rashiti, L., Shala, A., & Sopi, X. (2023). Digital Marketing In Retail Banking–Analysis Of Managers' Attitudes. *Business Management*(2 Year 2023), 23-46.

Sanfey, P., & Milatovic, J. (2018). *The Western Balkans in transition: diagnosing the constraints on the path to a sustainable market economy*. European Bank for Reconstruction and Development London.

Tafolli, F., & Grabner-Kräuter, S. (2020). Employee perceptions of corporate social responsibility and organizational corruption: Empirical evidence from Kosovo. *Corporate Governance (Bradford)*, 20(7), 1349–1370. DOI: 10.1108/CG-07-2020-0274

Terek, E., Nikolić, M., Vukonjanski, J., Gligorović, B., & Janković, B. (2015). The impact of media relations on certain organizational and business performances: Serbian case. *Public Relations Review*, 41(3), 370–372. DOI: 10.1016/j.pubrev.2015.04.004

Todorović, M. L., Petrović, D. Č., Mihić, M. M., Obradović, V. L., & Bushuyev, S. D. (2015). Project success analysis framework: A knowledge-based approach in project management. *International Journal of Project Management*, 33(4), 772–783. DOI: 10.1016/j.ijproman.2014.10.009

Toska, A., Ramadani, V., Dana, L.-P., Rexhepi, G., & Zeqiri, J. (2022). Family business successors' motivation and innovation capabilities: The case of Kosovo. *Journal of Family Business Management*, 12(4), 1152–1166. DOI: 10.1108/JFBM-11-2021-0136

Ulaj, G., & Hızıroğlu, M. (2024). THE INTELLECTUAL EVOLUTION OF EARLY INTERNATIONALIZATION: A BIBLIOMETRIC REVIEW OF THE KEY TOPICS AND TRENDS. 19th International Strategic Management Conference, Van Eck, N., & Waltman, L. (2010). Software survey: VOSviewer, a computer program for bibliometric mapping. *Scientometrics*, 84(2), 523–538.

Voza, D., Szewieczek, A., & Grabara, D. (2022). Environmental sustainability in digitalized SMEs: Comparative study from Poland and Serbia. *Serbian Journal of Management*, 17(1), 15–31. DOI: 10.5937/sjm17-36447

Williams, C. C., & Kosta, B. (2020). Evaluating the implications of starting-up unregistered on future firm performance: Evidence a 2019 survey in Albania. *Journal of Developmental Entrepreneurship*, 25(02), 2050010. DOI: 10.1142/S1084946720500107

Yener, M., Doğruoğlu, B., & Ergun, S. (2014). Challenges of Internationalization for SMEs and Overcoming these Challenges: A Case Study from Turkey. *Procedia: Social and Behavioral Sciences*, 150, 2–11. https://doi.org/https://doi.org/10.1016/j.sbspro.2014.09.002. DOI: 10.1016/j.sbspro.2014.09.002

Zupic, I., & Čater, T. (2015). Bibliometric methods in management and organization. *Organizational Research Methods*, 18(3), 429–472. DOI: 10.1177/1094428114562629

# Chapter 15
# Smart Guider on Historical Game Journey:
## Smart Scepter Design With Design Thinking Approach

**Hicran Hanım Halaç**
https://orcid.org/0000-0001-8046-9914
*Eskişehir Technical University, Turkey*

**Mehmet Bilge Kağan Önaçan**
*Istanbul Okan University, Turkey*

**Tolga Önel**
https://orcid.org/0000-0002-3256-8122
*Havelsan, Turkey*

## ABSTRACT

*Transferring cultural heritage to younger generations plays an important role in shaping and guiding the future of societies. In this context, the "Historical Game Journey (HGJ)" project, which is based on Information Technology (IT) infrastructure, was developed to transfer historical knowledge and cultural heritage awareness to young generations through gamification. The aim of this study is to design and develop a smart scepter as a prototype that will help children find targets during the tour within the scope of HGJ's IT infrastructure. Three different designs were prepared using the Design Thinking Approach, and the most suitable one was selected by conducting a survey with the students who will use the scepter. The scepter and the developed IT infrastructure can be utilized, with minor adjustments, in museums, orienteering competitions, tourist areas, and military campuses. Additionally, it is anticipated that the database created by tracking the smart scepter will contribute to smart city applications.*

DOI: 10.4018/979-8-3693-8181-6.ch015

## INTRODUCTION

Culture and cultural heritage are important for individuals' sense of identity, self-esteem, and honor. Elements of cultural heritage play a significant role in the formation and maintenance of both individual and societal identity. Every society from past to present has been blended with cultural, social, economic, and political influences inherited from the previous society. While some societies developed further by utilizing the scientific and technological opportunities provided by the time, some societies declined and ceased to exist. Correctly understanding, analyzing, and transferring the cultural and historical heritage of previous societies is inevitable for the development of the understanding of societies' and the whole world's culture. In Türkiye, the aim is to instill a national consciousness in primary school students that will ensure the preservation and development of culture, based on the fundamental elements that constitute Turkish culture (Gürdoğan-Bayır & Çengelci-Köse, 2019, p. 1830). The report of the Children and Culture Commission of the 3rd National Culture Council (March 3-5, 2017) by the Ministry of Culture and Tourism of the Republic of Türkiye mentions the necessity of teaching cultural heritage to children and emphasizes the importance of gamification in children's learning and family involvement in education (Halaç et al., 2022, p. 336).

Gamification is the application of game mechanics to non-game activities (Kunduracıoğlu, 2018, p. 7) and it improves learning motivation (Özkan & Samur, 2017). In the dictionary of the Turkish Language Association, a game is defined as an entertainment activity with certain rules that develops skills and intelligence and provides enjoyment, while also being an important means of socialization. Children rehearse what they will experience in society through games and toys, and in this way they socialize. Socialized members guarantee the future and continuity of society. It is stated that games and toys have a significant role as a means of deep-rooted communication and interaction for humanity (Vatandaş, 2020, pp. 913-914). Games and toys, which significantly impact children's ability to think, create, and be imaginative, have a very close relationship with culture. Toys represent both the cultural identity and heritage of the communities they belong to. As design elements, toys are always part of cultural continuity and have been shaped by cultural and historical changes within countries (Yusubova & Ural, 2023, p. 2548).

Toys are the tools for children's play and serve as objective stimuli. Due to the inseparable bond between games and toys, toys hold a fundamental position in shaping many games (Vatandaş, 2020, pp. 913-914). A smart toy, on the other hand, is a technologically enhanced physical toy built with a meaningful purpose. Smart toys are cognitive tools designed to meet children's needs, with aims such as increasing motivation and interest, enhancing retention, and developing higher-order thinking skills (Kara & Çağıltay, 2020; Soyupak & Soyupak, 2021).

The Historical Game Journey (HGJ) project (Halaç et al., 2022) supported by TÜBİTAK, involving researchers from various disciplines, and is based on an informatics technology infrastructure aims to increase children's interaction with historical sites alongside their parents within a game-based narrative context and to create awareness while helping them feel the historical texture and learn about cultural heritage in a tangible way. HGJ project can be briefly defined as an informatics technology infrastructure-based project that aims to teach cultural heritage and create awareness about it through gamification.

The abbreviation of the Turkish name for "Historical Game Journey" is "TOY". In ancient Turkish states, "toy" meant a council or assembly, and it also carried the meaning of a festival, celebration, or joyful gathering. Since the aim is to convey elements of Turkish culture to children, and because it is interesting and easy to remember, as well as relevant to the subject in its English meaning, TOY was chosen as the project name

(Halaç & Ayvaz, 2022). From this point onward in the study, the abbreviation TOY will be used to refer to "Historical Game Journey". In the literature, no studies have been found that:

- include children in cultural tourism,
- utilize gamification to raise awareness of cultural heritage,
- establish a technological infrastructure by combining different technologies in this gamification process, and
- collect data to be used in a city information system to identify user needs in specific areas along the travel route and provide suggestions for the functional transformation of the area. In this context, the motivation of the TOY project is to fill a significant gap both in the literature and in practice.

The project design is centered around smart scepters developed within the scope of this study, kiosks temporarily positioned in historical areas called Information and Communication Station (The abbreviation of the Turkish name for "Information and Communication Station" is "BILIG". In its literal meaning, "bilig" refers to wisdom or knowledge. In this study, the abbreviation BILIG is used to refer to "Information and Communication Station".) (Halaç & Ayvaz, 2022), information cards that children can obtain from the BILIG, and story-themed picture albums which are given to the children at the end of the tour. The child participating in TOY receives a smart scepter and an information card at the beginning of the tour. The information card contains clues about the target BILIG that the child needs to reach. While the child tries to reach the BILIG with the help of this clue, the smart scepter exchanges information with the BILIGs via RFID signals. As the child approaches the target BILIG, the number of LEDs lit on the scepter and the sound of the buzzer increase; as the child moves away, the number of LEDs and the sound decrease. In this way, the smart scepter helps the child find the target BILIG. When the child reaches the BILIG and touches it with his/her scepter, the BILIG provides information about the historical building, takes a picture of the child with the historical building in the background, and gives the child an information card. This information card contains details about the historical building, a traditional game to be played during the tour to next BILIG, and a map to reach the next target BILIG. Thus, by using gamification, it is aimed for the child to be more interested while traveling in the historical texture, to have fun while traveling, to learn while having fun, to make contact while learning, to ensure that the learned information is permanent, and for the child and the parent to spend quality time together.

Within the scope of the TOY project, it is envisaged that the child will carry a scepter in his/her hand during the tour. The words cane and scepter are often used interchangeably. However, the scepter is a straight support stick; it can be held from any part. The cane, on the other hand, has a handle to be held; the user is forced to hold it by the handle (Ekinci, 2022). In the administrative traditions of nations or states, the scepter has been seen as a symbol of power or a sign of dominance. In various religions and cultures, in all esoteric traditions, it has been considered a symbol of power, authority and/or religious-magical power (Dindi, 2021, pp. 108-110). In the past, much like soldiers carried swords, courtiers would carry ornate scepters during ceremonies. Viziers, beys, and pashas did not walk around without a staff. In the Ottoman Empire, until the Tanzimat period, scepters were primarily used by elderly men and women. However, during Sultan Abdul Hamid's reign, the scepter became more than just a support tool; it became a status symbol that distinguished the elite from commoners. Holding a scepter came to represent elegance and refinement. In ancient times, high-ranking individuals always carried a scepter, symbolizing rank and authority. So much so that mythological heroes and deities were often depicted holding a staff (Ekinci, 2022).

For the reasons listed below, it was decided that the scepter would be the object that ensures the child's communication and relationship with cultural heritage (places, artifacts, etc.) and that the child would carry it with interest until the end of TOY (Halaç & Ayvaz, 2022, pp. 331-332):

- Children tend to pick up and carry sticks they find while walking for reasons such as feeling more stable with a third leg, creating a sense of security by keeping a distance from what they discover, protecting themselves against potential dangers, and reaching the things that they cannot otherwise touch.
- A survey conducted with children found that 76% of them picked up and played with sticks they found in the places they visited.
- The stick figure is commonly used in traditional children's games.
- In mythology, theology, and history, a stick/scepter symbolizes support, power, and strength and is used by important figures.

The motivation for this study is the need to design a completely original smart scepter within the scope of the TOY project, one that would both attract children's interest and be enjoyable for them to carry, while also fulfilling the specified functions. The aim of this study is to design and prototype the aforementioned scepter. In this context, smart scepter alternatives were designed based on "radio frequency identification (RFID)", "near field communication (NFC)", and NodeMCU Technologies using the Design Thinking Approach. Prototypes were produced using a 3D printer, and the most suitable one for the project was selected through surveys conducted with the students who would use the scepter during the TOY tour.

In the subsequent sections of the study, the technologies used in the development of the scepter, the Design Thinking Approach, alternative scepter designs, the selection and prototyping of the suitable alternative, and the field application are discussed. The study is completed with a conclusion section that includes general evaluations and future studies.

## TECHNOLOGIES USED IN THE DESIGNED PRODUCT

Within the scope of this study, it was planned to produce the prototype of the smart scepter using Radio Frequency Identification (RFID), Near Field Communication (NFC), and NodeMCU technologies, and manufacture it using a 3D printer. The technologies to be used in the production of the smart scepter are briefly explained below.

### RFID Technology

Radio Frequency Identification (RFID) is a technology used to identify different objects individually and autonomously using radio frequency. The components of RFID are the reader, tag, and antenna. Readers receive information from the tags in the form of digital codes using radio waves. Tags store information and consist of an antenna and a microchip that hold the information. Antennas are used for communication between the tag and the reader. The communication between the reader antenna and the tag antenna is called coupling, which occurs in two ways: magnetic coupling and electromagnetic coupling. RFID tags are classified as shown in Figure 1 (Maraşlı & Çıbuk, 2015, pp. 250-254):

*Figure 1. Classification of RFID tags*

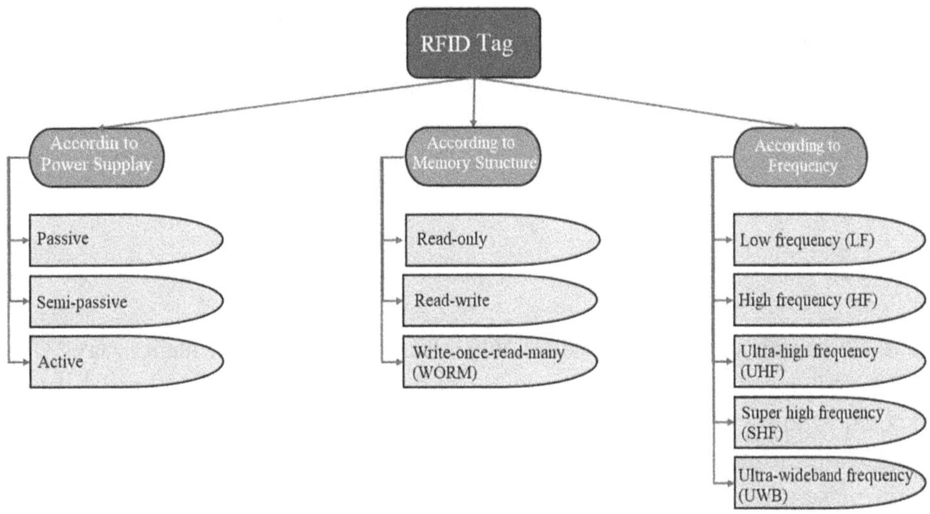


RFID tags are grouped as passive, semi-passive, and active according to their power supply. Passive tags do not have their own power source. They use power from the reader to energize the microchip and transmit data back to the reader and are inexpensive. Semi-passive tags have a small battery that helps power the microchip. They have a wider reading range, are more reliable, and offer faster response performance compared to passive tags. High-cost and high-performance active tags use their own power source to generate a response signal. They can transmit signals over longer distances (RFID Etiketler, n.d.; Maraşlı & Çıbuk, 2015).

RFID tags are also grouped according to memory structure as read-only, read-write, and write-once-read-many (WORM). Read-only tags are programmed with random IDs during manufacturing and cannot be changed afterward. These tags have limited storage capacity, low cost, and are generally of the passive type. Read-write tags can be read and written by the reader, have a memory capacity of 32-128 KB, are more expensive, and can be either active or passive. Write-once-read-many tags are programmed during production according to customer requirements, cannot be changed afterward, and have a memory capacity ranging from 128 bits to 1 KB (Maraşlı & Çıbuk, 2015, pp. 255-256; Yenigün et al., 2020, pp. 1599-1600).

RFID tags are grouped by frequency into low frequency (LF), high frequency (HF), ultra-high frequency (UHF), super high frequency (SHF), and ultra-wideband frequency (UWB). Low-frequency tags operate in the 120-140 kHz frequency range, have a reading distance of 1 cm to 2 meters, low data reading rates, and can operate at close range in challenging environments such as metal and liquid. High-frequency tags operate at 13.56 MHz, can be read between 20 cm and 1 meter, offer higher data reading rates compared to LF tags, but cannot be used in applications requiring high security. Ultra-high frequency tags operate in the 860-928 MHz frequency range and can be read from distances between 60 cm and 12 meters. Super high frequency tags operate at 2.45 GHz or 5.8 GHz, can be read up to 30 meters, have higher reading rates than UHF tags, and consume more energy. Ultra-wideband frequency tags operate in the 3.1-10.6 GHz frequency range, can send low-power signals over a wide band, have a reading distance of up to 200 meters, and are not affected by environmental conditions in precise readings (Maraşlı & Çıbuk, 2015, pp. 256-257; Yenigün et al., 2020, p. 1600). Wi-Fi-based RFID tags operate at a frequency of 2.4 GHz and have a range of around 250 meters in open areas.

Choosing the right tag in RFID applications is important. Appropriate selection is made by answering questions such as: "What is the surface to be tagged (metal, plastic, wood, etc.)?", "What should the reading distance be?", "What should the tag size be?", "In what environmental conditions (extreme heat, cold, humidity, indoors, outdoors, etc.) will it be used?", "How will the tag be attached (by sticking, riveting, etc.)?" (Yenigün et al., 2020, p. 1600), "What is the required amount of data?", and "Is there a need to rewrite the tag during the application?"

## NFC Technology

"Near Field Communication (NFC)", commonly referred to as NFC, is a technology that was initially developed and introduced by Sony and Philips. NFC was developed as a standard through the collaboration of Sony and NXP, aimed at using existing contactless technology in mobile devices and other electronic devices such as TVs, computers, refrigerators, etc. Contrary to popular belief, NFC is not a technology or product, but the name given to a standard (Webrazzi, 2011). Although NFC is technically a standard for near-field communication as defined by international protocols, the term "NFC Technology" is widely used in industry and literature to refer to the hardware, software, and applications that implement and utilize this standard. NFC is an emerging technology that builds upon RFID by incorporating an interface and protocol derived from RFID. This enables NFC devices to be part of the existing RFID ecosystem, ensuring compatibility with current RFID systems and standards (Motlagh, 2012, p. 10).

NFC is a short-range wireless communication technology based on RFID that allows easy, simple, and secure communication between two electronic devices. NFC technology provides data communication over a secure interface at low bandwidth (up to 424Kbit/s) and high frequency (13.56 MHz). Communication occurs when two NFC-compatible devices come into close proximity, typically 0-4 cm, offering significant security advantages. NFC technology supports data communication in three different operating modes: reader/writer mode, card emulation mode, and peer-to-peer mode. It is generally seen that smart environment applications operate in reader/writer mode, smart wallet applications in card emulation mode, and data exchange applications in peer-to-peer mode (Özdenizci et al., 2016). The differences in distance and data rate between NFC (which enables information sharing by establishing contactless, wireless communication between devices in close proximity to each other) and other existing wireless technologies are shown in Figure 2 (Motlagh, 2012, p. 11).

*Figure 2. The differences in distance and data rate between NFC and other existing wireless technologies (Motlagh, 2012, p. 11; Mobile Knowledge, 2016)*

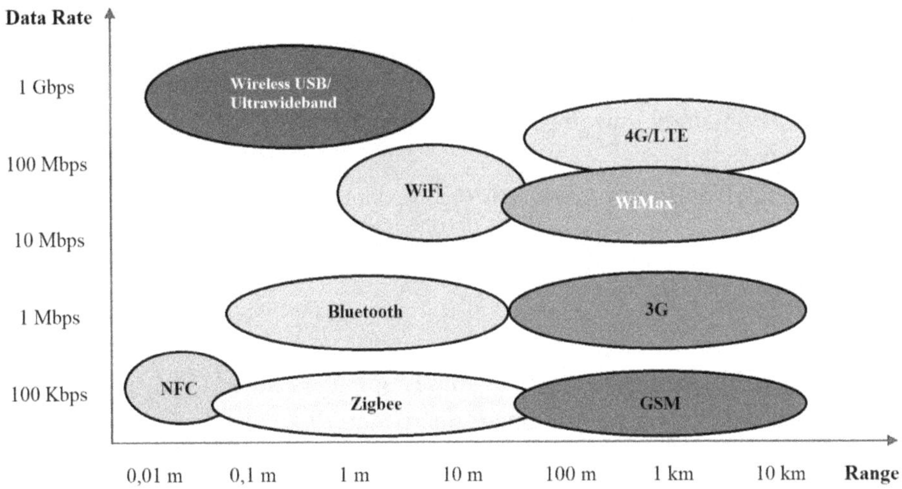


Due to its versatility, extremely small size, low cost and its presence in almost every smartphone produced today, NFC can be used in a wide variety of applications and devices. NFC is a contactless, secure wireless technology that connects people to the things around them. As opportunities for NFC technology continue to expand, some of the popular use cases currently available can be listed as follows ("Use cases", n.d.):

- **Access Control:** Systems for controlling access provide a secure and efficient way to manage entry to buildings, rooms, or restricted areas.
- **Automotive:** NFC technology is key in car access and ignition systems, allowing solutions that revolve around smartphones.
- **Customer Engagement:** NFC connects consumers to relevant information at the right moment, enabling interactions with brands, delivering offers and rewards, facilitating one-tap payments, and more.
- **Healthcare:** NFC in healthcare gives providers, caregivers, and patients access to essential information, improving safety and care quality by tracking supplies, medications, and other essentials.
- **Hospitality:** NFC technology allows seamless connections between guests and properties, offering keyless room access, contactless payments, and innovative experiences using smartphones, wearables, and affordable tags in a post-COVID world where travelers expect convenience.
- **Identity:** NFC plays a role in any place that requires identification and authorization, such as COVID vaccine passports, mobile driver's licenses, digital currencies, government IDs, and medical records.
- **IoT:** The Internet of Things (IoT) promises a future in which physical objects of all kinds—from household systems to health monitors—can collect and exchange data.
- **Mobility:** With NFC, a tap is all you need to start your journey anywhere. NFC technology has seamlessly improved MaaS (Mobility as a Service) and is transforming how you travel.

- **Payment:** Every day, millions of people use phones, watches, or wearables with NFC to pay for things as if using a wallet.
- **Retail:** The combination of commonly available NFC-enabled smartphones and versatile, easy-to-use NFC tags gives retailers a powerful tool to engage consumers with brands and increase conversions.
- **Transit:** Some of the world's busiest transit authorities have standardized on NFC technologies.
- **Wearables:** As a miniature, low-power, affordable technology, NFC tags and chips can find their way into almost everything.
- **Wireless Charging:** Transmitting power as well as data, the NFC Wireless Charging Specification currently supports induction charging up to 1W over a distance of up to 2cm.

## NodeMCU

Microcontrollers (MCU) can be thought of as small computers added to any physical object or space to give it “intelligence”. By being programmed, microcontrollers are devices that allow the control, management, and data collection of machines, either remotely or via direct connection. They contain a memory unit, a processor, and input/output units. In order to determine which MCU will work best with an application, it is important to know some of the following basic features of MCUs and what they do (Başçiftçi & Gündüz, 2019, pp. 63-64):

- **Bits:** Microcontrollers are usually categorized by the number of bits they offer, which affects how quickly they can perform calculations.
- **RAM:** RAM is fast-access memory that does not retain data when not powered. All MCUs come with some amount of RAM that allows actions to be performed quickly. The larger the capacity, the better, but additional RAM increases the cost of the MCU.
- **Flash:** Flash is computer memory that retains data when not powered and is very useful for features like offline storage.
- **GPIO:** GPIO stands for general-purpose input/output pins. These are the pins used to connect sensors and actuators to the MCU and to the internet. The number of pins can range from a few to hundreds, depending on the microcontroller.
- **Connectivity:** This refers to how the board (and application) connects to a network or the internet, via Wi-Fi, Ethernet, or another method.
- **Power Consumption:** Power consumption is critical for connected device applications, especially when the device must rely on a limited power source such as batteries or solar power.
- **Development Tools and Community:** It is important that the programs running on the chosen MCU have access to a mature set of tools, documentation, and community support to help create extensible projects.

NodeMCU is one of many prototyping and electronic development boards, such as Arduino and Raspberry Pi. NodeMCU is an open-source, easily programmable, low-cost, low-power consumption circuit board with dimensions of 48.4 x 25.5 mm, featuring an ESP8266 module. The ESP8266 Wi-Fi module enables easy connection to the internet (Sevinç, n.d.; Taşçıoğlu, 2021). NodeMCU comes with a built in USB connector. With a micro-USB cable, it can be connected NodeMCU devkit to one laptop and it can be flashed without any trouble. NodeMCU can be programmed in both LUA and Arduino languages so it can be used with development boards like Arduino or programmed directly using its onboard processor. It supports sending messages via the Message Queuing Telemetry Transport (MQTT) protocol and consumes low energy. The NodeMCU features 17 digital input/output pins and a reset button (Tekbaş, 2019, p. 35). An example of NodeMCU is presented in Figure 3.

*Figure 3. NodeMCU top view ("NODEMCU ESP 8266", n.d.)*

## Three-Dimensional (3D) Printer

A three-dimensional (3D) printer is a special printer that uses technology to transform a 3D model, drawn by the user on a computer, into a physical object by first converting it into an appropriate format and then sending it to the printer. A 3D printer creates products and parts layer by layer from the bottom up (Akbaba & Akbulut, 2021, p. 22). The method is based on adding material layer upon layer, which is why it is also called "additive manufacturing". In a part produced using additive manufacturing, up to 90% of raw material savings can be achieved compared to traditional methods like machining, casting, welding, and other conventional manufacturing techniques (Karagöz et al., 2021, p. 1187). Although the basic manufacturing techniques are the same, additive manufacturing methods are named according to the raw material used and the principle of layer bonding, such as Three-Dimensional Printing (3DP), Fused Deposition Modeling (FDM), Stereolithography (SLA), Laminated Object Manufacturing (LOM), Selective Laser Sintering (SLS)/Selective Laser Melting (SLM). These methods use liquid resin, polymers, polymer powders, and metal powders in the production of new products (Özsoy, 2019, p. 113).

The manufacturing process is divided into stages conducted by three different units: Computer-Aided Design (CAD), 3D printing software, and 3D printing machine. In the CAD unit, the model is drawn and converted to the ".STL" file format. In the 3D printing software unit, tasks such as ".STL" file repair, part positioning and placement, creating support structures for part manufacturing, slicing the model, determining processing parameters, and creating tool paths are performed. In the 3D printing machine unit, parts are manufactured. The manufacturing process starts with the design of a model in CAD software and ends with the production of the model in the machine (Özsoy, 2019, p. 113). To give the product its final shape, additional post-processing steps can be applied after manufacturing, depending on the 3D printing technology and material used, or based on the desired product characteristics (such as coloring, polishing, strength enhancement, surface smoothing, stress relief, etc.) (Karagöz et al., 2021, p. 1187).

In current 3D printing technologies, production is limited by the printing area. In this case, large-scale 3D printers are needed to produce very large parts in a single piece. However, it is possible to produce large parts using 3D printers with smaller print capacities (Cahoon, 2016). This method is based on the principle of producing large parts in smaller sections and then assembling them. These smaller parts, which will form the whole, are fixed together by interlocking or using intermediary parts (pins) and glued together (Köbeloğlu & Çetinkaya, 2019, p. 12).

3D printers are used in many areas of daily life. They are applied in a wide range of fields, including aviation, marine, automotive, medical applications, mold making, nano-composite production, the energy sector, film sector, the food industry, biomaterials and tissue engineering, reverse engineering, construction, textiles, education, art, and hobby applications (Karagöz et al., 2021, p. 1187; Köbeloğlu and Çetinkaya, 2019, p. 11; Sürmen, 2019, pp. 384-386).

## SMART SCEPTER DESIGN AND DEVELOPMENT

During the development phase of the smart scepter, meetings were held with a project team consisting of 1 project manager, 6 researchers, and 8 scholarship holders. Using the brainstorming method, the question "How can we produce a smart scepter that will visually attract the child's interest and functionally meet the needs?" was explored. For this purpose, Hwa et al.'s (2017, p. V) SCOPES approach was utilized to properly structure and frame the problem. SCOPES stands for the first letters of the English terms: Situation and/or Problem, Constraints, Objectives and Outcomes, People, Estimates, and Scopes. The framework drawn within the scope of SCOPES is presented in Table 1.

*Table 1. SCOPES evaluations*

| | | |
|---|---|---|
| S | SITUATION AND/OR PROBLEM | *"What is the SITUATION or PROBLEM that you are trying to address?"*<br>There is a need for an original scepter that will communicate with the BILIGs developed within the completely unique and original TOY project, and that the child can carry with interest throughout the entire tour. |
| C | CONSTRAINTS | *"What are the CONSTRAINTS when trying to address the situation or problem?"*<br>The constraints for the smart scepter have been determined as follows:<br>• It should have an attractive and different model.<br>• It should have lights to capture the child's interest and guide the child to the target through these lights.<br>• It should have an audio alert to guide the child to the target.<br>• It should pair with/assigned to the child and allow the BILIG to recognize the child.<br>• It should be resistant to impacts and falls.<br>• It should not be harmful to health.<br>• It should be able to communicate with the BILIGs within 150 meters.<br>• It should work for at least 2 hours (the maximum duration of the tour).<br>• It should be easy and quick to produce.<br>• The body should contain all components within it.<br>• It should weigh less than 500 grams so that it can be easily carried by the child.<br>• Its price should be under 20 USD as planned within the project. |
| O | OBJECTIVES AND OUTCOMES | *"What are the OBJECTIVES and intended OUTCOME of this design challenge?"*<br>The aim is to develop a smart scepter that the child will carry with interest, operate throughout the entire tour, maintain continuous communication with BILIG, and assist the child in finding new targets. The smart scepter in question aims to keep the child active, interested, and learning while having fun during the tour. |
| P | PEOPLE | *"Who are the PEOPLE that you are trying to help? Whose problem are you trying to address?"*<br>The smart scepter to be produced should appeal to primary school 3rd and 4th grade students who will participate in TOY. |
| E | ESTIMATES | *"What are the ESTIMATED resources required for this design challenge?"*<br>Skilled team members capable of developing the smart scepter both in software and hardware aspects, and hardware components that can be cost-effectively sourced from the market are considered potential resources for this research. Additionally, undergraduate, graduate, and doctoral students who can work within the scope of course projects are also considered to be utilized for this research. |
| S | SCOPE | *"Is there ample SCOPE to explore multiple alternatives to address the problem?"*<br>There is the possibility of producing multiple alternative products and being able to choose among them. |
| DESIGN CHALLENGE | | *"Frame the problem statement into 'How Might We...?'"*<br>How might we produce a smart scepter that will visually capture a child's interest and functionally meet the needs of the project? |

In order to design the smart scepter alternatives "Design Thinking Approach" was used. Design can be defined as an intentional process carried out to solve problems, meet needs, transform less desirable situations into preferred ones by improving conditions, or create new and useful things. Design Thinking Approach is intertwined with vague yet natural concepts such as emotions, needs, motivations, and behavioral factors. It carries certain characteristics of both art and science. Research into the ambiguous elements of the problem is determined through rational and analytical investigations. Scientific methods are used to analyze how users interact with products and to determine how the products function. In this way, users' needs are researched, previous solution experiences are examined, existing and potential future conditions specific to the product are considered, problem-related parameters are tested, and practical applications of alternative solutions are evaluated. Once a range of potential solutions is found, the final selection is determined through rational methods (Açık, 2024, pp. 162-163). Design Thinking represents the creative strategies that designers use during the design process. It can also be employed as an approach to address and solve problems more broadly than in professional design practice, and has been applied in business, social issues and product development (Parlar et al., 2017; Mutlu et al., 2014).

Within Design Thinking, a significant part of the problem-solving process involves the ability to synthesize knowledge from various sources. Therefore, Design Thinking has a multidisciplinary character. The Design Thinking Approach consists of five stages: empathize, define, ideate, prototype, and test (Wolniak, 2017, pp. 249-252). In this context, in the **"empathize" stage**, needs were identified, existing products in the market that could meet those needs were researched, similar products were compared, children—especially those in the area where the application would be done—were observed and their opinions were gathered from time to time, and brainstorming sessions were conducted. By temporarily adopting the user role, efforts were made to understand the needs, desires, emotions, and thoughts of the children who would use the designed product. Models of scepters used in ancient times, which supported and guided their users' every movement and symbolized power, were taken as examples. In the **"define" stage**, the smart scepter to be used in TOY was defined. In short, the smart scepter is a smart tool that the child can carry in his/her hand without getting bored during TOY, that will attract the child's attention and that can communicate with BİLIGs. In the **"ideate" stage**, assumptions were put forward for ideas that would create innovative solutions, and these assumptions were challenged. In this stage, the expected features of the product were revealed, and the design limits and constraints were determined. Alternative smart scepter designs that could answer the research question were created. Before moving on to the prototyping phase, the components of the smart scepter and the technologies to be used were determined, the details of which will be presented below. In this context, three different smart scepter designs that serve the same function but have different designs were developed, the details of which are presented in the following sections. In the **"prototype" stage**, prototypes of three different scepter designs were produced with the help of a 3D printer. In the **"test" stage**, the three alternative scepters whose prototypes were produced were tested according to the determined evaluation criteria. A survey was conducted with children to determine the most suitable alternative. According to the test and survey results, the three alternatives were compared, and the most suitable smart scepter was selected.

## Components of the Smart Scepter

The primary components of the smart scepter are planned as RFID tag, NFC tag, electronic hardware, software code, and the scepter body. The hardware for the smart scepter was selected by evaluating the alternatives currently available on the market according to criteria such as cost effectiveness, easy accessibility, functionality, widespread application, and the ability to meet the needs. Three different designs of the scepter body were created, and prototypes were produced using a 3D printer.

### RFID and NFC Tags

During the tour in the area, the smart scepter needs to communicate with BILIGs, and the scepter ID needs to be transmitted to BILIG. A Wi-Fi-based RFID tag was used for this purpose. Additionally, it is necessary to detect when the target point is reached and when the scepter touches BILIG, and to address the relevant person by name and take a photo in case more than one person reaches BILIG at the same time. To ensure this, an NFC tag with a 13.56 MHz frequency and a range of 0-4 cm was used.

## Electronic Hardware of the Smart Scepter

The smart scepter measures its distance to the wireless access point located in BILIG using the Radio Frequency (RF) signal strength up to 150 meters away in a semi-open area surrounded by historical buildings where the application is made and transmits its own ID information to the raspberry pi in BILIG via RF. As the scepter approaches BILIG, the RF signal strength increases, causing more LEDs on the scepter to light up and the buzzer to sound more frequently. When the scepter is 0-4 cm away from BILIG, a beep sound is emitted. The electronic hardware of the smart scepter given to the child by the central BILIG operator includes the pieces listed below as shown in Figure 4C:

1. Five LEDs and their resistors that will light up more as the child approaches the historical building, he/she needs to visit (Figure 4A).
2. One buzzer and its resistor to provide an audible warning as the child approaches the historical building (Figure 4A).
3. One shift register to allow the NodeMCU to control the LEDs (Figure 4A).
4. One voltage regulator to reduce the voltage from four AAA batteries to 3.3V, the operating voltage of the NodeMCU and other circuit elements (Figure 4A).
5. One on/off switch for the scepter (Figure 4A).
6. One NodeMCU (Figure 4B) for scepter control and RF communication are integrated as in Figure 4C.

*Figure 4. Electronic hardware of smart scepter*

*LEDs, buzzer, on-off switch, shift register, voltage regulator, and resistors* | *NodeMCU* | *Together with the battery case, all the electronic hardware of the smart scepter*

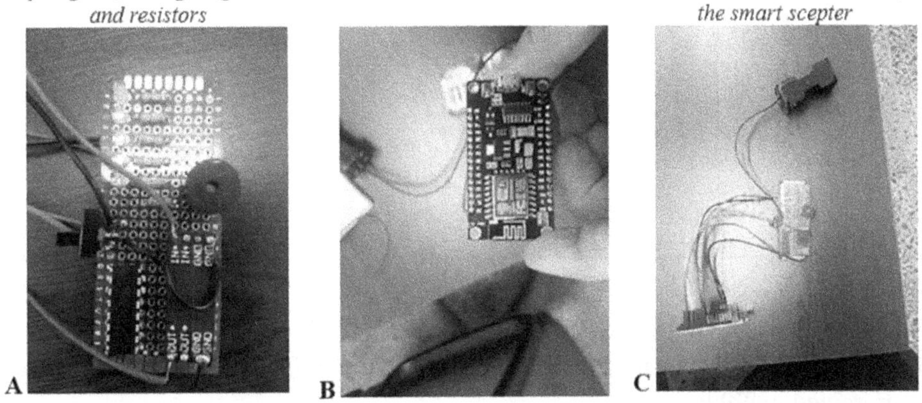

Electronic hardware was initially assembled on a breadboard to form the circuit. The NodeMCU, shift register, RFID reader, LEDs, buzzer, and batteries were appropriately connected. After securing the hardware connections, the coding process commenced.

## Software Code of the Smart Scepter

In the central BILIG software, the sequence of historical buildings to be visited by the child with the scepter is established by the central operator, and the child's name and surname are recorded. The scepter has two modes: Active and passive. In active mode, when the "Send" button is pressed, the software running on the NodeMCU on the scepter saves the station number to be visited in its dynamic memory as received from the central BILIG software. After the scepter reaches the target BILIG, the central BILIG sends the scepter its new target. Throughout the tour, the scepter follows the station number sent by the central BILIG and updates the target BILIG number with each transmission. The scepter software sends a heartbeat message every 15 seconds via the wireless network to inform the central BILIG software that it is active and functional. In passive mode, the sequence of stations to be visited, or the route, is loaded onto the scepter from the central BILIG on the participant's side. In this case, the scepter does not need to communicate with the central BILIG. The scepter guides the participant according to the signal received from the target station, following the predetermined route.

The software on the NodeMCU continuously monitors the signal strength of the wireless network service set identifier (SSID) of the station which the child with the scepter should visit. When the signal strength exceeds -90 dB (approximately 150 meters between the scepter and BILIG), one LED lights up; -80 dB (approximately 120 meters), two LEDs light up; -70 dB (approximately 90 meters), three LEDs light up; -60 dB (approximately 60 meters), four LEDs light up; and -50 dB (approximately 30 meters), five LEDs light up. When the signal strength exceeds -45 dB (approximately 10 meters between the scepter and BILIG), the buzzer starts to sound.

If the RFID/NFC tag on the scepter is brought within 2 cm of the RFID/NFC card reader in the BILIG, the station number in the dynamic memory is updated to the next station, and the buzzer sound stops. The NodeMCU board was programmed using the Arduino IDE interface. The pseudocode used in the scepter is presented below in Table 2.

*Table 2. Pseudocode running on the smart scepter*

```
loop
Search for nearby BILIGs
Connect to the BILIG with the highest signal strength
If the target station has not been received, obtain the target station from the connected BILIG
Control the LEDs and buzzer according to the signal strength received from the target BILIG station
If the target station is approached within less than 2 cm, obtain the next target station
endloop
```

The RFID/NFC reader system that will be included in BILIG so that the RFID tag and NFC tag information on the scepter can be read by BILIG is presented in Figure 5 and the pseudocode running in BILIG is presented in Table 3.

*Figure 5. RFID/NFC reader system*

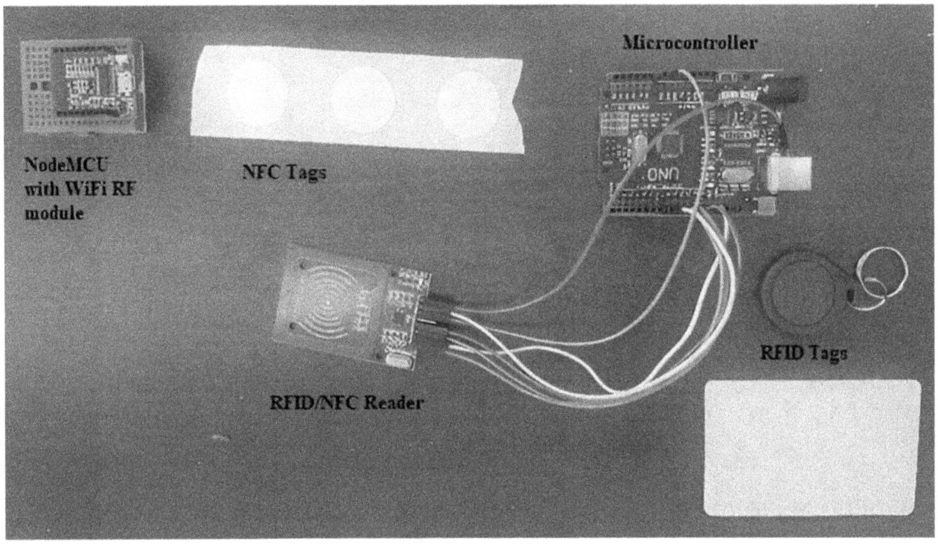


*Table 3. Pseudocode running on BILIG for reading RFID/NFC tag information*

```
loop
Get the ID information of the approaching new tag
If the approaching tag ID matches the expected tag ID for the station
Start the information flow
endloop
```

## Body of the Smart Scepter

The design of the smart scepter, which is one of the basic components of TOY and will keep the child in the game and attract their attention, is important. Because children attach special importance to toys; they see them as part of their games and an important tool for their own activities. They want to play with toys that interest them. For this reason, the shape and quality of the toy are important (Vatandaş, 2020, p. 919). The smart scepter to be used in TOY will guide the child to find the new target throughout the tour, interact with BILIG, and allow the child to take pictures with the historical building and get the information card containing the clue for the next target. For this reason, the smart scepter must have an attractive design that the child will not let go of throughout the tour.

In designing the smart scepter, designs were created in accordance with the framework drawn in SCOPES, as detailed above. Although initially, it was considered to produce the scepter from silicone and wood, it was decided to use a 3D printer with filament due to its practicality and speed. It was evaluated that the child's continuous interaction with the scepter could be ensured using colorful LEDs that light up one by one as the target is approached and a buzzer that increases its sound. In line with the determined framework and prominent views, initial sketch studies presented in Figure 6 were conducted.

*Figure 6. Sketch studies related to the scepter models*

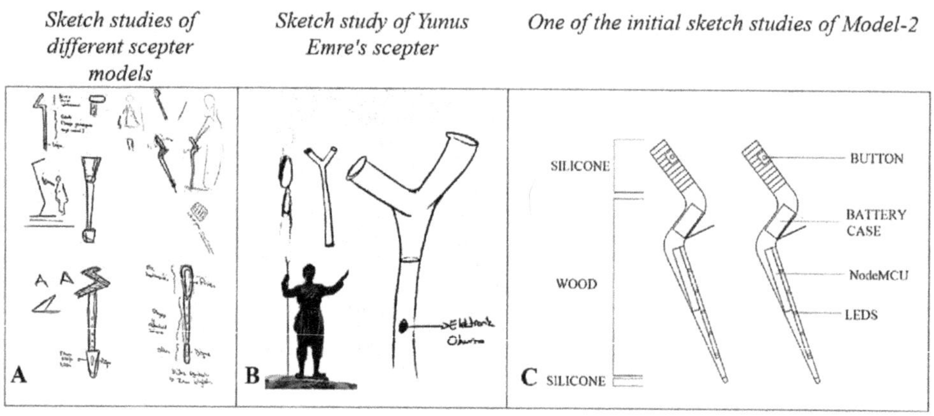


As a result of the brainstorming sessions and the proposed solutions, three alternative designs were produced. 3D drawings of the designs were made using AutoDesk Fusion 360 and SolidWorks programs and outputs were taken from the 3D printer. The outer wall of the scepter obtained in the digital environment was divided into suitable parts for the 3D printer and simple mechanical locking mechanisms were designed. Suitable element fixing slots were designed for the NodeMCU, battery case, shift register and buzzer belonging to the electronic hardware. Slots were opened on the scepters for the LEDs that light up according to the intensity of the SSID signal it receives and are planned to direct the user to BILIG. In addition, an NFC slot was designed at the end of the scepters for the NFC tag. The shapes, dimensions, and 3D printer outputs of the three alternative scepters are presented in Figure 7.

*Figure 7. The shapes, dimensions, and 3D printer outputs of the three alternative scepters*

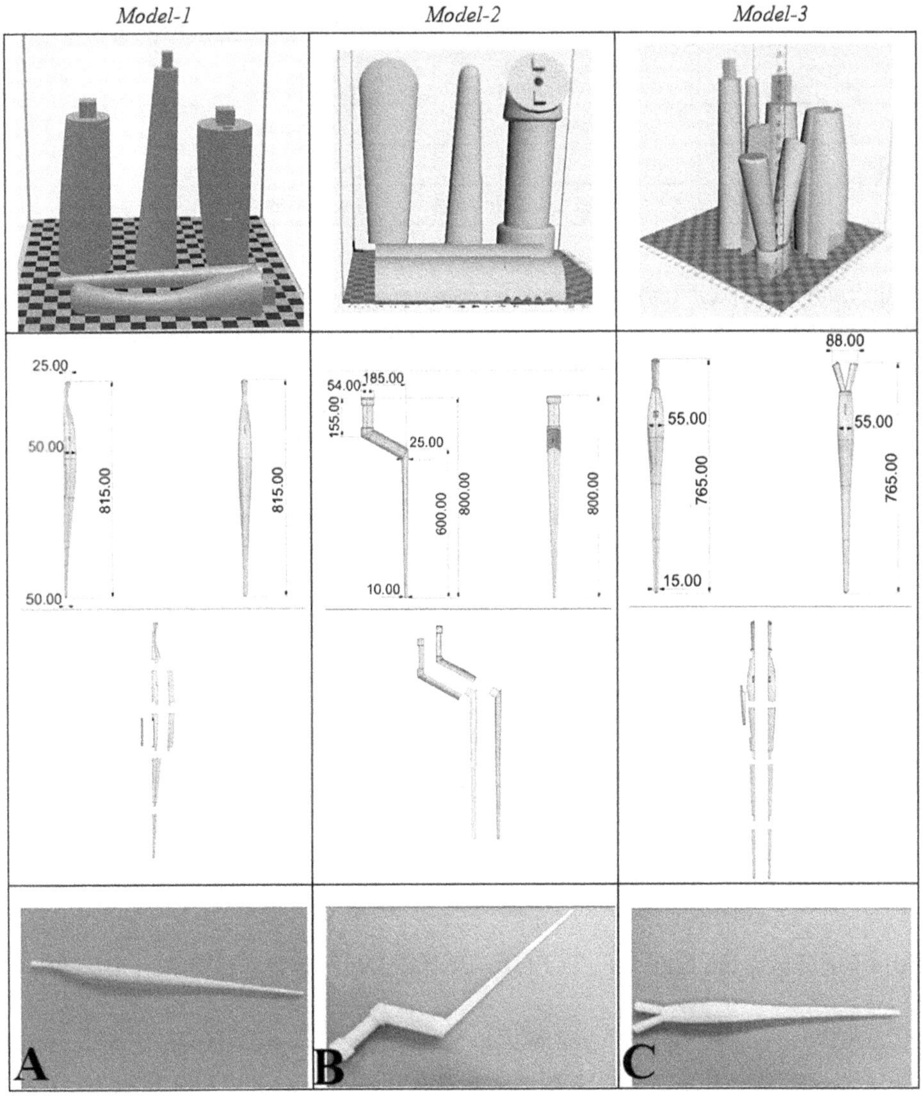


Information about the three alternative scepter models such as production times, the amount of filament used, weights and cost are presented in Table 4.

*Table 4. Information about the three alternative scepter models*

| Details | Model-1 | Model-2 | Model-3 |
|---|---|---|---|
| Production Time | 1 day 8h 1m 37s | 1 day 6h 07m 53s | 1 day 7h 02m 58s |
| Filament Consumption | ~ 115,06 meters/<br>~ 334,86 grams | ~ 107,38 meters/<br>~ 312,53 grams | ~ 109,94 meters/<br>~ 319,97 grams |
| Total Weight | ~ 365 grams | ~ 343 grams | ~ 350 grams |
| Flament Cost (USD) | ~ 3,81 | ~ 3,59 | ~ 3,65 |
| Total Cost (USD) | ~ 10,31 | ~ 10,09 | ~ 10,15 |

The three alternative scepters for which prototypes were produced were designed differently from each other. Scepter model-3 is inspired by Yunus Emre's scepter. Yunus Emre (born c. 1238, Turkey—died c. 1320, Turkey) is a poet and mystic who left a strong impact on Turkish literature ("Yunus Emre", n.d.). All parts of each scepter are manufactured to be easily assembled. Parts have been prepared for all equipment that will be included in the scepter. The handle part has been thinned and shaped to make it easier for the child to hold it.

During the testing phase, all three alternatives were tested for ease of use and functionality. The electronic hardware is the same in all three alternatives. After the short circuit tests of the electronic hardware, the reading success for the NFC and RFID tags was tested, and the average successful reading distances were determined. It was successfully observed that the number of LEDs lit, and the sound of the buzzer increased and decreased by increasing and decreasing the distance to the receiver in the BILIG. Mechanical force and strength tests were applied to the outputs produced via the 3D printer. During the tests, the target age group of the project was considered to determine ergonomic suitability, and the target age group was allowed to test the prototype to collect their opinions. At the end of the test studies, improvements and enhancements were made to the selected alternative model to be used in the application.

## SELECTION OF THE SCEPTER TO BE USED DURING THE APPLICATION

The selection of the scepter that children will use within the scope of the TOY project from the three prototypes that were tested is important because this smart scepter has an important role in TOY. For this reason, it is necessary to choose a suitable product that will be carried with interest by children throughout the tour. The methodology and survey study regarding the selection of the scepter are presented below.

### Methodology

A face-to-face survey method was used to select the appropriate scepter for use in TOY. Within the scope of the research, ethical approval was obtained from the Ethics Committee of Eskisehir Technical University Senate, with decision number 10/8, during the meeting held on June 01, 2022. The electronic components of all three alternative models were the same; therefore, the choice focused on the body design. At the beginning of the scepter selection period, the "Weighted Evaluation Criteria System" (Roy, 2014) method was deemed appropriate for selecting the suitable alternative, and the criteria were determined as performance, functionality, ease of production (production time, ease of assembly), cost, and children's interest. Since the electrical hardware was the same, performance and functionality were assumed to be identical for all three alternatives. As they were produced using the same method and materials (there were slight differences in production times, but this was negligible since only nine scepters would be produced within the project scope and there was sufficient time for production), the ease of production was also similar for all three alternatives and did not significantly impact the selection. The cost of each alternative was also comparable and within the planned budget. Therefore, the cost criterion was disregarded. Ultimately, the only significant criterion for selecting the suitable alternative was children's interest, and the best alternative was selected through the face-to-face survey with children. The details of the survey are presented in the next section.

## Survey Study

The research topic of TOY is related to sensitivity to cultural heritage. The choice of third and fourth-grade primary school students for the TOY application is significantly influenced by their tendency and suitability to understand, compared to previous grade levels, due to the lessons they receive and the characteristics of their developmental period. Since TOY will be applied to third and fourth-grade primary school students, the target group for the user surveys was selected as 3rd and 4th grade students (aged 8-11) studying at Eskişehir Mustafa Kemal Primary School/Middle School. The user survey consists of three sections. The first section aims to define the user profile. The second section is aimed at determining user preferences about the scepter design. The third section is related to determining the preferred scepter among alternatives. By asking children about their desires and preferences in scepter design, it is intended to consider user requests in the new prototypes to be produced. The survey aims to determine which scepter from the produced prototypes will be selected as the final product and to reach a scepter that will be used in the application phase of the TOY project, developed according to user requests and preferences.

### Defining the Participant Profile

The first three questions in the survey were asked to define the participant profile. In the first question, the participants were asked about their ages. 4% of the participants were 8 years old, 36% were 9 years old, 53% were 10 years old and 7% were 11 years old. In the second question, the participants were asked about their grades (grd). 40% of the participants were in the 3rd grade and 60% were in the 4th grade. In the third question, the participants were asked about their gender. Accordingly, 51% of the participants were female and 49% were male. The details of the participant profile are presented in Table 5.

*Table 5. Evaluation for defining the participant profile (age-gender-grade)*

| Age | Gender-Grade | | | | | | | |
|---|---|---|---|---|---|---|---|---|
| | Girl | Boy | Total | %Total | 3rd Grd | 4th Grd | Total | %Total |
| 8 | 3 | 3 | 6 | %4 | 6 | 0 | 6 | %4 |
| 9 | 31 | 27 | 58 | %36 | 50 | 8 | 58 | %36 |
| 10 | 46 | 40 | 86 | %53 | 8 | 78 | 86 | %53 |

continued on following page

*Table 5. Continued*

| Age | Gender-Grade | | | | | | | |
|---|---|---|---|---|---|---|---|---|
| | **Girl** | **Boy** | **Total** | **%Total** | **3rd Grd** | **4th Grd** | **Total** | **%Total** |
| 11 | 3 | 8 | 11 | %7 | 0 | 11 | 11 | %7 |
| Total | 83 | 78 | 161 | %100 | 64 | 97 | 161 | %100 |
| %Total | %51 | %49 | %100 | | %40 | %60 | %100 | |

## Determining Participant Preferences

Participants were asked what features they wanted the scepter to have. These included questions such as the color of the scepter, the color of the lights, etc. The information obtained from here was evaluated within the scope of improving the scepter.

## Determining the Preferred Scepter

To determine the preferences of the users, three scepters that were prototyped were put into contact with the children and they were asked which scepter they liked and preferred. As seen in Table 6, six users (4%) chose scepter number 1, 73 users (46%) chose scepter number 2, and 81 users (50%) chose scepter number 3.

*Table 6. User preferences for prototyped scepter*

| | **Model-1** | | **Model-2** | | **Model-3** | |
|---|---|---|---|---|---|---|
| Number of users who preferred | 6 | | 73 | | 81 | |
| | Girl | Boy | Girl | Boy | Girl | Boy |
| | 3 | 3 | 42 | 31 | 38 | 44 |
| | 3rd Grd | 4th Grd | 3rd Grd | 4th Grd | 3rd Grd | 4th Grd |
| | 2 | 4 | 31 | 42 | 31 | 50 |
| % of users who preferred | ~ 4 | | ~ 46 | | ~ 50 | |
| | Girl | Boy | Girl | Boy | Girl | Boy |
| | ~ 2 | ~ 2 | ~ 26 | ~ 20 | ~ 23 | ~ 27 |
| | 3rd Grd | 4th Grd | 3rd Grd | 4th Grd | 3rd Grd | 4th Grd |
| | ~ 1 | ~ 3 | ~ 20 | ~ 26 | ~ 19 | ~ 31 |
| Length | 8 | | 8,1 | | 8,1 | |
| Thickness | 6,8 | | 6,9 | | 7,6 | |
| Appearance | 5,2 | | 7,8 | | 8 | |

As a result of the participants' preferences, model-3 was selected as the scepter to be used within the scope of the project. Participants were asked to rate the alternative scepters for length, thickness, and appearance on a scale from 1 to 10 (best), and to choose one of the alternative scepters. The participants gave the highest scores for length, thickness, and appearance to the third alternative, and the majority of participants preferred model-3. It was determined that there was no significant difference based on gender or grade.

Participants were asked to choose one of the colors white, black, pink, and blue for the scepter, or to specify a different color. Five participants chose white, 70 chose black, 11 chose pink, and 32 chose blue. 44 participants specified a different color, and none of these different colors were chosen by more than seven participants. One boy participant chose pink, and five girl participants chose blue. The most preferred color, black, was chosen by 41 girl participants and 29 boy participants. The majority of both girls and boys preferred black. The scepters were produced in white to avoid increasing costs, as white filament was available. However, considering the commercial application of TOY, it should be evaluated whether to produce the scepters in black.

To determine the colors of the LED lights to be used in the scepter, participants were asked about their preferences for red, blue, and green. Accordingly, 52 participants (32%) preferred red, 54 participants (34%) preferred blue, and 55 participants (34%) preferred green as the LED light color. As a result of these close preferences, it was decided to use all three colors in the scepters to be produced.

After determining the participant preferences and determining the appropriate alternative, a total of nine scepters were produced with a 3D printer to be used during the application studies to be carried out in the Historical Odunpazarı Region. It was planned that six scepters would be used in the field simultaneously, while three would be kept as backups.

## IMPLEMENTATION AND DISCUSSION

The student sample to participate in the TOY application was determined using the convenience sampling approach (Saunders et al., 2009). This type of sampling approach was adopted because the sample selected for the research application consisted of primary school children, participation in the application was voluntary, and the legal permissions required by these processes. The number of students planned to be included in the sample was determined as 130 (50, 3rd grade students; 50, 4th grade students; and a group of 30 pilot students consisting of 3rd and 4th grade students) due to the project date and duration, feasibility, the fact that it was an event with family participation, and the event could not be carried out as planned due to weather conditions. After the posters distributed to the primary schools and the presentations made, the participants were first informed about the event, and then the participants were determined on a voluntary basis.

TOY field applications were held on August 12-13-14-16-19-20-21-27-29-30 and September 01, 2022 in Eskişehir Odunpazarı Historical City Center. Although 130 participants were initially planned, a total of 147 students, consisting of 79 third-grade and 68 fourth-grade students from various primary schools in Eskişehir, embarked on a historical game journey with their parents during this period. Even after the field application was completed, there were still requests to participate in TOY.

It was observed that the participating children carried the smart scepters in their hands throughout the tour. The most important problem observed in the scepters during the applications was the melting of the batteries due to a short circuit in a few scepters. Apart from this, a few minor corrections were made in the scepter software and the scepters were updated. The scepters that caused problems during the application were quickly replaced with scepters kept ready as backup. In general, TOY field applications were carried out successfully. In the interviews conducted at the end of the application, the participants (both students and parents) described TOY as an exciting, educational, and quality time-spending activity.

As for the scepter, the students found it eye-catching and a bit heavy, stating that they liked it, while the parents also found it eye-catching. The impact of TOY on students' learning of cultural heritage is being analyzed in a different study; it is not within the scope of this study.

TOY has a mobile infrastructure and is highly flexible. It can be easily configured in different locations, and the number of stations in the tour can be increased or decreased. Technically, there is no limitation on the number of stations (BILIG). The modem on a BILIG can support a maximum of 30 scepter connections simultaneously. Therefore, a maximum of 30 scepters can be connected to a BILIG at the same time. Consequently, the number of participants in the tour can be increased up to 30 at once. This number can be doubled by adding another modem to the BILIG or modems supporting around 200 connections can also be used. Details about the BILIGs are within the scope of another study; it is not covered in this study.

At the central BILIG, the sequence of stations that the scepter needs to visit is uploaded. As the participant approaches the station, he/she needs to visit, the number of LED lights on the scepter that light up and the intensity of the buzzer sound increase. By this way, the scepter guides the participant towards the target station. If there is an internet access point at the location of the BILIGs, the BILIGs can connect to the internet. If there is no internet access point, it needs to connect via GSM. After the scepter is touched to the BILIG, the BILIG takes a picture and sends this picture to the central BILIG via the internet. At the central BILIG, a story-themed picture album where the participant is the hero is prepared and given as a gift to the participant who complete the tour. If there is no internet connection, the pictures stored in BILIGs are collected at the end of the day, and the story-themed picture albums are sent to participants' addresses. It is evaluated that the most significant effort in setting up the TOY infrastructure in different cities or locations is the selection of stations, the preparation of information cards, and the writing of the story for the story-themed picture album.

It is considered that the scepters can be produced in different colors and designs based on feedback from participants. The setup and dismantling of the TOY infrastructure, as well as managing the application throughout the day, can be done by one person. It is evaluated that with 20-30% spare BILIGs and scepters available during the application, the application can run smoothly throughout the day. All the hardware that constitutes the TOY infrastructure, and consequently all the hardware of the scepter, are materials that can be easily obtained from the market. Assembly can also be done easily. Therefore, it is considered that there will be no difficulty in maintenance and upkeep.

Cultural heritage sites are under the responsibility of municipalities. Therefore, it is considered beneficial and appropriate for the TOY infrastructure to be funded by municipalities for promoting the city and raising awareness of cultural heritage. Through protocols and coordination between municipalities and schools or the Ministry of National Education, the participation in TOY for all primary school students in the city can be ensured according to a specific plan. The maintenance of the TOY infrastructure can be sustained with a nominal fee collected from participants, or the Ministry of National Education or municipalities can cover the maintenance costs.

## CONCLUSION AND RECOMMENDATIONS

In this study, information is given about design and prototype production of smart scepter. RFID and NFC tags positioned inside the scepter communicate with RFID and NFC readers positioned inside BILIGs. The scepter determines the distance depending on the signal strength and directs the user in the area to BILIG with the lights and sound warning system.

The scepters produced were successfully used in the TOY application, aside from a few minor issues. The mentioned scepter and the developed information infrastructure can be used with minor adjustments in museums, orienteering competitions, control of posts within military units of Armed Forces, ruins and tourist areas spread over large areas, and similar practical applications. The length, weight, shape, features, and functions of the scepter can be developed or modified based on user feedback or the area in which it will be used. Additionally, by tracking the smart scepter in archaeological sites and tourist areas, the management of the generated database could help plan and organize the traffic, activity areas, and streets in the area. In this way, it can make a significant contribution to smart city applications.

If the study is further developed, RFID tags with a broader distance perception or a different communication technology could be used for larger areas. In case of mass production, production methods like plastic injection, which offer cost-effective options for large-scale production, could be preferred instead of a 3D printer. Efforts could be made to reduce the weight and cost of the scepter, and scepters in different designs and colors could be prepared to offer participants a choice. Ultimately, the smart scepter can be integrated with a mobile device. Thus, energy efficiency could be increased by using low-energy communication technologies such as Bluetooth or Wi-Fi instead of radio frequency.

## ACKNOWLEDGMENT

We owe our gratitude to the managers and staff of Eskişehir Technical University (ESTÜ), Anadolu University (AÜ), Eskişehir Metropolitan Municipality, Odunpazarı Municipality, and primary schools in Eskişehir who have supported us throughout the entire project and never withheld their assistance. We also extend our thanks to the TÜBİTAK scholarship holders, doctoral, master's, undergraduate, and technical high school students who contributed to our project with great dedication.

This study was prepared as part of the "Historical Game Journey (HGJ) - Tarihsel Oyun Yolculuğu (TOY)" project, which was supported by TÜBİTAK under the National New Ideas and Products Research Support Program (1005), with the project number 118K117.

Within the scope of the research, ethical approval was obtained from the Ethics Committee of Eskisehir Technical University Senate, with decision number 10/8, during the meeting held on June 01, 2022 (Date: 02.06.2022, Number: E-87914409-050.06.04-73895).

## REFERENCES


Açık, C. (2024). Industrial Wood Product Design and Application with a Design Thinking Approach for Individuals with Learning Disabilities. *PLANARCH - Design and Planning Research*, 8(1), 162-167. DOI: .DOI: 10.54864/planarch.1417340

Akbaba, A., & Akbulut, E. (2021). 3 Boyutlu Yazıcılar ve Kullanım Alanları [3D Printers and Areas of Usage]. *ETÜ Sentez İktisadi ve İdari Bilimler Dergisi*, 3, 19–46.

Başçiftçi, F., & Gündüz, K. A. (2019). A Research for Microcontrollers Compatible to the Internet of Things. *Selcuk University Journal of Social and Technical Researches*, 18, 62–71.

Cahoon, S. (2016). *How to: Build large parts that exceed the build volume of your printer*. MatterHackers. https://www.matterhackers.com/articles/printing-outside-the-box-exceeding-the-build-volume-of-your-printer

Dindi, K. (2021). Tarih Felsefesi Bağlamında Hz. Musa'nın Asâsı -Mucize mi, Yoksa Hâkimiyet Sembolü mü? [Prophet moses' staff in the context of philosophy of history- Is it a miracle or a symbol of sovereignty?]. *Siyer Araştırmaları Dergisi*, 9, 108–110.

Ekinci, E. B. (2022). *Bastonun Gücü [The power of the cane]*. https://www.ekrembugraekinci.com/article/?ID=1249&bastonun-g%C3%BCc%C3%BC

Gürdoğan-Bayır, Ö., & Çengelci Köse, T. (2019). Kültürel miras ve korunmasına ilişkin ortaokul öğrencilerinin görüşleri [Secondary School Students' Views about Cultural Heritage and Preserving Cultural Heritage]. *Kastamonu Education Journal*, 27(4), 1827–1840. DOI: 10.24106/kefdergi.3393

Halaç, H. H., & Ayvaz, E. (2022). Kültürel Miras Öğretimi: Tarihsel Oyun Yolculuğu (TOY) [Teaching Cultural Heritage: Historical Game Journey (HGJ)]. *InProceedings of the 5th International Dede Korkut Conference of Turkish Culture, History and Literature*, İzmir, 330-333.

Halaç, H. H., Önaçan, M. B. K., Önel, T., & Ayvaz, E. (2022). Oyunlaştırma ile Kültürel Miras Farkındalığının Oluşturulması: Tarihsel Oyun Yolculuğu (TOY) [Creating Cultural Heritage Awareness with Gamification: Historical Game Journey (HGJ)]. *In Proceedings of the5th International Dede Korkut Conference of Turkish Culture, History and Literature*, İzmir, 334-338.

Hwa, L. C., Leow, J., Lau, J., Ho, A., & Yong, C. H. (2017). *Design thinking, the Guidebook*. Royal Civil Service Commission. https://www.rcsc.gov.bt/wp-content/uploads/2017/07/dt-guide-book-master-copy.pdf

Kara, N., & Çağıltay, K. (2020). Smart Toys for Preschool Children: A Design and Development Research. *Electronic Commerce Research and Applications*, 39, 1–11. DOI: 10.1016/j.elerap.2019.100909

Karagöz, İ., Danış Bekdemir, A., & Tuna, Ö. (2021). 3B Yazıcı Teknolojilerindeki Kullanılan Yöntemler ve Gelişmeler Üzerine Bir Derleme [A Review of Used Methods and Developments in 3D Printer Technologies]. *Düzce Üniversitesi Bilim ve Teknoloji Dergisi*, 9(4), 1186–1213. DOI: 10.29130/dubited.877423

Köbeloğlu, A., & Çetinkaya, K. (2019). 3B Yazıcılar ile Uzun Geometrili Parçaların Üretilebilirliği [Production of Long Geometric Parts With 3d Printers]. *International Journal of 3d Printing Technologies and Digital Industry*, 3(1), 11-18.

Kunduracıoğlu, İ. (2018). *Oyunlaştırma Kavramı Üzerine İçerik Analizi Çalışması [A content analysis on gamification concept]* (UMI No. 529715) [Master's Thesis, Balıkesir University, Institute of Science], Balıkesir, Türkiye. Council of Higher Education Thesis Center.

Maraşlı, F., & Çıbuk, M. (2015). RFID Teknolojisi ve Kullanım Alanları [RFID Technology and Application Areas]. *BEÜ Fen Bilimleri Dergisi*, 4(2), 249–275.

Motlagh, N. H. (2012). *Near Field Communication (NFC) A Technical Overview.* [Master's Thesis, University of Vaasafaculty of Technology, Telecommunication Engineering], Vaasa, Finland.

Mutlu, E., Parlar, Z., & Temiz, V. (2014). An Apparatus Design for High Speed Sealing Applications Based on Systematic Design Approach. *In Proceedings of 10th World Congress on Computational Mechanics (Blucher Mechanical Engineering Proceedings, 1(1))*, Sao Paulo, Brazil.

*NODEMCU ESP8266* (n.d.). https://joy-it.net/en/products/SBC-NodeMCU

Özdenizci, B., Ok, K., Aydın, M. N., & Coşkun, V. (2016). Yakın Alan İletişimi Teknolojisi [A Survey on Near Field Communication]. *Türkiye Bilişim Vakfı Bilgisayar Bilimleri ve Mühendisliği Dergisi*, 4(1). https://dergipark.org.tr/tr/pub/tbbmd/issue/22243/238785

Özkan, Z., & Samur, Y. (2017). Oyunlaştırma Yönteminin Öğrencilerin Motivasyonları Üzerine Etkisi [The Effect of Using Gamification on Students' Motivation]. *Ege Eğitim Dergisi*, 18(2), 857–886. DOI: 10.12984/egeefd.314801

Özsoy, K. (2019). Üç Boyutlu (3B) Baskı Teknolojisinin Eğitimde Uygulanabilirliği: Senirkent MYO Örneği [Usability of Three Dimensional (3D) Printing Technologies in Education: Senirkent MYO Case]. *Düzce Üniversitesi Bilim ve Teknoloji Dergisi*, 7(2), 111–123. DOI: 10.29130/dubited.436015

Parlar, Z., Soybora, E. K., Burhan, M. S., & Davaslıgil, S. (2017). Sistematik konstrüksiyon ve tasarım odaklı düşünme yaklaşımı ile yaratıcı kavramsal tasarım süreci: Küçük ev aleti tasarımı [Systematic design and design thinking approach for conceptual design process: small household appliance design]. *Sakarya Üniversitesi Fen Bilimleri Enstitüsü Dergisi*, 21(5), 1100–1109. DOI: 10.16984/saufenbilder.307260

*RFID Etiketler Nasıl çalışır? [How Do RFID Tags Work?].* RFIDmarket. (n.d.). https://www.rfidmarket.com.tr/blog/icerik/rfid-etiketler-nasil-calisir

Roy, R. K. (2014). *Strategy for Simultaneous Evaluation of Multiple Objectives.* MI, USA, Nutek, Inc., http://nutek-us.com/QITT07 - Overall Evaluation Criteria (OEC) Strategy.pdf

Sevinç, H. (n.d.). *ESP8266 ve Arduino ile Nesnelerin İnterneti [Internet of Things with ESP8266 and Arduino].* https://abms.com.tr/upload/product_datasheets/89c544826d965692a11bb9e1fcee5259fddf12c.pdf

Soyupak, O., & Soyupak, İ. (2021). Oyuncağın Akıllanması: Dijital Teknoloji Barındıran Oyuncakların Tasarımına Yönelik Bir Çerçeve Önerisi [Smarting the toy: A proposal for a framework for designing digital technology containing toys]. *Sanat&Tasarım*, 11(2), 468–480.

Sürmen, H. K. (2019). Eklemeli İmalat (3B Baskı): Teknolojiler ve Uygulamalar [Additive Manufacturing (3D Printing): Technologies and Applications]. *Uludağ Üniversitesi Mühendislik Fakültesi Dergisi*, 24(2), 373–392. DOI: 10.17482/uumfd.519147 373

Taşçıoğlu, Y. (2021, February 15). Nodemcu Nedir? NodeMCU Projeleri ile IoT Dünyasına Adım Atın! [What is Nodemcu? Step into the IoT World with NodeMCU Projects!]. *maker.robotistan Blog*. October 31, 2024, https://maker.robotistan.com/nodemcu-esp8266/#NodeMCU nedir? ESP8266 ile alakası nedir.

Tekbaş, M. (2019). Sağlık Kurumlarında Nesnelerin İnterneti Teknolojisinin Kullanımı: Bir Vaka Çalışması [The use of internet of things technology in health institutions: A case study]. (UMI No. 593832) [Master's Thesis, İstanbul University, Institute of Science] İstanbul, Türkiye. Council of Higher Education Thesis Center.

*Use cases*. NFC Forum. (n.d.). https://nfc-forum.org/learn/use-cases

Vatandaş, S. (2020). Oyun ve Oyuncak: Teknolojik ve Toplumsal Dönüşüm Sürecinde Oyun ve Oyuncağın Anlamsal ve İşlevsel Değişimi [Games and toys: Semantic and functional change of games and toys in the process of technological and social transformation]. *Süleyman Demirel Üniversitesi Vizyoner Dergisi*, 11(28), 913–930. DOI: 10.21076/vizyoner.674699

Webrazzi. (2011, February 19). *NFC Nedir, Ne Işe Yarar, Nasıl Kullanılır? [What is NFC, what does it do, how is it used?]*. Webrazzi. https://webrazzi.com/2011/02/19/nfc-teknolojisi-nedir-nfc-ile-neler-yapilabilir

Wolniak, R. (2017). The Design Thinking method and its stages. *Systemy Wspomaganıa W Inżynıerıı Produkcjı- Inżynieria Systemów Technicznych*, 6(6), 247-255.

Yenigün, R., Yıldız, A., & Uğur, L. (2020). RFID Kütüphane Sistemi İçin En Uygun RFID Etiketin AHP ve ANP Yöntemleriyle Belirlenmesi [RFID Library System Determination by AHP and ANP Methods]. *BEÜ Fen Bilimleri Dergisi*, 9(4), 1596–1608.

Yunus Emre. (n.d.). In *Encyclopedia Britannica*. https://www.britannica.com/biography/Yunus-Emre

Yusubova, N., & Ural, S. (2023). Bir Oyuncak Tasarımı Deneyinin Kültürel Kimlik Metodu Olarak Değerlendirilmesi [Evaluation of a Toy Design Experiment as a Method of Cultural Identity]. *International Academic Social Resources Journal*, 8(48), 2548–2560. DOI: 10.29228/ASRJOURNAL.68515

## KEY TERMS AND DEFINITIONS

**BILIG:** The abbreviation of the Turkish name for "Information and Communication Station". BILIG is a solar-powered, mobile kiosk positioned in front of the historical building to be visited during the TOY tour. It communicates with participants, provides verbal and visual information about the building, takes pictures, presents information cards, and can wirelessly communicate with other BILIGs.

**Cultural Heritage:** The totality of tangible, intangible, portable, and immovable values created by previous generations and can be passed down from generation to generation in a society.

**Design Thinking Approach:** A user-centered problem-solving approach that involves empathizing with users, defining problems, ideating solutions, prototyping the products, and testing the results by combining creativity and analytical thinking to develop innovative solutions.

**Gamification:** The application of game design elements and principles in non-game contexts to engage and motivate people to achieve specific goals.

**Smart City:** An urban area that leverages advanced technology, data, and IoT (Internet of Things) solutions to enhance residents' quality of life by improving infrastructure, optimizing resource management, and providing efficient services.

**Scepter:** A stick designed to be held from any part of its body. It serves multiple purposes: providing support as an additional leg, maintaining a safe distance when encountering new objects, offering protection against potential danger, reaching inaccessible points, and symbolizing power and authority beyond its utilitarian functions.

**TOY:** The abbreviation of the Turkish name for "Historical Game Journey". TOY is a project designed to create an educational model based on an information technology infrastructure, within a game-based narrative context, to increase children's interaction with historical areas, enable them to experience the historical texture, teach them about cultural heritage in a tangible way, and raise their awareness of cultural heritage.

**Wand:** A rod, stick or twig carried as a symbol of authority or used by a magician.

**Weighted Evaluation Criteria System Method:** A multi-criteria evaluation approach that normalizes and weights different criteria with varying units, quality characteristics, and relative importance to assess products or processes, producing a single numerical index (Weighted Target Score) for comparison.

# Compilation of References


Ab Wahid, R. (2019). Sustaining ISO 9001-based QMS in higher education: A reality? *The TQM Journal*, 31(4), 563–577. DOI: 10.1108/TQM-12-2018-0185

Abbas, S. M., Latif, M., & Sarwar, F. (2024). Digital Leadership and Innovative Work Behavior in IT Sector: The Mediating Role of Digital Entrepreneurial Orientation and Digital Organizational Culture. *Employee Responsibilities and Rights Journal*. Advance online publication. DOI: 10.1007/s10672-024-09503-7

Abdullahi, A. M., Hussein, H. A., Ahmed, M. Y., Hussein, O. A., & Warsame, A. A. (2024). The impact of education for sustainable development on university students' sustainable behavior: A case study from undergraduate students in Somalia. *Frontiers in Education*, 9, 1413687. Advance online publication. DOI: 10.3389/feduc.2024.1413687

Abdullah, N. A. S., Noor, N. L. M., & Ibrahim, E. N. M. (2013). Resilient Organization: Modelling The Capacity for Resilience. *International Conference on Research and Innovation in Information Systems*. DOI: 10.1109/ICRIIS.2013.6716729

Abelha, M., Fernandes, S., Mesquita, D., Seabra, F., & Ferreira-Oliveira, A. T. (2020). Graduate employability and competence development in higher education—A systematic literature review using PRISMA. *Sustainability (Basel)*, 12(15), 5900. DOI: 10.3390/su12155900

Åberg, C., Bankewitz, M., & Knockaert, M. (2019). Service tasks of board of directors: A literature review and research agenda in an era of new governance practices. *European Management Journal*, 37(5), 648–663. DOI: 10.1016/j.emj.2019.04.006

Abiddin, N., Ibrahim, I., & Aziz, S. (2022). Non-Governmental Organisations (NGOs) and Their Part towards Sustainable Community Development. *Sustainability (Basel)*, 14(8), 4386. Advance online publication. DOI: 10.3390/su14084386

Abukhait, R., Khattak, M. N., Shaya, N., & Ramanathan, U. (2023). The underlying mechanism between compulsory citizenship behaviors and employee innovative work behaviors and knowledge sharing: A moderated mediation model. *Frontiers in Psychology*, 14, 1128499. Advance online publication. DOI: 10.3389/fpsyg.2023.1128499 PMID: 36865361

Açık, C. (2024). Industrial Wood Product Design and Application with a Design Thinking Approach for Individuals with Learning Disabilities. *PLANARCH - Design and Planning Research*, 8(1), 162-167. DOI: .DOI: 10.54864/planarch.1417340

Adair, J. (2009). *Leadership for Innovation: How to Organize Team Creativity and Harvest Ideas*. Kogan Page.

Adams, R. B., & Ferreira, D. (2009). Women in the boardroom and their impact on governance and performance. *Journal of Financial Economics*, 94(2), 291–309. DOI: 10.1016/j.jfineco.2008.10.007

Adel, A. (2022). Future of Industry 5.0 in Society: HumanCentric Solutions, Challenges and Prospective Research Areas. *Journal of Cloud Computing (Heidelberg, Germany)*, 11(1), 1–15. DOI: 10.1186/s13677-022-00314-5 PMID: 36101900

Adhyaru, J. S., & Kemp, C. (2022). Virtual reality as a tool to promote well-being in the workplace. *Digital Health*, 8, 20552076221084473. DOI: 10.1177/20552076221084473 PMID: 35284084

Adil, A., & Kamal, A. (2018). Impact of Perceived Authentic Leadership and Psychological Capital on Burnout: Mediating Role of Psychological Ownership. *Psychological Studies*, 63(3), 243–252. DOI: 10.1007/s12646-018-0446-x

Aerts, K., Matthyssens, P., & Vandenbempt, K. (2007). Critical role and screening practices of European business incubators. *Technovation*, 27(5), 254–267. DOI: 10.1016/j.technovation.2006.12.002

Agarwal, R., & Dhar, V. (2014). Big data, data science, and analytics: The opportunity and challenge for IS research. *Information Systems Research*, 25(3), 443–448. DOI: 10.1287/isre.2014.0546

Agbo, F., Oyelere, S., Suhonen, J., & Tukiainen, M. (2021). Scientific production and thematic breakthroughs in smart learning environments: A bibliometric analysis. *Smart Learning Environments*, 8(1), 1. Advance online publication. DOI: 10.1186/s40561-020-00145-4

Agrawal, S., Agrawal, R., Kumar, A., Luthra, S., & Garza-Reyes, J. A. (2024). Can industry 5.0 technologies overcome supply chain disruptions?—A perspective study on pandemics, war, and climate change issues. *Operations Management Research : Advancing Practice Through Research*, 17(2), 453–468. DOI: 10.1007/s12063-023-00410-y

Aguilera, R. V. (2005). Corporate governance and director accountability: An institutional comparative perspective. *British Journal of Management*, 16(1), 39–53. DOI: 10.1111/j.1467-8551.2005.00446.x

Aguilera, R. V., Filatotchev, I., Gospel, H., & Jackson, G. (2008). An organizational approach to comparative corporate governance: Costs, contingencies, and complementarities. *Organization Science*, 19(3), 475–492. DOI: 10.1287/orsc.1070.0322

Ahlquist, J. (2023). *Digital Leadership in Higher Education: Purposeful Social Media in a Connected World*. Routledge. DOI: 10.4324/9781003444244

Ahmadian, S., Sesen, H., & Soran, S. (2017). Expanding the boundaries of compulsory citizenship behavior: Its impact on some organizational outputs. *Business and Economic Horizons*, 13(1), 110–118. DOI: 10.15208/beh.2017.08

Ahmed, F., Naqshbandi, M. M., Waheed, M., & Ain, N. U. (2024). Digital Leadership and Innovative Work Behavior: impact of LMX, Learning Orientation and Innovation Capabilities, Management Decision, Vol. ahead-of-print No. ahead-of-print. https://doi.org/DOI: 10.1108/MD-04-2023-0654

Ahmed, P. K., Shepherd, C. D., & Chen, J. (2022). Social sustainability and inclusive work environments in Industry 5.0. *Journal of Business Ethics*, 176(3), 423–439. DOI: 10.1007/s10551-022-05076-x

Ahmed, S., & Smith, E. (2023). The Future of Work: Adapting to Remote and Hybrid Models. *Abbottabad University Journal of Business and Management Sciences*, 1(01), 1–12.

Ainsworth, J. (2020). Feelings of ownership and volunteering: Examining psychological ownership as a volunteering motivation for nonprofit service organizations. *Journal of Retailing and Consumer Services*, 52, 101931. DOI: 10.1016/j.jretconser.2019.101931

Ajani, O. A., Gamede, B. T., & Bansal, R. (2024). Challenges and Opportunities of Integrating Industry 5.0 and Emerging Technologies in Higher Education for Enhancing Employability Skills. In Chakir, A., Bansal, R., & Azzouazi, M. (Eds.), *Industry 5.0 and Emerging Technologies. Studies in Systems, Decision and Control* (Vol. 565). Springer., DOI: 10.1007/978-3-031-70996-8_11

Akbaba, A., & Akbulut, E. (2021). 3 Boyutlu Yazıcılar ve Kullanım Alanları [3D Printers and Areas of Usage]. *ETÜ Sentez İktisadi ve İdari Bilimler Dergisi*, 3, 19–46.

Aksoy, M., Yilmaz, M. K., Tatoglu, E., & Basar, M. (2020). Antecedents of corporate sustainability performance in Turkey: The effects of ownership structure and board attributes on non-financial companies. *Journal of Cleaner Production*, 276, 1–11. DOI: 10.1016/j.jclepro.2020.124284

Al Sahaf, M. & Al Tahoo, L. (2021). Examining the key success factors for startups in the Kingdom of Bahrain, International Journal of Business Ethics and Governance, 9–49.

Alanazi, A. T. (2022). Digital Leadership: Attributes of Modern Healthcare Leaders. *Cureus*, 14(2), e21969. DOI: 10.7759/cureus.21969 PMID: 35282530

Albhirat, M. M., Rashid, A., Rasheed, R., Rasool, S., Zulkiffli, S. N. A., Zia-ul-Haq, H. M., & Mohammad, A. M. (2024). The PRISMA statement in enviropreneurship study: A systematic literature and a research agenda. *Cleaner Engineering and Technology*, 18, 100721. DOI: 10.1016/j.clet.2024.100721

Alcántara-Rubio, L., Valderrama-Hernández, R., Solís-Espallargas, C., & Ruiz-Morales, J. (2022). The implementation of the SDGs in universities: A systematic review. *Environmental Education Research*, 28(11), 1585–1615. DOI: 10.1080/13504622.2022.2063798

Alheeta, A. F., Al Adwanb, A., Areiqatc, A. Y., Zamild, A. M. A., & Saleh, M. A. (2021). The Effect of Leadership Styles on Employees' Innovative Work Behavior. *Management Science Letters*, 11, 239–246. DOI: 10.5267/j.msl.2020.8.010

Ali Nisar, Q., Haider, S., Waqas, A., Khan, W. A., & Selem, K. M. (2024). Cost of organizational citizenship behaviors: Serial mediation model of citizenship fatigue. *Management Research Review*, 47(6), 904–927. DOI: 10.1108/MRR-08-2023-0540

Ali, M. J. (2021). Understanding the 'g-index' and the 'e-index'. *Seminars in Ophthalmology*, 36(4), 139–139. DOI: 10.1080/08820538.2021.1922975 PMID: 33952018

Allegrini, M., & Greco, G. (2013). Corporate boards, audit committees and voluntary disclosure: Evidence from Italian Listed Companies. *The Journal of Management and Governance*, 17(1), 187–216. DOI: 10.1007/s10997-011-9168-3

Allen, T. D., French, K. A., Dumani, S., & Shockley, K. M. (2020). A cross-national meta-analytic examination of predictors and outcomes associated with work–family conflict. *The Journal of Applied Psychology*, 105(6), 539–576. https://doi.org/https://doi.org/10.1037/apl0000442. DOI: 10.1037/apl0000442 PMID: 31535873

Altuncu, Y., Oz Aktepe, S., & Islamoglu, G. (2012). Preliminary study for the development of uncertainty acoidance instrument in Turkey. *Journal of Business, Economics & Finance, 1*(4).

Al-Yazidi, A. S., Berri, J., & Mehedi Hassan, M. (2022). Novel hybrid model for organizations' reputation in online social networks. *Journal of King Saud University. Computer and Information Sciences*, 34(8), 5305–5317. DOI: 10.1016/j.jksuci.2022.01.006

Al-Yazidi, S., Berri, J., Al-Qurishi, M., & Al-Alrubaian, M. (2020). Measuring reputation and influence in online social networks: A systematic literature review. *IEEE Access : Practical Innovations, Open Solutions*, 8, 105824–105851. DOI: 10.1109/ACCESS.2020.2999033

Amabile, T. M., Conti, R., Coon, H., Lazenby, J., & Herron, M. (2004). Assessing the work environment for creativity. *Academy of Management Journal*, 39(5), 1154–1184. DOI: 10.2307/256995

Aminova, M. and Marchi, E. (2021). The role of innovation on start-up failure vs. its success, International Journal of Business Ethics and Governance, 41–72.

Anderson, H. J. (2017). Organizational-citizenship behavior. In Zeigler-Hill, V., & Shackelford, T. K. (Eds.), *Encyclopedia of Personality and Individual Differences* (pp. 1–3). Springer International Publishing., DOI: 10.1007/978-3-319-28099-8_788-1

Anderson, N., De Dreu, C. K. W., & Nijstad, B. A. (2004). The Routinization of Innovation Research: A Constructively Critical Review of the State-of-the- Science. *Journal of Organizational Behavior*, 25(2), 147–173. DOI: 10.1002/job.236

Anderson, N., Potočnik, K., & Zhou, J. (2014). Innovation and Creativity in Organizations: A State-of-the- science Review, Prospective Commentary, and Guiding Framework. *Journal of Management*, 40(5), 1297–1333. DOI: 10.1177/0149206314527128

Ansong, A. (2017). Corporate social responsibility and access to finance among Ghanaian SMEs: The role of stakeholder engagement. *Cogent Business & Management*, 4(1), 1385165. DOI: 10.1080/23311975.2017.1385165

Antonaci, F. G., Olivetti, E. C., Marcolin, F., Castiblanco Jimenez, I. A., Eynard, B., Vezzetti, E., & Moos, S. (2024). Workplace Well-Being in Industry 5.0: A Worker-Centered Systematic Review. *Sensors (Basel)*, 24(17), 5473. DOI: 10.3390/s24175473 PMID: 39275383

Apergi, L. A., Bjarnadottir, M. V., Baras, J. S., Golden, B. L., Anderson, K. M., Chou, J., & Shara, N. (2021). Voice interface technology adoption by patients with heart failure: Pilot comparison study. *JMIR mHealth and uHealth*, 9(4), e24646. https://doi.org/https://doi.org/10.2196/24646. DOI: 10.2196/24646 PMID: 33792556

Apriliyanti, I. D., & Alon, I. (2017). Bibliometric analysis of absorptive capacity. *International Business Review*, 26(5), 896–907. DOI: 10.1016/j.ibusrev.2017.02.007

Arayssi, M., Dah, M., & Jizi, M. (2016). Women on boards, sustainability reporting and firm performance. *Sustainability Accounting. Management and Policy Journal*, 7(3), 376–401.

Arena, C., Bozzolan, S., & Michelon, G. (2014). Environmental reporting: Transparency to stakeholders or stakeholder manipulation? An analysis of disclosure tone and the role of the board of directors. *Corporate Social Responsibility and Environmental Management.* Advance online publication. DOI: 10.1002/csr.1350

Aria, M., & Cuccurullo, C. (2017). bibliometrix: An R-tool for comprehensive science mapping analysis. *Journal of Informetrics*, 11(4), 959–975. https://doi.org/https://doi.org/10.1016/j.joi.2017.08.007. DOI: 10.1016/j.joi.2017.08.007

Arshi, T. A., Rao, V., Islam, S., & Morande, S. (2021). SECURE–a new business model framework for measuring start-up performance. *Journal of Entrepreneurship in Emerging Economies*, 13(3), 459–485. DOI: 10.1108/JEEE-02-2020-0043

Asante, K., Gyamfi, S., Amo-Boateng, M., & Peprah, F. (2024). Techno-economic analysis of solar PV electricity generation at the university of environment and sustainable development in Ghana. *Energy Reports*, 11, 659–673. DOI: 10.1016/j.egyr.2023.12.028

Ashman, H., Brailsford, T., Cristea, A. I., Sheng, Q. Z., Stewart, C., Toms, E. G., & Wade, V. (2014). The ethical and social implications of personalization technologies for E-lEarning. *Information & Management*, 51(6), 819–832. DOI: 10.1016/j.im.2014.04.003

Aslam, F., Aimin, W., Li, M., & Ur Rehman, K. (2020). Innovation in the era of IoT and industry 5.0: Absolute innovation management (AIM) framework. *Information (Basel)*, 11(2), 124. DOI: 10.3390/info11020124

Atar, E., Hossain, F., & Ullah, A. (2022). Syrian refugees in Turkey: exploring the role of I/NGOs in refugee crisis. Third World Quarterly(44, 231 - 245.), 231 - 245, https://doi.org/.DOI: 10.1080/01436597.2022.2144208

Atif, S. (2023). Analysing the alignment between circular economy and industry 4.0 nexus with industry 5.0 era: An integrative systematic literature review. *Sustainable Development (Bradford)*, 31(4), 2155–2175. DOI: 10.1002/sd.2542

Aureli, S., & Supino, E. (2017). Online reputation monitoring: An exploratory study on Italian hotel managers' practices. *International Journal of Hospitality & Tourism Administration*, 18(1), 84–109. DOI: 10.1080/15256480.2016.1264903

Avey, J., Luthans, F., & Youssef, C. M. (2010). The Additive Value of Positive Psychological Capital in Predicting Work Attitudes and Behaviors. *Journal of Management*, 36(2), 430–452. DOI: 10.1177/0149206308329961

Avolio, B., & Luthans, F. (2006). *The high-impact leader Authentic, resilient leadership that gets results and sustains growth*. McGraw-Hill.

Awad, E. M. (2024). *Managing Corporate Knowledge in the Digital Age: The Hidden Power*. International Technology Group Ltd.

Awan, M. R., & Mahmood, K. (2010). Relationship among Leadership Style, Organizational Culture and Employee Commitment in University Libraries. *Library Management*, 31(4/5), 253–266. DOI: 10.1108/01435121011046326

Ayoub, A. E. H., Almahamid, S. M., & Al Salah, L. F. (2023). Innovative Work Behavior Scale: Development and Validation of Psychometric Properties in Higher Education in the GCC Countries. *European Journal of Innovation Management*, 26(1), 119–133. DOI: 10.1108/EJIM-04-2021-0176

Ayres, R. U. (2000). On forecasting discontinuities. *Technological Forecasting and Social Change*, 65(1), 81–97. DOI: 10.1016/S0040-1625(99)00101-8

Ayyagari, R., Grover, V., & Purvis, R. (2011). Technostress: Technological Antecedents and Implications. *Management Information Systems Quarterly*, 35(4), 831–858. DOI: 10.2307/41409963

Azila-Gbettor, E. M., Mensah, C., & Abiemo, M. K. (2023). Compulsory citizenship behaviour and job outcome among unpaid interns: The buffering role of perceived co-worker support. *Higher Education. Skills and Work-Based Learning*, 14(1), 55–75. DOI: 10.1108/HESWBL-01-2023-0006

Bağış, M., Altınay, L., Kryeziu, L., Kurutkan, M. N., & Karaca, V. (2024). Institutional and individual determinants of entrepreneurial intentions: Evidence from developing and transition economies. *Review of Managerial Science*, 18(3), 883–912. DOI: 10.1007/s11846-023-00626-z

Baig, A. T., & Riaz, Z. (2021). Tracing an unyielding work compulsion: A moderated mediation model of abusive supervision and compulsory citizenship behavior. *Frontiers in Psychology*, 12, 746823. Advance online publication. DOI: 10.3389/fpsyg.2021.746823 PMID: 34912271

Bailey, D. E., & Kurland, N. B. (2002). A review of telework research: Findings, new directions, and lessons for the study of modern work. Journal of Organizational Behavior: The International Journal of Industrial. *Journal of Organizational Behavior*, 23(4), 383–400. DOI: 10.1002/job.144

Bai, S., & Zhao, Y. (2021). Startup investment decision support: Application of venture capital scorecards using machine learning approaches. *Systems*, 9(3), 55. DOI: 10.3390/systems9030055

Balaji, K. (2023, December). Exploring the Drivers and Effects on Supply Chain Resilience and Performance in an Emerging Market Using Artificial Intelligence. In 2023 3rd International Conference on Smart Generation Computing, Communication and Networking (SMART GENCON) (pp. 1-6). IEEE.

Balaji, K. (2023, June). Blockchain Based Banking Transactions Enabled by Big Data. In 2023 5th International Conference on Energy, Power and Environment: Towards Flexible Green Energy Technologies (ICEPE) (pp. 1-6). IEEE.

Balaji, K., Karim, S., Naidu, N. G., Venkatesh, T., & Ranjitha, P. V., & ChandraSekhar, S. (2023, June). Examining the Potential of Cryptocurrencies as An Asset Class-An Empirical Study. In 2023 International Conference on Applied Intelligence and Sustainable Computing (ICAISC) (pp. 1-6). IEEE.

Balaji, K. (2023, June). Unlocking the Potential of BI-Enhancing Banking Transactions Through AI&ML Tools. In *2023 International Conference on Applied Intelligence and Sustainable Computing (ICAISC)* (pp. 1-6). IEEE.

Balaji, K. (2024), "Artificial Intelligence for Enhanced Anti-Money Laundering and Asset Recovery: A New Frontier in Financial Crime Prevention," *2024 Second International Conference on Intelligent Cyber Physical Systems and Internet of Things (ICoICI)*, Coimbatore, India, 2024, pp. 1010-1016, DOI: 10.1109/ICoICI62503.2024.10696100

Balaji, K. (2024). Charting the Path to Global Prosperity: Unveiling the Impact and Promise of Sustainable Development. In Ordóñez de Pablos, P., Anshari, M., & Almunawar, M. (Eds.), *Harnessing Green and Circular Skills for Digital Transformation* (pp. 1–22). IGI Global., DOI: 10.4018/979-8-3693-2865-1.ch001

Balaji, K. (2024). Harnessing AI for Financial Innovations: Pioneering the Future of Financial Services. In Jermsittiparsert, K., Phongkraphan, N., & Lekhavichit, N. (Eds.), *Modern Management Science Practices in the Age of AI* (pp. 91–122). IGI Global., DOI: 10.4018/979-8-3693-6720-9.ch004

Balaji, K. (2024). The Nexus of Smart Contracts and Digital Twins Transforming Green Finance With Automated Transactions in Investment Agreements: Leveraging Smart Contracts for Green Investment Agreements and Automated Transactions. In Jafar, S., Rodriguez, R., Kannan, H., Akhtar, S., & Plugmann, P. (Eds.), *Harnessing Blockchain-Digital Twin Fusion for Sustainable Investments* (pp. 287–315). IGI Global., DOI: 10.4018/979-8-3693-1878-2.ch012

Balaji, K., & Babu, M. K. (2017). A study on the affect of technology on unplanned purchase behaviour among the customers across selected corporate retail chains of Andhrapradesh, India. *International Journal of Economic Research*, 14(4), 277–288.

Balaji, K., & Babu, M. K. (2017). A study on the role of the external and internal factors on consumer impulse buying behavior in selected retail outlets of Andhra Pradesh, India. *International Journal of Applied Business and Economic Research*, 15(4), 171–185.

Balaji, K., Karim, S., & Rao, P. S. "Unleashing the Power of Smart Chatbots: Transforming Banking with Artificial Intelligence," *2024 International Conference on Advances in Computing, Communication and Applied Informatics (ACCAI)*, Chennai, India, 2024, pp. 1-7, DOI: 10.1109/ACCAI61061.2024.10602456

Balaji, K., & Kishore Babu, M. (2016). A study on consumer shopping patterns in current retail scenario across selected retail stores in Andhra Pradesh, India. *International Journal of Economic Research*, 13(4), 1629–1640.

Baldwin, C. Y., & Clark, K. B. (2000). *Design Rules: The Power of Modularity*. MIT Press. DOI: 10.7551/mitpress/2366.001.0001

Barata, J., & Kayser, I. (2023) Industry 5.0 – Past, Present, and Near Future. *Procedia Computer Science*. vol 219: 778-788. ISSN 1877-0509. https://doi.org/DOI: 10.1016/j.procs.2023.01.351

Barata, J., & Kayser, I. (2024). How will the digital twin shape the future of industry 5.0? *Technovation*, 134, 103025. Advance online publication. DOI: 10.1016/j.technovation.2024.103025

Barca, M., & Hızıroğlu, M. (2009). 2000'li Yıllarda Türkiye'de Stratejik Yönetim Alanının Entellektüel Yapısı. *Eskişehir Osmangazi Üniversitesi İktisadi ve İdari Bilimler Dergisi*, 4(1), 113–148.

Barney, J., & Arikan, A. (2005). The resource-based view: Origins and implications. In (pp. 123-182). https://doi.org/DOI: 10.1111/b.9780631218616.2006.00006.x

Barney, J. B. (2001). Resource-based theories of competitive advantage: A ten-year retrospective on the resource-based view. *Journal of Management*, 27(6), 643–650. DOI: 10.1177/014920630102700602

Baron, R. M., & Kenny, D. A. (1986). The Moderator-Mediator Variable Distinction in Social Psychological Research: Conceptual, Strategic, and Statistical Considerations. *Journal of Personality and Social Psychology*, 51(6), 1173–1182. DOI: 10.1037/0022-3514.51.6.1173 PMID: 3806354

Barpanda, S., & Saraswathy, G. (2023). The impact of excessive workload on job performance of healthcare workers during pandemic: A conceptual mediation-moderation model. *IJMAR*, 10(1), 24–39. DOI: 10.18646/2056.101.23-002

Bartik, A. W., Bertrand, M., Cullen, Z. B., Glaeser, E. L., Luca, M., & Stanton, C. T. (2020). *How Are Small Businesses Adjusting to Covid-19? Early Evidence from a Survey No. w26989*. National Bureau of Economic Research. DOI: 10.3386/w26989

Bartlett, D., Mroczkowski, T. et al. (2020). Globalizing startups: Business development organizations in the Bay Area, Diversity, Innovation, and Clusters: Spatial Perspectives, 157.

Bartlett, W. (2009). Economic development in the European super-periphery: Evidence from the Western Balkans. *Economic annals, 54*(181), 21-44.

Bartlett, W. (2007). The Western Balkans. In *Varieties of capitalism in post-communist countries* (pp. 201–218). Springer. DOI: 10.1057/9780230627574_11

Bartsch, S., Weber, E., Büttgen, M., & Huber, A. (2021). Leadership Matters in Crisis-induced Digital Transformation: How to Lead Service Employees Effectively during the COVID-19 Pandemic. *Journal of Service Management*, 32(1), 71–85. DOI: 10.1108/JOSM-05-2020-0160

Başçiftçi, F., & Gündüz, K. A. (2019). A Research for Microcontrollers Compatible to the Internet of Things. *Selcuk University Journal of Social and Technical Researches*, 18, 62–71.

Bashir, M., Shaheen, K., Saleem, S., Bhutta, M. K., Abrar, M., & Jun, Z. (2019). The mediating role of psychological need thwarting in the relationship between compulsory citizenship behavior and psychological withdrawal. *Frontiers in Psychology*, 10, 2595. Advance online publication. DOI: 10.3389/fpsyg.2019.02595 PMID: 31849742

Bause, K., Radimersky, A., Iwanicki, M., & Albers, A. (2014). Feasibility studies in the product development process. *Procedia CIRP*, 21, 473–478. DOI: 10.1016/j.procir.2014.03.128

Bawuro, F., Shamsuddin, A., Wahab, E., & Chodozie, C. (2019). Prosocial Motivation and Innovative Behavior: An Empirical Analysis of Selected Public University Lecturers in Nigeria. *International Journal of Scientific & Technology Research*, 8(9), 1187–1194.

Bayarçelik, E. B., & Bumin Doyduk, H. (2020). Digitalization of business logistics activities and future directions. Ü. Hacıoğlu içinde, . Digital Business Strategies in Blockchain Ecosystems: Transformational Design and Future of Global Business, (s. 201-238).

Baykal, E. (2020). Effects of Servant Leadership on Psychological Capitals and Productivities of Employees. *Effects of Servant Leadership on Psychological Capitals and Productivities of Employees.*, 34, 273–291. DOI: 10.16951/atauniiibd.533275

Bear, A., & Fitzgibbon, M. (2005). Leadership in a not-for-profit world: a mixed toolbox. In Sims, R. R., & Quatro, S. A. (Eds.), *Leadership: Succeeding in the Private, Public, and Not-for-profit Sectors* (pp. 87–104). M.E. Sharpe.

Becker, B., & Gassmann, O. (2006). Corporate incubators: Industrial R&D and what universities can learn from them. *The Journal of Technology Transfer*, 31(4), 469–483. DOI: 10.1007/s10961-006-0008-6

Becker, G. S. (1992). Human capital and the economy. *Proceedings of the American Philosophical Society*, 136(1), 85–92.

Becker, G. S. (2009). *Human capital: A theoretical and empirical analysis, with special reference to education*. University of Chicago press.

Becker, T. E., & Kernan, M. C. (2003). Matching commitment to supervisors and organizations to in-role and extra-role performance. *Human Performance*, 16(4), 327–348. DOI: 10.1207/S15327043HUP1604_1

Bednar, P. M., & Welch, C. (2020). Socio-Technical Perspectives on Smart Working: Creating Meaningful and Sustainable Systems. *Information Systems Frontiers*, 22(2), 281–298. DOI: 10.1007/s10796-019-09921-1

Belloni, R. (2009). European integration and the Western Balkans: Lessons, prospects and obstacles. *Journal of Balkan & Near Eastern Studies*, 11(3), 313–331. DOI: 10.1080/19448950903152177

Benitez, J., Arenas, A., Castillo, A., & Esteves, J. (2022). Impact of Digital Leadership Capability on Innovation Performance: The Role of Platform Digitization Capability. *Information & Management*, 59(2), 103590. DOI: 10.1016/j.im.2022.103590

Bennis, W. (2013). Leadership in a Digital World: Embracing Transparency and Adaptive Capacity. *Management Information Systems Quarterly*, 37(2), 635–636.

Bentley, S. V., Naughtin, C. K., McGrath, M. J., Irons, J. L., & Cooper, P. S. (2024). The digital divide in action: How experiences of digital technology shape future relationships with artificial intelligence. *AI and Ethics*, 4(4), 1–15. DOI: 10.1007/s43681-024-00452-3

Berber, N., Aleksić, M., Slavić, A., & Jelača, M. S. (2022). The relationship between corporate social responsibility and corporate reputation in Serbia. *The Engineering Economist*, 33(3), 232–245. DOI: 10.5755/j01.ee.33.3.29316

Berger, M., Schäfer, R., Schmidt, M., Regal, C., & Gimpel, H. (2023). How to Prevent Technostress at the Digital Workplace: A Delphi Study. *Journal of Business Economics*. Advance online publication. DOI: 10.1007/s11573-023-01159-3 PMID: 38625156

Beverly, H. (2017). *Navigating your way to startup success*. Walter de Gruyter GmbH & Co KG. DOI: 10.1515/9781501507083

Beyhan, B., Akcomak, S., & Cetindamar, D. (2021). The Startup Selection Process in Accelerators: Qualitative Evidence from Turkey. *Entrepreneurship Research Journal*, 14(1), 27–51. DOI: 10.1515/erj-2021-0122

Bilir, C., Güngör, C., & Kökalan, Ö. (2020). Operations research/management science research in Europe: A bibliometric overview. *Advances in Operations Research*, 2020, 1–14. DOI: 10.1155/2020/1607637

Blau, P. M. (1964). Exchange and power in social life. *Sociological Inquiry*, 34(2). Advance online publication. DOI: 10.1111/j.1475-682X.1964.tb00583.x

Block, J., Fisch, C., & Rehan, F. (2020). Religion and entrepreneurship: A map of the field and a bibliometric analysis. *Management Review Quarterly*, 70(4), 591–627. DOI: 10.1007/s11301-019-00177-2

Bloom, N., Liang, J., Roberts, J., & Ying, Z. J. (2015). Does working from home work? Evidence from a Chinese experiment. *The Quarterly Journal of Economics*, 130(1), 165–218. DOI: 10.1093/qje/qju032

Blümel, E. (2013). Global challenges and innovative technologies geared toward new markets: Prospects for virtual and augmented reality. *Procedia Computer Science*, 25, 4–13. DOI: 10.1016/j.procs.2013.11.002

Boin, A., & Eeten, M. J. G. (2013). The Resilient Organization. *Public Management Review*, 15(3), 429–445. http://www.tandfonline.com/action/showCitFormats?doi=10.1080/14719037.2013.769856. DOI: 10.1080/14719037.2013.769856

Bolino, M. C., Klotz, A. C., Turnley, W. H., & Harvey, J. (2013). Exploring the dark side of organizational citizenship behavior. *Journal of Organizational Behavior*, 34(4), 542–559. DOI: 10.1002/job.1847

Bolino, M., Turnley, C., Gilstrap, W. H., & Suazo, J. B. (2010). Citizenship under pressure: What's a "Good Soldier" to do? *Journal of Organizational Behavior*, 31(6), 835–855. DOI: 10.1002/job.635

Bondanini, G., Giorgi, G., Ariza-Montes, A., Vega-Muñoz, A., & Andreucci-Annunziata, P. (2020). Technostress Dark Side of Technology in the Workplace: A Scientometric Analysis. *International Journal of Environmental Research and Public Health*, 17(21), 8013. DOI: 10.3390/ijerph17218013 PMID: 33143270

Bondarenko, T., Zhdanova, O., & Klimova, N. (2019). Multi-Criteria Mechanism for Selecting Projects by Fintech Accelerators, International Science and Technology Conference" FarEaston"(ISCFEC 2019), Atlantis Press, pp.6–10.

Bos-Nehles, A. C., & Veenendaal, A. A. R. (2017). Perceptions of HR Practices and Innovative Work Behavior: The Moderating Effect of an Innovative Climate. *International Journal of Human Resource Management*, 30(18), 2661–2683. DOI: 10.1080/09585192.2017.1380680

Boulouta, I. (2013). Hidden connections: The link between board gender diversity and corporate social performance. *Journal of Business Ethics*, 113(2), 185–197. DOI: 10.1007/s10551-012-1293-7

Bouzari, M., & Karatepe, O. M. (2017). Test of a mediation model of psychological capital among hotel salespeople. *International Journal of Contemporary Hospitality Management*, 29(7), 2178–2197. DOI: 10.1108/IJCHM-01-2016-0022

Bretas, V. P., & Alon, I. (2021). Franchising research on emerging markets: Bibliometric and content analyses. *Journal of Business Research*, 133, 51–65. DOI: 10.1016/j.jbusres.2021.04.067

Brett, J. (2019). *Evolving Digital Leadership: How to Be a Digital Leader in Tomorrow's Disruptive World*. Apress. DOI: 10.1007/978-1-4842-3606-2

Broadus, R. N. (1987). Toward a definition of "bibliometrics". *Scientometrics*, 12(5-6), 373–379. DOI: 10.1007/BF02016680

Brod, C. (1984). *Technostress: The Human Cost of the Computer Revolution*. Addison-Wesley.

Broo, D. G., Okyay, K., & Sait, S. M. (2022). Rethinking engineering education at the age of industry 5.0. *Journal of Industrial Information Integration*, 25, 100311. Advance online publication. DOI: 10.1016/j.jii.2021.100311

Brown, A., & Taylor, K. (2017). Enhancing supply chain resilience through employee involvement. *The Journal of Supply Chain Management*, 53(2), 45–60. DOI: 10.1111/jscm.12110

Brunner, M., Gonzalez-Castañé, G., & Ravesteijn, P. (2021). How Digital Leadership Competences and IT Capabilities Affect an Organization's Ability to Digitally Transform and Adopt New Technologies. *Journal of International Technology and Information Management*, 30(4), 7. Advance online publication. DOI: 10.58729/1941-6679.1526

Brynjolfsson, E., & McAfee, A. (2014) The second machine age: Work, progress, and prosperity in a time of brilliant technologies. W W Norton & Co. The second machine age: Work, progress, and prosperity in a time of brilliant technologies.

Büchi, G., Cennamo, N., Mittal, A., & Weill, P. (2020). Digital transformation of industrial ecosystems: Organizational resilience, adaptive workforce strategies, and human-centric technological integration. *Strategic Management Journal*, 41(8), 1511–1536. DOI: 10.1002/smj.3193

Budur, T., Abdullah, H., Rashid, C. A., & Demirer, H. (2024). The Connection Between Knowledge Management Processes and Sustainability at Higher Education Institutions. *Journal of the Knowledge Economy*. Advance online publication. DOI: 10.1007/s13132-023-01664-4

Burke, R., Koyuncu, M., Ashtakova, M., Eren, D., & Cetin, H. (2014). Hotel Star Ratings And Perceptions Of Servant Leadership And Service Quality Provided By Front-Line Service Workers In Four- And Five-Star Hotels In Turkey. An Exploratory Study. *Isguc The Journal of Industrial Relations and Human Resources*, 16(3), 3–9. DOI: 10.4026/1303-2860.2014.0251.x

Burt, G. (2007). Why are we surprised at surprises? Integrating disruption theory and system analysis with the scenario methodology to help identify disruptions and discontinuities. *Technological Forecasting and Social Change*, 74(6), 731–749. DOI: 10.1016/j.techfore.2006.08.010

Busulwa, R. (2023). *Navigating Digital Transformation in Management*. Routledge.

Cabrilo, S., & Dahms, S. (2018). How strategic knowledge management drives intellectual capital to superior innovation and market performance. *Journal of Knowledge Management*, 22(3), 621–648. DOI: 10.1108/JKM-07-2017-0309

Cahoon, S. (2016). *How to: Build large parts that exceed the build volume of your printer*. MatterHackers. https://www.matterhackers.com/articles/printing-outside-the-box-exceeding-the-build-volume-of-your-printer

Caillier, J. G. (2016). Does public service motivation mediate the relationship between goal clarity and both organizational commitment and extra-role behaviours? *Public Management Review*, 18(2), 300–318. DOI: 10.1080/14719037.2014.984625

Calderon-Monge, E., & Ribeiro-Soriano, D. (2024). *The Role of Digitalization in Business and Management: A Systematic Literature Review,* Review of Managerial Science. *Review of Managerial Science*, 18(2), 449–491. DOI: 10.1007/s11846-023-00647-8

Califf, C. B., Sarker, S., & Sarker, S. (2020). The Bright and Dark Sides of Technostress: A Mixed-Methods Study Involving Healthcare IT. *Management Information Systems Quarterly*, 44(2), 809–856. DOI: 10.25300/MISQ/2020/14818

Cameron, K. S., & Quinn, R. E. (1999). *Diagnosing and Changing Organizational Culture: Based on the Competing Values Framework*. Addison-Wesley.

Campbell, B. M., Sayer, J. A., & Walker, B. B., (2010). Navigating trade-offs: working for conservation and development outcomes. *Ecology and Society, 15*(2):16. [online] URL: http:// www.ecologyandsociety .org/vol15/iss2/art16/

Campus, G. (2021, January 19). *About Sustainability 2030*. University of Copenhagen. https:// sustainability2030.ku.dk/ucphs-approach/

Cantamessa, M., Gatteschi, V., Perboli, G., & Rosano, M. (2018). Startups' roads to failure. *Sustainability (Basel)*, 10(7), 2346. DOI: 10.3390/su10072346

Capital Markets Board. (2020). Sürdürülebilirlik İlkeleri Uyum Çerçevesi https://spk.gov.tr/data/63a17b1a8f95db0fa40e3309/s%C3%BCrd%C3%BCr%C3%BClebilirlik%20ilkeleri%20uyum%20cercevesi.pdf

Caputo, A., Molino, M., Cerato, B., & Cortese, C. G. (2023). Employer attractiveness: Two instruments to measure employer branding and reputation. *SAGE Open*, 13(3), 21582440231192188. Advance online publication. DOI: 10.1177/21582440231192188

Carayannis, E. G., & Morawska, J. (2023). University and Education 5.0 for Emerging Trends, Policies and Practices in the Concept of Industry 5.0 and Society 5.0. In Machado, C. F., & Davim, J. P. (Eds.), *Industry 5.0*. Springer., DOI: 10.1007/978-3-031-26232-6_1

Carayannis, E. G., & Morawska-Jancelewicz, J. (2022). The Futures of Europe: Society 5.0 and Industry 5.0 as Driving Forces of Future Universities. *Journal of the Knowledge Economy*, 13(4), 3445–3471. DOI: 10.1007/s13132-021-00854-2

Carroll, A. B. (1991). The pyramid of corporate social responsibility: Toward the moral management of organizational stakeholders. *Business Horizons*, 34(4), 39–48. DOI: 10.1016/0007-6813(91)90005-G

Carter, N., & Wilkinson, F. (2023, October 19). *Industrialization, Labor, and Life*. National Geographic Education. Retrieved October 7, 2024, from https://education.nationalgeographic.org/resource/industrialization-labor-and-life/

Carver, J. (2000). The opportunity for re-inventing corporate governance in joint venture companies. *Corporate Governance*, 8(1), 75–80. DOI: 10.1111/1467-8683.00182

Casey, D., & Sieber, S. (2016). Employees, sustainability and motivation: Increasing employee engagement by addressing sustainability and corporate social responsibility. *Research in Hospitality Management*, 6(1), 69–76. DOI: 10.2989/RHM.2016.6.1.9.1297

Castriotta, M., Loi, M., Marku, E., & Moi, L. (2021). Disentangling the corporate entrepreneurship construct: Conceptualizing through co-words. *Scientometrics*, 126(4), 2821–2863. DOI: 10.1007/s11192-020-03846-2

Cavus, N., & Aghamiri, S. (2023). Conceptual Intelligence, Digital Transformation, and Leadership Skills: Key Concepts for Modern Business Success. In Daimi, K., Alsadoon, A., & Coelho, L. (Eds.), *Cutting Edge Applications of Computational Intelligence Tools and Techniques* (pp. 231–253). Springer Nature. DOI: 10.1007/978-3-031-44127-1_11

Ceausu, I., Olaru, M., Ionescu, R., & Tohanean, D. (2018). Case study: Romanian startup accelerators—Startup selection and evaluation, 4th BASIQ International Conference on New Trends in Sustainable Business and Consumption Proceedings, pg, Volume 714.

Çera, G., Çera, E., Ribeiro, H. N. R., & Maloku, S. (2021). The role of trust in government and institutional environment in future business climate. *International Journal of Entrepreneurial Venturing*, 13(5), 425–442. DOI: 10.1504/IJEV.2021.119143

Chabane, B., Komljenovic, D., & Abdul-Nour, G. (2023). Converging on human-centred industry, resilient processes, and sustainable outcomes in asset management frameworks. *Environment Systems & Decisions*, 43(4), 663–679. DOI: 10.1007/s10669-023-09943-w

Chams, N., & García-Blandón, J. (2019). Sustainable or not sustainable? The role of the board of directors. *Journal of Cleaner Production*, 226, 1067–1081. DOI: 10.1016/j.jclepro.2019.04.118

Chand, R. (2023). Framework for identifying research gaps for future academic research. *IRA International Journal of Education and Multidisciplinary Studies*, 19(2), 160. DOI: 10.21013/jems.v19.n2.p12

Chaudhary, A., Cheema, A. U., Sheikh, L., & Islam, T. (2023). How does compulsory citizenship behavior disturb police employees' psychological health? The roles of work–family conflict and putting family first. *International Journal of Public Sector Management*, 36(4/5), 420–439. DOI: 10.1108/IJPSM-03-2023-0073

Che, X. (2015). *Effects of occupational stressors on nurses' safety performance and well-being: A within-individual study* [Doctoral dissertation, University of South Florida].

Cheng, L. Z. (2019). Compulsory citizenship behavior and facades of conformity with the mediating effect of work stress: A social exchange theory perspective. *[2019 aib southeast Asia regional conference: Us-China trade war, deglobalization, and international business (aibsear)].* AIB Southeast Asia Regional Conference - US-China Trade War, Deglobalization, and International Business, Cebu, PHILIPPINES.

Cheng, E. C. M., & Courtenay, S. M. (2006). Board composition, regulatory regime and voluntary disclosure. *The International Journal of Accounting*, 41(3), 262–289. DOI: 10.1016/j.intacc.2006.07.001

Chen, P., Xu, Y., Sparrow, P., & Cooper, C. (2021). Compulsory citizenship behaviour and work-family conflict: A moderated mediation model. *Current Psychology (New Brunswick, N.J.)*, 42(8), 6641–6652. DOI: 10.1007/s12144-021-01973-4

Chi, N.-W., Lin, C.-Y., Bruning, P. F., & Hung, Y. (2024). Forced to be a good citizen: Exploring the bright-and dark-side effects of daily compulsory citizenship behaviours on subsequent proactive helping and interpersonal deviance. *Journal of Occupational and Organizational Psychology*, 97(2), 647–671. DOI: 10.1111/joop.12486

Chiniara, M., & Bentein, K. (2016). Linking servant leadership to individual performance: Differentiating the mediating role of autonomy, competence and relatedness need satisfaction. *The Leadership Quarterly*, 27(1), 124–141. DOI: 10.1016/j.leaqua.2015.08.004

Choi, T.-M., Kumar, S., Yue, X., & Chan, H.-L. (2022). Disruptive Technologies and Operations Management in the Industry 4.0 Era and Beyond. *Production and Operations Management*, 31(1), 9–31. DOI: 10.1111/poms.13622

Chou, S. Y., Ramser, C., Chang, T., & Han, B. (2020). Emergence of interpersonal helping in times of crises: A theoretical model of prosperity and eradication of interpersonal helping in organizations. *Management Decision*, 58(10), 2257–2273. DOI: 10.1108/MD-08-2020-1041

Christensen, C. M. (1997). *The Innovator's Dilemma: When New Technologies Cause Great Firms to Fail*. Harvard Business Review Press.

Christopher, J. (2010). Corporate governance—A multi-theoretical approach to recognizing the wider influencing forces impacting on organizations. *Critical Perspectives on Accounting*, 21(8), 683–695. DOI: 10.1016/j.cpa.2010.05.002

Chun, R., & Davies, G. (2001). E-reputation: The role of mission and vision statements in positioning strategy. *Journal of Brand Management*, 8(4), 315–333. DOI: 10.1057/palgrave.bm.2540031

Cillo, V., Gregori, G. L., Daniele, L. M., Caputo, F., & Bitbol-Saba, N. (2022). Rethinking companies' culture through knowledge management lens during Industry 5.0 transition. *Journal of Knowledge Management*, 26(10), 2485–2498. DOI: 10.1108/JKM-09-2021-0718

Cioppi, M., Curina, I., Forlani, F., & Pencarelli, T. (2019). Online presence, visibility and reputation: A systematic literature review in management studies. *Journal of Research in Interactive Marketing*, 13(4), 547–577. DOI: 10.1108/JRIM-11-2018-0139

Ciucu-Durnoi, A., Delcea, C., Stănescu, A., Teodorescu, C., & Vargas, V. (2024). Beyond Industry 4.0: Tracing the Path to Industry 5.0 through Bibliometric Analysis. *Sustainability (Basel)*, 16(12), 5251. DOI: 10.3390/su16125251

Clarence, M., Devassy, V. P., Jena, L. K., & George, T. S. (2020). The effect of servant leadership on ad hoc schoolteachers' affective commitment and psychological well-being: The mediating role of psychological capital. *International Review of Education*, 67(3), 305–331. DOI: 10.1007/s11159-020-09856-9

Coldwell, D. A. L., & Callaghan, C. W. (2014). Specific organizational citizenship behaviours and organizational effectiveness: The development of a conceptual heuristic device. *Journal for the Theory of Social Behaviour*, 44(3), 347–367. DOI: 10.1111/jtsb.12046

Collevecchio, F., & Gionfriddo, G. (2023). Adopting a social purpose in for-profit firms: The role of the board of directors. *The International Entrepreneurship and Management Journal*, 19(3), 1467–1499. DOI: 10.1007/s11365-023-00879-w

Combs, J. G., Ketchen, J., David, J., Crook, T. R., & Roth, P. L. (2011). Assessing cumulative evidence within 'macro'research: Why meta-analysis should be preferred over vote counting. *Journal of Management Studies*, 48(1), 178–197. DOI: 10.1111/j.1467-6486.2009.00899.x

Contreras, F., Espinosa, J. C., Dornberger, U., & Acosta, Y. A. C. (2017). Leadership and Employees' Innovative Work Behavior: Test of a Mediation and Moderation Model. *Asian Social Science*, 13(9), 9–25. DOI: 10.5539/ass.v13n9p9

Çopani, D., & Kola, V. (2023). The Impact of Transformational Leadership in Relation to Job Performance in the Aviation Industry of Albania. *Proceedings of the 1st Bengkulu International Conference on Economics, Management, Business and Accounting (BICEMBA 2023)*

Cortellazzo, L., Bruni, E., & Zampieri, R. (2019). The Role of Leadership in a Digitalized World: A Review. *Frontiers in Psychology*, 10, 1938. DOI: 10.3389/fpsyg.2019.01938 PMID: 31507494

*Cost of a data breach 2024*. (n.d.). IBM. Retrieved October 9, 2024, from https://www.ibm.com/reports/data-breach

*Creating an inclusive workplace culture through diversity*. (2024, March 28). LinkedIn. Retrieved October 9, 2024, from https://www.linkedin.com/pulse/creating-inclusive-workplace-culture-through-diversity-lakshmi-kaul-kof8c

Croft, D. (2024) Guide: Industry 5.0. *Learn Lean* Sigma. [online] Available at: https://www.learnleansigma.com/guides/industry-5-0/

Crona, B., & Bodin, Ö. (2010). Power asymmetries in small scale fisheries: a barrier to governance transformability? *Ecology and Society, 15*(4):32. [online] URL: http://www. ecologyandsociety.org/vol15/iss4/art32/

Crossan, M. M., & Apaydin, M. (2010). A Multi-dimensional Framework of Organizational Innovation: A Systematic Review of the Literature. *Journal of Management Studies*, 47(6), 1154–1191. DOI: 10.1111/j.1467-6486.2009.00880.x

Csaszar, F., Nussbaum, M., & Sepulveda, M. (2006). Strategic and cognitive criteria for the selection of startups. *Technovation*, 26(2), 151–161. DOI: 10.1016/j.technovation.2005.01.010

Cuesta-Claros, A., Bonar, G., Malekpour, S., Raven, R., & Kestin, T. (2024). Uncovering perspectives on SDG integration for university transformations. *International Journal of Sustainability in Higher Education*, 25(6), 1252–1278. DOI: 10.1108/IJSHE-03-2023-0111

Curzi, Y., Fabbri, T., Scapolan, A. C., & Boscolo, S. (2019). Performance Appraisal and Innovative Behavior in the Digital Era. *Frontiers in Psychology*, 10, 1659. DOI: 10.3389/fpsyg.2019.01659 PMID: 31379682

Czikszentmihalyi, M. (1990). *Flow: The psychology of optimal experience*. Harper & Row.

Dabić, M., Maley, J., Dana, L.-P., Novak, I., Pellegrini, M. M., & Caputo, A. (2020). Pathways of SME internationalization: A bibliometric and systematic review. [</jrn>]. *Small Business Economics*, 55, 705–725.

Daily, C. M., & Dalton, D. R. (1994). Corporate governance and the bankrupt firm: An empirical assessment. *Strategic Management Journal*, 15(8), 643–654. DOI: 10.1002/smj.4250150806

Dalton, D. R., Daily, C. M., Certo, S. T., & Roengpitya, R. (2003). Meta-analyses of financial performance and equity: Fusion or confusion? *Academy of Management Journal*, 46(1), 13–26. DOI: 10.2307/30040673

Dalton, D. R., Daily, C. M., Ellstrand, A. E., & Johnson, J. L. (1998). Meta-analytic reviews of board composition, leadership structure, and financial performance. *Strategic Management Journal*, 19(3), 269–290. DOI: 10.1002/(SICI)1097-0266(199803)19:3<269::AID-SMJ950>3.0.CO;2-K

Damon, P. (2020). *Participants: nongovernmental organizations, including the private sector and academia* (4th ed.). Introduction to International Disaster Management.

Dandridge, T. (1979). Children are not little grown-ups: Small business needs its own organization theory. *Journal of Small Business Management*, •••, 17.

Daniel-Vasconcelos, V., Ribeiro, M., & Crisostomo, V. L. (2022). Does gender diversity moderate the relationship between CSR committees and sustainable development goals disclosure? Evidence from Latin American companies. *RAUSP Management Journal*, 57(4), 434–456. DOI: 10.1108/RAUSP-02-2022-0063

Davenport, T. H., & Ronanki, R. (2018). Artificial intelligence for the real world. *Harvard Business Review*, 96(1), 108–116.

Davidson, D. J. (2010). The applicability of the concept of resilience to social systems: Some sources of optimism and nagging doubts. *Society & Natural Resources*, 23(12), 1135–1149. DOI: 10.1080/08941921003652940

Davies, G., Chun, R., da Silva, R., & Ropert, S. (2004). A Corporate Character Scale to assess employee and customer views of organization reputation. *Corporate Reputation Review*, 7(2), 125–146. DOI: 10.1057/palgrave.crr.1540216

Davis, J., & Johnson, M. (2021). Human-AI collaboration and its impact on innovation performance. *Technology Management Review*, 34(1), 25–37. DOI: 10.1002/tmr.10435

De Andres, P., Azofra, V., & Lopez, F. (2005). Corporate boards in OECD countries: Size, composition, functioning and effectiveness. *Corporate Governance*, 13(2), 197–210. DOI: 10.1111/j.1467-8683.2005.00418.x de Deus, R. M., de Castro, R., Vieira, K. R. O., Leite, A. E., & Jabbour, C. J. C. (2015). The journey to sustainable universities: Insights from a Brazilian experience. *International Journal of Business Excellence*, 8(2), 146–159. DOI: 10.1504/IJBEX.2015.068205

de Mello, V. G., Kovaleski, J. L., Zola, F. C., Lima, F. R.Junior, Aragao, F. V., & De Genaro Chiroli, D. M. (2022). Proposal of a Fuzzy-QFD model for startup selection. *Technology Analysis and Strategic Management*, 52(3), 1395–1415.

Deci, E. L., & Ryan, R. M. (2000). The" what" and" why" of goal pursuits: Human needs and the self-determination of behavior. *Psychological Inquiry*, 11(4), 227–268. DOI: 10.1207/S15327965PLI1104_01

Delpechitre, D., Black, H. G., & Farrish, J. (2019). The Dark Side of Technology: Examining the Impact of Technology Overload on Salespeople. *Journal of Business and Industrial Marketing*, 34(2), 317–337. DOI: 10.1108/JBIM-03-2017-0057

Demirhan, D., Temel, S., & Durst, S. (2019). *The role of public entrepreneurship programs in fostering technology-based entrepreneurship: a Turkish case study, Societal Entrepreneurship and Competitiveness*. Emerald Publishing Limited.

Demir, K., Döven, G., & Sezen, B. (2019). Industry 5.0 and Human-Robot Co-working. *Procedia Computer Science*, 158, 688–695. DOI: 10.1016/j.procs.2019.09.104

Demirkiran, E., & Yonet, O. (2023). Are geert Hofstede's cultural dimensions correlated with pandemic statistics worldwide? *Gumushane University e-Journal of Faculty of Communication, 11*. https://dergipark.org.tr/en/download/article-file/3174748

Denysiuk, L. (2021). Success factors for corporate-startup collaboration, Technical Report, LBS Working Paper

Deprez, J., & Euwema, M. (2017). You Can't Always Get What You Want? Leadership Expectations of Intrapreneurs. *Journal of Managerial Psychology*, 32(6), 430–444. DOI: 10.1108/JMP-04-2016-0107

Derue, H., & Ribeiro-da-Silva, A. (2023). Therapeutic exercise interventions in rat models of arthritis. *Neurobiology of Pain*, 13, 100130. DOI: 10.1016/j.ynpai.2023.100130 PMID: 37179770

Diaz Tautiva, J. A., Rifo Rivera, F. I., Barros Celume, S. A., & Rifo Rivera, S. A. (2024). Mapping the research about organisations in the latin american context: A bibliometric analysis. *Management Review Quarterly*, 74(1), 121–169. DOI: 10.1007/s11301-022-00296-3

Dierendonck, D. (2011). Servant Leadership: A Review and Synthesis. *Journal of Management*, 37(4), 1228–1261. DOI: 10.1177/0149206310380462

Digital Marketing Institute. (2024). *Characteristics of Digital Leadership.* Retrieved at https://digitalmarketinginstitute.com/resources/lessons/digital-leadership_characteristics-of-digital-leadership_lxig#:~:text=What%20is%20Digital%20leadership%3F,part%20of%20your%20organizational%20culture

Dimov, D. (2010). Nascent entrepreneurs and venture emergence: Opportunity confidence, human capital, and early planning. *Journal of Management Studies*, 47(6), 1123–1153. DOI: 10.1111/j.1467-6486.2009.00874.x

Dindi, K. (2021). Tarih Felsefesi Bağlamında Hz. Musa'nın Asâsı -Mucize mi, Yoksa Hâkimiyet Sembolü mü? [Prophet moses' staff in the context of philosophy of history- Is it a miracle or a symbol of sovereignty?]. *Siyer Araştırmaları Dergisi*, 9, 108–110.

Donaldson, L., & Davis, J. H. (1991). Stewardship theory or agency theory: CEO governance and shareholder returns. *Australian Journal of Management*, 16(1), 49–64. DOI: 10.1177/031289629101600103

Dondi, M., Klier, J., Panier, F., & Schubert, J. (2021). *Defining the Skills Citizens Will Need in the Future World of Work*. Retrieved at https://www.mckinsey.com/industries/public-sector/our-insights/defining-the-skills-citizens-will-need-in-the-future-world-of-work#/

Donthu, N., Kumar, S., Mukherjee, D., Pandey, N., & Lim, W. M. (2021). Donthu, N., Kumar, S., Mukherjee, D.How to conduct a bibliometric analysis: An overview and guidelines. *Journal of Business Research*, 133, 285–296. DOI: 10.1016/j.jbusres.2021.04.070

Dragu, I. (2019). The evolution of corporate sustainability and corporate social responsibility towards the common goal of integrated reporting: Antecedents and perspectives for organizations and stakeholders. In Idowu, S. O., & Del Baldo, M. (Eds.), *Integrated Reporting, CSR, Sustainability, Ethics & Governance* (pp. 77–93). Springer., DOI: 10.1007/978-3-030-01719-4_4

Dreyer, J. (2024, August 07). *The 4 Types of Resilience in Action: Strengthening Your Mind and Body*. Jeanette Dreyer. https://www.jeanettedreyer.co.za/the-4-types-of-resilience-in-action/

Drishti, E., Kruja, D., & Curcija, M. (2016). An evaluation of the impact of entrepreneurship education on the entrepreneurship intentions in the Albanian late transition context. In *Routledge Handbook of Entrepreneurship in Developing Economies* (pp. 463–486). Routledge.

Drucker, P. F. (1985). *Innovation and Entrepreneurship: Practice and Principles*. Harper & Row.

Duan, W.-Y., Wu, T.-J., Wei, A.-P., & Huang, Y.-T. (2024). Reducing the adverse effects of compulsory citizenship behaviour on employee innovative behaviour via AI usage in China. *Asia Pacific Business Review*, •••, 1–21. DOI: 10.1080/13602381.2024.2332731

Duchek, S. (2020). Organizational resilience: A capability-based conceptualization. *Business Research*, 13(1), 215–246. DOI: 10.1007/s40685-019-0085-7

Dueholm Müller, S., Konzag, H., Agger Nielsen, J., & Bergsdóttir Sandholt, H. (2024). Digital Transformation Leadership Competencies: A Contingency Approach. *International Journal of Information Management*, 75, 102734. DOI: 10.1016/j.ijinfomgt.2023.102734

Dulewicz, V., & Herbert, P. (2004). Does the composition and practice of boards of directors bear any relationship to the performance of their companies? *Corporate Governance*, 12(3), 263–280. DOI: 10.1111/j.1467-8683.2004.00368.x

Dutot, V., & Castellano, S. (2015). Designing a measurement scale for E-Reputation. *Corporate Reputation Review*, 18(4), 294–313. DOI: 10.1057/crr.2015.15

Dyllick, T., & Hockerts, K. (2002). Beyond the business case for corporate sustainability. *Business Strategy and the Environment*, 11(2), 130–141. DOI: 10.1002/bse.323

Eberl, J. K., & Drews, P. (2021). *Digital Leadership – Mountain or Molehill? A Literature Review,* International Conference on Wirtschaftsinformatik 223–237. DOI: 10.1007/978-3-030-86800-0_17

EC. (2023). https://finance.ec.europa.eu/news/commission-adopts-european-sustainability-reporting-standards-2023-07-31_en

Edwards, M., & Hulme, D. (2014). *Non-governmental organisations-performance and accountability: Beyond the magic bullet.* Routledge. DOI: 10.4324/9781315070704

Egghe, L. (2006). Theory and practice of the g-index. *Scientometrics*, 69(1), 131–152. Advance online publication. DOI: 10.1007/s11192-006-0144-7

Eisenhardt, K. M. (1989). Building theories from case study research. *Academy of Management Review*, 14(4), 532–550. DOI: 10.2307/258557

Eisenmann, T. R. (2020). Determinants of early-stage startup performance: Survey results, Harvard Business School Entrepreneurial Management Working Paper, (21-057).

Eivazzadeh, N., & Nadiri, H. (2022). An empirical study to investigate the coercive management behavior: Evidence from academia. *E+M. Ekonomie a Management*, 25(1), 42–59. DOI: 10.15240/tul/001/2022-1-003

Ekinci, E. B. (2022). *Bastonun Gücü [The power of the cane].* https://www.ekrembugraekinci.com/article/?ID=1249&bastonun-g%C3%BCc%C3%BC

El Achkar, J. H., & Alsaba, M. (2024). *DYNAMIC INTEGRATION OF SUSTAINABILITY AND CLIMATE CHANGE IN ENGINEERING CURRICULA VIA CDIO. 20th International CDIO Conference*, Tunisia.

El Marrakchi, M., Bensaid, H., & Bellafkih, M. (2015b). Scoring reputation in online social networks. *10th International Conference on Intelligent Systems - Theories and Applications (SITA)*, 20-21 October 2015, Rabat, Morocco, pp. 1-6. https://DOI: 10.1109/SITA.2015.7358420

El Marrakchi, M., Bensaid, H., Bellafkih, M., & Bensaid, H. (2016). Intelligent reputation scoring in social networks: Use case of brands of smartphones. *11th International Conference on Intelligent Systems: Theories and Applications (SITA)*, 19-20 October 2016, Mohammedia, Morocco, pp. 1-6, https://DOI: 10.1109/SITA.2016.7772261

El Marrakchi, M., Bellafkih, M., & Bensaid, H. (2015a). *Towards reputation measurement in online social networks. 2015 Intelligent Systems and Computer Vision.* ISCV., DOI: 10.1109/ISACV.2015.7105540

Elangovan, U. (2021). *Industry 5.0: The Future of the Industrial Economy.* CRC Press., DOI: 10.1201/9781003190677

Elche, D., Ruiz-Palomino, P., & Linuesa-Langreo, J. (2020). Servant leadership and organizational citizenship behavior: The mediating role of empathy and service climate. *Journal of Business Research*, 110, 110–122.

Elezaj, S., & Ramaj, V. (2023). The Role of Innovation and Branding on Enterprise Sales Growth in Transition Countries. *Academic Journal of Interdisciplinary Studies, 12.*

Elson, C. (1995). Director compensation and the management captured board-the history of a symptom and a cure. *Southern Methodist Law Review*, 50, 127–174.

Emini, E., Ibraimi, S., & Rexhepi, G. (2023). The role of democratic leadership style and organisational learning in innovations and financial performance of enterprises. *International Journal of Environment. Workplace and Employment*, 7(3), 260–273. DOI: 10.1504/IJEWE.2023.135481

Erdogan, E., & Koohborfardhaghighi, S. (2019). Delivering a Systematic Framework for the Selection and Evaluation of Startups: *15th International Conference, GECON 2018*, Pisa, Italy, September 18–20, 2018, Proceedings, pp.151–159. DOI: 10.1007/978-3-030-13342-9_13

Ergul, A.S. & Kerse, G. (2024). The mediating role of organizational identification in the effect of compulsory citizenship behavior on employee silence: The case of Turkish (Konya Province) manufacturing industry. *Ekonomski vjesnik/Econviews, 37*(1), 127–138. https://doi.org/DOI: 10.51680/ev.37.1.9

Erhan, T., Uzunbacak, H. H., & Aydin, E. (2022). From Conventional to Digital Leadership: Exploring Digitalization of Leadership and Innovative Work Behavior. *Management Research Review*, 45(11), 1524–1543. DOI: 10.1108/MRR-05-2021-0338

Esen, T., Dahl, M. S., & Sorenson, O. (2023). Jockeys, horses or teams? The selection of startups by venture capitalists. *Journal of Business Venturing Insights*, 19, e00383. DOI: 10.1016/j.jbvi.2023.e00383

Espina-Romero, L., Guerrero-Alcedo, J., Goñi Avila, N., Noroño Sánchez, J. G., Gutiérrez Hurtado, H., & Quiñones Li, A. (2023). Industry 5.0: Tracking Scientific Activity on the Most Influential Industries, Associated Topics, and Future Research Agenda. *Sustainability (Basel)*, 15(6), 6. Advance online publication. DOI: 10.3390/su15065554

Estevam, E. J. G., & Kalinke, M. A. (2013). Recursos Tecnológicos e Ensino de Estatística na Educação Básica: um cenário de pesquisas brasileiras. *Rev. Bra. de Informática Na Educação, 21*(02).

European Commission. (2016). *Factories of the Future PPP: Towards Competitive EU Manufacturing*. EU Commission.

Evans, R., & Green, H. (2018). AI-driven data analytics for improved sustainability reporting. *Journal of Sustainable Development*, 11(4), 78–92. DOI: 10.5539/jsd.v11n4p78

Faliagka, E., Iliadis, L., Karydis, I., Rigou, M., Sioutas, S., Tsakalidis, A., & Tzimas, G. (2014). On-line consistent ranking on e-recruitment: Seeking the truth behind a well-formed CV. *Artificial Intelligence Review*, 42(3), 515–528. DOI: 10.1007/s10462-013-9414-y

Fama, E. F. (1980). Agency problems and the theory of the firm. *Journal of Political Economy*, 88(21), 288–307. DOI: 10.1086/260866

Farag, K., & Aktas, C. B. (2024). A survey of the most prevalent sustainability initiatives at universities. *International Journal of Sustainability in Higher Education, ahead-of-print*(ahead-of-print). DOI: 10.1108/IJSHE-07-2023-0285

Fenwick, M., McCahery, J. A., & Vermeulen, E. P. M. (2021). Will the World Ever Be the Same After COVID-19? Two Lessons from the First Global Crisis of a Digital Age. *European Business Organization Law Review*, 22(1), 125–145. DOI: 10.1007/s40804-020-00194-9

Fernandez-Feijoo, B., Romero, S., & Ruiz-Blanco, S. (2014). Women on boards: Do they affect sustainability reporting? *Corporate Social Responsibility and Environmental Management*, 21(6), 351–364. DOI: 10.1002/csr.1329

Fernandez-Gonzalez, A., Rodriguez-Sanchez, M., & Martinez-Lopez, J. (2024). Systemic resilience in organizational transformation. *Journal of Organizational Change Management*, 37(1), 88–107.

Ferrati, F. and Muffatto, M. (2019). A systematic literature review of the assessment criteria applied by equity investors, volume 1, pp.304–312.

Ferrati, F., Chen, H., & Muffatto, M. (2021). A Deep Learning Model for Startups Evaluation Using Time Series Analysis, F. Matos, M. Ferreiro, Rosa, and I. Salavisa, editors, Proceedings of 16th European Conference On Innovation & Entrepreneurship (Ecie, 2021), Vol 1, pp.311–320, Electr Network, Sep 16-17, 2021.

Ferreira, M., & Zambaldi, F. (2019). The mediating role of consumer engagement with the brand community and its effect on corporate reputation. *International Journal on Media Management*, 21(1), 45–64. DOI: 10.1080/14241277.2019.1585354

Filippucci, F., Gal, P., Jona-Lasinio, C., Leandro, A., & Nicoletti, G. (2024). The impact of Artificial Intelligence on productivity, distribution and growth: Key mechanisms, initial evidence and policy challenges.

Finger, M., & Samwer, O. (2013). *America's most successful startups: Lessons for entrepreneurs*. Springer Science & Business Media.

Fiorentino, R., Longobardi, S., & Scaletti, A. (2021). The early growth of start-ups: Innovation matters. Evidence from Italy. *European Journal of Innovation Management*, 24(5), 1525–1546. DOI: 10.1108/EJIM-02-2020-0057

Fombrun, C. J., Gardberg, N. A., & Sever, J. M. (2000). The Reputation QuotientSM: A multi-stakeholder measure of corporate reputation. *Journal of Brand Management*, 7(4), 241–255. DOI: 10.1057/bm.2000.10

Fombrun, C., Ponzi, L., & Newburry, W. (2015). Stakeholder Tracking and Analysis: The RepTrak® System for Measuring Corporate Reputation. *Corporate Reputation Review*, 18(1), 3–24. DOI: 10.1057/crr.2014.21

Foundation, N. R. (2016). *Research, Innovation and Enterprise (RIE) 2015 Plan*. Prime Minister's Office of Singapore.

Fowler, A. (2013). *Striking a balance: A guide to enhancing the effectiveness of non-governmental organisations in international development*. Routledge. DOI: 10.4324/9781315070735

Fraga-Lamas, P., Lopes, S. I., & Fernandez-Carames, T. M. (2021). Green IoT and Edge AI as Key Technological Enablers for a Sustainable Digital Transition towards a Smart Circular Economy: An Industry 5.0 Use Case. *Sensors (Basel)*, 21(17), 5745. Advance online publication. DOI: 10.3390/s21175745 PMID: 34502637

Franke, N., Gruber, M., Harhoff, D., & Henkel, J. (2006). What you are is what you like - similarity biases in venture capitalists' evaluations of start-up teams. *Journal of Business Venturing*, 21(6), 802–826. DOI: 10.1016/j.jbusvent.2005.07.001

Franke, N., Gruber, M., Harhoff, D., & Henkel, J. (2008). Venture capitalists' evaluations of start-up teams: Trade-offs, knock-out criteria, and the impact of VC experience. *Entrepreneurship Theory and Practice*, 32(3), 459–483. DOI: 10.1111/j.1540-6520.2008.00236.x

Freeman, R. E. (1984). *Strategic Management: A Stakeholder Approach*. Pitman Publishing.

Fuertes-Callén, Y., Cuellar-Fernández, B., & Serrano-Cinca, C. (2022). Predicting startup survival using first years financial statements. *Journal of Small Business Management*, 60(6), 1314–1350. DOI: 10.1080/00472778.2020.1750302

Fu, X., Yue, K., Liu, L., & Liu, L. (2016). Aggregating ordinal user preferences for effective reputation computation of online services. *2016 IEEE International Conference on Web Services (ICWS)*, San Francisco, CA, USA, 2016, pp. 554-561, DOI: 10.1109/ICWS.2016.77

Gagné, M., & Deci, E. L. (2005). Self-determination theory and work motivation. *Journal of Organizational Behavior*, 26(4), 331–362. DOI: 10.1002/job.322

Gajendran, R. S., & Harrison, D. A. (2007). The good, the bad, and the unknown about telecommuting: Meta-analysis of psychological mediators and individual consequences. *The Journal of Applied Psychology*, 92(6), 1524–1541. DOI: 10.1037/0021-9010.92.6.1524 PMID: 18020794

Galbreath, J. (2011). Are there gender-related influences on corporate sustainability? A study of women on boards of directors. *Journal of Management & Organization*, 17(1), 17–38. DOI: 10.5172/jmo.2011.17.1.17

Galletta, S., Mazzù, S., Naciti, V., & Paltrinieri, A. (2024). A PRISMA systematic review of greenwashing in the banking industry: A call for action. *Research in International Business and Finance*, 69, 102262. DOI: 10.1016/j.ribaf.2024.102262

Gann, L. (2024). *What is an h-index? How do I find the h-index for a particular author?* The University of Texas, MD Anderson Cancer Center. https://mdanderson.libanswers.com/faq/26221#:~:text=The%20h%2Dindex%20is%20calculated,cited%20at%20least%2017%20times

Ganz, M., Nohria, N., & Khurana, R. (2010). Leading change. In *Handbook of leadership theory and practice: A Harvard Business School centennial colloquium* (pp. 527–568). Harvard Business Review Press.

Gao, P., & Gao, Y. (2024). How Does Digital Leadership Foster Employee Innovative Behavior: A Cognitive–Affective Processing System Perspective. *Behavioral Sciences (Basel, Switzerland)*, 14(5), 362. DOI: 10.3390/bs14050362 PMID: 38785853

Garcia, A., Rodriguez, J., & Sanchez, L. (2024). Building resilience through human-centric risk management. *International Journal of Risk Management*, 29(1), 15–30. DOI: 10.1002/ijrm.12450

García-Lillo, F., Claver-Cortés, E., Úbeda-García, M., & Marco-Lajara, B. (2017). Exploring the intellectual structure of research on 'born globals' and INVs: A literature review using bibliometric methods. *Journal of International Entrepreneurship*, •••, 1–29.

Gartoumi, K. I. (2024). Five-Year Review of Blockchain in Construction Management: Scientometric and Thematic Analysis (2017-2023). *Automation in Construction*, 168, 105773. Advance online publication. DOI: 10.1016/j.autcon.2024.105773

Gbadegeshin, S. A., Al Natsheh, A., Ghafel, K., Mohammed, O., Koskela, A., Rimpiläinen, A., Tikkanen, J., & Kuoppala, A. (2022). Overcoming the valley of death: A new model for high technology startups. *Sustainable Futures : An Applied Journal of Technology, Environment and Society*, 4, 100077. DOI: 10.1016/j.sftr.2022.100077

Gerhardt, V., Dos Santos, J., Rubin, E., Neuenfeldt, A., & Siluk, J. (2021). Stakeholders'perception to characterize the start-ups' success. *Journal of Technology Management & Innovation*, 16(1), 38–50. DOI: 10.4067/S0718-27242021000100038

Ghobakhloo, M., Iranmanesh, M., Fathi, M., Rejeb, A., Foroughi, B., & Nikbin, D. (2024). Beyond Industry 4.0: A systematic review of Industry 5.0 technologies and implications for social, environmental and economic sustainability. *Asia-Pacific Journal of Business Administration, ahead-of-print*(ahead-of-print). DOI: 10.1108/APJBA-08-2023-0384

Ghobakhloo, M., Iranmanesh, M., Mubarak, M. F., Mubarik, M., Rejeb, A., & Nilashi, M. (2022). Identifying industry 5.0 contributions to sustainable development: A strategy roadmap for delivering sustainability values. *Sustainable Production and Consumption*, 33, 716–737. DOI: 10.1016/j.spc.2022.08.003

Ghobakhloo, M., Mahdiraji, H. A., Iranmanesh, M., & Sadeghi, V. J. (2024). From Industry 4.0 digital manufacturing to industry 5.0 digital society: A roadmap toward human-centric, sustainable, and resilient production. *Information Systems Frontiers*. Advance online publication. DOI: 10.1007/s10796-024-10476-z

Ghosh, R., Nachmias, S., Murdoch, D., & McGuire, D. (2024). Prioritizing humans: HRD's vital role in AI adoption for workplace success. *Human Resource Development International*, 27(3), 319–323. DOI: 10.1080/13678868.2024.2354627

Giannarakis, G. (2014). The determinants influencing the extent of CSR disclosure. *International Journal of Law and Management*, 56(5), 393–416. DOI: 10.1108/IJLMA-05-2013-0021

Gilli, K., Nippa, M., & Knappstein, M. (2023). Leadership Competencies for Digital Transformation: An Exploratory Content Analysis of Job Advertisements. *German Journal of Human Resource Management*, 37(1), 50–75. DOI: 10.1177/23970022221087252

Göçer, A., Fawcett, S. E., & Tuna, O. (2018). what does the sustainability-risk interaction look like? Exploring nuanced relationships in emerging economy sustainability initiatives. *Sustainability (Basel)*, 10(8), 2716. DOI: 10.3390/su10082716

Goh, M. H. (2024). https://blog.bcm-institute.org/operational-resilience/roles-and-responsibilities-for-board-of-directors-in-operational-resilience?hsCtaTracking=fdbeddea-0d0f-4f52-9a10-b6960c807070%7C04c707ba-642d-42b0-829c-0a73213e36d4

Goldring, D. (2015). Reputation orientation. *Marketing Intelligence & Planning*, 33(5), 784–803. DOI: 10.1108/MIP-11-2013-0183

Gomes, L. P., Caetano, M. O., Brand, S. M., Dai-Prá, L. B., & Pereira, B. N. (2023). Maintenance of an environmental management system based on ISO 14001 in a Brazilian private university, seeking sustainable development. *International Journal of Sustainability in Higher Education*, 24(2), 361–381. DOI: 10.1108/IJSHE-07-2021-0298

Goodwin, J., Rob, P., Freeston, M., Garland, D., Grahame, V., Kernohan, A., Labus, M., Osborne, M., Parr, J. R., Wright, C., & Rodgers, J. (2022). Caregiver perspectives on the impact of uncertainty on the everyday lives of autistic children and their families. *Autism*, 26(4), 827–838. DOI: 10.1177/13623613211033757 PMID: 34291688

Grabowska, S., Saniuk, S., & Gajdzik, B. (2022). Industry 5.0: Improving humanization and sustainability of Industry 4.0. *Scientometrics*, 127(6), 3117–3144. DOI: 10.1007/s11192-022-04370-1 PMID: 35502439

Graham, S. J., & Sichelman, T. S. (2016). *Intellectual property and technology startups: what entrepreneurs tell us, Technological Innovation: Generating Economic Results* (Vol. 26). Emerald Group Publishing Limited.

Greenhaus, J. H., & Allen, T. D. (2011). Work–family balance: A review and extension of the literature.

Greenleaf, R. (1977). *Servant leadership: a journey into the nature of legitimate power and greatness*. Poulist Press.

Gruber, M., MacMillan, I. C., & Thompson, J. D. (2013). Escaping the prior knowledge corridor: What shapes the number and variety of market opportunities identified before market entry of technology start-ups? *Organization Science*, 24(1), 280–300. DOI: 10.1287/orsc.1110.0721

Guarino, S. N. (2016). *"It's more unfair for me": The moderating role of equity sensitivity on the relationship between compulsory citizenship behavior and distributive justice* [Doctoral dissertation, Saint Louis University]. ProQuest Dissertations and Thesis Global.

Guerra Fernandes, J. A., Marques, C. S., Silva, R., & Martins, H. (2022). Ethnic entrepreneurship: A bibliometric review and future research agenda. *Strategic Change*, 31(4), 397–413. DOI: 10.1002/jsc.2516

Gupta, M., Shaheen, M., & Reddy, P. K. (2017). Impact of psychological capital on organizational citizenship behavior. *Journal of Management Development*, 36(7), 973–983. DOI: 10.1108/JMD-06-2016-0084

Gürdoğan-Bayır, Ö., & Çengelci Köse, T. (2019). Kültürel miras ve korunmasına ilişkin ortaokul öğrencilerinin görüşleri [Secondary School Students' Views about Cultural Heritage and Preserving Cultural Heritage]. *Kastamonu Education Journal*, 27(4), 1827–1840. DOI: 10.24106/kefdergi.3393

Gutiérrez-Ángel, N., Sánchez-García, J.-N., Mercader-Rubio, I., García-Martín, J., & Brito-Costa, S. (2022). Digital literacy in the university setting: A literature review of empirical studies between 2010 and 2021. *Frontiers in Psychology*, 13, 896800. Advance online publication. DOI: 10.3389/fpsyg.2022.896800 PMID: 36176798

Gutmann, T. (2023). Organizational design choices for corporate incubators. *IEEE Transactions on Engineering Management*, (99), 1–15. DOI: 10.1109/TEM.2023.3265511

Gutowski, T. G., Allwood, J. M., Herrmann, C., & Sahni, S. A. (2013). Global assessment of manufacturing: Economic development, energy use, carbon emissions, and the potential for energy efficiency and materials recycling, *Annual Review of Environment and Resources, 38* (81)-106.

Habeeb, S. (2019). A proposed instrument for assessing organizational citizenship behavior in BFSI companies in India. *Cogent Business & Management*, 6(1), 1–20. DOI: 10.1080/23311975.2019.1625702

Hackman, J. R., & Oldham, G. R. (1980). *Work Redesign*. Addison-Wesley.

Hair, J. F., Black, W. C., Babin, B. J., Anderson, R. E., & Tatham, R. L. (2005). *Multivariate Data Analysis* (6th ed.). Pearson Education, Inc.

Hair, J., Hult, G., & Sarstedt, M. (2017). *A premium on partial least squares structural equation modelling (PLS-SEM)*. SAGE.

Hakovirta, M., & Denuwara, N. (2020). Denuwara, N. How COVID-19 Redefines the Concept of Sustainability. *Sustainability (Basel)*, 12(9), 3727. DOI: 10.3390/su12093727

Halaç, H. H., Önaçan, M. B. K., Önel, T., & Ayvaz, E. (2022). Oyunlaştırma ile Kültürel Miras Farkındalığının Oluşturulması: Tarihsel Oyun Yolculuğu (TOY) [Creating Cultural Heritage Awareness with Gamification: Historical Game Journey (HGJ)]. *In Proceedings of the5th International Dede Korkut Conference of Turkish Culture, History and Literature*, İzmir, 334-338.

Halaç, H. H., & Ayvaz, E. (2022). Kültürel Miras Öğretimi: Tarihsel Oyun Yolculuğu (TOY) [Teaching Cultural Heritage: Historical Game Journey (HGJ)]. *InProceedings of the 5th International Dede Korkut Conference of Turkish Culture, History and Literature*, İzmir, 330-333.

Hamyeme, S., Belagra, F., & Bouzidi, F. (2024). The Effect of Implementing Servant Leadership Practices on the Adoption of Digital Transformation for Companies in the Telecommunications Sector. *Business Ethics and Leadership*. https://doi.org/.DOI: 10.61093/bel.8(3).26-42.2024

Hamzah, H., Hubeis, M., & Hendri, I. (2020). The effect of career development, justice organization and quality of work life to organizational commitment andiImplications to organizational citizenship behavior of employees at PT. *Perkebunan Nusantara XIII.International Review of Management and Marketing*, 10(3), 101–109. https://econjournals.com/index.php/irmm/article/view/10002. DOI: 10.32479/irmm.10002

Hanelt, A., Bohnsack, R., Marz, D., & Antunes Marante, C. (2021). A Systematic Review of the Literature on Digital Transformation: Insights and Implications for Strategy and Organizational Change. *Journal of Management Studies*, 58(5), 1159–1197. DOI: 10.1111/joms.12639

Harbeke, E., & Künlen, L. (2024, November 19). *The dawn of Industry 5.0*. https://www.rothschildandco.com/en/newsroom/insights/2024/10/the-dawn-of-industry-5.0/#:~:text=Industry%205.0%20redefines%20the%20purpose,and%20societal%20impact%2C%20Chart%203

Harjoto, M., Laksmana, I., & Lee, R. (2015). Board diversity and corporate social responsibility. *Journal of Business Ethics*, 132(4), 641–660. DOI: 10.1007/s10551-014-2343-0

Hart, S. L. (1995). A natural-resource-based view of the firm. *Academy of Management Review*, 20(4), 986–1014. DOI: 10.2307/258963

Hashai, N., & Zahra, S. (2022). Founder team prior work experience: An asset or a liability for startup growth? *Strategic Entrepreneurship Journal*, 16(1), 155–184. DOI: 10.1002/sej.1406

Hashim, M., Tlemsani, I., Mason-Jones, R., Matthews, R., & Ndrecaj, V. (2024) Higher education via the lens of industry 5.0: Strategy and perspective. *Social Sciences & Humanities Open*. vol 9. ISSN 2590-2911. https://doi.org/DOI: 10.1016/j.ssaho.2024.100828

Hasyim, H., & Bakri, M. (2024). Organizational Transformation in Adopting Hybrid Work Models: A Literature Review on Organizational Changes and Employee Readiness. *Jurnal Manajemen Bisnis*, 11(2), 1170–1182. DOI: 10.33096/jmb.v11i2.806

Hayes, A. F. (2013). *Introduction to Mediation, Moderation, and Conditional Process Analysis: A Regression-based Approach*. Guilford Publications.

Hector, O., & Cameron, R. (2023). Human-centric management: Nurturing talent, building culture, and driving organizational success. *The International Journal of Science in Society*, 5(4), 511–525. DOI: 10.54783/ijsoc.v5i4.809

Héder, M. (2017). From NASA to EU: The evolution of the TRL scale in Public Sector Innovation. *The Innovation Journal*, 22(2), 1–23.

He, P., Peng, Z., Zhao, H., & Estay, C. (2019). How and when compulsory citizenship behavior leads to employee silence: A moderated mediation model based on moral disengagement and supervisor-subordinate guanxi views. *Journal of Business Ethics*, 155(1), 259–274. DOI: 10.1007/s10551-017-3550-2

He, P., Wang, X., Wu, M., & Estay, C. (2018). Compulsory citizenship behavior and employee silence: The roles of emotional exhaustion and organizational identification. *Social Behavior and Personality*, 46(12), 2025–2047. DOI: 10.2224/sbp.7452

He, P., Zhou, Q., Zhao, H., Jiang, C., & Wu, Y. J. (2020). Compulsory citizenship behavior and employee creativity: Creative self-efficacy as a mediator and negative affect as a moderator. *Frontiers in Psychology*, 11, 1640. Advance online publication. DOI: 10.3389/fpsyg.2020.01640 PMID: 32793046

He, Q., Fu, J., Wu, W., & Pervaiz, S. (2022). Does compulsory citizenship behavior necessarily reduce employee? Work well-being? The role of relative deprivation and resource compensation based on compulsory citizenship behavior. *Psychology Research and Behavior Management*, 15, 1105–1119. DOI: 10.2147/PRBM.S321689 PMID: 35535130

Hermann, M., Pentek, T., & Otto, B. (2016). Design principles for industrie 4.0 scenarios. *System Sciences (HICSS)49th Hawaii International Conference* (pp. 3928-3937). IEEE.

Hermundsdottir, F., & Aspelund, A. (2021). Sustainability innovations and firm competitiveness: A review. *Journal of Cleaner Production*, 280, 124715. DOI: 10.1016/j.jclepro.2020.124715

Hernandez, M. (2012). Toward an understanding of the psychology of stewardship. *Academy of Management Review*, 37(2), 172–193. DOI: 10.5465/amr.2010.0363

Hernandez, P., Wong, H., & Patel, R. (2020). Leveraging digital tools for real-time sustainability reporting. *Journal of Environmental Management*, 269, 110810. DOI: 10.1016/j.jenvman.2020.110810

Herold, D. M., Fedor, D. B., Caldwell, S., & Liu, Y. (2008). The effects of transformational and change leadership on employees' commitment to a change: A multilevel study. *The Journal of Applied Psychology*, 93(2), 346–357. DOI: 10.1037/0021-9010.93.2.346 PMID: 18361637

Hillman, A. J., Cannella, A. A., & Paetzold, R. L. (2000). The resource dependence role of corporate directors: Strategic adaptation of board composition in response to environmental change. *Journal of Management Studies*, 37(2), 235–256. DOI: 10.1111/1467-6486.00179

Hillman, A. J., & Dalziel, T. (2003). Boards of directors and firm performance: Integrating agency and resource dependence perspectives. *Academy of Management Review*, 28(3), 383–396. DOI: 10.5465/amr.2003.10196729

Hillman, A. J., Withers, M. C., & Collins, B. J. (2009). Resource dependence theory: A review. *Journal of Management*, 55, 27–47.

Hirsch, J. E. (2005). An index to quantify an individual's scientific research output. *Proceedings of the National Academy of Sciences of the United States of America*, 102(46), 16569–16572. DOI: 10.1073/pnas.0507655102 PMID: 16275915

Hobfoll, S. E. (1989). Conservation of resources: A new attempt at conceptualizing stress. *The American Psychologist*, 44(3), 513–524. DOI: 10.1037/0003-066X.44.3.513 PMID: 2648906

Hobfoll, S. E., & Lilly, R. S. (1993). Resource conservation as a strategy for community psychology. *Journal of Community Psychology*, 21(2), 128–148. DOI: 10.1002/1520-6629(199304)21:2<128::AID-JCOP2290210206>3.0.CO;2-5

Hoch, J. E., Bommer, W. H., Dulebohn, J. H., & Wu, D. (2018). Do ethical, authentic, and servant leadership explain variance above and beyond transformational leadership? A meta-analysis. *Journal of Management*, 44(2), 501–552. DOI: 10.1177/0149206316665461

Hock-Doepgen, M., Montasser, J. S., Klein, S., Clauss, T., & Maalaoui, A. (2024). The Role of Innovative Work Behavior and Organizational Support for Business Model Innovation. *R & D Management*. Advance online publication. DOI: 10.1111/radm.12671

Hoekstra, E., & Peterson, S. (2005). Beyond Wall Street: leadership challenges unique to small private companies and entrepreneurial firms. Sims, R.R. and Quatro, S.A. (Eds), Leadership: Succeeding in the Private, Public, and Not-for-profit Sectors, M.E Sharpe, 46-64.

Hofstede, G. (1984). *Culture's consequences: International differences in work-related values*. Sage.

Hojdik, V., & Majtán, S. (2017). Online reputation management as an integral part of company business management. *Proceedings of the 2nd Annual International Scientific Conference of Business Economics, Management and Marketing (ISCOBEMM)*, Zajeci, Czech Republic, May 25-26, pp.76-83.

Hoogendoorn, S., Parker, S. C., & Van Praag, M. (2017). Smart or diverse start-up teams? Evidence from a field experiment. *Organization Science*, 28(6), 1010–1028. DOI: 10.1287/orsc.2017.1158

Hooper, D., Coughlan, J., & Mullen, M. (2008). *Structural Equation Modelling: Guidelines for Determining Model Fit*, Electronic Journal of Business Research Methods, 6(1), 53-60. Retrieved at http://arrow.dit.ie/cgi/viewcontent.cgi?article=1001&context= buschmanart.

Horvat, D., Jäger, A., & Lerch, C. M. (2024). Fostering innovation by complementing human competences and emerging technologies: An industry 5.0 perspective. *International Journal of Production Research*, •••, 1–25. DOI: 10.1080/00207543.2024.2372009

Hosftede, G. (2001). *Culture's Consequences: Comparing Values, Behaviors, Institutions, and Organizations Across Nations* (2nd ed.). Sage Publications.

*How to build organizational resilience: 6 proven steps*. (n.d.). Everbridge. Retrieved October 9, 2024, from https://www.everbridge.com/blog/how-to-build-organizational-resilience-six-proven-steps/

Howladar, M. H. R., & Rahman, M. M. (2021). Influence of servant leadership on organizational citizenship behavior: The role of organizational commitment. *International Journal of Research in Business and Social Science*, 10(1), 39–50.

Hoxhalli, G., Ulaj, G., & Kola, V. (2024). Immigrant Entrepreneurship in Europe: Insights from a Bibliometric Analysis. *International Journal of Management Science and Business Administration, 10*(6), 7-18. https://doi.org/. 2014.106.1001DOI: 10.18775/ijmsba.1849-5664-5419

Hristov, I., & Chirico, A. (2019). The Role of Sustainability Key Performance Indicators (KPIs) in Implementing Sustainable Strategies. *Sustainability (Basel)*, 11(20), 20. Advance online publication. DOI: 10.3390/su11205742

Hsu, H. E. (2010). The relationship between board characteristics and financial performance: An empirical study of United States initial public offerings. *International Journal of Management*, 27(2), 332–341.

Huang, C. C., You, C. S., & Tsai, M. T. (2012). A multidimensional analysis of ethical climate, job satisfaction, organizational commitment, and organizational citizenship behaviors. *Nursing Ethics*, 19(4), 513–529. DOI: 10.1177/0969733011433923 PMID: 22753457

Huang, N., Qiu, S., Yang, S., & Deng, R. (2021). Ethical leadership and organizationaş citizenship behavior: Mediation of trust and psychological well-being. *Psychology Research and Behavior Management*, 14, 655–664. DOI: 10.2147/PRBM.S311856 PMID: 34104011

Huang, S., Wang, B., Li, X., Zheng, P., Mourtzis, D., & Wang, L. (2022). Industry 5.0 and Society 5.0-Comparison, complementation and co-evolution. *Journal of Manufacturing Systems*, 64, 424–428. DOI: 10.1016/j.jmsy.2022.07.010

Hudakova, M., Urbancova, H., & Vnouckova, L. (2019). Key Criteria and Competences Defining the Sustainability of Start-Up Teams and Projects in the Incubation and Acceleration Phase. *Sustainability (Basel)*, 11(23), 6720. DOI: 10.3390/su11236720

Hung, T.-K., Lee, S.-C., Wu, Y.-S., & Hsieh, H.-M. (2022). Compulsory citizenship behavior and employees' contextual performance: Roles of perceived psychological safety and political skill. *Social Behavior and Personality*, 50(11), 1–13. DOI: 10.2224/sbp.11918

Hung, T.-K., Wang, C.-H., Tian, M., Lin, M., & Liu, W.-H. (2022). How to prevent stress in the workplace by emotional regulation? The relationship between compulsory citizen behavior, job engagement, and job performance. *SAGE Open*, 12(2), 21582440221105483. Advance online publication. DOI: 10.1177/21582440221105483

Huse, M., & Rindova, V. (2001). Stakeholders' expectations of board roles: The case of subsidiary boards. *The Journal of Management and Governance*, 5(2), 153–178. DOI: 10.1023/A:1013017909067

Husic, D. W. (2024). Reframing sustainability initiatives in higher education. *Sustainable Earth Reviews*, 7(1), 5. DOI: 10.1186/s42055-024-00076-9

Hussainey, K., Albitar, K., & Alkaraan, F. (2022). Corporate narrative reporting on industry 4.0 technologies: Does governance matter? *International Journal of Accounting and Information Management*, 30(4), 457–476. https://www.emerald.com/insight/1834-7649.htm. DOI: 10.1108/IJAIM-02-2022-0024

Hwa, L. C., Leow, J., Lau, J., Ho, A., & Yong, C. H. (2017). *Design thinking, the Guidebook*. Royal Civil Service Commission. https://www.rcsc.gov.bt/wp-content/uploads/2017/07/dt-guide-book-master-copy.pdf

Hyytinen, A., Pajarinen, M., & Rouvinen, P. (2015). Does innovativeness reduce startup survival rates? *Journal of Business Venturing*, 30(4), 564–581. DOI: 10.1016/j.jbusvent.2014.10.001

Ibrahim, M. S., & Saber, S. (2023). Machine learning and predictive analytics: Advancing disease prevention in healthcare. *Journal of Contemporary Healthcare Analytics*, 7(1), 53–71.

Ienciu, I. A., Popa, I. E., & Ienciu, N. M. (2012). Environmental reporting and good practice of corporate governance: Petroleum industry case study. *Procedia Economics and Finance*, 3, 961–967. DOI: 10.1016/S2212-5671(12)00258-4

Imran, F., Shahzad, K., Butt, A., & Kantola, J. (2020). Leadership Competencies for Digital Transformation: Evidence from Multiple Cases. In: Kantola, J., Nazir, S. & Salminen, V. (Eds.) *Advances in Human Factors, Business Management and Leadership:Proceedings of the AHFE 2020 Virtual Conferences on Human Factors, Business Management and Society, and Human Factors in Management and Leadership*, July 16-20, 2020, USA, 81-87. Advances in Intelligent Systems and Computing, Vol 1209. Cham: Springer. DOI: 10.1007/978-3-030-50791-6_11

*Industry 5.0 - European Commission*. (2022, January 10). Research and innovation. Retrieved October 7, 2024, from https://research-and-innovation.ec.europa.eu/research-area/industrial-research-and-innovation/industry-50_en

*Industry 5.0 Market Trends and Growth Opportunities for 2024 - 2030*. (2024, August 23). LinkedIn. Retrieved October 12, 2024, from https://www.linkedin.com/pulse/industry-50-market-trends-growth-opportunities-2024-hiyof

*Industry 5.0: Adding the human edge to industry 4.0*. (n.d.). SAP. Retrieved October 8, 2024, from https://www.sap.com/mena/insights/industry-5-0.html

Inglis, S., & Weaver, L. (2000). Designing agendas to reflect board roles and responsibilities: Results of a study. *Nonprofit Management & Leadership*, 11(1), 65–77. DOI: 10.1002/nml.11106

Insights, E. H. L. (2023, July 27). *Why Digital Leadership Is A Non-negotiable for Future Success*. Retrieved at https://hospitalityinsights.ehl.edu/digital-leadership-for-future-success

*Integrating Technology and Human Skills for Future Workplaces.* (2024, June 24). LinkedIn. Retrieved October 9, 2024, from https://www.linkedin.com/pulse/integrating-technology-human-skills-future-workplaces-mcdermott-fvu5f

International Financial Reporting Standards (IFRS). (2023). https://www.ifrs.org/issued-standards/ifrs-sustainability-standards-navigator/

Irizarry, J. L. (2022). Integrating Mindfulness in Public and Nonprofit Education Programs to Foster Social Equity. *Public Integrity*, 24(4–5), 504–516. DOI: 10.1080/10999922.2022.2034356

*ISO - International Organization for Standardization.* (2024). https://www.iso.org/home.html

*It's Time to Prioritize Your Work-Life Balance.* (2024, March 13). Harvard Online. Retrieved October 9, 2024, from https://www.harvardonline.harvard.edu/blog/prioritize-work-life-balance

Ivanov, D. (2023). The Industry 5.0 framework: Viability-based integration of the resilience, sustainability, and human-centricity perspectives. *International Journal of Production Research*, 61(5), 1683–1695. DOI: 10.1080/00207543.2022.2118892

Ivanović, D., Fu, H.-Z., & Ho, Y.-S. (2015). Publications from Serbia in the Science Citation Index Expanded: A bibliometric analysis. *Scientometrics*, 105(1), 145–160. DOI: 10.1007/s11192-015-1664-9

Jackling, B., & Johl, S. (2009). Board structure and firm performance: Evidence from India's top companies. *Corporate Governance*, 17(4), 492–509. DOI: 10.1111/j.1467-8683.2009.00760.x

Jacomo, P. (2017). Workforce Agility: Are you ready now? Future of work. [Online] [Cited 4.02.19] Available from the World Wide Web: URLhttps://www.digitalistmag.com/future-of-work/2017/01/09/workforce-agilityare-you-ready-now-04828683/

Jahmurataj, V., Ramadani, V., Bexheti, A., Rexhepi, G., Abazi-Alili, H., & Krasniqi, B. A. (2023). Unveiling the determining factors of family business longevity: Evidence from Kosovo. *Journal of Business Research*, 159, 113745. DOI: 10.1016/j.jbusres.2023.113745

Jáki, E., Major, F., & Molnár, E. (2022). *Key Competencies of Startup Teams Sought After by Investors.* DOI: 10.1007/978-3-030-81663-6_5

Jamali, D., Samara, G., & Meho, L. I. (2023). Determinants of research productivity and efficiency among the Arab world's accredited business schools. *Management Review Quarterly*, 1-33.

Janggu, T., Darus, F., Zain, M. M., & Sawani, Y. (2014). Does good corporate governance lead to better sustainability reporting? An analysis using structural equation modeling. *Procedia: Social and Behavioral Sciences*, 145, 138–145. DOI: 10.1016/j.sbspro.2014.06.020

Jan, M. A., Khan, F., Khan, R., Mastorakis, S., Menon, V. G., Alazab, M., & Watters, P. (2021). Lightweight Mutual Authentication and Privacy-Preservation Scheme for Intelligent Wearable Devices in Industrial-CPS. *IEEE Transactions on Industrial Informatics*, 17(8), 5829–5839. DOI: 10.1109/TII.2020.3043802 PMID: 33981186

Jano, D. (2023). Mapping Balkan–Southeast European studies. *Southeast European and Black Sea Studies*, 23(4), 801–817. DOI: 10.1080/14683857.2022.2153400

Janssen, O. (2000). Job Demands, Perceptions of Effort-Reward Fairness and Innovative Work Behaviour. *Journal of Occupational and Organizational Psychology*, 73(3), 287–302. DOI: 10.1348/096317900167038

Janssen, O. (2001). Fairness Perceptions as a Moderator in the Curvilinear Relationships between Job Demands, and Job Performance and Job Satisfaction. *Academy of Management Journal*, 44(5), 1039–1050. DOI: 10.2307/3069447

Jaskyte, K. (2004). Transformational Leadership, Organizational Culture, and Innovativeness in Nonprofit Organizations. *Nonprofit Management & Leadership*, 15(2), 153–168. DOI: 10.1002/nml.59

Javed, A., Shahzad, F., Rehman, S., Bin Zikria, Y., Razzak, I., Jalil, Z., & Xu, G. (2022). Future smart cities requirements, emerging technologies, applications, challenges, and future aspects. *Cities (London, England)*, 129, 103794. Advance online publication. DOI: 10.1016/j.cities.2022.103794

Jensen, M. C. (1993). The modern industrial revolution, exit, and the failure of internal control systems. *The Journal of Finance*, 48(3), 831–880. DOI: 10.1111/j.1540-6261.1993.tb04022.x

Jiang, Q., & Kurnitski, J. (2023). Performance based core sustainability metrics for university campuses developing towards climate neutrality: A robust PICSOU framework. *Sustainable Cities and Society*, 97, 104723. DOI: 10.1016/j.scs.2023.104723

Jin, X., & Hahm, S. (2019). The influence of high-power distance on turnover intention and emotional exhaustion among information technology workers in Korea: The mediating effects of compulsory citizenship behavior. *International Journal of Innovation. Creativity and Change*, 7(4), 262–278.

Jizi, M., Salama, A., Dixon, R., & Stratling, R. (2014). Corporate governance and corporate social responsibility disclosure: Evidence from the US banking sector. *Journal of Business Ethics*, 125(4), 601–615. DOI: 10.1007/s10551-013-1929-2

Jo, H., & Harjoto, M. (2011). Corporate governance and firm value: The impact of corporate social responsibility. *Journal of Business Ethics*, 103(3), 351–383. DOI: 10.1007/s10551-011-0869-y

Johnson, J. (2023). *Leadership in the Digital Age: Thriving in an Era of Constant Change*. Jeffrey Johnson.

Jones, M. (2023). Ethical AI and sustainable business practices in Industry 5.0. *Journal of Business Ethics*, 188(2), 345–359. DOI: 10.1007/s10551-023-05045-x

Jonsson, E. I. (2013). One role is not big enough: A multi-theoretical study of board roles in SMEs. *International Journal of Business Governance and Ethics*, 8(1), 50–68. DOI: 10.1504/IJBGE.2013.052741

Joseph, B., Walker, A., & Fuller-Tyszkiewicz, M. (2018). Evaluating the effectiveness of employee assistance programmes: A systematic review. *European Journal of Work and Organizational Psychology*, 27(1), 1–15. DOI: 10.1080/1359432X.2017.1374245

Judge, T. A., & Piccolo, R. F. (2004). Transformational and Transactional Leadership: A Meta-analytic Test of Their Relative Validity. *The Journal of Applied Psychology*, 89(5), 755–768. DOI: 10.1037/0021-9010.89.5.755 PMID: 15506858

Kabat-Zinn, J. (2023). Wherever you go, there you are: Mindfulness meditation in everyday life. Hachette UK.

Kagermann, H., Wahlster, W., & Helbig, J. (2013). *Recommendations for implementing the strategic initiative INDUSTRIE 4.0 Final report of the Industrie 4.0 Working Group*. Forschungs Union.

Kagnicioglu, C. H., & Ozdemir, E. (2017). *Evaluation of SMEs in Eskişehir within the context of industry 4.0. Procedia*. PressAcademia.

Kagzi, M., & Guha, M. (2018). Does board demographic diversity influence firm performance? Evidence from Indian-knowledge intensive firms. *Benchmarking*, 25(3), 1028–1058. DOI: 10.1108/BIJ-07-2017-0203

Kajtazi, K., Rexhepi, G., Sharif, A., & Ozturk, I. (2023). Business model innovation and its impact on corporate sustainability. *Journal of Business Research*, 166, 114082. DOI: 10.1016/j.jbusres.2023.114082

Kantur, D., & İşeri-Say, A. (2012). Organizational resilience: A conceptual integrative framework. *Journal of Management & Organization*, 18(6), 762–773. DOI: 10.5172/jmo.2012.18.6.762

Kaptan, Z. (2024). *A systematic literature review of compulsory citizenship behaviors: A bibliometric and meta-analysis study* [Master dissertation, Istanbul University]. Council of Higher Education Thesis Center.

Karagöz, İ., Danış Bekdemir, A., & Tuna, Ö. (2021). 3B Yazıcı Teknolojilerindeki Kullanılan Yöntemler ve Gelişmeler Üzerine Bir Derleme [A Review of Used Methods and Developments in 3D Printer Technologies]. *Düzce Üniversitesi Bilim ve Teknoloji Dergisi*, 9(4), 1186–1213. DOI: 10.29130/dubited.877423

Karakose, T., Kocabas, I., Yirci, R., Papadakis, S., Ozdemir, T. Y., & Demirkol, M. (2022). The Development and Evolution of Digital Leadership: A Bibliometric Mapping Approach-Based Study. *Sustainability (Basel)*, 14(23), 16171. DOI: 10.3390/su142316171

Kara, N., & Çağıltay, K. (2020). Smart Toys for Preschool Children: A Design and Development Research. *Electronic Commerce Research and Applications*, 39, 1–11. DOI: 10.1016/j.elerap.2019.100909

Karatepe, O. M., & Talebzadeh, N. (2016). An empirical investigation of psychological capital among flight attendants. *Journal of Air Transport Management*, 55, 193–202. DOI: 10.1016/j.jairtraman.2016.06.001

Karimi, J., & Walter, Z. (2015). The Role of Dynamic Capabilities in Responding to Digital Disruption: A Factor-based Study of the Newspaper Industry. *Journal of Management Information Systems*, 32(1), 39–81. DOI: 10.1080/07421222.2015.1029380

Karmaker, C. L., Bari, A. M., Anam, M. Z., Ahmed, T., Ali, S. M., Pacheco, D. A., & Moktadir, M. A. (2023). Industry 5.0 challenges for post-pandemic supply chain sustainability in an emerging economy. *International Journal of Production Economics*, 258, 108806. Advance online publication. DOI: 10.1016/j.ijpe.2023.108806

Karpie, A. (2018). Beyond Contingent Workforce Management: Embracing an Agile Workforce. [Online][Cited 3.02.19] Available from the World Wide Web: URL< http://spendmatters.com/2018/06/14/beyond-contingent-workforce managementembracing-an-agile-workforce/>

Kashyap, S., Joseph, S., & Deshmukh, G. K. (2016). Employee Well-Being, Life Satisfaction and the need for Work-Life balance. *Journal of Ravishankar University*, 22, 11–23. https://www.researchgate.net/profile/Gopal-Deshmukh/publication/311322121_Employee_Well-Being_Life_Satisfaction_and_the_need_for_Work-Life_balance/links/58419b8608aeda6968138468/Employee-Well-Being-Life-Satisfaction-and-the-need-for-Work-Life-balance.pdf

Katanic, S. (2021, July 21). *Effective Digital Leadership Is Key to Digital Transformation.* Retrieved at https://www.forbes.com/councils/forbesagencycouncil/2021/07/21/effective-digital-leadership-is-key-to-digital-transformation/

Kataria, A., Rashmi, K., & Rastogi, M. (2022). Fostering change-oriented OCBS: An analysis of India's IT talent. *Journal of Asia Business Studies.*

Kaya, B., & Karatepe, O. (2020). Does servant leadership better explain work engagement, career satisfaction and adaptive performance than authentic leadership? *International Journal of Contemporary Hospitality Management*, 32(6), 2075–2095. Advance online publication. DOI: 10.1108/IJCHM-05-2019-0438

Khakurel, J., Melkas, H., & Porras, J. (2018). Tapping into the wearable device revolution in the work environment: A systematic review. *Information Technology & People*, 31(3), 791–818. DOI: 10.1108/ITP-03-2017-0076

Khan, M., Haleem, A., & Javaid, M. (2023). Changes and improvements in Industry 5.0: A strategic approach to overcome the challenges of Industry 4.0. *Green Technologies and Sustainability, 1*(2).

Khan, M. J., Aslam, N., & Riaz, M. N. (2012). Leadership Styles as Predictors of Innovative Work Behavior. *Pakistan Journal of Social and Clinical Psychology*, 9(2), 17–22.

Khan, S., & Digout, J. (2017). The Corporate Reputation Reporting Framework (CRRF). *Corporate Reputation Review*, 21(1), 22–36. DOI: 10.1057/s41299-017-0041-4

Khitiri, B. (2017). Theories of corporate governance: Legal analysis *[TSU]*. *Journal of Law*, 2, 117–148.

Kiker, D., Callahan, J., & Kiker, M. (2019). Exploring the boundaries of servant leadership: A meta-analysis of the main and moderating effects of servant leadership on behavioural and effective outcomes. *Journal of Managerial Issues.*

Kilavuz, F. (2023). A bibliometric analysis of multicultural education research. *Sosyal Bilimler ve Eğitim Dergisi, 6* (Education Special Issue), 216-238. DOI: 10.53047/josse.1359321

Kim, M., Kim, S., Kim, J., Song, T. J., & Kim, Y. (2024). Do stakeholder needs differ?-Designing stakeholder-tailored Explainable Artificial Intelligence (XAI) interfaces. *International Journal of Human-Computer Studies*, 181, 103160. DOI: 10.1016/j.ijhcs.2023.103160

Kim, Y., & Park, H. (2020). Design thinking and its impact on sustainability in manufacturing. *Sustainability Science*, 15(1), 101–118. DOI: 10.1007/s11625-019-00810-5

Klašnja-Milićević, A., Vesin, B., Ivanović, M., & Budimac, Z. (2011). E-learning personalization based on hybrid recommendation strategy and learning style identification. *Computers & Education*, 56(3), 885–899. DOI: 10.1016/j.compedu.2010.11.001

Klein, A., Riekert, M., & Dinev, V. (2019). Accurate retrieval of corporate reputation from online media using machine learning. *Annals of Computer Science and Information Systems*, 43-46, 43–46. Advance online publication. DOI: 10.15439/2019F169

Klus, M. F., & Müller, J. (2021). The Digital Leader: What One Needs to Master Today's Organisational Challenges. *Journal of Business Economics*, 91(8), 1189–1223. DOI: 10.1007/s11573-021-01040-1

Klynveld Peat Marwick Goerdeler. (2020). *The time has come: The KPMG survey of sustainability reporting*. KPMG International.

Kmieciak, R. (2021). Critical Reflection and Innovative Work Behavior: The Mediating Role of Individual Unlearning. *Personnel Review*, 50(2), 439–459. DOI: 10.1108/PR-10-2018-0406

Knight, C., & Haslam, S. A. (2010). The relative merits of lean, enriched, and empowered offices: An experimental examination of the impact of workspace management strategies on well-being and productivity. *Journal of Experimental Psychology. Applied*, 16(2), 158–172. DOI: 10.1037/a0019292 PMID: 20565201

Kobayashi, K., Eweje, G., & Tappin, D. (2018). Employee wellbeing and human sustainability: Perspectives of managers in large Japanese corporations. *Business Strategy and the Environment*, 27(7), 801–810. DOI: 10.1002/bse.2032

Köbeloğlu, A., & Çetinkaya, K. (2019). 3B Yazıcılar ile Uzun Geometrili Parçaların Üretilebilirliği [Production of Long Geometric Parts With 3d Printers]. *International Journal of 3d Printing Technologies and Digital Industry*, 3(1), 11-18.

Kock, M., & Lynn, G. (2012). Lateral collinearity and misleading results in variance-based SEM: An illustration and recommendation. *Journal of the Association for Information Systems*, 13(7), 546–580. DOI: 10.17705/1jais.00302

Kohli, R., & Johnson, S. (2011). Digital Transformation in Latecomer Industries: CIO and CEO Leadership Lessons from Encana Oil & Gas (USA) Inc. *MIS Quarterly Executive*, 10(4), 141–156.

Komnenic, B., & Pokrajčić, D. (2012). Intellectual capital and corporate performance of MNCs in Serbia. *Journal of Intellectual Capital*, 13(1), 106–119. DOI: 10.1108/14691931211196231

Kor, B., Rodriguez Fernandez, D., & Acarturk, E. (2022). Antecedents of Individual Innovative Behavior in the Digital Era. *Proceedings - Academy of Management*, 2022(1), 16865. Advance online publication. DOI: 10.5465/AMBPP.2022.16865abstract

Kotras, B. (2020). Opinions that matter: The hybridization of opinion and reputation measurement in social media listening software. *Media Culture & Society*, 42(7-8), 1495–1511. DOI: 10.1177/0163443720939427

Kötting, M. (2020). Corporate incubators as knowledge brokers between business units and ventures: A systematic review and avenues for future research. *European Journal of Innovation Management*, 23(3), 474–499. DOI: 10.1108/EJIM-12-2017-0201

Kouzes, J. M., & Posner, B. Z. (2017). *The Leadership Challenge: How to Make Extraordinary Things Happen in Organizations*. John Wiley & Sons.

Kovac, N., Żmija, K., Roy, J. K., Kusa, R., & Duda, J. (2024). Digital divide and digitalization in Europe: A bibliometric analysis. *Equilibrium.Quarterly Journal of Economics and Economic Policy*, 19(2), 463–520. DOI: 10.24136/eq.2899

Koyuncu, M., Burke, R., Astakhova, M., Eren, D., & Çetin, H. (2014). Servant leadership and perceptions of service quality provided by front-line service workers in hotels in Turkey: Achieving competitive advantage. *International Journal of Contemporary Hospitality Management*, 26, 1083–1099. DOI: 10.1108/IJCHM-06-2013-0238

Kozubikova, L., Kotaskova, A., Dvorsky', J., & Kljucnikov, A. (2019). The impact of political factors' perception on the suitability of international business environment: The case of startups. *Economics & Sociology (Ternopil)*, 12(1), 61–79. DOI: 10.14254/2071-789X.2019/12-1/3

KPMG. (2022). *KPMG Guide to Digital Leadership: Developing Inspiring and Effective Digital Leaders at Every Level.* Retrieved at https://assets.kpmg.com/content/dam/kpmg/sa/pdf/2021/digital-leadership-guide.pdf

Kraja, Y. B., & Berberi, A. (2023). Female Entrepreneurs and Motivational Factors. *International Journal of Professional Business Review: Int.J. Prof. Bus. Rev.*, 8(5), 10.

Krasniqi, B. A. (2007). Barriers to entrepreneurship and SME growth in transition: The case of Kosova. *Journal of Developmental Entrepreneurship*, 12(01), 71–94. DOI: 10.1142/S1084946707000563

Kraus, S., Clauss, T., Breier, M., Gast, J., Zardini, A., & Tiberius, V. (2020). The economics of COVID-19: Initial empirical evidence on how family firms in five European countries cope with the corona crisis. *International Journal of Entrepreneurial Behaviour & Research*, 214(5), 26. DOI: 10.1108/IJEBR-04-2020-0214

Kreutzer, R. T., Neugebauer, T., & Pattloch, A. (2017). *Digital Business Leadership: Digitale Transformation – Geschäftsmodell - Innovation – Agile Organisation – Change-Management.* Springer Gabler. DOI: 10.1007/978-3-658-11914-0

Krings, D., Weber, K., & Schmidt, N. (n.d.). Dynamic resilience: Conceptual frameworks and empirical insights. *Strategic Management Journal*, 45(3), 212–235.

Krstić, J., & Ćorić, N. (2021). Public health communication: Skin cancer prevention implications. *Management: Journal of Sustainable Business and Management Solutions in Emerging Economies*, 29(1), 63–85. DOI: 10.7595/management.fon.2021.0036

Krstić, J., Reljić, M., & Filipović, S. (2019). Factors influencing electricity consumption: A review of research methods. *Management: Journal of Sustainable Business and Management Solutions in Emerging Economies*, 24(2), 13–22. DOI: 10.7595/management.fon.2018.0021

Kryeziu, L., Bağiş, M., Kurutkan, M. N., Krasniqi, B. A., & Haziri, A. (2022). COVID-19 impact and firm reactions towards crisis: Evidence from a transition economy. *Journal of Entrepreneurship. Management and Innovation*, 18(1), 169–196.

Kubickova, A., Dohnal, M., & Doubravsky', K. (2013). Qualitative decision–making a model of an investment into start-up companies. *International Journal of Technology Intelligence and Planning*, 9(3), 165–180. DOI: 10.1504/IJTIP.2013.059656

Kunduracıoğlu, İ. (2018). *Oyunlaştırma Kavramı Üzerine İçerik Analizi Çalışması [A content analysis on gamification concept]* (UMI No. 529715) [Master's Thesis, Balıkesir University, Institute of Science], Balıkesir, Türkiye. Council of Higher Education Thesis Center.

Kupiek, M. (2021). *Digital Leadership, Agile Change and the Emotional Organization: Emotion as a Success Factor for Digital Transformation Projects*. Springer Nature. DOI: 10.1007/978-3-658-33489-5

Kusio, T., Miskiewicz, R., Borowiecki, R., Fijałkowska, J., Rzepka, A., Gross-Gołacka, E., & Ristvej, J. (2023). Startups: The Global Context of Functioning and the Need for Innovation Openness. *Journal of Intercultural Management*, 15(3), 50–77. DOI: 10.2478/joim-2023-0011

L'Huillier, B. (2014). What does "corporate governance" actually mean? *Corporate Governance (Bradford)*, 14(3), 300–319. DOI: 10.1108/CG-10-2012-0073

Labaye, E., & Remes, J. (2015). Digital technologies and the global economy's productivity imperative. *Digiworld Economic Journal*, (100), 47.

Lakho, S., Farooqi, S. A., Zafar, F., & Siraj, S. (2024). Developing AI-Powered Chatbots for Mental Health Support. *Spectrum of engineering sciences, 2*(3), 179-199.

Lange, D., Lee, P. M., & Dai, Y. (2011). Organizational reputation: A Review. *Journal of Management*, 37(1), 153–184. DOI: 10.1177/0149206310390963

Lantada, A. D. (2022). Engineering Education 5.0: Strategies for a Successful Transformative Project-Based Learning. In Bouezzeddine, M. (Ed.), *Insights Into Global Engineering Education After the Birth of Industry 5.0.*, DOI: 10.5772/intechopen.102844

Larson, L., & DeChurch, L. A. (2020). Leading Teams in the Digital Age: Four Perspectives on Technology and What They Mean for Leading Teams. *The Leadership Quarterly*, 31(1), 101377. DOI: 10.1016/j.leaqua.2019.101377 PMID: 32863679

Laub, J. (1999). Assessing the servant organization: Development of the servant leadership. *Review of General Psychology*, •••, 326–341.

Laursen, K., & Foss, N. J. (2003). New human resource management practices, complementarities, and the impact on innovation performance. *Cambridge Journal of Economics*, 27(2), 243–263. DOI: 10.1093/cje/27.2.243

Leach, M. (Ed.). (2008). Re-framing resilience: a symposium report. STEPS Working Paper 13, STEPS Centre, Brighton, UK.

Leal Filho, W., Ribeiro, P. C. C., Setti, A. F. F., Azam, F. M. S., Abubakar, I. R., Castillo-Apraiz, J., Tamayo, U., Özuyar, P. G., Frizzo, K., & Borsari, B. (2024). Toward food waste reduction at universities. *Environment, Development and Sustainability*, 26(7), 16585–16606. DOI: 10.1007/s10668-023-03300-2 PMID: 37362965

Lee, J., Park, S., & Kim, H. (2015). Energy optimization through digital twin technology in industrial processes. *Energy*, 85, 88–98. DOI: 10.5855/ENERGY.2015.24.1.088

Lee, Y., Hsieh, Y., & Ma, C. (2011). A model of organizational employees' E-lEarning systems acceptance. *Knowledge-Based Systems*, 24(3), 355–366. DOI: 10.1016/j.knosys.2010.09.005

Leng, J., Sha, W., Lin, Z., Jing, J., Liu, Q., & Chen, X. (2023). Blockchained smart contract pyramid-driven multi-agent autonomous process control for resilient individualised manufacturing towards Industry 5.0. *International Journal of Production Research*, 61(13), 4302–4321. DOI: 10.1080/00207543.2022.2089929

Leng, J., Sha, W., Wang, B., Zheng, P., Zhuang, C., Liu, Q., Wuest, T., Mourtzis, D., & Wang, L. (2022). Industry 5.0: Prospect and retrospect. *Journal of Manufacturing Systems*, 65, 279–295. DOI: 10.1016/j.jmsy.2022.09.017

Leng, J., Zhong, Y., Lin, Z., Xu, K., Mourtzis, D., Zhou, X., Zheng, P., Liu, Q., Zhao, J. L., & Shen, W. (2023). Towards resilience in Industry 5.0: A decentralized autonomous manufacturing paradigm. *Journal of Manufacturing Systems*, 71, 95–114. DOI: 10.1016/j.jmsy.2023.08.023

Lengnick-Hall, C. A., Beck, T. E., & Lengnick-Hall, M. L. (2011). Developing a capacity for organizational resilience through strategic human resource management. *Human Resource Management Review*, 21(3), 243–255. Advance online publication. DOI: 10.1016/j.hrmr.2010.07.001

Lepojevic, V., Djordjevic, B., & Ivanovic-Djukic, M. (2018). Mediating effects of career stage on job-related characteristics-job satisfaction relationship. *The Engineering Economist*, 29(2), 215–225.

Liang, H. L. (2022). Compulsory citizenship behavior and facades of conformity: A moderated mediation model of neuroticism and citizenship pressure. *Psychological Reports*, 125(6), 1–21. DOI: 10.1177/00332941211031794 PMID: 34325551

Liang, H. L., Yeh, T. K., & Wang, C. H. (2022). Compulsory citizenship behavior and its outcomes: Two mediation models. *Frontiers in Psychology*, 13, 869744. Advance online publication. DOI: 10.3389/fpsyg.2022.869744 PMID: 35300160

Liang, H.-L. (2024). How and when authoritarian leadership affects compulsory citizenship behavior? A moderated mediation model of façade creation and leader-member exchange. *Current Psychology (New Brunswick, N.J.)*, 43(24), 1–13. DOI: 10.1007/s12144-024-05909-6

Liden, R., Wayne, S., Meuser, J., Hu, J., Wu, J., & Liao, C. (2015). Servant leadership: Validation of a short form of the SL-28. *The Leadership Quarterly*, 26(2), 254–269. DOI: 10.1016/j.leaqua.2014.12.002

Liden, R., Wayne, S., Zhao, H., & Henderson, D. (2008). Servant leadership: Development of a multidimensional measure and multilevel assessment. *The Leadership Quarterly*, 19(2), 161–177. DOI: 10.1016/j.leaqua.2008.01.006

Li, J., Weng, G., Yue, P., Li, C., & Wang, N. (2021). A scientometric review of tourism carrying capacity research: Cooperation, hotspots, and prospect. *Journal of Cleaner Production*, 325, 129278. Advance online publication. DOI: 10.1016/j.jclepro.2021.129278

Lin, C.-Y., & Chi, N.-W. (2022). Understanding why and when compulsory citizenship behaviors lead to subsequent destructive voice and citizenship behaviors: The retributive justice and impression management perspectives. *Human Performance*, 35(5), 303–322. DOI: 10.1080/08959285.2022.2121964

Lin, M., Chen, Z., Chen, R., & Fujita, H. (2021). Evaluation of startup companies using multicriteria decision making based on hesitant fuzzy linguistic information envelopment analysis models. *International Journal of Intelligent Systems*, 36(5), 2292–2322. DOI: 10.1002/int.22379

Linnenluecke, M. K. (2017). Resilience in business and management research: A review of influential publications and a research agenda. *International Journal of Management Reviews*, 19(1), 4–30. DOI: 10.1111/ijmr.12076

Lis, A., Bello, K., & Górka, J. (2021). Albania as an object and a context of research in economic sciences: Bibliometric analysis. *Ekonomia i Prawo.Economics and Law*, 20(1), 139–154.

Liu, F., Chow, I. H., & Huang, M. (2019). Increasing compulsory citizenship behavior and workload: Does impression management matter? *Frontiers in Psychology*, 10, 1726. Advance online publication. DOI: 10.3389/fpsyg.2019.01726 PMID: 31402890

Liu, Y., Zhao, H., & Sheard, A. (2017). Organizational citizenship pressure, compulsory citizenship behavior, and work–family conflict. *Social Behavior and Personality*, 45(4), 695–704. DOI: 10.2224/sbp.6064

Li, X., & Zheng, Y. (2014). The Influential Factors of Employees' Innovative Behavior and the Management Advices. *Journal of Service Science and Management*, 7(6), 446–450. DOI: 10.4236/jssm.2014.76042

Loke, R., & Lam-Lion, R. (2021). A company's corporate reputation through the eyes of employees measured with sentiment analysis of online reviews. *Proceedings of the 10th International Conference on Data Science, Technology and Applications*, 378-385. DOI: 10.5220/0010620600002993

Loke, R., & Reitter, W. (2021). Aspect based sentiment analysis on online review data to predict corporate reputation. *Proceedings of the 10th International Conference on Data Science, Technology and Applications (DATA)*, 343-352. DOI: 10.5220/0010607200002993

Long, L., Hui, L., Fook, G., & Zainon, W. M. N. (2017). A study on the effectiveness of tree-maps as tree visualization techniques. *Procedia Computer Science*, 124, 108–115. DOI: 10.1016/j.procs.2017.12.136

Longo, F., Padovano, A., & Umbrello, S. (2020). Value-Oriented and Ethical Technology Engineering in Industry 5.0: A Human-Centric Perspective for the Design of the Factory of the Future. *Applied Sciences (Basel, Switzerland)*, 10(12), 12. Advance online publication. DOI: 10.3390/app10124182

Loorbach, D. A., & Wittmayer, J. (2024). Transforming universities. *Sustainability Science*, 19(1), 19–33. DOI: 10.1007/s11625-023-01335-y

Luoma-aho, V., Canel, M., & Hakola, J. (2021). Public sector reputation and netpromoter score. *International Review on Public and Nonprofit Marketing*, 18(3), 419–446. DOI: 10.1007/s12208-021-00280-9

Luthans, F., Luthans, K., & Luthans, B. (2004). Positive psychological capital: Beyond human and social capital.

Luthans, F., Avolio, B., Avey, J., & Norman, S. (2007). Positive psychological capital: Measurement and relationship with performance and satisfaction. *Personnel Psychology*, 60(3), 541–572. DOI: 10.1111/j.1744-6570.2007.00083.x

Luthans, F., Luthans, K. W., & Luthans, B. C. (2004). Positive psychological capital: Beyond human and social capital. *Business Horizons*, 47(1), 45–50. DOI: 10.1016/j.bushor.2003.11.007

Lu, Y., Zheng, H., Chand, S., Xia, W., Liu, Z., Xu, X., Wang, L., Qin, Z., & Bao, J. (2022). Outlook on human-centric manufacturing towards Industry 5.0. *Journal of Manufacturing Systems*, 62, 612–627. DOI: 10.1016/j.jmsy.2022.02.001

Lv, W. D., Tian, D., Wei, Y., & Xi, R. X. (2018). Innovation Resilience: A New Approach for Managing Uncertainties Concerned with Sustainable Innovation. *Sustainability (Basel)*, 10(10), 3641. DOI: 10.3390/su10103641

Lv, X., Wang, Y., Liu, L., & Yin, S. (2024). Digital green innovation economy for Industry 5.0. *Sustainable Economies*, 2(1), 1. Advance online publication. DOI: 10.62617/se.v2i1.8

Ly, B., & Ly, R. (2024). Technostress in Times of Change: Unveiling the Impact of Leadership Styles in Cambodia's Public Organizations in the Wake of COVID-19. *Cogent Business & Management*, 11(1), 2331645. Advance online publication. DOI: 10.1080/23311975.2024.2331645

MacMillan, I. C., Siegel, R., & Narasimha, P. S. (1985). Criteria used by venture capitalists to evaluate new venture proposals. *Journal of Business Venturing*, 1(1), 119–128. DOI: 10.1016/0883-9026(85)90011-4

Madden, K. (2024, April 12). *The Tech-Savvy Executive: Overcoming Digital Anxiety in Leadership.* Retrieved at https://www.forbes.com/councils/forbescoachescouncil/2024/04/12/the-tech-savvy-executive-overcoming-digital-anxiety-in-leadership/

Maddikunta, P. K., Pham, Q.-V., B, P., Deepa, N., Dev, K., Gadekallu, T. R., Ruby, R., & Liyanage, M. (2022). Industry 5.0: A survey on enabling technologies and potential applications. *Journal of Industrial Information Integration*, 26, 100257. Advance online publication. DOI: 10.1016/j.jii.2021.100257

Madrid-Guijarro, A., & Durĕndez, A. (2024). Sustainable development barriers and pressures in SMEs: The mediating effect of management commitment to environmental practices. *Business Strategy and the Environment*, 33(2), 949–967. DOI: 10.1002/bse.3537

Mahmutaj, L. R., & Krasniqi, B. (2020). Innovation types and sales growth in small firms: Evidence from Kosovo. *South East European Journal of Economics and Business*, 15(1), 27–43. DOI: 10.2478/jeb-2020-0003

Majumdar, R., & Mittal, A. (2023). *Startup Financing: Some Evidence from the Indian Venture Capital Industry*. FIIB Business Review.

Malakyan, P. G. (2019). Digital Leader-followership for the Digital Age: A North American Perspective. In Franco, M. (Ed.), *Digital Leadership—A New Leadership Style for the 21st Century*. IntechOpen., DOI: 10.5772/intechopen.89820

Malek, J. & Desai, T. N. (2020). A systematic literature review to map literature focus of sustainable manufacturing. *Journal of Cleaner Production, 256,* 1-20 120345

Ma, N., Yao, X., & Wang, K. (2024). A complex network-based approach for resilient and flexible design resource allocation in industry 5.0. *Computers in Industry*, 159-160, 104108. Advance online publication. DOI: 10.1016/j.compind.2024.104108

Mankins, M. C., & Garton, E. (2017). *Time, Talent, Energy: Overcome Organizational Drag and Unleash Your Team s Productive Power*. Harvard Business Review Press.

Manning, B., Braam, G., & Reimsbach, D. (2019). Corporate governance and sustainable business conduct-effects of board monitoring effectiveness and stakeholder engagement on corporate sustainability performance and disclosure choices. *Corporate Social Responsibility and Environmental Management*, 26(2), 351–366. DOI: 10.1002/csr.1687

Mantello, P., & Ho, M. T. (2024). Emotional AI and the future of wellbeing in the post-pandemic workplace. *AI & Society*, 39(4), 1883–1889. DOI: 10.1007/s00146-023-01639-8 PMID: 36776535

Maraşlı, F., & Çıbuk, M. (2015). RFID Teknolojisi ve Kullanım Alanları [RFID Technology and Application Areas]. *BEÜ Fen Bilimleri Dergisi*, 4(2), 249–275.

Mariappanadar, S., & Hochwarter, W. A. (2022). A three-way synergistic effect of work on employee well-being: Human sustainability perspective. *International Journal of Environmental Research and Public Health*, 19(22), 14842. DOI: 10.3390/ijerph192214842 PMID: 36429568

Marien, M. (2014). The second machine age: Work, progress, and prosperity in a time of brilliant technologies. *World Futures Review*, 2(2), 174. DOI: 10.1177/1946756714541404

Marinović, N., Vlastelica, T., & Krstić, J. (2022). Evaluating digital corporate identity: Application of AHP method in website quality analysis. *Industrija*, 3/4(50), 55–74. DOI: 10.5937/industrija50-44052

Mark, G., Gudith, D., & Klocke, U. (2008, April). The cost of interrupted work: more speed and stress. In *Proceedings of the SIGCHI conference on Human Factors in Computing Systems* (pp. 107-110). DOI: 10.1145/1357054.1357072

Marsh, E., Perez Vallejos, E., & Spence, A. (2022). The Digital Workplace and Its Dark Side: An Integrative Review. *Computers in Human Behavior*, 128, 107118. DOI: 10.1016/j.chb.2021.107118

Martin, G., & Cooper, S. (2019). Social equity and human-centric innovation: Implications for corporate social responsibility. *Business & Society*, 58(2), 348–369. DOI: 10.1177/0007650317734871

Martini, B., Bellisario, D., & Coletti, P. (2024). Human-Centered and Sustainable Artificial Intelligence in Industry 5.0: Challenges and Perspectives. *Sustainability (Basel)*, 16(13), 5448. Advance online publication. DOI: 10.3390/su16135448

Marzi, G., Balzano, M., Caputo, A., & Pellegrini, M. M. (2024). Guidelines for Bibliometric-Systematic Literature Reviews: 10 steps to combine analysis, synthesis and theory development. *International Journal of Management Reviews*.

Mas-Tur, A., Kraus, S., Brandtner, M., Ewert, R., & Kürsten, W. (2020). Advances in management research: A bibliometric overview of the Review of Managerial Science. *Review of Managerial Science*, 14(5), 933–958. DOI: 10.1007/s11846-020-00406-z

Mayer, C. (2020). *Shareholderism Versus Stakeholderism – a Misconceived Contradiction. A Comment on "The Illusory Promise of Stakeholder Governance" by Lucian Bebchuk and Roberto Tallarita* (SSRN Scholarly Paper 3617847). DOI: 10.2139/ssrn.3617847

McIntyre, M. L., Murphy, S. A., & Mitchell, P. (2007). The top team: Examining board composition and firm performance. *Corporate Governance (Bradford)*, 7(5), 547–561. DOI: 10.1108/14720700710827149

McKinney, P. (2023, August 24). *Visionary Thinking: How Leaders Shape the Future*. Retrieved at https://www.philmckinney.com/visionary-thinking-how-leaders-shape-the-future/

McKinsey Global Institute (2021) *McKinsey Global Surveys, 2021: A Year in Review*. mckinsey-global-surveys-2021-a-year-in-review.pdf

McMurray, A. (2009). Leadership, climate, psychological capital, commitment, and wellbeing in a non-profit organization. *Leadership and Organization Development Journal*, •••, 436–457.

McNulty, T., & Pettigrew, A. (1999). Strategists on the board. *Organization Studies*, 20(1), 47–74. DOI: 10.1177/0170840699201003

Melewar, T. C., Dennis, C., & Foroudi, P. (2022). *Building corporate identity, image and reputation in the digital era*. Routledge.

Mellinas, J. P., & Martin-Fuentes, E. (2024). The Complex World of Online Reviews: Criteria for Establishing a Global Index for Accommodation. In Berezina, K., Nixon, L., & Tuomi, A. (Eds.), *Information and Communication Technologies in Tourism 2024. ENTER 2024. Springer Proceedings in Business and Economics*. Springer., DOI: 10.1007/978-3-031-58839-6_44

Merlano, C. A. (2024). Digital Leadership and Transformation in Contemporary Times. *International Journal of Digital Strategy, Governance, and Business Transformation*, 13(1), 1–20. Advance online publication. DOI: 10.4018/IJDSGBT.352047

Mesjasz-Lech, A., Kemendi, Á., & Michelberger, P. (2024). Circular manufacturing and Industry 5.0. Assessing material flows in the manufacturing process in relation to e-waste streams. *Engineering Management in Production and Services*, 16(1), 114–133. DOI: 10.2478/emj-2024-0009

Messmann, G. (2012). *Innovative Work Behaviour Investigating the Nature and Facilitation of Vocational Teachers' Contributions to Innovation Development.* Universität Regensburg, Unpublished Doctoral Dissertation.

Michalos, A. C. (2022). Corporate Social Responsibility in Universities and Sustainable Development. In Poff, D. C. (Ed.), *University Corporate Social Responsibility and University Governance* (pp. 75–104). Springer International Publishing., DOI: 10.1007/978-3-030-77532-2_4

Mi, L., Gan, X., Xu, T., Long, R., Qiao, L., & Zhu, H. (2019). A new perspective to promote organizational citizenship behaviour for the environment: The role of transformational leadership. *Journal of Cleaner Production*, 239, 118002. DOI: 10.1016/j.jclepro.2019.118002

Milkova, M., Andreichikova, O., & Andreichikov, A. (2018). Venture Capitalists decision making: Applying analytic network process to the startups' evaluation. *International Journal of the Analytic Hierarchy Process*, 10(1), 1–18. DOI: 10.13033/ijahp.v10i1.511

Miller, F., Osbahr, H., Boyd, E., Thomalla, F., Bharwani, S., Ziervogel, G., Walker, B., Birkmann, J., Van der Leeuw, S., Rockström, J., Hinkel, J., Downing, T., Folke, C., & Nelson, D. (2010). Resilience and vulnerability: complementary or conflicting concepts? Ecology and Society 15(3):11. [online] URL: https://www.ecologyandsociety.org/vol15/iss3/art11/

Miller, D., & Smith, K. (2018). Ethical frameworks for AI deployment in the workplace. *Journal of Business Ethics*, 152(4), 975–990. DOI: 10.1007/s10551-016-3340-1

Mirkamali, S. M., & Thani, F. N. (2011). A Study on the Quality of Work Life (QWL) among faculty members of University of Tehran(UT) and Sharif university of Technology (SUT). *Procedia: Social and Behavioral Sciences*, 29, 179–187. DOI: 10.1016/j.sbspro.2011.11.223

Mishra, N., & Bharti, T. (2023). Exploring the nexus of social support, work–life balance and life satisfaction in hybrid work scenario in learning organizations. The Learning Organization, ahead-of-print. https://doi.org/https://doi.org/10.1108/tlo-08-2022-0099

*MIT Sustainability*. (2023). https://sustainability.mit.edu/about

Mitchell, G. (2015). The Attributes of Effective NGOs and the Leadership Values Associated with a Reputation for Organizational Effectiveness. *Nonprofit Management & Leadership*, 26(1), 39–57. DOI: 10.1002/nml.21143

Mitsakis, F. V. (2020). Human resource development (HRD) resilience: A new 'success element'of organizational resilience? *Human Resource Development International*, 23(3), 321–328. DOI: 10.1080/13678868.2019.1669385

Modaresnezhad, M., Andrews, M. C., Mesmer-Magnus, J., Viswesvaran, C., & Deshpande, S. (2021). Anxiety, job satisfaction, supervisor support and turnover intentions of mid-career nurses: A structural equation model analysis. *Journal of Nursing Management*, 29(5), 931–942. https://doi.org/https://doi.org/10.1111/jonm.13229. DOI: 10.1111/jonm.13229 PMID: 33617110

Mohammadi, N., & Shafiee, M. (2022). How design thinking help us to select startups for the acceleration period? *Journal of Entrepreneurship in Emerging Economies*, 14(6), 1353–1368. DOI: 10.1108/JEEE-07-2021-0274

Mohammadi, N., & Shafiee, M. (2022). Predicting the success of seed-stage startups to enter the acceleration program and receive seed money. *International Journal of Entrepreneurial Venturing*, 14(2), 168–201. DOI: 10.1504/IJEV.2022.122654

Moher, D., Shamseer, L., Clarke, M., Ghersi, D., Liberati, A., Petticrew, M., Shekelle, P., & Stewart, L. A. (2015). Preferred Reporting Items for Systematic Review and meta-analysis Protocols (PRISMA-P) 2015 Statement. *Systematic Reviews*, 4(1), 1–9. DOI: 10.1186/2046-4053-4-1 PMID: 25554246

Molino, M., Ingusci, E., Signore, F., Manuti, A., Giancaspro, M. L., Russo, V., & Cortese, C. G. (2020). Wellbeing Costs of Technology Use during Covid-19 Remote Working: An Investigation Using the Italian Translation of the Technostress Creators Scale. *Sustainability (Basel)*, 12(15), 5911. Advance online publication. DOI: 10.3390/su12155911

Möllmann, J. (2023). More than a handshake–knowledge transfer in structured corporate–startup collaboration programs. *Journal of Knowledge Management*, 27(10), 2604–2624. DOI: 10.1108/JKM-03-2022-0222

Mondal, H., Deepak, K. K., Gupta, M., & Kumar, R. (2023). The h-Index: Understanding its predictors, significance, and criticism. *Journal of Family Medicine and Primary Care*, 12(11), 2531–2537. DOI: 10.4103/jfmpc.jfmpc_1613_23 PMID: 38186773

Money, K., & Hillenbrand, C. (2006). Using Reputation Measurement to Create Value: An Analysis and Integration of Existing Measures. *Journal of General Management*, 32(1), 1–12. DOI: 10.1177/030630700603200101

Montani, D., Gervasio, D., & Pulcini, A. (2020). Startup company valuation: The state of art and future trends. *International Business Research*, 13(9), 31–45. DOI: 10.5539/ibr.v13n9p31

Moore, D., Mccabe, G., & Bruce, G. (2013). *The basic practice of statistics* (6th ed.). W.H Freeman and Company.

Morgan, B. (2024). *The 8 Laws of Customer-focused Leadership: New Rules for Building a Business Around Today's Customer*. Harpers Collins Publishers.

Morrison, E. W. (1994). Role definitions and organizational citizenship behavior: The importance of the employee's perspective. *Academy of Management Journal*, 37(6), 1543–1567. DOI: 10.2307/256798

Moses, E., Che-Ahmad, A., & Abdulmalik, S. O. (2020). Board governance mechanisms and sustainability reporting quality: A theoretical framework. *Cogent Business & Management*, 7(1), 1–23. DOI: 10.1080/23311975.2020.1771075

Motlagh, N. H. (2012). *Near Field Communication (NFC) A Technical Overview.* [Master's Thesis, University of Vaasafaculty of Technology, Telecommunication Engineering], Vaasa, Finland.

Mourao, P. R., & Martinho, V. D. (2020). Forest entrepreneurship: A bibliometric analysis and a discussion about the co-authorship networks of an emerging scientific field. *Journal of Cleaner Production*, 256, 120413. Advance online publication. DOI: 10.1016/j.jclepro.2020.120413

Mourtzis, D., Panopoulos, N., Angelopoulos, J., Wang, B., & Wang, L. (2022). Human centric platforms for personalized value creation in metaverse. *Journal of Manufacturing Systems*, 65, 653–659. DOI: 10.1016/j.jmsy.2022.11.004

Movahed, A. B., Movahed, A. B., & Nozari, H. (2024). Opportunities and Challenges of Smart Supply Chain in Industry 5.0. In *Information Logistics for Organizational Empowerment and Effective Supply Chain Management* (pp. 108–138). IGI Global. DOI: 10.4018/979-8-3693-0159-3.ch006

Mozgovoy, V. (2019). Stress Pattern Recognition Through Wearable Biosensors in the Workplace: Experimental Longitudinal Study on the Role of Motion Intensity. *Proceedings - 6th Swiss Conference on Data Science, SDS 2019, 172740*, 37–45.

Mrugalska, B., & Wyrwicka, M. K. (2017). Towards lean production in industry 4.0. *Procedia Engineering*, 182, 466–473. DOI: 10.1016/j.proeng.2017.03.135

Mucha, S. (2020). Ethnic Albanian family businesses and COVID-19 pandemic: A gender-based comparison. *Journal of Family Business Management*, 12(1), 170–182. DOI: 10.1108/JFBM-07-2020-0074

Mukherjee, D., Lim, W. M., Kumar, S., & Donthu, N. (2022). Guidelines for advancing theory and practice through bibliometric research. *Journal of Business Research*, 148, 101–115. DOI: 10.1016/j.jbusres.2022.04.042

Mumford, M. D., & Gustafson, S. B. (1988). Creativity Syndrome: Integration, Application, and Innovation. *Psychological Bulletin*, 103(1), 27–43. DOI: 10.1037/0033-2909.103.1.27

Mumford, M. D., Scott, G. M., Gaddis, B., & Strange, J. M. (2002). Leading Creative People: Orchestrating Expertise and Relationships. *The Leadership Quarterly*, 13(6), 705–750. DOI: 10.1016/S1048-9843(02)00158-3

Muñoz-Bullon, F., Sanchez-Bueno, M. J., & Vos-Saz, A. (2015). Startup team contributions and new firm creation: The role of founding team experience. *Entrepreneurship and Regional Development*, 27(1-2), 80–105. DOI: 10.1080/08985626.2014.999719

Munsamy, M., Dhanpat, N., & Barkhuizen, E. N. (2023). The Development and Validation of a Digital Leadership Competency Scale. *Acta Commercii*, 23(1), a1057. DOI: 10.4102/ac.v23i1.1057

Murati-Leka, H. (2023). Kosovo's initial-stage venture capital market: Challenges and perspectives. *International Journal of Entrepreneurship and Small Business*, 50(1), 23–34. DOI: 10.1504/IJESB.2023.10058944

Musaigwa, M., & Kalitanyi, V. (2024). Effective leadership in the digital era: an exploration of change management. *Technology audit and production reserves*. https://doi.org/.DOI: 10.15587/2706-5448.2024.297374

Mustafa, I., Pula-Shiroka, J., Krasniqi, B. A., Ramadani, V., & Kryeziu, L. (2023). Informal Entrepreneurship in Kosovo: An Institutionalist Approach. In *Entrepreneurship Development in the Balkans: Perspective from Diverse Contexts* (pp. 151-169). Emerald Publishing Limited.

Muth, M. M., & Donaldson, L. (1998). Stewardship theory and board structure: A contingency approach. *Corporate Governance*, 6(1), 5–28. DOI: 10.1111/1467-8683.00076

Muthuraman, S., & Al-Haziazi, M. (2017). Examining the factors of organizational citizenship behavior with reference to corporate sectors in Sultanate of Oman. *International Review of Management and Marketing*, 7(1), 413–422.

Mutlu, E., Parlar, Z., & Temiz, V. (2014). An Apparatus Design for High Speed Sealing Applications Based on Systematic Design Approach. *In Proceedings of 10th World Congress on Computational Mechanics (Blucher Mechanical Engineering Proceedings, 1(1))*, Sao Paulo, Brazil.

Na'imah, T., & Nur, S. A. (2021). Job stress on teachers during the Covid-19 pandemic: The role of workload and organizational climate. *International Journal of Social Science and Human Research*, 4(10), 2763–2768.

Nahavandi, S. (2019). Industry 5.0-A Human-Centric Solution. *Sustainability (Basel)*, 11(16), 4371. Advance online publication. DOI: 10.3390/su11164371

Nastjuk, I., Trang, S., Grummeck-Braamt, J. V., Adam, M. T. P., & Tarafdar, M. (2024). Integrating and Synthesising Technostress Research: A Meta-analysis on Technostress Creators, Outcomes, and IS Usage Contexts. *European Journal of Information Systems*, 33(3), 361–382. DOI: 10.1080/0960085X.2022.2154712

Naumov, S. A. (2017). *Managing operational capabilities in startup companies*. Massachusetts Institute of Technology.

Nelson, D. R., N. Adger, & K. Brown. (2007). Adaptation to environmental change: contributions of a resilience framework. *Annual Review of Environment and Resources, 32*:395–419. http://dx.doi.org/. energy.32.051807.090348.DOI: 10.1146/annurev

Nerur, S. P., Rasheed, A. A., & Natarajan, V. (2008). The intellectual structure of the strategic management field: An author co-citation analysis. *Strategic Management Journal*, 29(3), 319–336. DOI: 10.1002/smj.659

Neubert, M. (2018). The impact of digitalization on the speed of internationalization of lean global startups. *Technology Innovation Management Review*, 8(5), 44–54. DOI: 10.22215/timreview/1158

Newman, A., Schwarz, G., Cooper, B., & Sendjaya, S. (2017). How servant leadership influences organizational citizenship behavior: The roles of LMX, empowerment, and proactive personality: JBE JBE. *Journal of Business Ethics*, 145(1), 49–62. DOI: 10.1007/s10551-015-2827-6

Nguyen, T., & Hoang, M. (2016). Cross-industry collaborations and human-centric innovation. *Journal of Innovation Management*, 4(3), 56–73. DOI: 10.24840/2183-0606_004.003_0005

Nikoloudis, C., Strantzali, E., & Aravossis, K. (2017). Applying the multi-criteria method Promethee II for the startup ranking during a business ideas competition, Proceedings of the 6th International Symposium on Operational Research "OR in the digital era—ICT challenges" Thessaloniki, Greece.

*NODEMCU ESP8266* (n.d.). https://joy-it.net/en/products/SBC-NodeMCU

Nonaka, I., & Takeuchi, H. (1995). *The Knowledge-Creating Company: How Japanese Companies Create the Dynamics of Innovation*. Oxford University Press. DOI: 10.1093/oso/9780195092691.001.0001

Normann, R. (1984). *Service Management: Strategy and Leadership in Service Business*. Wiley.

Norris, S. E. (2018). The business education of charismatic leaders and good soldiers. *International Journal of Adult Vocational Education and Technology*, 9(2), 11–29. DOI: 10.4018/IJAVET.2018040102

Noureldin, N., & Basuony, M. A. K. (2021). Females on board and sustainability performance in a developing country: Evidence from Egypt [Special issue]. *Corporate Ownership & Control*, 19(1), 288–298. DOI: 10.22495/cocv19i1siart6

Nourmohammadi, A., Fathi, M., & Ng, A. H. (2022). Balancing and scheduling assembly lines with human-robot collaboration tasks. *Computers & Operations Research*, 140, 105674. Advance online publication. DOI: 10.1016/j.cor.2021.105674

Nuortimo, K., Harkonen, J. & Breznik, K. (2024). Exploring corporate reputation and crisis communication. *Journal of Marketing Analitics*. DOI: 10.1057/s41270-024-00353-8

O' Daniel, M., & Rosenstein, A. H. (2008). *Professional communication and team collaboration* (Rg, H., Ed.). Agency for Healthcare Research and Quality (US)., https://www.ncbi.nlm.nih.gov/books/NBK2637/

Office, C. (2015). *Report on The 5th Science and Technology Basic Plan.* Cabinet Office of Japan.

Oh, H. K., Jung, J., Park, S., & Kim, S. W. (2020). A robust reputation system using online reviews. *Computer Science and Information Systems*, 17(2), 487–507. DOI: 10.2298/CSIS191122007O

Oke, A., Munshi, N., & Walumbwa, F. O. (2009). The Influence of Leadership on Innovation Processes and Activities. *Organizational Dynamics*, 38(1), 64–72. DOI: 10.1016/j.orgdyn.2008.10.005

*On the Importance of Human-Centricity and Data.* (n.d.). www3. weforum. org /docs /WE. Retrieved October 8, 2024, from https://www3.weforum.org/docs/WEF_On_the_Importance_of_Human_Centricity_2021.pdf

Oncioiu, I., Popescu, D.-M., Anghel, E., Petrescu, A.-G., Bîlcan, F.-R., & Petrescu, M. (2020). Online company reputation—A thorny problem for optimizing corporate sustainability. *Sustainability (Basel)*, 12(14), 5547. DOI: 10.3390/su12145547

Öner, Z. (2012). Servant leadership and paternalistic leadership styles in the Turkish business context: A comparative empirical study. *Leadership and Organization Development Journal*, 33(3), 300–316. DOI: 10.1108/01437731211216489

Onetti, A., Pepponi, F., & Pisoni, A. (2015, August). How the founding team impacts the growth process of early-stage innovative startups. *Sinergie Italian Journal of Management*, 33(May), 37–53.

Ongena, G., Morsch, P., & Ravesteijn, P. (2024). *Digital Leadership Competency to Enhance Digital Transformation.* International Journal of Innovation and Technology Management., DOI: 10.1142/S0219877024500421

Önhon, Ö. (2016). *The Relationship Between Organizational Climate for Innovation and Employees' Innovative Work Behavior; The Moderating Effects of Leadership Behavior; ICT Sector in Turkey.* T.C. Marmara Üniversitesi, Unpublished Doctoral Dissertation.

Organ, D. W. (1988). *Organizational citizenship behavior: The good soldier syndrome.* Lexington Books/D. C. Heath and Com.

Organ, D. W. (1988). Organizational citizenship behavior: The good soldier syndrome. Lexington books/DC heath and com.

Organ, D. W. (2014). *Organizational citizenship behavior: It's construct clean-up time.* Psychology Press.

Organ, D., Podsakoff, P., & MacKenzie, S. (2006). *Organizational citizenship behavior: Its nature, antecedents, and consequences.* Sage. DOI: 10.4135/9781452231082

Organisation for Economic Co-Operation and Development. (2023). *G20/OECD Principles of Corporate Governance 2023.* OECD Publishing., DOI: 10.1787/ed750b30-

Orrego, C., Villa, L. F., Sepúlveda-Cano, L. M., & Giraldo, M. L. M. (2021). Organizational online reputation measurement through natural language processing and sentiment analysis techniques. In Applied Computer Sciences in Engineering: 8th Workshop on Engineering Applications, WEA 2021, Medellín, Colombia, October 6–8, 2021 [Springer International Publishing.]. *Proceedings*, 8, 60–71.

Ortega-Rodríguez, C., Martín-Montes, L., Licerán-Gutiérrez, A., & Moreno-Albarracín, A. (2023). Nonprofit good governance mechanisms: A systematic literature review. *Nonprofit Management & Leadership*. Advance online publication. DOI: 10.1002/nml.21598

Osabiya, B. (2015). The effect of employees motivation on organizational performance. *Journal of Public Administration and Policy Research*, 7(4), 62–75. DOI: 10.5897/JPAPR2014.0300

Oxford University Press. (n.d.). *resilience noun - Definition, pictures, pronunciation and usage notes | Oxford Advanced Learner's Dictionary at OxfordLearnersDictionaries.com*. Oxford Learner's Dictionaries. https://www.oxfordlearnersdictionaries.com/definition/english/resilience

Ozaki, A. (2022). Human-Machine Collaboration in Advanced Manufacturing: Strategic Integration and Workforce Development. *Journal of Technology and Innovation Management*, 45(3), 112–129.

Ozdemir, V., & Hekim, N. (2018). Birth of industry 5.0: Making sense of big data with artificial intelligence, 'the Internet of things' and next-generation technology policy. *OMICS: A Journal of Integrative Biology*, 22(1), 65–76. DOI: 10.1089/omi.2017.0194 PMID: 29293405

Özdenizci, B., Ok, K., Aydın, M. N., & Coşkun, V. (2016). Yakın Alan İletişimi Teknolojisi [A Survey on Near Field Communication]. *Türkiye Bilişim Vakfi Bilgisayar Bilimleri ve Mühendisliği Dergisi*, 4(1). https://dergipark.org.tr/tr/pub/tbbmd/issue/22243/238785

Özhan, Ş., Ozhan, E., & Habiboglu, O. (2023). The analysis of brand reputation and willingness to pay price premium with regression analysis and classification algorithms. *Kybernetes*, Vol. ahead-of-print No. ahead-of-print. DOI: 10.1108/K-02-2023-0231

Özkan, Z., & Samur, Y. (2017). Oyunlaştırma Yönteminin Öğrencilerin Motivasyonları Üzerine Etkisi [The Effect of Using Gamification on Students' Motivation]. *Ege Eğitim Dergisi*, 18(2), 857–886. DOI: 10.12984/egeefd.314801

Özkeser, B. (2018). *Lean Innovation Approach in Industry 5.0*. The Eurasia Proceedings of Science, Engineering & Mathematics.

Ozkeser, B. (2018). Lean innovation approach in industry 5.0. *The Eurasia Proceedings of Science, Technology* [EPSTEM]. *Engineering & Mathematics*, 2, 422–428.

Özsoy, K. (2019). Üç Boyutlu (3B) Baskı Teknolojisinin Eğitimde Uygulanabilirliği: Senirkent MYO Örneği [Usability of Three Dimensional (3D) Printing Technologies in Education: Senirkent MYO Case]. *Düzce Üniversitesi Bilim ve Teknoloji Dergisi*, 7(2), 111–123. DOI: 10.29130/dubited.436015

Özsoylu, A. F. (2017). Industry 4.0. *Journal of Çukurova University Faculty of Economics and Administrative Sciences*, 1, 41–64.

Öztürk, O., Kocaman, R., & Kanbach, D. K. (2024). How to design bibliometric research: An overview and a framework proposal. *Review of Managerial Science*, •••, 1–29.

Ozyilmaz, A., & Cicek, S. S. (2015). How does servant leadership affect employee attitudes, behaviors, and psychological climates in a for-profit organizational context? *Journal of Management & Organization*, 21(3), 263–290. DOI: 10.1017/jmo.2014.80

Pactwa, K., Woźniak, J., Jach, K., & Brdulak, A. (2024). Including the social responsibility of universities and sustainable development goals in the strategic plans of universities in Europe. *Sustainable Development, n/a*(n/a). DOI: 10.1002/sd.2924

Padmaja, V., & Mukul, K. (2021). Upskilling and Reskilling in the Digital Age: The Way Forward for Higher Educational Institutions. In *Transforming Higher Education Through Digitalization*. CRC Press. DOI: 10.1201/9781003132097-15

Page, M. J., McKenzie, J. E., Bossuyt, P. M., Boutron, I., Hoffmann, T. C., Mulrow, C. D., Shamseer, L., Tetzlaff, J. M., Akl, E. A., Brennan, S. E., Chou, R., Glanville, J., Grimshaw, J. M., Hróbjartsson, A., Lalu, M. M., Li, T., Loder, E. W., Mayo-Wilson, E., McDonald, S., & Moher, D. (2021). The PRISMA 2020 statement: An updated guideline for reporting systematic reviews. *Systematic Reviews*, 10(1), 105906. DOI: 10.1186/s13643-021-01626-4 PMID: 33781348

Panagou, S., Neumann, W. P., & Fruggiero, F. (2024). A scoping review of human robot interaction research towards Industry 5.0 human-centric workplaces. *International Journal of Production Research*, 62(3), 974–990. DOI: 10.1080/00207543.2023.2172473

Paradkar, A., Knight, J., & Hansen, P. (2015). Innovation in start-ups: Ideas filling the void or ideas devoid of resources and capabilities? *Technovation*, 41, 1–10. DOI: 10.1016/j.technovation.2015.03.004

PAREKH, M. (n.d.). *Role of Leadership in Fostering Workplace Resilience*. KNOLSKAPE EDITORAL TEAM. https://knolskape.com/blog/role-of-leadership-in-fostering-workplace-resilience/#:~:text=Resilient%20leaders%20possess%20self%2Dawareness,being%20of%20their%20team%20members

Parent-Rocheleau, X., Bentein, K., & Simard, G. (2020). Positive together? The effects of leader-follower (dis)similarity in psychological capital. *Journal of Business Research*, 110, 435–444. DOI: 10.1016/j.jbusres.2020.02.016

Parlar, Z., Soybora, E. K., Burhan, M. S., & Davaslıgil, S. (2017). Sistematik konstrüksiyon ve tasarım odaklı düşünme yaklaşımı ile yaratıcı kavramsal tasarım süreci: Küçük ev aleti tasarımı [Systematic design and design thinking approach for conceptual design process: small household appliance design]. *Sakarya Üniversitesi Fen Bilimleri Enstitüsü Dergisi*, 21(5), 1100–1109. DOI: 10.16984/saufenbilder.307260

Parnitvitidkun, P. (2021). *Dimensions of Innovative Work Behavior in Digital Transformation,* KKBS Journal of Business Administration and Accountancy, 5(3), 69–96. Retrieved at https://so04.tci-thaijo.org/index.php/kkbsjournal/article/view/248992

Parnitvitidkun, P., Ponchaitiwat, K., Chancharat, N., & Thoumrungroje, A. (2024). Understanding IT Professional Innovative Work Behavior in the Workplace: A Sequential Mixed-methods Design. *Journal of Open Innovation*, 10(1), 100231. DOI: 10.1016/j.joitmc.2024.100231

Pasayat, A. K., Mitra, A., & Bhowmick, B. (2022). Determination of essential features for predicting start-up success: An empirical approach using machine learning. *Technology Analysis and Strategic Management*, 36(1), 1–19.

Pastoriza, D., & Ariño, M. A. (2008). When agents become stewards: Introducing learning in the stewardship theory. *1st IESE Conference on "Humanizing The Firm And The Management Profession" Barcelona, IESE Business School*, 1-17.

Paunović, M., Ružičić, M. M., & Moravčević, M. L. (2022). Business process innovations in family firms: Evidence from Serbia. *Journal of Family Business Management*, 13(1), 166–184. DOI: 10.1108/JFBM-03-2022-0044

Peixoto, B., Pinto, R., Melo, M., Cabral, L., & Bessa, M. (2021). Immersive virtual reality for foreign language education: A PRISMA Systematic Review. *IEEE Access : Practical Innovations, Open Solutions*, 9, 48952–48962. DOI: 10.1109/ACCESS.2021.3068858

Pena, I. (2002). Intellectual capital and business start-up success. *Journal of Intellectual Capital*, 3(2), 180–198. DOI: 10.1108/14691930210424761

Peng, Z., & Wan, Y. (2023). Generating business intelligence through automated textual analysis: Measuring corporate image with online information. *Chinese Management Studies*, 17(3), 545–572. DOI: 10.1108/CMS-07-2021-0318

Peng, Z., & Zhao, H. (2012). Does organization citizenship behavior really benefit the organization? Study on the compulsory citizenship behavior in China. *Nankai Business Review International*, 3(1), 75–92. DOI: 10.1108/20408741211201935

Perry, T., & Shivdasani, A. (2005). Do Boards Affect Performance? Evidence from Corporate Restructuring. *The Journal of Business*, 4(78), 1403–1432. DOI: 10.1086/430864

Peterson, R., & Wallace, K. (2023). Strategic frameworks for human-centric innovation. *Strategic Management Journal*, 44(1), 123–142. DOI: 10.1002/smj.3404

Pfeffer, J. (1987). A resource dependence perspective on intercorporate relations. *Intercorporate Relations: The Structural Analysis of Business*, 25-55.

Pfeffer, J., & Salancik, G. R. (1978). *The external control of organizations: A resource dependence perspective*. Harper & Row.

Philpot, S., & Roy, I. (2017, February 28). *Leadership Disrupted: Pushing the Boundaries- 2017 Global Human Capital Trends.* Retrieved at https://www2.deloitte.com/us/en/insights/focus/human-capital-trends/2017/developing-digital-leaders.html

Pierce, M., Hope, H., Ford, T., Hatch, S., Hotopf, M., John, A., & Abel, K. M. (2020). Mental health before and during the COVID-19 pandemic: A longitudinal probability sample survey of the UK population. *The Lancet. Psychiatry*, 7(10), 883–892. DOI: 10.1016/S2215-0366(20)30308-4 PMID: 32707037

Pierrakis, Y., & Owen, R. (2022). Startup ventures and equity finance: How do Business Accelerators and Business Angels' assess the human capital of socio-environmental mission-led entrepreneurs? Innovation. *Innovation (North Sydney, N.S.W.)*, 25(4), 371–395. DOI: 10.1080/14479338.2022.2029706

Pillay, N. (2024, November 11). Becoming a Digital Leader: Cultivating a Mindset for the Future. Retrieved at https://www.acumenmagazine.co.za/articles/becoming-a-digital-leader-cultivating-a-mindset-for-the-future-12750.html

Pinheiro, P., Putnik, G. D., Castro, A., Castro, H., Dal, B. F. R., & Romero, F. (2019). Industry 4.0 and industrial revolutions: An assessment based on complexity. *FME Transactions*, 47(4), 831–840. DOI: 10.5937/fmet1904831P

Pinheiro, R., Young, M., & Frigotto, M. L. (2022). *Towards Resilient Organizations and Societies*. Public Sector Organizations., DOI: 10.1007/978-3-030-82072-5

Pink, S., Quilty, E., Grundy, J., & Hoda, R. (2024). Trust, artificial intelligence and software practitioners: An interdisciplinary agenda. *AI & Society*, •••, 1–14. DOI: 10.1007/s00146-024-01882-7

Pintado, T. R., De Lema, D. G. P., & Van Auken, H. (2007). Venture capital in Spain by stage of development. *Journal of Small Business Management*, 45(1), 68–88. DOI: 10.1111/j.1540-627X.2007.00199.x

POAASA. (2024a). Kamu Gözetimi, Muhasebe ve Denetim Standartları Kurumu. https://www.kgk.gov.tr/SustainabilityDetailForm/11455/Raporlama%20Standartlar%C4%B1

POAASA. (2024b). Kamu Gözetimi, Muhasebe ve Denetim Standartları Kurumu. https://www.kgk.gov.tr/surdurulebilirlik

Podgórska, M., & Zdonek, I. (2024). Interdisciplinary collaboration in higher education towards sustainable development. *Sustainable Development (Bradford)*, 32(3), 2085–2103. DOI: 10.1002/sd.2765

Podsakoff, P. M., & MacKenzie, S. B. (1994). An examination of the psychometric properties and nomological validity of some revised and reduced substitutes for leadership scales. *The Journal of Applied Psychology*, 79(5), 702–713. DOI: 10.1037/0021-9010.79.5.702

Pollák, F., Dorcák, P., Markovič, P., & Soviar, J. (2019). Innovative approaches to the reputation management in the tourism sector. Innovation and transformation in a digital world (IDIMT-2019), September 4–6, Kutná Hora, Czech Republic, pp.285-292.

Pollák, F., Dorčák, P., Račeta, N., & Svetozarovová, N. (2016). Sustainable E-marketing of selected tourism subjects from the Mediterranean through active online reputation management. In *Leon-Garcia, A., et al. Smart City 360°. Lecture Notes of the Institute for Computer Sciences, Social Informatics and Telecommunications Engineering* (Vol. 166). Springer., DOI: 10.1007/978-3-319-33681-7_60

Pollák, F., & Markovič, P. (2022). Challenges for Corporate Reputation—Online Reputation Management in Times of Global Pandemic. *Journal of Risk and Financial Management*, 15(6), 250. DOI: 10.3390/jrfm15060250

Pollák, F., Soviar, J., & Svetozarovová, N. (2018). Selected approaches to sustainable development of corporate reputation - empirical study of online reputation management of subjects from the field of supply chain management. *8th Carpathian Logistics Congress on Logistics, Distribution, Transport and Management (CLC)*, 3-5 December, Prague, Czech Republic, pp. 324-329.

Ponzi, L. J., Fombrun, C. J., & Gardberg, N. A. (2011). RepTrak™ Pulse: Conceptualizing and validating a short-form measure of corporate reputation. *Corporate Reputation Review*, 14(1), 15–35. DOI: 10.1057/crr.2011.5

Pophal, L. (n.d.). *What Is Human AI Collaboration? | HR Glossary*. Visier. Retrieved October 9, 2024, from https://www.visier.com/blog/hr-glossary-what-is-human-ai-collaboration/

Popovic, G., Eric, O., & Stanic, S. (2020). Trade openness, institutions and economic growth of the western Balkans countries. *Montenegrin Journal of Economics*, 16(3), 173–184. DOI: 10.14254/1800-5845/2020.16-3.14

Popović-Pantić, S., Semenčenko, D., & Vasilić, N. (2020). Women Entrepreneurship in the Time of COVID-19 Pandemic: The case of Serbia. *Journal of Women's Entrepreneurship & Education.*

Porter, M. E., & Kramer, M. R. (2006). Strategy and society: The link between competitive advantage and corporate social responsibility. *Harvard Business Review*, 84(12), 78–92. https://hbr.org/2006/12/strategy-and-society-the-link-between-competitive-advantage-and-corporate-social-responsibility PMID: 17183795

Post, C., Rahman, N., & Rubow, E. (2011). Green governance: Boards of directors' composition and environmental corporate social responsibility. *Business & Society*, 50(1), 189–223. DOI: 10.1177/0007650310394642

Pradhan, R., Jena, L., & Bhattacharya, P. (2016). Impact of psychological capital on organizational citizenship behavior: Moderating role of emotional intelligence. *Cogent Business & Management*, 3(1), 3. DOI: 10.1080/23311975.2016.1194174

Pradhan, S., & Gupta, P. (2021). Abusive supervision and work-family conflict: An empirical investigation of Indian professionals. *International Journal of Conflict Management*, 32(3), 493–513. DOI: 10.1108/IJCMA-07-2020-0130

Prado-Lorenzo, J. M., & Garcia-Sanchez, I. M. (2010). The role of the board of directors in disseminating relevant information on greenhouse gases. *Journal of Business Ethics*, 97(3), 391–424. DOI: 10.1007/s10551-010-0515-0

Prahalad, C. K., & Hamel, G. (1990). The core competence of the corporation. *Harvard Business Review*, 68(3), 79–91. https://hbr.org/1990/05/the-core-competence-of-the-corporation

Prahalad, C. K., & Hamel, G. (2009). *The core competence of the corporation*. Routledge.

Pramana, A., Dalimunthe, Z., Gandakusuma, I., & Rizkianto, E. (2020). Evaluation Criteria of High-Flyer Tech Startup Investments by Venture Capital Firms in Indonesia, K. Soliman, editor, Education Excellence and Innovation Management: A 2025 Vision To Sustain Economic Development During Global Challenges, Int Business Informat Management Assoc, pp.4054–4062, 35th International-Business-Information-Management-Association Conference (IBIMA), Seville, SPAIN, APR 01-02, 2020.

Preacher, K. J., & Hayes, A. F. (2004). SPSS and SAS Procedures for Estimating Indirect Effects in Simple Mediation Models. *Behavior Research Methods, Instruments, & Computers*, 36(4), 717–731. DOI: 10.3758/BF03206553 PMID: 15641418

Pryor, C., & Howe, P. (2018). *Conform to the social norm: Why people follow what other people do*. The University of Melbourne. https://findanexpert.unimelb.edu.au/news/2944-conform-to-the-social-norm--why-people-follow-what-other-people-do

Puma Flores, M. J., & Rosa-Díaz, I. M. (2023). Online reputation for food sector exporters in the B2B context: The importance of sustainability. *Foods*, 12(20), 3862. DOI: 10.3390/foods12203862 PMID: 37893755

Qamar, F., & Soomro, S. A. (2023). Investigating the impact of servant leadership on service excellence: The mediating role of PsyCap as a personal resource and buffering role of conscientiousness. *Global Knowledge, Memory and Communication*.

Qin, G., & Zhang, L. (2024). How compulsory citizenship behavior depletes individual resources -a moderated mediation model. *Current Psychology (New Brunswick, N.J.)*, 43(2), 969–983. DOI: 10.1007/s12144-023-04386-7

Quarter, J., & Richmond, B. (2001). Accounting for social value in nonprofits and for-profits. *Nonprofit Management & Leadership*, 12(1), 75–85. DOI: 10.1002/nml.12106

Rademaker, T., Klingenberg, I., & Süß, S. (2023). *Leadership and Technostress: A Systematic Literature Review*. Management Review Quarterly., DOI: 10.1007/s11301-023-00385-x

Rafael, R., Shirley, A. J., & Liveris, A. (2014). *Rafael, R., Shirley, A. J., & Liveris, A. (2014). Report To The President Accelerating US Advanced Manufacturing. Report, US.* Washington DC: Report.

Ragu-Nathan, T. S., Tarafdar, M., Ragu-Nathan, B. S., & Tu, Q. (2008). The Consequences of Technostress for End Users in Organizations: Conceptual Development and Empirical Validation. *Information Systems Research*, 19(4), 417–433. DOI: 10.1287/isre.1070.0165

Raineri, N., Paille, P., & Morin, D. (2012). Organizational citizenship behavior: An intergenerational study.

Rajković, J., Nikolić, M., Ćoćkalo, D., Stojanović, E. T., & Kovačić, S. (2020). National culture and the entrepreneurial intentions of students in Serbia. *Journal for East European Management Studies*, 25(1), 105–141. DOI: 10.5771/0949-6181-2020-1-105

Ramadani, V., Gërguri, S., Dana, L.-P., & Tašaminova, T. (2013). Women entrepreneurs in the Republic of Macedonia: Waiting for directions. *International Journal of Entrepreneurship and Small Business*, 19(1), 95–121. DOI: 10.1504/IJESB.2013.054330

Ramadani, V., Hisrich, R. D., & Gërguri-Rashiti, S. (2015). Female entrepreneurs in transition economies: Insights from Albania, Macedonia and Kosovo. *World Review of Entrepreneurship, Management and Sustainable Development*, 11(4), 391–413. DOI: 10.1504/WREMSD.2015.072066

Ramadani, V., Rexhepi, G., Gërguri-Rashiti, S., Ibraimi, S., & Dana, L.-P. (2014). Ethnic entrepreneurship in Macedonia: The case of Albanian entrepreneurs. *International Journal of Entrepreneurship and Small Business*, 23(3), 313–335. DOI: 10.1504/IJESB.2014.065525

Rame, R., Purwanto, P., & Sudarno, S. (2024) Industry 5.0 and sustainability: An overview of emerging trends and challenges for a green future. *Innovation and Green Development*. 3(4). ISSN 2949-7531. https://doi.org/DOI: 10.1016/j.igd.2024.100173

Ramos, C. M. Q., & Casado-Molina, A.-M. (2021). Online corporate reputation: A panel data approach and a reputation index proposal applied to the banking sector. *Journal of Business Research*, 122, 121–130. DOI: 10.1016/j.jbusres.2020.08.061

Ramos-Rodríguez, A. R., & Ruíz-Navarro, J. (2004). Changes in the intellectual structure of strategic management research: A bibliometric study of the Strategic Management Journal, 1980–2000. *Strategic Management Journal*, 25(10), 981–1004. DOI: 10.1002/smj.397

Ramu, NB (2019) Management Challenges and Opportunities of Industry 5.0. *India's Changing Paradigm: Skills and Entrepreneurship for Global Competitiveness*. 62-68 (PDF) Management Challenges and Opportunities of Industry 5.0

Rani, S., Jining, D., Shoukat, K., Shoukat, M. U., & Nawaz, S. A. (2024). A Human–Machine Interaction Mechanism: Additive Manufacturing for Industry 5.0—Design and Management. *Sustainability (Basel)*, 16(10), 10. Advance online publication. DOI: 10.3390/su16104158

Ransbotham, S., Kiron, D., Gerbert, P., & Reeves, M. (2017). Reshaping business with artificial intelligence: Closing the gap between ambition and action. *MIT Sloan Management Review*, 59(1), 1–17.

Rantanen, A., Salminen, J., Ginter, F., & Jansen, B. J. (2020). Classifying online corporate reputation with machine learning: A study in the banking domain. *Internet Research*, 30(1), 45–66. DOI: 10.1108/INTR-07-2018-0318

Rao, K. K., Tilt, C. A., & Lester, L. H. (2012). Corporate governance and environmental reporting: An Australian study. *Corporate Governance (Bradford)*, 12(2), 143–163. DOI: 10.1108/14720701211214052

Rao, P. S. (2017). Human-centric innovation and disruptive industry trends. *Journal of Technology Management*, 32(2), 142–158. DOI: 10.1016/j.jtm.2016.10.001

Rashiti, L., Shala, A., & Sopi, X. (2023). Digital Marketing In Retail Banking–Analysis Of Managers' Attitudes. *Business Management*(2 Year 2023), 23-46.

Rasmussen, E. S., & Tanev, S. (2016). *Lean start-up: Making the start-up more successful, Start-up creation*. Elsevier. DOI: 10.1016/B978-0-08-100546-0.00003-0

Rastkhiz, S. E. A., Dehkordi, A. M., Farsi, J. Y., & Azar, A. (2018). A new approach to evaluating entrepreneurial opportunities. *Journal of Small Business and Enterprise Development*, 26(1), 67–84. DOI: 10.1108/JSBED-01-2018-0013

Ravasi, D., & Zattoni, A. (2006). Exploring the political side of board involvement in strategy: A study of mixed-ownership institutions. *Journal of Management Studies*, 43(8), 1671–1702. DOI: 10.1111/j.1467-6486.2006.00659.x

Ravichandran, A., Taylor, K., & Waterhouse, P. (2016). DevOps for Digital Leaders: Reignite Business with a Modern DevOps-Enabled Software Factory. New York: Springer. Science+Business Media. DOI: 10.1007/978-1-4842-1842-6

Raz, O., & Gloor, P. A. (2007). Size really matters—New insights for start-ups' survival. *Management Science*, 53(2), 169–177. DOI: 10.1287/mnsc.1060.0609

Rehman, A., & Umar, T. (2024). Literature review: Industry 5.0. Leveraging technologies for environmental, social and governance advancement in corporate settings. *Corporate Governance: The International Journal of Business in Society, ahead-of-print*(ahead-of-print). DOI: 10.1108/CG-11-2023-0502

Rehman, A., Ganesan, Y., & Haron, H. (2023). What is priority for organization: environmental, social and governance or sustainable corporate governance: literature review. In Çalıyurt, K. (Ed.), *History of Accounting, Management, Business and Economics, Accounting, Finance, Sustainability, Governance & Fraud: Theory and Application* (pp. 167–191). Springer. DOI: 10.1007/978-981-99-3346-4_8

*RESILIENCE | English meaning - Cambridge Dictionary*. (2024, October 2). Cambridge Dictionary. Retrieved October 8, 2024, from https://dictionary.cambridge.org/dictionary/english/resilience#google_vignette

Reuber, A. R., & Fischer, E. (2011). International entrepreneurship in internet-enabled markets. *Journal of Business Venturing*, 26(6), 660–679. DOI: 10.1016/j.jbusvent.2011.05.002

*RFID Etiketler Nasıl çalışır? [How Do RFID Tags Work?]*. RFIDmarket. (n.d.). https://www.rfidmarket.com.tr/blog/icerik/rfid-etiketler-nasil-calisir

Rhoades, D. L., Rechner, P. L., & Sundaramurthy, C. (2000). Board composition and financial performance: A meta-analysis of the influence of outside directors. *Journal of Managerial Issues*, 12(1), 76–91.

Rijwani, T., Kumari, S., Srinivas, R., Abhishek, K., Iyer, G., Vara, H., Dubey, S., Revathi, V., & Gupta, M. (2024). Industry 5.0: A review of emerging trends and transformative technologies in the next industrial revolution. *International Journal on Interactive Design and Manufacturing*. Advance online publication. DOI: 10.1007/s12008-024-01943-7

Ritz, A., Giauque, D., Varone, F., & Anderfuhren, S. (2014). From Leadership to Citizenship Behavior in Public Organizations: When Values Matter. *Review of Public Personnel Administration*, 34(2), 128–152. DOI: 10.1177/0734371X14521456

Riyanto, S., Endri, E., & Herlissha, N. (2021). Effect of work motivation and job satisfaction on employee performance: Mediating role of employee engagement. *Problems and Perspectives in Management*, 19(3), 162–174. DOI: 10.21511/ppm.19(3).2021.14

Rodríguez-Díaz, M., Alonso-González, R., Rodríguez-Voltes, C. I., & Rodríguez-Voltes, A. C. (2019). A rating of the online reputation balance in lodgings. *Administrative Sciences*, 9(3), 58. DOI: 10.3390/admsci9030058

Rodríguez-Díaz, M., Rodríguez-Díaz, R., Rodríguez-Voltes, A. C., & Rodríguez-Voltes, C. I. (2018). Analysing the relationship between price and online reputation by lodging category. *Sustainability (Basel)*, 10(12), 4474. DOI: 10.3390/su10124474

Rodríguez-Díaz, M., Rodríguez-Voltes, C. I., & Rodríguez-Voltes, A. C. (2018). Gap analysis of the online reputation. *Sustainability (Basel)*, 10(5), 1603. DOI: 10.3390/su10051603

Rompho, N. (2018). Operational performance measures for startups. *Measuring Business Excellence*, 22(1), 31–41. DOI: 10.1108/MBE-06-2017-0028

Rosak-Szyrocka, J., & Knop, K. (2024). Sustainable development Universities—Opportunities & challenges on the road to society 5.0 from the key stakeholder perspective. *PLoS One*, 19(8), e0308929. DOI: 10.1371/journal.pone.0308929 PMID: 39146253

Rosamond, E. (2020). From reputation capital to reputation warfare: Online Ratings, trolling, and the logic of volatility. *Theory, Culture & Society*, 37(2), 105–129. DOI: 10.1177/0263276419872530

Roy, R. K. (2014). *Strategy for Simultaneous Evaluation of Multiple Objectives*. MI, USA, Nutek, Inc., http://nutek-us.com/QITT07 - Overall Evaluation Criteria (OEC) Strategy.pdf

Rozanec, J. M., Novalija, I., Zajec, P., Kenda, K., Ghinani, H. T., Suh, S., & Soldatos, J. (2023). Human-centric artificial intelligence architecture for industry 5.0 applications. *International Journal of Production Research*, 20(20), 6847–6872. DOI: 10.1080/00207543.2022.2138611

Rust, R. T., Rand, W., Huang, M.-H., Stephen, A. T., Brooks, G., & Chabuk, T. (2021). Real-time brand reputation tracking using social media. *Journal of Marketing*, 85(4), 21–43. DOI: 10.1177/0022242921995173

Sachan, R., Chauhan, K., & Agarwal, V. (2024). Outlook on Upskilling and Reskilling Capacities for Industry 5.0. In Shrivastava, R., & Jain, K. (Eds.), *Humanizing Businesses for a Better World of Work* (pp. 1–16). Emerald Publishing Limited., DOI: 10.1108/978-1-83797-332-320241001

Sachsenmeier, P. (2016). Industry 5.0—The relevance and implications of bionics and synthetic biology. *Engineering (Beijing)*, 2(2), 225–229. DOI: 10.1016/J.ENG.2016.02.015

Saha, A. K., & Akter, S. (2013). Corporate governance and voluntary disclosure practices of financial non-financial sector companies in Bangladesh. *Journal of Applied Management Accounting Research*, 11(2), 45–61.

Sahebjamnia, N., Torabi, S. A., & Mansouri, S. A. (2015). Integrated business continuity and disaster recovery planning: Towards organizational resilience. *European Journal of Operational Research*, 242(1), 261–273. DOI: 10.1016/j.ejor.2014.09.055

Said, R., Zainuddin, Y. H., & Haron, H. (2009). The relationship between corporate social responsibility disclosure and corporate governance characteristics in Malaysian public listed companies. *Social Responsibility Journal*, 5(2), 212–226. DOI: 10.1108/17471110910964496

Sajuyigbe, A. S., Inegbedion, H. E., Ayeni, A. W., & Ighomereho, S. O. (2022). Compulsory citizenship behavior, work-life balance, and turnover intention in academia: Mediating effects of emotional intelligence. *Journal of Behavioral Science*, 17(2), 58–72.

Saksena, G., & Jha, A. (2024). Culture Essentials for Industry 5.0. In Sushil, N. R., & Joshi, R. (Eds.), *Flexibility, Resilience and Sustainability* (pp. 77–92). Springer Nature., DOI: 10.1007/978-981-99-9550-9_5

Salam, A. (2023). Navigating the Digital Landscape: Exploring the Interplay of Digital Leadership, E-Learning Anxiety, and Innovative Behavior. *Journal of Digitovation and Information System*, 3(1), 32–46. DOI: 10.54433/JDIIS.2023100020

Salanova, M., Llorens, S., & Cifre, E. (2013). The Dark Side of Technologies: Technostress Among Users of Information and Communication Technologies. *International Journal of Psychology*, 48(3), 422–436. DOI: 10.1080/00207594.2012.680460 PMID: 22731610

Salih, A. M. (2024). *Digital Leadership: Evidence from Theory and Practice*. Routledge.

Salomon, V. (2018). Strategies of startup evaluation on crowd investing platforms: The case of Switzerland. *Journal Of Innovation Economics & Management*, (26), 63–88. DOI: 10.3917/jie.pr1.0029

Sanfey, P., & Milatovic, J. (2018). *The Western Balkans in transition: diagnosing the constraints on the path to a sustainable market economy*. European Bank for Reconstruction and Development London.

Saniuk, S., Grabowska, S., & Straka, M. (2022). Identification of Social and Economic Expectations: Contextual Reasons for the Transformation Process of Industry 4.0 into the Industry 5.0 Concept. *Sustainability (Basel)*, 3(3), 1391. Advance online publication. DOI: 10.3390/su14031391

Santhi, A. R., & Muthuswamy, P. (2023). Industry 5.0 or industry 4.0S? Introduction to industry 4.0 and a peek into the prospective industry 5.0 technologies. *International Journal on Interactive Design and Manufacturing*, 17(2), 947–979. DOI: 10.1007/s12008-023-01217-8

Sarabadani, J., Jafarzadeh, H., & ShamiZanjani, M. (2017). Towards understanding the determinants of employees' E -learning adoption in workplace. *International Journal of Enterprise Information Systems*, 13(1), 38–49. DOI: 10.4018/IJEIS.2017010103

Sarioguz, O., & Miser, E. (2024). Artificial intelligence and participatory leadership: The role of technological transformation in business management and its impact on employee participation. *International Research Journal of Modernization in Engineering Technology and Science*, 6(2).

Sari, R., Dewanti, P., Fajar, M., Priantinah, D., & Pranesti, A. (2022). Development of Early Startup Companies' Valuation Model Based on Android Mobile Application: The Angel Investor's Perspective. *JOIV: International Journal on Informatics Visualization*, 6(2), 382–389. DOI: 10.30630/joiv.6.2.992

Sarkar, B. D., Shardeo, V., Dwivedi, A., & Pamucar, D. (2024). Digital transition from industry 4.0 to industry 5.0 in smart manufacturing: A framework for sustainable future. *Technology in Society*, 78, 102649. Advance online publication. DOI: 10.1016/j.techsoc.2024.102649

Sary, F. P., Dudija, N., & Moslem, M. (2023). Do Digital Competency and Self-leadership Influence Teachers' Innovative Work Behavior? *European Journal of Educational Research*, 12(3), 1449–1463. DOI: 10.12973/eu-jer.12.3.1449

Sato, Y., Tabuchi, T., & Yamamoto, K. (2012). Market size and entrepreneurship. *Journal of Economic Geography*, 12(6), 1139–1166. DOI: 10.1093/jeg/lbr035

Schaufeli, W. B., & Bakker, A. B. (2004). Job demands, job resources, and their relationship with burnout and engagement: A multi-sample study. Journal of Organizational Behavior: The International Journal of Industrial. *Journal of Organizational Behavior*, 25(3), 293–315. DOI: 10.1002/job.248

Schillemans, T., & Busuioc, M. (2015). Predicting public sector accountability: From agency drift to forum drift. *Journal of Public Administration: Research and Theory*, 25(1), 191–215. DOI: 10.1093/jopart/muu024

Schmidt, J. (2012). Do people in NGOs perform civic behavior? Organizational citizenship behavior in Polish NGOs – results of an empirical study. Tenth International Conference of the International Society for Third Sector Research (ISTR) Fondazione ForTeS - Fondazione Scuola di alta Formazione per il Terzo Settore. Italy.

Schneider, B., & Bowen, D. E. (1995). *Winning the Service Game*. Harvard Business Review Press.

Schumacker, R. E., & Lomax, R. G. (2010). *A Beginner's Guide to Structural Equation Modeling*. Routledge.

Scillitoe, J. L., & Birasnav, M. (2022). Ease of market entry of Indian startups: Formal and informal institutional influences. *South Asian Journal of Business Studies*, 11(2), 195–215. DOI: 10.1108/SAJBS-07-2019-0131

Scott, E. L., Shu, P., & Lubynsky, R. M.. (2015). *Are'better'Ideas More Likely to Succeed?: An Empirical Analysis of Startup Evaluation, Technical Report*. Harvard Business School.

Sekaran, U., & Roger, B. (2016). *Research methods for business* (7th ed.). John Wiley & Sons.

Şener, İ., Varoğlu, A., & Karapolatgil, A. A. (2016). Sustainability reports disclosures: Who are the most salient stakeholders? *Procedia: Social and Behavioral Sciences*, 235, 84–92. DOI: 10.1016/j.sbspro.2016.11.028

Senge, P. M. (1990). *The Fifth Discipline: The Art & Practice of The Learning Organization*. Doubleday.

Seppänen, P., Tripathi, N., Oivo, M., & Liukkunen, K. (2017). How Are Product Ideas Validated? The Process from Innovation to Requirements Engineering in Software Startups, Software Business: 8th International Conference, ICSOB 2017, Essen, Germany, June 12-13, 2017, Proceedings 8, Springer, pp.3-17.

Setó-Pamies, D. (2015). The relationship between women directors and corporate social responsibility. *Corporate Social Responsibility and Environmental Management*, 22(6), 334–345. DOI: 10.1002/csr.1349

Sevinç, H. (n.d.). *ESP8266 ve Arduino ile Nesnelerin İnterneti [Internet of Things with ESP8266 and Arduino]*. https://abms.com.tr/upload/product_datasheets/89c544826d965692a111bb9e1fcee5259fddf12c.pdf

Shad Manaman, H., Jamali, S., & AleAhmad, A. (2016). Online reputation measurement of companies based on user-generated content in online social networks. *Computers in Human Behavior*, 54, 94–100. DOI: 10.1016/j.chb.2015.07.061

Shafi, K. (2021). Investors' evaluation criteria in equity crowdfunding. *Small Business Economics*, 56(1), 3–37. DOI: 10.1007/s11187-019-00227-9

Shamma, H. M., El Masry, R., & Dutot, V. (2023). When online reputation drives consumers' online repurchase intentions: An Egyptian story. *Global Business Review*, 0(0), 09721509231155276. Advance online publication. DOI: 10.1177/09721509231155276

Shanahan, B. W., & Organ, J. (2022) Harnessing the Benefits of Micro Credentials for Industry 4.0 and 5.0: Skills Training and Lifelong Learning. *IFAC-PapersOnLine*. 55(39):82-87. ISSN 2405-8963. https://doi.org/DOI: 10.1016/j.ifacol.2022.12.015

Shankar, R. K., & Shepherd, D. A. (2019). Accelerating strategic fit or venture emergence: Different paths adopted by corporate accelerators. *Journal of Business Venturing*, 34(5), 105886. DOI: 10.1016/j.jbusvent.2018.06.004

Shao, C., Cui, P., Xun, P., Peng, Y., & Jiang, X. (2018). Rank correlation between centrality metrics in complex networks: An empirical study. *Open Physics*, 16(1), 1009–1023. https://doi.org/doi:10.1515/phys-2018-0122. DOI: 10.1515/phys-2018-0122

Sharma, A., & Singh, B. J. (2020). Evolution of Industrial Revolutions: A review [IJITEE]. *International Journal of Innovative Technology and Exploring Engineering*, 9(11), 66–73. DOI: 10.35940/ijitee.I7144.0991120

Sharma, L., Bulsara, H. P., Trivedi, M., & Bagdi, H. (2024). An analysis of sustainability-driven entrepreneurial intentions among university students: The role of university support and SDG knowledge. *Journal of Applied Research in Higher Education*, 16(2), 281–301. DOI: 10.1108/JARHE-11-2022-0359

Sharma, R., & Gupta, H. (2024). Harmonizing sustainability in industry 5.0 era: Transformative strategies for cleaner production and sustainable competitive advantage. *Journal of Cleaner Production*, 445, 141118. Advance online publication. DOI: 10.1016/j.jclepro.2024.141118

Sheninger, E. (2019). *Digital Leadership: Changing Paradigms for Changing Times*. Corwin Press.

Shin, Y. (2012). CEO ethical leadership, ethical climate, climate strength, and collective organizational citizenship behavior. *Journal of Business Ethics*, 108(3), 299–312. Advance online publication. DOI: 10.1007/s10551-011-1091-7

Shiroishi, Y., Uchiyama, K., & Suzuki, N. (2018). Society 5.0: For human security and well-being. *Computer*, 51(7), 91–95. DOI: 10.1109/MC.2018.3011041

Shishakly, R., Almaiah, M., Lutfi, A., & Alrawad, M. (2024). The influence of using smart technologies for sustainable development in higher education institutions. *International Journal of Data and Network Science*, 8(1), 77–90. DOI: 10.5267/j.ijdns.2023.10.015

Shu, C.-Y., Chiang, Y.-H., & Lu, C.-H. (2018). Authoritarian leadership supervisor support and workers' compulsory citizenship behavior. *International Journal of Manpower*, 39(3), 468–485. DOI: 10.1108/IJM-10-2016-0191

Simões, J., Ferreira, F., Peris-Ortiz, M., & Ferreira, J. (2020). A cognition-driven framework for the evaluation of startups in the digital economy: Adding value with cognitive mapping and rule-based expert systems. *Management Decision*, 58(11), 2327–2347. DOI: 10.1108/MD-09-2019-1253

Sinclair, H. (2024). *Digital Dawn: The Rise of New Business Realities*. Lars Meiertoberens.

Sindhwani, R., Afridi, S., Kumar, A., Banaits, A., Luthra, S., & Singh, P. L. (2022). Can industry 5.0 revolutionize the wave of resilience and social value creation? A multi-criteria framework to analyze enablers. *Technology in Society*, 68, 101887. Advance online publication. DOI: 10.1016/j.techsoc.2022.101887

Singh, K. (2014). Non- Governmental Organizations (NGOs) have become influential development agents in the developing world in recent decades through their so-called "sustainable" activities. *The Journal of American Science*, 11(1), 1–11.

Singh, P. (2022). *Using ICT and energy technologies for improving global engineering education*. Intech Open., DOI: 10.5772/intechopen.100097

Singh, R. (2021). Workforce development and continuous learning in Industry 5.0. *Journal of Vocational Behavior*, 89(1), 101–115. DOI: 10.1016/j.jvb.2021.103521

Skalicka, M., Zinecker, M., Balcerzak, A. P., & Pietrzak, M. B. (2023). Business angels and early stage decision-making criteria: Empirical evidence from an emerging market, Economic research-. *Ekonomska Istrazivanja*, 36(1), 25–50. DOI: 10.1080/1331677X.2022.2063920

Skare, M., Gavurova, B., & Polishchuk, V. (2023). A decision-making support model for financing start-up projects by venture capital funds on a crowdfunding platform. *Journal of Business Research*, 158, 113719. DOI: 10.1016/j.jbusres.2023.113719

Skočajić, I., Pavković, V., Krstić, J., Kostić-Stanković, M., Vlastelica, T., & Rajić, T. (2024). Urban tourism appeal: The effectiveness of communication channels and multimedia formats in creating tourists' expectations. *Sustainability (Basel)*, 16(11), 4552. DOI: 10.3390/su16114552

Smith, B. R., Kickul, J. R., & Wilson, F. (2010). *Entrepreneurial opportunity evaluation: a discrete choice analysis of financial and social entrepreneurial opportunity attributes, Values and Opportunities in Social Entrepreneurship*. Springer.

Smith, P. B., Dugan, S., Peterson, A. F., & Leung, W. (1998). Individualism: Collectivism and the handling of disagreement. A 23 country study. *International Journal of Intercultural Relations*, 22(3), 351–367. https://doi.org/https://doi.org/10.1016/S0147-1767(98)00012-1. DOI: 10.1016/S0147-1767(98)00012-1

Soares, J. O., Pina, J., Ribeiro, M., & Lopes, M. C. (2011). Quantitative vs. qualitative criteria for credit risk assessment. *Front. Finance Econ.*, 8(1), 69–87.

Sommer, R. M. (2014). *Relationship goals: Prioritizing personal fulfillment for lasting love*. TherapyIdeas. https://www.therapyideas.net/details/relationship-goals-prioritizing-personal-fulfillment-for-lasting-love/

Sommer, A. F., Hedegaard, C., Dukovska-Popovska, I., & Steger-Jensen, K. (2024, August). Industry 5.0 in Manufacturing: Enhancing Resilience and Responsibility through AI-Driven Predictive Maintenance, Quality Control, and Supply Chain Optimization. *international. Journal of Multidisciplinary Research*, 6(4), 815–828. DOI: 10.36948/ijfmr.2024.v06i04.25733

Song, H., Li, Y., Zhang, Q., & Cheng, Y. (2023). The moderating effects of trust and felt trust on the nonlinear relationship between compulsory citizenship behavior and counterproductive work behavior. *Psychology Research and Behavior Management*, 15(16), 2517–2531. DOI: 10.2147/PRBM.S413674 PMID: 37431432

Song, H., Yin, Q., Zhang, Q., & Li, Y. (2023). The impact of compulsory citizenship behavior on job performance of new-generation knowledge workers: The roles of ego depletion and relational energy. *Psychology Research and Behavior Management*, 28(16), 2367–2381. DOI: 10.2147/PRBM.S413932 PMID: 37404575

Sonnenfeld, J. A. (2002). What makes great boards great? *Harvard Business Review*, 80(9), 106–113. PMID: 12227143

Sousa, M. J., & Rocha, Á. (2019). Skills for Disruptive Digital Business. *Journal of Business Research*, 94, 257–263. DOI: 10.1016/j.jbusres.2017.12.051

Souza, M. A., González, M. O. A., & de Pinho, A. L. S. (2024). Maturity Model for Sustainability Assessment of Chemical Analyses Laboratories in Public Higher Education Institutions. *Sustainability (Basel)*, 16(5), 5. Advance online publication. DOI: 10.3390/su16052137

Soyupak, O., & Soyupak, İ. (2021). Oyuncağın Akıllanması: Dijital Teknoloji Barındıran Oyuncakların Tasarımına Yönelik Bir Çerçeve Önerisi [Smarting the toy: A proposal for a framework for designing digital technology containing toys]. *Sanat&Tasarım*, 11(2), 468–480.

Spagnoli, P., Molino, M., Molinaro, D., Giancaspro, M. L., Manuti, A., & Ghislieri, C. (2020). Workaholism and Technostress During the COVID-19 Emergency: The Crucial Role of the Leaders on Remote Working. *Frontiers in Psychology*, 11, 620310. Advance online publication. DOI: 10.3389/fpsyg.2020.620310 PMID: 33424730

Spears, L., & Lawrence, M. (2004). *Practicing Servant Leadership: Succeeding through trust, bravery, and forgiveness. San Francisco*. Jossey-Bass.

Spector, P. E. (2016). When more can become less high performance work systems as a source of occupational stress. In N. M. Ashkanasy, R. J. Bennett, & M. J. Martinko (Eds.), *Understanding the high performance workplace: The line between motivation and abuse,* 148–169. Routledge/Taylor & Francis Group.

Spender, J. C., Corvello, V., Grimaldi, M., & Rippa, P. (2017). Startups and open innovation: A literature. *European Journal of Innovation Management*, 20(1), 4–30. DOI: 10.1108/EJIM-12-2015-0131

Sposato, M. (2024). Digital Leadership in Organizations for Digital Transformation. In Espinosa, C., & Oliver, E. (Eds.), *Multidisciplinary Organizational Training of Human Capital in the Digital Age* (pp. 77–96). IGI Global Scientific Publishing.

Sreenivasan, A., & Suresh, M. (2023). Readiness of financial resilience in start-ups. *Journal of Safety Science and Resilience = An Quan Ke Xue Yu Ren Xing (Ying Wen)*, 4(3), 241–252.

Stan, O. M. (2018). Steps towards sustainability–human resource capital and employee wellbeing–benchmarking evidence. *Economics, Management, and Financial Markets*, 13(3), 290–300.

Steenkamp, H., & Rensburg, R. (2016). Harnessing stakeholder sentiment on social networking sites: A new conceptual framework for online reputation management. *Communicare*, 35(2), 55–84. DOI: 10.36615/jcsa.v35i2.1597

Stein, S. (2024). Universities confronting climate change: Beyond sustainable development and solutionism. *Higher Education*, 87(1), 165–183. DOI: 10.1007/s10734-023-00999-w

Stellenbosch. (2017). *How to measure your impact*. Stellenbosch University Library and Informantion Service. https://libguides.sun.ac.za/c.php?g=1199094&p=8770045

Stiles, P., & Taylor, B. (2001). *Boards at Work: How Directors View their Roles and Responsibilities.* Oxford University Press.

Stone-Romero, E. F., & Rosopa, P. J. (2008). The relative validity of inferences about mediation as a function of research design characteristics. *Organizational Research Methods*, 11(2), 326–352. DOI: 10.1177/1094428107300342

Stringer, L. (2016). *The Healthy Workplace: How to Improve the Well-Being of Your Employees---and Boost Your Company's Bottom Line*. Amacom.

Su, L., Chen, Y., & Li, Y. (2021). *Compulsory citizenship behavior leads to counterproductive work behavior: A multiple mediation path*. The 2021 12th International Conference on E-business, Management and Economics (ICEME 2021), July 17-19, 2021, Beijing, China (New York, NY: ACM) DOI: 10.1145/3481127.3481191

Subramaniam, S., & Janadari, N. (2020). Authentic leadership and organizational citizenship behaviour: The role of psychological capital. *International Journal of Productivity and Performance Management*.

Sudha, M. R., Malini, G. B. H., Sankar, R., Mythily, M., Kumaresh, P. S., Varadarajan, M. N., & Sujatha, S. (2025). Predictive modeling for healthcare worker well-being with cloud computing and machine learning for stress management. International Journal of Electrical & Computer Engineering (2088-8708), 15(1).

Sugiarto, A., Lee, C.-W., & Huruta, A. D. (2022). A Systematic Review of the Sustainable Campus Concept. *Behavioral Sciences (Basel, Switzerland)*, 12(5), 130. DOI: 10.3390/bs12050130 PMID: 35621427

Suhail, A., Haq, I. U., Azeem, M. U., & Vigoda-Gadot, E. (2024). Compulsory citizenship behavior, role overload, creativity and service-oriented voluntary behavior: Does generational difference have an impact? *Personnel Review*, 53(8), 2126–2146. Advance online publication. DOI: 10.1108/PR-12-2022-0894

Sundaramuthy, C., & Lewis, M. (2003). Control and collaboration: Paradoxes of governance. *Academy of Management Review*, 28(3), 397–415. DOI: 10.2307/30040729

Sürmen, H. K. (2019). Eklemeli İmalat (3B Baskı): Teknolojiler ve Uygulamalar [Additive Manufacturing (3D Printing): Technologies and Applications]. *Uludağ Üniversitesi Mühendislik Fakültesi Dergisi*, 24(2), 373–392. DOI: 10.17482/uumfd.519147 373

*sustainability noun - Definition, pictures, pronunciation and usage notes | Oxford Advanced Learner's Dictionary at OxfordLearnersDictionaries.com*. (n.d.). Oxford Learner's Dictionaries. Retrieved October 8, 2024, from https://www.oxfordlearnersdictionaries.com/definition/english/sustainability

Syed Alwi, S. F., & Da Silva, R. V. (2007). Online and offline corporate brand images: Do they differ? *Corporate Reputation Review*, 10(4), 217–244. DOI: 10.1057/palgrave.crr.1550056

Tafolli, F., & Grabner-Kräuter, S. (2020). Employee perceptions of corporate social responsibility and organizational corruption: Empirical evidence from Kosovo. *Corporate Governance (Bradford)*, 20(7), 1349–1370. DOI: 10.1108/CG-07-2020-0274

Tagscherer, F., & Carbon, C.-C. (2023). Leadership for Successful Digitalization: A Literature Review on Companies' Internal and External Aspects of Digitalization. *Sustainable Technology and Entrepreneurship*, 2(2), 100039. DOI: 10.1016/j.stae.2023.100039

Takewaki, I. (2020). New Architectural Viewpoint for Enhancing Society's Resilience for Multiple Risks Including Emerging COVID-19. *Frontiers in Built Environment*, 6, 143. DOI: 10.3389/fbuil.2020.00143

Tambe, P., Cappelli, P., & Yakubovich, V. (2019). Artificial intelligence in human resources management: Challenges and a path forward. *California Management Review*, 61(4), 1542. DOI: 10.1177/0008125619867910

Tao, F., Zhang, M., & Nee, A. Y. C. (Eds.). (2019). *Digital Twin Driven Smart Manufacturing*. Academic Press., DOI: 10.1016/B978-0-12-817630-6.00014-X

Tarafdar, M., Cooper, C. L., & Stich, J. (2017). The Technostress Trifecta - Techno Eustress, Techno Distress and Design: Theoretical Directions and An Agenda for Research. *Information Systems Journal*, 29(1), 6–42. DOI: 10.1111/isj.12169

Tarafdar, M., Pirkkalainen, H., Salo, M., & Makkonen, M. (2020). Taking on the "Dark Side" - Coping with Technostress. *IT Professional*, 22(6), 82–89. DOI: 10.1109/MITP.2020.2977343

Tarafdar, M., Pullins, E. B., & Ragu-Nathan, T. S. (2014). Technostress: Negative Effect on Performance and Possible Mitigations. *Information Systems Journal*, 25(2), 103–132. DOI: 10.1111/isj.12042

Tarafdar, M., Tu, Q., Ragu-Nathan, B. S., & Ragu-Nathan, T. S. (2007). The Impact of Technostress on Role Stress and Productivity. *Journal of Management Information Systems*, 24(1), 301–328. DOI: 10.2753/MIS0742-1222240109

Taşçıoğlu, Y. (2021, February 15). Nodemcu Nedir? NodeMCU Projeleri ile IoT Dünyasına Adım Atın! [What is Nodemcu? Step into the IoT World with NodeMCU Projects!]. *maker.robotistan Blog*. October 31, 2024, https://maker.robotistan.com/nodemcu-esp8266/#NodeMCU nedir? ESP8266 ile alakası nedir.

Tasdemir, C., & Gazo, R. (2020). Integrating sustainability into higher education curriculum through a transdisciplinary perspective. *Journal of Cleaner Production*, 265, 121759. DOI: 10.1016/j.jclepro.2020.121759

Tatineni, S. (2023). Cloud-Based Business Continuity and Disaster Recovery Strategies. *International Research Journal of Modernization in Engineering Technology and Science*, 5(11), 1389–1397.

Taweesangrungroj, A., Rattanabanchuen, R., & Sinthupinyo, S. (2022). A Decision-Making Model of Technological-Focused Government Agency Selection of Technological Start-Up Businesses. *Trends in Sciences*, 19(1), 1749–1749. DOI: 10.48048/tis.2022.1749

Team, R. C. (2023). _*R: A Language and Environment for Statistical Computing*_. Vienna, Austria. <https://www.R-project.org/>

Tekbaş, M. (2019). Sağlık Kurumlarında Nesnelerin İnterneti Teknolojisinin Kullanımı: Bir Vaka Çalışması [The use of internet of things technology in health institutions: A case study]. (UMI No. 593832) [Master's Thesis, İstanbul University, Institute of Science] İstanbul, Türkiye. Council of Higher Education Thesis Center.

Telli Danismaz, A. (2021). *Examination the role of the need to succeed and presenteeism in the relationship between compulsory citizenship behavior and organizational commitment* [Doctoral dissertation, The Council of Higher Education Thesis Center, Yildiz Technical University, Türkiye].

Tenório, M. M., Reinaldo, F. A. F., Góis, L. A., Lopes, R. P., & dos Santos, G., Junior. (2018). Elements of gamification in virtual learning environments: A systematic review. In *Teaching and Learning in a Digital World: Proceedings of the 20th International Conference on Interactive Collaborative Learning–Volume 2* (pp. 86-96). Springer International Publishing.

Terek, E., Nikolić, M., Vukonjanski, J., Gligorović, B., & Janković, B. (2015). The impact of media relations on certain organizational and business performances: Serbian case. *Public Relations Review*, 41(3), 370–372. DOI: 10.1016/j.pubrev.2015.04.004

Terho, H., Suonsyrjä, S., & Systä, K. (2016). The developers' dilemma: Perfect product development or fast business validation? Product-Focused Software Process Improvement: 17th International Conference, PROFES 2016, Trondheim, Norway, November 22-24, 2016, Proceedings 17, Springer, pp.571–579.

The United Nations. (n.d.). *Sustainability | United Nations*. The United Nations. https://www.un.org/en/academic-impact/sustainability

Thompson, S., & Haynes, M. (2017). The value of online seller reputation: Evidence from a price comparison site. *MDE. Managerial and Decision Economics*, 38(3), 302–313. DOI: 10.1002/mde.2777

Tigre, F. B., Curado, C., & Henriques, P. L. (2023). Digital Leadership: A Bibliometric Analysis. *Journal of Leadership & Organizational Studies*, 30(1), 40–70. DOI: 10.1177/15480518221123132

Tochia, C. (2021). How the digital workforce has re-defined boundary management and perceptions of technological tools on maintaining work-life balance (Doctoral dissertation, University of Southampton).

Todorović, M. L., Petrović, D. Č., Mihić, M. M., Obradović, V. L., & Bushuyev, S. D. (2015). Project success analysis framework: A knowledge-based approach in project management. *International Journal of Project Management*, 33(4), 772–783. DOI: 10.1016/j.ijproman.2014.10.009

*Top 9 ethical issues in artificial intelligence | World Economic Forum*. (2016, October 21). The World Economic Forum. Retrieved October 9, 2024, from https://www.weforum.org/agenda/2016/10/top-10-ethical-issues-in-artificial-intelligence/

Torres, C. C. (2021). Adaptation and Validation of Technostress Creators and Technostress Inhibitors Inventories in a Spanish-Speaking Latin American Country. *Technology in Society*, 66, 101660. DOI: 10.1016/j.techsoc.2021.101660

Toska, A., Ramadani, V., Dana, L.-P., Rexhepi, G., & Zeqiri, J. (2022). Family business successors' motivation and innovation capabilities: The case of Kosovo. *Journal of Family Business Management*, 12(4), 1152–1166. DOI: 10.1108/JFBM-11-2021-0136

Townsend, M., & Romme, A. G. L. (2024). The emerging concept of the human-centered organization: A review and synthesis of the literature. *Humanistic Management Journal*, 9(1), 53–74. DOI: 10.1007/s41463-024-00168-w

Tritoasmoro, I. I., Ciptomulyono, U., Dhewanto, W., & Taufik, T. A. (2024). Determinant factors of lean start-up-based incubation metrics on post-incubation start-up viability: Case-based study. *Journal of Science and Technology Policy Management*, 15(1), 178–199. DOI: 10.1108/JSTPM-12-2021-0187

Turel, O., & Gaudioso, F. (2018). Techno-stressors, Distress and Strain: The Roles of Leadership and Competitive Climates. *Cognition Technology and Work*, 20(2), 309–324. DOI: 10.1007/s10111-018-0461-7

Turner, B. L.II. (2010). Vulnerability and resilience: Coalescing or paralleling approaches for sustainability science? *Global Environmental Change*, 20(4), 570–576. DOI: 10.1016/j.gloenvcha.2010.07.003

Tutar, H., Nam, S., & Cagiltay, C. G. (2023). Bibliometric analysis and visual mapping of the articles published in the ILEF Journal from the beginning to the present [Başlangıcından Bugüne İLEF Dergisinde Yayınlanan Makalelerin Bibliyometrik Analizi ve Görsel Haritalandırılması]. *Kastamonu İletişim Araştırmaları Dergisi*, (10), 87–105. DOI: 10.56676/kiad.1163603

Ucok, D. I., & Erbay, E. O. (2022). Organizational citizenship behavior: The other side of the coin. *Marmara Üniversitesi İktisadi ve İdari Bilimler Dergisi*, 44(1), 162–182. DOI: 10.14780/muiibd.1135558

Udofia, E. (2024). *The Digital Leader: Demystifying Leadership in the Digital Transformation Era*. Xlibris.

Ulaj, G., & Hızıroğlu, M. (2024). THE INTELLECTUAL EVOLUTION OF EARLY INTERNATIONALIZATION: A BIBLIOMETRIC REVIEW OF THE KEY TOPICS AND TRENDS. 19th International Strategic Management Conference, Van Eck, N., & Waltman, L. (2010). Software survey: VOSviewer, a computer program for bibliometric mapping. *Scientometrics*, 84(2), 523–538.

Ulkhaq, M. M., & George Joseph, R. S. (2024). Students' attitudes towards campus sustainability: A comparison among three universities in Sweden. *Environment, Development and Sustainability*, 26(6), 16289–16313. DOI: 10.1007/s10668-023-03295-w

Uluturk, B. (2023). How Servant Leadership Influences Street-Level Bureaucrats' Work Engagement: The Mediating Roles of Motivating Language and Perceived Organizational Support. *Management Communication Quarterly*. Advance online publication. DOI: 10.1177/08933189231219708

Unaldi Baydin, N., Tiryaki Sen, H., Kartoglu Gurler, S., Dalli, B., & Harmanci Seren, A. K. (2020). A study on the relationship between nurses' compulsory citizenship behaviours and job stress. *Journal of Nursing Management*, 28(4), 851–859. DOI: 10.1111/jonm.13009 PMID: 32187768

*Understanding VR Training: A Comprehensive Guide*. (n.d.). PIXO VR. Retrieved October 12, 2024, from https://pixovr.com/what-is-virtual-reality-training/

Unhelkar, B., & Gonsalves, T. (2021). *Artificial Intelligence for Business Optimization: Research and Applications*. CRC Press. DOI: 10.1201/9781003120926

United Nations. (2015). The 17 goals. *United Nations Department of Economic and Social Affairs*. https://sdgs.un.org/goals

*Use cases*. NFC Forum. (n.d.). https://nfc-forum.org/learn/use-cases

Vaccaro, G., Cabrera, F., Pelaez, J. I., & Vargas, L. G. (2020). Comparison matrix geometric index: A qualitative online reputation metric. *Applied Soft Computing*, 96, 106687. DOI: 10.1016/j.asoc.2020.106687

Van den Berghe, L., & Levrau, A. (2013). *Fine-Tuning Board Effectiveness is Not Enough*. In: Kakabadse and Van den Berghe. Chapter 6. *How to Make Boards Work: An International Review, London: Palgrave Macmillan.*

Van den Heuvel, J., Van Gils, A., & Voordeckers, W. (2006). Board roles in small and medium-sized family businesses: Performance and importance. *Corporate Governance: An International Review, 14*(5), 467-485. https://doi.org/. 1467-8683.2006.00519.x.DOI: 10.1111/j

Van Eck, N., & Waltman, L. (2010). Software survey: VOSviewer, a computer program for bibliometric mapping. *Scientometrics*, 84(2), 523–538. DOI: 10.1007/s11192-009-0146-3 PMID: 20585380

van Erp, T., Carvalho, N. G. P., Gerolamo, M. C., Gonçalves, R., Rytter, N. G. M., & Gladysz, B. (2024). Industry 5.0: A new strategy framework for sustainability management and beyond. *Journal of Cleaner Production*, 461, 142271. DOI: 10.1016/j.jclepro.2024.142271

Varsha, P. S. (2023). How can we manage biases in artificial intelligence systems–A systematic literature review. *International Journal of Information Management Data Insights*, 3(1), 100165. DOI: 10.1016/j.jjimei.2023.100165

Vaswani, A., Shazeer, N., Parmar, N., Uszkoreit, J., Jones, L., Gomez, A. N., & Polosukhin, I. (2017). Attention Is All You Need. Advances in neural information processing systems, *31st Conference on Neural Information Processing Systems (NIPS 2017)*, Long Beach, CA, USA.

Vatandaş, S. (2020). Oyun ve Oyuncak: Teknolojik ve Toplumsal Dönüşüm Sürecinde Oyun ve Oyuncağın Anlamsal ve İşlevsel Değişimi [Games and toys: Semantic and functional change of games and toys in the process of technological and social transformation]. *Süleyman Demirel Üniversitesi Vizyoner Dergisi*, 11(28), 913–930. DOI: 10.21076/vizyoner.674699

Vigoda-Gadot, E. (2006). Compulsory citizenship behavior: Theorizing some dark sides of the good soldier syndrome in organizations. *Journal for the Theory of Social Behaviour*, 36(1), 77–93. Advance online publication. DOI: 10.1111/j.1468-5914.2006.00297.x

Vigoda-Gadot, E. (2007). Redrawing the boundaries of OCB? An empirical examination of compulsory extra-role behavior in the workplace. *Journal of Business and Psychology*, 21(3), 377–405. DOI: 10.1007/s10869-006-9034-5

von Berlepsch, D., Lemke, F., & Gorton, M. (2024). The importance of corporate reputation for sustainable supply chains: A systematic literature review, bibliometric mapping, and research agenda. *Journal of Business Ethics*, 189(1), 9–34. DOI: 10.1007/s10551-022-05268-x PMID: 36259069

Voza, D., Szewieczek, A., & Grabara, D. (2022). Environmental sustainability in digitalized SMEs: Comparative study from Poland and Serbia. *Serbian Journal of Management*, 17(1), 15–31. DOI: 10.5937/sjm17-36447

Wagner, C., Bublitz, A., & Kaloudis, A. (2024). Organizational resilience in the age of digital disruption. *The Journal of Business Strategy*, 45(2), 78–95.

Wagner, D. J. (2018). *Digital Leadership: Kompetenzen – Führungsverhalten - Umsetzungsempfehlungen*. Springer Fachmedien Wiesbaden GmbH. DOI: 10.1007/978-3-658-20127-2

Walker, D. J. (2018). Visualisation with treemaps and sunbursts in many-objective optimisation. *Genetic Programming and Evolvable Machines*, 19(3), 421–452. DOI: 10.1007/s10710-018-9329-0 PMID: 30956541

Walker, K. (2010). A systematic review of the corporate reputation literature: Definition, measurement, and theory. *Corporate Reputation Review*, 12(4), 357–387. DOI: 10.1057/crr.2009.26

Walsh, G., & Beatty, S. E. (2007). Customer-based corporate reputation of a service firm: Scale development and validation. *Journal of the Academy of Marketing Science*, 35(1), 127–143. DOI: 10.1007/s11747-007-0015-7

Walumbwa, F. O., Hartnell, C. A., & Oke, A. (2010). Servant leadership, procedural justice climate, service climate, employee attitudes, and organizational citizenship behavior: A cross-level investigation. *The Journal of Applied Psychology*, 95(3), 517–529. DOI: 10.1037/a0018867 PMID: 20476830

Wang, H., & Huang, Q. (2019). The dark side of feeling trusted for hospitality employees: An investigation in two service contexts. *International Journal of Hospitality Management, 76 (Part A)*, 122-131. https://doi.org/DOI: 10.1016/j.ijhm.2018.04.001

Wang, B., Liu, Y., Qian, J., & Parker, S. K. (2021). Achieving effective remote working during the COVID-19 pandemic: A work design perspective. *Applied Psychology*, 70(1), 16–59. DOI: 10.1111/apps.12290 PMID: 33230359

Wang, C.-H., Liang, H.-L., & Yu, Y.-C. (2024). How does workplace bullying lead to employee compulsory citizenship behavior and affect spouse well-being? Anger as the mediating role. *Current Psychology (New Brunswick, N.J.)*, 43(8), 7131–7143. DOI: 10.1007/s12144-023-04923-4

Wang, S., Liu, Y., Zhang, J., & Li, S. (2023). Why, how and when the double-edged sword of workplace friendship impacts differentiated organizational citizenship behavior: A relationship motivation theory approach. *Current Psychology (New Brunswick, N.J.)*, 42(16), 13838–13855. DOI: 10.1007/s12144-022-03818-0

Webrazzi. (2011, February 19). *NFC Nedir, Ne Işe Yarar, Nasıl Kullanılır? [What is NFC, what does it do, how is it used?]*. Webrazzi. https://webrazzi.com/2011/02/19/nfc-teknolojisi-nedir-nfc-ile-neler-yapilabilir

Weil, M. M., & Rosen, L. D. (1997). *TechnoStress: Coping with Technology @Work @Home @Play*. John Wiley & Sons.

Weiss, T., & Gordenker, L. (1996). *NGOs, the UN, and global governance*. Lynne Rienner. DOI: 10.1515/9781685855987

Wepener, M., & Boshoff, C. (2015). An instrument to measure the customer-based corporate reputation of large service organizations. *Journal of Services Marketing*, 29(3), 163–172. DOI: 10.1108/JSM-01-2014-0026

Westermann, A., & Forthmann, J. (2020). Social listening: A potential game changer in reputation management. How big data analysis can contribute to understanding stakeholders' views on organisations. *Corporate Communications*, 26(1), 2–22. DOI: 10.1108/CCIJ-01-2020-0028

Westhead, P., & Cowling, M. (1998). Family firm research: The need for a methodological rethink. *Entrepreneurship Theory and Practice*, 23(1), 31–56. DOI: 10.1177/104225879802300102

Westphal, J. D., & Bednar, M. K. (2005). Pluralistic ignorance in corporate boards and firms' strategic persistence in response to low firm performance. *Administrative Science Quarterly*, 50(2), 262–298. DOI: 10.2189/asqu.2005.50.2.262

*What Is Artificial Intelligence (AI)?* (n.d.). Google Cloud. Retrieved October 11, 2024, from https://cloud.google.com/learn/what-is-artificial-intelligence

*What is Blockchain? - Blockchain Technology Explained.* (n.d.). AWS. Retrieved October 11, 2024, from https://aws.amazon.com/what-is/blockchain/?aws-products-all.sort-by=item.additionalFields.productNameLowercase&aws-products-all.sort-order=asc

*What is Cloud Computing?* (n.d.). Google Cloud. Retrieved October 11, 2024, from https://cloud.google.com/learn/what-is-cloud-computing

Whiting, R. H., Hansen, P., & Sen, A. (2017). A tool for measuring SMEs' reputation, engagement and goodwill: A New Zealand exploratory study. *Journal of Intellectual Capital*, 18(1), 170–188. DOI: 10.1108/JIC-02-2016-0028

Williams, C. C., & Kosta, B. (2020). Evaluating the implications of starting-up unregistered on future firm performance: Evidence a 2019 survey in Albania. *Journal of Developmental Entrepreneurship*, 25(02), 2050010. DOI: 10.1142/S1084946720500107

Wolniak, R. (2017). The Design Thinking method and its stages. *Systemy Wspomaganıa W Inżynıerıı Produkcjı- Inżynieria Systemów Technicznych*, 6(6), 247-255.

World Bank. (2021, Jun. 22). 10 Years On, Turkey Continues Its Support for an Ever-Growing Number of Syrian Refugees. Retrieved Nov. 18, 2021, from https://www.worldbank.org/: https://www.worldbank.org/en/news/feature/2021/06/22/10-years-on-turkey-continues-its-support-for-an-ever-growing-number-of-syrian-refugees

World Business Council for Sustainable Development. (2020). *The state of corporate governance in the era of sustainability risks and opportunities*. World Business Council for Sustainable Development.

World Commission on Environment and Development. (1987). Our common future. *World Commission on Environment and Development, 383.*

World Economic Forum. (2021) *Annual Report 2020-2021*. Annual Report 2020-2021 | World Economic Forum

Wrede, S. J. S., Claassen, K., Rodil Dos Anjos, D., Kettschau, J. P., & Broding, H. C. (2023). Impact of Digital Stress on Negative Emotions and Physical Complaints in the Home Office: A Follow Up Study. *Health Psychology and Behavioral Medicine*, 11(1), 2263068. DOI: 10.1080/21642850.2023.2263068 PMID: 37818414

Wright, P. M., Dunford, B. B., & Snell, S. A. (2001). Human resources and the resource based view of the firm. *Journal of Management*, 27(6), 701–721. DOI: 10.1177/014920630102700607

Xie, H., & Lui, J. C. S. (2020). Mining deficiencies of online reputation systems: Methodologies, experiments and implications. *IEEE Transactions on Services Computing*, 13(5), 887–900. DOI: 10.1109/TSC.2017.2730206

Xifan, Y., Ma, N., Zhang, J., Wang, K., Yang, E., & Faccio, M. (2024). Enhancing wisdom manufacturing as industrial metaverse for industry and society 5.0. *Journal of Intelligent Manufacturing*, 35(1), 235–255. DOI: 10.1007/s10845-022-02027-7

Xu, X., Lu, Y., Vogel-Heuser, B., & Wang, L. (2021). Industry 4.0 and Industry 5.0—Inception, conception and perception. *Journal of Manufacturing Systems*, 61, 530–535. DOI: 10.1016/j.jmsy.2021.10.006

Xu, Z., & Suntrayuth, S. (2022). Innovative Work Behavior in High-tech Enterprises: Chain Intermediary Effect of Psychological Safety and Knowledge Sharing. *Frontiers in Psychology*, 13, 1017121. DOI: 10.3389/fpsyg.2022.1017121 PMID: 36353082

Yan, E., & Ding, Y. (2011). Discovering author impact: A PageRank perspective. *Information Processing & Management*, 47(1), 125–134. https://doi.org/https://doi.org/10.1016/j.ipm.2010.05.002. DOI: 10.1016/j.ipm.2010.05.002

Yang, J., Liu, Y., & Morgan, P. L. (2024). Human–machine interaction towards Industry 5.0: Human-centric smart manufacturing. *Digital Engineering*, 2, 100013. DOI: 10.1016/j.dte.2024.100013

Yasue, N., Mahmoodi, E., Zúñiga, E., & Fathi, M. (2025). Analyzing resilient performance of workers with multiple disturbances in production systems. *Applied Ergonomics*, 122, 104391. Advance online publication. DOI: 10.1016/j.apergo.2024.104391 PMID: 39342914

Yener, M., Doğruoğlu, B., & Ergun, S. (2014). Challenges of Internationalization for SMEs and Overcoming these Challenges: A Case Study from Turkey. *Procedia: Social and Behavioral Sciences*, 150, 2–11. https://doi.org/https://doi.org/10.1016/j.sbspro.2014.09.002. DOI: 10.1016/j.sbspro.2014.09.002

Yenigün, R., Yıldız, A., & Uğur, L. (2020). RFID Kütüphane Sistemi İçin En Uygun RFID Etiketin AHP ve ANP Yöntemleriyle Belirlenmesi [RFID Library System Determination by AHP and ANP Methods]. *BEÜ Fen Bilimleri Dergisi*, 9(4), 1596–1608.

Yıldız, A. (2018). Endüstri 4.0 ve akıllı fabrikalar. *Sakarya University Journal of Science*, 548-558.

Yildiz, B. (2022). The reliability and validity of the compulsory citizenship behaviors (CCBs) scale: Six-step R-based psychometrics protocol among nurses in Turkey. *Perspectives in Psychiatric Care*, 58(1), 395–403. DOI: 10.1111/ppc.12805 PMID: 33908632

Yildiz, B., & Elibol, E. (2021). Turnover intention linking compulsory citizenship behaviours to social loafing in nurses: A mediation analysis. *Journal of Nursing Management*, 29(4), 653–663. DOI: 10.1111/jonm.13200 PMID: 33128815

Yildiz, B., Kaptan, Z., Yildiz, T., Elibol, E., Yildiz, H., & Ozbilgin, M. (2023). A systematic review and meta-analytic synthesis of the relationship between compulsory citizenship behaviors and its theoretical correlates [Systematic Review]. *Frontiers in Psychology*, 14, 1120209. Advance online publication. DOI: 10.3389/fpsyg.2023.1120209 PMID: 37213371

Yildiz, B., Yildiz, H., & Ozbilgin, M. (2022). How do compulsory citizenship behaviors affect moral disengagement in organizations? Significance of anger toward the organization during the COVID-19 pandemic [Original Research]. *Frontiers in Psychology*, 13, 1038860. Advance online publication. DOI: 10.3389/fpsyg.2022.1038860 PMID: 36506970

Yin, B., & Luo, J. (2018). How Do Accelerators Select Startups? Shifting Decision Criteria Across Stages. *IEEE Transactions on Engineering Management*, 65(4), 574–589. DOI: 10.1109/TEM.2018.2791501

Yin, J., Ji, Y., & Ni, Y. (2023). Does "Nei Juan" affect "Tang Ping" for hotel employees? The moderating effect of effort-reward imbalance. *International Journal of Hospitality Management*, 109, 103421. DOI: 10.1016/j.ijhm.2022.103421

Yin, S., & Yu, Y. (2022). An adoption-implementation framework of digital green knowledge to improve the performance of digital green innovation practices for industry 5.0. *Journal of Cleaner Production*, 363, 132608. Advance online publication. DOI: 10.1016/j.jclepro.2022.132608

Yin, Y., Stecke, K. E., & Li, D. (2017). The evolution of production systems from Industry 2.0 through Industry 4.0. *International Journal of Production Research*, 56(1–2), 848–861. DOI: 10.1080/00207543.2017.1403664

Youness, C., & Valette-Florence, P. (2017). Online reputation scale development: A customer perspective. *Developments in Marketing Science:Proceedings of the Academy of Marketing Science*, 569–579. DOI: 10.1007/978-3-319-47331-4_109

Youness, C., Valette-Florence, P., & Assaf, C. (2024). Global corporate reputation: A projective qualitative approach from a customer perspective. *Qualitative Market Research*, 27(1), 108–128. DOI: 10.1108/QMR-04-2023-0052

Young, J. (2022). *Leadership Resilience in a Digital Age*. Routledge.

Youssef, A., & Mejri, I. (2023). Linking Digital Technologies to Sustainability through Industry 5.0: A bibliometric Analysis. *Sustainability*.

Yuan, F., & Khan, M. S. (2024). *Investigating the Impact of Digital Leadership on Innovation Performance of Public Universities in Yunnan, China,* Journal of Infrastructure. *Policy and Development*, 8(9), 7663. DOI: 10.24294/jipd.v8i9.7663

Yuan, F., & Woodman, R. (2010). The Role of Performance and Image Outcome Expectations. *Academy of Management Journal*, 53(2), 323–342. DOI: 10.5465/amj.2010.49388995

Yu, H., & Han, E. (2021). Developing a measure for online shopping mall reputation (OSMR). *Sustainability (Basel)*, 13(7), 3818. DOI: 10.3390/su13073818

Yunus Emre. (n.d.). In *Encyclopedia Britannica*. https://www.britannica.com/biography/Yunus-Emre

Yusubova, N., & Ural, S. (2023). Bir Oyuncak Tasarımı Deneyinin Kültürel Kimlik Metodu Olarak Değerlendirilmesi [Evaluation of a Toy Design Experiment as a Method of Cultural Identity]. *International Academic Social Resources Journal*, 8(48), 2548–2560. DOI: 10.29228/ASRJOURNAL.68515

Zahra, S., & Pearce, J. A.II. (1989). Boards of directors and corporate financial performance: A review and integrative model. *Journal of Management*, 15(2), 291–334. DOI: 10.1177/014920638901500208

Zaidan, E., Belkhiria, E., & Wazen, C. (2023). Universities of the Future as Catalysts for Change: Using the Sustainable Development Goals to Reframe Sustainability – Qatar University as a Case Study. In Al-Maadeed, M. A. S. A., Bouras, A., Al-Salem, M., & Younan, N. (Eds.), *The Sustainable University of the Future: Reimagining Higher Education and Research* (pp. 1–23). Springer International Publishing., DOI: 10.1007/978-3-031-20186-8_1

Zainal, D. (2013). A longitudinal analysis of Corporate Social Responsibility Reporting (CSRR) in Malaysia public listed firms: Pre- and post-mandatory CSRR requirement. *International Journal of Advanced Research in Management and Social Sciences*, 2(1), 245–262.

Zaki Ahmed, A., & Rodríguez-Díaz, M. (2020). Analyzing the online reputation and positioning of airlines. *Sustainability (Basel)*, 12(3), 1184. DOI: 10.3390/su12031184

Zeike, S., Bradbury, K., Lindert, L., & Pfaff, H. (2019). Digital Leadership Skills and Associations with Psychological Well-Being. *International Journal of Environmental Research and Public Health*, 16(14), 2628. DOI: 10.3390/ijerph16142628 PMID: 31340579

Zhang, K., & Aslan, A. B. (2021) AI technologies for education: Recent research & future directions. *Computers and Education: Artificial Intelligence*. vol 2. ISSN 2666-920X. https://doi.org/DOI: 10.1016/j.caeai.2021.100025

Zhang, W., Liu, W., Wu, Y., Ma, C., Xiao, X., & Zhang, X. (2022). How fear of external threats plays roles: An examination of supervisors' trait anger, abusive supervision, subordinate burnout and CCB. *International Journal of Environmental Research and Public Health*, 19(24), 16810. DOI: 10.3390/ijerph192416810 PMID: 36554690

Zhang, Y., Liao, J., & Zhao, J. (2011). Research on the organizational citizenship behavior continuum and its consequences. *Frontiers of Business Research in China*, 5(3), 364. DOI: 10.1007/s11782-011-0135-2

Zhao, S. (2024, May 7). *Employee-centered Industry 5.0 - Case analysis of Haier*. OAE Publishing Inc. Retrieved October 12, 2024, from https://www.oaepublish.com/articles/gmo.2023.122601

Zhao, H., Peng, Z., & Chen, H.-K. (2014). Compulsory citizenship behavior and organizational citizenship behavior: The role of organizational identification and perceived interactional justice. *The Journal of Psychology*, 148(2), 177–196. DOI: 10.1080/00223980.2013.768591 PMID: 24684078

Zhao, H., Peng, Z., Han, Y., Sheard, G., & Hudson, A. (2013). Psychological mechanism linking abusive supervision and compulsory citizenship behavior: A moderated mediation study. *The Journal of Psychology*, 147(2), 177–195. DOI: 10.1080/00223980.2012.680522 PMID: 23469477

Zhutiaeva, S. A., Usanov, A. Yu., & Selezneva, A. V. (2023). ESG Rankings to Confirm the Commitment of Universities to the SDGs. In Rumyantseva, A., Anyigba, H., Sintsova, E., & Vasilenko, N. (Eds.), *Finance, Economics, and Industry for Sustainable Development* (pp. 235–243). Springer Nature Switzerland., DOI: 10.1007/978-3-031-30498-9_21

Zulu, S. L., & Khosrowshahi, F. (2021). A Taxonomy of Digital Leadership in the Construction Industry. *Construction Management and Economics*, 39(7), 565–578. DOI: 10.1080/01446193.2021.1930080

Zuo, W. (2022). *The relationship between compulsory citizenship behavior and job involvement*. National Research TOMSK State University.

Zupic, I., & Čater, T. (2015). Bibliometric methods in management and organization. *Organizational Research Methods*, 18(3), 429–472. DOI: 10.1177/1094428114562629

Zwack, C., Haghani, M., Hollings, M., Zhang, L., Gauci, S., Gallagher, R., & Redfern, J. (2023). The evolution of digital health technologies in cardiovascular disease research. *npj. Digital Medicine*, 6(1), 1. DOI: 10.1038/s41746-022-00734-2 PMID: 36596833

# About the Contributors

**Alper Erturk** obtained his B.Sc. in Industrial Engineering from Turkish Naval Academy, received his M.Sc. in Information Technology Management (with distinction) from Naval Postgraduate School, CA, USA in 2000. He got his Ph.D. in Management Science from Gebze Technical University, Turkey in 2003. Very recently, he obtained his Post Graduate Diploma in Data Science and Business Analytics from Texas University McCombs Business School, USA in 2023. Prof. Erturk has been an active academician and researcher in Business Management & Analytics field for more than 15 years of experience in Turkey, the U.S., Belgium, Germany, Morocco, and Kuwait. Throughout his academic studies, he published 3 books, more than 30 articles, more than 10 book chapters and presented more than 30 papers in international academic conferences. He is an internationally recognized researcher with an h-index of 20 and i-index of 28. During his career, Prof.Ertürk achieved to receive many awards including "Most Cited Researcher of the year", "Outstanding Teaching Award", "Best Paper Award", as well as he was also a recipient of Fulbright Scholarship in 2019 and studied at Portland State University, OR, USA. Prof.Ertürk is currently working as a Full Professor and Chair of Management Department at Australian University – Kuwait since February 2022.

**Mehtap Özşahin** received her BA degree from Bogaziçi University, Faculty of Economics and Administrative Sciences in 2001. She had her masters and Ph.D. degrees in the field of Management from Gebze Institute of Technology, in 2005 and 2011 respectively. She has worked as a research assistant between the years of 2002-2013 at Gebze Institute of Technology and as an assistant professor between the years of 2014-2019 at Yalova University. She was promoted to associate professor position in 2020 and since has been working as an associate professor at Gebze Technical University. She has taught courses and conducted research in the fields of strategic management, leadership, digital transformation, business ethics, international business and organizational behavior. She has supervised 2 doctoral theses and 4 master's theses and nearly 50 master's projects. She has 20 journal articles published in international and national journals, 5 book chapters, and more than 35 scientific conference papers in national and international conferences and scientific meetings. She has held the co-chair (between the years of 2014-2021) and chair (since 2022) positions at International Strategic Management Conference, which is held annually for last 19 years. She also serves as a member of the organizing committee for two international conferences- International Strategic Management Conference and International Conference on Leadership, Technology, Innovation and Business Management since their inceptions in 2005 and 2011 respectively. She teaches courses in strategic management, international business, management and organization, management theories, business administration, business ethics, corporate social responsibility and career management areas.

**Vladimir Simović** is the Head of Digital Economics Department at the Institute of Economic Sciences (IES) in Belgrade, Serbia and Associate Professor at the Australian University, Kuwait (AU). The areas of his professional interests are digital marketing, digital entrepreneurship, digital competencies, and information systems in business. He is a project manager of the European ESF+ project on digital marketing competencies and the participant of European COST Action on Artificial intelligence in business with 15+ years of experience in research and teaching. He is the founder of several digital start ups in Serbia as well as a think tank dedicated to innovative learning practices.

***

**Ayfer Aksu** is currently pursuing her PhD in Management and Organization at Başkent University, Ankara. She serves as the Deputy Director of Internal Audit at the Ministry of Family and Social Services. She graduated from Hacettepe University in Ankara with a degree in Public Finance and completed her master's degree in the same university's Department of Finance. Previously, she worked as a Tax Inspector at the Ministry of Finance, served at the Financial Crimes Investigation Board, and worked as an internal auditor at the General Directorate of Foundations. She has expertise in auditing and holds the titles of Certified Internal Auditor (CIA), Certified Public Accountant (CPA-Turkey), Independent Auditor, and ISO 27001 Lead Auditor. From 2016 to 2022, she taught Internal Audit Practices to master's students at Ankara University as a lecturer. She provides training in auditing, governance, risk management, and internal control. She has one published article, a co-authored book chapter, and two conference papers.

**Ila Anand** is an Associate Professor and Head of the BBA Analytics department at CHRIST University's School of Business and Management. Holding a Ph.D. in her field, she brings extensive expertise in teaching, research, and academic administration. Her research focuses on emotions and consumer behavior, as well as sustainability. She has published papers with reputed international journals indexed in Scopus. A collaborative leader, Dr. Anand has held various leadership roles and excels in research, teaching, and academic writing.

**K. Balaji** is an Assistant Professor in Business and Management, Christ University, Bangalore. He did Ph.D. from KLU Business School, KL University,Vijayawada. He is having 12 years of teaching experience. He has to his credit 23 Research Articles published in reputed National and International Journals. He has participated and presented more than 12 papers in both National and International Seminars/Conferences and also attended more than 50 workshops/FDPS organized by various reputed organizations. He has also participated in more than 50 seminars / webinars organized by various reputed organizations. He has also attended in 6 Short Term Training programs.He has successfully conducted 3 webinars, one 5 day FDP and one International Conference on Reimaging marketing in New Normal. He is a ratified as Assistant Professor by both JNTUH, JNTU Anantapur and Sri Venkateswara University,Tirupati. His specialized areas include, Accounting and Financial management, Marketing Management, Retailing Management, Consumer Behavior studies, Entrepreneurship and Business Laws.

**Elif Bilginoğlu** completed her PhD in Management and Organization at Marmara University, Istanbul, Turkey. She is currently an Associate Professor who teaches in the Master's and Bachelor's Degree programs at Istanbul Bilgi University and Beykoz University. Her primary research interests include organizational behavior and management, with numerous publications focused on leadership training, development, and its impact on organizational effectiveness.

**Shivani Dhand** is an Associate Professor (14+ years of experience),a Certified SHRM faculty in the department of Mittal School of Business of Lovely Professional University.She is NLP(Neuro Linguistics Programming) Practioner She is also a member of the Indian Society for Training and Development (ISTD) and the Indian Society of Labour Economics. She is also a core committee member and Mentor of an NGO(Shalini Fellowship) Shivani Dhand has worked in an IT company as an HR. She has published 18 research papers in various journals which include Scopus-indexed, UGC care and peer-reviewed journals. She is a certified POSH trainer. She has worked with CPSC (Columbo Plan Staff College) Manila Philippines, and trained the faculty and Principals of various Institutions in Bhutan (2015). In 2016, She worked on one of the projects," Austria as an Innovation leader in EU in Austria and was awarded as best presentation and Excellent paper. Her research is situated in the field of Startups, HR Practices Human Resource Management, Entrepreneurship, and social entrepreneurship with a special focus on academic entrepreneurship. Shivani teaches several courses on Human Resource Management and Organisational Behaviour; Leadership. She teaches and developed a full E-content for Online education in the course "HR Analytics and was a guest lecturer in the "Entrepreneurship and Management" training. Shivani has delivered Lectures on Social Entrepreneurship. Completed two International Projects. Presented and published 13 papers at national and International Conferences. She has also served as a Training placement coordinator in Lovely Professional University. She has also invited as a Resource Person in the various faculty development programs sponsored by the Ministry of Human Resource Development, India. She has participated in 40+ conferences and seminars on data. Her experience includes lecturing in Bhutan, Austria, India, US. Research Publication: International: 13 National: 06 Authored Books:1 Patents: 3 Copyright: 2 Research Propsal:1 submitted

**Jean El Achkar** is an Assistant Professor of Petroleum Engineering at the Australian University in Kuwait and the Regional Coordinator for the Levant and Gulf at the Arab-German Young Academy of Sciences and Humanities (AGYA). In 2017, he earned dual PhDs, one in Chemical Engineering from the University of Southern Brittany, France, and the other in Biochemistry from Saint Joseph University, Beirut. His research expertise spans biofuel production, solid waste management, and wastewater treatment. His commitment to sustainability has garnered him international recognition and awards for his contributions to research and sustainability initiatives. Jean recently completed the Oxford Leading Sustainable Corporations Programme at Saïd Business School, University of Oxford, positioning him at the forefront of leadership in sustainability-driven corporate innovation.

**Hicran Hanım Halaç** graduated from the Department of Architecture at Anadolu University in 1996 and completed her master's degree in architecture at Gazi University in 2002. She received her doctorate degree from Anadolu University in 2010. She has held academic positions at Anadolu University and Eskişehir Technical University. She served as the Vice President of the department in 2012 and as the Vice Dean from 2017 to 2021. Her areas of interest include Architecture, Planning, Design, Conservation, Renovation, Restoration, Cultural Heritage, and more.

**Gentian Hoxhalli** currently serves as the Head of the Department of Mathematics and Statistics at Luarasi University. With over 10 years of experience in teaching, he specializes in the fields of Statistics,

Econometrics, and Applied Statistics. Dr. Hoxhalli has an extensive academic portfolio, having published numerous articles in scientific journals and presented at various conferences. He is also the author of three books in the field of statistics, further solidifying his expertise in this area. He is currently in the process of earning the academic title of Associate Professor and is completing his second PhD at Niccolò Cusano University in Rome, Italy, focusing on Governance and Business Administration. Dr. Hoxhalli's dedication to education and research underscores his significant contribution to the advancement of statistical sciences in both academic and professional domains.

**Muhammad Nawaz Iqbal** is an Academician, Researcher and Philosopher. He have almost 13 years of corporate experience and now serving as an Assistant Professor in department of Business Administration of Sir Syed university of Engineering and Technology, Karachi, Pakistan. He credited numerous publications in local and international journals and also credited two books in the field of Business Management.

**Helene Kordahji** heads the Quality and Planning Department at the Australian University in Kuwait. She is currently pursuing a DBA at the Clermont School of Business in France. Her research interests are in curriculum, pedagogy, classroom discourse, and the impact of education policy.

**Yusuf Maz** earned his B.Sc. in Mechanical Engineering from Middle East Technical University in 2020 and is expected to complete his M.Sc. in Management Engineering at Istanbul Technical University in 2024. Since 2021, Yusuf has been working as a Project Engineer at ASELSAN. His research focuses on startup evaluation criteria for corporate incubators.

**Mehmet Bilge Kağan Önaçan**, PhD, received his BS degree from the Naval Academy in 1993. He completed his first master's degree in the Computer Engineering Department at Boğaziçi University in 2002 and his second master's degree in Management and Organization at Selçuk University in 2008. He received his PhD degree from the Department of Business Administration at Ankara University in 2015. He worked as a lecturer, department head, and institute director at National Defense University. He is currently working at Simsoft, a company that develops simulators. At the same time, he is a lecturer in the Department of Information Systems and Technology at Istanbul Okan University. His areas of interest include Knowledge Management, Management Information Systems, Electronic Document Management Systems, e-Signature, Bridge Simulators, and more.

**Tolga Önel**, PhD, received his BS degree from the Naval Academy, Department of Electrical and Electronics Engineering, in 1995, and his MS and PhD degrees from the Computer Engineering Department at Boğaziçi University in 2002 and 2009, respectively. He worked as a lecturer and department head at National Defense University. He is currently employed at Havelsan, a defense technology company. His areas of expertise include computer networks, network-supported capabilities, sensor networks, data fusion, mobile networks, tactical communication systems, fuzzy logic systems, artificial intelligence, target detection and tracking systems, command and control systems, distributed systems, autonomous systems, the Internet of Things, intelligent environments, and more.

**Sakshi** is a Research Scholar in the department of Mittal School of Business of Lovely Professional University. She earned her master's degree in management from Maharshi Dayanand University, Rohtak, Haryana. She is pursuing her PhD in the field of human resource management.

**İrge Şener** received her bachelor's degree from the Faculty of Engineering at Middle East Technical University and her master's degree in Business Management from Bilkent University Faculty of Business Administration. She completed her PhD in the field of Strategic Management at Başkent University in 2011. She has work experience, mostly in the field of consultancy, in international, private and public Turkish companies operating in different sectors. She led or actively took part in many international and national projects in the field of strategic management. In addition, she worked as a researcher for the projects of 'The Scientific and Technolgical Research Council of Türkiye', ministries and various Development Agencies related to entrepreneurship, network structures and clustering. She has been working as a faculty member at Çankaya University Faculty of Economics and Administrative Sciences since 2011 and Director of Technology Transfer Office since 2023. Her research interests include strategic management, entrepreneurship, and both business and regional competitiveness.

**Gentjan Ulaj** is an Assistant Lecturer in Strategic Management at the University of New York Tirana and a PhD candidate at Istanbul University. His research interests include the internationalization of businesses, innovation, and the relationship between entrepreneurship and organizational development. With experience in both academia and business, Gentjan focuses on how small and medium-sized enterprises (SMEs) expand into global markets and the influence of institutional factors on entrepreneurship. He has presented his work at international conferences and has contributed to academic publications in management and business strategy.

**Abdülkadir Varoğlu** is a professor at Başkent University, Ankara. After graduating from the Turkish Military Academy as an officer with a bachelor's degree in business administration, he obtained his master's degree in business administration from Middle East Technical University and a PhD from Ankara University. Between 1984 and 2004, he held various positions at the Turkish Military Academy, including serving as a faculty member and the director of the Defense Sciences Institute. He also worked as a Human Resources Specialist at the Canadian Ministry of Defense for a period of one and a half years. At Başkent University, he served as the Head of the Department of Business Administration, Dean of the Faculty of Economics and Administrative Sciences, the Vice-Director of the Institute of Social Sciences, and the Vice-Rector. In addition, he has taught at several universities, academies, and the NATO School in Germany. He has numerous national and international articles and published books on topics such as strategic management, leadership, negotiation, international management, and military sociology.

**Nihan Yıldırım** is an associate professor in management engineering at Istanbul Technical University. She completed her dissertation in business administration at the Istanbul Technical University. Her research interests are technology and innovation management, management information systems, project management, entrepreneurship, and business data analytics. She is a board member of the ITU Social Innovation Center. Her research interests include technology and innovation management, entrepreneurship, social innovation, project management, strategic management, digital transformation, and data analytics.

**Bora Yildiz** is a Professor of Management at Faculty of Economics Department of Business Administration, Istanbul University. His main research domain is Organizational Behavior. He has also numerous national and international publications in the HRM, Management and Organization, Strategic Management, and Managerial Psychology areas. Along with these experiences he also participated in many national and international scientific organizations as an organizing committee member and Scientific community member. He has lectured different courses at the graduate and postgraduate degrees. He is also a member of Academy of Management.

**Uğur Yozgat** is a Professor of Management and Organization and Vice Rector at Nişantaşı University, Turkey. His research interests include strategic management, leadership, information systems management, knowledge management, communication, customer relationship management, performance management systems and decision making. He has several papers published in national, international, and SSCI journals and conference proceedings, and is in advisory board in many of them. In 2013 he was awarded by Turkish Academy of Social Sciences. Many of his research papers were awarded as best papers in conferences.

**Isam Zabalawi** is the President of the Australian University (AU). With a PhD in Electrical & Electronics Engineering from Leeds University, he is specialized in analog and digital signal processing and communication techniques. His interests include the communication industry, information technology, technology transfer and higher education development and reform. Professor Zabalawi is a well-published research scholar and prior to joining AU in 2017, held senior positions including President of The Arab Academy for Banking & Financial Sciences, Minister of Higher Education and Scientific Research in Jordan, Chancellor of the University of Sharjah (UAE), Chairman of the Higher Education Accreditation Council of Jordan, founding minister for establishing the German-Jordanian University and founding President of the International University for Science and Technology (IUST) in Syria 2005-2007. He is a Fellow of Engineers Australia and awarded the Engineering Executive credentials. Additionally, he is a fellow of The Institution of Engineering and Technology (IET) - United Kingdom and he is a fellow with the European Federation of National Engineering Associations (FEANI). He served as a Higher Education Reform Expert (HERE's) with the European Commission and Erasmus+ (Tempus) Office, Jordan.

# Index

## A



## B



## C



## D



## E



## G



## H

## J



## K



## M



## N



## O



## P



## R

## S



## T



## W

www.ingramcontent.com/pod-product-compliance
Lightning Source LLC
LaVergne TN
LVHW060355300926
849162LV00006B/1269